KT-210-063

THE ROUGH GUIDE TO

Cuba

written and researched by

Fiona McAuslan and Matt Norman

with additional contributions by

Claire Boobbyer

ROUGH GUIDES

roughguides.com

Contents

Introduction to
Cuba

Able to both confound and exceed expectations in equal measure, Cuba is an endlessly fascinating place. The archetypal tableau of revolutionary rhetoric, breathtaking beaches, classic cars gliding past faded colonial buildings and a population who dance on an endless ribbon of salsa and rum does of course exist, but for those prepared to dig beneath the dazzling surface, Cuba relinquishes so much more. Art Deco architecture peeks between the crumbling mansions; unobtrusive art galleries are filled with exciting contemporary art to rival the scenes of London, Los Angeles and New York; private restaurants hidden in backstreets throughout the country nudge Cuba towards the upper echelons of fine dining experiences; while a programme of arts festivals sees internationally renowned ballerinas, musicians and actors delight audiences for the modest reward of a state salary. Delve into the countryside and you'll find cloudforests and mountain ranges, birdwatching trails ripe for exploring, and panoramic plains filled with green-gold sugar cane that are a siren call for a growing number of visiting cyclists.

Even those who have visited Cuba previously will be amazed by the country of today. Since the 1990s, when the collapse of the Soviet Union (and the end of decades of subsidies to its communist outpost) saw Cuba descend into economic crisis, there has been a sense that this is a place on the cusp of a great political and cultural shift. There is no doubt that the economic reforms ushered in since 2008, when Fidel Castro handed over leadership to his younger brother Raul, have staked a marker in the fine Caribbean sand. With individuals now licensed to run a diverse range of businesses, there is an undeniable sense that Cuban commerce is awakening from a long hibernation: private taxi services, boutique restaurants, homestays, private tour companies and more are thriving – and becoming increasingly competitive.

ABOVE VIÑALES VALLEY

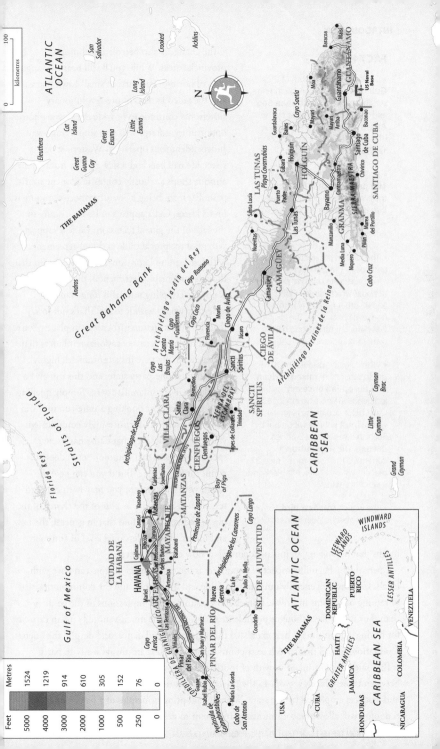

FACT FILE

- Cuba lies at the mouth of the **Gulf of Mexico** and is bound on the south by the **Caribbean Sea** and to the north and east by the **Atlantic Ocean**. It is the largest island in the Caribbean and covers 110,861 sq km.

- According to UNICEF, Cuba has a **100 percent adult literacy rate**, the highest in all of Latin America. **Life expectancy** at birth is 79 years, also the highest in Latin America.

- The Eastern province of **Granma** and one of Cuba's national newspapers are both named after the boat which carried Fidel Castro and 81 other rebels back home from exile back 1956. The boat itself was named after the original owner's grandmother.

- Ethnically, the population is predominantly of **mixed African and European ancestry**, as the indigenous Taíno who inhabited Cuba before Columbus's arrival were almost entirely wiped out by Spanish invasion and European diseases. The **population** is currently 51 percent mixed race, 37 percent white, 11 percent black and 1 percent Asian.

- The world's **smallest bird**, the bee hummingbird, is indigenous to Cuba.

The change is also percolating through provincial areas. While you'll still hear the languid clop of horse-drawn carts in small-town plazas, and the faded facades of pre-revolutionary storefronts continue to provide the classic photo opportunity, enterprise is also simmering away. Independent tour operators, Western-style streetside nail bars and a slew of new front-room antique shops are busily contesting for the tourist peso. Far from being a country whose economy is on its knees, Cuba appears to be flourishing in the face of the global recession; while a support system of reciprocal trade and fuel agreements with left-leaning Latin American states mean that, though undeniably detrimental, the US embargo is not the crippling force this long-standing adversary would wish it to be. That's not to say that the infrastructure isn't creaky in places. You're bound to come across occasional reminders that Cuba essentially remains a centralized, highly bureaucratic one-party state, and this can give a holiday here an unfamiliar twist. Simply queuing for a train ticket or booking a state-run tour can be unnecessarily and frustratingly complicated; you may well discover that Cuba has its own special logic, and that common sense doesn't count for much here. But if you can take the rough with the smooth, you may even come to regard such irritations as part of the charm of the place; and you'll also find that in general, the new and increasingly professional level of commerce means that organizing an independent trip is now easier than ever.

A perennially beguiling aspect of a stay here is the easy contact visitors can have with locals. Cubans are generally outgoing, sociable and hospitable, and the common practice of renting out rooms in private homes allow visitors closer impressions of the country than they might have thought possible in a short visit. The much-vaunted Cuban capacity for having a good time is best expressed through music and dance, and despite the queues, food rationing and free-speech restrictions, people in Cuba are always ready to party.

That said, the continued growth of tourism is cementing the two-tier earning power between those who now work in the private and tourist sectors and those like doctors and teachers employed by the state. Whether adopting principles of a free-market economy will allow the communist government to deliver its egalitarian agenda of wealth

CLOCKWISE FROM TOP LEFT BASKETBALL PLAYERS; HORSE-DRAWN CARRIAGE, GUARDALAVACA; CAPITOLIO BUILDING, HABANA VIEJA

redistribution remains to be seen. Similarly, no-one knows how the vestiges of present-day Cuba will endure in the face of recent change. One thing is for sure: immersing yourself in Cuba now is the best way to judge for yourself.

Where to go

No trip to Cuba would be complete without a visit to the potent capital, **Havana**. A unique and personable metropolis characterized by a small-town atmosphere, its time-warped colonial core, Habana Vieja, is crammed with architectural splendours, some laced with Moorish traces and dating as far back as the sixteenth century. Elsewhere there are handsome streets unspoiled by tawdry multinational chain stores and restaurants: urban development here has been undertaken sensitively, with the city retaining many of its colonial mansions and numerous 1950s hallmarks.

Together with the capital itself, most of Cuba's tourist attractions are concentrated in the provinces to the immediate east and west of Havana. The nature-tourism centres of **Artemisa** and **Pinar del Río** are popular destinations with day-trippers but also offer more than enough to sustain a longer stay. The most accessible resorts here are **Las Terrazas** and **Soroa**, focused around the subtropical, smooth-topped Sierra del Rosario mountain range, but it's the peculiarly shaped *mogote* hills of the prehistoric **Viñales Valley** that attract most attention, while tiny Viñales village is a pleasant hangout frequented by a friendly traveller community. Beyond, on a gnarled rod of land pointing out towards Mexico, there's unparalleled seclusion and outstanding scuba diving at **María La Gorda**.

There are **beach resorts** the length and breadth of the country but none is more complete than **Varadero**, the country's long-time premier holiday destination, two hours' drive east of Havana in **Matanzas province**. Based on a highway of dazzling white sand that stretches almost the entire length of the 25km **Península de Hicacos**, Varadero offers the classic package-holiday experience. For the tried-and-tested combination of watersports, sunbathing and relaxing in all-inclusive hotels, there is nowhere better in Cuba. On the opposite side of the province, the **Península de Zapata**, with its diversity of wildlife, organized excursions and scuba diving, offers a melange of different possibilities. The grittier **Cárdenas** and provincial capital **Matanzas** contrast with Varadero's made-to-measure appeal, but it's the nearby natural

CLASSIC AMERICAN CARS

Perhaps the most clichéd image of Cuba is of a **classic American car** rolling past a crumbling colonial building, and you don't have to spend long in the country to see why this image has become so ubiquitous. There are said to be around 60,000 vintage cars in Cuba, most of them still on the road and almost all of them imported from the factories of Detroit during the 1940s and 1950s, when the US was Cuba's most significant trade partner. After President Kennedy cut off all trade with Cuba via the 1962 economic embargo that exists to this day, car owners were compelled to keep their Buicks, Oldsmobiles, Chevrolets and Fords running. Unable to source replacement parts, proud owners have over the years become the most ingenious on the planet, culling pieces from Eastern Bloc Ladas, household appliances and even old tanks to keep their cars alive.

Author picks

Our hard-travelling authors visited every corner of Cuba, from the sandy beaches of the western tip to the verdant interior of the eastern rainforests, to bring you some unique travel experiences. These are some of their favourites.

Small theatres From inventiveness of sets executed with more flair than funds to the fluid beauty of the performers, a provincial theatre – such as Teatro La Caridad (see p.258) and Teatro Tomás Terry (see p.243) – or puppet show production at El Guiñol (see p.134) is a hidden cultural delight.

Antique and vintage collectables The land that not only froze in time but simultaneously got frozen out of numerous global markets has accumulated a mountain of antique decorative art, furniture and vintage memorabilia, which Cubans can now legitimately sell. Find the best places to uncover a gem in Havana (see p.135) and Trinidad (see p.291).

Our favourite casas particulares Whether it's eating a home-cooked meal, hanging out on the family veranda or taking a glimpse of domestic life, a homestay grants access to all that is idiosyncratic about Cuba. The owners of *Casa Muñoz* in Trinidad (see p.288), *Alojamiento Maite Valor Morales* in Morón (see p.316) and *El Cafetal* in Viñales (see p.175) all go the extra mile.

Alternative music venues All over the island, away from the spotlight that falls on the Casas de la Música and their ilk, are fantastically quirky venues like El Mejunje in Santa Clara (see p.266), artsy auditoriums such as the Casa de las Américas (see p.106) trendy clubs like *Sala Atril* in Havana (see p.133).

Baseball Cuban baseball parks are intimate and free of commercial distractions, while the crowds usually imbue a game with an infectious sense of fun, heightened by musical instruments around the grandstands. Catch a game at the Estadio Calixto García in Holguín (see p.358), the Estadio Sandino in Santa Clara (see p.266) and the Estadio Lationamericano in Havana (see p.138).

> Our author recommendations don't end here. We've flagged up our favourite places – a perfectly sited hotel, an atmospheric café, a special restaurant – throughout the guide, highlighted with the ★ symbol.

FROM TOP CASA MUÑOZ, TRINIDAD ; SANCTI SPÍRITUS PROVINCE, NEAR TRINIDAD

CUBAN RUM

When Carlos V issued a royal order in 1539 formalizing rum production, it secured **Cuban rum**'s place on the map. Today Cuba produces some of the world's most respected brands of rum, silky smooth modern varieties that have little in common with the harsh drink enjoyed by sixteenth-century pirates and renegades. Quality ranges from the most basic **white rum** widely used for mixing in cocktails (famously the mojito, the cuba libre and the daiquiri), to various **dark rums** aged in oak casks for different lengths of time, from around three years to as many as thirty, the latter of which sell for around $50CUC a bottle – and are best enjoyed neat or over a chunk of ice. Though Havana Club is the best known of all Cuba's rums, browsing the shelves of the convertible peso shops will reveal tempting but lesser-known varieties such as **Cubay**'s pleasantly sweet dark rum and **Ron Palma Mulata**, a good white rum that is slightly cheaper than its Havana Club equivalent. Among the finest Cuban rums are **Havana Club Gran Reserva** and **Santiago de Cuba Extra Añejo** – reputed to be the favourite tipple of Fidel Castro himself.

attractions of the **Bellamar caves** and the verdant splendour of the **Yumurí Valley** that provide the focus for most day-trips.

Travelling east of Matanzas province, either on the Autopista Nacional or the island-long Carretera Central, public transport links become weaker and picturesque but worn-out towns take over from brochure-friendly hot spots. There is, however, a concentration of activity around the historically precious **Trinidad**, a small colonial city brimming with symbols of Cuba's past, which attracts tour groups and backpackers in equal numbers. If you're intending to spend more than a few days in the island's centre, this is by far the best base, within short taxi rides of a small but well-equipped beach resort, the **Península de Ancón**, and the **Topes de Collantes** hiking centre in the **Sierra del Escambray**. Slightly further afield are a few larger cities: liveliest of the lot is sociable **Santa Clara**, with its convivial main square and thronging crowds of students, while laidback **Cienfuegos**, next to the placid waters of a sweeping bay, is sprinkled with colourful architecture, including a splendid nineteenth-century theatre. Further east, the workaday cities of **Sancti Spíritus** and **Ciego de Ávila**, both capitals of their namesake provinces, provide excellent stopoffs on a journey along the Carretera Central. Two of the most popular destinations in this part of the country, the luxurious resorts of **Cayo Coco** and **Cayo Guillermo**, are off the north coast of Ciego de Ávila province, featuring wide swathes of creamy-white beaches and tranquil countryside.

Continuing eastwards into **Camagüey province**, the smaller, rather remote resort of **Santa Lucía** is a much-promoted though less well-equipped option for sun-seekers, while there's an excellent alternative north of here in tiny **Cayo Sabinal**, with long empty beaches and romantically rustic facilities. Back on the Carretera Central, the romantic and ramshackle **Camagüey**, the most populous city in the central part of the island, is a sightseer's delight, fully meriting its UNESCO Heritage Site award, with numerous intriguing buildings and a lively nightlife, while the amiable city of **Holguín** is the threshold to the province of the same name, containing the biggest concentration of pre-Columbian sites in the country. On the northern coast of Holguín province, **Guardalavaca** (together with the neighbouring *playas* **Esmeralda**, **Pesquero** and luxurious **Turquesa**) is one of the country's liveliest and most attractive resorts, spread along a long and shady beach with ample opportunities for watersports.

FROM TOP BARBERSHOP, SANTIAGO DE CUBA CITY; AGROMERCADO, HAVANA

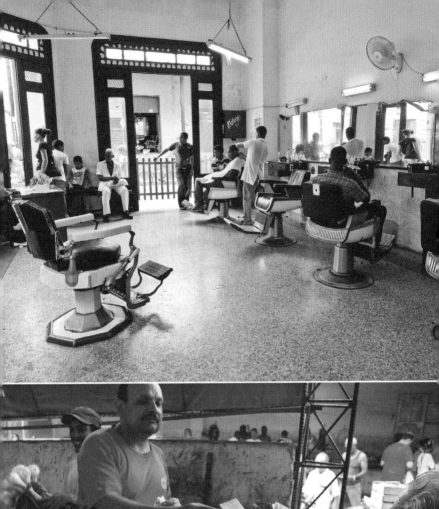

Forming the far eastern tip of the island, **Guantánamo province** is best known for its infamous US naval base, but the region's most enchanting spot is the jaunty coastal town of **Baracoa**. Isolated from the rest of the country by a high rib of mountains, this quirky, friendly town freckled with colonial houses is an unrivalled retreat popular with long-term travellers, and offers ample opportunities for revelling in the glorious outdoors.

Santiago de Cuba province, on the island's southeast coast, could make a holiday in itself, with a sparkling coastline fretted with golden-sand beaches such as **Chivirico**; the undulating emerald mountains of the **Sierra Maestra**, made for trekking; and **Santiago**, the country's most vibrant and energetic city after Havana. Host to Cuba's most exuberant **carnival** every July, when a deluge of loud, sweet and passionate sounds surges through the streets, the city's musical heritage is testified to by the fact that you can hear some of the best Cuban musicians here year-round. Trekkers and Revolution enthusiasts will want to follow the Sierra Maestra as it snakes west of here along the south coast into **Granma province**, offering various revolutionary landmarks and nature trails.

Lying off the southern coast of Artemisa province, **the Isla de la Juventud** is often overlooked, despite its immense though low-key charms. Easily explored over a weekend, the island promises leisurely walks, some of the best diving in the country and a personable capital town in Nueva Gerona. In the same archipelago is luxurious and anodyne **Cayo Largo**, the southern coastline's only sizeable beach resort.

When to go

Cuba has a hot and sunny tropical climate with an average temperature of 24ºC, but in the winter months of January and February the mercury can drop as low as 15ºC, and even lower at night. This is during the **dry season**, which runs roughly from November to April, when if you intend to go into the mountains it's advisable to pack something warmer than a T-shirt. If you visit in the summer, and more broadly between May and October, considered the **wet season**, expect it to rain on at least a couple of days over a fortnight. Don't let this put you off, though; although it comes down hard and fast, rain rarely stays for very long in Cuba, and the clouds soon break to allow sunshine through to dry everything out. Eastern Cuba tends to be hotter and more humid during this part of the year, while the temperature in the area around Trinidad and Sancti Spíritus also creeps above the national average. September and October are the most threatening months of the annual **hurricane** season that runs from June to November. Compared to other Caribbean islands and some Central American countries, however, Cuba has so far held up relatively well even in the fiercest of hurricanes, though rural areas are more vulnerable.

The **peak tourist season** in Cuba runs roughly from mid-December to mid-March, and all of July and August. Prices are highest and crowds thickest in high summer, when the holiday season for Cubans gets underway. As much of the atmosphere of the smaller resorts is generated by tourists, Cuban and foreign, out of season they can seem somewhat dull – although you'll benefit from lower prices. The cities, particularly Havana and Santiago, are always buzzing and offer good value for money throughout the year. Compared to the all-out celebrations in other countries, **Christmas** is a low-key affair in Cuba, with the emphasis on private family celebration. **New Year's Eve**, also the eve of the anniversary of the Revolution, is much more fervently celebrated. For **festivals**, July and August are the best times to be in Havana and Santiago, while the capital is also enlivened in November by the Latin American International Film Festival.

AVERAGE TEMPERATURES AND RAINFALL

	Jan	Feb	March	April	May	June	July	Aug	Sept	Oct	Nov	Dec
HAVANA												
Min/Max (°C)	18/26	18/26	19/27	21/29	22/30	23/31	24/32	24/32	24/31	23/29	21/27	19/26
Min/Max (°F)	64/79	64/79	66/81	70/84	72/86	74/88	76/90	76/90	76/88	76/84	70/81	66/79
Rainfall (mm)	71	46	46	58	119	165	125	135	150	173	79	58
PINAR DEL RÍO												
Min/Max (°C)	18/26	18/26	19/27	20/28	22/30	24/31	24/32	24/32	24/32	23/30	21/28	19/26
Min/Max (°F)	64/78	65/79	66/80	68/82	71/85	75/88	76/90	76/90	75/89	73/86	70/83	66/79
Rainfall (mm)	21	24	32	26	52	118	75	121	88	66	47	22
SANTIAGO DE CUBA												
Min/Max (°C)	20/30	20/30	22/30	23/31	24/32	25/32	25/33	25/33	25/33	24/32	23/32	22/30
Min/Max (°F)	69/86	69/86	71/86	73/87	75/89	77/90	77/92	77/92	77/91	75/90	73/89	71/87
Rainfall (mm)	74	43	53	58	140	102	69	94	107	193	94	81

25

things not to miss

It's not possible to see everything that Cuba has to offer in one visit, and we don't suggest you try. What follows is a selective taste of the country's highlights, from lively festivals to natural wonders and stunning architecture. All highlights have a page reference to take you straight into the text, where you can find out more.

1

1 BARACOA'S COUNTRYSIDE

Jewel of coastal eastern Cuba, tiny Baracoa makes an ideal base for exploring the verdant rainforest, mountain peaks and tranquil rivers dotted about this part of Guantánamo province.

2 PUNTA GORDA, CIENFUEGOS

The magnificently decorative Palacio del Valle is the icing on the cake during a wander around the broad avenues of this bayside district in laidback Cienfuegos.

3 CASA DE LA TROVA, SANTIAGO

Given Santiago's heritage as the birthplace of trova, it's unsurprising that the *Casa de la Trova* here is the country's top spot to listen and dance up a storm to traditional music, banged out by veteran and up-and-coming musicians alike.

4 **MUSEO PRESIDIO MODELO**
Page 439
Tour the isolated prison where Fidel Castro and his cohorts were incarcerated.

5 **VIÑALES**
Page 169
Particularly enchanting in the morning when mist rises from the valley floor, Viñales' prehistoric landscape is unforgettable.

6 **VILLA CLARA NORTHERN CAYS**
Page 272
The cays' stunning white-sand beaches sit in isolated splendour at the end of a narrow causeway.

7 **ALEJANDRO ROBAINA TOBACCO PLANTATION**
Page 181
This small but highly successful tobacco plantation offers refreshingly down-to-earth tours.

8 **HAVANA SALSA CLUBS**
Page 131
There's no better city in Cuba to see the biggest bands and join the hottest dancers on the salsa circuit.

9 **HAVANA JAZZ FESTIVAL**
Page 49
This lively festival is the perfect showcase for Cuba's jazz musicians.

10

11

12

13

10 HOTEL NACIONAL
Page 99

Wander around the cliff-edge gardens of this majestic hotel in the capital, or sip cooling cocktails on one of its elegant terraces.

11 LAS TERRAZAS, PINAR DEL RÍO
Page 157

Thickly wooded hillsides, grassy slopes and natural swimming pools make this idyllic eco-resort a great base for a few days' exploration.

12 PLAZA DE ARMAS BOOK MARKET
Page 136

The colourful stalls that wrap this lovely old square in paper offer a feast of fabulous vintage pre- and post-Revolution magazines, postcards, photos, posters and vinyl, from Cuba and the US.

13 HABANA VIEJA
Page 72

This well-preserved colonial centre boasts perfectly restored centuries-old buildings throughout its narrow streets and historic plazas.

14 HAVANA'S MALECÓN
Page 97

All the idiosyncrasies of Havana are on display here: the majestic and crumbling buildings, beatbox salsa, kissing couples and *jineteros*.

14

15 TRINIDAD OLD TOWN
Page 283

This much-visited sixteenth-century town is packed with colonial mansions and churches, threaded together by cobbled streets and compact plazas.

16 SANTIAGO IN JULY
Page 397

This is the best time to visit Cuba's second city, when its vibrant music scene boils over and the annual carnival brings fabulous costumes, excitement and song to the streets.

17 LA GUARIDA RESTAURANT
Page 126

Dine in style in Havana's most atmospheric paladar, where the excellent food is matched by Baroque surroundings, pre-revolutionary memorabilia and the aura of another age.

18 NECRÓPOLIS DE COLÓN
Page 110

Experience the quiet splendour of this extensive Havana cemetery and admire the grandiose mausoleums of the dead.

19 NATIONAL LEAGUE BASEBALL
Page 49

Take a seat alongside the exuberant crowds at one of the country's timepiece baseball stadiums.

24

25

 HERSHEY TRAIN
Page 214
This antiquated electric train slowly winds through the gentle countryside from Havana to Matanzas.

 LA PLATA MOUNTAIN TRAIL
Page 419
Bring Cuba's recent history to life with a day of mountain trekking to explore Fidel Castro's revolutionary base camps.

 CAVERNA DE SANTO TOMÁS
Page 178
A guided walk through these narrow underground chambers is a thrilling Tolkien-esque outing.

 **DIVING OFF THE SOUTHERN COASTLINE**
Page 50
The diving at María La Gorda, Punta Francés and the Jardines de la Reina is world-class.

24 CLASSIC AMERICAN CAR RIDE
Pages 34 & 197
Ride around Havana or Varadero in one of Gran Car's classic 1950s cars, a testament to both US engineering and Cuban ingenuity.

25 VARADERO BEACH
Page 192
Spend time lazing about on the longest, most impressive beach in Cuba, its golden sand backed by palm trees and fronted by unruffled blue-and-green waters.

Itineraries

Exploring Cuba can be bewitching and bewildering, and you can't cover the whole country in a single trip. Our Havana Grand Tour concentrates on the capital's main sights, while our other suggested routes focus on getting the most out of the country when you venture beyond Havana.

HAVANA GRAND TOUR

You could cram this tour of Havana's major sights into two days, but allow yourself three and there'll be plenty of time to soak up the atmosphere – and a mojito or two – along the way.

❶ Plaza de Armas The oldest and most animated of Habana Vieja's squares is where Havana established itself as a city in the second half of the sixteenth century – and it's been the barrio's heartbeat ever since. **See p.72**

❷ Obispo A microcosm of all that is changing in Havana, this pedestrianized thoroughfare is brimming with a lively mix of street vendors, open-fronted bars, neighbourhood hairdressers, secondhand bookstalls and artists' ateliers. See p.86

❸ Museo Nacional de Bellas Artes The country's most spectacular museum houses its largest art collection: revel in the history of Cuban art (and Cuba itself) seen through Spanish colonist portraits, Cuban painting and sculpture and Revolution-inspired work. See p.90

❹ Plaza de la Revolución Visit when the plaza is brimming with patriotic Cubans waving a sea of flags against a backdrop of sculptural tributes to Che Guevara, José Martí and Camilo Cienfuegos, and you'll have yourself the ultimate revolutionary photo opportunity. **See p.107**

❺ Casa de la Música Miramar Arguably the best of the city's music venues, hosting a consistently good programme of shows by Cuba's most popular musicians. **See p.133**

❻ La Esperanza Dine on Cuban delicacies in this fabulous paladar, where the owners have created a stunning interior design homage to the 1930s. **See p.128**

❼ Gran Teatro ballet Watch some of the world's finest prima ballerinas give mesmeric performances in an ornate building on the Parque Central; Carlos Acosta regularly takes to the boards here, too. **See p.134**

MOUNTAINS AND MOGOTES

Inland Cuba has natural treasures galore, and you could easily dedicate two weeks to trekking through the country's glorious forests, breathtaking mountains and verdant countryside.

❶ Las Terrazas A rich variety of birdlife flits through the fertile mixture of semitropical rainforest and evergreen forest on the slopes of the Sierra del Rosario mountain range. See p.157

❷ Viñales The jewel in the crown of western Cuba is the landscape in this striking national park, where rich red earth and lush tobacco fields contrast with the almost eerie Jurassic rock formations. **See p.169**

ABOVE VARADERO BEACH

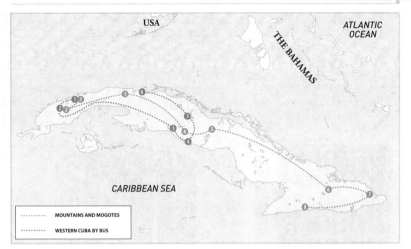

MOUNTAINS AND MOGOTES

WESTERN CUBA BY BUS

❸ Cuevas de Bellamar Venture over 50m below the surface and along hundreds of metres of atmospheric passageways in these awe-inspiring underground caves. **See p.218**

❹ Topes de Collantes This beautiful national park in the steep forested slopes of the Sierra del Escambray mountains has some excellent hiking trails. **See p.297**

❺ Boquerón The idyllic campsite here is tucked away down in the folds of the Jatibonico Sierra and framed by a halo of royal palms and banana groves alive with wildlife. **See p.319**

❻ Pinares de Mayarí Few venture into this beautiful and isolated pine forest, with a placid lake, majestic waterfall and intriguing Pre-Columbian caves hidden high above sea level. **See p.368**

❼ Baracoa Cradled by lush green mountains smothered in palm and cacao trees, and threaded with swimmable rivers, the Baracoan countryside is the perfect place to immerse yourself in the great outdoors. **See p.381**

❽ Sierra Maestra Even if you fall short of Pico Turquino, Cuba's geographical summit, a trek through the verdant peaks of the Sierra Maestra takes in stunning views, cloud forest vegetation and the mountain bases of Revolutionary rebels. **See p.420**

WESTERN CUBA BY BUS

Without your own transport, the key to seeing a good amount of the country's highlights on a seven day-long trip from Havana is to map out a journey along the long-distance bus routes.

❶ Las Terrazas This mountain retreat is just an hour from Havana by Víazul bus, but its forested hillsides and gentle attractions are a world away from the capital. **See p.157**

❷ Viñales From Las Terrazas, take a Víazul bus to the pretty rural village of Viñales, base for exploring prehistoric landscapes and caves. **See p.169**

❸ Cienfuegos From Viñales, hop on a Cubanacán-Transtur bus to the most laidback provincial capital in Cuba, with its bayside location, clean streets and open-plan neighbourhoods. **See p.242**

❹ Trinidad An hour and a half from Cienfuegos by Víazul bus, this is Cuba's most complete and intact colonial town. And with beaches just down the road, mountains not much further away and a glorious nearby valley, Trinidad makes a great base for exploring the region. **See p.278**

❺ Santa Clara Three hours from Trinidad by Víazul bus, this culturally rich city is the place to pay homage to Che Guevara. **See p.256**

❻ Varadero Use the Víazul service from Santa Clara to get to Cuba's most famous beach, where you can sunbathe for a day before heading back to Havana. **See p.192**

CASA DE LA TROVA, TRINIDAD

Basics

Getting there

Although Cuba is now firmly established on the Caribbean tourist circuit, there are not as many direct flights from the UK as one might expect, though there are plenty of airlines flying direct from elsewhere in Europe. Travelling from Canada couldn't be easier, with daily direct flights, but visiting Cuba from the US remains complicated due to the US trade embargo which includes restrictive laws on travel to the island. There are no direct flights from Australia.

Airfares to Cuba fluctuate according to season. **Fares** offered by big-name high-street **travel agents** are sometimes higher than those from smaller operators specializing in Latin America, which are also more familiar with details specific to Cuba, such as airport departure tax and tourist cards (see p.29).

Flights from the UK and Ireland

Since national carrier Cubana stopped flying **direct from the UK** in 2012, Virgin Atlantic is the only airline operating direct scheduled flights to Cuba, with two services a week from Gatwick. Return fares start from around £650 (including taxes) in low season but you'll be lucky to pay less than £800 in high season.

Various airlines fly to Havana **from London via European cities**, including Madrid, Paris, Amsterdam and Rome. **Air France** is the most versatile option, with daily flights from London Heathrow to Havana via Paris starting at around £700 in low season and £950 in high season. **Iberia** and KLM also fly from Heathrow, via Madrid and Amsterdam respectively, with similar seasonal prices. Other airlines flying direct from European cities include Cubana, KLM, Air Berlin and Air Europa. Though Cubana tends to offer the least expensive flights on the market, they have a justified reputation for overbooking, overzealous enforcement of the baggage weight limit and a relatively poor safety record.

No airline flies nonstop **from Ireland** to Cuba, and you'll usually fly first to London, Paris or Madrid.

Air France flies from Dublin via Paris from as little as €560 in low season and from around €760 in high season. Otherwise the best option is to buy a flight from London, Paris or Madrid and arrange flights from Ireland yourself.

Flights from the US

Despite the continuing embargo that Washington maintains on trade with Cuba, it is possible for US citizens to **fly direct from the US** to the island, but before booking a flight, whether direct or via a third country, you must first obtain a "**licence to travel**" (see box, p.28). Though licensed US travellers can now use direct charter flights from airports in Florida, New York and several other US cities, these flights are complicated, often take many weeks to arrange (as they require additional paperwork) and are usually more expensive than travelling via a third country. If you do choose to book a direct flight and have obtained a licence to travel, get in touch with Marazul (W marazulcharters.com) or ABC Charters (W abc-charters.com). However, it makes more sense to book a flight via Canada or Mexico (see below); just about every major US airline flies to both. However to travel on to Cuba legally from either country as a US citizen, you still need a licence.

Flights from Canada, Mexico and the Caribbean

Few countries have more flights to Cuba than Canada. Air Canada operates a daily service **from Toronto** to Havana and Varadero, with flights from other Canadian destinations going via Toronto. Cubana flies from Toronto and Montreal to Havana, Varadero, Cienfuegos, Santa Clara and Holguín, while the Panamanian carrier COPA Airlines also operates a daily service from Toronto to the Cuban capital. A number of other airlines fly chartered and scheduled flights from all over Canada. **Costs** can be as low as Can$370 in low season, though average fares are around the Can$600 mark, while in high season fares can go above Can$1000 but average at Can$700.

From Mexico, Cubana have regular direct flights from Mexico City to Havana for between US$300

OBTAINING PERMISSION TO TRAVEL TO CUBA

US citizens travelling to Cuba, no matter how they get there, must qualify for a "**licence to travel**". The stipulations for obtaining a licence have changed several times in the last fifteen years in the ongoing tug-of-war between the US government's conservative and liberal factions over the provisions and enforcement of the embargo, so it's always worth checking what the latest rules and definitions are at ⓦ treasury.gov or ⓦ havana.usint.gov. In 2011, for example, Washington expanded the possibilities for being granted a licence, allowing more people to travel for educational, cultural and religious purposes.

TRAVEL LICENCES

Currently there are two categories of licence: General and Specific. Confusingly, for a **General Licence** no application is necessary. If your trip fits into one of the categories which the US Government allows – usually travelling on behalf of an institution for educational, journalistic, diplomatic or religious purposes – then you can travel without having to make an application to the Treasury Department. Individuals travelling independently tend to have to apply for a **Specific Licence**, which is much more complicated. You'll need to send an application form and supporting documentation to the Office of Foreign Assets Control, US Department of the Treasury, Treasury Annex, 1500 Pennsylvania Ave NW, Washington DC 20220; for advice call ☏ 202 622 2480.

The various specialist US tour operators organizing legal tours to the island (see p.29) should be able to assist you in getting your licence and are the most useful sources of information and help.

You can also get **information** on licences from the Cuban government at the Cuban Interests Section at 2630 16th St NW, Washington DC 20009 (☏ 202 797 8518); or the Cuban Consulate Office at 2639 16th St NW, Washington DC 20009 (☏ 202 797 8609).

TRAVELLING WITHOUT A LICENCE

For US citizens, travelling to Cuba **without a licence** is illegal, whether you fly direct or via another country. However, some do bypass the legal obstacles by travelling via Canada, Mexico or other countries and buying **tourist cards** (see p.58) in those destinations to meet Cuban entry requirements, just like citizens of any other country. On request, Cuban authorities will stamp these cards instead of a passport on entering and leaving the island. Most US citizens who travel to Cuba illegally do not bring a stamped tourist card back to the US with them, as this in itself can serve as proof of a visit to Cuba. The penalty for travelling without a licence is a hefty fine and possible prison sentence.

---

and US$450 return in high season, staying consistently at around US$300 in low season; and from Cancún to Havana for between US$280 return in low season, and US$350 in high season. COPA and Aeroméxico also operate routes to Cuba, though they're not always direct and in 2012 Aeroméxico cancelled its flights from Cancún to the Cuban capital.

In the **Caribbean**, Cayman Airways fly from the Cayman Islands to Havana five times a week for around US$350 return throughout the year, or from Jamaica to Havana for closer to US$500.

Flights from Australia and New Zealand

Cuba is hardly a bargain destination from Australasia as there are no direct flights. The most easily available route **from Australia** is via Toronto with Air Canada, which costs around Aus$2000. A trip **from New Zealand** will involve a stop-over in either Canada, South America or Europe, with costs topping NZ$2500.

AIRLINES

Aeromexico ⓦ aeromexico.com.
Air Berlin ⓦ airberlin.com.
Air Canada ⓦ aircanada.com.
Air Europa ⓦ aireuropa.com.
Air France ⓦ airfrance.com.
Cayman Airways ⓦ caymanairways.com.
Copa Airlines ⓦ copaair.com.
Cubana ⓦ cubana.cu.
First Choice ⓦ firstchoice.co.uk.
Iberia ⓦ iberia.com.
KLM (Royal Dutch Airlines) ⓦ klm.com.
Thomson ⓦ thomson.co.uk.
Virgin Atlantic ⓦ virgin-atlantic.com.

A BETTER KIND OF TRAVEL

At Rough Guides we are passionately committed to travel. We believe it helps us understand the world we live in and the people we share it with – and of course tourism is vital to many developing economies. But the scale of modern tourism has also damaged some places irreparably, and climate change is accelerated by most forms of transport, especially flying. All Rough Guides' flights are carbon-offset, and every year we donate money to a variety of environmental charities.

AIRLINE OFFICES IN HAVANA

Aerocaribbean Calle 23 no.64 e/ Infanta y P, Vedado ☎ 7 879 7524.

Aeroflot Miramar Trade Center, 5ta Ave. e/ 70 y 80, Miramar ☎ 7 204 3200.

Aerogaviota Ave 47 no. 2814, e/ 28 y 34, Kohly, Playa ☎ 7 203 0686 & 0668.

Aeroméxico Calle 23 e/ Infanta y P, Vedado ☎ 7 830 9528.

Air Canada Calle 23 e/ Infanta y P, Vedado ☎ 7 836 3226.

Air Europa Miramar Trade Center, 5ta Ave y 78, Miramar ☎ 7 204 6904.

Air France Calle 23 no. 64 e/ Infanta y P, Vedado ☎ 7 833 2642.

Copa Airlines 5ta Ave y 76, Miramar ☎ 7 204 1111.

Cubana Calle 23 no. 64, Vedado ☎ 7 834 4446 to 49.

Iberia Miramar Trade Center, 5ta Ave y 76, Miramar ☎ 7 204 3444.

LTU Calle 23 no. 64, e/ Infanta y P, Vedado ☎ 7 833 3524 to 25.

Virgin Atlantic Miramar Trade Center Ave 3ra y 76, Miramar ☎ 7 204 0747.

AGENTS AND OPERATORS IN THE UK AND IRELAND

Cubaism UK ☎ 0800 298 9555, Cuba ☎ 7 863 9555, Ⓦ cubaism .com. With offices in both the UK and Havana, this agency knows Cuba inside out, offering flight bookings, tours, salsa holidays, transfers, car hire and tickets to cultural events.

Explore Worldwide UK ☎ 0845 013 1537, Ⓦ explore.co.uk. Big range of small-group tours, treks and expeditions centred on aspects of Cuba including Revolutionary trails, "backroads and beaches" and cycling (bikes provided).

Intrepid Travel UK ☎ 020 3147 7777, Ⓦ intrepidtravel.com. Small-group tours, including cycling trips, with the emphasis on cross-cultural contact and low-impact tourism. The various options combine Havana and the provinces.

Journey Latin America UK ☎ 020 8747 8315, Ⓦ journeylatin america.co.uk. Usually able to dig out some of the best-value flights to Cuba on the market. Offers reliable and well-planned escorted group tours and individual itineraries, several of which include staying in *casas particulares*.

North South Travel UK ☎ 01245 608291, Ⓦ northsouthtravel .co.uk. Friendly, competitive travel agency, offering discounted fares worldwide. Profits are used to support projects in the developing world, especially the promotion of sustainable tourism.

Travelmood Ireland ☎ 01 433 1040, Ⓦ travelmood.ie. Beach and city holidays and several themed tours from this Irish travel specialist.

AGENTS AND OPERATORS IN THE US AND CANADA

Center for Cuban Studies US ☎ 212 242 0559, Ⓦ cubaupdate .org. Assists US groups and individuals who are engaged in professional research, news-gathering, humanitarian or religious aid projects with travel to Cuba.

Cuba Education Tours US ☎ 1 855 687 2822, Ⓦ cubaexplorer .com. Experienced and highly recommended US tour operator dedicated solely to Cuba and run by a staff of mostly Cuban expats. One of their most attractive packages is their nine-day Havana Jazz Festival Tour.

Global Exchange US ☎ 415 255 7296, Ⓦ globalexchange.org. Human rights organization based in US which includes Cuba in its "Reality Tours" programme. Around a dozen different tours explore local culture, music, health, religion or agriculture.

Marazul Tours US ☎ 201 319 1054 or 800 223 5334, Ⓦ marazulcharters.com. Operates charter flights from the US to Cuba, coordinates group visits to the island and can help arrange travel licences and hotel accommodation as well.

Worldwide Quest Canada ☎ 416 633 5666, Ⓦ worldwidequest .com. Canadian specialists in nature and photo tours to Cuba, exploring various national parks, cays and mountain ranges as well as cities.

WoWCuba Canada ☎ 1 902 368 2453, US ☎ 1 800 969 2822, Ⓦ wowcuba.com. Long-established Canadian tour operator and Cuba specialist, offering well-planned bicycle, motorcycle, birdwatching and agriculture tours plus diving and fishing holidays.

Getting around

Though there is a reliable, good-value long-distance bus service, public transport in Cuba is generally slow, complicated and subject to frequent cancellations and delays. Improvements are creeping in but some services still work on a two-tier basis, with one service for convertible-peso-paying travellers and another, cheaper one for those paying in national pesos (foreign visitors are usually still obliged to pay in CUCs). Getting around the country efficiently means using buses or planes and, within cities, taxis in their various forms.

By bus

Given the relatively low percentage of car owners, Cuba's **buses** – known as *guaguas*, or omnibuses when referring to long-distance services – are at the heart of everyday Cuban life and by far the most commonly used form of transport, both within the cities and for interprovincial journeys.

Interprovincial buses

There are three separate services for **interprovincial routes**, Víazul and Conectando Cuba for foreign passport holders and CUC-paying Cubans, and Astro, a national-peso service reserved exclusively for Cubans.

The long-established **Víazul** (☎ 7 881 1413 & 5652, ⓦ viazul.com) is the more comprehensive of the CUC-charging bus networks, connecting most of the mainland provincial capitals. Though it also runs from smaller, touristy cities like Trinidad and Baracoa to the rest of the country, it doesn't serve a number of the most high-profile beach resorts, including Cayo Santa María and the northern cays in Villa Clara and Cayo Coco in Ciego de Avila. Nevertheless, it's still the quickest, most reliable and most hassle-free way to get about the country independently. **Tickets**, which are usually one-way, can be booked in advance at the offices of one of the three major Cuban travel agents Cubanacán, Cubatur and Havanatur (found in most provincial capital cities), and in some branches of Infotur, the national tourist information provider. As each office is allocated only a limited percentage of the total seats available, it's worth booking as far in advance as possible, particularly in the provinces outside Havana. You can also buy tickets at the bus stations themselves, but these often don't go on sale until an hour before the departure time; turning up more than an hour in advance will therefore usually give you no advantage, though your name may be taken down on a waiting list. If you're starting your journey somewhere other than a route terminus (such as Matanzas, between the termini of Havana and Varadero), you'll have to wait until the bus actually arrives before they'll sell you a ticket as they will have to wait to see if there are spaces. To avoid this scenario, book at least a day in advance. **Ticket prices** range from $6CUC for the 80km trip between Trinidad and Cienfuegos, to $51CUC for the fifteen-hour journey between Havana and Santiago. Children under 5 travel free, while those under 12 travel half price. You can also book tickets through the Víazul website before arriving in Cuba, though this must be done at least six days before the day of your bus journey.

The **Conectando Cuba** service, also known as **Cubanacán-Transtur** after the two companies that administer the service, differs from Víazul in that it picks you up and drops you off at hotels in the cities and towns that it serves, which are far fewer than the number covered by Víazul. While this means you avoid the hassle and expense of getting to and from the bus stations, it also means journey times can be much longer, as buses make more stops picking up passengers, especially in Havana where there could be stops at up to a dozen hotels. You can buy **tickets** at Cubanacán or Infotur no later than noon on the day before travel (no tickets are available on the day of travel), and you can specify the hotel from which you want to be picked up – note that it needn't be a hotel you're actually staying in. **Fares** are more or less the same as for Víazul services.

Both of Víazul and Connectado-Cuba buses are equipped with air conditioning, toilets and, in some cases, TV sets. They can get very cold, so remember to take a sweater with you; it's also worth bringing your own toilet paper.

Local bus services

While large numbers of foreign travellers use long-distance buses, very few use **local buses** as a means of getting around the country's towns and cities. The almost complete lack of information at bus stops, absence of timetables and the overcrowding are more than enough to persuade most visitors to stay well away. However, as most journeys cost less than half a national peso, you may be tempted to try your luck.

The only written **information** you will find at a bus stop is the numbers of the buses that stop there (and sometimes not even that). The front of the bus will tell you its final destination, but for any more detail you'll have to ask. Once you know which bus you want, you need to mark your place in the queue, which may not even appear to exist. The unwritten rule is to ask aloud who the last person is; so, for example, to queue for bus #232 you should shout *"¿Ultima persona para la 232?"* When the bus finally pulls up, make sure you have, within a peso, the right change – there's a flat fee of $0.40CUP.

By taxi

Taxis are one of the most popular expressions of private enterprise in Cuba. There are all kinds of different taxis, often outwardly indistinguishable from one another, and it sometimes seems that merely owning a car qualifies a Cuban as a taxi driver.

Tourist taxis

Though by no means exclusively for tourists, the official metered state taxis that charge in CUC are usually referred to as **tourist taxis** (or *turistaxis*), and are often modern Japanese and European cars as opposed to old American or Russian ones. Though most state taxis have a **meter**, many taxi drivers do not use them, not always for legitimate reasons. **Fares** range from $0.55CUC/km to $1CUC/km, with higher rates in Varadero and the other beach resorts than in the big cities. There are several other kinds of state-run taxis, many of them Ladas and charging in ordinary national pesos, but they are rarely used by foreign visitors and less likely still to stop for you if you're obviously not Cuban.

Private taxis

Huge numbers of **privately owned cars**, including a very high proportion of the American classics on the island, are run as taxis in Cuba. The local slang for these is *máquinas* or *almendrones*, though the latter is more usually used to describe communal taxis (see below), but in standard Spanish they are all called *taxis particulares*, literally **private taxis**.

Private taxis are licensed to charge either in national pesos or convertible pesos but there are no visible characteristics to distinguish between the two; none of them have meters. It is assumed that as a foreigner you will be paying in convertible pesos, whether or not the driver has the correct licence. Private taxis are not necessarily cheaper than state taxis and if you don't haggle the chances are you'll end up paying over the odds. The essential thing is that you **establish a price** before you start your journey.

Some drivers work interprovincial routes and wait at bus stations and some other fixed pick-up points, touting for business. Again, prices are always negotiable, but as a rough guide drivers carrying foreign passengers tend to charge around the same price per passenger as the equivalent Víazul bus fare (see p.30).

Communal taxis

Communal taxis, or **taxis colectivos** (more regularly referred to as **almendrones**), are more like bus services than regular taxis. They are usually privately owned vehicles, though there are some state-run *colectivos*, and generally they run along **specific routes**, both within and between towns and cities. There is no official mark or sign used to distinguish a *taxi colectivo* from the other kinds of taxi, or the route which it is operating along. However, drivers tend to wait with their car at the start of their route and shout out their final destination – if you see an old American car packed with passengers, it's most likely a *colectivo*. In most towns and cities there is usually a specific location, usually next door to a bus station, where *almendrones* waiting for long-distance passengers congregate, while in some cities, such as Santa Clara, there are **long-distance taxi** stations. Again, most long-distance *almendrones* operate along fixed routes, usually within a province (though there are interprovincial routes too). You may find it hard to flag down a *colectivo* as they are almost all registered to charge only in national pesos and sometimes don't expect non-Cubans to understand the system. There are fixed **fares** for most routes, usually $10CUP within a city, and around $20CUP for longer distances.

Bicitaxis and cocotaxis

Bicitaxis (also known as *ciclotaxis*) are three-wheeled bicycles with enough room for two passengers, sometimes three at a squeeze. In use all over the island, there are legions of these in Havana, where you won't have to wait long before one crosses your path. **Fares** are not all that different from tourist taxis, but again, negotiation is part of the deal. Around $1CUC/km should usually be more than enough.

Less common **cocotaxis**, sometimes called *mototaxis*, are aimed strictly at the tourist market and offer the novel experience of a ride around town semi-encased in a giant yellow bowling ball, dragged along by a small scooter. **Fares** in Havana have become standardized at $0.50CUC/km, but there will always be drivers looking to charge unsuspecting tourists a higher rate.

By train

At present, Cuba is the only country in the Caribbean with a functioning **rail system**, and although trains are slow (average top speed is 40km/hr) and subject to long delays and cancellations, they nevertheless provide a sociable form of travelling and a great way of getting a feel for the landscape as you journey around. You'll need your passport to **buy a ticket**, which, depending on which town you're in, you should do between an hour and five days before your date of departure, direct from the train station. (If you show up less than an hour beforehand, the ticket office will

HITCHHIKING

Hitching a lift is as common in Cuba as catching a bus, and is the main form of transport for some Cubans. The petrol shortages that followed the collapse of trade with the former Soviet Union in the early 1990s meant every available vehicle had to be utilized by the state, effectively as public transport. Thus a system was adopted whereby any private vehicle, from a car to a tractor, was obliged to pick up anyone hitching a lift. The yellow-suited workers employed by the government to hail down vehicles at bus stops and junctions on main roads and motorways can still be seen today, though their numbers have decreased significantly. Nevertheless, the culture of hitching, or **coger botella** as it is known in Cuba, remains, though drivers often ask for a few pesos these days. Crowds of people still wait by bridges and junctions along the major roads for trucks or anything else to stop. Tourists, though they are likely to attract a few puzzled stares, are welcome to join in.

almost certainly refuse to sell you a ticket.) You cannot buy tickets online or by phone, only in person as stations. Strictly speaking, all foreign travellers must pay for tickets in convertible pesos, but on some of the less-travelled routes you may get away with a national-peso ticket.

The **main line**, which links Havana with Santiago de Cuba via Santa Clara and Camagüey, is generally reliable and quite comfortable, though it will prove less appealing if you fail to bring your own toilet paper. Most of Cuba's major cities are served by this route, and while there are branch lines to other towns and cities and a few completely separate lines, any service not running directly between Havana and Santiago will be subject to frequent delays and cancellations, and even slower trains. The state tacitly discourages tourists from using some lesser-used branch lines, from cities such as Cienfuegos and Sancti Spíritus, as standards are so much lower than on the mainline, and instead nudges travellers toward the more profitable bus services.

The quickest of the two main line services, from Havana to Santiago, is known as the **Especial**. Sometimes referred to as the Tren Francés, it uses air-conditioned coaches imported from France, and offers two classes of seats. It leaves Havana once every three days and calls only at Santa Clara, Camagüey and Cacocum in Holguín province on the fifteen-hour journey to Santiago. An alternative service, the **Regular**, with no air conditioning and just one class of seating, leaves more frequently, usually four or five times a week. The two most notable routes beside the main line and its branch lines are the **Havana–Pinar del Río line**, one of the slowest in the country, and the **Hershey line** (see p.214), an electric train service running between Havana and Matanzas.

Fares from Havana to Santiago on the Especial are $62CUC for first-class seats and $30CUC for second-class; all tickets on the Regular service cost $30CUC. Examples of other fares are $6CUC for Havana to Pinar del Río and $32CUC for Havana to Guantánamo.

By car

Given the infrequency of buses on many routes and the fact that some significant destinations are completely out of reach of the bus and train networks, it makes sense to consider **renting a car** if you intend to do a lot of travelling around. Though it's relatively expensive to hire a car (cheapest rates are around $40CUC per day), traffic jams are almost unheard of and, away from the cities, many roads – including the motorways – are almost empty, meaning you can get around quite quickly. That said, driving on Cuban roads can be a bit of an anarchic experience (see p.33).

Renting a car

Most **car rental firms** in Cuba are state run, making the competition between them somewhat artificial: the two principal firms, Cubacar and Havanautos, now operate more or less as the same company from the same offices. Internationally recognized companies like Avis and Hertz do not exist in Cuba, but there are now one or two much smaller, **privately run operations** nudging into the market. The most significant of these is CarRental Cuba, whose vehicles come with or without chauffeurs; **prices** start at $55CUC a day. Prices from state-run companies start at $45–55CUC per day in high season (Dec 1–15, Jan–Apr, July & Aug).

Havanautos and Cubacar have the largest number of rental points throughout the island, though the other major rental company, REX, generally has flashier cars. It's well worth reserving a car at least a week in advance if you can – especially if you want one of the cheaper models, which tend to run out fast. You make a reservation with any of the state agencies through ⓦ transturcarrental.com.

All agencies require you to have held a **driving licence** from your home country (or an international driving licence) for at least a year and that you be 21 or older. You will usually be required to provide a **deposit** of between $200CUC and $250CUC.

CAR RENTAL AGENCIES

CarRental Cuba ☎ 52 83 4721 (mobile), ⓦ carrental-cuba.com.
Cubacar ☎ 7 835 0000, 273 2277, ⓦ transtur.cu.
Havanautos ☎ 7 835 0000, 273 2277, ⓦ havanautos.com.
Rex ☎ 7 835 6830, ⓦ rex.cu.

Driving in Cuba

Driving in Cuba is hazardous and patience-testing. **Road markings** and **street lighting** are rare and usually nonexistent on side roads, neighbourhood streets and even motorways, while the majority of roads, including the Autopista Nacional, have no cat's eyes either. **Potholes** are common, particularly on small country roads and city backstreets. Take extreme care on **mountain roads**, many of which have killer bends and few crash barriers. **Driving at night** anywhere outside the cities is dangerous, and to mountain resorts like Viñales or Topes de Collantes it's positively suicidal. Bear in mind also that push-bikes are very common on most roads in Cuba and rarely have any lights of their own. Most Cuban drivers use their **car horn** very liberally, particularly when overtaking and approaching crossroads. There's a brief glossary of driving terms in this book's "Language" section (see p.486).

To add to the confusion, away from the most touristy areas there is a marked **lack of road signs** which, coupled with the absence of detailed road maps, makes getting lost a probability. On journeys around provincial roads you will almost certainly have to stop and ask for directions, but even on the motorways the junctions and exits are completely unmarked. Be particularly vigilant for **railroad crossings**, common throughout the country, with a few actually sited on motorways. They are marked by a large X at the side of the road but otherwise you will be given no warning since there are no barriers before any crossings in Cuba. The accepted practice is to slow down, listen for train horns and whistles and look both ways down the tracks before driving across. Other things to look out for are permanently flashing yellow traffic lights at junctions, which mean you have right of way; a flashing red light at a junction means you must give way.

Petrol stations are few and far between (you can drive for up to 150km on the Autopista Nacional without passing one), and with no emergency roadside telephones it's a good idea to keep a canister of petrol in the boot, or at the very least make sure you have a full tank before any long journeys. Officially, **tourist cars** can only fill up at convertible-peso petrol stations, identifiable by the names Cupet-Cimex and Oro Negro, the two chains responsible for running them. They are manned by pump attendants and tipping is common practice. The cost of petrol at the time of writing was $1.73CUC per litre..

CAR RENTAL SCAMS AND HAZARDS

The most common hidden cost when renting a car in Cuba is a charge for the cost of the **petrol** already in the vehicle; if you are charged for this, however, then logically you should be able to return it with an empty tank. In general, it pays to be absolutely clear from the start about what you are being charged for to avoid any nasty surprises on returning the car.

Tampering with the **petrol gauge** is another popular trick – it's sometimes a good idea to take the car to a petrol station as soon as you've rented it and make sure the tank really is full before setting off on a long journey. By the same token, if you want your deposit back you should check the car over thoroughly before setting off to make sure every little scratch is **recorded** in the log-book by the agent.

You may find that if you pay by **credit card** – widely accepted in all rental agencies – the agent will ask you to pay for a small part of the overall cost (usually the insurance or petrol in the tank) in cash, as this will be the only way they can cream anything off – though note that this "scam" won't necessarily cost you anything extra.

You should also be aware that all rental cars come with easy-to-spot **tourist number plates**, so there is no hiding from *jineteros* and street entrepreneurs on your travels. However, these plates make it far less likely that anyone will steal your car, as Cubans driving tourist cars are more likely to attract the attention of the police. The plates are less of a deterrent, though, to people stealing your wheels or anything you have left inside the vehicle, so be particularly careful where you park (see box, p.34).

RENTING CLASSIC AMERICAN CARS

On the whole, **classic American cars** can only be rented with a chauffeur, effectively as taxis, from a state firm called **Gran Car**, based in Havana (☎ 7 648 7338) and Varadero (☎ 45 66 2454). The easiest way to do this is to go direct to their well-established taxi ranks (see p.34 and p.197). Since liberalization of private enterprise laws, however, individual car owners can rent out their pride and joy as a legitimate business. It's a little tricky tracking them down, though, as any advertising or presence on the web is rare – your best bet is to ask drivers at taxi ranks.

Major roads

Cuba's principal **motorway**, the **Autopista Nacional**, is split into two sections: the shorter one runs between Havana and the provincial capital of Pinar del Río and is marked on maps as the **A4**; the longer section between Havana and the eastern edge of Sancti Spíritus province is shown on maps as the **A1**. However, both are referred to simply as *el autopista*, literally "the motorway". The **speed limit** on the Autopista Nacional is 100km/hr.

The main alternative route for most long-distance journeys is the two-lane **Carretera Central**, marked on maps as **CC** – an older, more congested road running the entire length of the island, with an 80km/hr **speed limit**. This tends to be a more scenic option, which is just as well, as you can spend hours stuck behind slow-moving tractors, trucks and horse-drawn carriages. It is also the only major road linking up the eastern half of the island, and on a drive from Havana to Santiago de Cuba it becomes the nearest thing to a motorway from the eastern side of Sancti Spíritus province onwards.

There are more options for alternative routes in the western half of Cuba, where there are two other principal roads: the **Circuito Norte (CN)**, the quickest route between some of the towns along the northern coast, and the **Circuito Sur (CS)**, linking up parts of the southern coast. The Circuito Norte runs between Havana and Morón in Ciego de Avila and is the best road link between the capital and Varadero, a stretch better known as the **Vía Blanca**.

By plane

Tip to tip, Cuba is 1200km (745miles) in length and given the relatively slow road and rail routes, **domestic flights** offer a temptingly quick way of getting around. Of the three state-owned domestic airlines, Aerocaribbean operates the most routes. Almost all internal flights take off or land in **Havana** and there are very few cities or resorts that connect directly to anywhere other than the capital, though

PARKING

Car parks with meters are nonexistent in Cuba, and car parks themselves, outside of Havana, are few and far between. In the capital, there are a significant number of state- and privately-run car parks, the latter often makeshift affairs, sometimes in the ruins of old buildings – you could easily pass one without realizing it. Most of the large and luxurious hotels have their own car parks and they are often prepared to let non-guests use them if there's room.

Cuban car parks are always manned by **attendants**, to whom users pay a fee. A couple of convertible pesos are usually enough to cover a nightshift, but it makes sense to establish a price beforehand and to find out when the attendant's shift ends. If the car park is particularly crowded you may be asked to leave your keys in the event that your car needs to be moved to allow another driver out.

If you're staying in a *casa particular* or a smaller hotel, it's a good idea to ask where you can and should park your vehicle. Leaving it on the street is of course an option, but bear in mind that few (if any) car rental firms in Cuba offer insurance covering the cost of your wheels if they are stolen – a distinct possibility if you leave your car unattended overnight. Furthermore, the police have a tendency to look less favourably on any theft or damage to a vehicle if it is left anywhere other than a garage or a car park. At the very least you should look for someone who will watch your car for a fee; in most places even remotely touristy there will usually be someone in the habit of doing just that. In fact, even if you do leave your car unattended there is a decent chance that by the time you come back to it someone will be watching over it and maybe will have washed it – they will of course be expecting you to tip them.

you can fly direct from Varadero to Cayo Largo. Outside Havana the main **regional airports** are in Varadero, Santa Clara, Camagüey, Holguín and Santiago de Cuba, while Cayo Largo, Cayo Las Brujas and Cayo Coco all have their own airports handling flights specifically for the tourist industry.

Prices between the airlines are very similar, with return flights from Havana to Santiago de Cuba, one of the most expensive routes, costing around $260CUC, and to Nueva Gerona, one of the least expensive, around $90CUC. The best website for booking flights is Ⓦcubajet.com.

Cuban airlines have had a **poor safety record** over the last couple of decades. Many domestic routes use planes built in the 1970s and 1980s, some old Russian Antonov aircraft with a capacity of about fifty passengers.

DOMESTIC AIRLINES

Aerocaribbean ☎ 7 879 7524 & 7525, Ⓦfly-aerocaribbean.com.
Aerogaviota ☎ 7 203 0686 & 0668, Ⓦaerogaviota.com.
Cubana ☎ 7 834 4446, Ⓦcubana.cu

Cycling

Cycling tours are very popular in Cuba. However, though basic Chinese bikes are a common sight in all towns and cities, cycling for recreation or sport is not particularly popular among Cubans themselves. There are no proper cycling shops or bike rental agencies, and surprisingly few places renting or selling bikes and spare parts, though a few hotels do rent out bicycles. On the other hand, there are makeshift bicycle repair workshops all over the place and you'll rarely have to travel far within the cities before coming across what is known in Cuba as a *ponchera*, a makeshift puncture-repair workshop where the owner will usually offer basic bicylce repairs too.

The most straightforward long-distance cycling opportunities for visitors are **prepackaged cycling tours**. Several of the national tour operators (see below) offer *cicloturismo* packages, but you're generally better off booking with a foreign company. British firm Go Cycling Cuba (Ⓦgocycling cuba.com) is very professional, while McQueen's Island Tours (Ⓦmacqueens.com), a subsidiary of WoWCuba (see p.29), is another experienced operator, and are also the best equipped agency when it comes to **renting bikes in Cuba** for independent touring – though as with touring packages, you'll need to book your bike in advance. McQueen's has an office in the Kohly district of Havana and rents out mountain bikes and hybrids

for between $22CUC and $32CUC per day for between six and eleven days.

If you do intend to cycle in Cuba it's worth bringing your own padlock, as they are rarely supplied with rental bikes and are difficult to find for sale. Most Cubans leave their bikes in the commonplace *parqueos de ciclos*, located inside houses, ruined buildings or sometimes in outdoor spaces, where the owner will look after your bike for a national peso or two until you get back. Also worth packing if cycling around Cuba independently is a copy of *Bicycling Cuba* (see p.482).

AGENTS AND OPERATORS IN CUBA

Cubamar Viajes ☎ 7 833 2523, Ⓦcubamarviajes.cu. One of the smaller operators, responsible for running most of the country's *campismos*, offers some of its own unique off-the-beaten-track tours including cycling, trekking and bird watching.

Cubanacán ☎ 7 208 9920, Ⓦcubanacanviajes.com. Among the largest tourism entities in the country, Cubanacán has its fingers in almost every aspect of the tourist industry and has a suitably impressive portfolio of organized excursions and tours.

Cubatur ☎ 7 836 2259, Ⓦcubatur.cu. One of the most comprehensive programmes of excursions, with offices and *buros de turismo* all over the country; has the best website of all the tour operators, too.

Gaviota Tours ☎ 7 869 5774, Ⓦgaviota.tur.cu. With jeep and truck safaris in Matanzas province, or a helicopter trip from Havana to Cayo Levisa, Gaviota can provide something a little different as well as the more run-of-the-mill day-trips.

Havanatur ☎ 7 201 9800, Ⓦhavanatur.cu. Featuring offices all over Latin America, Europe and Canada, Havanatur is the only national Cuban travel agent that comes with an international reputation. Wide range of excursions and tours in every corner of the country.

Paradiso ☎ 7 832 9538 & ☎ 832 6928, Ⓦparadiso.cu. Specialists in "turismo cultural". In addition to historically and culturally oriented excursions, Paradiso provides music and dance classes, and stages special events such as music festivals.

Trinidad Travels ☎ 41 99 6444, Ⓦtrinidadtravels.com. One of the best of the relatively recently legalized privately run travel agents. As well as assistance with every aspect of visiting Cuba, it offers tours all over the country, and can tailor them to individual tastes in a way that the state-run agencies can't.

Accommodation

Broadly speaking, accommodation in Cuba falls into two types: hotels and casas particulares – literally "private houses". The hotels themselves divide into two relatively distinct groups: those run by wholly Cuban-owned chains, which are therefore state-run and owned; and those run by international chains.

ADDRESSES

Most **addresses** in Cuba indicate both the street on which the building is found and the two streets which it is between. For example, the address of a building on Avenida de Bélgica between the streets Obispo and Obrapía would be written Ave. de Bélgica e/ Obispo y Obrapía, e/ being an abbreviation of *entre* (meaning between). If a building is on a corner, then the abbreviation *esq*. (short for *esquina*) is used. So the address of a building on the corner of Avenida de Bélgica and Obispo would appear as Ave. de Bélgica esq. Obispo. You may also see this written as Ave. de Bélgica y Obispo. You should also look out for the use of the words *altos* and *bajos*, which indicate top-floor and ground-floor flats, respectively. When an address incorporates the Autopista Nacional or the Carretera Central, it may often include its distance from Havana. Thus the address Autopista Nacional Km 142 is 142km down the motorway from Havana. These distances are often marked by signs appearing every kilometre at the roadside.

Following the 1959 Revolution, streets in towns and cities throughout Cuba were **renamed** after people, places and events held in high esteem by the new regime. The old namescontinued to be used, however, and today most locals still refer to them. Where a name appears on a street sign it will almost always be the new name. Wherever addresses are written down they tend to also use the new name, though some tourist literature has now returned to using the old names. Where an address incorporating a renamed street appears in this book the new name will be used, with the old one in brackets.

Cuban hotel chains

The five principal **Cuban-owned chains** run most of the hotels in the country's cities and towns, and a fair few at beach resorts, particularly in Varadero. With any state hotel, knowing which hotel chain it belongs to will give you a fairly decent idea of what to expect, though in general the star ratings that the Cuban state assigns to its own hotels are very generous and fall below accepted international standards. **Islazul** (🖥 islazul.cu) operates most of the budget hotels, which are generally poorly maintained, sometimes with broken fixtures and fittings, leaky and noisy air-conditioning units and mediocre food. They compare very unfavourably with *casas particulares*, and usually cost at least twice as much. **Cubanacán** (🖥 hotelescubanacan .com) runs the mid-priced options, but some of their hotels (particularly its excellent Encanto-branded establishments) are better than the more expensive chains; Cubanacán is also responsible for most of the new or recently renovated hotels in the provinces, making them fairly dependable. The **Gran Caribe** (🖥 gran-caribe.com) and **Gaviota** (🖥 gaviota-grupo.com) portfolios consist mainly of large, supposedly more upmarket hotels, most of which are past their best but still offer a stay in a prestigious building or a prime location. **Habaguanex** (🖥 habaguanexhotels.com) hotels, which only exist in Havana, are the most reliably attractive and well-appointed state-run places, almost all of them in beautifully restored colonial buildings in the old town.

All these chains often offer very good deals via their websites and it's almost always worth **booking online in advance**.

Hostales

Run mostly by Habaguanex and Cubanacán, state-owned **hostales** are in fact boutique hotels, and often represent the best options in Cuba's provincial cities, though there are quite a few in Havana as well. Small, stylish and competitively priced when compared with standard state hotels, they are often housed in beautiful old buildings, and though rarely luxurious, they usually offer all the facilities you'd expect in a good-quality hotel, including decent restaurants and concierge services.

National-peso hotels

The cheapest accommodation in Cuba is a **national-peso state hotel**, most commonly found in less cosmopolitan towns away from the tourist

ACCOMMODATION PRICES

The prices published for all accommodation listed in this guide are for the cheapest available double or twin room during high season – usually mid-December to mid-March and all of July and August. During low season, some hotels lower their prices by roughly 10–25 percent. Advance online booking will often secure a significantly lower price, too.

centres. Although their nightly rates are sometimes the equivalent of a couple of convertible pesos, you get your money's worth. These are often extremely dilapidated properties, with bare-bones facilities: expect very poor bathrooms and ripped sheets on the beds. National-peso hotels are intended to be exclusively for Cubans, and the state does not promote them for visitor use. If you go to one you may well be told that all rooms are full, whether they actually are or not.

International hotel chains

Hotels operated by **international chains** are mostly found in Cuba's major beach resorts but there a few in Havana and other very touristy places. Though non-Cuban does not always mean better, the more upmarket foreign-run hotels do offer a superior level of service, and if you're used to reliable room service and staff that go the extra mile to make your stay pleasant, aim for a foreign chain.

Casas particulares

For many visitors, staying in Cuba's *casas particulares* is an ideal way to gain an insight into the country and its people. Many offer conditions far superior to the cheaper hotels and usually represent better value for money, while a few are downright upmarket. Their nearest equivalents are bed and breakfasts, but there is usually a stronger sense that you are staying in someone's home and there are rarely more than three rooms for rent. That said, a small number are more like boutique hotels, with as many as eight guest rooms, a clutch of staff and some truly impressive furnishings.

Casas particulares are found throughout Cuba – and they'll often as not find you, with **touts** (called *jineteros* or *intermediarios*) waiting in many towns to meet potential customers off the bus (see box below). You can identity a *casa* by the blue insignia (shaped like a capital I or sideways H) usually displayed near the front door; the same insignia in orange indicates the owners charge in national pesos and rent out rooms to Cubans only.

Given that most *casas particulares* rent out just a couple of rooms, you should always book in advance. Almost all houses have phones (though a few rely solely on mobiles), and most have email addresses too, but only a tiny minority have their own website. Booking ahead, however, is not always a guarantee that you will secure a room in the house

---

ACCOMMODATION TOUTS

The biggest drawback of staying in *casas particulares* is that you might have to run the gauntlet of the **touts**, also known as *jineteros* or *intermediarios*. Ostensibly, these are locals who work as brokers for a number of houses. In return they collect a commission (around $5CUC per night), which usually gets added to your nightly bill. In tourist hotspots, groups of local *casa* owners greet every Víazul bus arrival with pictureboards of their houses. Most are perfectly legitimate, but be aware of touts among them who, in the event that you say you have already booked a place, claim that it is full or has closed down – it's always a scam.

- Touts will often demand their commission from any *casa particular* to which they have taken customers – even when they have done little more than given directions. There is no way to avoid the attention of these people outright when you arrive in a town, and it can be incredibly frustrating when you feel besieged by people hassling you at every turn. There are, though, several ways to avoid falling prey to touts and thus having your accommodation bill increased unnecessarily.

- If you are approached, state that you have already organized accommodation, but don't disclose where. Often touts will arrive at your chosen house first and tell the owners that they have sent you themselves.

- Always book ahead and ask your hosts to meet you at the bus station with your name on a sign – many *casa* owners do this anyway.

- One of the best ways of finding a *casa particular* in another town is by referral. Most owners have a network of houses in other towns which they will recommend, and will often phone and make a reservation for you, or at the very least give you that house's card, though they may well collect a commission themselves for passing you on.

- If you need to ask for directions, ask for the street by name rather than the house you want to get to. Another trick to watch for is that *intermediarios* will pretend to direct you to the house of your choice but will actually take you to a totally different one, where their commission is better.

of your choice. Many house owners will not tell you when they're full; instead, they will allow you to turn up, and then escort you to another *casa particular* from which they will usually collect a commission. There's little you can do to circumvent this, but you can mention when you book that you would prefer not to be referred elsewhere. Two **useful websites** are ⓦ casaparticular.info, a comprehensive directory of houses and of other websites covering *casas particulares* in Cuba, and ⓦ cubacasas.net, which has been operating for many years and is generally reliable and up to date.

There is usually a high-season **going rate** in each city and town (generally $25–35CUC), which drops by $5CUC in low season. Few houses price their rooms outside of these established rates. You can also negotiate a lower rate for a longer stay. The law requires proprietors to register the names and passport numbers of all guests, and you are expected to enter your details into an official book as soon as you arrive. All payments are in cash.

Most *casas particulares* offer **breakfast** and an **evening meal** for an extra cost, which can be anything between $1CUC and $10CUC, with $5CUC the average. Make sure that you are clear about the cost of meals and agree to the rate at the start of your stay. Drinks will also be added to your bill, including those that you drink with your evening meal. Remember you'll also be charged for any bottled water you drink.

Campismos

Often overlooked by visitors to Cuba, **campismos**, quasi-campsites, are an excellent countryside accommodation option. Although not prolific, all provinces have at least one, often set near a river or small stretch of beach. While a number of *campismos* have an area where you can pitch a tent, they are not campsites in the conventional sense, essentially offering basic accommodation in rudimentary concrete cabins. Some have barbecue areas, while others have a canteen restaurant. They are all very **reasonably priced**, usually around $5–10CUC a night per cabin, though expect to pay more like $20CUC in more tourist-oriented areas. Although foreigners are welcome, this is one accommodation choice where Cubans actually have priority, and *campismos* are sometimes block-booked in June and July for workers' annual holidays. For more details contact Cubamar (☏ 7 833-2523 to 24, ⓦ cubamarviajes.cu), whose agents are listed throughout the guide. Cubamar also handles the hire of camper vans.

Food and drink

While you'll often be able to eat your fill of simply prepared, good food in Cuba, meals here are certainly not a gastronomic delight. Spices are not really used in cooking, and most Cubans have a distaste for hot, spicy food altogether. There is also a marked lack of variety and after two weeks in Cuba you'll be very familiar with the national cuisine. A few green shoots are poking through the culinary undergrowth, however, as a new wave of privately owned restaurants shakes things up.

Fluctuations in the food supply caused by Cuba's economic situation mean that restaurants and hotels can sometimes run short on **ingredients**; equally, imports of some foodstuffs are restricted due to the US embargo. As a consequence, you'll find the same platters cropping up time and again, and it's rare to find a restaurant that can actually serve everything on the menu, but perhaps in compensation for this, portion sizes tend to be massive. However, Cuba's culinary blandness is not all due to the embargo: there is a pervading conservative attitude to food here, with seemingly little desire to experiment with flavours and ingredients. That said, local produce is usually fresh and often **organic**. There is little factory farming in Cuba, and the food is not pumped full of hormones and artificial fertilizers – partly as a result of the tujikhe constraints of the Special Period, Cuba was a pioneer in the use of ecologically sound farming, all of which means that the ingredients do tend to be full of flavour.

As a general rule, always carry enough money to pay for your meal in **cash**. Although some of the top-end restaurants take credit cards, using this form of payment results in problems (real or created) so often that it's best avoided entirely.

State restaurants and cafés

Covering both convertible-peso and national-peso establishments, **state restaurants and cafés** differ greatly in quality – ranging from tasty meals in congenial settings to the simply diabolical. As a visitor you are more likely to stick to the convertible-peso places, which tend to have better-quality food and a wider range of options, including some international cuisine like Chinese and Italian; they also tend to be cleaner and generally more pleasant. The other viable option for decent meals

---

AVOIDING HIDDEN COSTS AND EXTRA CHARGES

Overcharging, particularly in state restaurants, is widespread in Cuba. Common-sense precautions include insisting that your bill is itemized, asking for the menu with your bill so you can tally the charges yourself, and always asking to see a menu that has prices listed alongside the dishes.

Paladars are less likely to get their maths wrong than state-run places, but are prone to **adjusting their prices** according to the type of customer (although this isn't an unheard-of practice in state restaurants either). There's often not a lot you can do about this, but bear in mind that it's most likely to occur if you've been guided to a restaurant by touts, who collar a commission from the owners; or sometimes if you're seen pulling up in a state taxi, so try to get dropped off a short distance away.

It's common for waiters to talk you through the menu, as opposed to showing you a **printed menu**, and though this might simply mean that the food on offer changes daily, it can also be a sign that you're being charged more than other diners – at the very least clarify prices when ordering.

---

are the restaurants in the tourist hotels, although the food they serve is sometimes quite removed from Cuban cuisine – with pizza and pasta dishes figuring heavily. **Service** in any kind of state restaurant is often characterized by a somewhat strained formality, even in some of the cheaper places. Though this can jar a little with your sense of expectation it's preferable to the almost non-existent service in fast-food restaurants such as the El Rápido chain, where cheap fried chicken, fries, hot dogs and burgers are served only when staff conversations have petered out.

National-peso restaurants, mostly located outside tourist areas, cater essentially to Cubans. While undeniably lower in quality than convertible-peso places, these are still worth checking out, as you can occasionally get a decent meal very cheaply. You should not have to pay more than locals do, so make sure your menu has prices listed in national pesos. They often run out of the popular choices quickly, so it's better to get to them early rather than later, particularly at lunchtime.

One of the most idiosyncratically Cuban **café chains** are the popular *Coppelia* ice-cream joints found all around the island. They are usually large, semi-outdoor affairs and dole out decent ice cream for a handful of national pesos, though some, like the main branch in Havana, also charge in CUCs.

Paladars

Legalized by the state in the 1990s in response to demand from Cubans keen to earn money through private enterprise, **paladars** (paladares in Spanish) offer visitors a chance to sample good Cuban home cooking in private residences, often the proprietor's house. A whole new wave of paladars have opened in the last few years following new laws that lifted all kinds of restrictions on where and how Cubans could run them. This has certainly raised the bar in terms of quality, as chefs previously shackled by laws banning all kinds of foodstuffs are now free to flex their skills and ideas in public. Though most paladars still stick to Cuban cooking, there a few signs of diversification too, with Japanese, Mexican and Swedish places opening up in recent years. The most striking improvement has been in the dining environments and atmospheres that the new owners have created, from authentic and stylish 1950s themes in spacious apartments to moody little grottos in old colonial buildings.

Prices vary more than they used to, and a main meal can cost anywhere between $3CUC and $25CUC, with the average about $9CUC. Although the menu will have few (if any) vegetarian options, paladars are more accommodating than state restaurants to ordering off the menu.

Cuban cuisine

Known as **comida criolla**, Cuban cuisine revolves around roast or fried pork and chicken accompanied by rice, beans and *viandas*, the Cuban word for root vegetables.

Popular national dishes include **ropa vieja**, shredded beef (or sometimes lamb) served as a kind of stew, prepared over a slow heat with green peppers, tomatoes, onions and garlic; **ajiaco** is another rich stew whose ingredients vary from region to region, but always includes at least one kind of meat, corn and usually some green vegetables; and **tasajo**, a form of fried dried beef. One particularly divine delicacy is **lechón**, or suckling

---

VEGETARIAN FOOD

Vegetarianism is still in its infancy in Cuba, where the idea is basically the more meat there is on a plate, the better. As a vegetarian your staple diet will be rice and beans, eggs, fried plantain, salads, omelettes and pizzas. Cubans often class *jamonada* (Spam) as not really meat and will often mix pieces into vegetarian dishes, so always remember to specify that you want something without meat (*sin carne*) and ham (*sin jamón*).

   Vegans will find that they will be extremely limited in what they can eat in Cuba. You'll generally be better off in paladars, where ordering off-menu is easier and most places serve rice, black beans and root vegetables such as potato and malanga.

---

pig, commonly marinated in garlic, onions and herbs before being spit- or oven-roasted. Meat and seafood is often cooked **enchilado**, meaning in a tomato and garlic sauce with mild chilli.

Invariably accompanying any Cuban meal are the ubiquitous **rice and beans** (black or kidney), which come in two main guises: **congrís**, where the rice and beans are served mixed (also known as *moros y cristianos*), and **arroz con frijoles**, where white rice is served with a separate bowl of beans, cooked into a delicious soupy stew, to pour over it. Other traditional accompaniments are **yuca con mojo** (cassava drenched in an oil and garlic sauce); fried **plantain**; mashed, boiled or fried **green bananas**, which have a buttery, almost nutty taste; **boniato**, a type of sweet potato; and a simple **salad** of tomatoes, cucumber, cabbage and avocado, the latter in season around August.

Lobster, **shrimp** and **fish** make it onto a lot of menus and are usually superbly fresh. As a rule of thumb, the simpler the dish the better it will be. Grilled or pan-fried fish is usually a safe bet, but a more complex dish like risotto will most often disappoint.

Fruit is generally eaten at breakfast and rarely appears on a lunch or dinner menu. The best places to buy some are the *agromercados*, where you can load up cheaply with whatever is in season. Particularly good are the various types of mangos, oranges and pineapples, while delicious lesser-known fruits include the prickly green soursop, with its unique sweet but tart taste, and the mamey – the thick, sweet red flesh of which is made into an excellent milkshake.

Street food

Street food is all the result of private enterprise. It's usually sold from front gardens, porches, windows, driveways and street trolleys, and these places are invariably the cheapest places to eat and an excellent choice for snacks and impromptu lunches, usually freshly made and very tasty. Dishes to look

out for include **corn fritters**, **pan con pasta** (bread with a garlic mayonnaise filling), and cheap **pizza** a good basic option though quality varies wildly. **Tamales** are prepared from cornmeal, peppers and onions, then wrapped in the outer leaves of the corn plant and steamed until soft. The somewhat bland taste is enlivened with a piquant red pepper sauce served on the side. It's wise to avoid home-made soft drinks, or at least ask if they have been prepared with boiled water (*agua hervida*) before sampling.

Meals

Breakfast in Cuba tends to be light, consisting of toast or, more commonly, bread eaten with fried, boiled or scrambled eggs. The better hotels do buffet breakfasts that cover cooked eggs and meats, cold meat and cheeses, and cereals; even if you're not a guest, these are a good option if you're hungry in the morning. It goes without saying you can expect to find *café con leche* – made with warm milk – on every breakfast table too.

Cubans tend to eat their main meal in the evening, usually a hearty dose of meat, rice, beans and *viandas*, but restaurant and paladar menus are pretty much the same at any time of the day.

Sweets and snacks

As you might expect from a sugar-producing country, there are several delicious **sweets** and **desserts** that you are more likely to find on a street stall than in a restaurant. Huge slabs of sponge cake coated in meringues are so popular at parties that the state actually supplies them free for children's birthdays up to the age of 15, to make sure no one goes without. Also good are **torticas**, small round shortcake biscuits; **cocos** or **coquitos**, immensely sweet confections of shredded coconut and brown sugar; and thick, jelly-like **guayaba** pasta, often eaten with cheese.

Convertible-peso stores and supermarkets stock **snack foods** of varying quality; in the better ones you can get decent Western potato chips, unimaginative cookies, olives, canned fish for sandwich fillers and some fruit, in addition to UHT long-life milk, breakfast cereals, sweets and chocolate. Most of these items are fairly expensive – you can run up a grocery bill of $10–15CUC for just a handful of simple ingredients, but after a few days of Cuban fare you may consider it a small price to pay.

Drink

If you like **rum** you'll be well off in Cuba: the national drink is available everywhere and is generally the most inexpensive tipple available – you can pick up a bottle for as little as $3CUC in supermarkets and hotels, while cocktails in bars only cost $2–4CUC. Havana Club reigns supreme as the best brand, but also look out for Santiago de Cuba, Caribbean Club and Siboney. White rum is the cheapest form, generally used in cocktails, while the darker, older rums are best appreciated neat. As well as the authorized stuff sold bottled in hotels and convertible-peso shops, there is also a particularly lethal bootleg white rum, usually just called street rum (*ron de la calle*), which is guaranteed to leave you with a fearful hangover and probably partial memory loss. Thick and lined with oily swirls, it is usually sold in most neighbourhoods in the bigger cities; *jineteros* will certainly know where to go, but don't let yourself be charged more than a couple of convertible pesos a litre if you're brave enough to try the stuff.

Apart from cigars and rum itself, Cuba's most famous export is probably its **cocktails**, including the ubiquitous **Cuba Libre** (see box below). Spirits other than rum are also available and are generally reasonably priced in all bars and restaurants, other than those in the prime tourist areas. The bottles on sale in many convertible-peso shops usually work out cheaper than in Europe.

Lager-type **beer** (*cerveza*) is plentiful in Cuba. The best known brands are Cristal, a smooth light lager, and Bucanero, a darker more potent variety. These are usually sold in cans and, less commonly, in bottles, for $2–2.50CUC. Beer on draught is less common in Cuba, although you can find it in some bars, all-inclusive resorts and national-peso establishments.

When drinking **water** in Cuba, it's a good idea to stick to the bottled kind, which is readily available from all convertible-peso shops and hotels – or follow the lead of prudent locals and boil any tap water you plan to drink (see p.43).

Canned **soft drinks**, called *refrescos*, are readily available from all convertible-peso shops, and in addition to Coke and Pepsi you can sample Cuba's own brands of lemonade (Cachito), cola (Tropicola, refreshingly less sugary than other cola drinks) and orangeade (the alarmingly Day-Glo Najita). Malta, a fizzy malt drink, is more of an acquired taste. Popularly sold on the street, *granizado* is a slush drink served in a paper twist and often sold from a push-cart; *guarapo* is a super-sweet frothy drink made from pressed sugar cane and mostly found at

---

CLASSIC CUBAN COCKTAILS

The origins of many **cocktails** are hotly disputed, from where they were first created to their proper original ingredients. There are, nevertheless, undoubtedly plenty of bona fide Cuban cocktails. The five Cuban classics listed here appear time and again on drinks menus throughout the country.

- **Cuba Libre** The simplest of Cuban cocktails, no more than white rum with cola and a twist of lime, is second only in popularity to the *mojito*. It was given its name ("Free Cuba") in 1902 after the country had broken free from Spanish colonial rule.

- **Daiquiri** There are countless variations on the daiquiri but the classic – as popularized by *La Floridita* and championed by Ernest Hemingway, who regularly visited that renowned bar in Old Havana – is made with white rum, Maraschino liqueur, sugar syrup, lime juice and crushed ice.

- **Mojito** The most famous Cuban cocktail, which came to prominence in *La Bodeguita del Medio* bar in Havana, is a refreshing combination of white rum, sugar, lime juice, soda water and mint.

- **Presidente** Gained fame during the years of American Prohibition in the 1920s and named in honour of Mario García Menocal, president of Cuba from 1912 to 1920. There are lots of recipes but the basic components are dark rum, curacao, white vermouth and a dash of grenadine.

- **Ron Collins** This is the Cuban version of the gin-based American Tom Collins, made here with white rum, sugar, lime, soda water and ice.

agromercados; while Prú is a refreshing speciality in eastern Cuba, fermented from sweet spices and a little like spiced ginger beer. If you are in a bar, fresh lemonade (*limonada natural*) is rarely advertised but almost always available for $1–2CUC.

Coffee, served most often as pre-sweetened espresso, is the beverage of choice for many Cubans and is served in all restaurants and bars and at numerous national peso coffee stands dotted around town centres. Cubans tend to add sugar into the pot when making it, so there is little chance of getting it unsweetened other than in hotels and tourist restaurants. Aromatic packets of Cuban ground coffee and beans are sold throughout the country, and it's well worth buying a few to take home.

Tea is less common but still available in the more expensive hotels and better restaurants – usually as an unsuccessful marriage of lukewarm water and a limp tea bag, or a very stewed brew.

Health

Providing you take common-sense precautions, visiting Cuba poses no particular health risks. In fact, some of the most impressive advances made by the revolutionary government since 1959 have been in the field of medicine and the free healthcare provided to all Cuban citizens. Despite all the investment, Cuba's health service has been hit hard by the US trade embargo, particularly in terms of the supply of medicines. It's essential to bring your own medical kit from home, including painkillers and any prescription drugs that you use, as availability is limited in Cuba.

No **vaccinations** are legally required to visit Cuba, unless you're arriving from a country where yellow fever and cholera are endemic, in which case you'll need a vaccination certificate. It is still advisable, however, to get inoculations for hepatitis A, cholera, tetanus and to a lesser extent rabies and typhoid. A booster dose of the hepatitis A vaccination within six to twelve months of the first dose will provide immunity for approximately ten years.

Bites and stings

Despite Cuba's colourful variety of fauna, there are no dangerously **venomous animals** on the island – the occasional scorpion is about as scary as it

gets, while the chances of contracting diseases from bites and stings are extremely slim. Cuba is not malarial and **mosquitoes** are relatively absent from towns and cities due to regular fumigation. They are, however, prevalent in many rural areas. Basic, common-sense **precautions** include covering your skin, not sitting out at dusk, closing windows at this time, and using DEET repellent.

There are occasional outbreaks of **dengue fever**, a viral infection spread by mosquitoes. It can occasionally be fatal, though usually only among the very young or old or those with compromised immunity; reported number of deaths in Cuba have been in single figures, and serious cases are rare. There's no vaccine, so prevention is the best policy. Avoid getting bitten by mosquitoes, and be aware that though more common after dusk, mosquitoes can strike throughout the day. **Symptoms** develop rapidly following infection and include extreme aches and pains in the bones and joints, severe headaches, dizziness, fever and vomiting. Should you experience any of the above symptoms, seek medical advice immediately – early detection and access to proper medical care eases symptoms and lowers fatality rates to below 1 percent.

More widespread wherever there is livestock, **ticks** lie in the grass waiting for passing victims and burrow into the skin of any mammal they can get hold of. Repellent is ineffective, so your best form of defence is to wear trousers tucked into socks. It is possible to remove ticks with tweezers, but make sure that the head, which can easily get left behind, is plucked out along with the body. Smearing them first with Vaseline or even strong alcohol leaves less of a margin for error. Minuscule **sand flies** can make their presence felt on beaches at dusk by inflicting bites that cause prolonged itchiness.

Cholera

A cholera outbreak in eastern Cuba in 2012 caused three fatalities, while another in Havana in early 2013 was the country's biggest outbreak in decades; dozens of people were infected, but none fatally so. As cholera appears in epidemics rather than isolated cases, you will probably hear about it should it be present when you visit. The disease is carried by contaminated water or food and is characterized by sudden attacks of diarrhoea with severe cramps and debilitation. Cholera can prove fatal if untreated, but foreign visitors are at a very low risk of contracting it.

Food and water

Due to the risk of parasites, drinking tap water is never a good idea in Cuba, even in the swankiest hotels. Whenever you are offered water, whether in a restaurant, paladar or private house, it's a good idea to check if it has been boiled – in most cases it will have been. **Bottled water** is available in convertible-peso shops and most tourist bars and restaurants.

Although reports of **food poisoning** are few and far between, there are good reasons for exercising caution when eating in Cuba. Food bought on the street is in the highest-risk category and you should be aware that there is no official regulatory system ensuring acceptable levels of hygiene. Self-regulation does seem to be enough in most cases, but you should still be cautious when buying pizzas, meat-based snacks or ice cream from street-sellers. Power cuts are common and there is no guarantee that defrosted food is not subsequently refrozen. National-peso restaurants can be equally suspect, particularly those in out-of-the-way places.

Sun exposure and heat issues

Cuba's humid tropical climate means you should take all the usual common-sense precautions: drink plenty of **water**, limit exposure to the **sun** (especially between 11am and 3pm) and don't use a sunscreen with a protection factor of less than 15, and if you're fair-skinned or burn easily, no lower than 25. You may find sunscreen difficult to find away from hotels and convertible-peso shops, so be sure to pack some before taking any trips into less-visited areas.

Hospitals, clinics and pharmacies

Don't assume that Cuba's world-famous **free health service** extends to foreign visitors – far from it. In fact, the government has used the advances made in medicine to earn extra revenue for the regime through a system of **health tourism**. Each year, thousands of foreigners come to Cuba for everything from surgery to relaxation at a network of anti-stress clinics, and these services don't come cheap. There are specific **hospitals** for foreign patients and a network of clinics, pharmacies and other health services targeted specifically at tourists, run by Servimed (w servimedcuba.com). The only general **hospital**

for foreigners, as compared to the smaller clinics found in around half-a-dozen cities and resorts across the island, is the Clínica Central Cira García in Havana (see p.140).

If you do wind up in hospital in Cuba, one of the first things you or someone you know should do is contact **Asistur** (T 7 866 4499, w asistur.cu), which usually deals with insurance claims on behalf of the hospital, as well as offering various kinds of assistance, from supplying ambulances and wheelchairs to obtaining and sending medical reports. However, for minor complaints you shouldn't have to go further than the **hotel doctor**, who will give you a consultation. If you're staying in a *casa particular* your best bet, if you feel ill, is to inform your hosts, who should be able to call the family doctor, the *médico de la familia*, and arrange a house-call. This is common practice in Cuba where, with one doctor for every 169 inhabitants, it's possible for them to personally visit all their patients.

There is no single **emergency number** for ringing an ambulance, but you can call 105 from most provinces and T 7 838 1185 or 838 2185 to get one in Havana. You can also try Asistur's emergency number (T 7 866 8339).

Pharmacies

There are two types of **pharmacy** in Cuba: national-peso places for the population at large; and **Servimed pharmacies** aimed primarily at tourists, charging in convertible pesos and usually located within a *clínica internacional*. Tourists are permitted to use the antiquated national-peso establishments but will rarely find anything of use besides aspirin, as they primarily deal in prescription-only drugs. The Servimed pharmacies only exist in some of the largest towns (as detailed throughout the guide), but even these don't have the range of medicines that you might expect.

MEDICAL RESOURCES

Canadian Society for International Health T 613 241 5785, w csih.org. Extensive list of travel health centres.

CDC T 1800 232 4636, w cdc.gov travel. Official US government travel health site.

International Society for Travel Medicine US T 1404 373 8282, w istm.org. Has a full list of travel health clinics.

Hospital for Tropical Diseases Travel Clinic UK w thehtd.org.

MASTA (Medical Advisory Service for Travellers Abroad) UK w masta.org for the nearest clinic.

Tropical Medical Bureau Ireland T 1850 487 674 w tmb.ie.

The Travel Doctor – TMVC T 1300 658 844, w tmvc.com.au. Lists travel clinics in Australia, New Zealand and South Africa.

Money

Cuba has two units of currency: the Cuban peso (CUP) and the Cuban convertible peso (CUC). While Cuban salaries are paid in CUP, the vast majority of foreign visitors use CUC, divided into centavos and, like the Cuban peso, completely worthless and unobtainable outside of Cuba.

The colour and images on **convertible peso banknotes** are distinct from those on regular pesos and the notes clearly feature the words *"pesos convertibles"*. The banknote **denominations** are 100, 50, 20, 10, 5, 3 and 1, while there are $1CUC, 50c, 25c, 10c and 5c coins. At the time of writing $1CUC was worth $24CUP, equivalent to £0.64, €0.76, Can$1.01 or US$1. The Cuban peso, which is also referred to as the **national peso** (*peso nacional* or *moneda nacional*), is divided into 100 centavos. Banknotes are issued in denominations of 50, 20, 10, 5, 3 and 1. The lowest-value coin is the virtually worthless 1c, followed by the 5c, 20c, 1-peso and 3-peso coins, the last adorned with the face of Che Guevara.

Hard currency is king in Cuba, and wherever you are it pays to always have at least some money in

cash. It's best to carry convertible pesos in **low denominations**, as many shops and restaurants simply won't have enough change. Be particularly wary of this at bus and train stations or you may find yourself unable to buy a ticket. If you do end up having to use a $50CUC or $100CUC note, you will usually be asked to show your passport for security. The slightest **tear** in any banknote means it is likely to be refused.

There is a 10 percent charge applied when exchanging US dollars in cash. **Scottish**, **Northern Irish** and Australian banknotes and coins cannot be exchanged in Cuba.

Credit cards, debit cards and ATMs

Visa and MasterCard **credit cards** and **debit cards** are more widely accepted than travellers' cheques for purchases. However, Maestro and Cirrus debit cards are not accepted at all, nor are any cards issued by a US bank or credit card company; American Express and Diners Club are generally unusable regardless of the country of issue. Although you'll generally be OK using cards in upmarket hotels, restaurants and touristy shops,

---

CONVERTIBLE OR NATIONAL PESOS?

Cuba's confusing dual-currency system has its own **vocabulary**, consisting of a collection of widely used terms and slang words (see p.491). The first thing to learn when trying to make sense of it all is that both national pesos and convertible pesos are represented with the dollar sign ($). Often common sense is the only indicator you have to determine which of the two currencies a price is given in when **written down**, but sometimes prices are specified as CUC, MN or CUP. Thus one national peso is sometimes written $1MN. In **spoken language**, the most common word for convertible pesos is simply CUCs (pronounced "kooks"). Other commonly used qualifiers are *divisas* for convertible pesos and *moneda nacional* for national pesos. However, many Cubans refer to either currency as pesos, in which case you may have to ask if they mean *pesos cubanos* or *pesos convertibles*.

The general rule for most visitors is to assume that everything will be paid for with convertible pesos. Ninety-nine percent of state-run hotels, many state-run restaurants, museums, most bars, nightclubs and music venues and the vast majority of products in shops are priced in **convertible pesos**, though you can use **euros** in one or two restaurants and other establishments. You'll be expected to use CUC to pay for a room in a *casa particular*, a meal in a paladar and most private taxi fares, though there is occasionally some flexibility.

Entrance to most cinemas and sports arenas, plus rides on local buses, street snacks and food from *agromercados* are all paid for with **national pesos**, while some shops away from the touristy areas stock products priced in national pesos too. There are also goods and services priced in **both currencies**. Usually this means the national peso charge applies only to Cubans, while non-Cubans pay the equivalent in convertible pesos, as is the case with tollgates on roads and museum entrance fees. However, in some instances tourists are merely advised rather than obliged to pay in convertible pesos, and by doing so occasionally enjoy some kind of benefit, such as being able to bypass a waiting list or queue. There are also services priced in national pesos which are the exclusive preserve of Cubans, such as Astro buses (see p.30) and some *casas particulares*.

when dealing with any kind of private enterprise, from paladars to puncture repairs, anything other than cash isn't worth a centavo. For most Cubans, plastic remains an unfamiliar alternative, and in most small- to medium-sized towns, cards are absolutely useless. Bear in mind also that power cuts are common in Cuba and sometimes render cards unusable.

The number of **ATMs** in Cuba is slowly increasing but there are still relatively few, and some of them only accept cards issued by Cuban banks. Among those that do accept foreign cards, very few take anything other than Visa, and again none accept cards issued by US banks. Most ATMs display stickers stating clearly the cards they accept. Those that take foreign cards are generally found in top-class hotels, branches of the Banco Financiero Internacional, the Banco de Crédito y Comercio and some CADECA *casas de cambio*.

As the CUC is not traded internationally, all transactions (including cash withdrawals) involving a foreign credit or debit card in Cuba will be converted into US dollars, for which a commission will be charged. At the current three percent rate, if you withdraw $100CUC from an ATM it will appear as US$103 on your transaction receipt. Some ATMs have a $200CUC withdrawal limit, including the commission charge, effectively making the limit $190CUC in most instances. There is no such limit if you withdraw cash through a bank teller, but the commission for this type of transaction is sometimes around one percent higher. Credit cards are more useful for obtaining **cash advances**, though be aware of the interest charges that these will incur. For most cash advances you'll need to deal with a bank clerk.

Travellers' cheques

Travellers' cheques are less convenient in Cuba than they are in many other countries. Although they are exchangeable for cash in many banks and bureaux de change (*cambios*), subject to a commission charge which ranges from three to six percent, a significant number of shops and restaurants refuse to accept them, and US-dollar travellers' cheques will be subject to an additional commission. Complicating matters further, most banks and *cambios* require a receipt as proof of purchase when cashing travellers' cheques. Also, make sure that your signature is identical to the one on the original cheque submitted: cashiers have been known to refuse to cash cheques with seemingly minor discrepancies.

Banks and exchange

Banking hours in Cuba are generally Monday to Friday 8am to 3pm, while a tiny minority of banks are open Saturday mornings. However, in touristy areas opening hours are sometimes longer for foreign currency transactions, referred to at banks as the "*servicio de caja especial*". Not all Cuban banks readily handle foreign currency transactions; those most accustomed to doing so are the Banco Financiero Internacional and the Banco de Crédito y Comercio, both with branches in all the major cities. Whether withdrawing money with a credit or debit card or cashing travellers' cheques, you'll need to show your passport for any transaction at a bank.

The government body CADECA runs the country's bureaux de change, known as **casas de cambio**, found in hotels, roadside kiosks and buildings that look more like banks. These establishments are where you should change convertible pesos into national pesos, though you can exchange foreign currency too and travellers' cheques, and use a Visa card or MasterCard to withdraw cash. They have more flexible opening hours than the banks – generally Monday to Saturday 8am to 6pm and Sunday 8am until noon. No commission is charged for buying national pesos.

Black market salesmen often hang around outside *casas de cambio* and may offer a favourable exchange rate or, sometimes more temptingly, the opportunity to buy pesos without having to queue. Although dealing with a black market salesman is unlikely to get you into any trouble, it could result in a prison sentence for the Cuban. You may also be approached by people on the street offering to exchange your money, sometimes at an exceptionally good rate. This is always a con.

Current exchange rates can be checked at Ⓦxe.com.

Financial difficulties

For any kind of money problems, most people are directed to **Asistur** (Ⓦasistur.cu), set up specifically to provide assistance to tourists with financial difficulties, as well as offering advice on legal and other matters. Asistur can arrange to have money sent to you from abroad as well as provide loans or cash advances. There are branches in a few of the big cities and resorts (see Directory in respective chapters).

Other than Asistur, the firm to contact if you have problems with your credit or debit cards is

FINCIMEX, which has offices in at least ten Cuban cities and can provide records of recent card transactions and shed light on problems such as a credit card being declined in a shop.

The media

All types of media in Cuba are tightly censored and closely controlled by the state. While this means that the range of information and opinion is severely restricted and biased, it has also produced media geared to producing (what the government deems to be) socially valuable content, refreshingly free of any significant concern for high ratings and commercial success.

Newspapers and magazines

There are very few **international newspapers** available in Cuba, and your only hope of finding any is to look in the upmarket hotels. Tracking down an English-language newspaper of any description, even in the hotels, is an arduous, usually unrewarding task and you're far better off looking online.

The main **national newspaper**, *Granma* (Ⓦ granma.cu), openly declares itself the official mouthpiece of the Cuban Communist Party. The stories in its eight tabloid-size pages are largely of a dry political or economic nature with some arts and sport coverage. Raúl Castro's speeches or Fidel Castro's musings are often published in their entirety and the international news has a marked Latin American bias. Articles challenging the official party line do appear, but these are usually directed at specific events and policies rather than overall ideologies. Hotels are more likely to stock the weekly *Granma Internacional*. Printed in Spanish, English, French, German, Italian, Turkish and Portuguese editions, it offers a roundup of the week's stories, albeit with a very pro-Cuban government spin. There are two other national papers: *Trabajadores* (Ⓦ trabajadores.cu), representing the workers' unions, and *Juventud Rebelde* (Ⓦ juventud rebelde.cu) founded in 1965 as the voice of Cuban youth. Content is similar, though *Juventud Rebelde*, in its Thursday edition, features weekly listings for cultural events and has more articles that regularly critique social issues.

Among the most cultured of Cuba's **magazines** is *Bohemia* (Ⓦ bohemia.cu), the country's oldest surviving periodical, founded in 1908, whose relatively broad focus offers a mix of current affairs, historical essays and regular spotlights on art, sport and technology. The best of the more specialized publications are the bimonthly *Revolución y Cultura* (Ⓦ www.ryc.cult.cu), concentrating on the arts and literature, and the tri-monthly *Artecubano*, a magazine of book-like proportions tracking the visual arts. There are a number of other worthy magazines, such as *La Gaceta de Cuba*, covering all forms of art, from music and painting to radio and television; *Temas* (Ⓦ temas.cult.cu), whose scope includes political theory and contemporary society; and *Clave*, which focuses on music.

Radio

There are nine national **radio** stations in Cuba, but tuning into them isn't always easy, as signal strength varies considerably from place to place. You're most likely to hear broadcasts from **Radio Taíno** (Ⓦ www.radiotaino.com.cu), the official tourist station, and the only one on which any English is spoken, albeit sporadically. Playing predominantly mainstream pop and Cuban music, Radio Taíno can also a useful source of up-to-date tourist information such as the latest nightspots, forthcoming events and places to eat. Its FM frequency changes depending on where you are in the country; in Havana, it's at 93.3FM.

Musically speaking, other than the ever-popular sounds of Cuban salsa, stations rarely stray away from safe-bet US, Latin and European pop and rock. The predominantly classical music content of Radio Musical Nacional is about as specialist as it gets; in Havana, it's at 99.1FM, but the frequency varies around the country.

Of the remaining stations there is little to distinguish one from the other. The exception is **Radio Reloj** (Ⓦ radioreloj.cu), broadcasting on 101.5FM, a 24-hour news station on air since 1947, with reports read out to the ceaseless sound of a ticking clock in the background, as the exact time is announced every minute on the minute; and **Radio Rebelde** (Ⓦ radiorebelde.cu), the station started in the Sierra Maestra by Che Guevara in 1958 to broadcast information about the rebel army's progress.

Television

There are five national **television channels** in Cuba: Cubavisión, Telerebelde, Canal Educativo, Canal Educativo 2 and Multivisión, all commercial-free but with a profusion of public service broadcasts, revolutionary slogans and daily slots commemorating historical events and figures. Surprisingly, given the sour relationship between Cuba and the US, **Hollywood films** are a TV staple, sometimes preceded by a discussion of the film's value and its central issues. The frequent use of Spanish subtitles as opposed to dubbing makes them watchable for non-Spanish speakers.

Cubavisión hosts a longstanding Cuban television tradition, the staggeringly popular **telenovela** soap operas, both homegrown and imported (usually from Brazil or Colombia). There are also several weekly music programmes showcasing the best of contemporary Cuban music as well as popular international artists. Saturday evenings are the best time to catch live-broadcast performances from the cream of the national salsa scene.

Telerebelde is the best channel for **sports**, with live national-league baseball games shown almost daily throughout the season, and basketball, volleyball and boxing making up the bulk of the rest. As the names suggest, both **Canal Educativo** channels are full of educational programmes, including courses in languages, cookery and various academic disciplines.

The newest channel, **Multivisión**, began broadcasting in 2008 with a schedule of predominantly foreign-made programmes, including films, Latin American soap operas, National Geographic documentaries and US cop shows and comedies. It has become enormously popular with Cubans.

Officially, **satellite TV** is the exclusive domain of the hotels, which come with a reasonable range of channels, though you won't find BBC or VOA. Cuba's international channel is Cubavisión Internacional, designed for tourists and showing a mixture of films, documentaries and music programmes.

Festivals

Cuba has some of the most highly regarded festivals in Latin America, and events like the Festival Internacional del Nuevo Cine Latinoamericano continue to grow in prestige and attract growing numbers of visitors. There are also plenty of lesser-known festivals celebrating Afro-Cuban dance, literature, ballet and other arts, and a whole host of smaller but worthwhile events in other provinces. Catching one of these can make all the difference to a visit to a less-than-dynamic town.

Cuba's main **carnival** takes place in Santiago de Cuba in July and is an altogether unmissable experience. As well as numerous parades featuring dramatically costumed carnival queens waving from floats, and more down-to-earth neighbourhood percussion bands, several stage areas are set up around the town where live salsa bands play nightly. Also worth checking out are the smaller carnivals held in Havana and other provincial towns, such as Guantánamo in late August, which feature parades and boisterous street parties as well. Below are listings for the main festivals and a selection of smaller events.

JANUARY

Liberation Day (Jan 1). This public holiday celebrates the first day of the triumph of the Cuban Revolution as much as the first day of the year, with street parties and free concerts throughout the country.

FEBRUARY

Feria Internacional del Libro de La Habana (Havana International Book Fair) Havana (mid/late Feb–early March;

FESTIVAL AND LISTINGS INFORMATION

It can still be frustratingly difficult to find accurate **information** on festivals, particularly away from the resort areas. The UNEAC website (ⓦwww.uneac.org.cu) is a useful resource, as are hotels, especially concerning events that they are hosting. To get information on events that have no dedicated website or email address, contact the local branches of Infotur in relevant towns and provinces.

Although the free monthly **listings magazine** *Cartelera* – only available, sporadically, in Havana from the larger hotels and branches of Infotur – carries information on a variety of Havanan goings-on, it is far from comprehensive and many local events, particularly those organized principally by and for Cubans, don't get a mention. The very best source of information is the excellent online magazine *Cuba Absolutely* (ⓦcubaabsolutely.com), with predominantly Havana listings. *Granma* newspaper has details of baseball games and is one of the only sources of television programming schedules, whilst *Juventud Rebelde* publishes cultural listings in its Thursday edition. Radio Taíno often broadcasts details of major shows and concerts as well as advertisements for the tourist in-spots. For less mainstream events the principal method of advertising is word of mouth, with posters and flyers rare.

 feriadellibro.cubaliteraria.cu). You'll find more books on Cuban politics and ideology at this citywide festival than you can shake a stick at, as well as new fiction and poetry, at the Fortaleza San Carlos de la Cabaña in Habana del Este (as well as at several bookshops across the capital). Events include discussions, poetry readings, children's events and concerts. Havana's Casa de las Américas also presents its literary prize during the festival period.

Festival del Habano (Cuban Cigar Festival) Havana and Pinar del Río (late Feb; festivaldelhabano.com). A commercialized festival promoting the Cuban cigar industry, but still a great event for any cigar enthusiast with visits to cigar factories and tobacco plantations, a trade fair and plenty of tastings.

MARCH

Festival Internacional de la Trova "Pepe Sánchez" Santiago de Cuba (usually March 19–24; cultstgo.cult.cu). Commemorating the life of the great nineteenth-century Santiaguero trova composer José "Pepe" Sánchez, this festival fills the town's streets, parks and most important music venues with the sounds of acoustic guitars and butter-smooth troubadours.

APRIL

Festival Internacional del Cine Pobre Gibara (mid-April; 7 838 3657, festivalcinepobre.com). Small coastal town Gibara hosts the annual International Low Budget Film Festival. As well as public screenings in the local cinema and on outside projectors, there's a competition for fiction and documentary films as well as an assortment of captivating exhibitions, recitals, seminars and concerts. See p.361.

International Urban Dance Festival: "Old Havana, City in Motion" Havana (mid-April; 7 860 4341, danzateatroretazos .cu). Rather than displays of breakdancing and body-popping, this festival, organized by the well-respected Retazos Dance Company, uses sites around Habana Vieja to show off contemporary dance choreography, with accompanying master classes, lectures, workshops and night-time jazz jams.

Bienal de La Habana (April–May; bienalhabana.cult.cu). This month-long biennale focuses on Cuban, Latin American, Caribbean, African and Middle Eastern artists. It takes place in dozens of galleries, museums and cultural centres all over the city, such as Pabellón Cuba and the Museo Nacional de Bellas Artes.

MAY

International Workers' Day (1 May). Known in Cuba simply by its date, Primero de Mayo is vigorously celebrated in this communist country. A crowd of around twenty thousand, waving banners and paper flags, march past dignitaries in front of the José Martí memorial in Havana, with similar parades taking place across the country, in a quintessentially Cuban celebration of national pride and workers' solidarity.

Romerías de Mayo San Isidoro de Holguín (May 2–8; www .romeriasdemayo.cult.cu). A yearly pilgrimage, Mass and three-day celebration of performing arts in this eastern city. See p.355.

Feria Internacional Cubadisco Havana (mid to late May; 7 832 8298, cubadisco.soycubano.com). A celebration of the local recording industry, in which Cuban musicians who have released albums in the preceding year compete for the title of best album. The finale is held at Salón Rosado de la Tropical Benny Moré.

JUNE

Festival Internacional "Boleros de Oro" Havana (late June; 7 832 0395, www.uneac.org.cu). The siren song of bolero, a musical genre born in Cuba in the nineteenth century, draws singers from all over Latin America for this week-long Havana festival organized by UNEAC. Concert venues usually include Teatro Mella and Teatro América in Havana as well as venues elsewhere in the country.

Camagüey Carnival Camagüey (mid June to late June). With over thirty outdoor stages and party areas set up throughout the city, and big stars like Adalberto Álvarez and his Orchestra in attendance, this is one of the worthier provincial carnivals. See p.339.

JULY

Fiesta del Caribe Santiago de Cuba (first week of July; 22 64 4793). Santiago's week-long celebration of Caribbean music and dance culture takes place at the beginning of July, with free concerts and dance displays in Parque Céspedes and throughout the city. See p.408.

Carnaval de Santiago de Cuba Santiago de Cuba (mid-July). Cuba's most exuberant carnival holds Santiago in its thrall for the last two weeks of July, with costumed parades and congas, salsa bands and late-night parties. Official dates are 18–27 but the week-long run-up is often just as lively. See p.397.

Carnaval de La Habana Havana (late July to early Aug). Usually lasting a week or so, the Havana carnival is a jubilant affair with many of the country's top bands playing to packed crowds throughout the city, and a weekend parade of floats working its way along the Malecón.

AUGUST

Simposio de Hip Hop Cubano Havana (late Aug). Superseding the former Festival de Rap, this five-day event, whose main venue is the Casa de Cultura de Plaza in Havana's Vedado district, has become a more studied affair with conferences, discussions and workshops but fortunately there are still live performances too, at venues around the city.

OCTOBER

Festival Internacional de Ballet de la Habana Havana (late Oct to early Nov; festivalballethabana.com). Held in even-numbered years and presided over by Alicia Alonso and the Cuban National Ballet. Recent highlights have included performances by visiting Cubans Carlos Acosta and José Manuel Carreño. Performances take place at the Gran Teatro and Teatro Mella.

Festival de Matamoros Son Santiago (mid to late Oct). This three-day festival, a tribute to the Santiago de Cuba nineteenth-century musician Miguel Matamoros, draws music stars from around the country for concerts, dance competitions, workshops and seminars. While the focus is on son, expect to see many other traditional styles of music, including salsa.

Havana International Theatre Festival Havana (Oct–Nov; ☎ 7 833 4581, ⓦ www.cubaescena.cult.cu). Excellent ten-day theatre festival showcasing classics and contemporary Cuban works as well as productions by theatre groups from Latin America, Europe and the US, with plenty of free street theatre in the city's open spaces as well.

NOVEMBER

Festival de la Habana de Música Contemporánea Havana (late Nov; ⓦ www.musicacontemporanea.cult.cu). A festival of classical and chamber music staged in venues around the city, such as the Casa de las Americas and the Convento de San Francisco de Asís.

Baila en Cuba – Encuentro Mundial de Bailadores y Academias de Baile de Casino y Salsa Havana (late Nov; ☎ 7 836 2124, ⓦ bailaencuba.com). A commercial event consisting of a week of concerts, workshops and classes showcasing and teaching Cuban dance styles. There's usually an impressive line-up of salsa bands too.

DECEMBER

Festival Internacional del Nuevo Cine Latinoamericano Havana (early Dec; ☎ 7 838 2841, ⓦ habanafilmfestival.com). One of Cuba's top events, this ten-day film festival combines the newest Cuban, Latin American and Western films with established classics, as well as providing a networking opportunity for leading independent directors and anyone else interested in film. Information, accreditation and programmes are available at the Hotel Nacional, from where the event is managed. It's well worth paying $40CUC accreditation, which gains you access to all screenings, seminars and talks and many after parties.

Havana International Jazz Festival Havana (mid-Dec; ☎ 7 862 4938). Organized by the Cuban Institute of Music and Cuban jazz legend Chucho Valdés, this is the powerhouse event in the local international jazz calendar. It consistently attracts an excellent line-up: Dizzy Gillespie, Charlie Haden and Max Roach have all played in the past, alongside Cuban luminaries such as Bobby Carcassés, Roberto Fonseca and of course Chucho Valdés himself. Venues across the city include Teatro Mella, Teatro Karl Marx, Teatro Amadeo Roldan, Teatro América and the Casa de la Cultura de Plaza.

Parrandas de Remedios Remedios, Villa Clara (Dec 24). An unusual and exuberant carnivalesque display of floats, fireworks and partying. See p.270.

Sports and outdoor activities

Cuba has an unusually high proportion of world-class sportsmen and women but its sporting facilities, for both participatory and spectator sports, lag some way behind the standards set by its athletes. Nevertheless, you can catch a game in the national baseball, basketball and soccer leagues for next to nothing, while Cuba is endowed with countless outstanding scuba-diving and fishing sites. Hiking and cycling are both popular outdoor activities for foreign visitors but access to either requires some advance planning.

Baseball

For some outsiders, the national **Cuban baseball league**, the Serie Nacional de Béisbol, isn't just one of the best leagues outside of the US to see world class players, but represents a nostalgic version of the game, harking back to a time when the sport elsewhere – particularly in the US – wasn't awash with money and spoiled by celebrity and commercialism. Every province has a team and every provincial capital a stadium, most of which were built in the 1960s or early 1970s, and are relatively intimate affairs, with the exception of Havana's 55,000 capacity Estadio Latinoamericano. Free of mascots, cheerleaders, obtrusive music blasted through PA systems and any form of commercial distraction, all the attention is instead on the game.

The national league adopted a new **season structure** in 2012. The first half of the season begins in November, as the sixteen teams play the first of their forty-five regular season games in an all against all contest. In March the top eight teams play a further forty-two games to qualify for

SPORTS LISTINGS AND INFORMATION

Finding out in advance about sporting events in Cuba is notoriously difficult. Most locals rely on word of mouth or are in-the-know fans, but for the foreign visitor there are very few publications carrying any useful **information**. The daily newspapers *Granma* and *Juventud Rebelde* usually have a page dedicated to sport, and you can sometimes garner information on forthcoming events from these. However, your best bet is to go **online**, even though Cuban sports websites are frequently out of service. The web-based sports publication *Jit* (ⓦ jit.cu) is the official mouthpiece of INDER (National Institute of Sport, Physical Education and Recreation), which has its own website (ⓦ inder.cu), and covers all Cuban plus some international sports.

play-offs, semifinals and finals in May. Traditionally, games start around 8pm during the week, but recently start times have been at 1.30pm for most games, both throughout the week and at weekends. Some stadiums now have special seating areas and higher admission costs (usually around $3CUC) for non-Cubans.

Dominant **teams** over the last decade have included Ciego de Avila, Industriales of Havana, Villa Clara and Santiago de Cuba. By far the best resource for anything relating to Cuban baseball, including season schedules and tournament information, is the website Ⓦ baseballdecuba.com.

Other spectator sports

The national **basketball** league, the Liga Superior de Baloncesto, generates some exciting clashes, even though most of the arenas are on the small side. There are only eight teams in the league, with Ciego de Avila the dominant force over the last decade. The basketball season usually takes place between November and January.

There is a national **football** (soccer) league as well, with its season running from October to February, followed by play-offs and finals in March. Pinar del Río, Villa Clara and Cienfuegos have been the most consistently strong teams over the last three decades. There are very few custom-built football stadiums, with many games taking place in baseball stadiums or on scrappy pitches with very little enclosure. Check the Ⓦ futbol-cubano.blogspot.com blog for league standings and the latest stories in Cuban football.

Scuba diving

Cuba is a **scuba-diving** paradise. Most of the major beach resorts, including Varadero (see p.206), Cayo Coco (see p.325), Santa Lucía (see p.341) and Guardalavaca (see p.362), have at least one **dive centre**, with numerous others all over the island, including several in Havana (see p.139). The most reliable dive sites are generally off the south coast where the waters tend to be clearer, away from the churning waves of the Atlantic Ocean, which affect visibility off Cuba's northern shores. For the **top dive spots** head for María La Gorda (see p.183) in southwestern Pinar del Río, Punta Francés (see p.441) on the southwestern tip of the Isla de la Juventud, and the Jardines de la Reina (see p.328) off the southern coastlines of Ciego de Avila. All three have been declared National Marine Parks by the Cuban government and as a result are protected from man-made abuses, particularly commercial fishing.

Diving in Cuba is worthwhile in any season, but during the hurricane season (June to November) and particularly in September and October, there is a higher chance that the weather will interfere and affect visibility. Among the **marine life** you can expect to see in Cuban waters are nurse sharks, parrotfish, turtles, stingrays, barracuda, tarpon, moray eels, bonefish, snapper and tuna. The best time to see whale sharks, arguably the highlight of any diving trip to the island, is in November, while in the spring the fish are in greater abundance. On the other hand, from late April to late May there is an increased chance of swimming into what Cubans call el caribé, invisible jellyfish with a severe sting, found predominantly off the southern coast of the island. To counter this you can either wear a full wetsuit or simply make sure you dive off the northern coastline at this time of year.

The principal **dive operator** in Cuba is Marlin (Ⓦ nauticamarlin.com), which runs most of the dive centres and many of the marinas. The only other significant players are Gaviota (Ⓦ gaviota-grupo .com), Cubanacán (Ⓦ cubanacan.cu) and Cubamar Viajes (Ⓦ cubamarviajes.cu). Most dive centres are ACUC certified, but a few are SSI or SNSI certified, and all offer courses accredited to one or more of these diving associations. There are countless opportunities for all levels of diving, from absolute beginners to hardened professionals, but the best place to start is in a hotel-based diving resort, where you can take your first lesson in the safety of a swimming pool. Typically, a beginners' course involving some theory, a pool lesson and an open-water dive costs $60–80CUC, while a week-long ACUC course costs in the region of $375CUC. For one single-tank dive expect to pay $30–40CUC.

Fishing

Cuba is now firmly established as one of the best **fishing** destinations in the Caribbean, if not the world. Largely free from the voracious appetite of the huge US fishing market and discovered only relatively recently by the rest of the world, Cuba's lakes, reservoirs and coastal areas offer all kinds of outstanding fishing opportunities.

Inland, bass are particularly abundant, especially at Embalse Hanabanilla (see p.274) in Villa Clara, Embalse Zaza in Sancti Spíritus and the several artificial lakes in Camagüey province, which afford them provide the best locations for **freshwater fishing**. The top Cuban destination for **fly-fishing** lies south of the Ciego de Avila and Camagüey coastlines at the Jardines de la Reina archipelago. This group of some 250 uninhabited cays, stretching for 200km at a distance fluctuating between 50km and 80km from the mainland, is regarded by some experts as offering the finest light-tackle fishing in the world. With commercial fishing illegal here since 1996, other than around the outer extremities, there are virtually untapped sources of bonefish and tarpon as well as an abundance of groupers and snappers. To get a look-in at the Jardines de la Reina archipelago, you will most likely have to go through one of the specialist foreign operators (see p.328) which have attained exclusive rights to regulate and organize the fishing here, in conjunction with the Cuban authorities. Fly-fishing is also excellent at the Peninsula de Zapata (see p.224). There are numerous other opportunities for saltwater fishing around Cuba, with **deep-sea fishing** popular off the northern coastlines of Havana (see p.139), Varadero (see p.200) and Ciego de Avila (see p.325), where blue marlin, sail fish, white marlin, barracuda and tuna are among the most dramatic potential catches.

There is no bad time for fishing in Cuban waters, but for the biggest blue marlin, July, August and September are the most rewarding months, while April, May and June attract greater numbers of white marlin and sail fish. The best bass catches usually occur during the winter months, when the average water temperature drops to 22°C.

Other than the considerable number of foreign tour operators who now offer specialist fishing trips to Cuba, hotels and marinas are the main points of contact for fishing in Cuba. Before you start, you will need a **fishing licence**, which costs $20CUC. Prices for ad-hoc freshwater fishing start at around $30CUC for four hours, while a four-hour off-shore fishing session for four fishermen typically costs between $250CUC and $300CUC.

Equipment for fishing, particularly fly-fishing, is low on the ground in Cuba, and what does exist is almost exclusively the property of the tour operators. Buying anything connected to fishing is all but impossible, so it makes sense to bring as much of your own equipment as you can.

Golf

Its associations with the pre-1959 ruling classes made **golf** something of a frowned-upon sport in Cuba once Fidel Castro took power. The advent of mass tourism, however, has brought it back, and though currently there are only two courses on the island there are plans for more. The biggest, best-equipped and most expensive is the eighteen-hole course run by the Varadero Golf Club (see p.204),

established in 1998. Less taxing are the nine holes of the Club de Golf Habana (see p.139), just outside the capital, the only course in the country that survived the Revolution.

Hiking

All three of Cuba's mountain ranges feature resorts geared toward hikers, from where **hiking routes** offer a wonderful way to enjoy some of the most breathtaking of Cuban landscapes. Designated hikes tend to be quite short – rarely more than 5km – and trails are often unmarked and difficult to follow without a guide. Furthermore, orienteering maps are all but nonexistent. This may be all part of the appeal for some, but it is generally recommended that you hire a **guide**, especially in adverse weather conditions. In the Cordillerra de Guaniguanico in Pinar del Río and Artemisa the place to head for is **Las Terrazas** (see p.157), where there is a series of gentle hikes organized mostly for groups. The **Topes de Collantes resort** (see p.297) in the Escambray Mountains offers a similar programme, while serious hikers should head for the **Gran Parque Nacional Sierra Maestra** (see p.420), host to the tallest peak in Cuba, Pico Turquino. To get the most out of hiking opportunities at these resorts you should make bookings in advance or, in the case of the Sierra Maestra, turn up early enough to be allocated a guide, as independent hiking is severely restricted.

Culture and etiquette

There are a few cultural idiosyncrasies in Cuba worth bearing in mind. Cubans tend to be fairly conventional in their appearance, and view some Western fashions, especially traveller garb, with circumspection, mainly because Cubans in similar dress (and there are a number around, particularly in Havana) are seen as anti-establishment. Anyone with piercings, dreadlocks or tattoos may find themselves checked rigorously at customs and occasionally asked to show their passport to the police.

Many **shops** restrict entrance to a few people at a time, and although as a tourist you may bypass the queue, you'll win more friends if you ask "¿el último?" (who's last?) and take your turn.

BATHROOM BREAK

Public toilets are few and far between in Cuba, and even fast-food joints often don't have a washroom. You're more likely to find bathrooms in hotels and petrol stations, but don't expect toilet paper to be supplied – carry your own. Train and bus stations usually have toilets, but conditions are often appalling. Cuban plumbing systems, be they in a *casa particular* or hotel, cannot cope with waste paper, so to avoid blockages remember to dispose of your paper in the bins provided.

Service charges of 10–12 percent are becoming increasingly common in state restaurants and in smarter paladars, most notably in Havana. In state restaurants where it is not included you should **tip** at your discretion; in paladars tips aren't expected but always welcome. There's no need to tip when you've negotiated a fare for a taxi, but you should normally tip when you use a state-run taxi.

Gay and lesbian travellers

Homosexuality is legal in Cuba and the age of consent is 16, though same-sex marriage remains illegal. Despite a very poor overall record on gay rights since the Revolution, there has been marked progress in the social standing and acceptance of gay men and women in Cuba since the early 1990s. That said, police harassment of gay men and particularly of transvestites is still quite common. Despite this, there are now significant numbers of openly gay men in Cuba, though gay women are far less visible. There is still a strong stigma attached to same-sex hand-holding or similar displays of sexuality, but freedom of expression for gay people is greater now than at any point since 1959. There are no official gay clubs and bars as such in Cuba but there are a few gay-friendly venues, particularly in Havana and Santa Clara.

Mariela Castro, the daughter of President Raúl, has emerged as a champion for gay rights in Cuba in recent years. As director of Cenesex, the National Centre for Sex Education, she has been instrumental in a number of initiatives designed to increase tolerance and awareness of gay issues. In 2007 Cenesex was behind the country's first official recognition and celebration of the International Day Against Homophobia.

There is no **pink press** in Cuba. The only magazine in which gay issues are regularly discussed is the rather academic *Sexología y Sociedad*, the quarterly magazine published by Cenesex.

Shopping

Though the range of consumer products available in Cuba's shops is slowly expanding, quality and choice are still generally poor – cigars, rum, music and arts and crafts remain the really worthwhile purchases here. The late 1990s saw the first modern shopping malls emerge, predominantly in Havana, but outside of these and a few of the grandest hotels, shopping comes with none of the convenience and choice you're probably used to. Almost all shops actually carrying any stock now operate in convertible pesos, but a pocketful of national pesos allows you the slim chance of picking up a bargain.

National-peso shops are often poorly lit and badly maintained, and some understandably won't allow foreign customers, giving priority to the national-peso-earning public. Though they are often half-empty, it's still possible to unearth the odd antique camera or long-since-deleted record, while others specialize in secondhand clothes. The most worthwhile are the **casas comisionistas,** the Cuban equivalent of a pawnbroker. These can be delightful places to poke around, frequently selling vintage and sometimes antique items, from furniture to pocket watches and transistor radios.

Cigars

With the price of the world's finest tobacco at half what you would pay for it outside Cuba, it's crazy not to consider buying some *habanos* (the term for **Cuban cigars**) while on the island. The national chain of **La Casa del Habano** stores accounts for most of the cigars sold in Cuba, with around ten outlets in Havana and lots more around the country, often in classy hotels; cigars are also sold in airports, gift shops and a lot of the less classy hotels, too. The industry standard is for cigars to be sold in boxes of 25, though you can find them in boxes of ten or fifteen, and miniatures in small tins too.

There are currently around thirty different **brands** of Cuban cigars. The biggest names and generally the most coveted: expect to pay upwards of $75CUC for a box of Cohiba, Montecristo, Partagás, Romeo y Julieta, H. Upmann and Hoyo de Monterrey cigars – and for the top dogs or rarest smokes, like Cohiba Esplendidos or Montecristo A, don't expect much change from $500CUC. Like

---

SHOP SECURITY MEASURES

In any convertible-peso shop where the locals outnumber the tourists you should be prepared for some idiosyncratic **security measures**, as hilarious as they are infuriating. Don't be surprised to be asked to wait at the door until another customer leaves, and don't expect to be able to enter carrying any kind of bag – you'll have to leave it at a *guardabolso*, with some identification, to be collected afterwards. These *guardabolsos* are similar to left-luggage offices and are usually located at the entrance to the building, but sometimes you'll have to search them out. If you purchase anything, make sure you pick up your receipt at the cash till, as your shopping will be checked against it at the exit. It's also possible that your carrier bag will be sealed with tape at the till only to be ripped open when you get to the door so that the contents can be checked – ripping it open yourself will leave not only your bag but the whole precious system in tatters. Bear in mind that there are **no refunds or exchanges** on any goods purchased anywhere.

---

most *habanos* brands, these are all hand-made, but if you're buying cigars as souvenirs or for a novelty smoke, you'd do just as well with one of the less expensive, machine-made brands. The most widely available are Guantanameras – though connoisseurs wouldn't touch them with a bargepole, at between $20CUC and $30CUC a box you can at least make a purchase without having to ring your bank manager. First-time smokers should start with a mild cigar and take it from there; it makes sense to try a machine-made brand given the lower cost, but of the hand-made brands Hoyo de Monterrey are relatively light.

If you leave Cuba with more than **fifty cigars**, you're theoretically required to make a customs declaration; and must also be able to show receipts for your purchases. Sometimes you may be asked to show receipts even for fewer than fifty cigars; if you can't, you risk having them confiscated. Although most travellers are not checked when leaving, you're obviously more at risk of having cigars confiscated if you've bought them on the black market (see box, p.54).

Rum

Along with cigars, **rum** is one of the longest-established Cuban exports and comes with a worldwide reputation. Although there are a few specialist rum shops around the island, you can pick up most of the recognized brands in any large supermarket without fear of paying over the odds. Rum is available in several different strengths, according to how long it was distilled; the most renowned name is Havana Club, whose least expensive type is the light but smooth Añejo Blanco, which will set you back $3–5CUC. The other, darker types increase in strength and quality in the following order: Añejo 3 Años,

Añejo Especial, Añejo Reserva, Añejo 7 Años, Cuban Barrel Proof and the potent Máximo Extra Añejo. Other brands to look out for include Caney, Mulata and a number of regional rums like Guayabita del Pinar, from Pinar del Río, and the excellent Santiago de Cuba. The maximum number of bottles permitted by Cuban customs is six.

Coffee

First introduced to the island by French plantation owners fleeing the 1798 Haitian revolution, **coffee** is one of Cuba's lesser-known traditional products. It's easy to find and excellent quality, mostly grown and cultivated without the use of chemicals in the rich soils and under the forest canopies of the three principal mountain ranges. Supermarkets are as good as anywhere to find it, but there are a few specialist shops in Havana and elsewhere. The top name is Cubita, but there are plenty of others like Turquino, from the east of the country, Serrano, and even a couple produced under cigar brand names Montecristo and Cohiba.

Books and music

The Cuban publishing industry is still recovering from the shortages of the Special Period (see p.464), and **bookshops** here are generally disappointing, with a very narrow range of titles. Stock is often characterized by nationalist and regime-propping **political texts**, from the prolific works of the nineteenth-century independence-fighter José Martí to the speeches of Fidel Castro, and other titles unwavering in their support of the Revolution. Perhaps more universally appealing are the **coffee-table photography books** covering all aspects of

BLACK MARKET CIGARS

The biggest business on the black market is selling **cigars** to foreign visitors, with the average price of a box representing at least as much as the average monthly wage. If you spend any time at all in a Cuban town or city you will inevitably be offered a box of cigars on the street. You can find boxes for as little as $10CUC, but no self-respecting salesman is likely to sell the genuine article at that price and they will almost certainly be fakes. Realistically, you should expect to pay between $20CUC and $40CUC, depending on the brand and type, for the real thing. Ideally you should ask someone you know, even just the owner of a *casa particular*; even if they don't have a direct contact, chances are they will be able to help you out – everyone knows someone who can get hold of a box of Cohibas or Monte Cristos.

SPOTTING FAKES

What makes a Cuban cigar a **fake** and what makes it **genuine** can be fairly academic, especially for smoking novices, and some fakes are so well made that it's difficult to tell the difference even once they're lit. If your cigars pass the following checks you'll know that you at least have some well-made copies.

- Genuine boxes should be sealed with three labels: a banknote-style label at the front, a smaller one reading *Habanos* in the corner and a holographic sticker.
- The bottom of the box should be stamped: *Habanos SA*, *Hecho en Cuba* and *Totalmente a mano*.
- A factory code and date should be ink-stamped on the base of the box.
- All the cigars in a box should be the same colour, shade and strength of smell.
- When the cigar is rolled between the fingers, no loose tobacco should drop out.
- There should only be extremely slight variations in the length of cigars, no more than a few millimetres.

life in one of the most photogenic countries in the world. There are both CUC and national-peso bookshops; the latter often stock academic texts as well as Cuban fiction, and are a good bet for back issues of Cuban magazines at bargain prices.

English-language books are few and far between, but two or three bookshops in Havana and at least one in Varadero and Santiago de Cuba have a handful of foreign-language titles, usually crime novels and pulp fiction.

Some of the most comprehensive catalogues of **CDs** are found in Artex stores, the chain responsible for promoting culture-based Cuban products. Most provincial capitals now have a branch, and there are several in Havana. Look out also for Egrem stores, run by one of the country's most prolific record labels and sometimes stocking titles hard to find elsewhere.

Arts and crafts

One of the most rewarding Cuban shopping experiences is a browse around the arts and crafts – or **artesanía** – markets. Cuba has its own selection of tacky tailored-to-tourism items, but if you want something a bit more highbrow there are plenty of alternatives, like expressive African-style wood carvings, a wide choice of jewellery, handmade

shoes and everything from ceramics to textiles. **Haggling** is par for the course and often pays dividends, but shopping around won't reveal any significant differences in price or product.

Look out also for the **BfC logo**, a seal of above-average quality and the trademark of the Fondos Cubanos de Bienes Culturales, shops selling the work of officially recognized local artisans. Artex shops also make a good port of call for crafts, though they tend to have more mass-produced items.

Antiques and vintage memorabilia

In recent years, with the expansion of private enterprise, Cuba's immensely rich bounty of **antique** and **vintage** furniture and memorabilia has come onto the open market. Though still quite hard to track down, the rewards for doing so are some extraordinary collections of books, maps, ceramics, glassware and jewellery, as well as Art Deco furniture and all sorts of 1950s memorabilia, from postcards and magazines to cabaret coasters, glasses and swizzle sticks. Look out also for 1970s revolutionary posters and collectable 1990s Cuban baseball cards. You'll find the richest vintage pickings in Havana (see p.135) and Trinidad (see p.291).

Travelling with children

Beach and placid waters aside, Cuba is not a country with an ample stock of entertainment for children. But what the country lacks in amenities, it makes up for in enthusiasm. By and large Cubans love children and welcome them everywhere, and having a kid or two in tow is often a passport to seeing a hidden side of Cuban social life. Practically speaking you'll be able to find things like nappies in the department stores of bigger towns and some of the hotel shops, though the quality might not be what you're used to. Baby wipes and nappy bags are less common so it's wise to bring your own. To get hold of baby food you may need to visit the larger supermarkets. The only milk widely available is UHT.

Make sure your **first-aid kit** has child-strength fever reducers, diarrhoea medicine, cold remedies, plasters and other medicines. These are available throughout the country but not always readily so and tend to be more expensive than at home. Plenty of child-friendly **sunscreen** is essential; the Caribbean sun is very hot, particularly during the rainy season (May–Oct). Remember also to bring lots of loose cotton clothing, plus a few long-sleeved tops and trousers to combat the brutal air conditioning in restaurants and buses. It's also a good idea to pack a raincoat and appropriate footwear, as sudden downpours are common even outside the rainy season. Bear in mind that with limited **laundry facilities** you may be hand-washing many garments, so take items that are easy to launder and dry.

Public **toilets** are scarce in Cuba (see p.52), and there are few places with dedicated **baby-changing facilities**.

In terms of **accommodation**, children under 12 can stay for half price in many hotel rooms and if no extra bed is required they may stay for free. Staying in a *casa particular* is a great way to give children a taste of Cuba beyond the tourist belt. Rooms often have extra beds for children and many households have pets and courtyards where children can play.

Eating out, children are made very welcome pretty much everywhere. Children's menus are on the rise but generally still scarce. Places with high chairs are similarly rare – most children sit on their parents' laps. Discreet breastfeeding in public is fine.

When travelling around Cuba with children, it's important to remember you'll often be dealing with long queues and sporadic schedules. Long bus journeys can be particularly exhausting and uncomfortable. If you plan on renting a car, bring your own **child or baby seat**, as rental companies never supply them and there are none in Cuba. Newer cars are fitted with three-point seat belts in the front and seat belts in the back.

Travel essentials

Costs

In general, Cuba is not a particularly cheap place to visit. An **average weekly budget** for two independent travellers sharing a room, who eat out and go out at night regularly, stay in cheap hotels or Cuban homes and move around the country using buses and trains, works out at around $425CUC – equivalent to £272, Can$429, US$425 or €323 at 2013 exchange rates. However, with some considerable effort and a willingness to sacrifice some quality and comfort, it is possible to get by on much less. The key to living on a **shoestring budget** is to stick as much as possible to national-peso goods and services, though often you'll be obliged to pay in convertible pesos (see p.44).

Given the prevalence of fresh-food markets, street vendors and house-front caterers, all of which accept national pesos, the biggest savings can be made when buying **food and drink**. Stick to the above and you can survive on just $40–50CUP per day, equivalent to less than $3CUC. In the more likely event that you eat in restaurants, paladars or *casas particulares*, $20–40CUC should cover breakfast, lunch and dinner.

You'll have to pay for **accommodation** in convertible pesos, since national-peso hotels are for Cubans only; *casas particulares* can be let to national-peso-paying Cubans or convertible-peso-paying foreigners, but not to both. You're unlikely to find a hotel room for less than $25CUC, though some of the older, more basic hotels that cater to Cubans as much as foreign visitors offer lower rates. Rooms in *casas particulares*, which are always doubles, generally cost between $20CUC and $35CUC, though for long stays in some places outside the capital, you may be able to negotiate a nightly price below $20CUC.

The cost of **public transport** is most flexible within the towns and cities, where local buses cost next to nothing, but most foreign visitors use taxis or tourist buses. When travelling long distances non-Cubans are, on the whole, obliged to use convertible-peso services, whether on buses, trains or planes. If you travel by Víazul bus, expect to pay between $10CUC and $50CUC for most journeys (for example, Havana to Varadero is $10CUC, Havana to Trinidad $25CUC and Havana to Santiago de Cuba $51CUC). Long-distance private taxis can sometimes work out cheaper than buses if you share them with three or four other hard-currency-paying travellers, with a 100km trip costing as little as $5–10CUC each (see p.31).

Though **museum entrance** costs are generally low, often only $1–2CUC, most places charge a larger sum, commonly between $2–5CUC, for the right to take photos, and as much as $25CUC to enter with a video camera.

Crime and personal safety

Crimes against visitors are on the rise in many Cuban cities, particularly Havana (including some violent crime), so it pays to be careful. That said, gun crime is virtually unheard of and murder rates are estimated to be way below those of most Latin American countries, though official crime statistics are kept under wraps by the Cuban government. In the vast majority of cases, the worst you're likely to experience is incessant attention from *jineteros*, but a few simple **precautions** will help ensure that you don't fall prey to any petty crime. While there's no need to be suspicious of everyone who tries to strike up a conversation with you (and many people will), a measure of caution is still advisable. You should always carry a photocopy of your **passport** (or the passport itself), as the police sometimes ask to inspect them.

The most common assault upon tourists is **bag-snatching** or **pickpocketing** (particularly in Habana Vieja), so always make sure you sling bags across your body rather than letting them dangle from one shoulder, keep cameras concealed whenever possible, don't carry valuables in easy-to-reach pockets and always carry only the minimum amount of cash. A common trick is for thieves on

bicycles to ride past and snatch at bags, hats and sunglasses, so wear these at your discretion. Needless to say, don't leave bags and possessions unattended anywhere, but be especially vigilant on beaches, where theft is common.

Other than this, watch out for **scams** from street operators. Never accept the offer of money-changers on the street, as some will take your money and run – literally – or try to confuse you by mixing up national pesos with convertible pesos, or palm you off with counterfeit notes. Exercise extra caution when using unofficial taxis, particularly when riding in a cab where "a friend" is accompanying the driver. Although you're unlikely to suffer a violent attack, you may well find yourself pickpocketed. This is a particularly common trick on arrival at the airport, where you should be especially vigilant. Even if you are on a tight budget, it's well worth getting a tourist taxi into the centre when you're loaded with all your valuables and possessions.

Some **hotels** are not entirely secure, so be sure to put any valuables in the hotel security box, if there is one, or at least stash them out of sight. Registered *casas particulares* are, as a rule, safe, but you stay in an unregistered one at your peril.

At airports, thefts from luggage during baggage handling both on arrival and departure are a significant possibility, so consider carrying valuables in your hand luggage, using suitcase locks and having bags shrink-wrapped before check-in.

Car crime

Though car theft is rare, **rental-car break-ins** are much more common. Take all the usual sensible **precautions**: leave nothing visible in your car – including items you may consider worthless like maps, snacks or CDs – even if you're only away from it for a short period of time. Furthermore, thieves are not just interested in your personal possessions but will break into and damage cars to take the radios, break off wing mirrors, wrench off spare parts and even take the wheels. To avoid this, always park your vehicle in a car park, guarded compound or other secure place (see box, p.34). Car rental agencies will be able to advise you on those nearest to you, or, failing that, ask at a large hotel. *Casa particular* owners will also be able to tell you where to park safely. If the worst happens and you suffer a **break-in**, call the rental company first, which should have supplied you with an emergency number. They can advise you how to proceed from there and will either inform the police themselves or direct you to the correct

---

POLICE

The **emergency number** for the Cuban police differs from place to place, though ☎ 106 has now become standardized in most provinces; see Directory listings throughout the guide.

JINETERISMO AND THE ESCORT INDUSTRY

As a general definition, the pejorative term **jinetero** refers to a male hustler, or someone who will find girls, cigars, taxis or accommodation for a visitor and then take a cut for the service. He – though more commonly this is the preserve of his female counterpart, a **jinetera** – is often also the sexual partner to a foreigner, usually for material gain.

Immediately after assuming power, Castro's regime banned prostitution and, officially at least, wiped it off the streets, with prostitutes and pimps rehabilitated into society. The resurgence of the tourist industry has seen prostitution slink back into business since the mid-1990s; however, in Cuba this entails a rather hazily defined exchange of services.

In the eyes of Cubans, being a *jinetero* or *jinetera* can mean anything from prostitute to paid escort, opportunist to simply a Cuban boyfriend or girlfriend.

As an obvious foreign face in Havana, you will often be pursued by persistent *jineteros* and *jineteras*. Many Cubans are desperate to leave the country and see **marrying a foreigner** as the best way out, while others simply want to live the good life and are more than happy to spend a few days or hours pampering the egos of middle-aged Westerners in order to go to the best clubs and restaurants and be bought the latest fashions.

Police sometimes stop tourists' cars and question Cuban passengers they suspect to be *jineteros* or *jineteras*, and *casas particulares* must register all Cuban guests accompanying foreigners (foreigners themselves are not penalized in any way).

police station. You must report the crime to be able to get a replacement car and for your own insurance purposes.

Women travellers

Though violent sexual attacks against female tourists are virtually unheard of, women travellers in Cuba should brace themselves for a quite remarkable level of attention. Casual sex is a staple of Cuban life and **unaccompanied women** are often assumed to be on holiday for exactly that reason. The nonstop attention can be unnerving, but in general, Cuban men manage to combine a courtly romanticism with wit and charm, meaning the persistent come-ons will probably leave you irritated rather than threatened. If you're not interested, there's no sure-fire way to stop the flow of comments and approaches, but decisively saying "no", not wearing skimpy clothing and avoiding eye contact with men you don't know will lessen the flow of attention a little. Even a few hours of friendship with a Cuban man can lead to pledges of eternal love but bear in mind that **marriage to a foreigner** is a tried-and-tested method of emigrating. Aside from this, women travelling in Cuba are treated with a great deal of courtesy and respect. The country is remarkably safe and you are able to move around freely, particularly at night, with more ease than in many Western cities, and you should encounter few problems.

Emergencies

Should you be unfortunate enough to be robbed and want to make an insurance claim, you must report the crime to the **police** and get a **statement**. Be aware, though, that the police in Cuba can be surprisingly uncooperative and sometimes indifferent to non-violent crime – they may even try to blame you for not being more vigilant. You must insist upon getting the statement there and then, as there is little chance of receiving anything from them at a later date. Unfortunately, the chance of your possessions being recovered is equally remote.

Following any kind of emergency, whether medical, financial or legal, you should, at some point, contact **Asistur** (☎7 866 4499, in emergencies call 24hr ☎866 8527, ⊕asistur.cu), the tourist-assistance agency. It has branches in most provincial capitals and can arrange replacement travel documents, help with insurance issues and recover lost luggage as well as provide a host of other services. In the case of a serious emergency, you should also notify your foreign consul (see p.58). US travellers should contact the US Interests Section in Havana (☎7 833 3551; see p.58).

Electricity

The **electricity supply** is generally 110V 60Hz, but always check, as in some hotels it is 220V, and in a significant number of *casas particulares* there is both. Plug adaptors and voltage converters are almost impossible to buy in Cuba, so if you intend to use electrical items from the UK or the rest of Europe, Australia or New Zealand, then you should, as a minimum, bring a plug adaptor and maybe voltage converter too.

Entry requirements

To enter Cuba, citizens of most Western countries must have a ten-year **passport**, valid for two months after your departure from Cuba, and an onward or return plane ticket. You'll also need a **tourist card** (*tarjeta del turista*), essentially a **visa**, which are valid for a standard thirty days for UK, US and Australasian citizens, and ninety days for Canadians, and must be used within 180 days of issue. Although you can buy tourist cards from Cuban consulates outside Cuba, some tour operators, airlines and travel agents can sell you one when you purchase your flight. Consulates can usually sell tourist cards instantly, but in some countries you may have to wait for a week. In addition to the completed application form, you'll need your passport (and sometimes a photocopy of its main page) plus confirmation of your travel arrangements, specifically a return plane ticket and an accommodation booking, though the latter is rarely checked. The charge if you go to the consulate in person in the UK is £15, in Canada Can$24, in Australia A$60, and in New Zealand NZ$30. For travellers flying via Mexico, tourist cards are available at Cuba-connecting airports for US$25. Postal applications are usually around twice as much. You will need to show your tourist card at customs on arrival and departure.

Once in Cuba, you can **renew a tourist card** for another thirty days for a fee of $25CUC, paid for in special stamps, which you can buy from banks. To do this consult a *buro de turismo*, found in the larger hotels, or one of the immigration offices in various provinces (listed throughout the guide). There is an office in Havana dedicated specifically to visa extensions (see p.140). When renewing your visa you will need details (perhaps including a receipt) of where you are staying.

Should you wish to stay longer than sixty days as a tourist (120 if you are Canadian) you will have to leave Cuban territory and return with a **new tourist card**. Many people do this by island-hopping to other Caribbean destinations or Mexico and getting another tourist card from the Cuban consulate there.

For full details of import and export regulations, consult the Cuban Customs website: Ⓦ www .aduana.co.cu.

DEPARTURE TAX

The airport departure tax, which must be paid by all travellers departing Cuba by plane, is $25CUC.

Embassies and consulates in Cuba

There are no consulates or embassies in Cuba for Australia or New Zealand. The local Canadian Embassy and the Australian Embassy in Mexico provide consular assistance to Australians and New Zealanders in Cuba.

Canada Embassy Calle 30 no. 518, Miramar ☎ 7 204 2516 & 2382, Ⓦ canadainternational.gc.ca/cuba.

South Africa Embassy Ave. 5ta no. 4201 esq. 42, Miramar ☎ 7 204 9671 & 9676.

UK Embassy Calle 34 no. 702–704, Miramar ☎ 7 204 1771.

US Special Interests Section Calzada e/ L y M, Vedado ☎ 7 839 4100, Ⓦ havana.usint.gov.

CUBAN CONSULATES AND EMBASSIES ABROAD

Australia Consulate-General Ground Floor, 128 Chalmers Street, Surry Hills, Sydney ☎ 02 9698 9797, 🖷 8399 1106.

Canada Embassy 388 Main St, Ottawa, Ontario K1S 1E3 ☎ 613 563 0141. Consulate-General in Montreal 4542–4546 Decarie Boulevard, Montreal H4A 3P2 ☎ 514 843 8897. Consulate-General in Toronto, Suite 401–402, 5353 Dundas Street West, Kipling Square, Toronto M9B 6H8 ☎ 416 234 8181.

Ireland Embassy 2 Adelaide Court, Adelaide Rd, Dublin ☎ 353 1475 0899.

New Zealand Embassy 35 Hobson Street, Thorndon, Wellington ☎ 4 472 3748.

South Africa Embassy 45 Mackenzie Street, Brooklyn 0181, Pretoria ☎ 12 346 2215.

UK Embassy and Consulate 167 High Holborn, London WC1 ☎ 020 7240 2488; 24hr visa and information service ☎ 0891 880 820.

Cuban Interests Section 2630 16th St NW, Washington DC 20009 ☎ 202 797 8518. Consulate Office, 2639 16th St NW, Washington DC 20009 ☎ 202 797 8609.

Insurance

Travel insurance covering medical expenses is essential when visiting Cuba. A typical travel insurance policy usually provides medical cover, as well as coverage for the loss of baggage, tickets and – up to a certain limit – cash or cheques, as well as cancellation or curtailment of your journey. Most of them exclude so-called dangerous sports unless an extra premium is paid. If you do take medical coverage, ascertain whether benefits will be paid as treatment proceeds or only after return home, and whether there is a 24-hour medical emergency number. If you need to make a claim, you should keep **receipts** for medicines and medical treatment, and in the event you have anything stolen, you must obtain an official statement from the police.

For all **insurance issues within Cuba**, including the purchase of policies, contact Asistur (☎7 866 4499, ☻asistur.cu), the tourist-assistance agency. It has branches in most provincial capitals (listed throughout the guide). Asistur may be the logical place to buy a policy for many **US citizens** as US insurance providers generally don't cover Cuba.

Internet

Getting **internet access** in Cuba is still not particularly easy or cheap and **wi-fi** barely exists at all outside of the upmarket hotels. There are cybercafés in all the major Cuban cities and resorts but usually just one or two, and in many towns there are none at all. Finding somewhere with a reliable, fast connection is an even greater challenge. The **hotels** offer the fastest and most robust connections but their rates can be exorbitant, commonly between $6CUC and $10CUC an hour. ETECSA, which runs the national telephone network, operates **Telepunto centres** where you can get online; there's one in most provincial capitals, but connections are often painstakingly slow and, particularly in Havana, you're sometimes better off at a hotel. Currently, charges in Telepuntos and Minipuntos are $0.10CUC/min with a minimum charge of $6CUC, giving you an hour online. Note that wherever you access the internet, you may occasionally be required to show a passport.

Having always been keen to control the flow of information to the Cuban public, the government has, unsurprisingly, restricted its citizens' access to the internet. However, though internet connections in private homes are illegal, some Cuban homes do have them, and anyone can go online in Telepuntos. Locals also have access to Cuban-based email accounts, and there is an increasing number of Cuban homes using email, mostly *casas particulares*. All hotels now have email addresses and online booking, but most restaurants do not.

Laundry

There are few public laundry services in Cuba. Most foreign visitors do their own or rely on the hotel service, although if you are staying in a *casa particular* your hosts are likely to offer to do yours for you for a small extra charge, usually $2–3CUC.

Mail

There's a good chance you'll get back home from Cuba before your postcards do. Don't expect **airmail** to reach Europe or North America in less than two weeks, while it is not unknown for **letters** to arrive a month or more after they have been sent. **Theft** is so widespread within the postal system that if you send anything other than a letter there's a significant chance that it won't arrive at all. You should also be aware that letters and packages coming into Cuba are sometimes opened as a matter of government policy.

Stamps are sold in both convertible and national pesos at post offices, white-and-blue post office kiosks (marked Correos de Cuba) and in many hotels ($CUC only at the latter). Convertible peso rates are reasonable at $0.75CUC for a postcard or letter to the US or Canada, $0.85CUC to Europe and $0.90CUC to the rest of the world. However, if you request **national-peso stamps**, which you are entitled to do, at between $0.40CUP and $0.75CUP for postcards and marginally more for letters, it can work out over fifteen times cheaper.

All large towns and cities have a **post office**, normally open Monday to Saturday from 8am to 6pm. Most provincial capitals and major tourist resorts have a branch with DHL (☻dhl.com) and EMS (☻ems.coop) **courier services**. Some of the larger hotels offer a full range of postal services, including DHL, EMS and the Cuban equivalent Cubanacán Express (☻cubanacan-express.cu), usually at the desk marked Telecorreos. What post offices there are in smaller towns and villages offer services in national pesos only and are more likely to be closed at the weekend.

If you're sending **packages** overseas, stick to DHL, by far the safest and most reliable option.

Maps

In general, Cuban maps are infrequently updated, a little unreliable and hard to find. The exception is the national road map book, the *Guía de Carreteras* ($10–12CUC), which covers the whole country and also carries basic street maps for many of the major cities – invaluable if you plan to make any long-distance car or bike journeys around the island. You can buy it in bookshops, tourist gift shops and some branches of Infotur. However, some minor roads are not marked on this or any other map and there is still a gap in the market for a fully comprehensive national road map or street atlas. Geographical and orienteering maps are nonexistent.

Opening hours and public holidays

Opening hours in Cuba are far from an exact science and should generally be taken with a generous pinch of salt. **Office** hours are normally 8.30am to 5pm, Monday to Friday, with one-hour lunchtime closures common, anytime between noon and 2pm. Standard opening hours for **state restaurants** and **paladars** are from noon to 11pm, but it's not unusual for places to close early, depending on the level of business. **Museums** are usually open Tuesday to Saturday from 9am to 6pm, and many also close for an hour at lunch. Those open on Sunday generally close in the afternoon. Expect museums, especially in Havana, to keep longer opening hours in July and August and sometimes in January, February and March too. **Shops** are generally open 9am to 6pm Monday to Saturday, a minority closing for lunch, while the shopping malls and department stores in Havana

---

NATIONAL HOLIDAYS

Jan 1 Liberation Day. Anniversary of the triumph of the Revolution.
May 1 International Workers' Day.
July 25–27 Celebration of the day of national rebellion.
Oct 10 Anniversary of the start of the Wars of Independence.
Dec 25 Christmas Day.

---

and Varadero stay open as late as 8pm. Sunday trading is increasingly common, with most places open until noon or 1pm, longer in the major resorts. Hotel shops stay open all day. **Banks** generally operate Monday to Friday 8am to 3pm, but this varies (see p.45). There is no culture of siesta in Cuba.

Phones

The chances are that it will be cheaper to use your mobile phone than a payphone to **ring abroad from Cuba**, though US travellers may encounter added complications. However, if you are making a call to a Cuban number then it's much more economical to use a **payphone**.

Mobile phones

Cubacel, part of national telecommunications company ETECSA (Ⓦetecsa.cu), is the sole **mobile phone service provider** in Cuba. If you intend to bring your own handset to Cuba you should check first whether or not your service provider has a roaming agreement with Cubacel, either by contacting your own provider or consulting the list on the ETECSA website. Most of the major British, Australasian and Canadian operators now have such agreements. Though restrictions on US telecommunications firms were lifted in 2009, allowing them to establish roaming agreements with Cuba, none have yet done so.

Renting or buying a mobile phone

The alternative to bringing your own handset is to rent or buy one in Cuba, which may be a necessity if your service provider does not have a roaming agreement with Cubacel or you have the wrong kind of mobile phone, though this is unlikely since the Cubacel network supports GSM phones, by far the most common type. There are over 35 Cubacel offices around the country, including representation in most Telepuntos (see p.59) and a few hotels. You can **rent a handset** for $6CUC a day. They offer temporary as well as permanent contracts to visitors and residents alike, but you are more likely to use the **pay-as-you-go** deals using prepaid cards. The prepaid service costs a daily rate of $3CUC for line rental and **call rates** within Cuba are $0.35CUC per minute or $0.09CUC per text message. You will also be charged receive calls if someone rings you from a land line. International call rates are currently $1.60CUC to anywhere in the Americas except Venezuela, $1.40CUC to Venezuela and

CALLING THE US

Whether from a mobile phone, landline or payphone, **calling the US from Cuba** is subject to a US-based tax, an extra cost of US$0.245min not included in the officially listed call rates.

$1.80CUC to the rest of the world. Prepaid cards are not widely available so make sure you stock up at Telepuntos.

Payphones

There are various kinds of **payphones** in Cuba, and several distinct ways that you can make and pay for calls. National **rates** for payphones are reasonable, starting at $0.05CUC/min for calls within the same province. International rates are exorbitant at $2CUC/min to the US or Canada; $2.60CUC/min to Central America and the Caribbean; $3.40CUC/min to South America; $4CUC/min to Spain, Italy, France and Germany; and $4.40CUC/min to the rest of the world.

Prepaid phone cards

Prepaid cards, known as **Chip cards** and priced in convertible pesos, can be bought from post offices, hotels, travel agents, some banks, Telepuntos (see p.59) and large walk-in phone booths known as Minipuntos. They only work in Chip card phones, most of which are coloured blue and found in hotels, Telepuntos, Minipuntos and other tourist establishments. They are available in denominations of $5CUC, $10CUC and $20CUC, and are straightforward phone cards which, once the credit has expired, are useless and can be thrown away.

Propia cards are sold in both national and convertible pesos and are compatible with all phones besides the Chip card phones. International calls are only possible with the convertible peso versions. There are an increasing number of phones aimed specifically at Propia users. They are grey and have no slot for coins. Propia cards are rechargeable, reusable and valid for six months, effectively phone credit accounts. Rather than inserting the card in a phone, when calling you enter the unique account code found on the card.

Coin-operated phones

The new generation of **coin-operated phones**, grey in colour and with a digital display, are an easy and cheap way to make a local call – international calls aren't permitted. They only accept national peso coins, in denominations of 5¢, 20¢ and $1CUP, and can also take Propia cards. Coin-operated phones can be hard to find and tend to be located outside in the street and rarely in call centres. There are also still some rusty old analogue payphones, especially in small towns, which only accept 5 centavo coins, have no digital display and have a slim chance of working at all.

Making calls

To **make a call** within the same province but to a different municipality you may need an **exit code** (*código de salida*) for the place from where you are making the call. Exit codes are available from the operator. If you are calling from a prepaid card phone simply dial ❶0 followed by the area code and number and this will put you through directly.

Some interprovincial calls are only possible through the operator. If you're consistently failing to get through on a direct line, dial ❶00 or 110.

You may see Cuban telephone numbers written as, for example, "48 7711 al 18", meaning that when

USEFUL NUMBERS AND CODES

- **Directory enquiries** ❶ 113.
- **National operator** ❶ 00 from most places, including major towns, cities and resort areas. The most common alternatives are ❶ 011 and ❶ 110.
- **International operator** The number for the international operator, which you'll need for reverse charge calls or if you are having problems connecting directly to a number outside Cuba, is either ❶ 012 (from Havana) or ❶ 180 (from outside Havana). A call connected via the international operator from a payphone incurs a higher call rate than normal.
- **International call prefix** ❶ 119. This code must precede the country code when making any international call.

- **Interprovincial area codes** These codes are provided with all phone numbers throughout this guide. When dialling, each code is preceded by the appropriate national grid prefix (*prefijo de teleselección nacional*), which is either ❶ 0 or ❶ 01 depending on where in the country the call is made from. The codes are printed in the telephone directories available in all Telepunto and Minipunto call centres.
- **Mobile phone codes** Cuban mobile phone numbers begin with a 5. When calling a mobile phone from a fixed phone, including payphones, the 5 is preceded by 0 (when calling from Havana) or 01 (when calling from outside Havana).
- **International dialling code for calls to Cuba** ❶ 53.

dialling the final two digits you may have to try all the numbers in between and including 11 and 18 before you get through.

Making an overseas phone call from a private phone in a house has its own special procedure and can be quite confusing, not to mention very costly – use a payphone if at all possible.

Time

Cuba is on **Eastern Standard Time** in winter and **Eastern Daylight Time** in summer. It is five hours behind London, fifteen hours behind Sydney and on the same time as New York.

Tourist information

The national tourist information network is **Infotur** (🌐 infotur.cu), and has desks in many hotels and at the larger airports and branches in most major cities and resorts, though many are rudimentary affairs. The friendly staff are generally willing to help with all sorts of queries, though they do try to steer visitors towards the state-run tourist apparatus. They carry a few basic guides and maps but are generally low on free literature and printed information. You can, however, book hotel rooms, rental cars, organized excursions and long distance bus tickets through them. Officially they do not supply information on paladars or *casas particulares*, though the staff are often willing to help with their own recommendations.

The three principal national **travel agents**, Cubanacán, Cubatur and Havanatur, have offices in most major cities and resorts and effectively double up as information offices, particularly in those places where there is no Infotur office. Though their principal aim is to sell you their own packages and organized excursions, the staff are accustomed to supplying any kind of tourist information. These agencies can also book hotel rooms and are usually the most convenient place to book Víazul bus tickets. Be aware that all information outlets and travel agents in Cuba, including Cuban websites, are run by the state and are unlikely to offer impartial advice on, for example, accommodation deals or places to eat.

With very little printed tourist literature it's well worth checking the internet for tourist information. The official Cuban sites, 🌐 cubaweb.cu and 🌐 dtcuba.com are worthwhile but foreign sites tend to be more reliable. Among the best are 🌐 cubaabsolutely.com, particularly good for Havana, and 🌐 cuba-junky.com.

An international network of tourist information offices is run by the **Cuban Tourist Board**. There are branches in several Latin American and European countries, including the UK, as well as in Canada and China.

CUBAN TOURIST BOARD OFFICES ABROAD

Canada 1200 Bay Street, Suite 305, Toronto M5R 2A5 🕿 416 362 0700, 🌐 gocuba.ca.

Mexico Darwin 68, piso 1, Colonia Anzures, Delegación Miguel Hidalgo, Mexico City 06100.

UK 154 Shaftesbury Avenue, London WC2H 8JT 🕿 020 7240 6655, 🌐 travel2cuba.co.uk.

Travellers with disabilities

Most of Cuba's upmarket hotels are well equipped for **disabled travellers**, each with at least one specially designed room and all the necessary lifts and ramps. However, away from the resorts there are very few amenities or services provided for people with disabilities, and in fact, you rarely see anyone in a wheelchair in the street in Cuba. Transport may prove the biggest challenge: the crowded public buses are not modified for wheelchair users, while the tourist buses do not have ramps. Using a taxi is the best option, as accessible car hire is difficult to find. Several taxi companies have people carriers that can accommodate wheelchair users.

Working and studying in Cuba

Working in Cuba as a foreign national is more complicated than in most countries, and anyone thinking of picking up a casual job on the island can pretty much forget it. All wages in Cuba are paid by the state in national pesos, so if the bureaucracy doesn't stop you the hourly rates probably will. The majority of foreign workers here are either diplomats or in big business, and the only realistic chance most people have of working is to join one of the voluntary brigades. **Studying** here is easier, as Spanish classes are offered at universities, by tour operators and also represent a significant niche in the private enterprise market.

If you plan to study or work in Cuba then you must have the relevant **visas** organized before you arrive. Students must have a **student visa** entitling them to stay in the country for longer than a month; these can be arranged through the Cuban consulate, though sometimes language schools can assist you with this.

Work

Working holidays in Cuba are organized in the US by the Venceremos Brigade (Ⓦ venceremosbrigade .net), in Canada by the Canadian Network on Cuba (Ⓦ canadiannetworkoncuba.ca) and in the UK by the Cuba Solidarity Campaign (Ⓦ cuba-solidarity .org.uk). Known as brigades, these organized volunteer groups usually spend two or three weeks working alongside Cubans on agricultural projects, living on purpose-built camps. There is a strong pro-government slant to the experience – which also involves visits to schools, hospitals and trade unions – but the opportunity to witness working conditions and gain a sense of the Revolution in action is nevertheless unique.

Study

There is an array of organizations that send people to Cuba to **study**, mostly to learn Spanish. You can, however, take Spanish classes independently without too much hassle. The most obvious place to go is the University of Havana, where the Faculty of Modern Languages has been running courses aimed specifically at foreign students and visitors for many years. The most basic **Spanish course** is an intensive one-week affair, with two-week, three-week and month-long options. You can also combine Spanish studies with courses in dance or Cuban culture, or even just study Cuban culture on its own. The university provides full-board on-campus accommodation for two weeks, including the cost of lessons. Courses start throughout the year on the first Monday of every month except August. For more details go to Ⓦ uh.cu/cursos-de-espanol or contact the Oficina de Servicios Académicos Internacionales at ☎ 7 870 4667 or 0584, Ⓔ alexeis@rect.uh.cu. Similar courses are run at just about every principal university in the country, most of them found in the provincial capital cities.

Aside from the universities, the best way to arrange a proper course of Spanish classes in Cuba is through professional organizations based outside the country, like Caledonia (Ⓦ www.caledonia languages.co.uk) or Cactus Language (Ⓦ cactus language.com).

Havana

CLASSIC CARS OUTSIDE THE HOTEL
NACIONAL, VEDADO

1

Havana

Havana is an enchanting and captivating city, with the twists and turns of its compelling history and rich culture laid bare in the surprising diversity of its architecture and kaleidoscope of citizens. Nowhere is there uniformity, with the hotchpotch of buildings and people presenting a different set of stop-and-stare images on every street. Policemen on military service lean against Soviet-era Brutalist office blocks; adherents of Santería, dressed all in white, stroll past Neo-Gothic churches; queues of smart, elderly socialites form outside Art Deco theatres; and taxi drivers in baseball caps tout rides in their fifty-year-old Buicks and Chevrolets in front of Neoclassical shop fronts. In the centre especially, almost every street seems to have an intriguing story to tell, whether one of colonial grandeur, bygone glamour, economic hardship or revolutionary change – and sometimes all of these, wrapped up in just one block.

The past and the present are closely interwoven all over this sprawling metropolis, with tenement buildings moulded from the mansions of imperial counts, 1950s department store signs hanging over entrances to community centres and government agencies occupying eighteenth-century convents. An infectious vitality pervades every neighbourhood, as life in Havana unfolds unselfconsciously and in plain view: front doors are left open, washing is hung out on balconies, domino players sit at tables on the kerb, conversations are shouted between buildings and families watch TV in exposed street-side living rooms. Even in the most touristy parts of the city, which double up as residential neighbourhoods, the locals make their presence felt.

Havana's diverse districts mark distinct eras in the capital's evolution. What was once contained within seventeenth-century city walls now forms the most captivating section of harbourside **Habana Vieja**, the old city, and the capital's tourist centre. Soldered on to Habana Vieja is gritty, lively **Centro Habana**, often bypassed by visitors on their way to more tourist-friendly parts of town but home to the most striking and

MALECÓN SWIMMERS

Highlights

❶ Museo Nacional de Bellas Artes The best and largest art collection in Cuba, displayed in two marvellous and contrasting buildings. See p.90

❷ Malecón in Centro Habana Havana's sociable seafront promenade is overlooked by a multitude of lovely buildings. See p.97

❸ Hotel Nacional This luxurious twin-towered hotel still embodies 1930s glamour. See p.99

❹ Café Laurent Penthouse views, 1950s decor and fine cuisine at one of the best of the city's new paladars. See p.127

❺ Hurón Azul For traditional Cuban music, from bolero to son, this fabulous arts centre is unmissable. See p.132

❻ Gran Teatro Enjoy the world-renowned Cuban National Ballet and other dance companies in a fittingly magnificent building. See p.134

❼ Plaza de Armas book market An Old Havana mainstay, with stacks of vintage magazines, rare political posters and other collectables. See p.136

❽ Playa Santa María del Mar Cuba's take on a city beach is lively, unaffected and bags of fun. See p.144

HIGHLIGHTS ARE MARKED ON THE MAPS ON P.68 & PP.70–71

1

idiosyncratic section of Havana's oceanfront promenade, the **Malecón**. Sharing the Malecón with Centro Habana is **Vedado**, heart of the city borough of Plaza, its attractive, leafy, open plan neighbourhoods blessed with most of the city's abundant theatres, cabarets, nightclubs and cinemas. From here you could walk the couple of kilometres to the vast and famous **Plaza de la Revolución**, with giant monuments to two icons of the Cuban struggle for independence, Che Guevara and José Martí. Beyond Vedado to the west, on the other side of the Río Almendares, **Miramar** ushers in another change in the urban landscape. Modelled on mid-twentieth-century Miami, this part of the city comes into its own at night, with some of Havana's most sophisticated restaurants and best music venues scattered around the leafy streets.

Brief history

Havana's success and riches were founded on the strength and position of its **harbour** – the largest natural port in the Caribbean. However, the original **San Cristóbal de la Habana** settlement, established on July 25, 1515, St Christopher's Day, was actually founded at modern-day Batabanó, on the south coast of what is now Mayabeque province. It wasn't until November 25, 1519, that the city was relocated to the banks of the large bay known as the **Bahía de la Habana**.

Port, bridge and gateway

The early settlement began to ripple out into what is now Habana Vieja, with the first streets established down on the waterfront between the present-day Plaza de Armas and Plaza de San Francisco. However, it was with the discovery of a deep, navigable channel

HAVANA HASSLE

While Havana puts the hotels, restaurants, shops and clubs of all the other Cuban cities to shame, hanging around outside most of these places, and patrolling the streets in between them, are legions of *jineteros* – street hustlers and opportunists. The government now takes the high levels of **tourist harassment** here very seriously, posting policemen all over Habana Vieja and the streets around the *Habana Libre* hotel, areas where *jineterismo* has traditionally been most concentrated. Even so, many foreign visitors are still surprised by what can seem like an onslaught of touts peddling anything from cigars and taxi rides to a place to stay and a young woman to stay with.

Habana Vieja, the old town, is not only a magnet for *jineteros* but is also the **bag-snatching** centre of the city, with an increasing number of petty thieves working the streets, so take the usual precautions. Even at night, however, there is rarely any violent crime.

through the treacherous shallow waters between Cuba and the Bahamas that Havana really took off as a major city, becoming a bridge between Spain and the New World thanks to its strategic location on the newly established **trade routes**.

As the Spanish conquistadors plundered the treasures of the Americas, Havana became the meeting point for the **Spanish fleet** on its way back across the Atlantic. For several months of the year, ships returning from all over the Americas laden with precious cargoes would slowly gather at the port until a force strong enough to deter possible **pirate attacks** in the Caribbean had been assembled. An infrastructure of brothels, inns and gambling houses sprang up to cater for the seamen, and the port itself became a target for frequent attacks by buccaneers.

Fortification and free trade

In 1558, after consolidating shipping operations by making Havana the only Cuban port authorized to engage in commerce, Spain started a long period of fortification with the construction of the first stone fort in the Americas, the impressive **Castillo de la Real Fuerza**. Work started on the **Castillo de San Salvador de la Punta** and the formidable **Castillo de Los Tres Reyes del Morro** in 1589 and was finally completed in 1630. Three years later a protective wall began to be built around the city, and was completed in 1740.

Assaults on the city persisted, however, and in 1762 Havana fell to the **British**. The free trade that the port enjoyed during its brief eleven months of occupation – the British swapped Havana for Florida – kick-started the island's **sugar trade**; previously restricted to supplying Spain, it was now open to the rest of the world. Spain wisely kept British trade policies intact and the consequential influx of wealthy Spanish sugar families propelled Havana into a new age of affluence.

The building booms

The **nineteenth century** was a period of growth, when some of the most beautiful buildings around Habana Vieja were constructed and the city enjoyed a new-found elegance. At the same time, crime and political corruption were reaching new heights, causing many of the new bourgeoisie to abandon the old city to the poor and to start colonizing what is now Vedado. By the 1860s the framework of the new suburbs stretching west and south was in place.

In 1902, after the **Wars of Independence**, North American influence and money flowed into the city, and the first half of the twentieth century saw tower blocks, hotels and glorious Art Deco palaces like the Edificio Bacardí built as the tourist industry boomed. Gambling flourished, run by American gangsters like Meyer Lansky, who aimed to turn Havana into a Caribbean Las Vegas.

Equality, decay and rebirth

The **Revolution** put an abrupt end to all this decadence, and throughout the 1960s the new regime cleaned the streets of crime and prostitution, laying the basis for a socialist

1

HAVANA

— – – · Municipal boundary

Habana Bus Tour:
- Route T1 & stop
- Route T2 & stop
- Route T3 & stop

Monumento General
Calixto García
Casa de las
Américas
Teatro
Amadeo
Roldán
Galerías
de Paseo
Hotel
Meliá Cohiba

Parque
José Martí
US
Interests
Section
Hotel
Presidente
Memorial
a las Víctimas
del Maine
Hotel
Nacional
Museo de
la Danza
Pabellón
Cuba
VEDADO
Coppelia
Hotel Habana Libre
Hotel
Habana
Libre
Museo
Napoleónico
Museo de Artes
Decorativas
Universidad
de la Habana

Parque
John Lennon
Casa de
la Amistad
PLAZA DE LA REVOLUCIÓN
Estadio
Juan Abrantes
Castillo
del Príncipe

Puente
de Hierro
AVENIDA ZAPATA
Sala Polivalente
Ramón Fonst

KOHLY
Cementerio
Colón
Necrópolis de Colón
Teatro
Nacional
Plaza De La
Revolución
Astro Terminal
de Omnibus
Nacionales

Puente Almendares
Puente
Almendares
PLAZA DE LA
REVOLUCIÓN
Biblioteca
Nacional
Memorial
José Martí

Club
Almendares
PLAYA
Bosque de
la Habana
Estad
Latín
americar

Parque
Zoológico
de 26

Viazul Terminal
de Omnibus
CERRO

NUEVO
VEDADO

CALZADA DEL CERRO

Ciudad
Deportiva

500
metres

Parque Lenin (9km), Airport (12km) & Jardin Botanico Nacional (15km)

Club Habana (8km) & Marina Hemingway (10km)

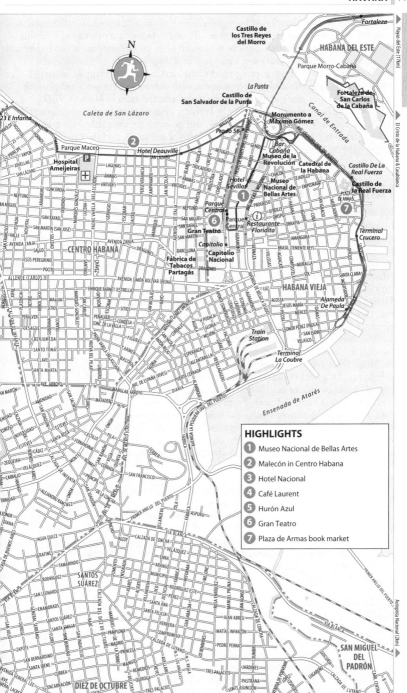

HIGHLIGHTS

1 Museo Nacional de Bellas Artes

2 Malecón in Centro Habana

3 Hotel Nacional

4 Café Laurent

5 Hurón Azul

6 Gran Teatro

7 Plaza de Armas book market

1

capital. Fine houses, abandoned by owners fleeing to the US, were left in the hands of servants, and previously exclusive neighbourhoods changed face overnight. With the emphasis on improving conditions in the countryside, city development was haphazard and the **post-Revolution years** saw many fine buildings crumble while residential overcrowding increased, prompting Fidel Castro to take action. Happily, since the 1990s there have been steady improvements, with redevelopment work recapturing some of the former glory, especially in the worst-affected areas of Habana Vieja.

Today there is a growing **prosperity** in Havana, evident from fancy restaurants full of locals, increasingly well-appointed houses, and new cars on the roads. However, many of its citizens still live in poverty on a minimum of resources, and the capital shines a bright light on the growing inequalities in Cuba today.

Habana Vieja

No other area in Havana gives such a vivid and immediate impression of the city's history as **Habana Vieja** (Old Havana). Cobbled plazas, shadowy streets, colonial mansions, leafy courtyards, sixteenth-century fortresses and architecture famously ravaged by time and climate are all remarkably unmarred by modern change or growth. Ironically, however, the very lack of urban development between the 1960s and 1990s, which allowed the historical core to be so untouched, was the same force that allowed for the area's subsequent decay. The huge **restoration project** of this UNESCO World Heritage Site that began some 25 years ago is visibly still underway today, and though there are now one or two whole streets almost completely lined by beautifully renovated buildings, much work remains. But though its central streets are heaving with visitors, Habana Vieja is no sanitized tourist trap, and the area buzzes with a frenetic sense of life and a raw sense of the past – for every recently restored colonial building, there are ten crumbling apartment blocks packed with residents. And in the side-streets, neighbours chat through wrought-iron window grills and schoolchildren attend classes in former merchants' houses.

Habana Vieja's main sightseeing area is relatively compact and made for exploring **on foot**. Although the narrow streets and eclectic architecture lend a sense of wild disorder, the straightforward grid system is very easy to navigate. The **Plaza de Armas** is the core of the historic old city and the logical starting point for touring the district, with numerous options in all directions, including the prestigious **Plaza de la Catedral** three blocks away to the north and the larger but equally historic **Plaza Vieja** five blocks to the south.

For the other unmissable sights head from the Plaza de Armas up **Obispo**, Habana Vieja's busiest street, to the **Parque Central**. The wide boulevards and grand buildings on this western edge of Habana Vieja differ in feel from the rest of the old town, and belong to an era of reconstruction heavily influenced by the United States, most strikingly in the **Capitolio** building. Some of the most impressive museums are here, including the **Museo de la Revolución** and the **Museo Nacional de Bellas Artes**, Cuba's best and biggest art collection.

Plaza de Armas

The oldest of Habana Vieja's squares, the **Plaza de Armas** is where Havana established itself as a city in the second half of the sixteenth century, and for most of the eighteenth and nineteenth centuries it was the seat of government in Havana. It still boasts some distinguished colonial buildings, several of which now house museums, most notably the **Museo de la Ciudad**. The three brick streets that form the edges of the plaza and, uniquely, its single wooden one are dominated by Havana's biggest and best secondhand **book market** (see p.136), enclosing the square's bushy central gardens with

HAVANA'S NEW AND OLD STREET NAMES

Some streets in Havana have both a post-Revolution and a pre-Revolution name. Locals normally refer to the older, pre-Revolution names, while street signs and some maps give only the new ones. Below are the most important of these distinctions.

OLD NAME	NEW NAME
Avenida del Puerto	Avenida Carlos Manuel de Céspedes
Avenida de Rancho Boyeros	Avenida de la Independencia
Belascoaín	Padre Varela
Cárcel	Capdevila
Carlos III	Avenida Salvador Allende
Egido	Avenida de Bélgica (southern half)
Galiano	Avenida de Italia
Malecón	Avenida Antonio Maceo
Monserrate	Avenida de Bélgica (northern half)
Monte	Máximo Gómez
Paseo del Prado	Paseo de Martí
Paula	Leonor Pérez
Reina	Avenida Simón Bolívar
San José	San Martín
Someruelos	Aponte
Teniente Rey	Brasil
Vives	Avenida de España
Zulueta	Agramonte

the buzz of commerce. Often seething with tourists, and bathed in live music wafting over from the restaurant in one corner, this is the beating heart of the old town for most visitors.

El Templete

Baratillo e/ Nico López y O'Reilly, Plaza de Armas • Daily 9am–6.30pm • $2CUC

In the northeastern corner of Plaza de Armas, the incongruous classical Greek architecture of **El Templete**, a curious, scaled-down version of the Parthenon in Athens, marks the exact spot of the foundation of Havana and the city's first Mass in 1519. The building itself was established in 1828; the large ceiba tree which now stands within its small gated grounds is the last survivor of the three that were planted here on that inaugural date. Inside the tiny interior, two large **paintings** depict these two historic ceremonies, both by nineteenth-century French artist Jean Baptiste Vermay, whose work can also be seen inside the Catedral de la Habana.

Museo de la Ciudad

Tacón no.1 e/ Obispo y O'Reilly, Plaza de Armas • Daily 9am–6.30pm • $3CUC, $4CUC with guided tour • ☎ 7 861 5779

The robust yet refined **Palacio de los Capitanes Generales** on the western side of Plaza de Armas was the seat of the Spanish government from the time of its inauguration in 1791 to the end of the Spanish–American War in 1898. It's now occupied by one of Havana's best museums, the **Museo de la Ciudad**, which celebrates the original building itself as well as the city's colonial heritage in general. Highlights on the ground floor include a fantastic nineteenth-century **fire engine** and a collection of **horse-drawn carriages**. Upstairs, among rooms that have been restored to their original splendour, is the magnificent **Salón de los Espejos** (Hall of Mirrors), lined with glorious gilt-looking mirrors, ornate candlestick holders and three huge, ostentatious crystal chandeliers. Next door is the slightly less striking **Salón Verde**, also known as the Salón Dorado (Golden Hall), where the governor would receive guests amid golden furniture and precious porcelain. Completing the triumvirate of the building's most impressive rooms

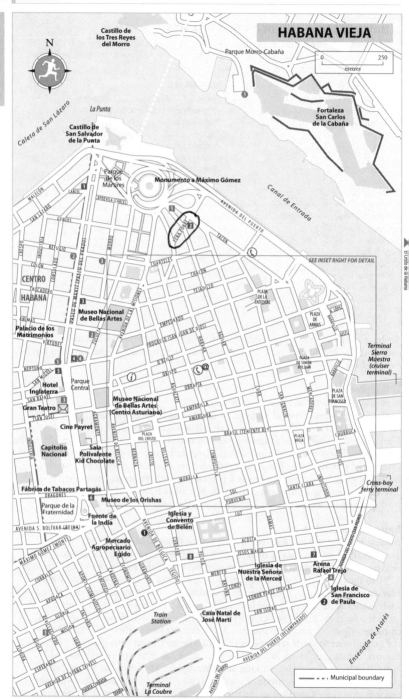

HABANA VIEJA

Castillo de
los Tres Reyes
del Morro

Parque Morro-Cabaña

0   250
metres

Fortaleza
San Carlos
de la Cabaña

La Punta

Caleta de San Lázaro

Castillo de
San Salvador
de la Punta

Canal de Entrada

Parque
de los
Mártires

Monumento a Máximo Gómez

AVENIDA DEL PUERTO

MALECÓN

CÁRCEL

CAPDEVILA (CÁRCEL)

TACÓN

SAN LÁZARO

GENIOS

MORRO

SEE INSET RIGHT FOR DETAIL

El Litoral de la Habana

REFUGIO

COLÓN

CENTRO

CUARTELES

TROCADERO

HABANA

CHACÓN

TEJADILLO

PLAZA
DE LA
CATEDRAL

PLAZA
DE
ARMAS

**Museo Nacional
de Bellas Artes**

ANIMAS

EMPEDRADO

**Palacio de los
Matrimonios**

VIRTUDES

PROGRESO (SAN JUAN DE DIOS)

PLAZA
DE SIMÓN
BOLÍVAR

Terminal
Sierra
Maestra
(cruiser
terminal)

NEPTUNO

O'REILLY

SAN MIGUEL

OBISPO

**Hotel
Inglaterra**

SAN RAFAEL

OBRAPÍA

(SAN JOSÉ)

Gran Teatro

Parque
Central

OBRAPÍA

PLAZA
DE SAN
FRANCISCO

**Museo Nacional
de Bellas Artes
(Centro Asturiano)**

LAMPARILLA

AMARGURA

Cine Payret

PLAZA
DEL CRISTO

BRASIL (TENIENTE REY)

PLAZA
VIEJA

CHURRUCA

**Capitolio
Nacional**

**Sala
Polivalente
Kid Chocolate**

Fábrica de Tabacos Partagás

Cross-bay
ferry terminal

DRAGONES

MURALLA

SANTA CLARA

6 **Museo de los Orishas**

SOL

Parque de la
Fraternidad

PORVENIR

**Fuente
de la India**

**Iglesia y
Convento
de Belén**

LUZ

AVENIDA S. BOLÍVAR (REINA)

ACOSTA

**Mercado
Agropecuario
Egido**

JESÚS MARÍA

MAXIMO GÓMEZ (MONTE)

CORRALES

8

MERCED

**Iglesia de
Nuestra Señora
de la Merced**

7

**Arena
Rafael Trejo**
4

APODACA

CONDE

**Iglesia de
San Francisco
de Paula**
2

GLORIA

CONDE PÉREZ (PAULA)

SAN ISIDRO

**Train
Station**

**Casa Natal de
José Martí**

MISIÓN

ESPERANZA

Ensenada de Atarés

AVENIDA DEL PUERTO (DESAMPARADOS)

**Terminal
La Coubre**

— - - · Municipal boundary

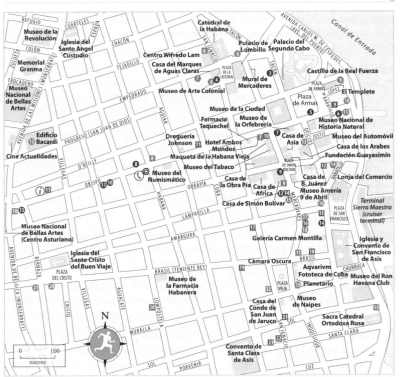

ACCOMMODATION		EATING		NIGHTLIFE	
Ambos Mundos	10	Al Medina	13	Adagio	3
Los Balcones	22	A Prado y Neptuno	5	Café Taberna	11
Beltrán de Santa Cruz	21	La Barca	10	Casa de la Cultura	
Casa de Eugenio Barral		Bodegón Onda	14	Julián del Casal	5
García	7	La Bodeguita del Medio	7	Patio Amarillo	6
Casa de Fefita y Luís	1	Café La Barrita	12	Sala de Conciertos Antigua	
Casa de Juan y Margarita	13	Café El Escorial	19	Iglesia San Francisco de Paula	4
Casa de Martha y Yusimi	8	Café del Oriente	16		
Casa de Migdalia		El Chanchullero	20	SHOPS & MARKETS	
Caraballé Martín	23	Doña Blanquita	2		
Casa de Pablo y Lidia	20	Doña Eutimia	8	Antiguo Almacenes	
Chez Nous	19	La Imprenta	15	San José	2
Conde de Villanueva	14	Hanoi	21	Boloña	7
Florida	11	El Mesón de la Flota	18	Casa del Café	6
Los Frailes	18	La Moneda Cubana	6	Casa del Habano	12
El Mesón de la Flota	16	Museo del Chocolate	17	Casa del Ron y del	
Palacio del Marqués de		Nao	11	Tabaco Cubano	13
San Felipe y Santiago		El Portico	4	Feria de Arte Obispo	10
de Bejucal	15	Prado	3	Galería Manos	11
Parque Central	4	La Tasca	1	Galería Victor Manuel	4
Raquel	17	El Templete	9	Guayabera Habanera	3
San Miguel	2			Habana 1791	9
Santa Isabel	9	DRINKING		Librería Caballero	
Saratoga	6	Café Lamparilla	9	de París	14
Sevilla	3	Café El Lucero	1	Longina	8
Telégrafo	5	Dos Hermanos	13	Mercado Egido	1
Valencia	12	Factoría Plaza Vieja	12	Plaza de Armas	
		El Floridita	10	Book Market	5
		Lluvia de Oro	8		
		Plaza de Armas	7		
		Sloppy Joe's	2		

1

is the sumptuous **Salón del Trono** (Throne Room) which, with its dark-red, satin-lined walls, was intended for royal visits, though no Spanish king or queen ever visited colonial Cuba.

Palacio del Segundo Cabo

O'Reilly esq. Tacón, Plaza de Armas • ☎ 7 861 5779

The construction of the elegant, stern-faced **Palacio del Segundo Cabo** began in 1770; its Baroque architecture is typical of Cuban buildings of that era. Along with the adjacent Palacio de los Capitanes Generales, it formed part of the remodelling of the Plaza de Armas ordered under the governorship of the Marqués de la Torre. Its original purpose was as the Royal Post Office; it didn't become the residence of the Segundo Cabo, the second-highest ranking official on the island, until 1854. It has since been used by a host of institutions, including the Tax Inspectorate, the Supreme Court of Justice and the Cuban Geographical Society, and is currently undergoing lengthy renovations with no known reopening date.

Museo Nacional de Historia Natural

Obispo no.61 esq. Oficios, Plaza de Armas • Tues 1.30–5pm, Wed–Sun 10am–5.30pm • $3CUC, $4CUC with guide • ☎ 7 863 9361

The **Museo Nacional de Historia Natural** is, on an international scale, an unremarkable and rather diminutive natural history museum. Nevertheless, it is one of the biggest and best of its kind in Cuba, and one of the only museums in Habana Vieja suitable for children. Housed in what was the US Embassy building in the 1930s, mammals of the five continents occupy the back rooms on the ground floor, where light and sound effects bring the cluttered displays to a semblance of life. **Cuban species** are displayed upstairs, including the prehistoric manjuarí fish, iguanas, bats and various birds. In an adjoining building, the **sala infantil** offers a space for kids with crayoning tables, games, story books and a somewhat macabre stuffed-baby-animal petting area.

Museo de la Orfebrería

Obispo no.113 e/ Oficios y Mercaderes, Plaza de Armas • Tues–Sun 9am–6.30pm • $1CUC • ☎ 7 863 9861

A few doors along on Obispo from the Museo Nacional de Historia Natural is the **Museo de la Orfebrería**, worth a twenty-minute scoot round. This building was a colonial-era workshop for the city's prominent goldsmiths and silversmiths and now displays some of their work, alongside an eclectic set of **gold** and **silver** pieces from around the world. As well as pocket watches, ceremonial swords and vases there are some fantastic, ostentatious old clocks. A jewellery shop is also located in the same building.

Castillo de la Real Fuerza

O'Reilly e/ Ave. del Puerto y Tacón, Plaza de Armas • Tues–Sat 9.30am–5pm, Sun 9.30am–12.30pm • Free • ☎ 7 864 4488

A heavy-set sixteenth-century fortress surrounded by a moat, the **Castillo de la Real Fuerza** was built in 1577 to replace a more primitive fort that stood on the same site but was destroyed by French pirates in 1555. The oldest construction still standing in Havana today, the impressive building never really got into its role as protector of the city. Set well back from the mouth of the bay, it proved useless against the English, who took control of Havana in 1762 without ever coming into the firing range of the fortress's cannon.

Museo Castillo de la Real Fuerza

The castle's 6m-thick stone walls make an atmospheric setting for the **Museo Castillo de la Real Fuerza**, an excellent display of Cuba's naval history. The first room is littered with interesting relics mainly found on or near the site, like pre-Columbian stone axes, a bayonet clumped with rust and a fascinating model of the castle itself. These are a good warm-up act for rooms further into the castle's depths, which are stuffed with **treasure** culled from the colonies and destined for Spain. Fat silver discs as big as dinner plates and 22-carat gold bars almost 30cm long, bearing marks from the mines of Lima and Potosí, glitter in one display cabinet while another is filled with Spanish marriage necklaces and other jewellery. Elsewhere, the museum's attention is turned to the **ships** themselves. All labels are in Spanish but the scale models of galleon ships, alongside comprehensive exhibits detailing life on board for sailors, can be easily appreciated without them.

The belltower

In the castle's upper level there are more model boats, including some modern liners, but the real draw is the rooftop view over the eastern bay and also the **belltower**, complete with the original bell used to warn Habaneros of approaching pirates. Cresting the tower is a copy of the **Giraldilla weathervane** – a bronze statue of a woman, named after the Giralda tower in Seville, which is that city's symbol. The original is now in the Palacio de los Capitanes Generales, following its deposition in the 1926 hurricane.

Oficios

The oldest street in the city, **Oficios** heads south from the Plaza de Armas through the Plaza de San Francisco and down to the port road on the southern side of Habana Vieja. Flanked by colonial residences, the three blocks between the two plazas make up its most travelled section and are lined with several small **museums**, a few shops, a couple of restaurants and a hotel.

Casa de los Árabes

Oficios no.16 e/ Obispo y Obrapía • Tues–Sat 9.30am–5pm, Sun 9am–1pm • Free or donation • ☎ 7 861 5868

A former religious school, the **Casa de los Árabes** building was constructed in the seventeenth century, and is one of the most striking single examples of the Moorish influence on Spanish – and therefore Cuban – architectural styles. It tends to outshine the sketchy collection of Arabian furniture and costumes found in its corridor-room, which is set up like a Marrakesh market and features fabrics and rugs hanging from the walls and ceilings.

Museo del Automóvil

Oficios no.13 e/ Jústiz y Obrapía • Tues–Sat 9.30am–5pm, Sun 9am–1pm • $1CUC • ☎ 7 863 9942

Across the street from the Casa de los Árabes, and of wider appeal, is the **Museo del Automóvil** where, among the two dozen or so cars parked inside, dating mostly from the first half of the twentieth century, the **1902 Cadillac** is one of the most attention-grabbing. The **1981 Chevrolet** donated by the Peruvian ambassador and a number of other models deliver a rather succinct history of the automobile, which one can't help feeling should be more comprehensive given the number of old cars still on the streets in Cuba.

Plaza de San Francisco

Two blocks beyond the Museo del Automóvil, Oficios opens out onto the **Plaza de San Francisco**, opposite the colourful **Terminal Sierra Maestra**, where the two or three luxury cruise ships that include Cuba in their Caribbean tour come to dock. With the main port road running the length of its west side and two of its main buildings given over to offices – including, on the north side, the theatrical five-storey **Lonja del Comercio**, built in 1909 – the square is the most open and functional of Habana Vieja's main plazas, and the one you're least likely to linger in.

1

Iglesia y Convento de San Francisco de Asís

Oficios e/ Churruca y Amargura, Plaza de San Francisco • ☎ 7 862 3467

Taking up the entire southern side of Plaza de San Francisco is the **Iglesia y Convento de San Francisco de Asís**, built in 1739 on the site of an older structure, which from 1579 was one of the most prestigious religious centres in Havana, a kind of missionary school for Franciscan friars who set off from here for destinations throughout Spanish America.

Museo de Arte Sacro

Iglesia y Convento de San Francisco de Asís • Mon–Sat 9am–6pm, Sun 9am–1pm • $2CUC, or $3CUC with English-speaking guide, photos $2CUC • ☎ 7 862 9683

Wonderfully restored in the early 1990s, the San Francisco de Asís monastery now contains the neatly condensed **Museo de Arte Sacro**, featuring religious art and silverware, church furniture and pottery found on the site, as well as the cope and shoes worn by the first Auxiliary Bishop of Cuba, Dionisio Rezino y Ormachea (1645–1711). However the real pleasure here comes from wandering around the beautifully simple **interior**, admiring the solid curves of the north cloister, and climbing the wooden staircase up the 46m belltower for magnificent **views** across the bay and over most of Habana Vieja.

Galería Carmen Montilla

Oficios no.162 e/ Brasil y Amargura • Mon–Sat 9.30am–5pm • Free • ☎ 7 866 8768

Opposite the entrance to the Iglesia de San Francisco is the **Galería Carmen Montilla**, a delightful colonial townhouse restored in the mid-1990s from scratch by Carmen Montilla Tinoco, a Venezuelan artist and friend of Fidel Castro. Used for exhibitions of Cuban and overseas artists alike, Tinoco's own surreal and sometimes morbid paintings hang on the interior balcony.

Museo del Ron Havana Club

Ave. del Puerto (San Pedro) no.262 esq. Sol • Mon–Thurs 9am–5.30pm, Fri–Sun 9am–4.30pm • $7CUC • ☎ 7 861 8051

A couple of blocks south of the Plaza de San Francisco on the port road is one of Havana's more engaging museums, the **Museo del Ron Havana Club**, a showpiece for the country's sizeable rum industry. Tracing the history and production methods behind this 400–year-old liquor, the lively **tour** (with guides who speak English, French, German and Italian) offers one of the city's few modern museum experiences, with slick presentation and interactive exhibits. Passing through darkened atmospheric rooms, the tour is designed to follow the rum-making process in sequential order, charting the transformation of sugar cane into Cuba's national drink. On the walk round you will see historical and contemporary rum-making machinery, and a captivating model of a sugar mill, and smell the odours from bubbling tanks full of fermenting molasses. You finish up in a fully functioning replica of a 1930s **bar**, where you're given a sip of the brew itself. There is also a shop selling the full range of Havana Club rums.

Sacra Catedral Ortodoxa Rusa

Ave. del Puerto (San Pedro) esq. Santa Clara • Daily 9am–5.45pm • Free

Standing out like a sore thumb on the Avenida del Puerto and a dead ringer for a fairytale fortress, the **Sacra Catedral Ortodoxa Rusa Nuestra Señora de Kazán**, to give it its full name, is one of the most unexpected sights in Habana Vieja. With hemispherical domes and a cylindrical base typical of neo-Byzantine architecture, this Russian Orthodox cathedral (the only one of its kind in Cuba) was inaugurated on October 19, 2008. There are thought to be between five and ten thousand Russians in Havana, most of whom moved here during the 1960s and 1970s, a time of enthusiastic economic and cultural exchange between Cuba and the Soviet Union. The temptation to look inside such a

1

strikingly unique building is hard to resist but, perhaps surprisingly, the interior is memorable mostly for its simplicity. The starkness of the white-walled, white marble-floored **nave**, accessed via the pleasant little courtyard up the steps at the rear, is punctuated by three golden chandeliers and a gleaming gold altar, full of painted saints and angels, but otherwise there is very little to avert your gaze.

Plaza de la Catedral and around

The **Plaza de la Catedral**, just a couple of blocks northwest of the Plaza de Armas, is one of the most historically and architecturally consistent squares in the old city. Perfectly restored and pleasantly compact, it's enclosed on three sides by a set of symmetrical eighteenth-century aristocratic residences. The first houses were built on the site – which was swampland when the Spanish found it – around the turn of the sixteenth century. It wasn't until 1788 that the Plaza de la Ciénaga (Swamp Square), as it was then known, was given its current moniker, after the Jesuit church on its north face was consecrated as a cathedral.

Catedral de la Habana

Empedrado no.156 e/ San Ignacio y Mercaderes, Plaza de la Catedral • Mon–Fri 10.30am–3pm, Sat 10.30am–2pm • Free, belltower $1CUC

The striking yet surprisingly small **Catedral de la Habana**, hailed as the consummate example of the Cuban Baroque style, dominates the Plaza de la Catedral with its swirling detail, curved edges and cluster of columns. Curiously, however, the perfect symmetry of the detailed exterior was abandoned in the design of the two **towers**, the right one noticeably and unaccountably wider than the left. The **interior** features a set of grandiose framed portraits by French painter Jean Baptiste Vermay (copies of originals by artists such as Rubens and Murillo), commissioned by Bishop José Díaz de Espada in the early nineteenth century to replace those works he considered to be in bad taste. One of the cathedral's principal heirlooms, a funeral monument to Christopher Columbus said to have contained his ashes, now stands in the cathedral in Seville, where it was taken when the Spanish were expelled from Cuba in 1898. A spiral stone staircase leads to the top of the **belltower**, where the views take in the Capitolio and the other side of the bay.

Museo de Arte Colonial

San Ignacio no.61 esq. Plaza de la Catedral • Daily 9am–7pm, doors close 6.30pm • $2CUC, guided tour $1CUC extra, photos $2CUC • ☎ 7 862 6440

Opposite the cathedral, the Casa de los Condes de Casa Bayona, built in 1720, houses the **Museo de Arte Colonial**, a comprehensive collection of mostly nineteenth-century furniture and ornaments. The predominantly European-made artefacts include elaborately engraved mahogany dressers and a petite piano. One room is full of colourful **vajillas**, plates engraved with the family coat of arms of counts and marquises from Cuba. It was customary in colonial aristocratic circles to give one of these *vajillas* to your hosts whenever visiting the house of fellow nobility.

Statue of Antonio Gades

Leaning against one of the stone pillars under the arches on the east side of Plaza de la Catedral is a life-sized bronze statue by José Villa Soberón of **Antonio Gades**, one of the greatest Spanish ballet dancers and choreographers of modern times, to whom the revival of Flamenco is attributed. Gades was also a committed communist and passionate supporter of the Revolution.

Casa del Marques de Aguas Claras

San Ignacio no.54 esq. Empedrado, Plaza de la Catedral • Restaurant noon–midnight; café 24hr • ☎ 7 867 1034

Sharing the northwestern corner of the Plaza de la Catedral with the cathedral, and host to the *El Patio* restaurant and café, is the **Casa del Marques de Aguas Claras**, the most sophisticated of the plaza's colonial mansions. You'll have to eat at the overpriced restaurant to get a proper look inside, where a serene fountain-centred courtyard is encompassed by pillar-propped arcs and coloured-glass portals.

Palacio de Lombillo

Empedrado no.151 esq. Mercaderes, Plaza de la Catedral • Mon–Fri 9am–5pm & Sat 9am–1pm

The **Palacio de Lombillo** dates from 1741 and was originally home and office to a sugar-factory owner. Much of it is closed to the public, but you can pop inside via the door on Empedrado and take a peek at the patio or scale the broad staircase.

Taller Experimental de Gráfica

Callejón del Chorro no.62, Plaza de la Catedral • Mon–Fri 9am–4pm • Free • ☎ 7 862 0979

At the end of Callejón del Chorro, a short cul-de-sac on the southwestern corner of the plaza, is the low-key **Taller Experimental de Gráfica**, an artists' workshop, gallery and market. The specialism here is etching and engraving, and the lithographs and stencil art displayed (and on sale) are more innovative and original than much of what you'll see in the arts and crafts shops around Habana Vieja. You can chat to the artists themselves, who are either busy at work in the open workshop or standing by their displays trying to make sales.

Centro de Arte Contemporáneo Wifredo Lam

San Ignacio esq. Empedrado • Mon–Sat 10am–5pm • $2CUC

In the shadow of the cathedral, the **Centro de Arte Contemporáneo Wifredo Lam** has a gallery with temporary exhibitions, sometimes of quite off-centre contemporary art, including photography, painting and sculpture.

Mercaderes

Bookended by the Plaza de la Catedral and the Plaza Vieja is **Mercaderes**, the most heavily trodden and interesting route between these two old squares, full of small museums and simple but pleasing distractions. Along with Oficios, this is one of the oldest streets in Havana and one of the most historically evocative in Habana Vieja, and almost every building on its six blocks has now been restored or renovated. The most densely packed sightseeing section is south of Obispo, where a museum, gallery, hotel or café occupies almost every building. Halfway along, the cafés gathered around the diminutive **Plaza de Simón Bolívar** are ideally located for a drink in the shade as you tour the area.

The Mural de Mercaderes

Mercaderes e/ Empedrado y O'Reilly

Within a block of the Plaza de la Catedral on Mercaderes is the giant **Mural de Mercaderes**, portraying 67 figures from Cuban arts and politics. Pictured as a group standing outside and on the balconies of a classic colonial Cuban building, they include Carlos Manuel de Céspedes (nineteenth-century revolutionary), José de la Luz y Caballero (nineteenth-century philosopher), Jean Baptiste Vermay (French painter whose work appears in the cathedral and in El Templete on the Plaza de Armas) and José Antonio Echeverría (1950s student leader and revolutionary).

Maqueta de la Habana Vieja

Mercaderes no.114 e/ Obispo y Obrapía • Daily 9am–6pm • $1.50CUC • ☎ 7 866 4425

The **Maqueta de la Habana Vieja** is an enthrallingly detailed model of the old city, including the bay and Habana del Este. Made up of some 3500 miniature buildings, the cityscape took three years to construct and occupies the larger part of the single room you can visit here. You should be able to pinpoint a few hotels, the main squares and the largest buildings, like the Capitolio. Each scheduled viewing is accompanied by a lighting sequence meant to replicate a day in the life of Habana Vieja and comes complete with the sounds of birdsong and car horns; if you listen carefully enough you should be able to make out the voice of someone offering to sell you a box of cigars.

Museo del Tabaco

Mercaderes no.120 e/ Obispo y Obrapía • Tues–Sat 9am–5.15pm, Sun 9am–12.45pm • Free or donation • ☎ 7 861 5795

A few doors along from the Maqueta de la Habana Vieja, a narrow staircase leads up almost directly from the street to the **Museo del Tabaco**, a surprisingly small collection of smoking memorabilia given Cuba's heritage in this industry. Stretched over five pokey rooms are modest collections of ashtrays, pipes and snuff boxes as well as a slightly more substantial set of twentieth-century lighters in all kinds of shapes and designs, from miniature telephones to a dinky piano and a machine gun. There's a cigar shop next door.

Casa de Asia

Mercaderes no.111 e/ Obispo y Obrapía • Tues–Sat 9.30am–4.45pm, Sun 9.30am–12.45pm • Free or donation

Another of the small museums on Mercaderes, the long narrow rooms of the **Casa de Asia** hold a hotchpotch of items from numerous Asian countries. The diversity of what's on display means that most visitors will find at least one thing to catch their eye, whether it's the samurai-style sword from tenth-century Laos, the model boats from Bangladesh or the metal statuette of the Hindu deity Shiva Nataraja.

Plaza de Simón Bolívar

One block from Obispo on Mercaderes, a mixed group of museums and galleries huddles around the **Plaza de Simón Bolívar**, a delightful and cosy little square consisting of exuberant gardens squeezed up against the surrounding buildings and crisscrossed by pathways. A **statue** of Simón Bolívar (see box, p.82) looks down from a plinth, and at the back of the square are the tables of a café based over the other side of Obrapía, the street hugging the square's northern border and dissecting Mercaderes.

Casa de Benito Juárez

Obrapía esq. Mercaderes • Tues–Sat 9.30am–5pm, Sun 9am–12.30pm • Free or donation • ☎ 7 861 8166

Facing the plaza from the Obrapía side is the occasionally worthwhile **Casa de Benito Juárez**, also known as the **Casa de México**. The two rooms set aside for temporary exhibitions of Mexican photography, painting or craftwork tend to be the more interesting sections, but are not always in use.

Fundación Guayasimín

Obrapía no.111 e/ Mercaderes y Oficios • Tues–Sat 9.30am–4.45pm, Sun 9am–12.45pm • Free or donation • ☎ 7 861 3843

The sparse interior of the **Fundación Guayasimín** displays paintings by the Ecuadorean artist and friend of Fidel Castro Oswaldo Guayasimín (1919–99). The works on display include a portrait of Fidel Castro which the painter presented to him on his seventieth birthday. The house was originally set up as a studio and apartment for Guayasimín himself, and the the bedroom and dining room are still intact.

Casa de Simón Bolívar

Mercaderes no.156 e/ Obrapía y Lamparilla • Tues–Sat 9am–4.30pm, Sun 9am–12.30pm • Free or donation • ☎ 7 861 3988

The **Casa de Simón Bolívar** details the life and times of the Venezuelan known as "El Libertador de las Américas" (see box, p.82). Significant or symbolic events in Bolívar's life – such as his birth, baptism and even his first sexual experience – are rendered via a series of often comically cartoonish clay models. Display screens in a separate room go into more depth, with useful written explanations in English, and there are also prints of some great paintings from the period that provide a lively visual context, plus an art gallery upstairs.

1

SIMÓN BOLÍVAR AND LATIN AMERICAN INDEPENDENCE

One of the few people in history to have had a country named after him, the man who put Bolivia on the map is also one of the most enduring and highly regarded icons of Latin America. **Simón Bolívar** was lauded for his prominent role in the independence struggles of the early nineteenth century, not least by Hugo Chávez, whose Bolivarian Revolution was inspired by the man who is remembered as the "Liberator of the Americas".

Born into an aristocratic family on July 24, 1783, in Caracas, Venezuela, Bolívar had lost both his parents by the age of 9. Sent to Europe for the final years of his formal education, he returned to Venezuela in 1802 a married man. His wife, the daughter of a Spanish nobleman, died of yellow fever within a year of the wedding and, grief-stricken, he returned to Europe and immersed himself in the writings of Montesquieu, Jean Jacques Rousseau and other European philosophers. It was under such influences in Paris and Rome that Bolívar developed a passion for the idea of American independence.

He returned once again to Venezuela in 1807, just as the Spanish Crown was forced into a loosening of its grip on the American colonies, following the Napoleonic invasion of Spain. Bolívar was to be the single most influential man during the ensuing **Spanish–American wars of independence**, as state by state South and Central America broke free of their colonial shackles. Involved personally in the liberation of five of these countries, including Venezuela, perhaps the most important and heroic of all the military campaigns that he waged was the taking of **New Granada** (modern-day Colombia). Against all the odds he led an army of some 2500 men through the Andes, enduring icy winds and assailing the seemingly nonnegotiable pass of Pisba. When Bolívar and his men descended into New Granada the colonial army was completely unprepared, and on August 10, 1819, after victory at the battle of Boyacá, they marched triumphantly into Bogotá.

On September 7, 1821 **Gran Colombia** (a state covering much of modern day Colombia, Panama, Venezuela, Ecuador, northern Peru and the northwest of Brazil) was created, with Bolívar as president. Though his goal of creating a federation of South American nations along the lines of the USA ultimately failed, tarnishing his contemporary reputation before he died in 1830, Bolívar's legacy was already cemented in history. By 1833 the Spanish American wars of independence, in which he had played such a prominent role, concluded with every mainland Spanish American country from Argentina to Mexico free of colonial rule, leaving Spain clinging onto just the Philippines, Puerto Rico and Cuba.

Casa de Africa

Obrapía no.157 e/ Mercaderes y San Ignacio • Tues–Sat 9.15am–4.45pm, Sun 9am–1pm • Free • ☎ 7 861 5798

Just a few paces away from the Plaza de Simón Bolívar is the standout museum in the vicinity, the **Casa de Africa**, a three-floor showcase for African and Afro–Cuban arts, crafts and culture. Many of the tribal artefacts, traditional artworks, sculptures and statues here once belonged to Fidel Castro, most of them given to him by leaders of the African countries he visited. Among the most arresting exhibits are two fantastic life-size wooden sculptures of large birds from the Ivory Coast and a marvellous sculpted depiction of a royal procession from Benin, featuring a pipe-smoking chieftain being carried on a hammock.

Casa de la Obra Pía

Obrapía esq. Mercaderes • Tues–Sat 10.30am–5.30pm, Sun 9am–1pm • Free or donation • ☎ 7 861 3097

Opposite the Casa de Africa, and distinguished by its ornately framed front entrance, is the eclectic **Casa de la Obra Pía**. An expansive seventeenth-century mansion with a spacious central patio, it's now a somewhat underused museum space. The interior architecture and original features of the house are the real draws, though they are well complemented by the substantial set of exhibits **upstairs**. Many of the rooms are impressively complete: the master bedroom, for example, is full of Rococo and Renaissance-style furniture, including an impressively grand bed and a cot designed to resemble an old boat. The threadbare displays **downstairs**, in the two rooms devoted to Alejo Carpentier (1904–80), Cuba's most famous novelist, are too limited to hold a broad appeal.

Museo Armería 9 de Abril

Mercaderes e/ Obrapía y Lamparilla • Mon–Sat 9am–6pm • Free • ☎ 7 861 8080

As the original 1950s sign outside indicates, **Museo 9 de Abril** was once an *armeria*, or gun store, but is now a one-room museum with display cabinets full of pistols, machetes, rifles, knives and various other weapons. It is more renowned, though, as a monument to what happened here on **April 9, 1958**, when, following calls for a general strike led by Fidel Castro, four rebels were killed trying to raid the store. There are photos of those who died as well as a few documents and newspaper articles from the time.

Plaza Vieja

Despite its name, **Plaza Vieja**, at the southern end of Mercaderes, is not the oldest square in Havana, having been established at the end of the sixteenth century after the creation of the Plaza de Armas. It became the "Old Square" when the nearby Plaza del Cristo was built around 1640, by which time Plaza Vieja had firmly established itself as a centre for urban activity, variously used as a marketplace and festival site. Most of its beautifully restored, porticoed buildings, however, were built in the eighteenth and nineteenth centuries, long after its foundation.

Today, more than any of the other principal old town squares, it reflects its original purpose as a focus for the local community, with some of the buildings around its colourful borders still home to local residents and others occupied by educational and cultural institutions. This has been one of the most redeveloped spots in Habana Vieja over the last decade, now repaved and distinguished with a central fountain, a museum, a planetarium, an arts centre and primary school, a rooftop camera obscura and some decent shops, restaurants and cafés, including one of the best places for a drink in Habana Vieja, the *Factoría Plaza Vieja* (see p.129). The only significant edifice yet to be restored, in the southeastern corner, is the Art Nouveau Palacio Cueto. Built between 1906 and 1908, it became a stunning hotel in the 1920s and is set to be one again if the renovations ever finish, having started around a decade ago.

For many visitors the Plaza Vieja is as far south in Habana Vieja as they are likely to wander, as the neighbourhood beyond is markedly short on specific sights. However, for a true taste of the old town as it was prior to the current tourism boom this part of the city is worth investigating.

Cámara Oscura

Brasil (Teniente Rey) esq. Mercaderes, Plaza Vieja • Daily 9am–5.30pm • $2CUC • ☎ 7 862 1801

In the northeastern corner of Plaza Vieja, where Mercaderes crosses Brasil, is the **Cámara Oscura**, a captivating ten-minute tour of Habana Vieja and the bay through a 360-degree-rotating telescopic lens. At the top of the seven-storey Gómez Vila building, built in 1933 and one of only two post-colonial edifices on the square, this impressive piece of kit can pick out sights and scenes from all over the old city in entertainingly close detail.

Fototeca de Cuba

Mercaderes no.307 e/ Brasil (Teniente Rey) y Muralla, Plaza Vieja • Tues–Sat 10am–5pm • Free • ☎ 7 862 2530

On the same side of the square as the Cámara Oscura, the **Fototeca de Cuba** is an underused and often understocked photography gallery with two rooms of temporary exhibitions. Both Cuban and international themes, subjects and photographers feature, and past exhibitions have ranged from portraits of Fidel Castro to showcases of National Geographic photography.

1

Planetario

Mercaderes e/ Brasil (Teniente Rey) y Muralla, Plaza Vieja • Wed–Sat 9.30am–5pm • $10CUC • ☎ 7 865 9544

Opened in 2009, the Havana **planetarium**, largely funded by the Japanese government, is on a smaller scale than versions in many cities around the world but is still one of the more impressive things to go and see in Habana Vieja, especially for kids. The four floors of rooms chart a journey through the cosmos, from the Big Bang (represented by a light and sound display) onwards. In the main hall is a three-dimensional representation of the **solar system**, with the giant sun, sensibly, at its centre. Other highlights include the **Space Theatre**, providing projections of stars, constellations and meteor showers and, on the fourth level, an observatory.

Museo de Naipes

Muralla esq. Inquisidor, Plaza Vieja • Tues–Sat 9.30am–4.45pm, Sun 9am–1pm • Free • ☎ 7 860 1534

Occupying the oldest building on Plaza Vieja, the **Museo de Naipes** takes a cursory but colourful look at the evolution and culture of **playing cards**. Decks of cards from around the world and down the years are neatly laid out in display cases, grouped into loose themes such as commerce and culture, and accompanied by related paraphernalia. Many are from Spain – not surprisingly, since most of what is here was donated by the Fundación Diego de Sagredo, a Madrid-based cultural and architectural institution who part-funded the museum's creation.

Casa del Conde de San Juan de Jaruco

Muralla esq. San Ignacio, Plaza Vieja • Gallery and shop Mon–Sat 9am–5.30pm, Sun 9am–1pm

On the southwestern corner of Plaza Vieja is the **Casa de los Condes de Jaruco**, dating from 1737 and one of the most important examples of eighteenth-century Cuban residential architecture, with its numerous stained-glass *vitrales* and interior friezes. It now houses a commercial art gallery and a dinky gift shop.

Aqvarivm

Brasil (Teniente Rey) e/ Oficios y Mercaderes • Thurs–Sat 9am–5pm, Sun 9am–1pm • $1CUC • ☎ 7 863 9493

About half a block east of Plaza Vieja is the tiny **Aquarium de Habana Vieja**, officially known as **Aqvarivm**. Its dimly lit interior contains eight rather unspectacular fish tanks, each teeming with fish from all over the world. The rarest species here – and certainly the strangest in appearance – is the prehistoric *manjuarí*, looking every bit the living fossil that it is, with its elongated body and protruding jaws lined with three sets of teeth.

Museo de la Farmacia Habanera

Brasil (Teniente Rey) e/ Compostela y Habana • Daily 9am–5pm • Free • ☎ 7 866 7556

In between Plaza Vieja and the residential Plaza del Cristo is the **Museo de la Farmacia Habanera**, housed in the old Farmacia La Reunión, a huge pharmacy established in 1853 that stayed in business until the Revolution in 1959. Restored to the impressive splendour of its heyday, it features an extravagantly adorned ceiling and walls lined with finely carved wooden cabinets brimming with hundreds of porcelain jars, which would once have contained the medicinal mixtures sold here. Some of the nineteenth-century laboratory apparatus used to make these mixtures, including a bizarre contraption once used to treat skin inflammations, is exhibited to the rear of the building. There are still concoctions for sale here, including natural medicines, some herbs and spices and more prosaic products like toothpaste and Alka-Seltzer.

STREET PERFORMERS, PLAZA VIEJA (P.83) >

1

Obispo and around

Linking the Plaza de Armas with Parque Central to the west is **Obispo**, Habana Vieja's busiest, most animated street and home to its thickest concentration of **shops** and **bars**. Redeveloped almost in its entirety since the mid-1990s, this narrow pedestrianized thoroughfare is almost always crowded with a lively, sometimes hectic mix of street vendors, bar touts, Cuban shoppers and foreign visitors. An endless stream of people pour in and out of the open-fronted bars, shops, neighbourhood hairdressers, hotels, restaurants and front-room galleries, or browse the secondhand bookstalls, haggle with the CD bootleggers and queue at the banks and phone centre.

Hotel Ambos Mundos

Obispo no.153 esq. Mercaderes • Room 511 open daily 10am–5pm • $2CUC • ☎ 7 860 9530

A Havana classic built between 1923 and 1925, the *Hotel Ambos Mundos* (see p.119) is most famous as Ernest Hemingway's Cuban base for ten years from 1932, from where he allegedly wrote *Death in the Afternoon* and embarked on *For Whom the Bell Tolls*. The hotel's rooftop-garden restaurant and bar (see p.129) is one of the best places for a **drink** in the old city and is open to non-guests. On the way up in the original 1920s cage-elevator, stop off on the fifth floor and visit **Room 511**, where Hemingway stayed. The original furniture and even his typewriter have been preserved, and there's usually a guide on hand to answer any questions.

Farmacia Taquechel

Obispo no.155 e/ San Ignacio y Mercaderes • Daily 9.30am–6.30pm • Free • ☎ 7 862 9286

Founded in 1898, **Farmacia Taquechel** is one of Habana Vieja's triumvirate of prestigious nineteenth-century pharmacies, along with the Droguería Johnson (see below) and La Reunión (see p.84). Restored in 1996, the fully functioning but clearly tourist-focused pharmacy specializes in natural medicines and displays admirable attention to period detail: from the shelves of porcelain medicine jars down to the cash register, there isn't a piece out of place.

Droguería Johnson

Obispo no.260 esq. Aguiar • Daily 9am–5pm • Free • ☎ 7 862 0311

Founded in 1886, the **Droguería Johnson** moved from O'Reilly, a block to the north, to this more commercially lucrative location on Obispo in 1914. Completely renovated after a fire in 2006 closed it down for the rest of the decade, it now has a mixture of original features and brand new elements modelled on the original design. The striking fifty-foot dark wood counter runs the length of the marble-floored building, while hundreds of elegant porcelain medicine jars line the floor-to-ceiling display cases.

Museo del Numismático

Obispo no.305 e/ Habana y Aguiar • Tues–Sat 9.15am–4.45pm & Sun 9am–1pm • $1CUC • ☎ 7 861 5811

Halfway along Obispo, in a grandiose, pillar-fronted building, is the **Museo del Numismático**, whose collection of coins, medals and banknotes over two floors is more interesting than you might think, acting as a window on events and personalities in Cuban history. For example, the medals for the highest order of merit under both the pre- and post-Revolution regimes, displayed here, are emblazoned with the face of José Martí (see p.109), testament to his wide political appeal.

Edificio Bacardí

Ave. de Bélgica (Monserrate) no.261 e/ Empedrado y San Juan de Dios

Undoubtedly one of the finest Art Deco buildings in Cuba is the **Edificio Bacardí**, two blocks north of the end of Obispo. Twelve storeys high, and finished in shiny red granite and enamelled terracotta, its construction was completed in 1930. It stood as a symbol of the wealth and influence of the Bacardí empire (see p.398), founded by the

1

famous rum family from Santiago. A statue of the familiar bat logo crowns the central tower but the company no longer operates in Cuba and today it is predominantly an office building. The best way to enjoy its sumptuous interior is to visit *Café La Barrita* on the mezzanine level just off the lobby (see p.124). Unofficially, a $1–2CUC tip will allow you to take the lift to the top and enjoy the knockout views.

Parque Central

Just beyond the western end of Obispo is the grandest square in Habana Vieja. The **Parque Central** sits at the halfway point of the Paseo del Prado, running along the border between Habana Vieja and Centro Habana. In the late nineteenth and early twentieth centuries this area saw many colonial buildings demolished and replaced with flamboyant palaces, imposing Neoclassical blocks and some of the finest hotels ever built in the city, many of them still standing today around the square's borders. Mostly shrouded in shade, the square lies within shouting distance of one of Havana's most unforgettable landmarks, the **Capitolio Nacional**. Though the traffic humming past on all sides is a minus, the grandeur of the surrounding buildings lends the square a stateliness quite distinct from the residential feel which pervades elsewhere in Habana Vieja.

The Gran Teatro

Paseo del Prado e/ San Rafael y San José, Parque Central • Guided tours $2CUC; guides are allocated at the ticket booth midway between the two entrances • ☎ 7 861 7391

The attention-grabber on the Parque Central is undoubtedly the **Gran Teatro**, an explosion of balustraded balconies, colonnaded cornices and sculpted stone figures striking classical poses. The theatre complex is made up of two parts: the nineteenth-century theatre building itself and the former **Centro Gallego**, or Galician Centre, which was built around the theatre in 1915 at the same time as the exterior and is now largely used for ballet rehearsals and lessons. It's well worth taking a guided tour to marvel at the sumptuous Neoclassical **interiors** of both buildings. Particularly stunning is the recently restored double marble staircase in the Centro Gallego.

Hotel Inglaterra

Paseo del Prado no.416 esq. San Rafael, Parque Central • ☎ 7 860 8594

In the thick of the commotion on the Parque Central is the renowned **Inglaterra**, the oldest hotel in the country, having been opened in 1856; past guests include Antonio Maceo (see p.456), who lodged here in 1890 during a five-month stay in Havana. The pavement café out front is one of the few places around the park where you can sit and take it all in, though you are unlikely to be able to do so in peace.

Capitolio Nacional

Paseo del Prado e/ San José y Dragones

Just beyond the southwestern corner of the Parque Central, and visible above the Gran Teatro on the same corner, looms the familiar-looking neo-classical dome of the **Capitolio Nacional**. Bearing a striking resemblance to the Capitol Building in Washington DC (though little is made of this in Cuban publications), its solid, proudly columned front dominates the local landscape. The interior architecture and design are truly stunning and impressively complex in style, though as it's currently closed for extensive and lengthy restoration, the public may not get another proper look at it for years. From the vast and magnificent entrance hall, the two resplendent main debating chambers with their breathtaking gold-and-bronze Rococo-style detail, the ornate Italian Renaissance-style Salón Baire and the Biblioteca Martí (supposedly a replica of the Vatican library), so many of its rooms are marked by extravagant,

1

ornate detail. Built in just three years by several thousand workers, it was opened in 1929 amid huge celebrations. It was the seat of the House of Representatives and the Senate prior to the Revolution and from 1960 functioned as the headquarters of the Ministry for Science, Technology and the Environment. Today it is principally a tourist attraction.

Paseo del Prado

Cutting through the Parque Central's western edge and marking the border between Habana Vieja and Centro Habana is the **Paseo del Prado**, one of the old town's prettiest main streets. Also known as the Paseo de Martí, but more often simply as **El Prado**, its reputation comes from the boulevard section north of the park, beginning at the *Hotel Parque Central* and marching down to the seafront. A wide walkway lined with trees and stone benches bisects the road, while on either side are the hundreds of columns, arches and balconies of the mostly residential neocolonial buildings, painted in a whole host of colours. Encouragingly, despite its position in the city's touristic centre, El Prado still belongs to the locals and is usually overrun with newspaper sellers and children playing ball games.

Parque de la Fraternidad

The network of lawns dissected by paths and roads immediately to the south of the Capitolio is the **Parque de la Fraternidad**, the biggest expanse of open land in Habana Vieja and the city's largest transport hub. Alive with buses, taxis and people, only a few of them stopping to sit on the park's benches, the sense of commotion here overrides all else. With so much traffic and so many roads to cross, few visitors bother spending much time in the park itself, though there are a couple of curiosities and, on the eastern side, the magnificent **Hotel Saratoga** (see p.120) and the quirky **Museo de los Orishas**.

It wasn't until 1928 that the park took its current form and name, constructed as part of the sixth Pan-American Conference that took place in Havana. This was when the centrepiece – a huge, encaged ceiba tree, the **Arbol de la Fraternidad Americana** – was planted, using soil brought from every country that attended the conference. In addition, busts of some of the continent's most revered leaders were installed, including Abraham Lincoln, Simón Bolívar and Benito Juárez, the first indigenous president of Mexico.

The Fuente de la India

Parque de la Fraternidad

Stranded on what has effectively become a traffic island, on the Prado side of the Parque de la Fraternidad, a monument known as the **Fuente de la India** has become one of the symbols of the city. Erected in 1837, an Amerindian woman in a feather headdress sits atop this marble monument holding the city's coat of arms, flanked by four fierce-looking fish. The woman is **La Noble Habana**, who, according to popular legend, greeted the Spanish colonialists who first arrived at the port in 1509 with a gesture that appeared to refer to the bay and uttered the word "habana" – thus spawning the name of the city.

Museo de los Orishas

Paseo del Prado e/ Máximo Gómez (Monte) y Dragones, Parque de la Fraternidad • Daily 9am–5pm • $10CUC for solo visitors, or $6CUC per person if there's more than one, $3CUC for students • ☎ 7 863 5953

At the southern end of El Prado, housed within the Asociación Cultural Yoruba de Cuba headquarters (a focal point and meeting place for the capital's Santería community) is the **Museo de los Orishas** or "Museum of the Gods". This unusual though slightly overpriced museum is populated with full-size terracotta statues of the best-known Afro–Cuban deities, each one full of personality and set in its own representative scene. With the

SANTERÍA AND CATHOLICISM

Walking the streets of Havana you may notice people dressed head-to-foot in white, a bead necklace providing the only colour in their costume. These are practitioners of **Santería**, the most popular of Afro–Cuban religions, and the beads represent their appointed **orisha**, the gods and goddesses at the heart of their worship.

With its roots in the religious beliefs of the Yoruba people of West Africa, Santería spread in Cuba with the importation of slaves from that region. Forbidden by the Spanish to practise their faith, the slaves found ways of hiding images of their gods behind those of the Catholic saints to whom they were forced to pay homage. From this developed the **syncretism** of African *orishas* with their Catholic counterparts – thus, for example, the Virgen de la Caridad del Cobre, the patron saint of Cuba, embodies the *orisha* known as Oshún, the goddess of femininity, in part because both are believed to provide protection during birth. Similarly, Yemayá, goddess of water and queen of the sea – considered the mother of all *orishas* – is the equivalent of the Virgen de Regla, whom Spanish Catholics believed protected sailors. Other pairings include San Lázaro, patron saint of the sick, with Babalu-Ayé, Santa Bárbara with Changó, and San Cristóbal with Aggayú. There are some four hundred Afro–Cuban *orishas* in all.

assistance of the on-hand English-speaking guide, this is both a straightforward and fascinating insight into the main deities, as well as some of the practices, which form the basis of this earthy, colourful faith. There are also activities here open to the public, including dance performances; details can be found on the notice board in the entrance hall. A restaurant-cum-caféteria on site serves African–Cuban food.

Southern Habana Vieja

South of the Parque de la Fraternidad and Plaza Vieja, the tourist sights almost instantly die out and Habana Vieja takes on a more workaday character, dotted with churches, food markets, *casas particulares* and a couple of old convents among all the apartment buildings, in an area so far largely untouched by the huge restoration projects. There are a couple of specific points of interest, but aimless wandering is the order of the day round here, with the shadowy, crowded streets offering an undiluted taste of life in Old Havana.

Casa Natal de José Martí

Paula no.314 e/ Picota y Egido • Tues–Sat 9.30am–5pm, Sun 9.30am–12.30pm • $1.50CUC • ☎ 7 861 3778

Two blocks east of the Parque de la Fraternidad is the Avenida de Bélgica, a main road leading down to the most tangible and best-kept tourist attraction in this part of town, the **Casa Natal de José Martí**. This modest two-storey house was the birthplace of Cuba's most widely revered freedom fighter and intellectual, though he only lived here for the first three years of his life. Dotted with the odd bit of original furniture, the rooms of this perfectly preserved blue-and-yellow house don't strive to re-create domestic tableaux, but instead exhibit photographs, documents, some of Martí's personal effects and other items relating to his tumultuous life (see box, p.109). The eclectic set of memorabilia includes a plait of his hair, his bureau and a watch chain given to him by pupils of a Guatemalan school where he taught. There are images of his arrest, imprisonment and exile on the Isla de Pinos (now the Isla de la Juventud), and details of his trips to New York, Caracas and around Spain.

Iglesia de San Francisco de Paula

Avenida del Puerto, opposite the eastern end of Leonor Pérez • Mon–Sat 9am–5pm • Free • ☎ 7 860 4210

With an unusual squat shape and a distinct lack of uniformity via arched stone walls protruding from one side, the **Iglesia de San Francisco de Paula** looks somewhat cobbled together. The church was once the chapel of a hospital for poor and homeless women,

1

first established in 1664 but then completely rebuilt after being damaged by a hurricane in 1730. In 1946, it had passed into private ownership and the hospital was demolished, leaving the apparently designless structure left standing today. Nowadays it's used for classical and orchestral **concerts** (see p.131), but you can pop in during the day to appreciate the simple, compact and delicately restored grey stone interior, where a few splashes of colour are provided by modern paintings of biblical scenes and an almost abstract stained-glass window.

Museo Nacional de Bellas Artes

Tues—Sat 9am—5pm, Sun 10am—2pm • $5CUC for one building, $8CUC for both • Guided tour $2CUC per building • ☎ 7 861 5777 & 862 0140 • ⊕ museonacional.cult.cu

Set along the broad avenues that fill the relatively open spaces on the western edge of Habana Vieja, the **Museo Nacional de Bellas Artes** is the most impressive and spectacular of Havana's museums and by far the largest art collection in the country, with its collection divided between two completely separate buildings, two blocks apart. The museum stands head and shoulders above the vast majority of its city rivals, presented and put together with a degree of professionalism still quite rare for this kind of attraction in Cuba. The large and rather plain-looking Art Deco **Palacio de Bellas Artes** is the showcase for exclusively Cuban art, offering a detailed examination of the history of Cuban painting and sculpture, including everything from portraits by Spanish colonists to Revolution-inspired work – though pre-Columbian art is notably absent. Artists from the rest of the world are represented in the **Centro Asturiano**, with an impressive breadth of different kinds of art, including Roman ceramics and nineteenth-century Japanese paintings.

No English translations have been provided for any of the titles in either building, which can be a hindrance to fully appreciating some of the works on display – particularly in the ancient art section, where it's not always clear what you are looking at. Both buildings have **bookshops** where you can buy good-quality, Spanish-only guides to their collections ($12CUC each), invaluable if you have an interest in the context and background of the paintings.

Palacio de Bellas Artes

Trocadero e/ Zulueta y Ave. de las Misiones (Monserrate)

No other collection of **Cuban art**, of any sort, comes close to the range and volume of works on display in the beautifully lit, air-conditioned **Palacio de Bellas Artes**, a two-minute walk north along Agramonte from the Parque Central. The collection spans five centuries but has a far higher proportion of twentieth-century art, though given the dearth of colonial-era painting around the island the museum can still claim to best represent the country's artistic heritage.

The best way to tackle the three-floor, chronologically ordered collection is to take the lifts up to the top floor and walk around clockwise. From a set of relatively ordinary colonial-era portraits and landscapes there is an abrupt leap into the twentieth century, the most substantial and engaging part of the collection. Among the most famous of the paintings is *Gitana Tropical* (Tropical Gypsy) by **Victor Manuel García** (1897–1969), one of the first Cuban exponents of modern art. His evocative yet simplistic portrait of a young native American woman is a widely reproduced national treasure. Paintings by other Cuban greats such as **Wifredo Lam** (1902–82) and **Fidelo Ponce de León** (1895–1949) are succeeded by art from the 1950s, 1960s and 1970s respectively, and then finally a section dedicated to works produced since 1979. This includes installation art, sculptures and, in the work of **Raúl Martínez** (1927–95), an example of a very Cuban take on pop art.

It's worth having a drink at the **caféteria** on the ground floor just to sit beside the pleasant open courtyard, where there are a few modern sculptures dotted about. Before leaving, check the notice board in the entrance hall for upcoming **events** in the museum, often in its 248-seat theatre.

Centro Asturiano
San Rafael e/ Zulueta y Ave. de las Misiones (Monserrate)

In contrast to the Art Deco simplicity of the Palacio de Bellas Artes, the interior of the stately **Centro Asturiano**, on the east border of the Parque Central, is a marvel to look at in itself. Housing the international collections of the Museo de Bellas Artes, this grandiose building is plastered with balcony-supported columns and punctuated with carved stone detail. The entrance hall with its wide marble staircase is a real knockout, punctuated by thick pillars and, looming above, spacious balustraded balconies from which you can admire the stunning stained-glass ceiling.

The exhibits are divided up by **country of origin**, with the largest collections by Italian, French and Spanish artists, on the fifth, fourth and third floors respectively. There are one or two standouts among the more mundane British, German, Dutch and Flemish collections, all on the **fifth floor**, such as *Kermesse* by Jan Brueghel (the younger), one of the only internationally famous artists in this section. The painting depicts a peasant scene with all sorts of debauchery going on, a focus typical of his work.

Elsewhere you can see **ancient art** from Rome, Egypt, Greece and Etruria, including vases, busts, and most notably the coffin from a 3000-year-old tomb; a small room of nineteenth-century Japanese paintings and, sketchiest of all, a haphazard set of Latin American and North American paintings.

Museo de la Revolución
Refugio no.1 e/ Zulueta y Ave. de las Misiones (Monserrate) • Daily 9am–5pm • $5CUC, guided tour $2CUC, $2CUC for Granma memorial only • ☎ 7 862 4091

Next to a small piece of the old city wall is Havana's most famous museum, the **Museo de la Revolución**. Triumphantly housed in the sumptuous presidential palace of the 1950s dictator General Fulgencio Batista, the museum manages to be both unmissable and overrated at the same time. The events leading up to the triumph of the Revolution in 1959 are covered in unparalleled detail, but a clear narrative of what happened is lost in the sometimes disjointed displays, and your attention span is unlikely to last the full three storeys. Visitors work their way down from the top floor, which is the densest part of the museum. Rooms are grouped chronologically into historical stages, or **etapas**, from *Etapa Colonial* to *Etapa de la Revolución*, though the layout is a bit higgledy-piggledy in places, making it unclear what point in the timeline you have reached.

The Revolutionary War and the urban insurgency movements during the 1950s were surprisingly well documented photographically and it's at this stage of the story that the exhibits are most engaging. Among them are the classic photos of the campaign waged by Castro and his followers in the Sierra Maestra and the sensationalist **Memorial Camilo-Che**, a life-sized wax model of revolutionary heroes Camilo Cienfuegos and Che Guevara. However, even serious students of Cuban history may overdose on models of battles and firearms exhibits also found in this section.

Much of the second floor is given over to tiresome depictions of battle plans and the "construction of Socialism", bringing the story up to the present. It's the **interior of the building** itself, built between 1913 and 1917 during the much-maligned "pseudo-republic" era, that is most captivating on this floor. There's the gold-encrusted Salón Dorado; the lavish dining room of the old palace when it was occupied by General Batista; the dignified furnishings of the Presidential Office (used by all the presidents of Cuba from 1920 to 1965); and the wonderfully colourful **mural** on the ceiling of the Salón de los Espejos.

1

Granma Memorial
Daily 9am–5pm • $2CUC, not including Museo de la Revolución

Joined to the Museo de la Revolución building, but located to the rear in the fenced-in gardens of the palace, is the **Granma Memorial**, where the boat which took Castro and his merry men from Mexico to Cuba to begin the Revolution is preserved in its entirety within a giant glass case. Also here are military vehicles (whole or in bits, depending on which side they belonged to) used during the 1961 Bay of Pigs invasion, and a poignant pink marble monument to those who died in the revolutionary struggle. A flame rising from a single Cuban star is surrounded by the words "*Gloria eternal a los heroes de la patria nueva*" (Eternal glory to the heroes of the new fatherland).

Castillo de San Salvador de la Punta and around
Ave. del Puerto esq. Paseo del Prado • Tues–Sat 9.30am–5.30pm, Sun 9am–1pm • Free

Hogging most of La Punta, the paved corner of land at the entrance to the bay, the sixteenth-century fortress of **Castillo de San Salvador de la Punta** is one of the oldest military fortifications in the city. Construction began in 1589 at the same time as that of El Morro (see p.93), and together these two forts formed the city's first and most important line of defence. Save for a few cannon, there's very little to see inside San Salvador de la Punta, as the museum previously housed here was moved following repeated storm damage, though the ramparts afford modest views along the Malecón and over to El Morro.

La Punta itself caps one end of the official border between Habana Vieja and Centro Habana. Right next to the busy junction where the Malecón meets the Avenida del Puerto, its position is less than enchanting, though it still attracts groups of chattering locals and youngsters, who gather to throw themselves off the Malecón into the rocky pools that jut out from the sea wall here.

Monumento a Máximo Gómez
On a giant traffic island between La Punta and the rest of Habana Vieja is the Neoclassical **Monumento a Máximo Gómez**, one of the grandest memorials in Havana. Dedicated to the venerated leader of the Liberation Army in the nineteenth-century Cuban Wars of Independence, the statue has the general sitting on a horse held aloft by marble figures representing the People.

Parque de los Mártires
Over the road from the Monumento a Máximo Gómez is the pretty little **Parque de los Mártires**, marking the spot where the notorious prison, the **Cárcel de Tacón**, built in 1838, once held such political prisoners as José Martí. It was mostly demolished in 1939, and all that remains are two of the cells and the chapel in what is little more than a large concrete box.

Parque Morro-Cabaña
Carretera de la Cabaña, Habana del Este • Daily 8am–11pm • $1CUC • Transport options include the ferry (see p.93), a taxi ($3–5CUC from Habana Vieja) or the Habana Bus Tour from the Parque Central (see p.116); get off at the first stop after the tunnel on the route to the Playas del Este.

While many visitors don't make it to the **Parque Morro-Cabaña**, across the bay from Habana Vieja, those who do are rewarded by the uncrowded sights of an impressive, sprawling complex of fortifications that, along with the two fortresses in Habana Vieja, comprised the city's colonial defence system. A stalwart part of both the Havana skyline and timeline, the two fortresses here dominate the view across the channel into the harbour, and mark key events and periods in the city's history. Beyond the forts, further

CROSS-BAY FERRIES

Used very little by tourists, the rudimentary **cross-bay ferry services** that link Habana Vieja with Casablanca and Regla on the eastern side of the bay represent a cheap and pleasant (but slow) way of getting to the Parque Morro-Cabaña. Ferries leave from a small jetty opposite the Russian Orthodox Cathedral on San Pedro in Habana Vieja, two minutes' walk from the Plaza de San Francisco and the main Sierra Maestra Terminal. Bikes are not permitted. The ferry runs daily between 6am and 11pm, and the fare is $0.10CUP; departures are outlined below.

Habana Vieja to: Casablanca (every 30min; 10min); Regla (every 30min; 20min).
Casablanca to: Habana Vieja (every 30min; 10min).
Regla to: Habana Vieja (every 30min; 20min).

into the bay, a gargantuan statue of Christ, **El Cristo de La Habana**, was one of the last public works completed before Cuba was taken over by Fidel Castro and his revolutionary – and subsequently atheist – government.

Of the several **restaurants** and **bars** in and around this military park, the best is *La Tasca* (see p.125), a delightful spot for lunch or dinner.

Castillo de los Tres Reyes Magos del Morro

Parque Morro-Cabaña • Daily 8am–8.30pm • $5CUC, $6CUC with guide, extra $2CUC for lighthouse

Crowning the low cliffs of the rocky headland that marks the entrance to the Bahía de la Habana is the imposing **Castillo de los Tres Reyes Magos del Morro**, more commonly known as **El Morro**. This castle was built between 1589 and 1630 to form an impeding crossfire with the Castillo de San Salvador de la Punta (see p.92) on the opposite side of the bay, a ploy that failed spectacularly when the English invaded overland in 1762 and occupied the city for six months.

Once you get beyond the bar, shop and the exhibition room laid out with scale models of Cuban forts just off the central courtyard, the castle has an eerie, just-abandoned feel. The cavernous billet rooms and cannon stores are empty but in near-perfect condition, while the easy-to-follow layout and peaceful, uncluttered spaces lend themselves to wandering around at your own pace. Particularly fine are the broad castle **ramparts** studded with rusted cannon and offering splendid views on all sides. There are even better views from the summit of the **lighthouse**, built on the cliff edge in 1844, over two centuries after the rest of the fortress had been completed.

Fortaleza San Carlos de la Cabaña

Parque Morro-Cabaña • Daily 10am–10pm • $5CUC before 6pm, $8CUC after 6pm, guide $1CUC extra

Situated roughly 500m further into the Bahía de la Habana from El Morro, the **Fortaleza San Carlos de la Cabaña** needs a half day to do it justice. Despite containing a much larger number of things to see and do within its grounds, its wide-open spaces, benches and trees, along with a garden area, make it the more relaxing of the two forts. Built to be the most complex and expensive defence system in the Americas, the fortress was started in 1763 as soon as the Spanish traded the city back from the English. However, its defensive worth has never been proved, as takeover attempts by other European powers had largely died down by the time it was finished in 1774.

You can see why it took so long to finish after touring the extensive grounds, akin to a small village complete with a chapel, spacious lawns, several more recently installed cafés and restaurants, and impeccable cobbled streets lined with houses where soldiers and officers were originally billeted – now a miscellany of workshops, touristy arts-and-crafts stores and a number of small **museums**. Among these

1

THE HERSHEY TRAIN FROM HAVANA

Aside from the Cristo de La Habana statue, the only other diversion in Casablanca is the terminus of the **Hershey train** (see p.116), one end of Cuba's only electric train service (the other is in the provincial capital of Matanzas). Regularly used by Cubans travelling to stations in Mayabeque and Matanzas, the line is not an official tourist attraction, but the loveable little trains, built in the 1940s, are a great way to take a slow, relaxing ride through picturesque landscape to Canasí (see p.233), Jibacoa (see p.234) or all the way to the city of Matanzas (see p.214), which takes about three hours and costs just under $3CUC.

one- and two-room museums is a weaponry and armoury collection, a set of colonial-era furniture once in practical use at the fortress and a commemoration of the 1961 Bay of Pigs invasion and the 1962 Cuban Missile Crisis, featuring some dramatic photographs from the time. The **Ceremonia del Cañonazo**, in which soldiers in nineteenth-century uniforms fire the cannon at 9pm every evening, is entertaining enough to stick around for.

El Cristo de La Habana

Daily 8am–11pm • $1CUC, free if you show a ticket for Parque Morro-Cabaña • The best way to get here from Habana Vieja is the cross-harbour ferry (see box, p.93), which docks close by

On the hill above the picturesque village of Casablanca, 1km southeast from the entrance to the Fortaleza San Carlos de la Cabaña, is **El Cristo de La Habana**, a 17m-high Christ figure commissioned by Marta Batista, wife of the dictator, and sculpted from Italian marble by Jilma Madera in 1958. Although impressive close-up, where you can ponder the massive scale of the sandaled feet and the perfectly sculpted hands, said to weigh a tonne each, there's precious little to do on the hillside other than admire the **views** over Havana. The best perspective of the statue itself is from Habana Vieja, especially in the evening, when you can gaze across the bay and enjoy its floodlit grandeur.

Centro Habana

For many visitors the crumbling buildings and bustling streets of **Centro Habana**, crammed between the hotel districts of Habana Vieja and Vedado, are glimpsed only through a taxi window en route to the city's more tourist-friendly areas. Yet this no-frills quarter has a character all of its own, as illuminating and fascinating as anywhere in the capital. Its late eighteenth- and nineteenth-century neighbourhoods throb with life, particularly around San Rafael and Avenida de Italia, renowned shopping streets where many of the most glamorous department stores were located before the Revolution (see box, p.96), when the Avenida de Italia was known as Galiano, the name most locals still use. Near the southern end of Galiano is **El Barrio Chino**, Havana's Chinatown, small by international standards but still a busy focal point for the area.

For the most part, Centro Habana is not that attractive on the surface. Full of broken sewage systems, potholed roads and piles of rubbish, it isn't for the faint-hearted, and hasn't yet enjoyed the degree of investment and rejuvenation lavished on Habana Vieja. However, the famous **Malecón** seafront promenade is starting to regain its former glory, with many of its buildings given face-lifts in recent years, and there's nowhere in the city that feels more alive. Centro Habana's streets buzz with people and non-stop noise, ringing with an orchestra of street vendors shouting their wares, *bicitaxis* blasting their sound systems, schoolchildren's screams and doorstep politics.

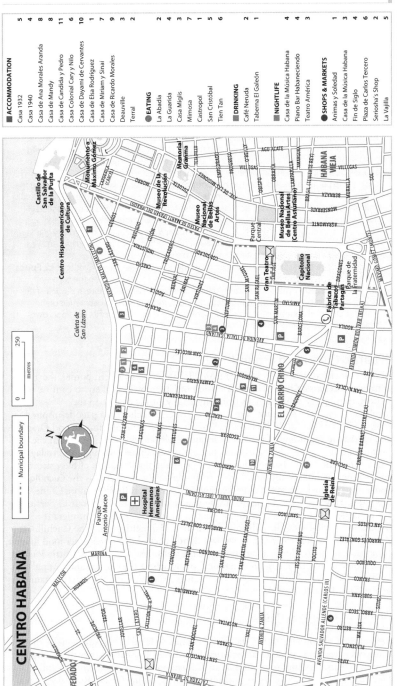

CENTRO HABANA

1

STORE DETECTIVE

During the 1950s, Havana's most prestigious shopping destination was the Centro Habana intersection where San Rafael and Neptuno converged with Galiano. At its heart, on the corner of San Rafael and Galiano, stood **El Encanto**, the most renowned of the department stores, occupying an entire block and boasting the patronage of Hollywood stars like Lana Turner, John Wayne and Errol Flynn. In 1961 the store, which by this time had been nationalized, was burned to the ground, the result of a bomb attack in the tumultuous early years of the Revolution.

Five decades later and general neglect coupled with the effects of the US trade blockade has left the area sorely dilapidated, and instead of swanky shopfronts, it's now peppered with a selection of artless hard-currency stores and murkily lit peso shops. Rather than unearthing great retail finds, the real pleasure here is spotting the vestiges of a glamorous past in the old shop signs, marble pavements, faded interiors and elaborate tiled frontages that dazzle amid the ruins. In particular, look out for the **Hotpoint mosaic** on San Rafael esq. Industria; and the stylish flourish of lettering spelling out **Fin de Siglo** along the building on the corner of Aguila and San Rafael, once a fancy five-floor department store featuring a hair salon decorated with floor-to-ceiling mirrors, now the scene of a huge, jam–packed ground-floor market selling secondhand clothing and other goods; and the **Flogar** logo imprinted on the dusty glass frontage of the large, half-empty store at Galiano no.42, where once mannequins displayed the latest fashions in the Macy's-style window displays.

The only department store to have been fully redeveloped since the Revolution is **La Epoca**, reborn a little less than a half-a-century after it first moved into its home on the corner of Galiano and Neptuno in 1954, becoming the third largest department store in Havana at the time, employing over four hundred staff. Locals flock here today to buy counterfeit brand clothing, electrical goods and homewares, though the current design of its five floors owes more to modern supermarkets than the chic interiors of yesteryear.

El Barrio Chino and around

About a block inside Centro Habana from Habana Vieja's western border, the grand entrance to **El Barrio Chino**, Havana's version of Chinatown, is likely to confuse most visitors, as it's placed three blocks from any visibly ethnic change in the neighbourhood. The **entrance**, a rectangular concrete arch with a pagoda-inspired roof, is south of the Capitolio Nacional, on the intersection of Amistad and Dragones, and marks the beginning of the ten or so square blocks which, at the start of the twentieth century, were home to some ten thousand Chinese immigrants. Today only a tiny proportion of El Barrio Chino, principally the small triangle of busy streets comprising Cuchillo, Zanja and San Nicolás – collectively known as the **Cuchillo de Zanja** – three blocks west of the arched entrance, is discernibly any more Chinese than the rest of Havana. Indeed, the first thing you are likely to notice about El Barrio Chino is a distinct absence of Chinese people, the once significant immigrant population having long since dissolved into the racial melting pot. The Cuchillo de Zanja itself does, however, feature its own tightly packed little backstreet food market, composed mostly of simple fruit and vegetable stalls. It's lined with eccentric-looking restaurants, many still charging in national pesos, where the curious and unique mixture of tastes and styles is as much Cuban as Asian. Among the better restaurants here is *Tien Tan* (see p.126).

Fábrica de Tabacos Partagás
Industria no.50 e/ Dragones y Barcelona

Behind the Capitolio (see p.87) stands the **Fábrica de Tabacos Partagás**, one of the country's oldest and largest cigar factories, founded in 1845 and currently undergoing lengthy repairs. Up until its closure in 2012 it employed some 750 workers and produced twelve brands of cigars, including Cohiba, Monte Cristo, Romeo y Julieta, Bolívar and Partagás itself. The fascinating **tours** here should be reinstated when the factory finally reopens, though knowing when this will be is anyone's guess; the last time it shut down for repairs in 1989 it was closed for two years. The cigar store just inside the entrance remains open.

Iglesia de Reina

Ave. Simón Bolívar (Reina) no.461–463 e/ Padre Varela (Belascoaín) y Gervasio • Daily 8am–noon & 3–5pm • Mass daily 8am & 4.30pm • Free

Well away from any tourist traffic, a block away from the Avenida Salvador Allende, one of Centro Habana's broadest thoroughfares, sits the magnificent church locally known as the **Iglesia de Reina**. The tallest church in the country, with a spire rocketing out from a block of worn-out neocolonial apartment buildings, it was built between 1914 and 1923 and is officially known as the Parroquia del Sagrado del Corazón de Jesús y San Ignacio de Loyola. Its unlikely location in the grime of Centro Habana, with heavy traffic passing by outside, contrasts effectively with its Neo-Gothic splendour and makes a wander through its imposing entrance irresistible. Inside, a second surprise awaits, as the church's **interior** is infinitely more impressive than that of Habana Vieja's much more heavily visited cathedral: the cavernous vaulted roof of the three naves is supported by colossal columns and the huge central altar incorporates a dazzling array of detail. Wherever you look, something catches the eye, from the skilfully sculpted scenes etched into the central pillars to the stained-glass windows at different levels on the outer walls.

The Malecón and around

The most picturesque way to reach Vedado from Centro Habana or Habana Vieja is to stroll down the famous **Malecón** sea wall, which snakes west along the coastline from La Punta for about 4km. It's the city's defining image, and ambling along its length, drinking in the panoramic views, is an essential part of the Havana experience. But don't expect to stroll in solitude: the Malecón is the capital's front room and you won't be on it for long before someone strikes up a conversation. People head here for free entertainment, particularly at night when it fills up with guitar-strumming musicians, vendors offering cones of fresh-roasted nuts, and star-gazing couples, young and old alike. In recent years it's grown in popularity for the city's expanding clique of gays and transvestites, who put its sinuous length to good effect as a nightly catwalk and meeting place, especially the area close to the *Hotel Nacional* in Vedado. In the daytime it's crowded with schoolchildren (intent on hurling themselves into the churning Atlantic), wide-eyed tourists and anglers climbing down onto the rocks below.

The Centro Habana section, referred to on street signs as the **Malecón tradicional**, has been undergoing tortoise-paced renovations for around two decades now. Lined with colourful neo colonial buildings, it's the oldest, most distinct and characterful section in the city, though – potholed and sea-beaten – it looks much older than its hundred or so years. Construction began in 1901, after nearly a decade of planning, and each decade saw another chunk of wall erected until, in 1950, it finally reached the Río Almendares. Today there are a few places worth stopping in for their enjoyable sea views. The best of these is *Café Neruda* (see p.129), *Taberna El Galeón* (see p.129), *Castropol* (see p.126) and the *La Abadía* tapas bar (see p.126).

Centro Hispanoamericano de Cultura

Malecón no.17 e/ Paseo del Prado y Capdevila (Cárcel) • Mon–Sat 9.30am–5pm • ☎ 7 860 6282

A seafront arts centre in a wonderful Neoclassical building, the **Centro Hispanoamericano de Cultura** stages art exhibitions, book and poetry readings and, on Saturday afternoons, live music performances. There's also a library and a small cinema but it's worth just taking a quick wander around the beautifully restored building, one of the few open to the public on the Malecón that isn't a hotel, restaurant or bar.

1

Parque Antonio Maceo

On the western edge of Centro Habana, a few blocks from Vedado, the Malecón passes in front of the **Parque Antonio Maceo**, often referred to simply as the Parque Maceo, an open concrete park and one of the most attractive public spaces in Centro Habana. Overlooked by the best hospital in the country, the towering Hospital Hermanos Ameijeiras, the park is marked in the centre by a statue of Antonio Maceo, the Cuban general and hero of the Wars of Independence. The only other monument the **Torreon de San Lázaro**, a solitary little turret, little more than a curiosity but dating all the way back to 1665, making it 250 years older than the park itself. Once part of the city's defence system, it's now stuck in the corner of the park where Marina intersects with the Malecón. There's a small playground here and the park attracts scores of kids and chattering adults every evening, which is the best time to visit.

Callejón de Hamel

Four blocks west from the Parque Maceo on San Lázaro, a wide alleyway known as the **Callejón de Hamel** has been converted into an intriguing and cultish monument to Afro–Cuban culture. Often featured in Cuban music videos, this bizarre backstreet is full of **shrines**, cut into the walls and erected along the sides, brimming with colour and a mishmash of decorative and symbolic images. The backdrop is an abstract **mural** painted by Salvador González in 1990, when it was decided that it was high time for a public space dedicated to Afro–Cuba. A few chairs and tables make up a tiny café at one end and the alley also features a small studio workshop selling smaller pieces of art done by González. On Sundays from around 11am, Callejón de Hamel becomes a venue for **Santería ceremonies**, mini street festivals in which participants dance passionately to the rhythm of rumba in a frenetic atmosphere, accentuated by chants invoking the spirits of the *orishas*. The alley becomes overrun with visitors – not to mention *jineteros* – and the event has unfortunately become slightly contrived, though it's still a very accessible way to experience one of the most engaging expressions of Santería.

Vedado

The cultural heart of the city, graceful **Vedado** draws the crowds with its palatial hotels, contemporary art galleries, exciting (and sometimes incomprehensible) theatre productions and live music concerts, not to mention its glut of restaurants, bars and nightspots. Loosely defined as the area running west of Calzada de Infanta up to the Río Almendares, Vedado is less ramshackle than other parts of the city. Tall 1950s buildings and battered hot rods parked outside glass-fronted stores lend the downtown area a strongly North American air, contrasted with the classical ambience of nineteenth-century mansions; the general impression is of an incompletely sealed time capsule, where the decades and centuries all run together.

Vedado is fairly easy to negotiate, laid out on a grid system divided by four main thoroughfares: the broad and handsome boulevards Avenida de los Presidentes (also called Calle G) and Paseo, running north to south, and the more prosaic Linea and Calle 23 running east to west. The most prominent sector is modern **La Rampa** – the name given to a busy section of Calle 23 immediately west from the Malecón, as well as the streets just to the north and south. Presenting a rather bland uniformity that's absent from the rest of Vedado, it's a relatively small space, trailing along the eastern part of the Malecón and spanning just a couple of streets inland. A little to the south of La Rampa proper is the elegant **Universidad de La Habana**, attended by orderly students who personify the virtues of post-Revolution education.

Southwest of the university is the **Plaza de la Revolución**, with its immense monuments to Cuban heroes José Martí, Ernesto "Che" Guevara and, more recently

1

HAVANA FROM A HEIGHT

With its architecturally distinct neighbourhoods dating from separate eras, Havana looks stunning from above, but since the city is laid out on relatively flat land, you have to go to the southern outskirts or over to the eastern side of the bay for hills high enough to afford a decent **view**. There are, however, numerous tall buildings open to the public dotted around the city proper, with fabulous vistas across the boroughs. The best of these are detailed below.

Cámara Oscura Plaza Vieja, Habana Vieja. Catch a view of Havana from the roof terrace or get a "guided tour" of parts of the city through a telescopic lens. See p.83.

Edificio FOCSA Calle 17 no.55 e/ M y N, Vedado. The restaurant at the top of the city's tallest apartment building offers a winning combination of food and great views. See p.101.

Habana Libre Calle L e/ 23 y 25, Vedado. You'll have to eat at the restaurant or pay the nightclub's entrance fee to get up to the top of this famous Havana hotel – but either way, it's worth it. See p.122.

Iglesia de San Francisco de Asís Plaza de San Francisco, Habana Vieja. Climb the wooden staircase to the top of the church belltower and enjoy a great perspective of the old city. See p.78.

Memorial José Martí Plaza de la Revolución, Vedado. An obligatory part of the tourist circuit, the memorial offers the best vantage point for bird's-eye views of Havana, reaching as far as the western suburbs. See p.107.

Saratoga and Parque Central hotels Paseo del Prado, Habana Vieja. The most blissful way to view the city from above is by lounging in one of these two rooftop hotel swimming pools. See pp.119–120.

Torre del Oro Roof Garden, Hotel Sevilla Trocadero no.55 e/ Paseo del Prado y Agramonte (Zulueta). One of the swankiest restaurants in the city, in a cavernous balustraded hall with marble floors and towering windows – the food is only average, but the views across the city are superb. See p.120.

added, Camilo Cienfuegos. Although generally considered part of Vedado, Plaza de la Revolución (also known just as Plaza) is actually the municipality to which the Vedado neighbourhood belongs, and with its huge utilitarian buildings has a flavour quite distinct from the other parts of Vedado. The uncompromisingly urban landscape of the plaza itself – a huge sweep of concrete – is a complete contrast to the area's other key attraction, the atmospheric **Necrópolis de Cólon**, a truly massive cemetery.

In the part of Vedado north of Calle 23 up to the Malecón, west to the Río Almendares and east roughly as far as the Avenida de los Presidentes, the backstreets are narrow and avenues are overhung with leaves. Many of the magnificent late- and post-colonial buildings here – built in a mad medley of Rococo, Baroque and Neoclassical styles – have been converted into state offices and museums. Particularly noteworthy is the **Museo de Artes Decorativas**, an exhausting collection of fine furniture and *objets d'art*. Further west from the Malecón, dotted around Linea, Paseo and the Avenida de los Presidentes, are several excellent galleries and cultural centres. Not to be missed is the **Casa de las Américas**, a slim and stylish Art Deco building that was set up to celebrate Pan-Americanism.

La Rampa

Halfway along the Malecón's length an artificial waterfall, at the foot of the *Hotel Nacional* precipice, marks the start of **La Rampa** (The Slope), the road into the centre of Vedado. Once the seedy pre-revolutionary home of Chinese theatres, casinos and pay-by-the-hour knocking shops, La Rampa is now lined with airline offices and official headquarters, its seedy side long gone (or at least well hidden).

Set on a bluff above the Taganana cave (see box, p.101) and with a magnificent view of the ocean, the landmark **Hotel Nacional** (see p.122) is home to a princely tiled lobby, and an elegant colonnaded veranda looking out to sea across an expanse of well-tended lawn commandeered by tame guinea fowls. The perfect cinematic backdrop for a *mojito*, it was built in 1930 and quickly became a favourite with

1

VEDADO

0 — 500
metres

- - - Municipal boundary

N

Monumento General Calixto García
Parque Deportivo José Martí
US Interests Section
PLAZA ANTI-IMPERIALISTA
Memorial a las Víctimas del Maine
Casa de las Américas
SEE INSET BELOW
Centro Cultural Bertold Brecht
Museo de la Danza
Hotel Nacional
Museo Abel Santamaría
Teatro Hubert de Blanck
El Gran Palenque
Teatro Mella
Museo de Artes Decorativas
Cine Riviera
Universidad de la Habana
J.A. Mella Memorial
Museo Napoleónico
Museo Antropológico Montané & Museo de Ciencias Naturales Felipe Poey
Estadio Juan Abrantes
Parque John Lennon
Quinta de los Molinos & Museo Máximo Gomez
Castillo del Principe
AVE. SALVADOR ALLENDE (CARLOS III)
Puente de Hierro
Sala Polivalente Ramón Fonst
AVENIDA ZAPATA
Cine Chapelín
AVENIDA ZAPATA
Memorial Ernesto "Che" Guevara
Memorial Camilo Cienfuegos
Astro Terminal de Omnibuses Nacionales
Teatro Nacional
PLAZA DE LA REVOLUCIÓN
Biblioteca Nacional
Necrópolis de Colón
Museo & Memorial José Martí

SHOPS

Agromercado Calle 19 y A	5
Arte Malecón	1
Belkis	6
Casa del Habano	12
Galería Juan David	10
Galería Habana	2
Habana Sí	13
ICAIC	8
Ibrain Portieles	9
Librería Centenario del Apóstol	3
Librería Fernando Ortíz	4
Mercado de La Rampa	11
Mirtha	7

EATING

1830	7	G Café	2
Los Amigos	10	El Gran Añejo	1
Café Laurent	11	Gringo Viejo	4
Cafetería La Rampa	13	La Torre	9
Casa de Adela	5	Unión Francesa	6
Coppelia	12	La Veranda	8
Decameron	3		

DRINKING

Aire Mar	12	La Fuente	5
Café Bar Madrigal	9	Opus Bar	3
El Emperador	14	La Torre	15
Fresa y Chocolate	10		

NIGHTLIFE

Cabaret Parisién	13	El Guiñol	16
Café Cantante Mi Habana	11	Hurón Azul	6
Casa de la Amistad	8	No Se Lo Digas a Nadie	2
Casa de la Cultura de Plaza	7	Salón Rojo	17
Delirio Habanero		Teatro Amadeo Roldán	4
Piano Bar	11	Turf Club	1
Galería Juan David		La Zorra y El Cuervo	18
El Gato Tuerto	12		

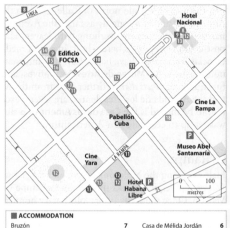

LINEA
Hotel Nacional
Edificio FOCSA
Cine La Rampa
Pabellón Cuba
Museo Abel Santamaría
Cine Yara
LA RAMPA
Hotel Habana Libre

0 — 100
metres

ACCOMMODATION

Bruzón	7	Casa de Mélida Jordán	6
Casa de Aurora Ampudia	8	Casa de Silvia Vidal	5
Casa de Conchita García	11	Habana Libre	12
Casa de Leydiana Navarro Cardoso	10	Nacional	9
Casa de Magda	4	Presidente	2
Casa Matilde	1	Riviera	3

visiting luminaries – among them Ava Gardner, Winston Churchill, Josephine Baker and John Wayne – and more recently has added the likes of Naomi Campbell and Jack Nicholson to its clientele.

Edificio FOCSA
Calle M esq 17

Considered variously as a feat of engineering or a monolithic eyesore, the giant Y-shaped luxury apartment block **Edificio FOCSA** looms over the heart of Vedado like a giant chunk of honeycomb. When built in 1956 this was the second-tallest concrete building in the world; it exemplified modern living with a cinema, supermarket, shops and even a television studio within. According to Alfredo José Estrada in his book *Havana: Autobiography of a City*, by the 1960s the building was know as "*edificio coño*" (roughly equivalent to the "Oh my God!" building) because of the stunned reaction of visiting country bumpkins. Following the Revolution, it housed Soviet personnel whose lack of respect, according to locals, resulted in widespread disrepair. By the early 1990s vultures nested in crumbling eyries, a snapped cable in the deteriorated elevator resulted in a fatal accident in 2000, and the state stepped in with a repair programme that has restored much of the building's former glory. Today FOCSA has one of Vedado's better shopping complexes at ground level, while *La Torre* restaurant (see p.127) on the 33rd of the building's 35 floors boasts panoramic views over the Malecón and beyond.

Memorial a las víctimas del Maine
Malecón y Linea

Just to the north of the *Hotel Nacional* stands the striking **Memorial a las víctimas del Maine**, erected in memory of 260 crew members of the US battleship *The Maine*, which was blown up in Havana harbour on February 15, 1898 (and so is studiously ignored by Cuban maps and guidebooks).

   Following the Revolution, crowds attacked the monument, toppling and destroying the heavy iron eagle that once perched on the top (the wings are displayed in the Museo de la Ciudad, while the head is in the US Special Interests Section canteen). The present government has stamped its presence with the terse inscription: "To the victims of *The Maine*, who were sacrificed by imperialist voraciousness in its zeal to seize the island of Cuba from February 1898 to 15 February 1961".

US Interests Section
Calzada e/ L y M • ☎ 7 839 4100, ⊛ havana.usint.gov

Straddling the entire block formed by Calzada, L, M and the Malecón is the **US Interests Section**, the organization that has acted in lieu of a US embassy since diplomatic relations between Cuba and the US ended in 1961. The somewhat

---

TAGANANA CAVE

You can enter the **Taganana cave** (Mon–Sat 9am–5pm; free) through the *Hotel Nacional* grounds, where a small display charts the history of the cave and its rocky outcrop. It was named after a character created by novelist Cirilo Villaverde, whose story placed the fictional Indian Taganana there after seeking refuge from pursuing conquistadors. The natural cave and its vantage point overlooking the seafront were capitalized upon by the Spanish, who built the Batería de Santa Clara battery on it in 1797 and then in 1895 positioned two cannon here for use during the Wars of Independence. Following the war, the battery was expanded and converted into military barracks, which remained until the 1930s when the area was earmarked for a showcase hotel. The cave's final moment of glory came during the Missile Crisis in 1962, when Che Guevara and Castro decamped here with suitable military artillery in preparation for an air defence of the capital.

1

monolithic modernist building was built as the US Embassy by architect firm Harrison and Abramovitz in 1953.

Plaza Anti-Imperialista

Deliberately built to obscure as much as possible of the US Interest Section building, of which it sit directly in front, the **Plaza Anti-Imperialista** is a huge, sweeping space under a series of metal suspension arches like the ribs of a giant carcass. Many of the supports are covered in plaques bearing the names and quotes of Cubans and non-Cubans who have supported the country's struggle for self-determination and independence over the last century or so.

Museo Abel Santamaría

Calle 0 esq. Calle 25 • Mon–Fri 10am–5pm, Sat 10am–1.30pm • Free

Tucked away in an unassumingly residential corner just east of La Rampa is one of Havana's smallest museums, the **Museo Abel Santamaría**. It was here in 1952 that Abel Santamaría, his sister Haydee Santamaría, Fidel Castro and others planned the attack on the Moncada barracks (see p.400). Following the unsuccessful attack, Abel was captured and tortured to death on Batista's orders. In tribute to him, his simply decorated apartment has been preserved as it was on his final days living there.

Coppelia

Calle 23 esq. L • ☎ 7 832 6184 • Tues–Sun 11am–11pm

In the middle of an attractive park dotted with weeping figs and rubber trees is Havana's mighty ice-cream emporium, **Coppelia**, the flagship branch of this national chain. Looking like a giant space pod, with a circular white chamber atop a podium, the multi-chamber restaurant was designed by Mario Girona in 1966 as an eating place with prices within the reach of every Cuban. It was named Coppelia by Celia Sánchez (see p.423) after her favourite ballet of the same name. Serving over a thousand customers a day, it's a city institution, hugely popular with locals, who regularly wait in line for over an hour – though, contrary to its egalitarian ethics, there is now a separate fast-track parlour to the left of the main entrance, catering for those paying in convertible pesos. Cuban film buffs will recognize the park from the opening scenes of Tomás Gutiérrez Alea's seminal 1993 film, *Fresa y Chocolate*. To appreciate the space-age architecture fully, go up to *La Torre* restaurant (see p.127) for a panoramic view.

Universidad de La Habana

San Lázaro y L

Regal and magnificent, the **Universidad de La Habana** sits on the brow of the Loma Aróstegui Hill, three blocks or so south of La Rampa, overlooking Centro Habana.

SQUARING UP

Also known as Plaza de la Dignidad, the Plaza Anti-Imperialista open-air auditorium was hurriedly constructed in 2000 as a forum for Fidel Castro's protestations and invective during the furore surrounding the flight to the US (and eventual return) of schoolboy **Elián Gonzáles**. In January 2006, North American diplomats began displaying messages about human rights via an electronic **ticker-tape** on the side of the building facing the plaza; the US termed this as an attempt to break Cuba's "information blockade"; Fidel Castro denounced it as a "gross provocation". Later that year the Cuban authorities retorted by erecting **138 black flags** facing the ticker tape, each decorated with a white star and said to symbolize Cubans who have died as a result of violent acts against the country by unsympathetic regimes since the Revolution began in 1959. US diplomats subsequently announced in 2009 they would desist from displaying inflammatory messages. Today the plaza is as often used for free music concerts as speeches.

Founded in 1728 by Dominican monks, the university originally educated Havana's white elite; blacks, Jews, Muslims and mixed-race peoples were all banned, though by an oversight surprising for the time, women weren't, and by 1899 one-seventh of its students were female. It counts among its **alumni** many of the country's famous political figures, including Cuban liberator José Martí, independence fighter Ignacio Agramonte, and Fidel Castro, who studied law here in 1945. Originally based in a convent in Habana Vieja, it was secularized in 1842 but did not move to its present site, a former Spanish army barracks, until 1902, spreading out across the grounds over the next forty years. Today, the university is an awesome collection of buildings and home to some of the city's most unusual **museums**.

The scene of countless student protests, including one led by Julio Antonio Mella in 1922 (see p.458), the university was long seen as a hotbed of youthful **radicalism**. Guns were stashed here during the Batista administration, when it was the only site where political meetings could take place unhindered. The present administration, however, keeps the university on a firm rein and firebrand protests are no more, though its politicized past is evoked in some quirky details scattered throughout the grounds. These include the original American **tank** captured during the civil war in 1958 and placed here by the Union of Young Communists as a tribute to youth lost during the struggle, and, opposite, an "**owl of wisdom**" made of bits of shrapnel gleaned from various battle sites. Still a respected seat of learning, the university today has a rather serious air: earnest students sit on the lawn and steps in front of faculty buildings locked in quiet discussion, while inside a library-like hush reigns.

Memorial a Julio Antonio Mella

The rubbly pile of oversized grey and whitewashed concrete blocks, near the foot of a sweeping stone staircase capped by twin observation points, is actually the **Memorial a Julio Antonio Mella**, a modern tribute to this former student, political agitator and founder of the Communist Party, thought to have been murdered for his beliefs. Off to one side, a bust captures his likeness while the words on the main column are his: "To fight for social revolution in the Americas is not a utopia for fanatics and madmen. It is the next step in the advance of history." At the top of the stairs, beyond the lofty entrance chamber, lavishly fêted with Corinthian columns, lies the Ignacio Agramonte courtyard, with a central lawn scattered with marble benches and bordered on four sides by grandiose faculty buildings.

Museo de Ciencias Naturales Felipe Poey

Felipe Poey building, Patio de los Laureles • Mon–Fri 9am–noon & 1–4pm • $1CUC

To the left of the university's main entrance is the **Museo de Ciencias Naturales Felipe Poey**, the most bewitching of all the campus buildings, with a beautiful central atrium from which rises a towering palm twisted with vines. Named after an eminent nineteenth-century naturalist, and with the musty atmosphere of a zoologist's laboratory, the dimly lit room holds an assortment of stuffed, preserved and pickled animals. The highlight is the collection of **Polymita snails' shells**, delicately ringed in bands of egg-yolk yellow, black and white, while other notables are a (deceased) whistling duck, a stuffed armadillo and Felipe Poey's death mask, incongruously presented along with some of his personal papers. If you have young children, you might want to check out the kids' corner, where you can pet the stuffed duck, squirrel and iguana.

Museo Antropológico Montané

Felipe Poey building, Patio de los Laureles • Mon–Fri 9am–4.00pm • $1CUC

Those unmoved by the charms of taxidermy can press on from the Museo de Ciencias Naturales up the right-hand staircase along the cloistered balcony to the **Museo Antropológico Montané**, home to an extensive collection of pre- Columbian pottery

1

and idols from Cuba and elsewhere. Though padded out with apparently indiscriminately selected pieces of earthenware bowls, the collection contains some beautifully preserved artefacts, like the Peruvian Aztec pots adorned with alligator heads and the fierce stone figurine of the Maya god Quetzalcoatl, the plumed serpent, tightly wrapped in a distinctive clay coil design. Star attractions include a **Taíno tobacco idol** from Maisí in Guantánamo; roughly 60cm tall, the elongated, grimacing, drum-shaped idol with shell eyes is believed to have been a ceremonial mortar used to pulverize tobacco leaves. Also fascinating is the delicate reproduction of a Haitian two-pronged **wooden inhaler** carved with the face of a bird, which the Taíno high priest would use to snort hallucinogenic powder in the Cohoba ceremony, a religious ritual for communicating with the dead. Finally, check out the stone **axe** found in Banes, Holguín, which is engraved with the stylized figure of Guabancex, a female deity governing the uncontrollable forces of nature, her long twisted arms wrapped around a small child.

Museo Napoleónico

San Miguel no.1159 esq. Ronda • Tues–Sat 9.30am–5pm, Sun 9.30am–1pm • Tours in English, Spanish and French $2CUC • ☎ 7 879 1412

Just behind the university, the **Museo Napoleónico** boasts an eclectic array of ephemera on the French emperor, spread over four storeys of a handsome nineteenth-century house. The collection was gathered at auction by Orestes Ferrara, an Italian ex-anarchist who became a colonel in the rebel army of 1898 and subsequently a politician in Cuba. Ranging from state portraits, *objets d'art* and exquisite furniture to military paraphernalia and sculpture, it should appeal to anyone with even a passing interest in the era. The renovated museum was reopened in 2012 with great pomp and ceremony by Alix, Princess Napoleon, a descent of the man himself.

Central Vedado

West of the university grounds lies **Central Vedado**, quieter than the boisterous La Rampa area and more scenic than Plaza de la Revolución. To walk through these silent, suburban streets, once the exclusive reserve of the wealthy, is one of the richest pleasures Havana holds, the air scented with sweet mint bush and jasmine. At night, the stars, untainted by street lamps, form an eerie ceiling above the swirl of ruined balconies and inky trees. No less attractive in the daytime, with few hustlers, it is also one of the safest areas to stroll, and the added attraction of several museums will give extra purpose to a visit.

Museo de Artes Decorativas

Calle 17 no.502 e/ E y D • Tues–Sat 10.30am–6pm, Sun 9am–noon • $2CUC, $3CUC with guide, photos $3CUC • ☎ 7 832 0924

A fifteen-minute walk west from the university, the beautifully maintained **Museo de Artes Decorativas** contains one of the most dazzling collections of pre-revolutionary decorative arts in Cuba. The mansion in which it's set was built towards the end of 1920s as the private estate of the Count and Countess of Revilla de Camargo, who fled Cuba in 1961, whereupon it was appropriated by the state as the ideal showcase for the nation's cultural treasures. With its regal marble staircase, glittering mirrors and high ceilings, it is a perfect backdrop for the sumptuous, if overwrought, collection of Meissen and Sèvres china, *objets d'art* and fine furniture – a tantalizing glimpse of Vedado's past grandeur. The nine rooms are **themed** according to period, style and function, with some significantly more distinct and coherent than others, particularly those that most faithfully replicate their original purpose, when the house was lived in, such as the largely unaltered bathroom. **Guides** are knowledgeable and friendly but tend to bombard you with information, and with such a massive collection in so small a space you may feel more comfortable setting your own agenda and seeing the rooms unattended.

To the left of the grand entrance hall, the **Salón Principal** (Main Room), richly panelled in gold and cream, is full of lavish Rococo ornaments, like the pair of stylishly ugly eighteenth-century German dog-lions, while the **Chinese Room** next door is dominated by large, intricately screen-printed wooden panels. Upstairs, the rooms are gathered around a majestic balconied hall, among them a fabulous **bathroom** with a marble bathtub inset in the wall. Don't miss the fascinating framed **photographs** hanging in the upstairs hallways depicting over-the-top banquets and high-society social functions that took place in the house itself in the 1940s and 1950s, alongside pictures of the treasures stashed by the owners in the basement.

Parque John Lennon

For an ambling detour, head further up Calle 17 until you reach Calle 6 and **Parque John Lennon**, so named for the sculpture, created in 2000 by José Villa Soberón, of the eponymous musician seated on one of the park benches. It's a pretty good likeness and more or less life-sized. Although Lennon never came to Cuba, the Beatles have always been wildly popular here, so much so that it's not uncommon to hear people claiming to have learnt English through listening to their songs. Perhaps proving his popularity, Lennon's trademark circular glasses have been prised off by souvenir hunters several times, and now the sculpture is protected at night by an armed guard. Every year on December 8 – the anniversary of Lennon's death – there is a combination vigil and jamming session, though recent years have seen attendance dwindle from former crowds to a mere handful of devotees.

Museo de la Danza

Linea no.251 esq. G • Tues–Sat 10am–5pm • $2CUC• ☎ 7 831 2198

A few blocks away north of the Museo de Artes Decorativas, the **Museo de la Danza** charts the history of the ballet in Cuba and elsewhere via an immense amount of exhibits crammed into a small colonial house. Though the displays struggle to maintain a clear focus, the common thread is **Alicia Alonso**, Cuba's most famous prima ballerina, and every effort has been made to relate exhibits to her. That said, twentieth-century Russian ballet, and particularly **Anna Pavlova**, is given its own spotlight, with an embroidered cape worn by Pavlova, photos of her and a poster from a 1917 production of *El Gallo de Oro* (*Le Coq D'Or*) in which she starred. Some of the best exhibits are found in the museum's back room, where original preliminary sketches for costumes and stage sets are exhibited. The final and largest rooms are devoted entirely to Alonso and the **Ballet Nacional de Cuba**, which was founded by Alonso herself, her husband Fernando and his brother Alberto in 1948 and is widely recognized as one of the top ballet companies in the world.

Galería Habana

Linea e/ E y F • Mon–Fri 10am–4.30pm, Sun 9am–1pm• Free • ☎ 7 832 7101, ⓦ galerihabana.com

A short detour west from the Museo de la Danza to brings you to the unprepossessing doorway (at the base of an apartment block) of one of Havana's longest-standing and most respected art spaces: **Galería Habana**. Established in 1962 to showcase Cuban talent, several of the country's most celebrated artists are represented here. With white walls and marble floor, the airy and minimal gallery perfectly frames the work of masters like the late **Wifredo Lam**'s Afro–Cuban Surrealism and **Pedro Pablo Oliva**'s dreamy mysticism. Younger contemporary artists include the collective **Los Carpinteros**, whose architectural installations mix sly humour and social commentary. Exhibitions change every three months, with many pieces offered for sale. Those with several thousand euro to spare can also snap up a slice of Cuban art history for themselves at November's **Subasta Habana** auction (ⓦ subastahabana.com), which the gallery runs annually at the *Hotel Nacional*.

1

Casa de las Américas

Avenida de los Presidentes, esq. Calle 3ra • Mon–Thurs 10am–5pm, Fri 10am–4pm • Free • ☎ 7 838 2706, ⓦ casadelasamericas.org

The **Casa de las Américas** is housed in a dove-grey Art Deco building inlaid with panes of deep blue glass. Previously a private university, it was established as a cultural institute in 1959 – with its own publishing house, one of the first in the country – by the revolutionary heroine Haydee Santamaría to promote the arts, history and politics of the Americas. Since then, its promotion and funding of visual artists, authors, playwrights and musicians has been successful enough to command respect throughout the continent and to attract endorsement from such international literary figures as Gabriel García Márquez.

Today it hosts regular conferences, musical performances and talks, many of which are open to the general public and a few of which take place outside of the building's regular opening hours. The monthly programme of events is published on the website and is also available from the reception hall or the Librería Cayuela, the building's small bookshop. It's worth ringing in advance before you visit, as attendance at some events is by prior arrangement only. Outside of these events, visitors are restricted either to the bookshop, the ground-floor reception area that sometimes hosts small art exhibitions or, most worthwhile of all, the lovely little **Galería Latinoamericana** on the first floor.

Galería Latinoamericana

Mon–Thurs 10am–5pm, Fri 10am–4pm • $2CUC

This understated **Galería Latinoamericana** stages high-quality bimonthly exhibitions, showcasing anything from painting and sculpture to photography and film-poster art from other Latin American countries.

Galería Mariano

Calle 15 no.607 e/ B y C • Tues–Sat 10am–5pm • $2CUC

Ten blocks away from the main building, the Casa de las Américas operates another gallery, the **Mariano**, where exhibitions tend to be of ornamental arts and handicrafts from all over Latin America and the Caribbean.

Monumento General Calixto García

Within view of Casa de las Américas on the Malecón is the aristocratic **Monumento General Calixto García**. Set in a walled podium, it's an elaborate tribute to the War of Independence general who led the campaign in Oriente, and shows him dynamically reining in his horse surrounded by friezes depicting his greatest escapades, which would warrant closer inspection were it not widely used as a public toilet.

Avenida de los Presidentes

Bisecting Vedado from broadly north to south, the **Avenida de los Presidentes** (aka Calle G) is one of the suburb's main arteries, connecting the Malecón area to the southern side of Municipio Plaza. The avenue is at its most beautiful between the sea and Calle 27, a wide boulevard lined with lawns, benches and trimmed topiary bushes, and statuesque houses rising amid the trees on either side. Sculptures, statues and tributes to an assortment of presidents are interspersed along its length. At the southeastern foot of the Aróstegui hill, Avenida de los Presidentes intersects with Avenida Salvador Allende (also known as Carlos III), which heads east towards Centro Habana. Set back from this traffic-clogged avenue are the romantic remains of the **Quinta de los Molinos** tobacco mill estate, currently closed for renovation at the time of writing.

Castillo del Príncipe

Ave. de los Presidentes

At the foot of the José Miguel Gómez memorial the wide pedestrian-friendly boulevard comes to an abrupt halt; to explore further, those on foot must negotiate

1

AVENIDA DE LOS PRESIDENTES' STATUES

On a white plinth near the northern end are the remnants of a statue of Cuba's first president, **Tomás Estrada Palma**, one of the two presidents after whom the avenue is named. Torn down in a wave of anti-American feeling in 1959 as a response to his role in signing the Cuban–American Treaty that leased Guantánamo Bay to the US government in 1903, all that remains of the statue are his feet.

Further along, the tributes become more international. Among non-Cubans honoured are Chile's socialist president and friend of Fidel Castro, **Salvador Allende**, and Mexican president and national hero **Benito Juárez**. Perhaps less expected is the statue of US president **Abraham Lincoln**, in the grounds of the Abraham Lincoln School on the west side of the avenue between calles 17 and 19.

The second of the avenue's original presidents is at the southern end of the boulevard. Framed by several metres of impressive curved marble colonnade adorned with Neoclassical figures, the statue of **José Miguel Gómez** is redolent of bombastic pomp and self-glorification. Cuba's second president, whose term was dogged by accusations of corruption, he was also removed from his plinth in the early 1960s, though was mysteriously returned to it in 1999.

the narrow dust track that runs alongside the busy flow of traffic heading over the brow of the Loma Aróstegui hill. Almost completely obscured by trees and shrubs lining the sharp banks of the hill to the right is the **Castillo del Príncipe** (closed to visitors). Something of a curiosity, if only because of its notable absence from official tourist literature and maps, the castle was built between 1767 and 1779 by the Spanish military engineer Don Silvestre Abarca, who also designed the Fortaleza San Carlos de la Cabaña (see p.93).

The castle's various bulwarks, warehouses and offices provided ample space for the thousand soldiers billeted there in the late eighteenth century. Though it never proved its mettle when under attack, the castle's fortifications – not to mention underground dungeons and galleries – were formidable enough to warrant its conversion into one of Havana's most notorious prisons in the early nineteenth century. The tables were turned in the early years of the Revolution when counter-revolutionaries, including several captured during the Bay of Pigs invasion, were incarcerated here. The prison was subsequently converted into its rather esoteric present-day use as a ceremonial unit for the armed forces in the 1970s.

Plaza de la Revolución

At the southwest corner of the Quinta de los Molinos grounds, the Avenida de los Presidentes becomes Avenida de Ranchos Boyeros and continues south for about 1km to the **Plaza de la Revolución**. For much of the time the plaza comes as a bit of a letdown, revealing itself to be just a prosaic expanse of concrete bordered by government buildings and the headquarters of the Cuban Communist Party. You'll find a more animated scene if you coincide your visit with May Day or other annual parade days, when legions of loyal Cubans, ferried in on state-organized buses from the *reparto* apartment blocks on the city outskirts, come to wave flags and listen to speeches at the foot of the José Martí memorial. Tourists still flock here throughout the year to see the plaza's tri-fold attractions: the **Memorial Ernesto "Che" Guevara**, **Memorial José Martí** and the **Memorial Camilo Cienfuegos**.

Memorial José Martí
Plaza de la Revolución

Although widely seen as a symbol of the Revolution, the star-shaped **Memorial José Martí** had been in the pipeline since 1926 and was completed a year before the

1

Revolution began. Its 139m marble super-steeple is even more impressive when you glance up to the seemingly tiny crown-like turret, constantly circled by a dark swirl of birds. Near the base sits a 17m **sculpture** of Martí (see box opposite), the eloquent journalist, poet and independence fighter who missed his chance to be Cuba's first populist president by dying in his first ever battle against the Spanish on April 11, 1895. Carved from elephantine cubes of white marble, the immense monument captures Martí hunched forward in reflective pose.

Museo José Martí

Plaza de la Revolución • Mon–Sat 9am–4.30pm • Museum $3CUC, museum and lookout $4CUC, photos $1CUC

Behind the statue of José Martí, the stately ground floor of the memorial tower houses the exhaustive **Museo José Martí**, which charts Martí's career mainly through letters and photographs. The lavish entrance hall, its walls bedecked with Venetian mosaic tiles interspersed with Martí's most evocative quotes, certainly befits a national hero and is the most impressive aspect of a museum that tends to stray off the point at times. The most eye-catching exhibit is close to the entrance to the first room: a replica of Simón Bolívar's diamond-studded **sword**, which was given to Fidel Castro by Venezuelan President Hugo Chávez in 2000.

The exhibits

The second room holds **photographs** of Martí in Spain, Mexico and North America along with an assortment of **artillery**, most notably Martí's six-shooter Colt revolver engraved with his name, and the Winchester he took with him into his only battle. A temporary exhibition space in the fourth room showcases work by local artists, while music *peñas* with local crooners singing boleros and the like take place in a small function room on the first and third Saturday of the month.

The lookout point

When you've finished in the museum, take the lift to the top floor and the highest **lookout point** in Havana – on a clear day you can see the low hills in the east and out as far as Miramar in the west. The room is divided into segments corresponding to the five spines of its star shape, so you can move around to take in five separate views.

Memorial Ernesto "Che" Guevara

Plaza de la Revolución

On the opposite side of the square to the north, the ultimate Cuban photo opportunity is presented by the **Memorial Ernesto "Che" Guevara**, a stylized steel frieze replica of Alberto "Korda" Gutierrez's famous photo of Guevara, titled *Guerrillero Heroico* – the most widely recognized image of him. The sculpture that you see now on the wall of the Ministry of Interior building, where Guevara himself once worked, was forged in 1993 from steel donated by the French government. Taken on March 5, 1960, during a memorial service for victims of the La Coubre freighter explosion on Calle 23, Korda's photograph, with Guevara's messianic gaze fixed on some distant horizon and hair flowing out from beneath his army beret, embodies the unwavering, zealous spirit of the Revolution. It was only in 1967, after his capture and execution in Bolivia (see p.261), that the photo passed into iconography, printed on T-shirts and posters throughout the 1970s as an enduring symbol of rebellion.

Korda, who died in 2001, famously received no royalties from the image, and even gave its wide dissemination his blessing. As a lifelong supporter of the Revolution and Guevara's ideals, he believed that spreading the image would allow Guevara's ideals to spread alongside it, which neatly allows for the image's commercial use in Cuba itself.

JOSÉ MARTÍ

Almost every Cuban town, large or small, has a bust or a statue of **José Martí** somewhere, , and if they don't already know, it doesn't take long for most people who spend any time touring round Cuba to start wondering who he is. Born José Julián Martí y Pérez to Spanish parents on January 28, 1853, this diminutive man, with his bushy moustache and trademark black bow tie and suit, came to embody the Cuban desire for self-rule and was a figurehead for justice and independence, particularly from the extending arm of the US, throughout Latin America.

ANGRY YOUNG MAN

An outstanding pupil at the San Anacleto and San Pablo schools in Havana, and then at the Instituto de Segunda Enseñaza de la Habana, Martí was equally a man of action, who didn't take long to become directly involved in the **separatist struggle** against colonial Spain. Still a schoolboy when the first Cuban War of Independence broke out in 1868, by the start of the following year he had founded his first newspaper, **Patria Libre**, contesting Spanish rule of Cuba. His damning editorials swiftly had him pegged as a dissident, and he was arrested a few months later on the trivial charge of having written a letter to a friend denouncing him for joining the Cuerpo de Voluntarios, the Spanish volunteer corps. Only 16 years old, Martí was sentenced to six years' hard labour in the San Lázaro stone quarry in Havana. Thanks to the influence of his father, a Habaneran policeman, the sentence was mitigated and the now-ailing teenager was **exiled** to the Isla de la Juventud, then known as the Isla de Pinos, and finally to Spain in 1871.

Martí wasted no time in Spain, studying law and philosophy at the universities in Madrid and Zaragoza, all the while honing his literary skills and writing **poetry**, his prolific output evidenced today in the countless compendiums and reprints available in bookshops around Cuba. One of his poems, taken from the collection *Versos Sencillos* (Simple Verses), was adapted and became the official lyrics of the song *Guantanamera*, a Cuban anthem.

FORMING IDEAS

By 1875 he was back on the other side of the Atlantic and reunited with his family in **Mexico**. Settling down, however, was never an option for the tireless Martí, who rarely rested from his writing or his agitation for an independent Cuba and social justice throughout Latin America. Returning to Havana briefly in 1877 under a false name, he then moved to **Guatemala** where he worked as a teacher and continued his writings. Among his students was the daughter of Guatemalan president Miguel García Granados, who fell in love with Martí but whose love went unrequited. Martí returned again to Cuba in 1878 and during another brief stay he married Carmen Zayas Bazán, with whom he had a son that same year. By 1881 he was living in **New York**, where he managed to stay for the best part of a decade. His years in New York were to prove pivotal. Initially swept away by what he perceived to be the true spirit of freedom and democracy, he soon came to regard the US with intense suspicion, seeing it as a threat to the independence of all Latin American countries.

CHARGING TO BATTLE

The final phase of Martí's life began with his founding of the **Cuban Revolutionary Party** in 1892. He spent the following three years drumming up support for Cuban **independence** from around Latin America, raising money, training for combat, gathering together an arsenal of weapons and planning a military campaign to defeat the Spanish. In April 1895, with the appointed general of the revolutionary army, Máximo Gómez, and just four other freedom fighters, he landed at Playitas on Cuba's south coast. Disappearing into the mountains of the Sierra Maestra, just as Fidel Castro and his rebels were to do almost sixty years later, they were soon joined by hundreds of supporters. On May 19, 1895, Martí went into **battle** for the first time and was shot dead almost immediately. Perhaps the strongest testament to José Martí's legacy is the esteem in which he is held by Cubans on both sides of the Florida Straits, his ideas authenticating their vision of a free Cuba and his dedication to the cause an inspiration to all.

1 **Memorial Camilo Cienfuegos**

Plaza de la Revolución

Erected in 2009 on the front of the Ministry of Informatics and Communications on the east side of the square is Enrique Ávila's 100-ton steel sculpture of **Camilo Cienfuegos**, in a similar style to the Che image, includes the words "*Vas bien Fidel*". This somewhat obsequious tagline is a reference to a reply that Cienfuegos gave to Fidel Castro at the victory rally on January 8, 1959: "How am I doing?" asked Castro. "You're doing fine, Fidel," came the reply.

Necrópolis de Colón

Avenida Zapata • Daily 8am–5pm • $1CUC

Five blocks northwest from Plaza de la Revolución along tree-lined Paseo, there's a worthwhile detour to the left at the Zapata junction: the **Necrópolis de Colón**, one of the largest cemeteries in the Americas. With moribund foresight the necropolis was designed in 1868 to have space for well over a hundred years' worth of corpses, and its neatly numbered "streets", lined with grandiose tombstones and mausoleums and shaded by large trees, stretch out over five square kilometres. A tranquil refuge from the noise of the city, it is a fascinating place to visit – you can spend hours here seeking out the graves of the famous, including the parents of José Martí (he is buried in Santiago), celebrated novelist Alejo Carpentier, Alberto "Korda" Gutierrez and a host of revolutionary martyrs.

CAMILO CIENFUEGOS – HERO OF THE REVOLUTION

Good looking, personable and a formidable soldier, **Camilo Cienfuegos** was one of the most significant rebels in the revolutionary struggle. Born in Havana to Spanish anarchists, Cienfuegos did not share the wealthy middle-class background of other key rebels and accounts of his early life are characterized by financial struggles. He enrolled in the Escuela Nacional de Bellas Artes in 1940 but lack of money forced him to leave and work as an apprentice in the El Arte fashion store in Havana.

EARLY ACTIVISM

Cienfuegos became active in the underground student movement against Fulgenico Batista and was wounded during a protest in 1955. Shortly afterwards, sick of the police harassment that identification as a student rebel warranted, he left Cuba for the US and then Mexico.

It was in **Mexico** that he met Fidel Castro and decided to join forces with his revolutionary expedition. An apocryphal tale has it that the *Granma* boat, ready to set sail from Mexico to the motherland (see p.460), was already overloaded with would-be rebels, and Cienfuegos was only granted last-minute passage because he was deemed so thin that the extra weight would be of no bearing.

MILITARY BRILLIANCE

Surviving the rebels' initial catastrophic battle, Cienfuegos went on to be one of the rebel army's most successful generals, attaining the rank of **comandante** in 1957. His most significant victory was in winning the key **Battle of Yaguajay** in Santa Clara province in December 1958, which impelled Batista's forces to surrender a crucial garrison helping cement the revolutionary success.

FATAL DISAPPEARANCE

Following the revolution, Cienfuegos continued in a military role, quashing anti-Castro uprisings. Whether he would have played a more political role in the new Cuban order is open to speculation. Within a year of victory, on October 28, 1959, his **plane disappeared** over the ocean during a night flight from Camagüey to Havana, and after a search failed to reveal any trace of the remains, he was declared dead. Cienfuegos was feted as one of the heroes of the Revolution, and even today schoolchildren throw flowers into the seas and Cuban rivers in his honour on the anniversary of his disappearance.

The main avenue sweeps into the cemetery past tall Italian marble tombstones, including a copy of Michelangelo's *Pietà*. Particularly noteworthy is the **mausoleum**, just behind the main avenue on Calle 1 y Calle D; draped with marble maidens depicting justice and innocence, it holds the remains of a group of medical students executed in 1871 on the charge of desecrating the tomb of a Spanish journalist.

In the southern half of the cemetery, marked by large plots of as yet unused land, veterans of the Revolution, including luminary figures Celia Sánchez, July 26 Movement leader and companion to Fidel Castro, and poet Nicolás Guillén, lie in an extensive and faintly austere **pantheon house** just off the main avenue.

Octagonal chapel

In the centre of the necropolis is the Romanesque **octagonal chapel**, opened in 1886. Masses are held every day at 8am but the chapel is also open at varying times during the day. You should seize the chance to peek inside and admire the luminous German stained-glass windows and, towering above the altar, Cuban artist Miguel Melero's fresco *The Last Judgement*.

The tomb of Amelia Goyri de la Hoz

Close to the octagonal chapel at Calle 1 e/ F y G and always engulfed by a cornucopia of flowers and guarded by an attendant, the tomb of **Amelia Goyri de la Hoz** and her child is an arresting sight. A Habaneran society woman, Goyri de la Hoz died in childbirth on May 3, 1901, and was buried with her child, who survived her by only a few minutes, placed at her feet. During a routine exhumation the following year, she was supposedly found to be cradling the child in her arms. The story spread immediately. Goyri de la Hoz was dubbed **La Milagrosa** (The Miracle Worker) and the event was attributed to the power of a mother's love working beyond the grave. Soon *La Milagrosa* was attributed with universal healing powers, and to this day supplicants queue round the block to have their wishes granted. A strict etiquette controls the ritual: to stand a chance of success you must first knock on the tombstone three times with the brass handles to alert the saint within, then cover the tomb with flowers before mentioning the wish and, finally, leave without turning your back.

Miramar and the western suburbs

Home to the city's flashiest neighbourhoods, **Miramar and the western suburbs** comprise Havana's alter ego, replete with sleek Miami-style residences, swish new business developments and brash five-star hotels. Among the last sections of the city to be developed before the Revolution, this is where the wealth was then concentrated, and it's slowly trickling back through a growing clique of international investors and wealthy foreign residents. The area still has its share of broken sewage systems, unlit streets and overcrowded buses, but a gentler pace of life exists throughout the western suburbs, calmed by the broad avenues and abundance of large drooping trees.

Though there is an **aquarium**, one or two small **museums** and plenty of wonderful houses and embassies to gawp at, most visitors to this part of the city come here for the **nightlife** and **entertainment**, particularly the famous **Tropicana** cabaret (see p.133), as well as for the area's swanky international **restaurants** and its upmarket **paladars**, which between them offer the most diverse and sophisticated eating options in Havana. You'll have to go all the way to the western extremities to find the only proper beach, at **Club Habana** and, just beyond that, **Marina Hemingway**, where boat trips and diving expeditions are the main draw.

The whole area west of the **Río Almendares** is occasionally mistakenly referred to as Miramar, but this is in fact the name only of the oceanfront neighbourhood closest to Vedado, the two linked together by a tunnel under the river. Most of this western

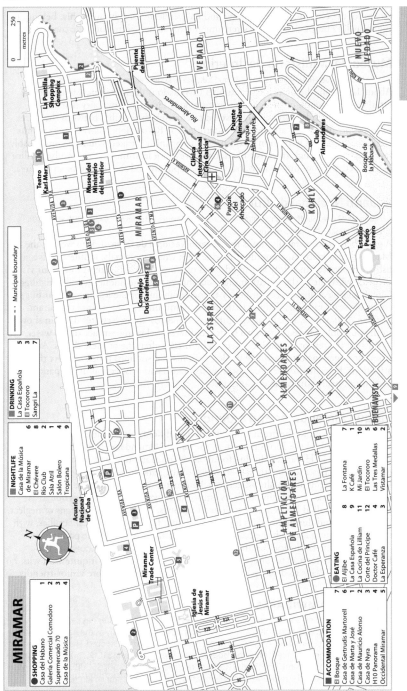

MIRAMAR

● SHOPPING

Casa del Habano	1
Galeria Comercial Comodoro	2
Supermercado 70	3
Casa de la Música	4

■ NIGHTLIFE

Casa de la Música de Miramar	6
El Chévere	8
Rio Club	2
Sala Atril	4
Salon Bolero	1
Tropicana	9

■ DRINKING

La Casa Española	5
El Tocororo	3
Sangri La	7

■ ACCOMMODATION

El Bosque	7
Casa de Gertrudis Martorell	6
Casa de Marta y José	1
Casa de Mauricio Alonso	2
Casa de Nyra	4
H10 Panorama	4
Occidental Miramar	5

■ EATING

El Aljibe	8	La Fontana	7
La Casa Española	9	K Café	1
La Cocina de Lilliam	11	Mi Jardin	10
Corte del Principe	12	El Tocororo	6
Doctor Café	4	Las Tres Medallas	5
La Esperanza	5	Vistamar	3

Infotur, Club Habana (4km) & Marina Hemingway (5.5km)

1

section of the city, including Miramar and its even leafier neighbour **Kohly**, belongs to the sprawling borough of **Playa**, stretching out for some 15km along the coast.

Museo del Ministerio del Interior

Calle 14 e/ 3ra y 5ta • Tues–Fri 9am–5pm, Sat 9am–3.30pm • $2CUC, with guide $3CUC, photos $5CUC • ☏ 7 202 1240

About 1km from the mouth of the tunnel to Vedado is the **Museo del Ministerio del Interior**, the museum of the Cuban secret services. Housed in two airy Miramar mansions, the displays are mainly devoted to charting the conflict between the secret services and alleged US attempts to undermine the Revolution. Many of the exhibits comprise billboards written in Spanish, so non-Spanish speakers will find considerably less of interest, though there is still enough here – not least the first ever Cuban police dog stuffed and mounted – to warrant a quick spin around should you be in the area.

Acuario Nacional de Cuba

Avenida 3ra esq. 62 • Tues–Sun 10am–6pm; dolphin shows 11am, 3pm & 5pm; sea-lion shows noon & 4pm • $7CUC adults, $5CUC children • ☏ 7 202 5871, ⓦ acuarionacional.cu

A good bet for some family fun is the **Acuario Nacional de Cuba**, 1.5km west of the Maqueta de la Habana, an outdoor marine park where mammals, reptiles, birds and fish are showcased in wildly varying degrees of animation. You should time your visit to coincide with one of the twenty-minute **dolphin shows**, the unquestionable highlight here, featuring as many as eight highly trained dolphins; or the less spectacular but still enjoyable sea lion shows. Failing that, stop here for lunch at the on-site **restaurant**, *El Gran Azul*, where, usually at 1.30pm, you can enjoy an underwater dolphin show from your table, viewed through a huge window set below the surface of the water.

Much of the rest of the park can seem a bit lifeless after one of these shows. Away from the larger enclosures, where turtles, pelicans and sea lions usually attract the most attention, there are dozens of uninspiring fish tanks and this section of the park by itself is not really worth the entrance fee.

Parque Almendares and around

South of Miramar, in the green and hilly suburb of **Kohly** and alongside an attractive and open stretch of the Río Almendares, the **Parque Almendares** is the only decent-sized city park in Havana. Running for about 400m along the river, its tangle of palms, giant weeping figs and pine trees coats much of the park in a dense woodland, filling it with dappled light and an almost eerie enchantment, especially at dusk. This moody charm is enhanced by wishing wells, twisting pathways and iron benches but is tempered by scuffed lawns and abandoned buildings, along with other signs of neglect. At weekends and during holidays it's a popular spot frequented by local families, with salsa reverberating through the park from speakers arrayed around the parking lot.

The park is the landscaped section of a much larger forested area known as the **Bosque de la Habana**, extending over 2km along the river, most of it quite wild with no obvious paths. Plans to develop the woodlands and make them more visitor-friendly

---

PARQUE ALMENDARES ACTIVITIES

As well as providing a welcome expanse of greenery, Parque Almendares has several **activities** to choose from. This is an ideal place for a picnic, particularly as the park's sole café, situated in the centre (Tues–Sun 10am–5pm), is somewhat sparsely stocked. The river, though dirty, makes a good venue for **rowing boats** (Tues–Sun 10am–6pm; $1CUC/hr), while a **crazy golf course** (Tues–Sun 10am–5pm, $1CUP), pony rides (no fixed times, $5CUP), a playground and an aviary make the park one of the better attractions in Havana for children.

are slowly getting underway, but for now the woods and parkland offer a slice of the countryside right in the heart of the city.

Club Almendares

28A esq. 49B • Daily 10am–6pm • $10CUC, includes $8CUC *consumo* to spend on food and drink

Just out of sight of the Parque Almendares, around a corner a couple of hundred metres up the road, is **Club Almendares**, an outdoor leisure complex featuring bars, restaurants and a snack bar, as well as games rooms and a swimming pool. Popular with Cubans, it's a lively spot, though the facilities suffer from being somewhat run down.

Club Habana

Daily 7.30am–9pm • $10CUC Mon–Fri, $15CUC Sat & Sun • ☎ 7 204 5700 • Take the Habana Bus Tour (route T2, see p.116); if driving follow Avenida 5ta from the tunnel 8km to the seafront neighbourhood of Flores

Several kilometres west of Miramar is **Club Habana**, an upmarket leisure and business complex based in and around an enormous stately mansion. Most significantly, it is also the site of Havana's only proper city **beach**, as well as some of the best sports facilities in the city. Prior to the Revolution, this was the Havana Biltmore Yacht and Country Club, whose members were drawn predominantly from the Cuban aristocratic classes and the wealthy US business community, and it maintains an air of exclusivity today, with membership costs prohibitively high for most Cubans.

The palm-lined 200m sandy **beach** is a real treat compared to anything else this close to the city centre, and given the entrance cost, it's usually pretty deserted. With several half-decent eateries on site and three **swimming pools**, this is the best place in Havana to spend a whole day of pure undisturbed escapism. The palatial clubhouse is prosaically dominated by business facilities but does feature a wall of intriguing photographs depicting the club and its members pre-1959.

ARRIVAL AND DEPARTURE **HAVANA**

BY PLANE

JOSÉ MARTÍ INTERNATIONAL AIRPORT

All international flights land at José Martí International Airport (information ☎ 7 266 4133 & 649 5666; switchboard ☎ 7 275 1200 & 266 4644), about 16km south of the city centre.

Facilities The vast majority of international passengers are deposited at terminal 3 (☎ 7 649 0410), where most airport services are concentrated, including a few shops, a restaurant and a bureau de change, while there are car rental desks in each of the three terminals.

Getting to Havana Since there is no public transport linking the rest of Havana directly with the airport, you'll almost certainly have to take a taxi into town; the standard fare for the half-hour journey into Havana is $25CUC but you may be able to negotiate a reduction if you're determined enough; it's also quite common to share cabs with other travellers as an way of reducing costs.

Destinations Baracoa (4 weekly; 3hr); Bayamo (2 weekly; 2hr); Camagüey (6 weekly; 1hr 30min); Cayo Coco (1 daily; 2hr 30min); Cayo Largo (1 daily; 50min); Cayo Las Brujas (1 daily; 1hr 5min); Ciego de Avila (1 weekly; 1hr 25min); Guantánamo (4 weekly; 2hr 25min); Holguín (2 daily; 1hr 10min–1hr 40min); Nueva Gerona (1 daily; 40min); Santiago de Cuba (2 daily; 2hr).

BY BUS

VÍAZUL BUSES

Essentials You're most likely to be dropped off at the Víazul terminal (☎ 7 881 1413, ext 101 or 881 5652), on Avenida 26 across from the city zoo. From here, an excellent Víazul-run minibus taxi service will take you to Habana Vieja ($6CUC), Centro Habana ($5CUC) or Vedado ($3CUC); if there are more than three of you, the charge is $2CUC per person wherever you're going. Otherwise, you'll have to catch a regular taxi into town; expect to pay around $5–8CUC, depending on the taxi, for the drive to Habana Vieja.

Terminal de Omnibus Nacionales The main long-distance bus station is the Terminal de Omnibus Nacionales (switchboard ☎ 7 870 9401; convertible-peso ticket office ☎ 7 870 3397; information ☎ 7 879 2456), at Avenida Independencia esq. 19 de Mayo, near the Plaza de la Revolución. The vast majority of arrivals here are Astro buses, reserved exclusively for Cubans, but foreign travellers do sometimes arrive and depart here. The centre of Vedado is a twenty-minute walk away, the #P12 and #P16 buses (see p.117) stop nearby on their way into the centre; a taxi fare to Habana Vieja should cost $3–4CUC.

Tickets Víazul bus tickets can be bought in advance at any branch of the travel agents Havanatur, Cubanacán or Cubatur (see p.142) and from branches of Infotur (see p.118).

1

Destinations Bayamo (3 daily; 13hr); Camagüey (6 daily; 8hr 15min); Ciego de Ávila (4 daily; 7hr); Cienfuegos (3 daily; 4hr 20min); Holguín (3 daily; 12hr); Las Terrazas (1 daily; 1hr 30min); Las Tunas (4 daily; 11hr); Matanzas (4 daily; 2hr 10min); Pinar del Río (2 daily; 3hr); Sancti Spíritus (4 daily; 6hr); Santa Clara (4 daily; 4hr 30min); Santiago de Cuba (4 daily; 15hr 30min); Trinidad (3 daily; 6hr); Varadero (4 daily; 3hr 10min); Viñales (2 daily; 3hr 40min).

CUBANACAN-TRANSTUR BUSES

Essentials Also known as Conectando Cuba, this service picks up and drops off passengers from designated hotels in Habana Vieja, Vedado and Miramar. To buy tickets go to Infotur (see p.118) or a Cubanacán travel agent (see p.142). Destinations Camagüey (1 daily; 10hr); Ciego de Avila (1 daily; 8hr); Cienfuegos (1 daily; 5hr); Holguín (1 daily; 13hr); Pinar del Río (1 daily; 3hr 30min); Santiago de Cuba (1 daily; 15hr); Trinidad (1 daily; 7hr); Varadero (1 daily; 3hr); Viñales (1 daily; 4hr 40min).

BY TRAIN
ESTACIÓN CENTRAL DE FERROCARRILES

Essentials Trains pull in at the main terminal of the Estación Central de Ferrocarriles (☎7 860 9448 & 862 1920) in southern Habana Vieja. The Parque Central is just under 1km from here. Several local buses (see p.117) stop close to the station, including the #P4 and #P5, but hauling a lot of luggage onto a crowded Havana bus isn't much fun. There are often private cabs outside the station and the occasional tourist taxi, though you're more likely to find a *bicitaxi*. Taxi fares to Parque Central in Habana Vieja should be around $3CUC and to Vedado around $5CUC.

Tickets Train tickets are sold at the much smaller Terminal La Coubre (☎7 864 6041 & 862 1006), 200m down the road from the main terminal on Avenida del Puerto. You'll

need to get here by 8.30am a whole five days before your date of travel, and expect to join a large queue.

Schedules and routes Long-distance services are patchy at best, with trains running roughly every other day; check at the station to find out the current situation. There is also a very limited suburban train network that reaches out to the outskirts of rural Havana and into Mayabeque and Artemisa provinces.

Destinations Cacocum in Holguín (6–9 weekly; Camagüey (8–12 weekly; 9–14hr); Ciego de Avila (6–9 weekly; 7–11hr); 13–14hr); Matanzas (9–11 weekly; 2hr); Pinar del Río (every other day; 6hr); Sancti Spíritus (every second day; 11hr); Santa Clara (12–14 weekly; 5–7hr); Santiago de Cuba (4–5 weekly; 15hr).

HERSHEY TRAINS

Essentials The other train terminal in the city is at one end of the Hershey line, the only electric train service in Cuba. It connects Havana to the city of Matanzas, the terminal at the other end of this line. The station is in Casablanca, on the eastern side of the harbour, near the Parque Morro-Cabaña. There are dozens of tiny stations along the route but trains only stop sporadically at most of them. The most expensive ticket is $3CUC.

Destinations Canasí (4 daily; 2hr 20min); Guanabo (4 daily; 40min); Hershey (4 daily; 1hr); Jibacoa (4 daily; 2hr); Matanzas (4 daily; 3hr); San Antonio (4 daily; 2hr 45min).

BY BOAT

Terminal Sierra Maestra A tiny minority arrive on one of the very few cruise ships that dock in Havana every week. Those that do will disembark at the Terminal Sierra Maestra (☎7 866 6524 & 862 1925), facing the Plaza de San Francisco in Habana Vieja.

GETTING AROUND

Havana has a poor **public transport** system, with no metro, a skeletal municipal train network and an overcrowded bus service. You will almost certainly find yourself having to use a **taxi** at least once, though this is not such a bad thing when the car is a 1955 Chevrolet.

BY BUS
HABANA BUS TOUR

Essentials Though this service is ostensibly for touristic tours of the city, it actually offers a decent alternative to the public bus system, and with a timetabled schedule, route maps at bus stops and guaranteed seats, it offers a lot that the regular municipal system doesn't – albeit for a greater cost. The T1 ($3CUC) runs between the Parque Central and the Plaza de la Revolución; the T2 ($1CUC) between the Plaza de la Revolución and Marina Hemingway; and the T3 ($3CUC) between the Parque Central and the Playas del Este.

Tickets and schedules Tickets for each route are valid all day and are sold on board. Though there are designated bus stops, you can flag buses down anywhere on their routes. In theory the service runs daily from 9am to 9pm at half-hourly intervals, but in reality this varies; you may sometimes wait an hour or more, while last buses set off as early as 7pm.

PUBLIC BUSES

Essentials The public bus system, divided between the Metrobús and Omnibus Metropolitanos networks, is how the majority of residents (but only a tiny minority of foreign visitors) get around Havana. Though both networks are still

METROBÚS ROUTES

ROUTE NUMBER		ROUTE
P1	(for Miramar)	San Miguel del Padrón–Playa
P2	(for Museo Hemingway)	Cotorro–Vedado
P3	(for Guanabacoa)	Habana del Este–Vedado
P4	(for Kohly)	Playa–Terminal de Trenes (Habana Vieja)
P5	(for Miramar)	Playa–Terminal de Trenes (Habana Vieja)
P6	Vedado–Arroyo Naranjo	
P7	(for Museo Hemingway)	Parque de la Fraternidad (Habana Vieja)–Cotorro
P8	(for Parque Morro-Cabaña)	Habana del Este–Arroyo Naranjo
P9	(for Tropicana and Kohly)	Marianao–Diez de Octubre
P10	Diez de Octubre–Playa	
P11	(for Parque Morro-Cabaña)	Habana del Este–Vedado
P12	(for Santiago de las Vegas)	Santiago de las Vegas–Parque de la Fraternidad
P13	Santiago de las Vegas–Diez de Octubre	
P14	(for La Lisa)	Playa–Parque de la Fraternidad (Habana Vieja)
P15	(for Guanabacoa)	Habana del Este–Parque de la Fraternidad (H.V.)
P16	(for Santiago de las Vegas)	Santiago de las Vegas–Vedado
PC	(for Parque Lenin)	Habana del Este–Playa

characterized by overcrowding and long waits, the Metrobús service is more regular and the easier of the two to use. Its buses – most of them Chinese-made bendy buses – are distinguishable by their route names, all beginning with "P". The front of the vehicle will tell you its final destination, but for any more detail you'll need to consult the route map posted inside.

Fares and network hubs Fares are a flat fee of $0.40CUP and you won't receive any change, no matter the value of the coin or note you pay with. The major bus hubs are the Parque de la Fraternidad in Habana Vieja, the network of roads between the Parque Maceo and the Hospital Hermanos Ameijeiras in Centro Habana, and Coppelia in Vedado.

BY TAXI

STATE TAXIS

There are plenty of official metered state taxis. It shouldn't take long to flag one down in the main hotel districts and particularly along the Malecón. For a 24-hour pick-up service, ring Cubataxi (☎ 7 855 5555 & 877 5762).

Taxi ranks There are taxi ranks on the Paseo del Prado at the Parque Central in Habana Vieja, and outside the hotels *Habana Libre* on Calle L and *Nacional* on Calle O in Vedado.

PRIVATE TAXIS AND COLECTIVOS

As with the rest of Cuba, Havana is full of privately owned taxis, mostly huge, 1950s American cars operating as *taxis colectivos* (aka *almendrones*; see p.31). The main routes are along Neptuno in Centro Habana, and Calle L and Linea in Vedado. You should be able to flag one down anywhere along these roads, though some drivers may ignore you since most are licensed only to carry Cubans; be prepared to negotiate a fare.

Taxi ranks At the Parque de la Fraternidad and opposite the face of the Capitolio building, *colectivos* form a huge, jumbled taxi rank, some of them transporting passengers to the city limits and beyond.

GRAN CAR TAXIS

The only state-run taxi using classic American cars is Gran Car (☎ 7 873 1411). These taxis congregate at the Parque Central in Habana Vieja and outside the Hotel Nacional in Vedado, though you can call for one and even request your preferred model – they are generally in outstanding condition.

Fares Fares are higher than normal taxis but you won't have to share with anyone else and you can also rent a car and chauffeur for tours around the city. Prices start at $25CUC an hour or $125CUC for a whole day; fares for single journeys are negotiable.

BICITAXIS AND COCOTAXIS

Bicitaxis Three-wheeled, two-seater bicycle cabs, *bicitaxis* are found all over Havana but are not necessarily any cheaper than cars; a 2km ride is likely to cost $3–5CUC.

Cocotaxis Swelling Havana's taxi ranks even further are *cocotaxis*, three-wheeled motorscooters encased in large yellow spheres, usually found waiting outside the *Hotel Inglaterra* and the *Hotel Nacional*. You pay no extra for their novelty value, with fares currently officially set at $0.50CUC per kilometre, considerably cheaper than many normal state taxis – though their safety record is less than great.

BY CAR

Generally speaking, if you stay put in Havana, car rental (see p.32) is a relatively expensive way of getting around.

1

But with many of the city's day-trip destinations poorly connected by public transport, renting a car can save you a lot of time and hassle. The car-rental agencies have desks in the lobbies of most of the four- and five-star hotels; be warned, though, that booking a car in advance is often difficult as demand frequently outweighs supply.

CAR RENTAL

Habana Vieja Cubacar (☎ 7 866 0284) and REX (☎ 7 862 6343) both have offices at the Terminal Sierra Maestra opposite the Plaza de San Francisco

Miramar Go to Cubacar at Ave. 3ra y 28 in Miramar (☎ 7 204 3356).

Vedado You can find Cubacar at Paseo esq. 3ra in Vedado (☎ 7 833 2164) and REX at Linea esq. O, just off the Malecón (☎ 7 836 7788 & 835 6830)

CAR PARKS

There are official state-run car parks at Ave. de Italia (aka Galiano) esq. Ave. Simón Bolívar (daily 8am–8pm), near the Habana Vieja border in Centro Habana, and at Calle O e/ 23 y 25 (daily 24hr) in Vedado. Rates are $0.50CUC/hr.

BY SCOOTER

There are surprisingly few scooter rental outlets in the city and most are located within hotel complexes either in the western suburbs or right outside the city at the Playas del Este. There is a Cubanacán Motoclub branch at the Dos Gardenias commercial complex, at Ave. 7ma esq. 26, in Miramar and further west at the *Hotel Comodoro*, at Ave. 3era esq. 84.

BY BICYCLE

Though the wide spread of Havana's main tourist districts means travelling by bicycle can be quite tiring, it is a fantastic way to see the city and there are special lanes for cyclists on many of the main roads. However, despite the huge number of bicycles in Havana, specialist bicycle shops do not exist. Your best option is to rent a bicycle through a *casa particular*, quite a common practice, or book through a specialist travel agent (see p.29) well in advance.

BY HORSE AND CARRIAGE

You can pick up a horse and carriage at the Plaza de San Francisco in Habana Vieja. Fares are negotiable but a tour of Habana Vieja is usually $10CUC.

INFORMATION

Tourist information Infotur (🖭 infotur.cu), the national tourist information network, operates several information centres in Havana. The two principal offices are at Obispo no.521 e/ Bernaza y Villegas in Habana Vieja (daily 8.30am–7pm; ☎ 7 866 3333 & 863 6884) and in Miramar at Ave. 5ta y 112 (daily 9am–6pm; ☎ 72 04 7036).

Maps For the best choice of maps and guides, head for the Boloña bookshop at Mercaderes no.115 e/ Obispo y Obrapía, Habana Vieja (Mon–Fri 8.30am–5pm, Sat 8.30am–noon; ☎ 7 831 3625).

Listings For a brief rundown of what's on, look for listings publications *Cartelera* and *Mi Habana* in hotel lobbies and

Infotur offices. In Habana Vieja, look out also for the "Programa Cultural" noticeboards installed in the plazas, which carry details of upcoming concerts, exhibitions, workshops and the like.

Websites The only comprehensive music, theatre, festival and arts listings for the Havana are online. The best site is Cuba Absolutely (🖭 cubaabsolutely.com), covering a broad spectrum of events and not tied to a state-sponsored agenda. Try also the "Cartelera" sections of La Jiribilla (🖭 lajiribilla.cu) and Opus Habana (🖭 opushabana.cu), the latter for Habana Vieja venues only.

ACCOMMODATION

Accommodation in Havana is abundant and, as in the rest of Cuba, splits into two distinct categories, hotels and *casas particulares* (private houses). From sumptuous boutique-style houses to more bijou apartment rooms, the city boasts a fantastically broad range of **casas particulares** which, broadly speaking, grow more luxurious the further west you venture. All areas, however, possess a significant number of *casas* that are far classier than the cheapest hotels, and it's a mistake to assume that a stay in a house means a compromise in comfort. And as there are only one or two **hotels** with rooms for less than $50CUC a night, *casas particulares* have practically cornered the budget market, which they do with such panache and comfort that there really is no need to seek out budget hotels at all. On the other hand, if you want a pool, international food and all the mod cons, very few houses can compete with the classier hotels.

BOOKINGS, RATES AND AVAILABILITY

You can usually find a hotel room on spec, but you'd do well to make a **reservation**, particularly in high season (roughly July–Aug and Dec–March). Similarly, it's always worth making a reservation in a *casa particular*.

Prices are negotiable in all areas, depending on how long you intend to stay and how hard you're prepared to bargain – it's wise to agree on the price at the start of your stay. The majority of places will provide breakfast for an extra $3–5CUC a day.

MOB HOTELS

Many of Havana's most glorious hotels, especially those in Vedado, were built in the 1950s with a casino attached and the funds for their construction put up by members of the American **Mafia**, who were busy building an empire in the Cuban capital. With a booming tourist economy, a shortage of top class hotel rooms and American mobsters queuing up to take advantage of lax Cuban gambling laws, Cuban President Fulgencio Batista, in cahoots with the Mob, passed Hotel Law 2074 in 1955. This provided tax exemptions to any hotel providing tourist accommodation and guaranteed government financing and a gaming licence to anyone willing to invest $1 million or more in hotel construction, or $200,000 for the building of a nightclub. An unprecedented boom in hotel and casino construction followed as the Havana Mob expanded its portfolio, which already included the *Hotel Nacional*, the *Sevilla Biltmore* and the *Hotel Comodoro*, establishing landmark hotels like the *Habana Hilton*, the largest hotel in Havana when it opened in 1958, renamed the *Habana Libre* after the Revolution; the seafront *Hotel Deauville*, built in 1957 by Santo Trafficante, the Florida crime boss and long-time investor in Cuba; the luxurious *Hotel Riviera*, inaugurated in late 1957, having been conceived and funded by Meyer Lansky, the Don of the Havana-based mob; and the *Capri*, which also opened in 1957 and where the Mob installed the Hollywood tough-guy actor George Raft as a meeter-and-greeter, the personification of the hotel and casino industry in 1950s Havana, with its mixture of celebrity glamour and gangster backing.

HABANA VIEJA

Handy for many of the key sights and well served by restaurants and bars, Habana Vieja's hotels are very popular. Many are essentially small boutique places, with ten to twenty rooms in charismatic colonial-era properties. *Casas particulares* here are almost exclusively in apartments rather than houses, and while they're decidedly less spacious than those further west, their proximity to the main sights and attentive owners make them an excellent choice.

HOTELS

Ambos Mundos Obispo no.153 esq. Mercaderes ☏ 7 860 9530, ⓦ hotelambosmundos-cuba.com; map pp.74–75. This stylishly artistic 1920s hotel, where Ernest Hemingway stayed between 1932 and 1939, is bang in the middle of the most visited part of Habana Vieja. It features an original metal cage lift and a fantastic rooftop terrace. Rooms are well equipped and comfortable. $175CUC

Beltrán de Santa Cruz San Ignacio no.411 e/ Muralla y Sol ☏ 7 860 8330, ⓦ habaguanexhotels.com; map pp.74–75. Located in the thick of the old city but just off the main tourist circuit, this handsomely converted family townhouse – with balconied hallways, wide stone staircase and courtyard – has a relaxed vibe. $145CUC

★ **Conde de Villanueva** Mercaderes esq. Lamparilla ☏ 7 862 9293 to 94, ⓦ habaguanexhotels.com; map p.74–75. Also known as the *Hostal del Habano*, this is a cigar smoker's paradise with its own cigar shop, an attic-like smokers' lounge and the freedom to puff away throughout the premises. Despite its relatively small size this place packs in several other charming communal spaces, including a courtyard heaving with plants and a fantastic cellar-style restaurant. $175CUC

★ **Florida** Obispo no.252 esq. Cuba ☏ 7 862 4127, ⓦ habaguanexhotels.com; map pp.74–75. The restoration of this aristocratic and splendid building has been impressively detailed and complete. There's a perfect blend of modern luxury and colonial elegance with marble floors, iron chandeliers, birds singing in the airy stone-columned central patio and potted plants throughout. Incorporates an adjoining building known as the *Hotel Marqués de Prado Ameno*. $200CUC

Los Frailes Brasil (Teniente Rey) no.8 e/ Mercaderes y Oficios ☏ 7 862 9383 & 9293, ⓦ hotellosfrailescuba.com; map pp.74–75. Unique in character, this moody little place is themed on a monastery, with staff dressed as monks. The low-ceiling staircase, narrow central patio and dim lighting work well together to create a serene and restful atmosphere, while the rooms are very comfortable. $145CUC

El Mesón de la Flota Mercaderes e/ Amargura y Brasil (aka Teniente Rey) ☏ 7 863 3838, ⓦ habaguanexhotels .com; map pp.74–75. Similar in size and character to a traditional inn, this well-priced *hostal* has just five spacious rooms, all with simple but attractive stained-wood furnishings. The whole ground floor is occupied by a rustic and noisy Spanish restaurant (see p.125). $145CUC

Palacio del Marqués de San Felipe y Santiago de Bejucal Oficios esq. Amargura, Plaza de San Francisco ☏ 7 864 9191, ⓦ hotelmarquesdesanfelipe.com; map pp.74–75. One of the area's newest boutique hotels, this is a charming colonial conversion based around a narrow central patio with an atrium roof. Breakfasts are particularly good, and rooms are clean and high spec, if a little cold and artless. $240CUC

★ **Parque Central** Neptuno e/ Paseo del Prado y Agramonte (Zulueta), Parque Central ☏ 7 860 6001, ⓦ hotelparquecentral-cuba.com; map pp.74–75. This luxury five-star is Habana Vieja's largest hotel. Its justified reputation for good service attracts business travellers and holidaymakers alike, while its elegant interior – particularly the wonderful leafy lobby – is a real knockout. Rooms are sumptuously comfortable, there are two classy restaurants, a gym and a marvellous roof terrace featuring a café and swimming pool. **$320CUC**

Raquel Amargura esq. San Ignacio ☎7 860 8280, ⓦhotelraquel-cuba.com; map pp.74–75. Handsome and sleek with Art Deco touches, this is an unexpectedly upmarket hotel given its low-key side-street location. A cage lift, metal chandeliers and a glass ceiling revealing the first floor contribute to the sophisticated finish. **$200CUC**

San Miguel Cuba esq. Peña Pobre ☎7 862 7656 & 863 4029, ⓦhabaguanexhotels.com; map pp.74–75. Though it's set well back from the water's edge, this is the only hotel in Habana Vieja facing the bay and the sea, views of which are best enjoyed from the rooftop terrace café. The building itself is rather plain, though there are ostentatious touches such as the lavishly framed mirrors. **$200CUC**

Santa Isabel Baratillo no.9 e/ Obispo y Narciso López, Plaza de Armas ☎7 860 8201, ⓦhotelsantaisabel.com; map pp.74–75. One of the most exclusive of Habana Vieja's hotels, this impressively restored eighteenth-century building features colonial-style furnishings in all the rooms, and a fountain in the idyllic arched courtyard. **$280CUC**

★ **Saratoga** Paseo del Prado no.603 esq. Dragones ☎7 868 1000, ⓦhotel-saratoga.com; map pp.74–75. The interior of this super-plush hotel is dripping with lavishness, and the sleek bars and ritzy lounge areas give the impression of a Humphrey Bogart movie set. The modern facilities include a rooftop pool, a gym and a solarium, while rooms feature pseudo-antique furnishings, DVD players and internet connections, and there's wi-fi is throughout. **$310CUC**

Sevilla Trocadero no.55 e/ Paseo del Prado y Agramonte (aka Zulueta) ☎7 860 8560, ⓦhotelsevilla-cuba.com; map pp.74–75. A large, refined yet fading hotel, dating from 1908 and built in an eclectic mix of architectural styles. It possesses one of Havana's most spectacular restaurants, the *Roof Garden*, and the old town's largest pool. Rooms are spacious, well equipped and comfortable, but some could do with a sprucing up. **$210CUC**

Telégrafo Paseo del Prado no.408, esq. Neptuno ☎7 861 1010, ⓦhoteltelegrafo-cuba.com; map pp.74–75. Built from the shell of a nineteenth-century hotel, this fine four-star is a mostly modern construction incorporating some of the building's original features, such as the interior brick arches. A slightly quirky atrium café is at its heart and rooms are very comfortable, though perhaps less stylish than the elegant exterior might suggest. **$200CUC**

Valencia Oficios no.53 esq. Obrapía ☎7 867 1037, ⓦhabaguanexhotels.com; map pp.74–75. Plain but pleasant rooms in a beautiful building that feels more like a large country house than a small city hotel. Attractions include a cobbled-floor courtyard with hanging vines. Shares its facilities with *El Comendador*, located next door. **$175CUC**

CASAS PARTICULARES

Los Balcones San Ignacio no.454 e/ Sol y Santa Clara ☎7 862 9877; map pp.74–75. With its polished and perfectly preserved vintage furniture and décor, this plush first-floor apartment could pass for a colonial art museum. Run by an elderly couple, there are two high-standard bedrooms with their own balconies and large bathrooms, though neither is en suite. **$35CUC**

★ **Casa de Eugenio Barral García** San Ignacio no.656 e/ Jesús María y Merced ☎7 862 9877, ⓔfabio .quintana@infomed.sld.cu; map pp.74–75. Deep in southern Habana Vieja, this large and exceptional apartment is spotlessly clean and brimming over with precious furniture and curios. A sensational roof terrace garden is a terrific spot for lounging, and the five luxurious double bedrooms are exquisitely and ornately furnished with antiques. **$35CUC**

Casa de Fefita y Luís Prado no.20, apto. B, 5to piso e/ San Lázaro y Cárcel ☎7 867 6433, ⓔfefita_luis @yahoo.com; map pp.74–75. Situated on the fifth floor of this superbly located apartment block, the two simple en-suite rooms for rent both have great views across the bay. A windowed terrace balcony is perfect for long breakfasts. **$35CUC**

Casa de Juan y Margarita Obispo no.522, apto. 5 e/ Bernaza y Villegas ☎7 867 9592, ⓔeislerlavin@yahoo.es; map pp.74–75. A tightly packed fourth-floor apartment on Habana Vieja's busiest street, close to numerous bars and restaurants and rented in its entirety by the nonchalant landlord. One of the two simple rooms has a balcony looking over the street. The door to the building is just inside a clothes shop entrance, next door to the tourist information office. Bedroom **$30CUC**; whole apartment **$60CUC**

Casa de Martha y Yusimi Jesús María no.312 (bajos) e/ Picota y Curazao ☎7 867 5005, ⓔdelfin.marrero @infomed.sld.cu; map pp.74–75. Right near the train station, with two rooms. One is ideal for self-caterers, with a neatly designed kitchenette and dining area; the other is a smaller, snug space. Both have the freedom of the communal plant-lined central patio. **$30CUC**

Casa de Migdalia Caraballé Martín Santa Clara no.164, apto. F, e/ Cuba y San Ignacio ☎7 861 7352, ⓔcasamigdalia@yahoo.es; map pp.74–75. Opposite the Convento de Santa Clara, this large, airy apartment contains two pleasant double rooms and another with three single beds, all benefiting from plenty of natural light. **$30CUC**

Casa de Pablo y Lidia Compostela no.532 e/ Brasil (Teniente Rey) ☎7 861 2111; map pp.74–75. A spacious

1

upstairs colonial-era apartment with a huge two-part lounge leading into a colourful patio corridor off which the two bedrooms are located. There's also a very spacious but largely bare roof terrace suitable for sunbathing. Pablo (who speaks English) and Lidia are an older, very welcoming and friendly couple. $30CUC

★ **Chez Nous** Brasil (aka Teniente Rey) no.115 e/ Cuba y San Ignacio ☎ 7 862 6287, ✉ cheznous@ceniai .inf.cu; map pp.74–75. Outstanding *casa particular* with a majestic exterior and an impressive interior, dignified by perfectly preserved nineteenth-century furnishings. Two superb balconied rooms are on the first floor, while from the central patio a spiral staircase leads up to the fabulous roof terrace where there's another very comfortable, contrastingly modern room with en-suite bathroom and its own porch. $30CUC

CENTRO HABANA

As reflected in their rates, the hotels in Centro Habana are less luxurious than Habana Vieja, thought they do boast some stunning views over the Malecón and the ocean beyond. *Casas particulares* are almost exclusively in apartments rather than houses, and though they are generally cheaper than their competitors in Habana Vieja and Vedado you are not necessarily sacrificing space or comfort, as many of the best houses here offer plenty of both. There are none of the gardens or green spaces that you'll find in Vedado or Miramar but the location, handy for both Habana Vieja's sights and Vedado's restaurants and nightlife, is arguably as convenient as anywhere.

HOTELS

Deauville Ave. de Italia (Galiano) esq. Malecón ☎ 7 866 8813, 🌐 islazul.cu; map p.95. It's all about the location at this basic, high-rise hotel on the seafront, where many of the rather tired rooms have fantastic views of the Malecón, Habana Vieja and Vedado. The dinky sixth-floor swimming pool is the only pool in the area. $72CUC

★ **Terral** Malecón esq. Lealtad ☎ 7 860 2100, 🌐 habaguanexhotels.com; map p.95. The city's newest seafront hotel, this sleek, modernist affair is a great place to stay. Of the fourteen comfortable rooms, twelve have sea-facing balconies with fabulous views, and all are furnished and decorated with a touch of 1980s minimalism, heavy on the blacks and whites; there's also a rooftop terrace. $175CUC

CASAS PARTICULARES

★ **Casa 1932** Campanario no.63 (bajos) e/ San Lázaro y Lagunas ☎ 7 863 6203, 🌐 casa1932.com; map p.95. The Jazz Age is still alive inside this remarkable, tightly packed ground-floor apartment brimming with pre-Revolution photos, advertising signs, furniture and other paraphernalia. The treasure-trove of interwar antiques includes a 1930s cash register, a gramophone and the dark-coloured hardwood

beds, wardrobes and chests in the three excellent bedrooms. En-suite bathrooms, TV, fridge and a/c provide the modern comforts. An unforgettable place. $35CUC

Casa 1940 San Lázaro no.409 e/ Manrique y Campanario ☎ 7 863 7437 & 864 5246, ✉ casahabana @gmail.com; map p.95. You can rent the whole of this zesty apartment, one block from the Malecón, or just one of the two simple but stylish and clean double rooms. Some nice touches – like the photos of 1950s Havana, a collection of vintage snuff boxes and some attractive old furniture – provide splashes of character. A good option for families. Room $35CUC; apartment $60CUC

Casa de Ana Morales Aranda Neptuno no.519, apto. 3 e/ Campanario y Lealtad ☎ 7 867 9899, ✉ ana .morales@infomed.sld.cu; map p.95. A comfortable second-floor flat where the huge, stylish bedroom comes with a street-side balcony. The owners are friendly and speak English. $25CUC

Casa de Candida y Pedro San Rafael no.403 (bajos) e/ Manrique y Campanario ☎ 7 867 8902, ✉ candidacobas @yahoo.es; map p.95. Two double rooms in a modest ground-floor flat with a dinky hidey-hole patio near the back of the house. The down-to-earth owners also rent a whole apartment upstairs, which is spacious, if a little sparse, and comes with a neat little kitchen. The whole place is notable for its informal, family atmosphere. Rooms $25CUC; apartment $50CUC

Casa Colonial Cary y Nilo Gervasio no.216 e/ Concordia y Virtudes ☎ 7 862 7109, ✉ orixl@yahoo.es; map p.95. An elegant but – thanks to its likeable elderly owners – unpretentious and very spruce ground-floor apartment where three guest rooms, with en-suite bathrooms and antique furniture, help to fill the considerable space. A very pleasant place to stay. $30CUC

Casa de Dayami de Cervantes San Martín (San José) no.618, e/ Escobar y Gervasio ☎ 7 873 3640, ✉ lchavao @infomed.sld.cu; map p.95. Homely two-level apartment where guests are given the run of the upstairs floor, which features a roof terrace at either end and two neat and cosy bedrooms. The owners are a friendly family, one of whom speaks English. $25CUC

★ **Casa de Elsa Rodríguez** Malecón no.51 esq. Cárcel, apto. 9, 9no piso ☎ 7 861 8127, ✉ elsamalecon@yahoo .es; map p.95. Wonderful apartment up on the ninth floor of a seafront building. Both of the spacious en-suite guest rooms have excellent views and memorable touches such as Art Deco armchairs and Art Nouveau glass lampshades. The elegant and arty communal areas include a comfy, conservatory-style side-room next to the lounge, with perfect views of the fortifications on the eastern side of the bay. $35CUC

Casa de Mandy Neptuno no.519, apto. 4, e/ Campanario y Lealtad ☎ 7 862 8400, ✉ neptuno519 @yahoo.es; map p.95. An extremely likeable, laidback option run by an astute landlord, this quiet flat, tucked away at the back of an apartment building, is distinctive for the uniformity and excellent condition of its original Art Deco furnishings. $25CUC

★ **Casa de Miriam y Sinaí** Neptuno no.521 e/ Campanario y Lealtad ⓣ7 878 4456, ⓔsinaisole@yahoo.es; map p.95. Run by one of the friendliest, hardest-working landladies in the city and her sociable English-, Italian- and German-speaking daughter, this is a fantastic, smartly furnished first-floor apartment with an enchanting central patio filled with rocking chairs, plants and a fountain. The two comfortable double bedrooms both have hotel-standard bathrooms, and one has a balcony. There's a separate independent apartment next door too if you want complete privacy. Room $25CUC; apartment $50CUC

Casa de Ricardo Morales Campanario no.363, apto. 3 e/ San Miguel y San Rafael ⓣ7 866 8363, ⓔmoralesfundora@yahoo.es; map p.95. Ideal for anyone looking for privacy and security, this thoughtfully decorated first-floor apartment (fitted with an alarm) is rented out in its entirety. There's a spacious, well-equipped kitchen, two comfy double bedrooms with connecting bathroom and a homely lounge-diner with a TV, large sofa, balcony and decorative items from Mexico. One room $30CUC; two rooms $50CUC

VEDADO

Quiet, leafy Vedado is a more relaxed place to stay than further east in the city, although you'll need transport to visit Habana Vieja. One-time playground of North America's rich and famous, the best of the hotels here date from the pre-Revolution era, and while some of their rooms could do with a refurb, the restaurants, pools and lounging areas give a real sense of the insouciance of yesteryear. Vedado *casas particulares*, among them some of the city's most elegant nineteenth- and early twentieth-century residences, tend to be spacious and quiet, often with gardens and patios.

HOTELS

★ **Habana Libre** Calle L e/ 23 y 25 ⓣ7 834 6100, ⓦsolmeliacuba.com; map p.100. This stylish Vedado landmark, with stunning atrium and exterior mosaic by Amelia Pelaez, has three restaurants, a terrace pool, a business centre and good-quality rooms with all mod cons. A great choice even if some amenities have seen better days. $250CUC

★ **Nacional** Calle 0 esq. 21 ⓣ7 836 3564, ⓦhotelnacionaldecuba.com; map p.100. One of Havana's best-looking hotels, with the air of an Arabian palace particularly evident in the main lobby where Moorish tiles and beamed ceiling create a splendid backdrop. The rooms are sensitively decorated with reproduction furnishings while the swimming pools, health and fitness facilities, cabaret and open-air garden-terrace make this a fine choice. There are also three decent restaurants and cafés on site. $187CUC

Presidente Calzada no.110 esq. Ave. de los Presidentes ⓣ7 838 1801, ⓦhotelesc.com; map p.100. Vedado's most charismatic hotel, retaining many original features from its 1928 inauguration. The small lobby is a delight, with marble flooring and enormous teardrop chandeliers, while the rooms complement the general feel with antique furniture, views over the city and marble bathrooms. The buffet restaurant is unlikely to be the highlight of your stay, however. $210CUC

Riviera Paseo y Malecón ⓣ7 836 4051, ⓦhotelhavanariviera.com; map p.100. Built by the Mafia in the 1950s as a casino hotel, the *Riviera* retains much of that era's style. Many original features – like its long, sculpture-filled lobby, rooms boasting original furniture and Copa Room cabaret – capture the retro vibe. Regular online offers can work out at a quarter of the rack rate price here. $125CUC

CASAS PARTICULARES

★ **Casa de Aurora Ampudia** Calle 15 no.58 (altos) e/ M y N ⓣ7 832 1843; map p.100. Two double a/c rooms, one with its own living room and en-suite bathroom, in a beautiful colonial house within a stone's throw of the Malecón. Two expansive balconies each have fantastic sea views. Aurora, Luis and Aurora's son Nelson are among the friendliest and most helpful owners in the city, and the delicious and inventive meals cooked by ex-chef Luis are an added pleasure. $25CUC

Casa de Conchita García Calle 21 no.4 e/ N y O, apto. 74 ⓣ7 832 6187; map p.100. One of the most popular choices in this beautiful Rococo block, with two very clean and modern rooms tended to by a friendly and helpful host. If Conchita has no spaces she will be able to direct you to the best of the rest in the building. $35CUC

Casa de Leydiana Navarro Cardoso Calle N, no.203 (bajos) e/ 19 y 21 ⓣ7 835 4030, ⓔcarloshf@infomed.sld.cu; map p.100. Every effort has been made to equal hotel service and mod cons in the two rooms here, with fridges stocked with minibar treats, television, fan and faux colonial furniture. There's a large terrace overlooking the Edificio FOCSA on which to take breakfast. $30CUC

Casa de Magda Calle K, no.508 (bajos) e/ 25 y 27 ⓣ7 832 3269, ⓔdorarguez@infomed.sld.cu; map p.100. The elaborate Baroque furniture, chandeliers and china lions adorning this house are worthy of a decorative arts museum. The two rooms both have a/c and en-suite bathrooms; one is particularly splendid, with a king-sized mahogany bed and matching wardrobe. A wide porch out front is perfect for people-watching. Some English is spoken. $25CUC

★ **Casa Matilde** Calle 13 no.106 e/ L y M apto 3 1er Piso ☎ 7 832 9959, ✉ matildeportela@hotmail.com; map p.100. Four spacious a/c rooms, each with their own bathroom and several of which are newly decorated, in a pleasant first-floor apartment in a beautiful Art Deco block full of original features. Some English is spoken by the friendly owner, who is also a font of Cuban social and political knowledge and opinion. **$30CUC**

★ **Casa de Mélida Jordán** Calle 25 no.1102 e/ 6 y 8 ☎ 7 836 1136, ✉ melida.jordan@gmail.com; map p.100. A big, stylish house set back from the road and surrounded by a marble veranda overlooking a garden filled with roses and ferns. Both of the rooms are beautifully furnished and have a private bathroom. The largest has twin beds and the other has a double, although an extra bed can be added. English is spoken and there are various extra services available. A superb choice. **$30CUC**

★ **Casa de Silvia Vidal** Paseo no.602 e/ 25 y 27 ☎ 7 833 4165, ✉ silviavidal602@yahoo.es; map p.100. An ornate stained-glass window at the top of the marble staircase and mahogany period furniture make this one of the city's most regal *casas particulares*. The four double rooms, one with an extra bed for a child, each has its own bathroom and air conditioning. The lush garden and conservatory are an added bonus. **$35CUC**

MIRAMAR AND THE WESTERN SUBURBS

Replete with Western-style luxury, Miramar's slick, towering hotels represent the best the city has to offer, and though not very convenient for sightseeing, they all operate a regular shuttle service to Habana Vieja. Miramar's *casas particulares* are also in a league of their own, with several offering independent apartments complete with dining areas, living space and, in some cases, swimming pools – and an increased price tag to match.

HOTELS

El Bosque Ave. 28A e/ 49A y 49C, Reparto Kohly, Playa ☎ 7 204 9232, 🌐 gaviota.com; map p.113. In a leafy suburb overlooking the eponymous Bosque de la Habana wood, this affordable hotel is the perfect retreat from the city. Some of the basic but well-maintained rooms have views over the wood itself. Amenities include a pool. **$72CUC**

H10 Habana Panorama Ave. 3ra y 70, Miramar, Playa ☎ 72 04 0100, 🌐 h10hotels.com; map p.113. A cosmopolitan and stylish high-rise hotel featuring a marble lobby bedecked with greenery. A fitness centre, pre-pay wi-fi throughout, a piano bar and a huge pool with a bar make for a stress-free stay. **$135CUC**

Occidental Miramar Ave. 5ta e/ 72 y 76 Miramar, Playa ☎ 7 204 3584, 🌐 occidental-hoteles.com; map p.113. Despite its uninspiring facade, the sleek interior and smooth, professional service make this an excellent choice. Facilities include a business centre, a top-class gym, squash and tennis courts and huge pool. Rooms have all mod cons including wi-fi, and there's a choice of three restaurants. **$140CUC**

CASAS PARTICULARES

★ **Casa de Gertrudis Martorell** Ave. 7ma no.6610 e/ 66 y 70, Miramar, Playa ☎ 7 202 6563, ✉ reservas @habitacionhabana.com; map p.113. A perfect marriage of high-class comfort and facilities, with restrained, subtle decoration and furnishings, this *casa particular* knocks the socks off most hotels for sheer luxury. Complete with a huge terrace, the whole top floor is rented in its entirety, and features three bedrooms with king-size beds and original paintings by renowned Cuban artists. The ground floor has three equally palatial individual rooms. Rooms **$70CUC**; top floor apartment **$250CUC**

Casa de Marta y José Calle 6 no.108 apto 6 e/ 1ra y 3ra ☎ 7 209 5632; map p.113. A friendly place with two rooms, each with bath. A balcony with a sea view and fantastic home-cooked meals make this a fine choice. **$50CUC**

Casa de Mauricio Alonso Calle A no.312 apto. 9 e/ 3ra y 5ta, Miramar, Playa ☎ 7 203 7581, ✉ masexto @infomed.sld.cu; map p.113. The major selling point of this stylish retro penthouse apartment is its view over the ocean and Havana. One of the spacious rooms has its own bathroom, while the other two share. Fresh orange juice every morning and city tours are just some of the services offered by the very friendly English-speaking owner. **$30CUC**

Casa de Nyra Ave. 3ra no.1607 e/ 16 y 18, Miramar, Playa ☎ 7 202 4028; map p.113. Stylish South Beach-inspired apartment with a marble floor leading out to a fantastic patio and garden. There are three rooms, each with a minibar, fan and a/c; one is en suite while the other two share a bathroom. **$40CUC**

EATING

Eating out in Havana is on the up. A new wave of **paladars** has given the dining scene a lease of life, particularly in Centro Habana and Habana Vieja, where standards have long lagged behind those set in Vedado and Miramar. Traditional Cuban food does still dominate, but paladar owners are becoming more ambitious and innovative, creating alternative menus and designing memorable, eye-catching interiors. The best **state restaurants** and many of the superior paladars are in Vedado and Miramar, still the home of the city's finest dining and where you are more likely to have a truly unforgettable meal out. The capital's **cafés** are often indistinguishable from restaurants, serving meals as much as drinks, and there are also a few places more akin to coffee shops, worth searching out if you are looking for a relaxing, hassle-free snack or drink.

1

BREAKFAST VENUES

There aren't many cafés or restaurants offering decent **breakfasts** in Havana, and though it's usually best to stick to your hotels or *casa particular*, there are some places worth getting up and out for. The best are listed below.

Cafetería La Rampa Hotel Habana Libre, Calle 23 esq. L, Vedado ☎ 7 834 6100; map p.100. A good choice of breakfast platters in this US-style diner, from traditional Cuban featuring pork and rice to the full American for $8CUC. Breakfast daily 24hrs.

El Pórtico Hotel Parque Central, Paseo del Prado esq. Neptuno, Habana Vieja ☎ 7 860 6627; map pp.74–75. The marvellous lobby café at this five-star hotel, full of classic colonial charm, serves top-notch continental breakfasts of cakes, croissants, toast and fruit for $7.50CUC or all of the above plus smoked salmon, eggs, bacon, ham, chorizo, cheese, milk and yoghurt for $12CUC. Breakfast daily 8am–noon.

Prado Hotel Park View Colón esq. Morro, Habana Vieja ☎ 7 861 3293; map pp.74–75. Breakfast with views all the way over to Vedado from this seventh-floor hotel restaurant. When there are a sufficient number of hotel guests a buffet is laid on here, available to non-guests for $5CUC per person. Otherwise it's bread, fruit and eggs. Breakfast daily 7–10am.

La Veranda Hotel Nacional Calle O esq. 21, Vedado ☎ 7 836 3564; map p.100. The buffet breakfast in the basement of this fabulous hotel is unbeatable for sheer scale and choice, with everything you would hope to see in a classic English or American spread, plus loads of extras including cereal, fruit, sweets and bread. All-you-can-eat for $13CUC. Breakfast daily 7–10am.

HABANA VIEJA AND PARQUE MORRO-CABAÑA

CAFÉS

Café La Barrita Edificio Bacardí, Ave. de las Misiones e/ San Juan de Dios y Empedrado ☎ 7 862 9325 ext.119; map pp.74–75. Hidden away on the mezzanine level behind the foyer of the Bacardí building, this stylish Art Deco café is a comfortable and congenial little hideout and a great spot to take a break. Good-value snacks, too. Daily 9am–6pm.

Café El Escorial Plaza Vieja ☎ 7 868 3545; map pp.74–75. A dependable coffee shop with a covered terrace facing the square and a rustic interior decorated in earthy tones. As well as over 25 varieties of coffee, they serve coffee cocktails and coffee ice cream as well as other sweets, like cheesecake. Daily 9am–10pm.

Museo del Chocolate Mercaderes esq. Amargura ☎ 7 866 4431; map pp.74–75. Despite the name this is more a café than a museum, and one where they serve only chocolate drinks and sweets, all made from Cuban cocoa. Order a deliciously thick hot chocolate while you watch the sweets being made at the back. Daily 9am–10pm.

STATE RESTAURANTS

Al Medina Oficios no.12 e/ Obispo y Obrapía ☎ 7 867 1041; map pp.74–75. Main dishes such as *pollo musukán* and *samac libanés* sound more Middle Eastern than they taste but the food here still offers a welcome break from the norm. More unique are the mixed meze combinations ($10CUC and $15CUC), which include falafel, fatoush, tabbouleh and less-than-authentic hummus. You can dine inside, where there's a wooden-beam ceiling, brick archways and glass lanterns, or in a canopied courtyard. Daily noon–midnight.

⭐ **A Prado y Neptuno** Paseo del Prado (aka Paseo de Martí) esq. Neptuno ☎ 7 860 9636; map pp.74–75. Always buzzing with punters and the place to come for some of the best pizzas ($5–13CUC) in the city. There's a good selection of pasta and seafood on the menu, but the pizzas are the sensible choice here, with plenty of varieties. Well suited to large, noisy groups. Daily noon–midnight.

La Barca Ave. Carlos Manuel de Céspedes (aka Ave. del Puerto) esq. Obispo ☎ 7 866 8807; map pp.74–75. Sister restaurant to the outstanding *El Templete* next door, the cooking here is not nearly as refined but is less expensive and more traditionally Cuban, making it a good place to try classics like skewered lobster and shrimp ($10CUC) or Creole-style smoked pork ($12CUC). The breezy open-air location on the port road is enhanced by views of the fortifications on the east side of the bay. Daily noon–midnight.

Bodegón Onda Hotel El Comendador Obrapía no.55 esq. Baratillo ☎ 7 867 1037; map pp.74–75. At the end of a side street, this dinky tapas joint should be more popular than it is, given the decent quality and excellent value of its two or three set meals (all priced under $5CUC) and small selection of tapas. The standard of cooking is higher than much pricier places nearby and the now departed Spanish chef appears to have left his mark; the bean and chickpea stew is particularly successful. Daily noon–11pm.

La Bodeguita del Medio Empedrado e/ San Ignacio y Cuba ☎ 7 867 1374; map pp.74–75. One of the city's most famous restaurants – and busiest tourist traps – still has some appeal. Beyond the often impossibly crowded bar is an enthralling labyrinth of rooms, the walls caked in scribbled messages and photos of celebrity customers. The food isn't bad for such a touristy place, mostly classic national dishes like *ropa vieja* ($12CUC) or cod in Creole sauce ($13CUC). Daily noon–11.30pm.

Café del Oriente Oficios no.112 esq. Amargura, Plaza de San Francisco ☎7 860 6686; map pp.74–75. A ritzy, high-class restaurant where the bow-tied waiters serve delicacies like steak tartare ($18CUC), roast rabbit ($12.50CUC) and lobster thermidor ($27CUC). The lunchtime menu has cheaper, more familiar dishes like pasta and chicken, but the Orient Express-style decor, live piano music and 1930s aristocratic ambience are perfectly suited to a late-night dinner. Daily noon–midnight.

Hanoi Brasil (aka Teniente Rey) esq. Bernaza ☎7 867 1029; map pp.74–75. This rustic place, with its small rooms and tightly packed trellis-roof courtyard, is one of the cheapest state restaurants in old Havana, with basic set meals for $4.95CUC; the most expensive item on the menu is the lobster, shrimp and fish mixed grill for just $12.95CUC. Any pretence that this is a Vietnamese restaurant has long since disappeared – this is standard, inexpensive Cuban food. Daily 11.45am–midnight.

La Imprenta Mercaderes no.208 e/ Lamparilla y Amargura ☎7 864 9581; map pp.74–75. A mixture of excellent value tapas – stuffed potatoes, tortilla or fish fritters ($1.25CUC each) – and carefully cooked, attractively presented mains such as salted shrimp ($8CUC) and slices of beef ($9.55CUC), served in a handsome, airy building full of earthy tones and decorative nods to its previous incarnation as a nineteenth-century printing house. Daily noon–10.30pm.

El Mesón de la Flota Mercaderes e/ Amargura y Brasil (aka Teniente Rey) ☎7 863 3838; map pp.74–75. Spanish–Cuban cuisine in a tavern-type restaurant, with nightly flamenco performances on a central stage. There's a tasty selection of cheap tapas ($1–5CUC), including fried chickpeas, squid and three types of tortilla, which double up as starters for the mostly seafood main dishes, among which is a good-value lobster with tropical fruits ($12CUC). Daily noon–11pm.

La Tasca Parque Morro-Cabaña ☎7 860 8341; map pp.74–75. Occupying a fabulous waterside terrace right on the edge of the most attractive stretch of the bay, this restaurant works equally well by day or by night, though after dark the lights of Habana Vieja on the opposite shore provide a particularly romantic backdrop. The three house specials – a paella ($19CUC), a mixed grill ($18CUC) and a kebab-style dish ($24CUC) – each combine seafood with meat, and are prepared with a professional simplicity. Daily noon–10pm.

★ **El Templete** Ave. Carlos Manuel de Céspedes (Ave. del Puerto) no.12–14 esq. Narciso López ☎7 866 8807; map pp.74–75. The gourmet seafood at this harbourfront restaurant is the finest and tastiest in Habana Vieja, thanks in large part to the Basque head chef. From delicious salads and starters like octopus *a la gallega* (boiled and garnished with paprika, salt and oil) to mouthwatering mains such as cod *a la vizcaína*, in a garlic, chilli and onion sauce, almost everything on the menu stands out and delivers. Mains are around $14CUC. Daily noon–midnight.

PALADARS

★ **El Chanchullero** Brasil e/ Bernaza y Cristo, Plaza del Cristo ☎7 872 8227; map pp.74–75. A great example of Havana's new breed of paladars, this trailblazing, trendy, laidback little place on the old town's only untouristy square is closer to a backstreet Madrid tapas bar than the more formal set-ups that traditionally characterize the city's restaurants. Juicy portions of great-value chicken, pork or shrimp are served in earthenware bowls, not with the usual rice and beans, but perfectly dressed salads instead. Mains $3–4.50CUC. Daily 1pm–midnight.

Doña Blanquita Paseo del Prado no.158 e/ Colón y Refugio ☎7 867 4958; map pp.74–75. Overlooking El Prado from the terrace balcony of a roomy first-floor apartment, and serving a wide selection of well-cooked, generously portioned *comida criolla* dishes ($7–12CUC), particularly pork and chicken, with plenty of extras, too. Daily noon–10pm.

★ **Doña Eutimia** Callejón del Chorro no.60c, Plaza de la Catedral ☎7 861 1332; map pp.74–75. By far the best of the new paladars around the Plaza de la Catedral. There's nothing unusual on the menu but national culinary trademarks like roast chicken ($7CUC) and fish *enchilado* ($8CUC) are cooked to an excellent standard, as are starters like malanga fritters and croquettes (both $2CUC). Tables sit snugly together in the artistically decorated and very sociable interior. Reservations recommended. Daily noon–11pm.

La Moneda Cubana Empedrado e/ Mercaderes y Plaza de la Catedral ☎7 861 5304; map pp.74–75. Offers set lunches for between $16CUC and $20CUC, such as garlic shrimp and aromatic herbs ($20CUC) and beef with onion in a red wine sauce ($18CUC). Best in the daytime when the lovely split-level roof terrace with views over to the ramparts on the other side of the bay lifts this place – in both senses – above the nearby state restaurants, though it lacks the personal touch of many other paladars. Daily noon–midnight.

Nao Obispo no.1 e/ San Pedro y Baratillo ☎7 867 3463, ⓦ naobarpaladar.com; map pp.74–75. Opened in 2012, the imaginative interior and atmosphere mark this paladar as one of the new breed, but it seems not everyone in the kitchen got the memo. Some of the food, like starters of unusually good-quality grilled sausage ($4CUC) and a bread basket ($3CUC), break refreshingly with the worst of the old Cuban norms; but the humongous lump of roast chicken ($6CUC) and basic croquettes ($3CUC) do not. Choose carefully, ask how each dish is cooked and served, and your visit will be a happy one. Daily noon–midnight.

1

EAT TO THE BEAT: TOP FIVE PLACES FOR LIVE MUSIC AND A MEAL

It's actually quite hard to avoid live music when eating out in Havana, but there are some restaurants that offer more than just the ubiquitous – and sometimes very good – guitar-strumming, maraca-shaking trio. For more of a show or something a little different, try **Café Taberna**, where one of the many incarnations of the Buena Vista Social Club play nightly (see p.131); **El Mesón de la Flota**, where the flamenco music is accompanied by a fabulous dance performance (see p.125); **El Tocororo**, where meals are accompanied by an excellent jazz band (see p.128); the **Cabaret Parisien** in *Hotel Nacional*, for a full music and dancing extravaganza (see p.132); or **El Gato Tuerto**, a cross between a club and a restaurant where they've been crooning since before the Revolution (see p.132).

CENTRO HABANA

STATE RESTAURANTS

La Abadía Malecón no.410 e/ Manrique y Campanario ☎7 864 4432; map p.95. Well-presented tapas, most priced between $1CUC and $3CUC, in a casual stopoff under canvas-covered metal arches over the road from the sea wall. The stuffed red peppers, tuna *empanadas*, fried chickpeas with sausage and garlic mushrooms are all very appetizing. Daily noon–midnight.

Castropol Malecón no.107 e/ Genio y Crespo ☎7 861 4864; map p.95. Run by an Asturian emigrant society, the upstairs balcony of this seafront restaurant is a great place to eat at dusk, with views over to El Morro lighthouse and several Vedado landmarks. As well as the usual, perfectly decent Cuban beef, chicken, fish and shrimp offerings are some worthwhile departures from the norm, especially among the starters, like Serrano ham filled with cheese and raisins ($5.95CUC), smoked salmon ($5.20CUC) and lobster *ceviche* ($6.90CUC). Downstairs, in the cheaper *taberna*, you can order pizza, pasta and grilled food. Daily noon–midnight.

★ Tien Tan Bulevar del Barrio Chino (aka Cuchillo) no 17 e/ Rayo y San Nicolás ☎7 863 2081; map p.95. Perhaps the best in China Town, *Tien Tan* has an extensive and well-priced menu with many authentic dishes expertly prepared by Shanghai-born chefs. Delicious starters like dumplings ($2CUC) and noodle soup with shrimp are equalled by mains like Foo Yung chicken ($7CUC). Pretty Chinese lanterns and red tablecloths, plus a good mix of Cubans and visitors, add to the pleasant atmosphere. Daily 11am–11pm.

PALADARS

★ Casa Miglis Lealtad no.120 e/ Animas y Lagunas ☎7 864 1486, ⓦ casamiglis.com; map p.95. This stylish Swedish place right in the thick of run-down Centro Habana is one of the most surprising and welcome additions to the city's eating-out scene. The menu, which includes nods to Cuban, Greek and Mexican cooking, does nevertheless provide the city's only opportunity to eat *skagen* (Sweden's take on prawns on toast; $6CUC) or meatballs with mashed potato and lingonberries ($8CUC), both authentic and flavourful. The problem is sourcing the ingredients – expect a few shakes of the head when you place your order. Daily noon–midnight.

★ La Guarida Concordia no.418 e/ Gervasio y Escobar ☎7 866 9047, ⓦ laguarida.com; map p.95. This renowned paladar has long been an obligatory stop off for visiting celebrities, from Queen Sofía of Spain to Jay Z, and is worth every penny of its higher-than-average prices ($12–20CUC for mains). The meat and fish menu breaks with all the national norms, and the dishes – like rabbit lasagne, salmon in a spring onion sauce with bacon, and sugar-cane tuna glazed with coconut – brim with flavour and originality. Set in the aged apartment building where the acclaimed *Fresa y Chocolate* was filmed, the decor is eye-catchingly eclectic and the moody ambience in the three rooms perfect for a long-drawn-out meal. Reservations are essential. Daily noon–midnight.

Mimosa Salud no.317 e/ Gervasio y Escobar ☎7 867 1790; map p.95. This neighbourhood pizzeria has locals queuing at the door and though (as far as the quality of the food goes) this slightly flatters to deceive, the pizzas ($2.85–6.50CUC) are way above the Cuban average, made to your desired thickness and with a huge variety of toppings. Cosy dining booths line the narrow reception area, which opens out into a more spacious room, alls dimly lit under low ceilings and with a moody, basement feel. Daily noon–midnight.

★ San Cristóbal San Rafael no.469 e/ Lealtad y Campanario ☎7 867 9109 & 860 1705; map p.95. Perfectly presented juicy and saucy Creole cuisine, including succulent "country-style pork slices" ($7CUC), lots of hearty beef dishes ($9.50–22CUC) and some chicken options ($7.50–15CUC). The knock-out interior consists a lovely, leafy narrow terrace and three captivating dining rooms, two heaving with pictures. A feast for the eyes and stomach. Daily noon–midnight.

VEDADO

CAFÉS

Cafetería La Rampa Habana Libre, Calle 23 esq. L ☎7 834 6100; map p.95. This bright spot with a long diner-style counter overlooks the lively La Rampa junction.

Great shakes and pasta along with some bizarre sandwich combinations like parmesan, parsley and Baileys to tickle your fancy. Daily 24hrs.

★ **Coppelia** Calle 23 esq. L ☎ 7 832 6184; map p.100. Havana's massive ice-cream emporium contains several cafés and an open-air area (you pay in national pesos in the former, convertible pesos in the latter), serving rich sundaes in exotic flavours like coconut, mango and guava. Tues–Sun 11am–10pm.

★ **G Café** Ave. de los Presidentes esq. 23 (no phone); map p.100. Faux wicker chairs, an abundance of greenery and the crowds of students from the med school nearby give this lovely café a bohemian feel. Lemon tea, cappuccino and cocktails are all served (you pay in national pesos), while the poetry bookshop at the back offers a lending service, for something to read while you drink. Daily 9am–6pm.

El Gran Añejo Meliá Cohiba, Paseo e/ 1ra y 3ra ☎ 7 833 3636; map p.100. Large comfortable sofas, wi-fi and smooth service – plus a great selection of cakes for afternoon tea – make this hotel café an ideal place to catch a slice of luxury for a few hours. Daily noon–midnight.

STATE RESTAURANTS

1830 Malecón no.1252 esq. 20 ☎ 7 838 3090; map p.100. A sumptuous colonial house complete with antique furniture, chandeliers and an expansive patio. The food lives up to the surrounds with well-prepared choices including duck in orange sauce and chicken breast with honey and lemon sauce. Cuban dishes like *ropa vieja* are also superb, priced at $7–12CUC and well worth the splurge. There are also salsa nights here. Daily noon–midnight.

La Torre Edificio FOCSA, piso 33, Calle 17 no.55 esq. M ☎ 7 838 3088; map p.100. Mesmerizing views from atop the city's second-tallest building mean you don't really notice the plain interior here. The above-average prices are just about matched by the standard of cuisine, which tends towards choice meat and seafood, prepared with successful simplicity. The pheasant in apple sauce ($25CUC) and oven-cooked cod ($16CUC) all hit the spot, while pork chops ($9CUC) are one of the few less expensive dishes. Daily noon–11.30pm.

★ **Unión Francesa** Calle 17, no.861, e/ 4 y 6 ☎ 7 832 4493; map p.100. Set in a nineteenth-century mansion, this is possibly the most atmospheric and peaceful place to eat in the heart of Vedado. There are three floors to choose from, with alfresco tables overlooking Parque Lennon and a patio at the top lined with antique cabinets and a floral canopy. Friendly and attentive staff serve creative dishes like chicken with glazed pineapple or an orange sauce. A main course and sides is around $8CUC. As a bonus the cocktails are freely poured too. Daily noon–midnight.

PALADARS

Los Amigos Calle M no.253 e/ 19 y 21 ☎ 7 830 0880; map p.100. Tasty lunchtime choices include rice and beans or *ajiaco* stew and possibly the best home-made chips in Havana. It's always busy so reservations are recommended (though you can wait on the patio outside if you prefer. They also do a takeaway service – you supply the container. Daily noon–midnight.

★ **Café Laurent** Calle M No. 257 e/ 19 y 21 ☎ 7 832 6890; map p.100. This airy penthouse papered with 1950s magazines and filled with white furniture is one of the best of Havana's new wave of restaurants. Mains like beef meatballs or fish in salsa verde are beautifully presented and taste as good as they look, while starters are delicate and inventive. Eat out on the balcony and enjoy the stunning views over Vedado and the ocean. Mains are $8.50–12.50CUC. Reservations recommended. Daily noon–midnight.

Casa de Adela Calle F no.503 e/ 23 y 21 ☎ 7 832 3776; map p.100. Filled with plants, cooing birds and ethnic artefacts, this gem of a restaurant has a throwback bohemian feel. There's no menu here – instead, you pay $25CUC per person for a large selection of taster dishes, including delicious chorizo with coconut, meatballs, and malanga fritters with peanuts. Reservations essential. Daily 1–4pm & 6.30–11pm.

★ **Decameron** Linea, no.753 e/ Paseo y 2 ☎ 7 832 2444; map p.100. The decor and ambience here are inspired and low-key, with pendulum clocks lining the walls, soft lighting and cane-backed chairs. A mix of Italian, Cuban and European food contributes to the cosmopolitan air. The *ropa vieja* is one of the city's best; duck comfit with guava is delicious and beautifully presented. Prices are reasonable too, with most dishes falling in the $6–10CUC bracket. Strong and sweet *mojitos*, plus attentive service, round things off nicely. Daily noon–midnight.

Gringo Viejo Calle 21 no.454 e/ E y F ☎ 7 831 1946; map p.100. Traditional Cuban dishes like garlic octopus, *ropa vieja*, *frijoles negros* and fried chickpeas perfectly complement contemporary choices such as chicken with pineapple sauce and stewed lamb (mains $6–13CUC). There's a competent wine list, too. If you can forgive the slightly impersonal staff, this is one of the better mid-range restaurants in town. Reservations recommended. Daily noon–11pm.

MIRAMAR AND THE WESTERN SUBURBS
CAFÉS

K Café Teatro Karl Marx, Ave. 1ra e/ 8 y 10, Miramar, Playa ☎ 7 203 0801; map p.113. One of the area's most popular spots, this large and lively café in the lobby of a huge theatre serves coffees and cocktails as well as sandwiches and pizzas. Child seats (and portions) are an added bonus for parents. Daily noon–midnight.

STATE RESTAURANTS

El Aljibe Ave. 7ma e/24 y 26, Miramar, Playa ☏ 7 204 1584; map p.113. El Aljibe offers a touch of luxury, with an ambient open-air setting and a fabulous wine cellar that make it a top choice for diners in the mood for pushing the boat out. The food pulls no surprises, but it is tasty. House specialities include the beef *brocheta* and roast chicken, and there's plenty of it. Main dishes $15–30CUC. Daily noon–midnight.

La Casa Española Ave. 7ma esq. 26, Miramar, Playa ☏ 7 206 9644; map p.113. The dining rooms in this mock medieval fort are a real knockout, with beautiful mosaic-tiled floors and Mudéjar motifs and furnishings. Starters include *chorizo a la cerveza*, while mains range from salmon in cider to lamb in red wine sauce or slices of pork in sherry, with two courses averaging between $9CUC and $16CUC. Daily noon–11pm.

★ **El Tocororo** Calle 18 esq. Ave. 3ra, Miramar, Playa ☏ 7 204 2209; map p.113. Atmospheric restaurant with first-class service and imaginative Cuban dishes, including smoked salmon in a tapenade dressing with okra and raisins, or *cerdo a la camagueyana*, a traditional pork dish from Camagüey. A fantastic six-piece band performs in the evenings. Prices are generally upwards of $12CUC for a main course. Reservations advisable. Daily noon–midnight.

PALADARS

★ **La Cocina de Lilliam** Calle 48 no.11311 e/ 13 y 15, Miramar, Playa ☏ 7 209 6514, ⊕ lacocinadelilliam.com; map p.113. Expats and ex-presidents (check out Jimmy Carter's thank-you letter in the menu) patronize this discreet and luxurious restaurant, with tables set in a beautiful garden. The food is very good, with the malanga fritters, the black rice and octopus and the ginger ice cream particular standouts. Expect to pay around $70CUC for dinner for two. Tues–Sat noon–3pm & 7–11pm.

★ **Corte del Principe** Calle 9na esq. a 74 Playa (no phone); map p.113. Run by Italian expat Sergio and overlooking an expansive park, Havana's most authentic Italian restaurant is an absolute gem. Sun-dappled terrace tables are spread with fresh baked bread, home-made linguine with pesto, spaghetti carbonara and paper-thin Parma ham. A credible wine list adds to the gastronomic delight. Tues–Sun noon–3pm & 7–11pm.

★ **Doctor Café** Calle 28 no.111 e/ 1ra y 3ra, Miramar, Playa ☏ 7 203 4718; map p.113. Little touches like warm home-made bread, plus the big flavours in the exquisitely cooked seafood and meat dishes on a constantly changing menu, reflect the owners' insistence on the freshest ingredients. The professionalism extends to the friendly and attentive service, and the setting is pleasant, split between a convivial garden patio and a small stone-floor dining room. Starters $4–6CUC; mains $8–12CUC. Daily noon–midnight.

★ **La Esperanza** Calle 16 no.105 e/ 1ra y 3ra, Miramar, Playa ☏ 7 202 4361; map p.113. The owner of this fabulous restaurant has created a 1930s homage to the house's previous owner, the eponymous Esperanza. The creative menu is expertly prepared and includes chicken in soy and ginger sauce or grilled aubergine au gratin with oregano. Prices for starters are $4–12CUC, and mains are no more than $13CUC. Reservations essential. Mon–Sat 7–11pm.

La Fontana Calle 46 no.305 esq. 3ra, Miramar, Playa ☏ 7 202 8337; map p.113. A lively restaurant specializing in barbecued and grilled platters, equally popular with the Cuban bohemian set and foreigners. The food is almost as good as the atmosphere, with large portions of octopus ($10CUC), pork chops ($8CUC) and ribs ($8CUC) on the menu. Daily noon–12.30pm.

Mi Jardín Calle 66, no.517 esq. 5ta B, Playa ☏ 7 203 4627; map p.113. This atmospheric Mexican–Italian paladar serves mains ($2.50–10CUC) such as *totopos con frijole* (refried beans with cheese, hot pepper sauce and tacos) and *pollo en mole* (chicken in a savoury chocolate sauce), which are perfectly presented and rich with complex flavours. Seating is out in the pretty garden patio or in a dining room with marble floor and Mexican artwork. Reservations recommended. Daily noon–midnight.

Las Tres Medallas Calle 20 no. 313 e/ Ave 3ra y Ave 5ta ☏ 05 265 5337 (mobile) ; map p.113. Thin-crust pizzas and expertly prepared *comida criolla* including beef in red wine, chicken supreme and grilled lobster and prawns, served on an appealing terrace bedecked with hanging palms. The late-night bar here is also worth a visit. The *tres medallas* refer to the three medals won by Cuban Olympic volleyball champion Mireya Luis Hernadez, the owner's wife. Tues–Sun noon–midnight.

Vistamar Ave. 1ra no.2206 e/ 22 y 24, Miramar, Playa ☏ 7 203 8328; map p.113. Relatively posh shorefront paladar with sea views from its first-floor dining room and around a dozen variations on the fresh fish, pork and chicken dishes that appear on the official menu (mains $8–10CUC). The unofficial menu, which can feature lobster, shrimp and beef, is equally good, as are the crisp and well-dressed salads. Daily noon–midnight.

DRINKING

There are surprisingly few straight-up bars in Havana. Most **drinking venues** are part bar, part café, offering rum, beer, coffee and tea in equal measure, while many also serve light meals (some of these are listed with restaurants). They are invariably small, single-room venues and many in Habana Vieja feature live music. A bar crawl in Havana can involve a lot of walking, as there are very few areas with a concentrated buzz – it often makes sense to find a likeable venue and stay there. **Obispo** in Habana Vieja can lay claim to the biggest concentration of drinking spots – and of *jineteros* – while the nearby **Plaza de la Catedral** district is also quite lively at night. In **Vedado**, the *Habana Libre* hotel is the best starting point for evening drinking, and the *Riviera* hotel is another good option, while the **La Rampa** area has a good clutch of bars and clubs that heat up after 11pm. It's also worth checking out theatre bars and gardens in Vedado (see p.132) for atmospheric and discerning tipples even if you haven't attended a performance. However, for sheer joie de vivre you can't beat taking some beers or a bottle of rum down to the **Malecón** and mingling with the crowds beneath the stars.

HABANA VIEJA

Café Lamparilla Lamparilla e/ Mercaderes y San Ignacio ☎7 864 9580; map pp.74–75. Decent draught beer served at tables spread out almost the entire length of this narrow block, as well as at the narrow bar inside. There is also a short food menu. Daily noon–midnight.

Café El Lucero Cuba no.2 esq. Aguiar ☎7 862 2550; map pp.74–75. Both informal and quite grand, with five pillars propping up its front-of-house roadside terrace, and a spiral staircase leading up and away from the passing traffic to the atmospheric second level with its low ceiling and low-set windows. A long list of cocktails, none costing more than $2.50CUC, feature on the excellent drinks menu. Daily 10am–midnight.

Dos Hermanos San Pedro no.304 esq. Sol ☎7 861 3514; map pp.74–75. A restaurant and classic turn-of-the-century bar opposite the more run-down section of the Terminal Sierra Maestra. Take a stool at the sleek antique saloon bar counter, with its dark wood panelling, for an authentic prohibition-era rum session. Daily noon–midnight.

★ **Factoría Plaza Vieja** San Ignacio esq. Muralla, Plaza Vieja ☎7 866 4453; map pp.74–75. Not only is this one of the few places in Havana where you can get a beer on tap, but the deliciously smooth house tipple is brewed on the premises, served by the glass ($2CUC) or in communal five-glass dispensers ($10CUC). No wonder this corner of the square is always buzzing. You can order food too, like pork, fish and lobster. Daily noon–midnight.

El Floridita Monserrate esq. Obispo ☎7 867 1300; map pp.74–75. Home of the Cuban daiquiri, this was one of Hemingway's favourite hangouts. The comfy chairs, flowery wallpaper and velvet curtains make it feel like a posh living room, albeit one crammed with tourists sampling an expensive range of fifty-odd cocktails, including fifteen types of daiquiri. Meals here are unjustifiably expensive. Daily 11.30am–midnight.

Lluvia de Oro Obispo esq. Habana ☎7 862 9870; map pp.74–75. One of the liveliest and most reliably busy bars in Habana Vieja, with live bands playing throughout the day and night to almost equal numbers of tourists and *jineteros*. Daily 9am–1am.

Plaza de Armas Hotel Ambos Mundos, Obispo no.153 esq. Mercaderes ☎7 860 9530; map pp.74–75. This fabulous rooftop patio-bar gives a great perspective on the Plaza de Armas and the surrounding neighbourhood. Lolling on the tasteful garden furniture among the potted plants is as relaxing an option as you could wish for in Habana Vieja. There's a restaurant up here too. Daily noon–11pm.

Sloppy Joe's Ánimas esq. Zulueta ☎7 866 7157; map pp.74–75. Once a mecca for American prohibition-era visitors to the island, this legendary saloon bar, having closed in 1965, was reborn in 2013, authentically replicating the original interior including the famously long dark mahogany bar. The cocktails are excellent and the sense of 1950s Havana quite special. Daily noon–midnight.

CENTRO HABANA

Café Neruda Malecón no.355 e/ San Nicolás y Manrique ☎7 864 4159; map p.95. In a gap between seafront apartment buildings is this outdoor café, one of the most pleasant drinking spots on the Malecón. Features a lawn, park benches and tables protected from the wind by panes of glass sealing the place off from the street. Hot and cold drinks plus light snacks. Daily noon–midnight.

Taberna El Galeón Malecón e/ Manrique y Campanario (no phone); map p.100. The only real bar on the Malecón's best stretch, and one of the best places for a light meal or snack. You can sit out on a colonnaded porch or huddle into the tightly packed, understated interior.

VEDADO

Aire Mar Hotel Nacional, Calle O esq. 21 ☎7 836 3564; map p.100. Seasoned visitors swear a cooling daily *mojito* on the palatial terrace bar of this hotel is the way to beat the languid afternoon heat. The *Salón de la Fama* bar just inside is a bit tackier, but intriguing for all the photos of the hotel's famous guests. Daily 10am–2am.

★ **Café Bar Madrigal** Calle 17 no. 809 e/ 2 y 4 ☎7 831 2433; map p.100. Epitomizing the direction in which modern Havana is headed, this bar is redolent of hipster trysts and late-night cool. Raw brick walls are hung with film posters, old box brownie cameras and Cuban artwork, while the bar is well stocked with local and international favourites. Tapas is served and bands regularly play. Tues–Sat 6pm–midnight, Fri & Sat 6pm–4am.

★ **El Emperador** Edificio FOCSA, Calle 17 e/ M y N ☎7 832 4998; map p.100. This classy little 1950s bar hidden at the foot of the FOCSA building succeeds where so many others fail, with sultry lighting, hushed tones and a long marble bar serving perfect cocktails to a discreet

1

LOBBY GROUP

Habana Vieja has some fantastically elegant hotels, and the most arresting feature in many of them is the **lobby**. The enchanting cafés and bars that occupy many of these lobbies are ideal spots for escaping the humidity and hassle of the city streets, relaxing, sipping drinks, snacking or simply enjoying the magnificent setting. Below are a five of the best, all of them open to non-guests.

Ambos Mundos (see p.119). The epicentre of the most visited part of Habana Vieja, and perfectly located for a rest as you tour the old city. The lobby is often filled with the sounds of boleros and chachachas coming from the grand piano in the corner, and there's a sociable feel, with people constantly milling around. Daily 24hrs.

Los Frailes (see p.119) A small, narrow and very simple lobby with a bar at one end and an almost sombre vibe, with the lights permanently on an evening setting, several low-slung couches and a resident clarinet quartet playing soothing tunes. Great place for a sneaky snooze. Daily 7am–midnight.

Parque Central (see p.119). Protected from the cacophony of the Parque Central, the delightful, leafy *El Pórtico* café is the perfect spot to recharge or wind down. Tea, coffee and alcoholic drinks are on offer

alongside sandwiches, salads, tapas and sweets. Daily 8am–3am.

Saratoga (see p.120) The fantastic atrium café and bar on the lobby's mezzanine level mixes Art Deco lamps, lights and other fixtures and fittings with colonial chic. A large coffee menu, a good selection of spirits, breakfasts, sandwiches and tapas can all be savoured from the comfy chairs and couches. Daily 24hrs.

Sevilla (see p.120) The lobby in this classic Havana hotel, which blends into the pretty *Patio Sevillano* café, is a little worn around the edges, but this increases the sense of pre-Revolution authenticity. Full of slouch-inducing chairs and dotted with photos from its mafia-owned heyday, relaxing here comes with a dose of history. Daily 24hrs.

---

clientele. Throw in the live piano music and this becomes one to return to again and again. Daily 7pm–1.30am.

Fresa y Chocolate Calle 23 e/ 10 y 12 **☎**7 836 2096; map p.100. This unassuming bar, with a glass arched roof and an entrance overgrown with greenery, is the hangout of choice for Cuban soap stars and musicians. Live bands play in the evening and attract an arty crowd. Daily 9am–11pm.

La Fuente Calle 13 e/ F y G (no phone); map p.100. The crowd is mostly Cuban at this open-air café/bar. Tables clustered around a water feature and musicians plucking out impromptu tunes add to the relaxed vibe. Daily 11am–midnight.

★ **Opus Bar** Teatro Amadeo Roldán Calzada esq. D **☎**7 836 5429; map p.100. A good-looking, narrow bar with the air of a glam VIP departure lounge, all big squashy easy-chairs and sultry lighting. The available liquors include the fifteen-year-old Gran Reserva Havana Club, plus there's a good range of cocktails. While it gets busier between 8pm and 1am, this rather sophisticated hideout is best for a laidback drink rather than a thumping night out. Daily 3pm–3am.

La Torre Edificio FOCSA, piso 33, Calle 17 no.55 esq. M **☎**7 832 2451; map p.100. Set on the top floor of the tallest apartment building in the city, with floor-to-ceiling windows that negate the need for anything more than the long wooden bar, a couple of plants and simple seating. A wide selection of cocktails ($2–3CUC) and other alcoholic drinks plus bar snacks. Daily noon–midnight.

MIRAMAR

La Casa Española Ave. 7ma esq. 26, Miramar, Playa **☎**7 206 9644; map p.113. There's a café, bar and rooftop views to enjoy, spread around the five floors of this mock fortress complete with suits of armour and mock-medieval paraphernalia inside. Tasty Spanish dishes such as paella are served alongside Cuban-style lobster, pork and prawns. Daily noon–midnight.

★ **El Tocororo** Calle 18 esq. Ave. 5ta, Miramar, Playa **☎**7 204 2209; map p.113. This superb restaurant (see p.128) has an equally alluring bar, in a separate room from the dining area, where musicians often play until late, entertaining drinkers having a post-meal *mojito*. One of the few proper bars in Miramar – non-diners are welcome. Daily noon–2am.

Sangri La Calle 42 esq. Calle 21 (no phone); map p.113. Hip little basement hangout with white banquette seating and an expanse of dark flecked marble. Strong cocktails and understated background tunes attract a well-heeled international crowd. Daily noon–2am.

NIGHTLIFE AND ENTERTAINMENT

Havana's **nightlife** doesn't jump out at you, but instead works its magic from isolated corners all over the city, in secluded clubs, hidden courtyards, theatre basements and on hotel rooftops. Spontaneous nights out are difficult as there's no single area with much of a buzz and the headline venues are widely dispersed. The only way to find out who is playing, and where, are the fliers (usually cheap photocopies) at Infotur offices (see p.118) and in hotel lobbies, promoting club nights and live musical. As schedules are so unreliable it's wise to call the venue itself.

CLUBS, CABARETS AND LIVE MUSIC

Many of the biggest and brashest clubs and cabarets are found in the mansions and hotels of Vedado and Miramar; outside its restaurants, Habana Vieja is surprisingly low on clubs and music venues. Whatever the venue, a night out almost always involves some form of live music, with numerous small concert venues and plenty of places where you can enjoy a meal with a performance (see box, p.130). Modern salsa, timba and reggaeton dominate the city's music scene and though styles such as trova, bolero and son are regularly performed at bars, cafés and restaurants, they are less common in concert venues and nightclubs.

HABANA VIEJA

Adagio Paseo del Prado esq. San Rafael ☎ 7 861 6575; map pp.74–75. In one of the street-facing halls of the Gran Teatro, this unusual place offers an alternative to traditional Cuban music with a programme of opera singers, vocal harmony singing groups and live piano in a venue that feels a bit like a bar in a corporate hotel, with its marble floor, black-and-white colour scheme and underlit, mirror-backed bar. Free. Daily 7–11pm.

Café Taberna Mercaderes esq. Brasil (aka Teniente Rey) ☎ 7 861 1637; map pp.74–75. The food at this restaurant is nothing to shout about but the music is excellent and performed nightly. One of the resident bands is billed as the Buena Vista Social Club, and

though you won't recognize anyone from the world-famous album bearing that name, the music is in exactly the same vein. Entry is $35CUC, and includes a meal and two drinks; shows start at 9.30pm. Daily 11am–midnight.

Casa de la Cultura Julián del Casal Revillagigedo no.162 e/ Gloria y Misión ☎ 7 863 4860; map pp.74–75. Well off the beaten track and aimed primarily at locals, the programme of daytime and evening events at this cultural community centre includes live music – rumba features heavily, but there's also a monthly trova ranging from bolero and tango to rumba and reggaeton. Visit the building to get the weekly programme. Entrance free. Concerts usually daily from 8pm.

Patio Amarillo San Ignacio no.22 e/ Empedrado y Tejadillo ☎ 7 864 2426; map pp.74–75. Traditional Cuban music is performed nightly on the miniature stage of this small tables-and-chairs venue just off the Plaza de la Catedral. More subdued than its equivalents on raucous Obispo. Free. Daily 8–10.30pm.

Sala de Conciertos Antigua Iglesia San Francisco de Paula Ave. del Puerto esq. San Ignacio ☎ 7 860 4210; map pp.74–75. This diminutive church hosts classical and orchestral concerts at weekends; there's usually a schedule just inside the door. Arrive half an hour before performance times. Some concerts are free, others cost up to $5CUC. Usually Fri & Sat from 7pm.

THE TROPICANA

Not for nothing were the female dancers of the **Tropicana** described in their heyday as *Las Diosas de Carne* (goddesses of the flesh). There is something quite idolatrous about the spectacle of intricately painted showgirls clad in feathers, sequins and elaborate headdresses commanding the stage of the most famous cabaret in the world.

Evolving to cater to the north American tourist trade, **Cuban cabaret** really started when nightclub owner Victor de Correa cut a deal with casino operators Rafael Mascaro and Luis Bular and relocated the dance troupe and musicians from his successful nightclub Edén Concert, to the rented grounds of Guillermina Pérez Chaumont's stately villa in Havana's Marianao. The new business partners renamed the cabaret Tropicana in reference to the lush vegetation that would characterize their outdoor cabaret; and with a winning combination of dazzling musical shows and high-stakes casino, the club went from strength to strength.

Its heyday was in the 1950s, when the famous Arcos de Cristal glass-walled stage opened. The 1950s also saw cabaret-casinos open in various venues across Havana including at the *Havana Hilton*, the *Riviera* and the *Nacional* hotels – all of which still operate cabarets to this day. Following the Revolution all cabarets were nationalized and the mob, which had grown to have a large commercial interest in the cabarets, were expelled from the country.

Today the standard of both house band and dancers at the Tropicana is phenomenal, with the troupe often including several dancers who narrowly failed to make the grade at the Cuban national ballet. While some might find the sexist nature of scanty costumes and provocative dances somewhat hard to swallow, there's no denying that this spectacle is a quintessential Cuban experience.

1

CENTRO HABANA

Casa de la Música Habana Ave. de Italia (aka Galiano) no.155 e/ Neptuno y Concordia ☏7 860 8297 & 862 4165; map p.95. One of the top live music and club venues in Havana, with large and raucous queues forming outside every weekend and often during the week as well. All the biggest and most talked-about names in Cuban salsa, reggaeton and cubaton play here. Entrance $5–25CUC. Performances Mon–Thurs & Sat–Sun 5–9pm & 11pm–3am, Fri 4–8pm & 11pm–3am.

Piano Bar Habaneciendo Ave. de Italia (aka Galiano) e/ Neptuno y Concordia ☏7 862 4165; map p.95. A relatively smart venue, though not snobbishly so, where punters can enjoy all types of Cuban music, both traditional and popular. Above the *Casa de la Música Habana* and under the same management, thus guaranteeing that big names such as Laritsa Bacallao and Coco Freeman perform here. Entrance $5–10CUC. Wed–Fri 5–9pm, Sat 4–9pm, Sun 3–8pm.

Teatro América Ave. de Italia (aka Galiano) no.253 e/ Concordia y Neptuno, Centro Habana ☏7 862 5416; map p.95. Smaller than its more renowned counterparts, this humble but happening theatre lends itself well to the comedy shows, live jazz and traditional music performances that are its mainstays. Entrance $5CUC.

VEDADO

Cabaret Parisién Hotel Nacional, Calle O esq. 21 ☏7 836 3663; map p.100. The city's most renowned cabaret after *Tropicana*, staged in a custom-built cabaret theatre with a long history. Productions are usually well attended and contain all the ridiculous costumes and musical styles you would hope for, and last for about two hours. Entrance $35CUC, and from $55CUC with dinner. Daily 9pm–2am.

Café Cantante Mi Habana Teatro Nacional de Cuba, Paseo y 39, Plaza de la Revolución ☏7 879 0710; map p.100. One of the top clubs for Havana's salsa, timba and merengue enthusiasts. Top artists like Paulito FG and Los Van Van sometimes headline here, while regulars include Maikel Blanco y Su Salsamayor, one of the most popular Cuban salsa bands of recent years; prices depend on who's playing but are upwards of $10CUC, with a cheaper Thursday matinee. Arrive before 11pm at weekends, when the small basement gets jam-packed and the queue can be enormous. Tues–Sat 4pm–4am.

Casa de la Amistad Paseo no.406 esq. 17 ☏7 830 3114; map p.100. Resident troubadour groups perform well-executed salsa, son and boleros in the majestic grounds of a Rococo building that was once a private house. Saturdays are livelier with old-school salsa. Entrance free during the week, or $5–7CUC at weekends. Mon & Wed–Fri 9am–6pm, Tues & Sat 9am–1am.

Casa de la Cultura de Plaza Calzada 909 esq. 8 ☏7 831 2023; map p.100. There is no end to the activities at this off-the-beaten-track culture house, from theatre and poetry readings to every type of music Havana offers. Every week there's a choice of bolero, hip-hop, rumba and feelin'. With flamenco evenings and dance or art classes also available, this is a wonderful venue for those looking to immerse themselves in community-based culture. Usually free. Tues–Sun 6–11pm.

Delirio Habanero Piano Bar Teatro Nacional de Cuba, Paseo y 39, Plaza de la Revolución ☏7 878 4273; map p.100. This sultry and atmospheric late-night jazz hangout is popular with Cuban sophisticates and visitors alike, with low-key piano music, live bands nightly (10.30pm–3am) and rumba on Sundays. Limited table space makes reservations essential at weekends. Entrance $5CUC. Daily 10pm–6am.

★ **El Gato Tuerto** Calle O e/ 17 y 19 ☏7 838 2696; map p.100. This pre-Revolution, beatnik jazz bar, whose name translates as the "one-eyed cat", has kept its cool edge despite a complete renovation, and offers one of the best nights out in the area. Excellent live feelin' is played nightly from midnight, though for a slightly older crowd, and there's a stylish eating area upstairs. Entry is free but subject to a $5CUC minimum *consumo*. Daily 10pm–4am.

★ **Hurón Azul** UNEAC Calle 17 no.351 e/ Ave. de los Presidentes y H ☏7 832 4152; map p.100. It's always worth checking out the programme posted outside this beautiful Vedado mansion, home to the Writers' and Artists' Union. Regular events include bolero (Sat 9pm–2am), nueva trova alternated with rumba (Wed from 5pm) and son or rumba (Sun from 5pm). In addition there are various art exhibitions, fashion shows and festivals on the grounds throughout the week, and you can sometimes catch such luminaries as Pablo Milanés in concert. Entrance $5CUC. Daily 5pm–2am.

No Se Lo Digas a Nadie Café Teatro Bertol Brecht Calle 13 no. 259 esq. Calle I ☏7 832 9359; map p.100. This basement of this recently refurbished theatre houses one of the hippest music venues in the city, with performances by the likes of Frank Delgado, Qba Libre, Raul Paz and Síntesis. As the name – "Don't tell anyone" – implies, it's still something of an in-the-know secret. Opening hours are somewhat informal so it's worth calling ahead to check. Tues, Thurs & Fri 10.30pm–2.30am.

★ **Salón Rojo** Calle 21 esq. N ☏7 834 6560; map p.100. One of Havana's hottest nightspots, often host to big-hitting Cuban acts like Charanga Habanera and Havana D´ Primera, this is an atmospheric venue with seating sloping down towards the stage and a dancefloor from which people spill over to dance in the aisles. Entrance $5–10CUC. Daily 10pm–4am.

Teatro Amadeo Roldán Calzada esq. D, Vedado ☏78 32 4521; map p.100. Recently renovated, this is the home of the National Symphony Orchestra and one of the best places to hear classical music in Havana. The orchestra always plays at weekends (Fri 9pm, Sat 5pm, Sun 4pm).

There are opera, choral, soloists and some jazz programmes most weeknights between 6pm and 8pm, but you should check in advance. $5–10CUC.

Turf Club Calzada esq. F ☎7 836 2120; map p.100. This great basement club playing reggaeton, electro and salsa has a predominantly Cuban clientele – and the occasional international DJ like Gilles Peterson. There's little hassle and a separate seating area away from the dancefloor makes for a relaxing vibe. If the salsa doesn't get you up and dancing, the house special – Rociante Horse, or Red Bull with whisky – will. Entrance $3CUC. Daily 10pm–3am.

La Zorra y El Cuervo Calle 23 no.155 e/ N y O ☎7 833 2402; map p.100. A cool and stylish basement venue, with contemporary decor and a European feel, which puts on superior live jazz shows each night. It doesn't heat up until the band starts at 11pm. Entrance $10CUC. Daily 10pm–late.

MIRAMAR AND THE WESTERN SUBURBS

Casa de la Música de Miramar Calle 20 esq. 35, Miramar, Playa ☎7 202 6147; map p.113. One of the most animated nightspots in Havana, this *casa de la música* is worth the trip out to Miramar. The mansion in which it's set is beautiful, and regular bands have included Bamboleo, Adalberto Alvarez and Paulo FG – however it can be quite cruisey. If you want a table it's advisable to book in advance. Entrance $10–25CUC. Daily 5–9pm & 11pm–4am.

★ **El Chévere** Club Almendares, Calle 49C esq. 28A, Kohly, Playa; map p.113. A favourite venue for many of the city's salsa schools, this friendly, open-air salsa club has a large dancefloor and stage under a high roof. Cubans and foreigners mix amicably, with *jineterismo* frowned upon and a strict door policy. Cuban dance enthusiasts and learners should make a beeline here. Entrance $2CUC. Wed 6–11pm.

Río Club Calle A e/ Ave. 3ra y Ave. 3ra, Miramar, Playa ☎7 206 4219; map p.113. Popularly known as *El Johnny*, this large split-level club currently attracts a boisterous college-age crowd with a soundtrack of international dance music and contemporary Cuban sounds. Entrance $5CUC. Daily 10pm–3am.

★ **Sala Atril** Teatro Karl Marx, Ave. 1ra e/ 8 y 10, Miramar, Playa ☎7 206 7596; map p.113. A great venue for easy access to some of Havana's less well-represented music scenes in a relatively intimate stage venue attracting a diverse, trendy crowd. The programme of events represents an interesting cross-section of mostly modern and alternative Cuban music. The layout includes private booths and an outdoor terrace. Entrance $5CUC. Daily 10pm–3am.

Salón Bolero Complejo Dos Gardenias, Ave. 7ma esq. 26, Miramar, Playa ☎7 204 2353; map p.113. Upstairs in a restaurant and bar complex, the *Salón Bolero* is a saloon bar where exponents of bolero entertain subdued crowds seven nights a week. For a laidback evening of music,

enjoyed from tables gathered around a small stage, this is a good option. Entrance $5CUC. Daily 10pm–3am.

Tropicana Calle 72 no.504 Marianao ☎7 267 1717; map p.113. Possibly the oldest and most lavish cabaret in the world, Cuba's unmissable, much-hyped open-air venue hosts a pricey extravaganza in which class acts and a ceaseless flow of dancing girls, (under)clad in sequins, feathers and frills, regularly pull in a full house. Starts at 8.30pm with the show at 10–11pm, followed by dancing. You can arrange all-inclusive bus trips from most hotels. Booking is essential. Entrance $70–90CUC. Tues–Sun 8.30pm–dawn.

CINEMA

Cinema is very popular in Havana, and there are plenty of atmospheric fleapits dotted around the city. They may be run-down – air conditioning often breaks and the smell of the toilets can be an unwelcome distraction – but a refreshing lack of anonymous multiplexes makes for an idiosyncratic experience. Most screen a selection of Cuban, North American and European films, with the English-speaking ones generally subtitled in Spanish or, if you're unlucky, badly dubbed. Programmes can change daily, and cinema listings daily in *Granma* newspaper. As a visitor you will probably be charged in convertible pesos ($2–3CUC), but it's a small price to pay for the experience.

Cine Actualidades Ave. de Bélgica no.362 e/ Animas y Virtudes, Habana Vieja ☎7 861 5193. Havana's first cinema, this small venue now offers one of the more varied monthly programmes.

Cine Chaplin Calle 23 e/ 10 y 12, Vedado ☎7 831 1101. The Chaplin may be small but it's one of Havana's most important cinemas, showing classic and modern Cuban films.

Cine La Rampa Calle 23 esq. O, Vedado ☎7 878 6146. Although the auditorium is a bit run-down, the entrance and atrium in brass and marble is rather stunning. Mostly North American and European films on show.

Cine Payret Paseo del Prado esq. San José, Habana Vieja ☎7 863 3163. The best spot in Habana Vieja to see Cuban films and the occasional Hollywood blockbuster.

Cine Riviera Calle 23 e/ G y H, Vedado ☎7 830 9564. A stylish cinema, painted cobalt blue, that shows a range of Cuban and international films.

Cine Yara Calle L esq. 23, Vedado ☎7 832 9430. A large, old-fashioned auditorium showing the latest Spanish and Cuban releases, with a small video room showing special-interest films.

THEATRE AND DANCE

Supported and overseen by the state since the Revolution, theatre and dance have flourished in Havana, and as affordable arts became a national tenet under Castro, ticket prices are low (though note that Cubans pay in CUP, while visitors are charged in CUC). Performances are of very high standard, and contrary to expectations, political opinions are often fairly freely expressed. Though a good level of Spanish is needed to get the most out of theatre performances, it's nevertheless worth checking out at least one show on your trip. Companies like Teatro Buendía (☎7 881 6689) and Teatro de la Luna (☎7 879 6011) have attracted international acclaim for their work.

Ballet Cuba also has one of the world's finest ballet companies, the Ballet Nacional de Cuba (✆www .balletcuba.cult.cu), which was founded in 1948 by prima ballerina and Cuban heroine Alicia Alonso. Performances might be slightly shabbier round the edges than aficionados are accustomed to, but are still an enriching cultural experience.

Folklórico dance From open-air street performances (particularly around Habana Vieja) to minutely choreographed shows in theatres, the city also has plenty of *folklórico* dance, which celebrates Afro–Cuban culture. Many of the major theatres have regular performances by companies like the state-funded Conjunto Folklórico Nacional de Cuba (✆www.folkcuba.cult.cu) and excellent contemporary dance company Danza Contemporánea de Cuba (✆dccuba.com), which worked with Carlos Acosta on his internationally acclaimed Tocororo show.

THEATRE AND DANCE VENUES

Callejón de Hamel e/ Hospital y Aramburu, Centro Habana (no phone). The best-known Afro–Cuban dance location in the city (see p.98) now has a slightly offputting staged feel, attracting more *jineteros* than dancers, but the rumba ceremonies that take place here every Sunday in this quirky pedestrianized block of Centro Habana are still a sight to behold.

Centro Cultural Bertold Brecht Calle 13 no.259 e/ J y I, Vedado ☎7 832 9359. Two auditoria which feature theatre including musicals and farces (Fri & Sat 8.30pm) and a matinee (Sun), as well as performances for kids

(Sat & Sun 11am) and comedy (Tues 8.30pm). Entrance $1–3CUC.

El Gran Palenque Calle 4 no.103 e/ Calzada y 5ta Vedado ☎7 833 4560. Home to the Conjunto Folklórico Nacional de Cuba, which puts on rumba and other Afro–Cuban dance performances on the patio. The regular Peña de la Rumba is a highly charged, energetic affair with group and individual dancers plus audience participation. It's well worth the entrance fee and takes place at 3pm on Sat. $5CUC.

Gran Teatro Paseo del Prado esq. San Rafael, Habana Vieja ☎7 861 3096. This outstandingly ornate building on the Parque Central is the home of the Ballet Nacional de Cuba but also hosts operas and contemporary dance pieces. The biannual Festival Internacional de Ballet de la Habana takes place here in October, and there's a season of Spanish ballet each August. Otherwise, there are performances most weeks (usually Fri–Sun), most starting around 8pm, earlier on Sun. Entrance is around $10CUC.

★ **El Guiñol** Calle M e/ 17 y 19 ☎7 832 6262. Resourceful and inventive puppet theatre, aimed at children but magical enough to be enjoyed by all. Renowned local writers and actors are often part of the production team. Regular performances Sat & Sun 11am and 5pm.

Teatro Karl Marx Calle 1ra e/ 8 y 10, Miramar ☎7 830 0720. Impressively ugly 1960s building hosting all kinds of music and dramatic arts events, including international rock concerts and classical theatre. Definitely worth checking what's on. Entrance $5–15CUC.

Teatro Mella Linea no 657, e/ A y B ☎7 833 8696. This large theatre puts on many performances by the Conjunto Folklórico Nacional de Cuba as well as comedy, theatre and variety shows. Fri and Sat 8pm, Sun 5pm. Entry $10CUC.

Teatro Nacional de Cuba Calle Paseo y 39, Plaza de la Revolución ☎7 879 6011. Havana's biggest theatre puts on some of the city's best events all year round, from ballet to guitar and jazz. Spanish-speakers should check out the avant-garde drama, especially during the February theatre festival.

SHOPPING

Havana stands out, refreshingly for some, as one of the few capitals in the West whose centre is not dominated by a **shopping district** – Obispo, in Habana Vieja, is as close as it gets. Elsewhere, although new malls and boutiques are mushrooming steadily around the city, the general standard of merchandise is quite low, with rum, cigars, coffee and crafts the exceptions. For everything else the large hotels and the Artex and Caracol state chain stores have some of the best-quality products. Standard opening hours are Monday to Saturday 9am to 6pm; only a tiny minority of shops stays open after 7pm. Some shops are open all Sunday but most either don't open or close at lunchtime. Havana still has a significant number of **national-peso shops**, especially in Centro Habana, mostly half-empty and stocking used, old or shoddy goods – the fading signs and barely stocked outlets along Avenida de Italia stand as testament to a bygone era.

ARTS AND CRAFTS

Havana's street markets tend to overstock with Che Guevara-themed memorabilia, paintings of old American cars, black coral jewellery and wooden sculptures. However, if you're prepared to put in the hours you can find

the occasional sculpture, piece of jewellery or handmade item of clothing that stands out from the rest. Markets tend to close on a Sunday or a Monday (rarely both), and generally trade between 9am and 6pm.

Antiguo Almacenes San José Ave. del Puerto, Habana

Vieja; map pp.74–75. In a huge nineteenth-century warehouse right on the harbourfront, this is the largest arts and crafts market in the city. There is strikingly little that stands out, but for the sheer volume of paintings, jewellery, Che hats, leather bags, T-shirts, instruments and handicrafts it can't be beat. There are several cafés and a *casa de cambio*. Daily 10am–8pm.

★ **Arte Malecón** Calle D e/ 1ra y 3ra, Vedado (no phone); map p.100. Quality paintings, ceramics and other handicrafts, including items engraved or printed with images from the Museo de Bellas Artes, plus a decent DVD and CD department in a set of attractive little rooms also featuring a bar and café.

Feria de Arte Obispo Obispo e/ Compostela y Aguacate, Habana Vieja; map pp.74–75. Around fifteen stalls in the ruins of an old building on the main shopping street in the old town, selling ornamental gifts, clothing, jewellery and ceramics. Daily 10am–7pm.

Galería Habana Linea no.460 e/ E y F, Vedado ☎ 7 832 7101, ⊛ galerihabana.com; map p.100. One of Havana's most internationally respected galleries always has an impressive collection of contemporary art on display and for sale. Mon–Fri 10am–4.30pm, Sun 9am–1pm.

Galería Manos Obispo no.411 e/ Aguacate y Compostela, Habana Vieja ☎ 7 860 8577; map pp.74–75. Run by the Asociación Cubana de Artesanos Artistas (a seal of good quality), with an eclectic mix of items including photographs, cigar boxes, bags, shoes, woodcarvings, ceramics and jewellery. Daily 10am–7pm.

Galería Victor Manuel San Ignacio no.56, Plaza de la Catedral, Habana Vieja ☎ 7 866 9268; map pp.74–75. A relatively high standard of merchandise including Art Nouveau lamps, photographs of Havana, jewellery and sculptures. Daily 9am–9pm.

Mercado de La Rampa La Rampa e/ M y N, Vedado; map p.100. The miscellaneous merchandise at this small craft market includes pumpkin-seed necklaces, handmade leather items and imported clothes. Tues–Sun 9am–7pm.

BOOKS AND POSTERS

Secondhand bookstalls are popular in Havana. Most are tiny affairs set up in doorways and front rooms, but some –

VINTAGE SHOPPING IN HAVANA

In the early days of the Revolution, wealthy Havana families buried their prized possessions in cellars before fleeing the country, hoping to return when the revolutionary government had been ousted. Others stayed, clinging onto their valuables in what became the land that consumer culture forgot. Recent economic liberalization has allowed the owners of these treasures to come out from behind the once closed doors of their sumptuous Vedado mansions, or set up stalls in Centro Habana markets, and become legitimate **antique** and **vintage furniture** and **art** dealers. Serious collectors will be knocked out by the Art Deco furniture and huge chandeliers on sale; easier to fit in your suitcase are collectable glasses, drinks trays or cocktail stirrers from the famous 1950s cabarets and casinos; or, more widely available are cigar box artwork, film posters and mid-century black-and-white postcards or photographs. Many items are in remarkably good condition, but don't expect a bargain – most antique dealers know the value of their stock. The list below represents some of the best places to find vintage goods in Havana.

Belkis Calle 2 no.607 e/ 25 y 27, Vedado ☎ 7 830 4124; map p.100. An entire Vedado mansion turned over to antique dealing with an overwhelming selection of pre-revolutionary glassware, colonial-era ceramics, crockery and art, a varied collection of furniture and small collectable items like compact mirrors, costume jewellery and brooches. No fixed opening hours; ring to arrange a visit.

Fin de Siglo San Rafael e/ Ave. de Italia (Galiano) y Aguila, Centro Habana; map p.95. A corner of this huge market houses three stalls selling antique books and maps, 1950s postcards, cigar-box artwork, records and collectables, including compact mirrors, and jewellery boxes. Ask if you want something in particular – not everything is on display. Daily 9am–6pm.

Ibrain Portieles Torres Calle 35 no.251 e/ 4 y 6, Vedado (no phone); map p.100. Ibrain specializes in

Cuban and colonial-era lamps and Art Deco furniture. He also sells ceramics, glassware and small collectables such as antique hand mirrors. No fixed opening hours.

Mirtha Calle 6 no.601 e/ 25 y 27, Vedado ☎ 7 836 0695 or ☎ 05 34 68397 (mobile); map p.100. Two rooms packed with colonial-era chandeliers, an impressive and varied selection of artwork, religious artefacts and large colourful ceramics, all available for international shipping. No fixed opening hours; ring to arrange a visit.

La Vajilla Ave. de Italia (Galiano) esq. Zanja, Centro Habana ☎ 7 862 4751; map p.95. The ground floor of this *casa comisionista* (aka pawnshop) is filled with beautiful Art Deco and antique furniture; upstairs, there's a sizeable range of chandeliers, lamps and decorative glassware. Mon–Sat 9am–6pm, Sun 9am–1pm.

1

such as the one at the Plaza de Armas – are more substantial. Bookshops are also the city's principal sellers of stationery and collectible Cuban film posters.

Boloña Mercaderes esq. Obispo, Habana Vieja (no phone); map pp.74–75. The publishing arm of the Oficina del Historiador de la Ciudad has its own, very small, specialist shop carrying an excellent selection of books, magazines and pamphlets on the history and reconstruction of Havana, particularly Habana Vieja. Mon–Sat 10am–7pm, Sun 9am–1pm.

★ **Librería Caballero de París** Plaza de San Francisco, Habana Vieja (no phone); map pp.74–75. A fantastic stock of political and propagandist posters from the 1960s, 1970s and 1980s, featuring the battle cries and slogans of the Revolution against striking images. Prices tend to be upwards of $30CUC. Film and pre-Revolution posters, books, photos and magazines and lots of old political texts are also on offer. Daily 8am–10pm.

Librería Centenario del Apóstol Calle 25 no.164 e/ 0 y Infanta, Vedado ☎7 835 0805; map p.100. A tightly packed national-peso secondhand bookstore, with piles of magazines from Cuba and around the world plus old maps and travel guides. Also very heavy on socio-political literature and Cuban fiction. Daily 9am–9pm.

Librería Fernando Ortiz Calle L esq. 27, Vedado ☎7 832 9653; map p.100. One of the city's widest selections of books on history and politics in English and Spanish, as well as a decent selection of novels. Mon–Sat 9am–6pm, Sun 9am–1pm.

★ **Plaza de Armas Book Market** Plaza de Armas, Habana Vieja; map pp.74–75. Havana's largest book market, with stalls running all the way around the plaza. Among the revolutionary pamphlets, Che Guevara tomes and the occasional novels you can find vintage Cuban and US tourist brochures, postcards and lifestyle magazines, some reflecting life before Castro, plus copies of rare books and all sorts of other collectors' items like revolutionary posters and Cuban film art. Starting prices are high – be prepared to haggle. Daily 9am–6pm.

CIGARS AND RUM

The Casa del Habano chain accounts for most of the cigars sold in Cuba and is well represented all over Havana. Many of the top-class hotels have their own cigar shops; among the best are the *Conde de Villanueva* and *Parque Central* in Habana Vieja and the *Meliá Cohiba*, *Habana Libre* and the *Nacional* in Vedado. Specialist rum shops are much less common but many of the cigar shops also sell rum.

★ **Casa del Habano** 5ta y 16 Ave. 5ta. no.1407 esq. Calle 16, Miramar ☎7 204 7973; map p.113. An

---

TOP FIVE CIGAR LOUNGES AND SMOKING ROOMS

Even if you don't smoke, there is an allure to the world of **Cuban cigars**, with its kudos-bearing brand names such as Montecristo and Cohiba, its world famous patrons from Winston Churchill to Jack Nicholson, and all its stylish trappings, like the artistic cigar labels and the smart box designs. There is no better place to immerse yourself in this world than in Havana's **cigar lounges** and **smoking rooms**, mostly attached to cigar shops, With dignified furnishings, a subdued atmosphere and neat little bars, they provide the perfect setting for the slow consumption of a Churchill or Double Corona. Whether you're testing a cigar before a purchase or enjoying the smokes you've just bought, you'll have to light up to sit down in one, but you don't have to be an aficionado to enjoy these smoking dens. Five of the best are listed below.

Casa del Habano 5ta y 16 Ave. 5ta. no.1407 esq. Calle 16, Miramar. An array of smoking spaces, including a "private sales" room with tiled floor and high-backed chairs, a bar with wicker furniture and a cigar-friendly restaurant make this one of the best places to sit down and test your smokes in the city. Mon–Sat 10am–6pm, Sun 10am–1pm.

Casa del Habano Hotel Conde de Villanueva Mercaderes no.202 esq. Lamparilla, Habana Vieja ☎7 862 9293. The inconspicuous mezzanine-level entrance, low ceilings and dimmed lights make you feel like you're in on a secret here. At one end of the slender shop is an easy-chair lounge, at the other a very cool bar – you won't find a more atmospheric place to smoke a cigar in all of Havana. Daily 10am–7pm.

Casa del Habano Club Habana Ave. 5ta e/ 188 y 192, Flores, Playa ☎7 204 5700. The spacious wood-panelled back room at this sports and social club has artwork on the walls, a bar and comfortable leather furniture. Daily 9am–5pm.

Casa del Habano Hotel Nacional, Calle 0 esq. 21, Habana Vieja ☎7 836 3564. At the back on the basement level of this two-floor shop is the *salón de fumadores*, with two wicker three-piece suites and a bar. Daily 10am–6pm.

Casa del Habano Hotel Meliá Habana Ave. 3ra e/ 76 y 80, Miramar, Playa ☎7 204 8500. There are large, comfortable leather sofas in the centre of this cigar shop, next to an eye-catching curved bar with a great selection of Scotch, plus an open-air seating area and a quiet smoking room off in the back. Daily 10am–7pm.

impressive cigar shop in a posh mansion, with an extensive range of brands (including some rare or collectible cigars) in floor-to-ceiling cabinets, plus all kinds of smoking accessories. Mon–Sat 10am–6pm, Sun 10am–1pm.

Casa del Habano Hotel Conde de Villanueva, Mercaderes no.202 esq. Lamparilla, Habana Vieja ✆ 7 862 9293; map pp.74–75. The most memorable and moodiest cigar shop in Havana (see box, p.136), the stock here is excellent and the shop is run by one of Cuba's foremost *torcedors* (master cigar rollers), Reynaldo Jímenez. Daily 10am–7pm.

Casa del Habano Hotel Habana Libre, Calle L e/ 23 y 25, Vedado; map pp.74–75. The largest cigar store in Cuba, with an extensive range of *habanos*, an open smokers lounge and a bar. Daily 10am–8pm.

Casa del Ron y del Tabaco Cubano Obispo e/ Bernaza y Ave. de Bélgica, Habana Vieja ✆ 7 866 8911; map pp.74–75. One of the best selections of rum under one roof in the whole of Havana, and a decent range of *habanos* too. Mon–Sat 10am–7pm, Sun 10am–6pm.

SHOPPING MALLS AND DEPARTMENT STORES

Though unimpressive by international standards, Havana's modern shopping malls house some of the better shops in the city outside the hotels. Most of the more upmarket complexes are found in Miramar and Vedado.

Galería Comercial Comodoro Ave. 3ra e/ 80 y 84, Miramar ✆ 7 204 6177; map p.113. Havana's largest and most upmarket shopping mall is also the city's most pleasant place to shop, flanked by lawns, pavement cafés and outdoor eateries. There are around thirty stores, many of them clothes shops, as well as specialists in jewellery, watches, perfume and cigars. Mon–Sat 10am–6pm, Sun 9am–1pm.

Plaza de Carlos Tercero Ave. Salvador Allende (aka Carlos Tercero) e/ Arbol Seco y Retiro, Centro Habana ✆ 7 873 6370 & 6373; map p.95. This four-floor no-frills mall is usually swarming with customers and has a food court, a number of clothing and shoe shops, plus homewares and a cigar store. Mon–Sat 10am–6pm, Sun 10am–2pm.

FOOD SHOPS AND MARKETS

Farmers who have supplied their government quota are allowed to sell their surplus produce in *agromercados* (farmers' markets), where everything is fresh and you generally find more variety than you do in hotels and restaurants. Everything is sold in national pesos and is fantastically cheap – a pound of tomatoes will only set you back around $6CUP, while oranges go for $2CUP each. Most of the large food markets have a CADECA *casa de cambio* on hand where you can change convertible pesos into national currency. Make sure you take a plastic bag in which to carry your goodies, as these are never provided – though you may find someone selling them for $1CUP each.

Agromercado Calle 19 y A Vedado; map p.100. The

prettiest of Havana's *agros*, this picturesque market sells meat, flowers, honey and dry goods like rice and beans alongside heaps of fresh fruit and vegetables. Tues–Sun 7am–6pm.

Animas y Soledad Animas e/ Soledad y Arambura, Centro Habana; map p.95. One of the largest *agromercados* in Centro Habana. Daily 7am–6pm.

Casa del Café Obispo esq. Baratillo, Plaza de Armas, Habana Vieja ✆ 7 866 8061; map pp.74–75. Specialist coffee shop, though there are cigars and rum for sale here too. Daily 10am–7pm.

Mercado Egido Ave. de Bélgica, e/ Corrales y Apodaca, Habana Vieja; map pp.74–75. This is the daddy of food markets – a huge indoor space selling fruit and vegetables, spices, honey, rice, beans and meat as well as a few household goods like soap and razor blades. Daily 7am–7pm.

Supermercado 70 Ave. 3ra e/ 66 y 70, Miramar ✆ 7 204 2890; map p.113. The biggest supermarket in Havana, but still surprisingly low on variety. There's a fresh meat counter and a better-than-average selection of dairy products. Mon–Sat 9am–6pm, Sun 9am–1pm.

MUSIC AND FILM

Havana's music stores are all relatively small, and the range of CDs a little disappointing for a city so intrinsically associated with music and musicians. But as stock tends to consist only of music recorded on the island by Cuban labels, you'll find obscure gems in the more niche genres, like Cuban hip-hop and rumba, alongside numerous salsa, son, bolero and reggaeton albums you're unlikely to come across anywhere else. Music shops also double up as suppliers of DVDs and videos. Bootleg sellers of CDs and DVDs, actually legal businesses in Cuba, now proliferate all over the city but particularly on Obispo in Habana Vieja and San Rafael in Centro Habana.

Casa de la Música Habana Ave. de Italia (aka Galiano) e/ Concordia y Neptuno, Centro Habana ✆ 7 860 9640; map p.95. Run by Egrem, the nation's principal record label, this small store has self-service listening facilities and a slightly more discerning selection of CDs than some others in Havana. Mon–Sat 10am–6pm, Sun 9am–1pm.

Casa de la Música Miramar Calle 20 esq. 35, Miramar, Playa ✆ 7 204 1980; map p.113. One of the best nightclubs in Havana also has a music shop with a good stock of CDs plus musical instruments for sale. Mon–Sat 10am–6pm.

Galeria Juan David Cine Yara, Calle L esq. 23, Vedado (no phone); map p.100. Tiny commercial outlet for the Cuban film industry selling videos, film-poster art and similarly decorated souvenirs like umbrellas. Mon–Sat 9am–6pm.

Habana Sí Calle L esq. 23, Vedado ✆ 7 838 3162; map p.100. One of the widest and best-organized ranges of CDs in town, precisely divided into genres. Also carries books and a decent collection of Cuban films on video and DVD. Mon–Sat 9am–6pm.

1

★ **ICAIC Centro Cultural Cinematográfico** Calle 23 no.1155 e/ 10 y 12, Vedado ☎7 830 4579; map p.100. An excellent source of cool screen-printed film posters, plus cult films on video (including many by Tomás Gutiérrez Alea), and some specialist film publications, mainly in Spanish. Mon–Sat 9am–6pm.

Longina Obispo no.360 e/ Habana y Compostela, Habana Vieja ☎7 862 8371; map pp.74–75. The most conveniently located music shop for sightseers, though the choice is narrower than elsewhere. Does better with its array of musical instruments. Mon–Sat 10am–6pm, Sun 10am–1pm.

Seriosha Neptuno no.408 e/ San Nicolás y Manrique, Centro Habana ☎7 862 5477; map p.95. A little crate-diggers' paradise for collectors of Latin and easy-listening music on vinyl, all priced in Cuban pesos. Mon–Sat 9am–6pm.

CLOTHING AND PERFUME

The quality of Cuban-made clothing is generally very poor, though the numerous T-shirt specialists, most of them found in hotels such as the Habana Libre, tend to offer a better cut of cloth.

Guayabera Habanera Tacón no.18 e/ Plaza de Armas y Empedrado, Habana Vieja (no phone); map pp.74–75. The best selection of the classic Cuban shirt, the *guayabera*, in the city. Mon–Sat 9am–6pm.

Habana 1791 Mercaderes no.156 e/ Obrapia y Lamparilla, Habana Vieja ☎7 861 3525; map pp.74–75. This unique shop sells perfumes like those used during the eighteenth and nineteenth centuries in Cuba, handmade from flowers and plant oils, for between $5CUC and $20CUC. Mon–Sat 9am–6pm, Sun 9am–1pm.

SPORTS AND OUTDOOR ACTIVITIES

You only need to spend a few hours wandering the streets of any part of the capital to appreciate the prominent role that **sport** plays in the lives of Habaneros. Fierce arguments strike off every evening on basketball courts all over the city, and you'll rarely see an open space, at any time of the day, not hosting a game of baseball or football. On a professional level, Havana is the finest place for live sport in Cuba, with teams in all the national leagues and a number of large stadia. Entrance to most sports arenas is only $1–2CUP and booking in advance is unnecessary and rarely possible.

BASEBALL

Estadio Latinoamericano The city's national-league baseball team, Industriales, traditionally the most successful team in Cuba, plays at the 55,000-capacity Estadio Latinoamericano (☎7 870 8175) at Pedro Pérez no.302 e/ Patria y Sarabia in Cerro, the city borough south of Centro Habana and Vedado.

Essentials To catch a game all you need do is turn up and pay at the gate. You may have to sit in a special tourist section, for which you'll be charged around $3CUC. The big crowds usually only come out for the most important confrontations, and especially when they play their arch rivals Santiago de Cuba. The most reliable and detailed source for game schedules is the website ⓦ baseballdecuba.com.

BASKETBALL

Essentials The local basketball team, Capitalinos, spends the winter months (usually Jan–April) in weekly combat

---

MULTI-SPORT SPECTATOR VENUES

Havana has a number of **multi-sport arenas** and **stadiums**, with baseball the only sport enjoying the luxury of its own exclusive stadium. As event information is so hard to get hold of and individual team websites all but nonexistent, one of the best ways to stay informed is to contact the venues themselves.

Coliseo de la Ciudad Deportiva Vía Blanca y Ave. de Rancho Boyeros, Cerro ☎7 648 5000. This 15,000-capacity arena, built in 1957, is part of a huge sports complex of the same name. Volleyball is most frequently played here, though gymnastics, martial arts, boxing and occasionally basketball also take place.

Estadio Panamericano Ave. Monumental Km 4 1/2, Habana del Este. The huge Complejo Panamericano sports complex, not all of it open to the public, was originally built to host the 1991 Pan American Games. The centrepiece Estadio Panamericano (☎7 795 4140) athletics stadium has also staged football matches in recent years.

Sala Polivalente Kid Chocolate Paseo del Prado e/ Brasil y San Martín, Habana Vieja ☎7 862 8634. Opposite the Capitolio Nacional, this rickety old sports hall is best known for staging boxing matches, but also hosts basketball, wrestling, badminton and five-a-side football. Event programmes are posted on a noticeboard at the entrance.

Sala Polivalente Ramón Fonst Ave. de Rancho Boyeros e/ Bruzón y 19 de Mayo, Plaza de la Revolución ☎7 881 4296. Used predominantly for basketball, this arena has also hosted volleyball, handball, gymnastics and fencing.

1

TOP FIVE SWIMMING POOLS

There's only one proper beach in Havana itself, so if you want to swim or sunbathe without travelling the 15km to the Playas del Este (see p.144), you'll need to find yourself a **swimming pool**. The city has a few municipal public pools, but these are often not filled and are so unreliable that you're almost always better off aiming for one of the hotel or tourist-complex pools listed below. Non-guests have to pay to use hotel pools, but the cost usually includes a *consumo*, which you can use to buy food and drink; you may also be asked to show a passport.

Club Almendares Calle 49B, Kohly. Some 200m from Parque Almendares, this is a fairly small but very sociable pool with various eating and recreation facilities. Entry $10CUC, includes $8CUC *consumo*. Daily 10am–6pm.

Hotel Nacional Calle O esq. 21, Vedado. This hotel has two pools, a small, rectangular one used by swimmers, and a more classic freeform hotel pool used by splashers and paddlers. Entry $18CUC, includes $13CUC *consumo*. Daily 10am–6pm.

Hotel Occidental Miramar Ave. 5ta e/ 72 y 76 Miramar, Playa. One of the largest pools in Miramar. The $20CUC entry includes $17CUC *consumo*. Daily 10am–6pm.

Hotel Riviera Paseo y Malecón, Vedado. The only hotel pool with diving boards, this is also the most evocative of the pre-Revolution era, barely changed since it opened in the late 1950s. Entry $10CUC, includes $10CUC *consumo*. Daily 10am–6pm.

Hotel Saratoga Paseo del Prado no.603 esq. Dragones, Habana Vieja. The rooftop pool here affords not only a great place to kick back but some of the best available views of Habana Vieja and certainly of the Capitolio Nacional and the Parque de la Fraternidad. Entry $10CUC, includes $8CUC *consumo*. Daily 9am–6pm.

with the other seven teams in the Liga Superior de Baloncesto (LSB), the national league. Advance information on games is hard to find, a situation not helped by irregular timing of the league from season to season. Your best bet is either to ask around or to contact one of the relevant arenas (see box, p.138). Over the years games have been played variously at the Sala Polivalente Ramón Fonst, the Ciudad Deportiva and the Sala Polivalente Kid Chocolate. Games usually begin around 6pm.

FOOTBALL

Essentials The home of football in Havana is the Estadio Pedro Marrero (☎ 7 209 5428) at Ave. 41 no.4409 e/ 44 y 46 in Marianao in the western suburbs, where the more popular and successful of the city's two league teams – Ciudad de la Habana – and the national team play most of their matches. Games tend to kick off between 3pm and 5pm but match schedules have been highly irregular in recent seasons, with games taking place on any day of the week.

GOLF

Essentials The Club de Golf Habana (daily 8am–9pm; ☎ 7 649 8918) runs the only golf course in the city. Located on the Carretera de Vento just off the airport road, the Avenida de Rancho Boyeros, this basic nine-hole course covers an area of less than one square kilometre. Green fees are $20/30CUC for nine/eighteen holes with caddy hire at

$3/6CUC respectively; trolley hire is $5CUC and club hire is $10CUC, while for another $10CUC you can get a golf lesson. The complex also features a tennis court ($2CUC per person), bowling alley, pool and restaurant.

DIVING AND FISHING

Marinas Havana has two marinas, the Marina Hemingway at Ave. 5ta y Calle 248 (☎ 7 204 5088) in the far western suburbs of Santa Fe in Playa (you'll need your passport for any trip from here, as it's an international port of entry), and Marina Tarará at Vía Blanca Km 18 in Habana del Este (☎ 7 796 0242). Most of the fishing, diving and sailing in the waters around Havana is arranged through one of these two, both run by Marlin (Ⓦnauticamarlin.com), and offering a very similar set of packages and the same prices.

Diving The La Aguja dive centre at the Marina Hemingway (daily 10am–5pm; ☎ 7 204 1150) offers dives at the twenty or so sites that line the Playa coastline, including a couple of shipwrecks, coral walls and small caves, and charges $40CUC for one dive or $60CUC for two on the same trip. For all diving enquiries at Marina Tarará contact the marina itself.

Fishing Both marinas offer deep-sea fishing (*pesca de altura*); trips for four people cost $300/400/500CUC for four/six/eight hours, including all equipment and bait, a fishing instructor and crew plus some on-board drinks. Bottom-fishing (*pesca a fondo*) trips are also available, starting at $170CUC for four hours (min four people).

DIRECTORY

ATMs Machines accepting Visa and MasterCard can be found at some CADECA *casas de cambio*, including the one

at Obispo no.257 e/ Aguiar y Cuba in Habana Vieja (daily 5am–1am) and at Calle 23 e/ L y K in Vedado, and at some banks, such as the Banco de Crédito y Comercio at Amargura esq. Mercaderes in Habana Vieja.

Embassies The vast majority of embassies and consulates (see p.58) are based in Miramar.

Internet The most efficient internet services are in the cybercafés of the hotels *Inglaterra* at Paseo del Prado esq. San Rafael ($6CUC/hr) and the *Florida* (daily 11am–8pm; $6CUC/hr; see p.119), both in Habana Vieja, and the business centres in the *Saratoga* and *Parque Central* hotels in Habana Vieja (see pp.119–120), and the *Habana Libre* and *Nacional* hotels in Vedado (see p.122), where the charges are between $7CUC/hr and $10CUC/hr. For free wi-fi, head for the lobby bars of *Hotel Saratoga*.

Launderettes Lavandería Aster at Calle 34 no.314 e/ Ave. 3ra y Ave. 5ta in Miramar (Mon–Fri 8am–5pm & Sat 9am–noon; ☎7 204 1622); $4CUC per load.

Medical care There is no single emergency number for ringing an ambulance, but you can call ☎105 or ☎7 838 1185 & 2185 to get one. You can also contact Asistur, the tourist assistance agency, on its emergency number (☎7 866 8339). One of the best hospitals, run predominantly for foreigners, is the Clínica Internacional Cira García in Miramar at Calle 20 no.4101 esq. Ave. 41 (☎7 204 4300 to 4309).

Money and exchange There are CADECA *casas de cambio* at Obispo no.257 e/ Aguiar y Cuba (Mon–Sat 8am–9pm & Sun 8–11am) and at Baratillo esq. Oficios (Mon–Sat 8.30am–4pm & Sun 8.30–11.30am) in Habana Vieja; at Calle 23 e/ L y K in Vedado (Mon–Sat 9am–4.30pm & Sun 9–11.30am); and at Ave. 5ta e/ 40 y 42 (Mon–Sat 9am–4.30pm & Sun 9am–noon) in Miramar. The *casa de cambio* (daily 8am–noon & 1–7pm) at *Hotel Nacional* in Vedado stays open late, most notably on Sundays. The banks most accustomed to foreign currency transactions include branches of the Banco Financiero Inter-nacional at Oficios esq. Brasil (aka Teniente Rey) (Mon–Fri 8am–3pm) in Habana Vieja; Calle 25 e/ L y M (Mon–Fri 8am–3pm)

inside the *Habana Libre* in Vedado; and Ave. 1ra e/ 0 y 2 (Mon–Fri 8am–3pm) in Miramar.

Pharmacies Farmacia Internacional, at Ave. 41 no.1814, esq. 20, in Miramar (☎7 214 4744; Mon–Fri 9am–6pm, Sat 9am–noon), and at the Clínica Internacional Cira García (see above), also in Miramar, are two of the best-stocked in Havana. In Habana Vieja try the Farmacia Taquechel on Obispo no.155 e/ Mercaderes y San Ignacio, which stocks basic pain-relief tablets including aspirin but specializes in natural medicines. In Vedado, the Retinosis Pigmentaria clinic on Calle L no.151 (☎7 833 3599; Mon–Fri 9am–6pm) has good supplies, while there are small pharmacies in the *Nacional* (☎7 836 3564 ext.798) and *Habana Libre* (☎7 834 6187) hotels.

Police There are police stations at Dragones esq. Agramonte in Habana Vieja, and at Dragones e/ Lealtad y Escobar (☎7 862 4412) in Centro Habana. In an emergency ring ☎106.

Post offices and stamps Post offices are at Paseo del Prado esq. San Martín (daily 8am–7pm), on the border of Habana Vieja and Centro Habana; Calzada de Infanta esq. Concordia, Centro Habana (Mon–Fri 8am–6pm), just a few metres from Vedado; and Calle 23 esq. C in Vedado itself (Mon–Fri 8am–6pm & Sat 8am–noon). You can buy stamps at the store on Obispo e/ Villegas y Bernaza, Habana Vieja (Mon–Sat 9am–5pm).

Telephones For mobile phone rental and the city's largest banks of public telephones go to the ETECSA Telepunto centres at Obispo esq. Habana in Habana Vieja (daily 8.30am–7pm), which also has internet access; and Aguila no.565 esq. Dragones in Centro Habana (daily 8.30am–7pm). Smaller ETECSA Minipuntos are located at Tacón esq. Chacón in Habana Vieja and at Calle P esq. 23 in Vedado.

Visas and tourist cards To renew and extend tourist cards and visas go to the office at Factor esq. Final in Nuevo Vedado (Mon–Fri 8.30am–3pm). Arrive early and expect delays.

Around Havana

Havana's **suburbs** stretch out for miles, and though they are technically within the city's political boundaries, they feel far removed – a sense that's reinforced by the extremely poor public transport links. The best beaches, notably the top-notch **Playas del Este**, are to the east, past the uncomplicated towns of **Cojímar** and **Guanabacoa**. The neatly packaged **Museo Ernest Hemingway**, the writer's long-time Cuban residence, lies **south** of Havana, as do the picturesque landscaped expanses of **Parque Lenin** and the impressive **Jardín Botánico Nacional**.

GETTING AROUND

By public transport, car or taxi The tourist bus service, the Habana Bus Tour (see p.116), is the best way of getting to the Playas del Este and the rest of Habana del Este. For

HAVANA'S OUTER BOROUGHS

the rest of the outlying boroughs you'll either need your own transport, be prepared to pay for a taxi or tackle the Metrobus system (see box, p.117).

1

East of Havana

Taking the tunnel in Habana Vieja under the bay and heading east on the Vía Monumental, past El Morro and parallel to the coast, leads you straight to **Cojímar**, a fishing village famed for its Hemingway connection. Past here the road dips inland to become the Vía Blanca and passes Villa Panamericana, the village built to support the 1991 Pan American Games, and runs south towards **Guanabacoa**, a quiet provincial town with numerous attractive churches and a fascinating religious history. For many, the big attraction east of Havana will be the boisterous **Playas del Este**, the nearest beaches to the city, where clean sands and a lively scene draw in the crowds.

With the exception of the route to the beach, scarcity and unreliability of **public transport** becomes even more pronounced once outside the city proper, and you'll need a car to see many of these sights.

Cojímar

Just 6km east of Havana, the tiny fishing village of **COJÍMAR** is a world apart from the bustling city – tailor-made for enjoying such simple pleasures as watching fishing boats bob about in the calm, hoop-shaped bay, or wandering the tidy, bougainvillea-fringed streets.

Cojímar's sole claim to fame revolves around one of its late residents, **Gregorio Fuentes**, the first mate of Ernest Hemingway's boat *The Pilar*, who also claimed to be the old man upon whom Hemingway based Santiago, the protagonist of his Pulitzer- and Nobel Prize-winning novel *The Old Man and the Sea*. Up until the late 1990s Fuentes could be seen sitting outside his house or in *La Terraza de Cojímar* restaurant, charging US$10 for a consultation with fans eager for Hemingway stories. When Fuentes died in 2002, aged 104, it marked the end of an era and one of the last personal links with Hemingway.

Monumento a Hemingway

Playing up its connections to Ernest Hemingway, Cojímar pays homage to the writer in the **Monumento a Hemingway**, a weatherbeaten construction close to the small *malecón*, which looks a bit like a tiny circular Acropolis. In the middle is Hemingway himself, represented by a rather meagre brass bust, made from boat fittings donated by local fishermen. The whole thing has the air of an oversized misplaced garden ornament.

Torreón de Cojímar

Overhanging the water's edge, the **Torreón de Cojímar** fort, built between 1639 and 1643 as part of the Spanish colonial fortification, is so small it looks rather like a well-crafted toy. A squat and sturdy building, with sharp, clean angles and Moorish sentry boxes, it was designed by the engineer Juan Bautista Antonelli – who also designed the not-dissimilar El Morro castle in the Parque Morro-Cabaña – as an early-warning system for attacks on Havana harbour, and only needed to accommodate a couple of sentries rather than a whole battalion. Even so, it was usually left unmanned, a defensive weakness fully exploited by the British in 1762, who bombarded it with cannon-fire, routed the peasants' and slaves' attempts at retaliation and romped off to capture the city. The fort is still in military use, so there's no access to the building, although you're free to examine the outside.

ARRIVAL AND DEPARTURE — COJÍMAR

By bus Cojímar is served by the #58 bus which leaves from Prado, by the mouth of the tunnel in Habana Vieja; the fare is $0.20CUP.

By taxi A taxi from Havana will cost around $15CUC one-way.

EATING

La Terraza de Cojímar Calle 152 no. 161 ☎ 7 766 5150. Cojímar's flagship restaurant is airy, pleasant and full of black-and-white photos of Hemingway and Fuentes, although the food isn't all it could be: go for the simple dishes. Reservations are recommended as the place is sometimes booked out by bus tours. Daily noon–10pm.

Guanabacoa

Less than 2km inland from the Vía Monumental turn-off to Cojímar is **GUANABACOA**, a little town officially within the city limits but with a distinctly provincial feel. The site of a pre-Columbian community and later one of the island's first Spanish settlements, it is historically important, though its disproportionately large number of churches and the strong tradition of Afro–Cuban religion, a result of its position as an important centre for slave trade, hold the most appeal for visitors.

Museo Histórico de Guanabacoa

Martí no.108 e/ Quintin Bandera y E.V. Valenzuela • Mon & Wed–Sat 9.30am–4.30pm • $2CUC • ☎ 7 797 9117

Guanabacoa's most coherent and impressive attraction is the **Museo Histórico de Guanabacoa**, two blocks from the understated main square, Parque Martí. The interest lies in the collection of cultish objects relating to the Afro–Cuban religious practices of **Santería**, **Palo Monte** and the **Abakuá Secret Society**. One room is moodily set up to reflect the mystic environment in which the *babalao*, the Santería equivalent of a priest, performs divination rituals, surrounded by altars and African deities in the form of Catholic saints. Equally poignant are the representations of Elegguá, one of the most powerful of Afro–Cuban *orishas*, with their almost threatening stares. There are also some interesting bits and pieces, including furniture and ceramics, relating to the town's history. It's worth calling ahead before you visit as the opening hours are erratic.

Guanabacoa's churches

Guanabacoa's five **churches** make up the remainder of its sights, and though none has reliable opening times there's usually a staff member on hand willing to let you wander inside. The most accessible and intact are the run-down **Iglesia Parroquial Mayor** on Parque Martí, with its magnificent, though age-worn, gilded altar; the eighteenth-century **Iglesia de Santo Domingo** and adjoining monastery, on the corner of Lebredo and Santo Domingo, with a lovely leafy courtyard; and the huge monastery, now a school, attached to the still-functioning **Iglesia de San Francisco**, a block south of Martí on Quintin Bandera.

ARRIVAL AND DEPARTURE — GUANABACOA

By bus The #P15 bus from the Parque de la Fraternidad in Habana Vieja cuts right through the centre of town; the fare is $0.20CUP.

1

Playas del Este

Fifteen kilometres east of Cojímar, the Vía Blanca reaches Havana's nearest beaches – Playa Santa María del Mar, Playa Boca Ciega and Playa Guanabo, collectively known as the **Playas del Este**. Hugging the Atlantic coast, these three swathes of fine sand form a long, twisting ochre ribbon that vanishes in the summer beneath the crush of weekending Habaneros and tourists. There's not a whole lot to distinguish between the beaches, geographically, although as a general rule the sand is better towards the western end.

If you're based in Havana, the excellent self-catering and hotel **accommodation** here makes this area a good choice for a mini-break. Those craving creature comforts should head for the big hotels in Santa María, while budget travellers will find the best value in the inexpensive hotels and *casas particulares* in Guanabo. Although a number of restaurants serve cheap meals, these all tend to be much the same, and your best bet is to eat at one of the two paladars in Guanabo; otherwise, see if one of the *casas particulares* can recommend somewhere.

ARRIVAL AND DEPARTURE
PLAYAS DEL ESTE

By bus The excellent Habana Bus Tour company's #T3 runs a regular service that picks up and drops off at several hotels along the Santa María strip roughly every thirty minutes from 9am to 9pm. An unlimited-use day ticket costs $5CUC; it's worth bearing in mind that the route gets extremely busy in summer, particularly on the last Havana-bound buses of the day.

By taxi A metered taxi from the centre of Havana as far as Guanabo will cost $15–20CUC.

Playa Santa María del Mar

Sun loungers $2CUC/day, massage roughly $5–7CUC/30min, catamaran rental $8CUC/30min, snorkelling equipment $3CUC/hr

Because of its proximity to Havana, **Playa Santa María del Mar**, usually just called Santa María, is the busiest and trendiest of the eastern beaches, with boombox reggaeton, watersports and beautiful bodies on sun-loungers. It extends for about 4km from the foot of Santa María Loma, a hill to the south of the Río Itabo, with the bulk of hotels dotted around the main Avenida de las Terrazas, just behind the beach. Arguably the most attractive of the three beaches, with golden sands backed by grasslands and a few palm trees, it's also the most touristy and can feel a bit artificial.

The beach has plenty of sun-loungers and is patrolled by eager beach masseurs, and there are various **activities** on offer – though sadly you'll see more empty beer cans than fish if you go snorkelling.

ACCOMMODATION
PLAYA SANTA MARÍA DEL MAR

Atlántico Ave. de las Terrazas, no. 10 ☎7 797 1085, ⓦhotelesc.es. Although the building is a bit outdated, this large and friendly all-inclusive (drinks included too) is your best choice for Santa María accommodation. Facilities

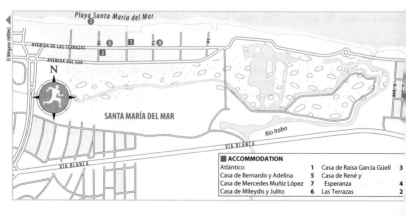

■ ACCOMMODATION			
Atlántico	1	Casa de Raisa García Güell	3
Casa de Bernardo y Adelina	5	Casa de René y	
Casa de Mercedes Muñiz López	7	Esperanza	4
Casa de Mileydis y Julito	6	Las Terrazas	2

include tennis courts, a beachfront pool with kids' area, gym and internet. There's also a free shuttle to Havana. **$150CUC**

Las Terrazas Ave. de las Terrazas e/ 11 y 13 ☎ 7 797

1203. Spacious and airy apartments in a complex, some with views over the beach. Each room has a TV and fridge, and there are two pools in the grounds. Good value for groups. **$44CUC**

EATING AND DRINKING

With thatch-hut **beach bars** at intervals along the sand and roving vendors selling rum-laced coconuts, there's no shortage of refreshments. A big convertible-peso shop on Avenida de las Terrazas sells the makings of a **picnic**, although the prices are higher than for goods in Havana, so you'd do well to bring what you need with you.

La Caleta Ave. de las Terrazas s/n (no phone). Central to the beach, this open-air restaurant has a thatched-palm roof, music at weekends and a lively air. The decent menu includes lobster brochette for $8CUC and pork dishes for $5CUC. Daily 8.30am–6pm.

Don Pepe Ave de las Terrazas ☎ 7 976 0700. This open-sided restaurant makes an airy retreat from the midday sun. *Comida criolla* and pizzas are served slowly, though

with a smile. Rather incongruously, there is a roving magician. Daily 10am–10pm.

Mégano Santa María beach ☎ 7 797 1670. At the western end of the beach, this is the best of the few cafés dotted around and is generally well stocked with drinks, ice cream and pork/rice dinners for around $5CUC. Daily 8.30am–6pm.

Playa Boca Ciega

A bridge across the Río Itabo connects Santa María to **Playa Boca Ciega**, also known as Playa Mi Cayito. A paucity of public facilities make this the least user-friendly of all the beaches. However, the beautiful sherbet-yellow beach is open to all, and the waters around the estuary mouth are usually quite busy and cheerful, with kids and adults paddling and wading in the river currents. Further west, towards Santa María, the beach is popular with the gay community.

Playa Guanabo

Far more pleasant than Playa Boca Ciega is laidback **Playa Guanabo**, roughly 2.5km to the east, where the sun-faded wooden houses and jaunty seaside atmosphere go a long way to compensate for the slightly poor brownish-sand beach. With fewer crowds and no big hotels, it feels much more authentic than Santa María, especially towards the east end of town where tourism has hardly penetrated at all. While not idyllic, it still has its charms: palm trees offer welcome shade, and if you're not bothered about the odd bit of seaweed, this is a refreshingly unaffected spot to hang out.

As most tourists stay on the better beaches further west, Guanabo is pretty much left to the Cubans, with many residents commuting daily from here to Havana. Avenida 5ta, the appealing main street, has a clutch of cafés and shops, including a

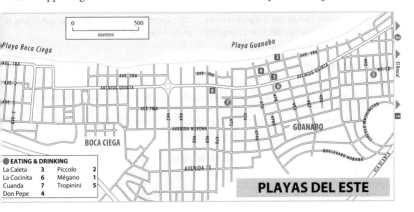

EATING & DRINKING			
La Caleta	3	Piccolo	2
La Cocinita	6	Mégano	1
Cuanda	7	Tropinini	5
Don Pepe	4		

PLAYAS DEL ESTE

1

convertible-peso shopping precinct selling sweets, toys and sportswear, while around the side streets and near the beach are a couple of excellent paladars. The Banco Metropolitano on Avenida 5ta has a cash machine.

ACCOMMODATION   PLAYA GUANABO

Casa de Bernardo y Adelina Calle 478 no.306 e/ 3ra y 5ta ☎ 7 796 3609, ✉ bernardo@infomed.sld.cu. One a/c room with a private bathroom, an adjoining sitting room, a dining area and a kitchen with a fridge. The balcony with a sea view is a bonus. **$30CUC**

Casa de Mileydis y Julito Calle 468 no.512 e/ 5ta y 7ma ☎ 7 796 0100. One a/c apartment in a *casa particular*, close to the beach, with TV and small bathroom. Has a pretty garden and a porch where you can relax, plus extremely hospitable owners. **$30CUC**

Casa de Raisa García Güell Ave. 3ra no.47801 e/478 y 480 Guanabo ☎ 7 796 2878, ✉ danielyero@infomed .sld.cu. This beautiful house has a sun-dappled patio filled with plants and two massive en-suite rooms. It's close to the beach, and there's space for parking too. **$30CUC**

Casa de René y Esperanza Ave. 3ra no. 47607 e/476 y 478 ☎ 7 796 3867, ✉ jcparra@infomed.sld.cu. The double room, with its own kitchen, boasts a wide terrace with a sea view. **$25CUC**

EATING AND DRINKING

La Cocinita Calle 5ta e/ 178 y 180 (no phone). This open-sided bar is the liveliest spot in town, with a live band most nights. It's safe enough but can feel a little edgy at times due to the groups of raucous men who patronize it. Daily noon–midnight.

Cuanda Calle 472 esq. 5ta D (no phone). A basic restaurant dishing up reasonable meals on the pork, salad, rice and beans theme. At $3.50CUC for a main, it's pretty good value. Daily noon–midnight.

Piccolo Calle 5ta, no. 50206 e/ 502 y 504 ☎ 7 796 4300.

Exposed brickwork and a stone floor give this paladar a rustic feel. A decent stab at Italian food has been made, with highlights including spaghetti and pesto sauce ($7.50CUC) and pizzas. Daily noon–midnight.

Tropinini Calle 5ta Ave. no.49213 e/ 492 y 494 (no phone).Breakfast at this excellent paladar is a wholesome combination of eggs, toast and fruit juice, while lunch and dinner consist of pork, chicken or spaghetti served with fried green bananas and salad for $5–6CUC. Easily the best choice in the area. Daily noon–midnight.

Brisas del Mar

Some 4km east of Guanabo is the virtually deserted **Brisas del Mar**. Were it not for the outstanding *casa particular* practically built on the strand, this lovely stretch of clean sand would make for an awkward day-trip. However, it's well worth making an overnight stay to experience the near solitude so rare in Playas del Este and to enjoy the hospitality of one of the best *casas particulares* in the entire province.

ACCOMMODATION   BRISAS DEL MAR

★ **Casa de Mercedes Muñiz López** Calle F no.4 e/ 24 y Lindero, Brisas del Mar, Guanabo ☎ 7 796 5119. The two simple but thoughtfully decorated rooms in a building that backs onto an almost private stretch of beach make for the perfect coastal idyll. One room has its own lounge and

both have their own bathroom. The lovely owners serve delicious home-cooked meals on a sun terrace and will come and collect you from Guanabo centre when you arrive. There's even an outdoor shower to wash off sand as you leave the beach. **$35CUC**

South of Havana

Heading south of Havana, the city fades in fits and starts, the buildings dying out only to reappear again almost immediately among the trees and green fields which bind this area together. Numerous satellite towns dot the semi-urban, semi-rural landscape, distinctly provincial in character yet close enough to Havana to be served by municipal bus routes. The best of what there is south of the city is all within a 30km drive of the city centre.

The airport road, the **Avenida de Rancho Boyeros**, also known as the **Avenida de la Independencia**, is the easiest route to most of the day-trip destinations this side of the capital. It makes sense to visit at least a couple of these on the same day, since they are all difficult to get to by public transport and in many cases the distances between them

1

are short. A near-perfect preservation of the great writer's home in Havana, the **Museo Ernest Hemingway**, is the most concrete option and one of the few that stands up well by itself. The relative proximity of **Parque Lenin** – an immense park – to the **Parque Zoológico Nacional** and the sprawling **Jardín Botánico Nacional**, over the road from **ExpoCuba**, makes these a convenient combination for anyone looking for an activity-packed day out.

Museo Ernest Hemingway

Mon–Sat 10am–5pm • $5CUC • ☎ 7 692 0176 & 693 1186 • Take Metrobus #P7 bus from the Parque de la Fraternidad in Habana Vieja or the #P2 from the junction between Calle 23 and Avenida de los Presidentes in Vedado; it's a 10min walk from the bus stop in San Francisco de Paula

Eleven kilometres southeast of Habana Vieja, in the suburb of San Francisco de Paula, is **Finca La Vigía**, an attractive little estate centred on the whitewashed late-nineteenth-century villa where Ernest Hemingway lived for twenty years until 1960. Now the **Museo Ernest Hemingway**, it makes a simple but enjoyable excursion from the city, and is also visitable on a organized tour (see p.142). On top of a hill and with splendid views over Havana, this single-storey colonial residence, where Hemingway wrote a number of his most famous novels, has been preserved almost exactly as he left it – with drinks and magazines strewn about the place and the dining-room table set for guests. Brimming with character, it's a remarkable insight into the writer's lifestyle and personality, from the numerous stuffed animal heads on the walls and the bullfighting posters to the bottles of liquor and the thousands of books lining the shelves in most of the rooms, including the bathroom. The small room where his typewriter is still stationed was where Hemingway did much of his work, often in the mornings and usually standing up. Frustratingly, you can't actually walk into the rooms but must view everything through the open windows and doors; by walking around the encircling veranda, however, you can get good views of most rooms. In the well-kept **gardens**, which you can walk round, surrounded by bamboo, Hemingway's fishing boat is suspended inside a wooden pavilion; the graves of four of his dogs are next to the empty swimming pool. You can also scale the **lookout tower** and take in the fantastic 360-degree vistas from its roof terrace.

Note that the museum closes when it rains, to protect the interior and grounds, so try to visit on sunny days.

Parque Lenin

Ave. San Francisco (Calle 100) • June–Sept Wed–Sun 9am–5pm; July & Aug Tues–Sun 9am–5pm • Free • Information ☎ 7 643 1165, switchboard ☎ 7 644 3026 • Metrobuses on routes #P13 and #PC (see p.117) pass closest to the park, but do not stop at the park itself; to drive there, follow signs from Ave. de Rancho Boyeros

Roughly a twenty-minute drive south of the city, about 3km east of the José Martí airport, are the wide open grounds of **Parque Lenin**, a cross between a landscaped urban park and a rolling tract of untouched wooded countryside. Founded in 1972, this was once a popular escape for city residents who came here to picnic, ride around on horseback or on the park's own steam train, and enjoy the other facilities, including

---

ACTIVITIES IN PARQUE LENIN

A horseback ride is a great way to explore the park's large spaces; you can hire horses ($3CUC/hr) from the **Centro Ecuestre**, signposted at the first right-hand turn as you enter from the city side, though there are also locals offering rides on their own horses nearby – be prepared to haggle. It's in this northern half of the park where you'll find the **Parque Mariposa** (entrance $1CUP, rides $1–6CUP), a Chinese-designed amusement park built in 2007. Though unspectacular, this is nonetheless one of Havana's best attractions for young children, with over twenty different rides including bumper cars, a swinging pirate ship, a water slide, a rollercoaster and a 42m-high Ferris wheel.

1

restaurants and cafeterias, swimming pools, a small art gallery, boats and fairground rides. The deterioration in public transport since the early 1990s led to a sharp drop in visitors, and today a pervasive air of abandon blows around the park, with many of the facilities, including the train and pools, now closed and in disrepair. Nonetheless, its sheer size (almost eight square kilometres) and scenic landscape make Parque Lenin a great place for a picnic, a wander or just a breath of fresh air, and there are still a couple of basic restaurants here. The park's attractions are spread quite sparsely, so it can be a tiring place to explore on foot; roads around the park allow you to explore by car.

South of the park's central reservoir, the Presa Paso Sequito, is the **Galería Amelia Peláez** (Tues–Sun 9am–5pm; free), a small art gallery that stages temporary exhibitions; nearby is the semi-abandoned and quite surreal **aquarium** where, in over sixty small tanks, you can see all sorts of fish, crabs, turtles and even a couple of crocodiles; and the park's most famous monument, the 9m-high **marble bust of Lenin**.

Parque Zoológico Nacional

Ave. Varona Km 3.5, Capdevila, Boyeros • Wed–Fri 10am–3.30pm, Sat & Sun 10am–4.30pm • $4CUC adults, $3CUC children, plus $5CUC to enter with your own car • ☏ 7 644 1870

A perpetually half-finished safari park in between the Ave. Rancho Boyeros and Parque Lenin, the **Parque Zoológico Nacional** features a small lake and two completed enclosures. Herbivores of the African savannah, including elephants, rhinos, giraffes and zebras, roam about in the **Pradera Africana** enclosure, while the park's twenty or so lions are in the **Foso de Leones**, a huge grass- and tree-lined pit. Both enclosures usually allow excitingly close contact with the animals. However, the majority of the various species here, mostly big cats and apes, are kept in cramped conditions in the so-called **Area de Reproducción**. The zoo opened in 1984, partly in response to the need for improved conditions for the animals cooped up in Havana's smaller, inner-city zoo, but there is still some way to go before these ambitions are fully realized.

If you don't want to walk or drive about the park, you can ride one of the free **tour buses** that leave from just inside the main entrance every thirty minutes or so; guides are on board to talk you through the attractions, but don't count on an English-speaker.

Jardín Botánico Nacional

Carretera del Rocío, 4km south of the entrance to Parque Lenin, Calabazar • Daily 9am–4pm • $1CUC • Tours $3CUC in own vehicle, $4CUC for 1hr 30min tractor-bus tour • Tractor-bus tours (1–2hr) leave every hour or so from just inside the main entrance, near the information office • ☏ 76 97 9159, ⓦ uh.cu/centros/jbn/

A sweeping expanse of parkland showcasing a massive variety of plants and trees, the **Jardín Botánico Nacional** is the prettiest, most pleasant and most worthwhile of the attractions on Havana's southern outskirts of the city. Laid out as a savannah rather than a forest, the grounds are split into sections according to continent. Highlights include the collection of 162 surprisingly varied species of palm, the cacti in the **Pabellones de Exposiciones** greenhouse-style buildings and the meticulously landscaped **Japanese Garden**, donated by the Japanese government on the thirtieth anniversary of the Revolution in 1989. The restaurant near the Japanese Garden is also the best place to stop for lunch.

FERIA INTERNACIONAL DE LA HABANA

For one week every year, usually the first week in November, ExpoCuba hosts the **Feria Internacional de la Habana** (ⓦferiahavana.com), an international trade fair. This is by far the best time to visit ExpoCuba as commercial enterprises from around the world come to exhibit their products and promote their services, creating a livelier atmosphere and a more exciting range of exhibits. There are fashion shows, concerts and all kinds of goods on display, as well as a pitch for many of the capital's more famous restaurants.

Though you can explore the park yourself, a lack of printed literature and plaques means you'll learn far more by booking an organized excursion from the city (see box, p.142) or taking the **guided tour**, whether in the tractor-bus or by having a guide in your own car. There's usually at least one English-speaking guide available, but it's worth noting that the tractor-bus tours do not necessarily cover the whole park.

ExpoCuba

Carretera del Rocío • Wed–Sun 9am–5pm, closed Sept–Dec, except for special events • $1CUC • Rollercoaster $0.50CUC, boating $1CUC

On the other side of the Carretera del Rocío, directly opposite the Jardín Botánico Nacional, what looks like a well-kept industrial estate is in fact **ExpoCuba**, a permanent exhibition of the island's endeavours in industry, science, technology and commerce since the Revolution. Despite its impressive scope, displays are a little dry and the hordes of children here on school trips tend to be more interested in riding on the mini rollercoaster and boating on the small lake. There are various cafeterias and a restaurant with great views.

Santiago de las Vegas

Metrobus #P12 runs from Parque de la Fraternidad in Habana Vieja

With a history dating back to the late seventeenth century and a population of around 35,000, **SANTIAGO DE LAS VEGAS**, 2km south of José Martí airport, is one of Havana's more noteworthy satellite towns. That said, there are few specific sights beyond the attractive central square and the modest national hockey stadium, both just off the main street, but if you're on your way to the church and pilgrimage point in El Rincón (see below) you may want to stop here for a bite to eat or a stroll to get a feel for Cuba beyond the big city.

The Santuario de San Lázaro

El Rincón, 2km south of Santiago de las Vegas on the main road, the Carretera Santiago de las Vegas • Daily 7am–6pm • Free

Ten kilometres south of central Havana, the **Santuario de San Lázaro**, on the edge of the tiny village of **El Rincón**, is the final destination of a **pilgrimage** made by thousands of Cubans every December. Amid scenes of intense religious fervour, pilgrims come to this gleaming, lovingly maintained church to ask favours of San Lázaro, whose image appears inside, in exchange for sacrifices (see box below). Throughout the year, though, people come here to cut deals with the saint and lay down flowers or make a donation, and the road through the village is always lined with people selling flowers and statuettes. Sitting peacefully in the grounds of an old hospital, the church itself is striking only for its immaculate simplicity, though there are several fine altars inside.

EL DÍA DE SAN LÁZARO

On December 17, the road between Santiago de las Vegas and El Rincón is closed as hordes of people from all over Cuba come to ask favours of **San Lázaro** in exchange for a sacrifice, or to keep promises they have already made to the saint. Some have walked for days, timing their **pilgrimage** so that they arrive on the 17th, but the common starting point is Santiago de las Vegas, 2km down the road. The most fervent of believers make their journey as arduous as possible, determined that in order to earn the favour they have asked for they must first prove their willingness to suffer. In the past people have tied rocks to their limbs and dragged themselves along the concrete road to the church; others have walked barefoot from much further afield; while others bring material sacrifices, often money, as their part of the bargain.

Artemisa and Pinar del Río

VIÑALES VALLEY

Artemisa and Pinar del Río

Despite their relative proximity to Havana, the provinces of Pinar del Río and Artemisa (the latter newly created in 2010) are a far cry from the noise, pollution and hustle of the capital. This is a distinctly rural region, where the laidback towns and even Pinar's regional capital of Pinar del Río are characterized by a markedly provincial feel. The major attractions are well away from the population centres, the majority situated in and around the green slopes of the Cordillera de Guaniguanico, the low mountain range that runs like a backbone down the length of the landscape. Famous for producing the world's finest tobacco (that most time-consuming of crops), Pinar del Río is stereotyped as a province populated by backward country folk, and is the butt of a string of national jokes. Life here unfolds at a subdued pace, and its hillside and seaside resorts are well suited to unfettered escapism.

Hidden within the **Sierra del Rosario**, the relatively compact eastern section of the *cordillera*, the peaceful, self-contained mountain retreats of **Las Terrazas** and **Soroa** are billed slightly inaccurately as ecotourism centres, but provide perfect opportunities to explore the tree-clad hillsides and valleys. Heading west along the *autopista*, which runs parallel with the mountain range along the length of the province, there are a few low-key attractions to the north. It's unlikely you'll want to make much more than a fleeting visit to any one of them, unless you're in search of the healing qualities of the spa at **San Diego de los Baños**, a small village straddling the border between the Sierra del Rosario and the western section of the *cordillera*, the **Sierra de los Organos**. Although the area is host to a large park and a set of caves of both geological and historical interest, their considerable potential is mostly untapped through neglect and isolation.

Most visitors instead head straight for Pinar del Río's undoubted highlight, the **Viñales valley**, where the flat-topped mountains, or *mogotes*, give the landscape a unique, prehistoric look and feel. While heavily visited, Viñales remains unspoilt and the village at its centre, full of simple houses with rooms to rent out to tourists, has an uncontrived air about it. Easily visited out on a day-trip from Havana, there's also enough to see away from Viñales's official sights for a longer, more adventurous stay. Conveniently close to the valley is the secluded little beach on serene **Cayo Jutías**, while on the same northern coastline is the more substantial but even more remote **Cayo Levisa**, better suited for a longer visit and for diving.

You'll need to be pretty determined to get to the country's westernmost locations, which are beyond Pinar del Río's provincial capital, where the *autopista* ends, and more

MARÍA LA GORDA

Highlights

❶ Baños de San Juan Perfect for picnics or a midday bathe, this delightful river haven above Las Terrazas also has a unique set of tree houses on stilts where you can stay the night. See p.158

❷ Hiking at Las Terrazas Guided hikes from here are the best way to delve into the sierra. See p.159

❸ Cabaret Rumayor One of the best cabarets outside Havana, this glitzy open-air show is the essence of hedonistic Cuba. See p.168

❹ Viñales The unique humpbacked mogote hills, prehistoric caves and friendly vibe in the village all make this an unmissable stopoff. See p.169

❺ Gran Caverna de Santo Tomás The most complex cave system in Cuba, plunging into a hillside on eight different levels and surprisingly easy to visit. See p.178

❻ Cayo Jutías The reputation of this virtually untouched islet is growing, so catch it at its natural best while you can. See p.178

❼ María La Gorda Fine white-sand beaches backed by pine woods and world-class diving make the sojourn to Cuba's western tip worth the effort. See p.183

HIGHLIGHTS ARE MARKED ON THE MAP ON P.154

PINAR DEL RÍO

HIGHLIGHTS

1. Baños de San Juan
2. Hiking at Las Terrazas
3. Cabaret Rumayor
4. Viñales
5. Gran Caverna de Santo Tomás
6. Cayo Jutías
7. María La Gorda

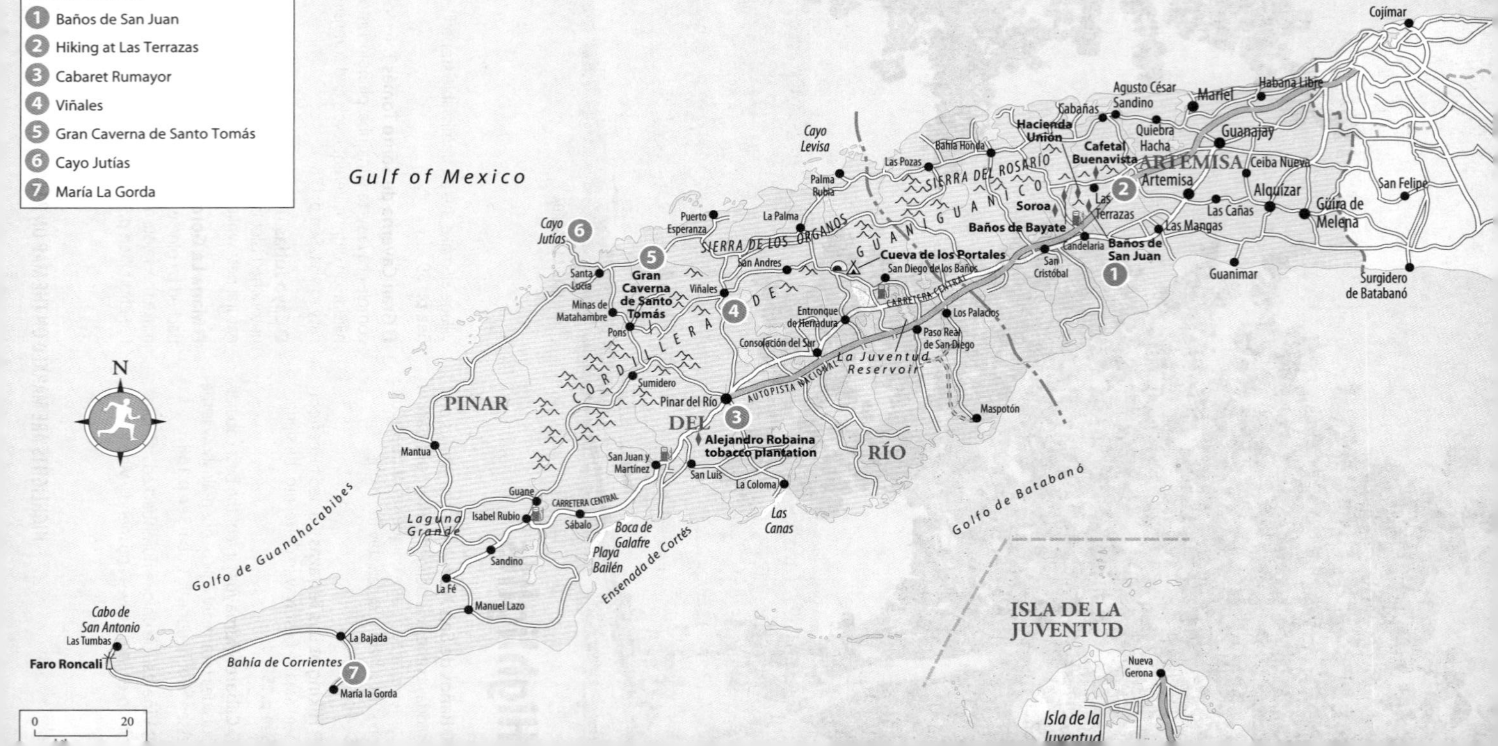

Gulf of Mexico

ISLA DE LA JUVENTUD

Golfo de Batabanó

Golfo de Guanahacabibes

Bahía de Corrientes

or less out of reach unless you rent a car or book an official excursion. If you make it, you'll find the serene and scenic patchwork landscape of the Vuelta Abajo region, said to produce the finest tobacco leaves in the world and home to some internationally renowned tobacco plantations, including the **Alejandro Robaina**, which is one of the few you can easily visit. The modest beaches of **Playa Bailén** and **Boca de Galafre** and the small tourist site at **Laguna Grande** provide quick detours if you want to break up the journey to **María La Gorda**, whose fine sandy shores, crystal-clear waters, outstanding scuba diving and fantastic sense of out-of-reach tranquillity are the real justification for coming all this way.

2

| **GETTING AROUND** | **ARTEMISA AND PINAR DEL RÍO** |

As with much of Cuba, relying on **public transport** in Artemisa and Pinar del Río is a hazardous, patience-testing business. Much of these two provinces are quite simply out of range of any of the public services, which, where they do exist, are more often than not extremely unreliable.

By bus Víazul provides a daily bus service from Havana to Pinar del Río city and then north to Viñales (2 daily; 3hr).

By train Very few visitors ever take the train from Havana into Pinar del Río (3-4 weekly; 6hr), as it's notoriously slow and doesn't make any useful stops except for the city itself; the other towns which it stops in are at least a few kilometres from anywhere worth visiting.

By car For any kind of independent travel in and around the Sierra del Rosario or the eastern half of the Sierra de los Organos, you'll need your own car, which you will have to rent in Havana, Viñales or Pinar del Río city. Most drivers speed their way through the province on the four-lane *autopista nacional* (marked on most road maps as A4), which comes to an end at the city of Pinar del Río. You can pick it up around 5km south of Avenida 5ta in Miramar, Havana. Running roughly parallel is the Carretera Central, a slower option which begins its route in La Lisa, the western suburb south of Playa, and takes you closer to the mountains and gives better views of the surrounding landscape. The most scenic, slowest and least travelled route of all is along the northern coastline. Once past Pinar del Río city, the Carretera Central is the only major road.

Eastern Artemisa

With its verdant fields, expansive reservoirs and lush plantations all glistening in the sunlight, it's no surprising to learn that **Eastern Artemisa** is known as the **Jardín de Cuba** (Garden of Cuba), an area of great fertility where bananas, sugar cane, citrus fruits and tobacco flourish in the rich red ferric soil. It's a somnambulant area, with a couple of passing attractions like the photogenic town of **San Antonio de los Baños** and the poetic decay of **Antiguo Cafetal Angerona**. The area had a brief moment of infamy thanks to Mariel on the northern coast. The nearest port to the US, it was from here that some 125,000 Cubans left the island in 1980 in what was known as the **Mariel Boatlift** (see p.464).

San Antonio de los Baños

Of all the small towns in Artemisa, **SAN ANTONIO DE LOS BAÑOS**, about 20km south of Havana's western suburbs and a 45-minute drive from Habana Vieja, is the only one that merits more than a fleeting visit. A riverside hotel with good opportunities for swimming and boating, an engaging museum and a countryside park provide at least a day's worth of laidback activity. The town itself has the undisturbed, nonchalant feel that characterizes so much of Cuba's interior, with an archetypal shady square and residential streets largely free of traffic.

Museo de Humor

Calle 60 e/ 41 y 45 • Tues–Sat 10am–6pm, Sun 9am–1pm • $2CUC • ☎ 47 38 2817

Based in a colonial home, the entertaining **Museo de Humor** has a small permanent exhibition charting the history of graphic humour in Cuba – the caricatures of national and international figures are particularly engaging. The best time to visit, however, is when the museum hosts one of several national and international **competitions** of comic art, when the best entries are displayed. The two most prestigious competitions, the **Salón de Humorismo y Sátira** and the **Bienal Internacional del Humorismo Gráfico**, take place in alternate years starting in March or April and lasting as late as August. If you're coming all this way specifically for the museum, it's worth ringing in advance, as it sometimes closes for days at a time to mount exhibitions.

2

Museo de Historia
Calle 66 e/ 41 y 45 • Tues–Sat 10am–6pm, Sun 9am–1pm • $1CUC • ☎ 47 38 2539

Situated on a quiet street, the modest **Museo de Historia** has a relatively diverse collection that includes some great photographs of local bands from the 1920s and 1930s as well as a room of colonial furniture. The museum was closed for refurbishment at the time of writing but is likely to reopen in late 2013.

ARRIVAL AND DEPARTURE	SAN ANTONIO DE LOS BAÑOS
By car The simplest route from Havana is to follow the Avenida de Rancho Boyeros to the first major junction heading south from the city, then turn west onto the Pinar	del Río road, the *autopista nacional*. Head west for 9km to reach another major junction, for the Autopista del Mediodía, which heads south for the 17km to San Antonio de los Baños.

ACTIVITIES	
Boating You can rent rowing boats ($1CUC/hr), motorboats ($3CUC/hr) and pedalos ($1CUC/hr) from a café (daily 9am–5pm) on a terrace on the banks of the	Río Ariguanabo; from the grounds of *Las Yagrumas* hotel, head down to a bend in the river where you'll see the freestanding building.

ACCOMMODATION	
Las Yagrumas ☎ 47 38 4460, ✉ gerencia@yagrumas .co.cu. A family-oriented hotel catering predominantly to Cubans, who are usually here in large numbers. Based	around a large pool, the palm-fringed grounds slope down to a bend in the Río Ariguanabo. **$42CUC**

Antiguo Cafetal Angerona

Before crossing the provincial border into Pinar del Río, it's worth taking a detour to the **Antiguo Cafetal Angerona**, a nineteenth-century coffee plantation 6km west of the town of Artemisa. Here, where 750,000 coffee plants once grew, you'll find the derelict ruins of the Neoclassical mansion where the owner – a German named Cornelio Souchay – resided, as well as the slave quarters and a 10m-high watchtower, all of it now in the grip of advancing vegetation. Legend has it that Souchay used the seclusion of the plantation to engage in a clandestine interracial affair with a black Haitian woman named Ursula Lambert, away from the gossip and prejudice of the city. Nowadays the site is occasionally visited by tour groups, but you're more likely to be the only visitor wandering about.

Sierra del Rosario

Heading west on the *autopista nacional*, the first attractions you'll come to, just inside the provincial border, are Artemisa's star attractions, the isolated mountain valley resorts at Las Terrazas and Soroa. These are by far the best bases from which to explore the densely packed forest slopes of the protected **Sierra del Rosario**, but only **Las Terrazas** can uphold the claim popularized in tourist literature of connecting tourism with conservation and the local community. Considerably smaller but no less popular than Las Terrazas, **Soroa**'s compact layout makes it more accessible to day-trippers from Havana.

The sierra was declared a Biosphere Reserve by UNESCO in 1985, acknowledgement in part for the success of the reforestation project of the 1970s (see p.157), and visitors are encouraged to explore their surroundings using official **hiking routes**. There's a comprehensive programme of guided hikes at Las Terrazas and some gentler but still rewarding walks around Soroa. Though sometimes referred to as such, the peaks of the Sierra del Rosario don't quite qualify for mountain status, the highest point reaching just under 700m, and although there is some fantastic scenery, it's rarely, if ever, breathtaking.

LAS TERRAZAS & SOROA

■ ACCOMMODATION		● EATING	
Hotel Moka	1	El Bambu	4
Hotel Moka cabins	3	Baños de Bayate	3
Hospedaje Estudio de Arte	5	Casa del Campesino	2
Villas Moka	2	Fonda de Mercedes	1
Villa Soroa	4	El Romero	1

Las Terrazas

Daily 9am–5pm • $4CUC • ⓦ lasterrazas.cu

A wonderfully harmonious resort and small working community, **LAS TERRAZAS**, 74km southwest of Havana, is one of the most important ecotourism sites in the country. About 2km beyond the tollbooth on the main access road, where you pay your entry fee unless you're staying at the resort's solitary hotel, there are right- and left-hand side-roads in quick succession. The right turn leads to Rancho Curujey, a visitor centre for both tour groups and independent travellers, while the left turn leads several hundred metres down to the **village**, a well-spaced complex of red-roofed bungalows and apartment blocks, beautifully woven into the grassy slopes of a valley, at the foot of which is a man-made **lake**. The housing is perched on terraced slopes that dip steeply down into the centre of the Las Terrazas community, forming a smaller, more compact, trench-like valley within the valley-settlement itself. Though the cabins look as if they're meant for visitors, they belong to the resident population of around a thousand.

The final stretch of the main road leads up to the other tollbooth (where you won't get charged if you already paid at the Havana end) on the western border of the resort, immediately after which a left turn will take you on the road to Soroa and back to the *autopista*.

Brief history

The Las Terrazas community was founded in 1971, with its residents encouraged to play an active role in the preservation and care of the local environment. They formed the backbone of the workforce, whose first task was a massive government-funded **reforestation project** covering some fifty square kilometres of the Sierra del Rosario. As well as building the village itself, this project entailed planting trees along terraces dug into the hillside, thus guarding against erosion and giving the place its name. This was all part of a grander scheme by the government to promote self-sufficiency and education in rural areas, one of the promises of the Revolution. Today a large proportion of the community works in tourism, some as employees at the hotel and others as owners of the small businesses that have been set up in response to the growing numbers of visitors.

THE SIERRA DEL ROSARIO'S BIRDS

A mixture of semitropical rainforest and evergreen forest, the Sierra del Rosario is home to a rich variety of **bird species**, fifty percent of which are endemic to this region. Among the more notable of the seventy-or-so species here are the white-and-red Cuban trogon or *tocororo*, Cuba's national bird, and the Cuban grassquit, known in Spanish as the *tomeguín del Pinar*.

Las Terrazas village workshops

Several sets of steps lead from the *Hotel Moka* back down the slopes into the Las Terrazas village, where small, low-key **workshops** have been set up inside some of the apartment-block buildings. Local artists produce pottery, silkscreen prints, paintings and other crafts and artwork, which you can buy or simply watch being made; though a tad contrived, the latter is still quite engaging.

Plaza Comunal

On one side of the gaping trench that separates the two halves of the Las Terrazas village, the **Plaza Comunal** boasts benches, trees and modest views of the lake and valley. It's a focal point for local residents, and gets quite sociable in the evenings.

Peña de Las Terrazas Polo Montañez

Daily 9am–5pm • $2CUC

Down on the edge of the lake, a signposted right-hand turn from the road into the village leads to the small **Peña de Las Terrazas Polo Montañez** museum. Indistinguishable to all the others from the outside, this cabin was where one of Cuba's most heralded musicians of recent times, **Polo Montañez**, lived and gave impromptu concerts before he was killed in a car accident in November 2002. The simple little four-room museum exhibits some of Montañez's personal effects, including his guitars; his bedroom has been left as it was when he lived here.

Cafetal Buenavista

Daily 9am–4pm • Free

A turning next to the Las Terrazas tollbooth at the Havana end of the resort leads to the **Cafetal Buenavista**, an excellent restoration of a nineteenth-century coffee plantation and the final destination for some of the official hikes in the area (see box opposite). French immigrants who had fled Haiti following the 1791 revolution established over fifty coffee plantations across the sierra, but this is the only one to be almost fully reconstructed. The superbly restored stone house, with its high-beamed ceilings, now holds a restaurant, with the food cooked in the original kitchen building behind. The terraces on which the coffee was dried have also been accurately restored, and the remains of the slaves' quarters are complete enough to give you an idea of the incredibly cramped sleeping conditions they experienced.

Baños de San Juan

Daily dawn–dusk • $4CUC, free if you if you show a receipt from the Las Terrazas checkpoint

From the south side of Las Terrazas village, at the junction where the road to the hotel begins, another road leads off in the opposite direction for the **Baños de San Juan**, a

---

ACTIVITIES IN LES TERRAZAS

As well as hiking (see box opposite), there are several other activities on offer in Les Terrazas. Most thrilling is an aerial **canopy tour** (daily 9am–6pm; $25CUC) of the village on one-man seats suspended from steel cables 25m above the ground. It starts from a platform in the woodlands around the hotel and extends for 800m all the way down to the boating house, the Casa de Botes, on the edge of the lake, stopping at several other platforms along the way. Bookings are taken at the *Hotel Moka* or the Casa de Botes.

More sedate options include **horseriding**, booked at the *Hotel Moka* (daily 9am–6pm; $5CUC/hr). The various set rides include 2hr excursions to the *Casa del Campesino* (see p.160) and the Baños de San Juan, a 3hr ride to the Cafetal Buenavista and a couple of 2hr rides, including one that scales the nearby Loma de Taburete. If you want an even more subdued pastime, you can rent **rowing boats** (daily 9am–6pm; $3CUC/hr) on the lake. The Casa de Botes, where boats are moored, is easy to find just off the main road through the village.

delightful spot featuring natural pools, riverside picnic tables, a simple restaurant and some even simpler cabins providing rudimentary accommodation. From here it's a hop and a skip down to the river, where a footbridge takes you over the water to the paths zigzagging both ways along the river's edge, mingling with tiny tributaries branching off from the main river, creating a network of walkways punctuated by paved clearings where you can stop and sit under matted roofs. Following the route downstream leads to the focal point here, a small set of clear, natural **pools** fed by dinky waterfalls – ideal for a bit of midday bathing.

2

Hacienda Unión

Set back from the banks of Rio San Juan about 2km from the Las Terrazas checkpoint, is the neighbouring **Hacienda Unión**, one of the area's partly reconstructed nineteenth-century coffee plantations. A stone path leads down the slope and onto the right-hand fork of the same dirt track that branches off from the main road. There is nothing to restrict you from wandering down and taking a look around the broken stone walls of

---

RANCHO CURUJEY AND HIKING AT LAS TERRAZAS

There is no better or more accessible way to experience the diversity and beauty of the Sierra del Rosario than the official **hiking routes** and **nature trails** around Las Terrazas. Of varying lengths and difficulty, each is characterized by a different destination of historical or ecological interest, and collectively they offer the most comprehensive insight available into the region's topography, history, flora and fauna. All hiking here must be arranged through the Oficinas de Reservaciones y Coordinación at **Rancho Curujey** (☎48 57 8555).

To reach Rancho Curujey from Havana and the west, take the signposted right-hand turnoff from the main through-road just before the left turn that leads to the village and hotel. The centre can supply you with a guide – without which you are not permitted to follow any of the trails through this protected area – and tailor a programme or just a day of walking to your requirements. For groups of six people or more, guides usually cost around $10CUC per person on a pre-booked excursion, though prices vary depending on the size of the group and your specific needs, and can reach $30–40CUC. You may be able to join another visiting group if you call a day in advance, or if you arrive before 9am. The *Hotel Moka* works closely with Rancho Curujey and can arrange hiking packages for guests.

HIKING ROUTES AND NATURE TRAILS

Cascada del San Claudio (20km) The longest hike offered here lasts a whole day, or around eight to ten hours, and is a gruelling affair, scaling the hills looming over to the northwest of the complex and down the other side to the San Claudio River.

El Contento (8km) This pleasant, easy-going hike descends into the valley between two of the local peaks and joins the Río San Juan. It passes the La Victoria ruins, another of the area's old coffee plantations, as well as fresh and sulphurous water springs, and reaches its limit at the Baños de San Juan, a beautiful little set of pools and cascades where you can bathe.

Loma del Taburete (7km) One of the tougher hikes, this route climbs some relatively steep inclines on the way up a 453m-high hill (from the peak of which there are views all the way over to the coast) then slopes down to the Baños de San Juan on the other side, where the hike concludes.

Sendero Las Delicias (3km) This trail finishes up at the Cafetal Buenavista and takes in a viewpoint at the summit of the Loma Las Delicias, from where there are some magnificent panoramic views.

Sendero La Serafina (4km) A nature trail ideal for birdwatching, leading uphill through rich and varied forest. Guides can point out some of the 73 bird species that inhabit the sierra, such as the endemic catacuba and the enchanting Cuban nightingale.

Valle del Bayate (7km) On the road to Soroa, 6km from Las Terrazas, a dirt track next to the bridge over the Río Bayate follows the river into the dense forest. Passing first the dilapidated San Pedro coffee plantation, this undemanding trail arrives at the Santa Catalina plantation ruins, a peaceful spot where you can take a dip in the natural pools.

the plantation, which has at least kept enough of its structure to be recognizable as what it was two centuries ago. The circular grinding mill, with its cone-shaped roof and stone base, is the most intact section and the easiest to spot. The majority of the space here has been given over to the cultivation of various flowers and plants, divided up into small, rock-lined plots forming an attractively laid out if somewhat rudimentary **garden**.

Baños de Bayate

On the main through-road for Las Terrazas, 3km past the turning for the *Casa del Campesino* restaurant, another dirt track, this one more of a bone-rattler than the last, winds down about 1km to a section of forest-shrouded river known as the **Baños de Bayate**. The depth and clearness of the water at this lovely spot provides a perfect opportunity to cool off from the jungle's humidity, although its tranquillity is sometimes broken by the screams and shouts of young swimmers leaping into the river.

ARRIVAL AND INFORMATION — LAS TERRAZAS

By car Las Terrazas is reached by a signposted 8km turnoff at Km 51 of the *autopista nacional*. Once through a thickly wooded landscape, you continue up to a junction where, a few metres after a left turn, you'll reach a tollbooth marking the beginning of the main through-road to the resort.

Tourist information The Rancho Curujey visitor and information centre (☎ 48 57 8555) has maps of the resort, and can help with almost any activity around Las Terrazas.

ACCOMMODATION

Hotel Moka cabins Baños de San Juan ☎ 48 57 8600. Set back from the river, at the foot of some grassy slopes breaking up the woodlands here, are five rooms (known as *cabañas rusticas*) for rent via *Hotel Moka*. They're no more than roof-covered platforms on stilts, aimed squarely at the backpacker set, with no furniture and about enough space to lay a couple of sleeping bags down. **$25CUC**

★ **Hotel Moka** Comunidad Las Terrazas ☎ 48 57 8600, ⊛ hotelmoka-lasterrazas.com. This peaceful hillside hideaway about 1km northwest of the checkpoint is well worth a visit even if you're not staying, as non-guests can make use of the restaurant and the pool ($3CUC/day). The graceful main building hugs the surrounding trees, which in some places actually grow through the structure itself. There's an adjoining bar and moderately priced restaurant serving typical Cuban food, while the swimming pool and tennis courts are set further back. **$81CUC**

Villas Moka Hotel Moka Comunidad Las Terrazas ☎ 48 57 8600, ⊛ hotelmoka-lasterrazas.com. If you prefer to be among the locals and don't mind having to walk a bit further to use the *Hotel Moka*'s facilities, you can stay in one of the five *villas comunitarias* down by the lake. These are effectively *casas particulares* run by the hotel, and are the only way you can stay in a family home here. **$81CUC**

EATING AND DRINKING

El Bambú Baños de San Juan (no phone). On the riverbank looking over the waterfalls, this rustic café serves simple, inexpensive Cuban food. Daily 9am–7pm.

Baños de Bayate restaurant Baños de Bayate (no phone). This outdoor restaurant by the river is perfect for a post-swim plate of grilled pork or chicken, though you'll be hard pushed to find much else. Expect to pay around $6CUC for a meal. Daily 9am–dusk.

Casa del Campesino Las Terrazas ☎ 48 57 8555. Just beyond the left-hand turn for the hotel and village off the main through-road, a sign indicates the short dirt track to this secluded little woodland ranch housing a restaurant. You can just have a drink or choose from the simple *comida criolla* menu, though you may have to wait a little while for the latter, especially if you arrive before 1pm. You'll need bug repellent to combat the rapacious mosquitoes. Daily 8am–9pm.

Fonda de Mercedes Las Terrazas village ☎ 48 57 8647. A few buildings along from *El Romero*, this open-air restaurant-cum-paladar on a roof-covered balcony platform serves top-notch Cuban cuisine with a real home-cooked flavour; main dishes are between $5CUC and $8CUC. The house special is a traditional recipe from Camagüey province called *aporreado de ternera*, a veal stew made with aromatic herbs and spices. Daily 9am–9pm.

★ **El Romero** Las Terrazas village ☎ 48 57 8555. In an apartment building near the steps leading down from the hotel, with a unique menu of organic, vegetarian dishes such as a creamy cold pumpkin and onion soup, bean-filled crêpes and chickpea balls marinated in onion and garlic. Small tapas-style portions are $3–5CUC; larger meals $9–15CUC. Daily 9am–9pm.

Soroa

Sixteen kilometres southwest of Las Terrazas, the tiny village of **SOROA** nestles in a long narrow valley. Although a cosy spot, access into the hills is limited and the list of attractions brief, meaning the resort is best suited to a shorter break than a prolonged visit.

El Salto
Daily dawn–dusk • $3CUC

Most of what you'll want to see is within ten minutes' walk of Soroa, but if you've driven up from the *autopista*, the first place you'll get to, 100m or so from the *Villa Soroa* hotel, is the car park for **El Salto**, a 20m-high waterfall. Though a relatively modest cascade, a dip in the refreshing waters is a fitting reward for the half-hour walk through the woods to reach it; take the dirt track from the car park.

El Mirador de Soroa
Horses can be arranged at *Villa Soroa* for $3CUC per person

Signposted from the El Salto car park, the scenic viewpoint of **El Mirador de Soroa** is the more challenging of the two hills in the area, and you may well feel like a massage (see below) after the thirty-minute hike up along an increasingly steep and narrow (though shady) dirt track. While there are a number of possible wrong turns on the way up, you can avoid getting lost by simply following the track with the horse dung – many people choose to ride up on horseback. At the summit you'll find vultures circling the rocky, uneven platform and impressive views over the undulating peaks of palm-smothered hills.

Banos Romanos
Daily 9am–4pm • Treatments from $5CUC • ☎ 48 52 3534

On the way up to El Mirador de Soroa, a sign points over a small bridge towards the **Baños Romanos**, located in an unassuming stone cabin; massages, cold sulphurous baths and other treatments including acupuncture can be arranged here through the *Villa Soroa* hotel.

El Castillo de las Nubes

El Castillo de las Nubes is the more developed of Soroa's two hilltop viewpoints and the only one you can drive to. The road up to its summit, which you'll have to follow even if you're walking up as there are no obvious trails through the woods, starts from between the car park for El Salto and the hotel. On foot, it shouldn't take more than twenty minutes to reach the hilltop, where there is a perfect lookout spot from the deserted stone house at the end of the road – from here you can see all the way to the province's southern coastline.

Jardin Botanico Orquideario de Soroa
Daily 9am–4pm • $3CUC • ☎ 48 57 2558

At the foot of the road up from the El Salto car park to the Soroa summit, the **Jardin Botanico Orquideario de Soroa** is a well-maintained botanical garden specializing in orchids and spreading across 35,000 square metres. Currently used by the University of Pinar del Río, it was constructed in 1943 by Tomás Felipe Camacho, a wealthy lawyer and botanist from the Canary Islands. Until his death in 1960, Camacho dedicated his time to the expansion and glorification of the *orquideario*, travelling the world in search of different species. The obligatory tours are a little rushed, but you get to see flowers, plants, shrubs and trees from around the globe, including some seven hundred species of orchid, in grounds radiating out from a central villa where Camacho lived.

ARRIVAL AND DEPARTURE   SOROA

By car The turning from the *autopista* is marked by the first gas station en route to Pinar del Río from Havana, but you can also get there direct from Las Terrazas along the linking road without returning to the motorway.

ACCOMMODATION

Hospedaje Estudio de Arte Carretera a Soroa, Km 8.5 ☎ 48 59 8116, ✉ infosoroa@hvs.co.cu. On the right some 500m past *Villa Soroa*, this *casa particular* is an affordable alternative to the hotel. Located in a pleasant household owned by local artist Jesus Gastell Soto and his wife Aliuska, the one air-conditioned room has its own bathroom. **$25CUC**

Villa Soroa Carretera a Soroa, Km 8 ☎ 48 52 3534, ✉ recepcion@hvs.co.cu. The best place to stay in Soroa, this is a well-kept complex encircling a swimming pool, with comfortable, modern-looking cabins. Three- to six-hour guided treks starting at $6CUC per person into the surrounding hillside are available. **$53CUC**

San Diego de los Baños and around

West of Soroa along the *autopista* lie a number of relatively entertaining detours, all within a forty-minute drive of the main road. If you are driving – which is the best option, given no bus routes currently operate to this area from Havana or Pinar del Río city – it's easy to cover them all in a single day. The place you're most likely to spend a night, or at least stop for a meal, is the sleepy town of **San Diego de los Baños**, famous for its health spa, which is said to be the best in the country, though there are now several more modern, upmarket hotel-spas on the island offering better facilities (minus the same range of therapies).

The box-like exterior of the spa contrasts strikingly with the flourishing forests on the other side of the river. When you've had your fill of the waters, you might want to rent bikes and motorbikes at the hotel, or arrange hiking and fishing trips into the hundred square kilometres of protected **woodlands** just a leisurely stroll away. There's not much else to do in San Diego de los Baños, though you could wander around the village to the leafy little square, with its creaking seesaws and swings and church; or spend a few hours in the **cinema**, next door to the *Hotel Mirador*.

From here it's only a short drive to the area's other two attractions: **Parque La Güira**, a rambling country park, and, slightly further north, the **Cueva de los Portales**, a modestly impressive cave that cuts a dramatic hole straight through the Loma de los Arcos, and which was once the military headquarters of Che Guevara and his army.

Balneario San Diego

Mon–Sat 8am–5pm, Sun 8am–noon • Bathing from $4CUC; treatments from $20CUC • ☎ 48 54 8880, ✉ tsalud@sermed.cha.cyt.cu

Perched above the river that cuts along the edge of San Diego de los Baños, the **Balneario San Diego**'s reputation for medicinal powers dates back to 1632, when a slave, forced into isolation because of ill health, took an afternoon dip in the natural springs here and was supposedly instantly cured. Word rapidly spread and the country's infirm began to flock here to be healed. By 1844 a town had been established to provide for the visitors, and eventually a rather utilitarian health spa was built to house the waters, though this didn't take its current shape until after the Revolution. Nowadays most visitors are tourists, or Cubans on a prescribed course of treatment, as well as for beauty therapy, though you can just take a wallow in the waters. Popular treatments include acupuncture, medicinal mud and apitherapy (the therapeutic use of bee products), a field in which Cuba is reportedly a pioneer.

ARRIVAL AND DEPARTURE   SAN DIEGO DE LOS BAÑOS

By car San Diego de los Baños is 40km west of Soroa on the *autopista*: at Km 100, take the right-hand turning, follow this to its conclusion and then take the right turn (signposted to San Cristóbal); some 12km along, you'll reach the Balneario San Diego.

ACCOMMODATION AND EATING

Hotel Mirador Calle 23 final ☎ 48 77 8338, ✉ carpeta @mirador.sandiego.co.cu. Beautifully set in small-scale landscaped gardens, the pleasantly furnished rooms and overall tranquillity make this the perfect place to stay while visiting the spa; in fact, many of its guests are here on a treatment-plus-accommodation package deal. Qualified

medical specialists work with staff across the road and can arrange consultations and courses of treatment. **$32CUC**
Restaurante Terraza Hotel Mirador ☉ 48 77 8338.

The *Hotel Mirador* restaurant is the only place you can rely on for a meal, offering a selection of fish, meat and basic spaghetti dishes. Daily 7–9am & noon–10pm.

Cueva de los Portales

To drive here, take the heavily potholed road north of Parque La Güira for 10km before turning at the sign to the now-abandoned *Cabaña Los Pinos.*

The gaping hillside corridor known as **Cueva de los Portales** was the suitably remote **former headquarters** of Che Guevara and his army during the Cuban Missile Crisis of October 1962. It was declared a national monument in 1987, and it is its historical rather than geographic significance that will impress. Anyone can drive up and wander in free of charge, and, when you're in the area, it's well worth thirty minutes of your time. If you're lucky, there'll be a guide about to offer a free tour of the complex, though undoubtedly a tip would be appreciated.

The solitary road from Parque La Güira leads all the way to the turning for the cave, a right turn as you are heading north from the park. Then, from a clearing in the woods a stone path leads into and through a wide-open tunnel, the full length of which is visible from outside the high arching entrance. Through the arch, running parallel with the path, is the **Río Caiguanabo**, a tributary of the Río San Diego, which swirls into a natural pool perfect for a post-inspection dip. Off to the side is the headquarters cave itself, a giant chamber adorned with imposing stalactites and stalagmites. Inside are some intriguing remnants of Guevara's occupation – the stone table where he worked and played chess, an unfinished little breeze-block hut that acted as his office and some stone staircases and paths hewn out of the rock.

ACCOMMODATION · CUEVA DE LOS PORTALES

Campismo Los Portales ☉ 48 49 7347. Though the eleven newly renovated, spick-and-span cabins are primarily for Cubans, they are sometimes rented out to tourists, providing there's space. All are equipped with only the bare minimum of comfort requirements, but everything is in good nick. Among the fittingly simple facilities are a four-table restaurant and a games room with a pingpong table. **$10CUC**

Pinar del Río city

Stranded out on the far side of the westernmost province in Cuba at the end of the *autopista*, **PINAR DEL RÍO** is, quite simply, a backwater of a city. Close to some more alluring destinations – particularly Viñales, just 25km to the north, but also María La Gorda and the beaches Boca de Galafre and Playa Bailén to the south – the city works best as a base for exploring this half of the province. Despite its 125,000-strong population, Pinar del Río has the feel of a much smaller place, its central streets more reminiscent of a residential neighbourhood than a town centre.

Despite being the capital of the province, Pinar del Río is comparatively undeveloped for tourism: none of the international or upmarket hotel chains is represented here, nightlife is limited and dining options and the museums could do with a rethink. On the other hand, countless *casas particulares* are spread all over the city. You'll need no more than a couple of days to get to know the place inside out, and in fact very few visitors spend even that long here. The highlight is the **Fábrica de Tabacos Francisco Donatién**, a diminutive cigar factory offering illuminating tours, while the *Cabaret Rumayor* offers a taste of classic Cuban entertainment whose extravagance feels somewhat out of place in this less-than-cosmopolitan town. If you do find yourself here for any length of time you're probably best spent seeking out a paladar or *casa particular* to suit your taste and retreating to one of these, or lounging around the pool and grounds of the *Hotel Pinar del Río*, away from the attentions of the *jineteros* (see box, p.165).

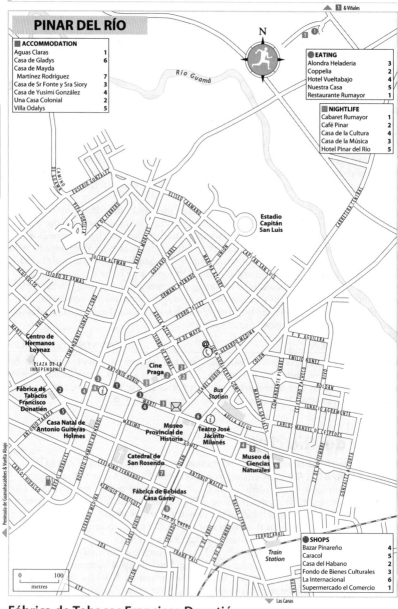

PINAR DEL RÍO

ACCOMMODATION

Aguas Claras	1
Casa de Gladys	6
Casa de Mayda Martínez Rodríguez	7
Casa de Sr Fonte y Sra Siory	3
Casa de Yusimi González	4
Una Casa Colonial	2
Villa Odalys	5

EATING

Alondra Heladería	3
Coppelia	2
Hotel Vueltabajo	4
Nuestra Casa	5
Restaurante Rumayor	1

NIGHTLIFE

Cabaret Rumayor	1
Café Pinar	2
Casa de la Cultura	4
Casa de la Música	3
Hotel Pinar del Río	5

SHOPS

Bazar Pinareño	4
Caracol	5
Casa del Habano	2
Fondo de Bienes Culturales	3
La Internacional	6
Supermercado el Comercio	1

Fábrica de Tabacos Francisco Donatién

Antonio Maceo no.157 • Mon–Fri 9am–noon &1–4pm, Sat 9am–noon • $5CUC; buy tickets from Casa del Habano • ☎ 48 77 3069

Two blocks southeast of the roadbound Plaza de la Independencia, the **Fábrica de Tabacos Francisco Donatién** is the city's premier attraction and home of Vegueros cigars, a lesser-known brand but one that's well respected among connoisseurs. Compared to the Partagás factory in Havana, however, this place is tiny and the brief guided tour (available in English or French) much less illuminating, though the intimate non-mechanized workshop offers a genuine insight into the care and skill involved in producing some of the world's finest cigars.

Casa del Habano

Antonio Maceo no.162 • Mon–Fri 9am–noon &1–4pm, Sat 9am–noon

A selection of cigar brands is sold in the Fábrica de Tabacos Francisco Donatién shop, but there's a wider choice in the **Casa del Habano** over the road, an excellent **cigar shop**. All the best Cuban brands are on sale, and there's a smart little smokers' lounge as well as a café out the back.

2

Fábrica de Bebidas Casa Garay

Isabel Rubio • Mon–Fri 9am–5pm, Sat 9am–1pm • $1CUC • ☎ 48 75 2966

Four blocks south of Martí is the **Fábrica de Bebidas Casa Garay** rum factory, founded in 1891 and where the popular Guayabita del Pinar brand is produced. The entrance charge includes a ten-minute guided tour of the three rooms and courtyard that make up the compact factory, beginning in the back room (where barrels of fermenting molasses create a potent smell) and finishing in the claustrophobic bottling and labelling room. Unsurprisingly, bottles of Guayabita are on sale, and you get a free sample of both the dry and sweet versions to help you make your decision.

Museo Provincial de Historia

Martí e/ Isabel Rubio y Colón • Mon–Fri 8.30am–4.30pm, Sat 9am–1pm • $1CUC • ☎ 48 75 4300

The more central of the two museums on Martí is the **Museo Provincial de Historia**. It contains some interesting bits and pieces – including pre-Columbian tools and bones, and displays on the history of tobacco, coffee and slavery in the province – but overall is too disparate to present any kind of coherent narrative about the region. As with all history museums in Cuba, the Revolution is overemphasized.

Museo de Ciencias Naturales

Martí esq. Comandante Pinare • Tues–Sat 9am–4.30pm, Sun 8–11.30am • Free • ☎ 48 75 3087

Down at the quiet eastern end of Martí, the Palacio de Guach contains the **Museo de Ciencias Naturales**. This eclectic building is the most architecturally striking in the city,

---

PINAR DEL RÍO'S JINETEROS

Pinar del Río could not be described as a tranquil city, thanks to the increasingly aggressive nature and disproportionately large number of **jineteros** who thrive here away from the attentions of the state, which generally focuses on Havana and the more popular tourist locations. As a result, levels of pestering and prostitution are surprisingly high. Foreign visitors, particularly those in rental cars or on Víazul buses, are often surrounded by touts within minutes of arrival and are likely to attract what can become a tiring level of persistent attention throughout their time in the city.

The problem is particularly tiresome when you're looking for **accommodation**. Some *jineteros* have adopted particularly aggressive techniques, going as far as following you to the door of a house and claiming that no one lives there or that it's full, just as the owner approaches to let you in. With this in mind, be careful if asking directions, particularly from young men who offer to take you to the address. Many house owners have complained of touts demanding commission even when the guests have actually arrived independently. If you got there on your own, make it clear to the house owner that you did not get their address from a tout; it can also help to let the tout know you will be doing this.

its arches mottled with dragons and other monstrous figures and the whole place riddled with elaborate chiselled detail. Inside, each room has a specific theme, and although the ocean and plant rooms seem to be made up of whatever the museum could get its hands on, like bottled fruits and some miscellaneous dried leaves, there are more complete collections of butterflies, moths, exotic insects, shells and birds. Kids will enjoy the convincing giant stone tyrannosaurus and stegosaurus in the courtyard, where there's also a mural depicting other prehistoric creatures.

ARRIVAL AND DEPARTURE
PINAR DEL RÍO

By car Arriving in Pinar del Río by car is a breeze, as the *autopista* leads straight into the middle of town. You should be particularly mindful of your speed when entering the city, as one or two of the waiting touts who line the main road are sometimes willing to stand in the middle of the street and flag you down with false urgency; drive on by, as they rarely have anything useful to tell you.

By bus Arriving by bus, whether Astro or Víazul, you'll be dropped at the Terminal de Omnibus on Adela Azcuy (☎ 48 75 2572), one block from Martí. The station is within walking distance of most of the hotels and a good

number of *casas particulares*; although there are usually plenty of private taxis outside the station, they are usually looking to fill their cars for long-distance journeys.
Destinations Havana (2 daily; 3hr); Viñales (2 daily; 40min).

By train In the unlikely event that you arrive by train, be prepared for a walk from the small station (☎ 48 75 2272), which is four blocks south of Martí, as there are rarely any taxis there.
Destinations Boca de Galafre (1 daily; 1hr 30min); Havana (1 daily; 5hr); Playa Bailén (1 daily; 1hr 45min); San Cristóbal (1 daily; 3hr).

GETTING AROUND

On foot The city centre is manageable on foot and it's unlikely you'll stray more than three or four blocks either side of Martí.

By car or scooter Most of the city's car rental agencies operate from the *Pinar del Río* hotel at the end of Martí, just before the *autopista*. Cubacar has a desk here (8am–6pm; ☎ 48 77 8278) and at *Hotel Vueltabajo*, Martí no.103, esq. Rafael Morales (8am–6pm; ☎ 48 75 9381).

Havanautos (daily 8am–6pm; ☎ 48 77 8015) rents scooters and has an office in the car park of the hotel. Transtur rents cars from an office in the *Hotel Vueltabajo* (daily 8am–6pm; ☎ 48 77 8078).

By taxi The only taxi rank in town is outside the *Pinar del Río* hotel; otherwise call Turistaxi ☎ 48 76 3481 or Transtur ☎ 48 77 8278.

INFORMATION AND TRAVEL AGENCIES

Infotur The most useful and most central information office, based at *Hotel Vueltabajo*, José Martí (Mon–Sat 9am–5.45pm; ☎ 48 75 9381), offering general information about the region as well as hotel reservations, car rental, guided city tours and excursions to many of the province's highlights.

Cubanacán Also on Martí (Mon–Sat 8am–noon & 1–5pm; ☎ 48 75 0178) and offering hotel reservations, car rental, guided city tours and excursions.

Cubatur Less than a block from the main street on Rosario e/ Martí y Máximo Gómez (Mon–Fri 8am–noon & 1–5pm, Sat 8am–noon; ☎ 48 77 8405), with maps and glossy but uninformative guides to the province as well as tours and car rental.

Havanatur bookshop At Martí esq. Colón (Mon–Fri 8am–noon & 1.30–5pm, Sat 8am–noon & 1–4pm; ☎ 48 79 8494); services include hotel reservations, car rental, guided city tours and excursions.

ACCOMMODATION

Of the five **hotels** in town, three are officially for Cuban nationals. There's a plethora of **casas particulares** on offer, though, several within walking distance of the train station along Comandante Pinares. Unfortunately there are equal numbers of **jineteros** (see p.165).

HOTELS

Aguas Claras Carretera de Viñales ☎ 48 77 8426. Some 7.5km from Pinar del Río, this is by far the most attractive place to stay in or near the city (though only worth it if you have your own car). Tucked into the trees, the leafy, landscaped cabin complex is out of walking distance from anything other than open countryside, but offers a higher class of comfort than anywhere else. There's a pool, a

decent restaurant and organized excursions to all the provincial highlights. $50CUC

★ **Hotel Vueltabajo** Martí no.103, esq. Rafael Morales ☎ 48 75 9381, ⊕ islazul.cu. Without doubt the prettiest hotel in town, this delightful little place is easily the most comfortable option in the centre. The stylish colonial facade, with its dinky balustraded, canopy-covered balconies, is complemented by a handsome, simple interior

2

ORGANIZED EXCURSIONS FROM PINAR DEL RÍO

One of the best reasons to stay in Pinar del Río is to use it as a base for **excursions** into the nearby countryside. The national travel agents Havanatur, Cubanacán and Cubatur offer a number of day-trips, along with some one- and two-night stays, to the province's main tourist spots as well as a selection of hard-to-get-to attractions. As public transport is particularly poor within Pinar del Río province, an organized excursion is often the only (and certainly the easiest) way to get to these destinations if you don't have your own vehicle. Even if you do have a car, the poor roads, lack of maps and road signs, and basic remoteness involved in many journeys here mean the various excursions detailed below are all the more useful. What follows is a list of small selection of packages currently offered by Havanatur and Cubanacán. Prices shown are generally for three people or fewer; there are price reductions for groups of more than three.

Cayo Levisa One of the area's most popular day-trips is to the small resort on this offshore cay. Cubanacán offers a list of different packages, starting at $29CUC per person, which includes a welcome cocktail and snack.

Gran Caverna de Santo Tomás Both Havanatur and Cubanacán offer tours of the extensive cave systems near Viñales valley, costing $18CUC per person (minimum two people).

María La Gorda One- and two-night stays offered by Havanatur to the end-of-the-line María La Gorda beach resort where fishing, snorkelling and diving are the order of the day; $190CUC per person, minimum two people. A transfer-only deal is also available at $27CUC for a return ticket.

Tobacco Tour The day-trip to the Vuelta Abajo region (see p.181), taking in a tobacco farm, a UBPC (farming cooperative) and the cigar factory back in Pinar del Río is run by Havanatur and Cubanacán, and costs $50CUC per person.

Viñales The basic tour does not include lunch but does cover all the main sights in Viñales valley, such as the Mural de la Prehistoria and the Cueva del Indio; it costs $48CUC per person with Cubanacán.

full of polished wood, shining floors and reasonably well-appointed rooms. $65CUC

CASAS PARTICULARES

⭐ **Casa de Gladys** Ave. Comandante Pinares no.15 e/ Martí y Máximo Gómez ☎ 48 77 9698, ✉ casadegladys @gmail.com. Both the rooms for rent in this huge house next to the Museo de Ciencias Naturales have double beds and en-suite bathroom, and there are some memorable furnishings, like the matching colonial-style wardrobe, bed and dresser in one room. Secure parking for two cars and a fantastic backyard complete with a fountain. $20CUC

Casa de Mayda Martínez Rodríguez Isabel Rubio no.125 e/ Antonio Maceo y Ceferino Fernández ☎ 48 75 2110, ✉ mayda16@princesa.pri.sld.cu. An orderly, well-maintained mini-apartment with a spacious roof terrace, all set atop the friendly owners' house. It's well suited to a romantic couple, with more privacy than most other places and plenty of comfort. There's a garage and the owners' son speaks English. $20CUC

Casa de Sr Fonte y Sra Siory Martí no.49C e/ Gerardo Medina e Isabel Rubio ☎ 48 77 5958, ✉ poty @correodecuba.cu. Two rooms on their own floor at the top of a well-maintained house. Both are en suite and have

a/c. It's cool and quieter than you would expect inside and there's a bar area too. $20CUC

Casa de Yusimí González Martí no.164 e/ Ave Cmdte Pinares y Calle Nueva ☎ 48 75 2818. A complete apartment with two air-conditioned rooms, a kitchen with hob, and a pleasant living room with a balcony overlooking a lively road complete with passing horse-drawn carriages. Rooms $25CUC, whole apartment $50CUC

Una Casa Colonial Gerardo Medina no.67 e/ Isidro de Armas y Adela Azcuy ☎ 48 75 3173. The nearest thing to a privately run hotel in Pinar del Río, there are officially three rooms for rent here, though several more are on standby in case the legal limit is changed again. The rooms, many with en-suite bathrooms, are gathered around a lovely patio garden where there's a tiny restaurant area and an impressive outdoor jacuzzi. There's space for three cars in the garage. $25CUC

Villa Odalys Martí 158 e/ Ave. Comandante Pinares y Calle Nueva ☎ 48 75 5212. A large en-suite room at the back of the house with hot water, a/c, fridge and black-and-white TV. Ideal for those seeking privacy, while also very sociable (if that's your preference), with three people living in the house and plenty of young people always about. $25CUC

EATING

Since the 2011 changes in private enterprise law, many new venues have opened in Pinar del Río and the eating scene has been upgraded from dire to mediocre. The state-run **restaurants** lack both variety and ambience, with a concentration of

2

particularly poor ones right in the centre on Martí. You'll fare slightly better with paladars, but it's still worth paying the extra to have meals included if you are staying at a *casa particular*.

Alondra Heladeria Martí esq. Rafael Morales (no phone). This ice-cream parlour is more expensive than *Coppelia* – for which you get a few more frills, sprinkles and cocktails umbrellas in your sundae. Daily noon–midnight.

Coppelia Gerardo Medina e/ Antonio Rubio y Isidro de Armas (no phone). Good-value ice cream: standard flavours are chocolate or strawberry, and more exotic options like chocolate ripple and guava are available intermittently. Daily noon–midnight.

Hotel Vueltabajo Martí no.103 esq. Rafael Morales ☎ 48 75 9381. The canteenish restaurant at the best hotel in town falls way short of the decent standard set by the hotel itself, but it's very cheap and as reliable an option as any. Basic pizzas and pastas for less than $2CUC, and a few fancier, slightly pricier (yet dodgier) meat dishes, such as *"pollo a la gordon blue"*, make up the bitty menu. Daily 7–9.30pm.

Nuestra Casa Colón no.161 e/ Ceferino Fernández y 1ero de Enero. Surrounded by the branches of a mature tree, the novel setting of this rooftop-cum-treehouse paladar (reached via a stepladder) is the main talking point here. The spoken menu is limited to simple but filling fish, pork or chicken dishes; expect to pay $8CUC for a main meal. Closed Sun. Daily 7pm–midnight.

Restaurante Rumayor Carretera Viñales Km 1 ☎ 48 76 3007. Next door to the cabaret of the same name, the city's biggest and best restaurant boasts a large, rustic dining hall adorned with African tribal imagery and a spacious shady garden where there are *folklórico* dance shows on weekdays at around 10.30pm. Popular with locals, the sensibly priced Cuban cuisine includes the recommended *pollo ahumado a la Rumayor* (wood-smoked chicken). Reservations essential. Tues–Sun noon–11pm.

NIGHTLIFE AND ENTERTAINMENT

Don't expect much **nightlife** until the weekend, when Pinar del Río's main streets buzz with young people. That said, there is a reasonable spread of live music venues, and if you're here over a weekend, it's worth investigating the programme at the theatre; although in Spanish, performances here offer an authentic insight into Cuban culture.

LIVE MUSIC VENUES

★ **Cabaret Rumayor** Carretera Viñales Km 1 ☎ 48 76 3051. Like most cabarets in Cuba, the show here is drenched in gaudy 1970s-style glamour, and the open-air setting adds to the drama of a seemingly endless sequence of song-and-dance routines from tearful ballads to button-busting showtime numbers. Definitely worth a look, particularly if you don't fancy shelling out on the more expensive counterparts in bigger venues. Entry $5CUC including some drinks. Fri & Sat 10pm–late.

Café Pinar Gerardo Medina e/ Antonio Rubio y Isidro de Armas. The one place in town that can generally be relied upon to deliver a buzz, though the music here – often played live – doesn't get going until 11pm or so, by which time the place is typically bumping with dressed-up locals. Free entry. Daily 8pm–2am.

Casa de la Cultura Martí no.65 e/ Rafael Morales y Rosario ☎ 48 75 2324. There are regular bolero and danzón nights here as well as a *peña campesina*, a traditional rural Cuban song and dance. Entrance is usually free. Sun 8pm–2pm.

Casa de la Música Gerardo Medina ☎ 48 75 4794. Staged in an open-air courtyard, the pleasantly entertaining unpretentious son, bolero and salsa shows here cater to an undemanding audience. Free entry. Performances usually start at around 9pm. Daily 7pm–midnight.

CLUBS

Hotel Pinar del Río Martí ☎ 48 75 5070. Just before the *autopista*, this is the only real nightclub in town, with slick decor and a playlist that mixes reggaeton, salsa and pop. Entry is $5CUC. Tues–Sun 10pm–late.

THEATRES

Teatro José Jacinto Milanés Martí no.60 e/ Recreo y Colón ☎ 48 75 3871. This elegant nineteenth-century venue has a regular programme of theatre and comedy as well as international and national dance shows. Highlights include local slapstick comedians and inventive contemporary theatre productions, often with quasi-political themes.

SHOPPING

Bazar Pinareño Martí no.28 e/ Gerardo Medina y Isabel Rubio. A small but worthy collection of Cuban music CDs is complemented by some screen-printed film and propaganda posters. Daily 9am–5pm.

Caracol Maceo esq. Antonio Tarafa. You'll find a good selection of Cuban music CDs here. Daily 9am–5pm.

Fondo de Bienes Culturales Martí esq. Gerardo Medina. This market has quite a good range of nut and seed jewellery, plus ugly leather sandals and clay figurines. Daily 9am–5pm.

La Internacional Martí esq. Colón. A small selection of books that may be of interest to foreign visitors, including

some specialist guide books, coffee-table photography and some English–Spanish dictionaries.
Supermercado el comercio Martí Oeste y Arenado.

This is the best of the several supermarkets on Martí, this one sellings groceries, toiletries and cheap clothing. Mon–Sat 9am–5pm, Sun 9am–noon.

DIRECTORY

Baseball The 14,000-capacity Estadio Capitán San Luis (☎ 48 75 4290), near the road to Viñales Pinar del Río, has one of the most successful baseball teams in the national league, with games usually played Tues–Thurs & Sat from 7.30pm start, and Sun from 4pm.

Internet and telephone The local ETECSA Telepunto at Gerardo Medina no.127 esq. Juan Gualberto Gómez (daily 8.30am–6.30pm) has several internet terminals and six phone booths.

Medical help Hospital Abel Santamaria, Carretera Central Km 3 ☎ 48 76 4660. Ring ☎ 48 76 2317 for an ambulance.

Money and exchange The best bank for foreign currency transactions and credit-card withdrawals is the Banco Financiero Internacional at Gerardo Medina no.46 e/ Isidro de Armas y Martí (Mon–Fri 8am–3pm). Banco de Crédito y Comercio has branches at Martí no.32 e/ Isabel Rubio y Gerardo Medina (Mon–Fri 8am–noon & 1.30–3pm) and

Martí e/ Rosario (Ormani Arenado) y Rafael Morales (same hours). The CADECA *casas de cambio* are on Gerardo Medina e/ Antonio Rubio y Isidro de Armas and Martí no.46 e/ Isabel Rubio y Gerardo Medina (both Mon–Sat 8.30am–5.30pm, Sun 8.30am–12.30pm).

Pharmacy The only pharmacy for tourists is in the *Pinar del Río* hotel.

Police Dial ☎ 48 75 2525, or 116 in case of emergency.

Post office The main branch is at Martí esq. Isabel Rubio, where you can send and receive faxes and make photocopies.

Swimming pools The pool at the *Hotel Pinar del Río*, at the end of Martí just before the *autopista* ($2–3CUC; ☎ 48 75 5070) is your best bet for poolside lounging within the town. Non-guests can also use the pool at the *Aguas Claras* hotel, 7.5km from Pinar del Río at Carretera de Viñales ($2CUC; ☎ 48 77 8426).

The Viñales valley

An official **national park** and by far the most visited location in Pinar del Río, the jewel in the province's crown is the valley of **VIÑALES**, with its fantastically located accommodation, striking landscapes and an atmosphere of complete serenity. Though only 25km north of Pinar del Río city, the valley feels very remote, with a lost-world quality that's mainly due to the unique *mogotes*, the boulder-like hills that look as if they've dropped from the sky onto the valley floor. These bizarre hillocks were formed by erosion during the Jurassic period, some 160 million years ago. Rainfall slowly ate away at the dissolvable limestone and flattened much of the landscape, leaving a few survivors behind, their lumpy surface today coated in a bushy layer of vegetation. Easily the most photographed examples are the **Mogote Dos Hermanas** or "twin sisters", two huge cliffy mounds hulking next to one another on the west side of the valley, with acres of flat fields laid out before them serving to emphasize the abruptness of these strange explosions of rock. For the archetypal **view** of the valley, head for the viewing platform at the *Hotel Jazmines*, a few hundred metres' detour off the main road from Pinar del Río, just before it slopes down to the valley floor.

Laidback locals and a sensitive approach to commercialization ensure that Viñales retains a sense of pre-tourism authenticity absent from other popular destinations. The tourist centres and hotels are kept in isolated pockets of the valley, often hidden away behind the *mogotes*, and driving through it's sometimes easy to think that the locals are the only people around. Most of the population lives in the small **village** of Viñales, which you'll enter first if you arrive from the provincial capital or Havana, and where there are plenty of *casas particulares*. It's also one of the few places in the country that acts as a hub for independent travellers and is a good place to hook up with travel buddies. From the village it's a short drive to all the official attractions, most of which are set up for tour groups, but it's still worth doing the circuit just to get a feel of the valley and a close look at the *mogotes*. If time is limited, concentrate your visit on the **San Vicente** region, a valley within the valley and home to the **Cueva del Indio**, the most comprehensive accessible cave system in Viñales. Also in San Vicente are the **Cueva de San Miguel** and **El Palenque de los**

2

Cimarrones, the latter a much smaller cave leading through the rock to a rustic encampment where runaway slaves once hid, but now set up to provide lunchtime entertainment for coach parties. Difficult-to-explore and little-visited **Valle Ancón** lies on the northern border of this part of the valley. On the other side of the village, the **Mural de la Prehistoria** is by far the most contrived of the valley's attractions.

The valley supports its own **microclimate**, and from roughly June to October it rains most afternoons, making it a good idea to get your sightseeing done in the mornings. Mosquitoes are also more prevalent at this time of year and insect repellent is a definite must for any visit.

Viñales village

Considering the number of tourists who pass through it, the conveniently located village of **VIÑALES** is surprisingly undeveloped for tourism, with only one official state restaurant, no hotels in the village itself (though several close by) and very few amenities in general. Nestled on the valley floor, simple tiled-roof bungalows with sunburnt paintwork and unkempt gardens huddle around the pine-lined streets, with only the occasional car or tour bus disturbing the laidback atmosphere as it plies its way up and down the main street of Salvador Cisnero, which slopes gently down either side of a small square where you'll find all but one of the town's noteworthy buildings. Despite the village's diminutive size, there's no shortage of people offering you a place to stay or a taxi, though this doesn't constitute any kind of hassle. There's a genuine charm to the village, though there's actually little here to hold your attention for very long.

Casa de la Cultura

Salvador Cisnero • Mon 4–9pm, Tues–Thurs & Sat–Sun 10am–9pm, Fri 2–9pm • Free

The village's main square is home to the **Casa de la Cultura**, which dates from 1832 and houses a small, sporadically active theatre on the second floor. You're free to take a quick peek upstairs, where there's still some old colonial-style furniture.

Galería de Arte

Salvador Cisnero • Daily 8am–11pm • Free

Next door to the Casa de la Cultura, the diminutive **Galería de Arte** displays small collections of paintings by local artists. Most are somewhat mawkish acrylic landscapes of the Viñales valley, though there's a handful of more original abstracts thrown in for good measure.

Jardín Botánico de Caridad

C.P. Esperanza • Daily 8am–5pm • Free

A five-minute walk north from the plaza just beyond the end of Salvador Cisnero, the most intriguing of the village's attractions is the densely packed garden referred to as the **Jardín Botánico de Caridad**. A gate adorned with pieces of real fruit marks the easily missable entrance of these almost fairy-tale grounds, the property of two sisters whose small brick cottage sits in the middle. The compact, shady garden is a botanist's dream, squeezing in all kinds of trees, shrubs and plants – papaya, begonias, orchids, mango and starfruit trees and many others. One of the sisters is usually around to help you pick your way through, explaining and identifying all the plants and noting many of their medicinal qualities, making it clear that there is order among this seeming chaos.

Museo Adela Azcuy

Salvador Cisnero no.115 • Tues–Sat 9am–10pm, Sun 8am–noon • $1CUC

Heading west down Salvador Cisnero from the plaza is the lightweight though relatively engaging municipal museum, the **Museo Adela Azcuy**. Its four small rooms

present an eclectic picture of local history, geology and culture, as well as bits and pieces of tourist information. Exhibits include a mock-up of the wall of a *mogote* and a short corridor dressed up to resemble a cave chamber, complete with stalactites. There is also a scant set of objects relating to the one-time occupant of the house, **Adela Azcuy** herself, one of the few women to fight in armed combat and be hailed in Cuba as a heroine of the nineteenth-century Wars of Independence.

ARRIVAL AND DEPARTURE

VIÑALES VILLAGE

By bus All buses pull up opposite the main square, outside the Víazul ticket office (☎ 48 79 3195) at Salvador Cisnero no.63a. From here all the *casas particulares* in the village are within walking distance, but to get to any of the hotels you'll need to catch a taxi or the local tourist bus.

Destinations Viñales to: Havana (2 daily; 4hr 30min); Pinar del Río (2 daily; 40min).

By minibus transfer An appealingly hassle-free way to get to the capital and beyond, minibus transfers can be booked through any of the travel agents in the village, or through the Víazul ticket office on Salvador Cisnero. The only set fares are for the daily services to to Havana — $15CUC direct, or $20CUC for the scenic routes via Soroa or the north coast — and to Cienfuegos ($30CUC), Trinidad ($37CUC) and María La Gorda ($25CUC). As there are often more prospective passengers than seats on the Havana-bound services, it's wise to book your onward journey several days prior to travel, particularly in peak seasons.

GETTING AROUND

By car Car rental is available from Havanautos (☎ 48 79 6390) at the petrol station on Salvador Cisnero on the northeastern edge of town. There's also Cubacar (☎ 48 79 6060), in the Cubanacán office on Salvador Cisnero opposite the square.

By tourist bus The easiest way of getting around is on the hop-on, hop-off Viñales Bus Tour, an extremely convenient minibus service with stops at all the tourist attractions and hotels. It runs daily from 10am (or 9am in high season) to 7pm and begins at the bus stop just outside the main square on Salvador Cisnero. Tickets cost $5CUC, can be bought on the bus itself, and are valid for a whole day.

By scooter The best place for scooter rental is Palmares Motoclub (daily 8.30am–8pm; $12CUC/2hr, $23CUC per day), opposite the *Casa de Don Tomás* restaurant on Salvador Cisnero. You can also try Havanautos at the petrol station on Salvador Cisnero, or Cubanacán at Salvador Cisnero no.63c. Charges at both start at $10CUC/hr or $15CUC/3hr.

By bike Cubanacán, Salvador Cisnero no.63c, rents out bikes for $1CUC/hr or $5CUC per day. You can also rent mountain bikes from Palmares (see above) for similar prices.

By taxi Transtur (☎ 48 79 6060).

INFORMATION, TRAVEL AGENCIES AND TOURS

Information Centro de Visitantes Viñales's visitor centre (daily 9am–6pm; ☎ 48 79 6144, Ereservas@pnvinales.co.cu), on the road into the village from Pinar del Río at Carretera a Viñales Km 23, has a few rather dull geographical displays and a panoramic viewing platform overlooking the valley. It also offers various activities including hiking and horseriding ($5CUC an hour) and eco excursions (see box below).

Infotur The office at Salvador Cisnero no.63b (Mon–Sat

8.30–4.45pm; ☎ 48 79 6263) offers local information from helpful staff and good quality maps.

Cubanacán At Salvador Cisnero no.63c (daily 8.30am–12.30pm & 1.30–9pm, usually closes early Sept–Oct and April–May; ☎ 48 79 6393), and with a similar set of services to Havanatur.

Havanatur The biggest national travel agent, at Salvador Cisnero no.84 (daily 8am–10pm, usually closes early Sept–

ACTIVITIES AROUND VIÑALES

Paradiso (see p.174) can arrange **dance classes** and **percussion lessons** (both $5CUC/hr; 2hr minimum as well as **horseriding** around the valley, as do Havanatur (see above) and the hotels (all $5CUC/hr; 3hr minimum). There are also plenty of local residents who, for a fee, can fix you up with an unofficial tour through the valley by horse – you won't have to ask around for long before someone obliges, assuming the price is right.

Though **rock climbing** has become increasingly popular in Viñales over the last ten years, it is still not state-approved and there are no official guides or routes. The rather politically biased US website ⓦ cubaclimbing.com has some good information on tried and tested routes in the region, though it's not updated regularly. There are long-standing plans to establish official climbing routes, so check with the Centro de Visitantes (see above) for the latest information.

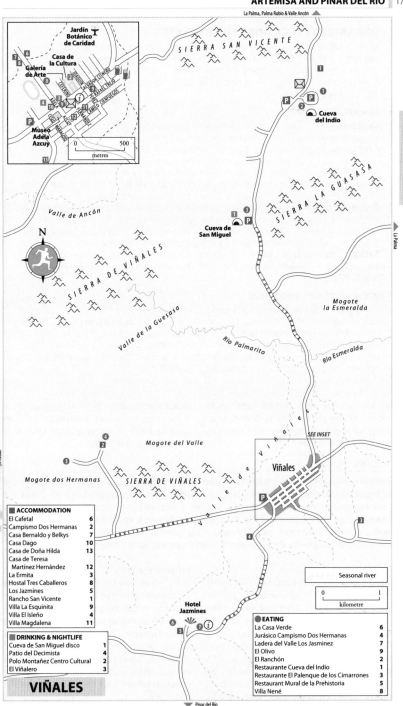

La Palma, Palma Rubio & Valle Ancón

2

La Palma

Pinar del Río

VIÑALES

Jardín Botánico de Caridad

Casa de la Cultura

Galería de Arte

Museo Adela Azcuy

Cueva del Indio

Cueva de San Miguel

Valle de Ancón

SIERRA SAN VICENTE

SIERRA LA GUASASA

SIERRA DE VIÑALES

Mogote la Esmeralda

Valle de la Guesasa

Río Palmarito

Río Esmeralda

Mogote del Valle

Mogote dos Hermanas

SIERRA DE VIÑALES

Valle de Viñales

Viñales

Hotel Jazmines

0   500
metres

N

Seasonal river

0   1
kilometre

ACCOMMODATION

El Cafetal	6
Campismo Dos Hermanas	2
Casa Bernaldo y Belkys	7
Casa Dago	10
Casa de Doña Hilda	13
Casa de Teresa	
Martínez Hernández	12
La Ermita	3
Hostal Tres Caballeros	8
Los Jazmines	5
Rancho San Vicente	1
Villa La Esquinita	9
Villa El Isleño	4
Villa Magdalena	11

DRINKING & NIGHTLIFE

Cueva de San Miguel disco	1
Patio del Decimista	4
Polo Montañez Centro Cultural	2
El Viñalero	3

EATING

La Casa Verde	6
Jurásico Campismo Dos Hermanas	4
Ladera del Valle Los Jasminez	7
El Olivo	9
El Ranchón	2
Restaurante Cueva del Indio	1
Restaurante El Palenque de los Cimarrones	3
Restaurant Mural de la Prehistoria	5
Villa Nené	8

2

ORGANIZED EXCURSIONS FROM VIÑALES

All the travel agents in the village offer very similar and similarly priced excursions, day-trips and transfers around Viñales and the rest of the province. Though there are sometimes slight variations depending on whether you opt for Havanatur, Paradiso or Cubanacán, the packages listed here are available at all three, with Cubanacán tending to be slightly more expensive; all prices below are per person.

ORGANIZED TOURS

Cayo Jutías This subdued offshore cay is actually so easy to get to that you're better off visiting independently if you have your own car. $22CUC with lunch included.

Cayo Levisa This daily excursion is an uncomplicated way of getting over to the more developed but less accessible of the two visitor-friendly cays in the province. The cheapest option covers transportation only; lunch is included for the more expensive choice. $15–40CUC.

Pinar del Río A day-trip to the provincial capital, including a visit to the cigar factory. $35–39CUC.

Recorrido por Viñales A tour of the valley that takes in all the major attractions, with lunch included. It's particularly worthwhile if you fancy eating outside the village or hotels, as many of the restaurants around the valley tailor their meal times to suit visiting tour groups. $28–35CUC; add $5CUC an hour extra if you want to do the tour on horseback.

Sendero por el valle This three-hour hike from the village into the valley is a great way to explore beyond the roads that most visitors stick to, visiting a tobacco plantation along the way. $10CUC.

WALKING TOURS AND HIKES

The staff at the Museo Adela Azcuy (see p.170) organize walking tours in the valley setting off daily at 9am and 3pm (1–4hrs; $8CUC per person). The **Centro de Visitantes** (see p.172) offers various hikes around the valley with an ecological slant, including trips to a tobacco plant and a traditionally run farm, excursions through areas of endemic wildlife and a walk through the centre of a *mogote* called Cueva Silencio. Treks start at 9am and 2pm from the centre, last between two and a half and three hours and all cost $6CUC.

Oct and April–May; ☏48 79 6262, Evinales@cimex .com.cu), offering one-day visits to locations around Viñales and beyond (see box above) and a useful long-distance minibus service (see p.172).

Paradiso Various cultural activities and excursions, as well as horseriding trips and dance classes (see p.172) are available to book from the office at Salvador Cisnero no.76 (daily 8am–4pm; ☏48 79 6164).

ACCOMMODATION

There's an even spread of good places to **stay** in the Viñales valley, with options to suit all tastes and budgets, from two of the best-situated and most attractive hotels in Cuba to a surprising abundance of *casas particulares*, many of which have views of the *mogotes*. Finding the latter shouldn't be a problem, as most have signs outside and buses dropping tourists in Viñales village are usually met by a crowd of locals equipped with business cards; but note that despite the large number of rooms, demand often far outweighs supply and the whole village is sometimes full to capacity by 7pm – make sure you book *casas particulares* during the day. Mosquito repellent is a must if you're going to stay in one of the places on the valley floor.

HOTELS

★ **La Ermita** Carretera de Ermita Km 2 ☏48 79 6071, ✉reserva@vinales.hor.tur.cu. Gorgeous open-plan hotel in immaculate grounds high above the valley floor providing panoramic views of the San Vicente valley and out beyond the *mogotes*. The tidy complex features three dignified apartment blocks with columned balconies, a central pool, a tennis court, a wonderful balcony restaurant and a comprehensive programme of optional activities and excursions including horseriding, trekking and birdwatching. Rooms are tasteful and reasonably well equipped. **$92CUC**

Los Jazmines Carretera a Viñales Km 25 ☏48 79 6205, ✉reserva@vinales.hor.tur.cu. There are stunning views of the most photographed section of the valley from virtually every part of the hotel complex, including the elegant colonial-style main building and its balconied restaurant. The rooms themselves (some in a separate, more modern block and a few in red-roofed cabins) could do with a makeover, the restaurant food is very poor and the whole place is past its prime, but the unbeatable hillside location does make up for it all. **$99CUC**

CASAS PARTICULARES

⭐ **El Cafetal** Adela Azcuy norte final ☎ 52 23 9175. Nestled in the lee of the mountains with a beautiful view of the countryside, this idyllic spot has two rooms, each with two beds and en-suite bathrooms. The garden, complete with mango trees and coffee plants, is bedecked with hammocks from which to soak up the atmosphere. The owners can organize rock climbing, walk and horseriding tours. **$20CUC**

Casa Bernaldo y Belkys Adela Azcuy norte no.36 ☎ 53 74 6729, ✉ casabernardoybelkys@correodecuba.cu. One well-appointed room in a quiet house with a sparkling new bathroom. An attractive breakfast area has views over the mountains. **$20CUC**

Casa Dago Salvador Cisnero no.100 ☎ 48 79 3173. This place used to be a respected paladar, a fact reflected in the high quality of food still on offer. Run in a relatively businesslike fashion, it has a reception room with a tiny bar where the innumerable photos of people laughing and smiling testify to the renowned entertainment skills of the singing, guitar-strumming and piano-playing owner. There is one clean, well-kept room with two double beds, a/c and a modernized bathroom. **$20CUC**

Casa de Doña Hilda Casa no.4, Carretera a Pinar del Río ☎ 48 79 6053. There is one room for rent in this mini-home complex, with its own small bungalow next to the main house with en-suite bathroom and a fridge. A large dirt courtyard joins it all together and there is a drive where you can safely park your car. The host, Hilda, cooks some of the best food in town. **$20CUC**

Casa de Teresa Martínez Hernández Camilo Cienfuegos no.10 e/ Adela Azcuy y Seferino Fernández ☎ 48 69 5518. Just one room with en-suite bathroom to rent in this attractive and compact *casa particular*, but with capacity for up to three people it's ideal for a family. There's a terrace from which to view the sunset too. **$25CUC**

⭐ **Hostal Tres** Caballeros Sergio Dopico no.20 ☎ 48 79 6166, ✉ cl9aaq@frcuba.co.cu. Two a/c rooms, each with en-suite bathroom, in a lovely house on one of the roads that leads out of the village into the countryside. A terrace overlooks the *mogotes* while there are also front and back verandas. **$20CUC**

Villa La Esquinita Rafael Trejo no.18 e/ Mariana Grajales y Joaquín Pérez ☎ 48 79 6303. One of the a/c rooms for rent in this spruced-up house has three beds – two double and one single – while the other has two beds and is en suite, with a fridge. Outside is a bountiful fruit and vegetable plot, and a menagerie of animals. **$25CUC**

⭐ **Villa El Isleño** Carretera a Pinar del Río ☎ 48 79 3107. Right on the edge of the village and one of the first houses you'll come to if you've driven from the provincial capital, this handsome place offers two excellent double rooms in a separate block out the back with its own terrace. The backyard shares a border with a tobacco field and there are views of the Mogote Dos Hermanas. **$25CUC**

Villa Magdalena Rafael Trejo no.41 esq. Ceferino Fernández ☎ 48 79 6029. One of the only colonial houses in the village backstreets, with a grand-looking, pillar-lined porch. Both double rooms have a/c and en-suite bathrooms, and one has a walk-in closet. A large, friendly family lives here. **$25CUC**

EATING

With so many people having opened up excellent new **paladars**, even those with jaded palates should find something to delight in Viñales. The village streets are peppered with interesting places to eat throughout the day and evening – there's even a **vegetarian option**. In response to the competition *casas particulares* have upped their game too, so if you decide to dine where you're staying you'll generally be assured an excellent meal – and prices are generally lower than at paladars, too. State restaurants, and the places in the hotels, are best avoided, however.

⭐ **La Casa Verde** 50m from Hotel Los Jazmines ☎ 05 22 38626. Genial proprietors, a great location in a tropical garden overlooking the mountains and an abundance of well-prepared food make this one of the most popular paladars in the area. A wide array of *comida criolla* is served, with the perfectly cooked fresh fish and succulent lobster particularly good; mains are around $6CUC. Sides include sweet potato chips and rice and beans. Home-grown coffee and rum are often included on the house, too. Daily 11am–11pm.

Ladera del Valle Los Jasminez Carretera a Viñales Km 23 ☎ 58 18 8998. Within sight of the Centro de Visitantes, this paladar in an atmospheric clapboard house with a thatched roof serves solid and dependable *comida criolla*. Dishes include barbecued pork and chicken roasted to a turn on an open grill, as well as lobster. Meat mains are around $5CUC, with lobster $8CUC. Despite the long advertised hours, ring first if arriving very late. Daily 24hr.

⭐ **El Olivo** Salvador Cisnero no.89 ☎ 48 69 6654. Arguably the best of the new crop of central paladars, *El Olivo* combines ambience, attentive service and an interesting menu. The menu is largely Spanish and Italian, with choices like Andalucian pork skewers, roast back of lamb with vegetables and chicken in white wine all reasonably well executed. Vegetarians are catered for too with a number of interesting small plates including fresh cheese with dressing, mixed grilled vegetables and *gazpacho*. Daily noon–10pm.

⭐ **Villa Nené** Adela Azcuy Norte no.35 ☎ 01 52 23 8897, ✉ villanene@correodecuba.cu. Vegetarian dishes (around $8CUC) are the speciality of the house in this pretty paladar cum *casa particular*. Succulent cassava, boiled then sautéed in garlic, is particularly delicious, while the roasted pumpkin side is also worth sampling. Cocktails are also a

treat, courtesy of a trained barman. Reservations are recommended. Daily 11am–11pm.

DRINKING AND NIGHTLIFE

Cueva de San Miguel disco Km 32 Carretera a Puerto Esperanza ✆ 48 79 3203. For nightlife on the valley floor, some 4km north of Viñales village, your only real option is this show and cheesy disco, which has a quieter bar attached. Lack of demand, especially in low season, means it's worth checking in advance before you go; ring or enquire with one of the travel agents for details. Thurs–Sun 10pm–12.30am.

Patio del Decimista Salvador Cisneros no.102 (no phone). Streetside bar where musicians sit strumming on the patio. Live stage shows take place daily at 9pm. Free entry. Daily 10am–2am.

Polo Montañez Centro Cultural Salvador Cisneros

esq. Joaquin Pérez (no phone). The village's biggest and best spot for live music is this semi-covered outdoor venue tucked away in a corner of the central square. Nightly shows of mostly traditional Cuban music begin at 9pm and are followed by recorded salsa and disco until the place closes down, usually no later than 2am and often earlier. Daily 11am–2am. Entrance $2CUC.

El Viñalero Salvador Cisnero (no phone). The strains of the house guitar band can often be heard throughout the day on this amiable spot a block from the main square. There is often live traditional music in the larger patio at the rear once they stop serving food in the evening. Free entry. Daily 10am–12am.

DIRECTORY

Internet and telephone ETECSA office, Ceferino Fernández no.3 e/ Salvador Cisnero y Rafael Trejo, Viñales village.

Money and exchange In Viñales village, Banco de Crédito y Comercio, at Salvador Cisnero no.58 (Mon–Fri 8am–noon & 1.30–3pm, Sat 8–11am), can handle credit-card transactions and cash travellers' cheques, as can the *casa de cambio* at Salvador Cisnero no.92 (Mon–Sat

8.30am–4pm, Sun 8.30–11.30am), where you can also purchase pesos.

Police station Salvador Cisnero no.69.

Post office Ceferino Fernández e/ Salvador Cisnero y Rafael Trejo.

Swimming pool The pool at *La Ermita* is open to the public at $7CUC/person, $6CUC of which can be spent on food and drink.

Mural de la Prehistoria

Mogote Dos Hermanas • Daily 8am–7pm • $2CUC

Less than 1km to the west of Viñales village, the valley floor's flat surface is abruptly interrupted by the magnificent hulking mass of the Mogote Dos Hermanas. It plays host to the somewhat misleadingly named **Mural de la Prehistoria**, hidden away from the main road down a narrow side turning. Rather than the prehistoric cave paintings that you might be expecting, the huge painted mural, measuring 120m by 180m and desecrating the face of one side of the *mogote*, is in fact a modern depiction of evolution on the island, from molluscs to man. It's impressive only for its size, with garish colours and lifeless images completely out of tune with this otherwise humble yet captivating valley. The mural was commissioned by Fidel Castro and painted in the early 1960s.

ACCOMMODATION AND EATING

Campismo Dos Hermanas ✆ 48 79 3223. Hidden away within the jagged borders of the surrounding *mogotes*, on the road to the Mural de la Prehistoria, this recently renovated *campismo* is better equipped than most, despite having no a/c or fans in its neat, well-kept white cabins. On the spacious site are a TV room, games room, bar and restaurant, swimming pool and a regional museum, as well as a nightly disco. The cheapest of the state-run options, this is the place to come if you want to share your stay with Cuban holidaymakers, but be prepared for the constant blare of music in peak season. **$10CUC**

Jurásico Campismo Dos Hermanas ✆ 48 79 3223.

MURAL DE LA PREHISTORIA

Decent *comida criolla*, including a tasty roast chicken special, served in the intimate white-walled dining room of a pleasant tile-roof lodge, with a dinky patio out front where you can also eat. Mains from $5CUC. Daily 8am–4pm.

Restaurant Mural de la Prehistoria ✆ 48 79 6260. The bar, restaurant and souvenir shop just off to the side of the mural do nothing to alleviate the place's contrived nature, although it's not an unpleasant spot to have a drink and a bite to eat. The speciality pork cooked "Viñales style", roasted and charcoal-smoked, is the highlight on an otherwise limited menu. Daily 9am–5pm.

Cueva de San Miguel
6km northwest of Viñales • Daily 9am–4pm • $1CUC

By taking the left-hand fork at the petrol station at the northeastern end of the village, you can head out of Viñales through the heavily cultivated landscape to the narrower, arena-like San Vicente valley, around 2km away. Just beyond the *mogotes* that stand sentry-like at the entrance to the valley is the **Cueva de San Miguel**, also called the Cueva de Viñales. Unmissable from the road, the cave's gaping mouth promises drama and adventure, but it's disappointingly prosaic, with unnecessarily loud music blaring from a **bar** just inside the entrance which, though a bit tacky, does provide a welcome break from the sun.

2

El Palenque de los Cimarrones
Cueva de San Miguel • Daily 9am–4pm • $1CUC

You can pay extra to investigate past Cueva de San Miguel's bar and venture down a corridor that disappears into the rock, emerging after just 50m or so at **El Palenque de los Cimarrones**. This reconstruction of a runaway slave (*cimarron*) settlement provides limited insight into the living conditions of the African slaves who, having escaped from the plantations, would have sought refuge in a hideout (*palenque*) such as the one on display here. There's little more than some cooking implements and a few contraptions made of sticks and stones, though there are some original pieces used by the slaves. You're left to guess what each one was used for and, although there is a small plaque declaring its authenticity, it's not even made clear whether this was actually the site of an original *palenque*.

EATING   EL PALENQUE DE LOS CIMARRONES

Restaurante El Palenque de los Cimarrones Valle de San Vicente ☎ 48 79 6290. This large restaurant set under round *bohío* roofs caters predominantly to lunchtime tour groups, but the food is better than you might expect.

Traditional Cuban roast chicken and pork dishes (around $8CUC) are cooked in appetizing seasonings, though the serving staff dressed as runaway slaves are somewhat less savoury. Daily 11am–6pm.

Cueva del Indio
6km north of Viñales village • Daily 9am–5pm • $5CUC, boat ride extra

From the Cueva de San Miguel it's a two-minute drive or a twenty-minute walk north to San Vicente's most captivating attraction, the **Cueva del Indio**. Rediscovered in 1920, this network of caves is believed to have been used by the Guanahatabey Amerindians, both as a temporary refuge from the Spanish colonists and – judging by the human remains found here – as a burial site. Well-lit enough not to seem ominous, the cool caves nevertheless inspire a sense of escape from the humid and bright world outside. There are no visible signs of Indian occupation: instead of paintings, the cave walls are marked with natural wave patterns, testimony to the flooding that took place during their formation millions of years ago. Only the first 300m of the large jagged tunnel's damp interior can be explored on foot before a slippery set of steps leads down to a subterranean river. It's well worth paying the extra peso for the **boat ride** here, where a guide steers you for ten minutes through the remaining 400m of explorable cave. The boat drops you off out in the open, next to some souvenir stalls and a car park around the corner from where you started.

EATING   CUEVA DEL INDIO

El Ranchón ☎ 48 79 3200. A small footbridge leads from the cave car park across the river to a restaurant hidden behind the trees, where the set meal, featuring grilled pork, costs $11CUC. Daily noon–4pm.

Restaurante Cueva del Indio Cueva del Indio ☎ 48 79 6280. Canteen on the path leading up to the caves'

entrance, bearing close resemblance to a school dining hall and with a slight Indo-Cuban slant to the Creole cooking on offer, which includes *tortas de yuca* (a cassava bread) and *ajiaco* (a traditional Cuban stew) alongside the usual roast chicken and fried pork. Mains around $8CUC. Daily 11am–6pm.

Valle Ancón

A few hundred metres up the road from the Cueva del Indio, just past an isolated post office, is the *Rancho San Vicente* cabin complex. About 500m further, a left turn leads to the last stop in Viñales, the **Valle Ancón**. Mostly untouched by tourism, this least-visited and unspoilt of the valleys in Viñales is also the most complicated to explore and can become uncomfortably muddy in the rain. There's a small village of the same name, plenty of coffee plantations and a number of hard-to-find caves and rivers, but the rewards are usually outweighed by the effort needed to get there.

ACCOMMODATION   **VALLE ANCÓN**

Rancho San Vicente ☎ 48 79 6201, ✉ reserva@vinales .hor.tur.cu. Opposite the abandoned *Hotel Ranchón*, on the way out of San Vicente towards the Valle Ancón, with twenty attractive and comfortable a/c cabins spread out around the site's gentle, wooded slopes. There's a swimming pool and a bathhouse offering massage and mud therapy. **$80CUC**

Cayo Jutías and Cayo Levisa

The nearest beaches to Viñales are the two cays, **Jutías** and **Levisa**, that lie off the northern coast of Pinar del Río province. Both are easily accessible by car and relatively undeveloped, so if you're looking for white-sand beaches without the contrived air that's part and parcel of the all-inclusive resorts elsewhere in the country, the cays are ideal.

Cayo Jutías

Just off the north coast of this part of Pinar del Río province (a 60km drive north and west from Viñales) is **Cayo Jutías**, a secluded island hideout that's relatively untouched compared to most of the other tourist magnets in the region. Besides the road ploughing through the middle of the low-lying thicket that covers most of the cay, the only signs of construction are a wooden restaurant at the start of the 3km of **beach** on the north side, and an old metal lighthouse built in 1902. The beach itself is admittedly

---

GRAN CAVERNA DE SANTO TOMÁS

An impressive and complicated set of caves set in the limestone rock of a hulking *mogote*, the magnificent **Gran Caverna de Santo Tomás** (daily 8.30am–3pm; $8CUC, including a 1hr tour with lamp and helmet) makes a good day-trip from the Viñales valley. The most extensive cave system in Cuba, with 46km of caves, it attracts serious speleologists and small tour groups alike, but happily it has not yet become overrun with visitors. To book a visit to the caves ring Fran Vegerano in Viñales village (☎ 48 79 3145) or, alternatively, Havanatur or Cubanacán (see p.172), both of which sell day-trips from the village for around $20CUC.

Seventeen kilometres along the road west from Viñales village is the clearly marked turn-off for **El Moncada**, a scattering of houses that shares a sheltered valley with the caves. From the turn-off, a pine-lined road leads down into the valley and the first right-hand turn off this leads through El Moncada village and up to a specialist school, the Escuela Nacional de Espeleologia Antonio Núñez (daily 8.30am–5pm; no phone), which doubles as a visitor centre with a tiny museum (free) and provides basic **accommodation** ($20CUC per person) in a four-room, cement-walled bungalow with breakfast and dinner included. Most people, unless they are experienced splunkers, are taken into either level six or seven of the **eight levels**, the mouths of which are semi-hidden up a rocky, forested slope from where there are fabulous views of the valley. Highlights of the walk – which covers 1km of chambers – include surprising cave winds, bats flying about and underground pools. The knowledgeable guides point out easy-to-miss plants, deposits of guano and, on level six, a replica of a **mural**. The mural is part of the evidence, as is the 3400-year-old skeleton found here, that these caves were once the refuge of the Guanahatabeys, the original inhabitants of Cuba.

a little scrappy in places and rarely more than 3m wide, but this does nothing to spoil the place's edge-of-the-world appeal – this may well be the best spot in Cuba to lie back and do absolutely nothing.

ARRIVAL AND DEPARTURE
CAYO JUTÍAS

By car Driving to the cay from Viñales is surprisingly easy, as the route is well marked. Follow the signposted road out of Viñales village to the Mogote Dos Hermanas until you reach the tiny village of Pons, where you take the signposted right-hand turn. The road surface deteriorates as you twist and turn onto another village, Minas de Matahambre, from where you head for Santa Lucía,

following the signs to Cayo Jutías all the way, until you reach the causeway linking the cay to the mainland where, at a tollbooth, there is a $5CUC charge for foreign visitors, or $5CUP for Cubans.

By organized tour Havanatur (☎ 48 79 6262; see p.172) runs trips from Viñales for $22CUC per person, which includes lunch.

ACTIVITIES

Watersports A hut by the beach restaurant rents out fairly shabby snorkelling equipment ($2.50CUC/hr or $5CUC/per day) and small kayaks ($1CUC/hr for a single, $2CUC/hr for a double), as well as sun loungers and

sunshades ($1CUC each). You can also explore the local coral reef on an outboard motorboat ($5CUC per person).

Sports The watersports hut also offers volleyball or football on sandy beachside pitches ($5CUC per person).

ACCOMMODATION AND EATING

Camping The only way to spend a night on the cay (though very rarely does anyone do this) is to camp – be sure to bring plenty of insect repellent, as the mosquitoes come out in force in the evening.

Beach restaurant (no phone). A wooden restaurant at the start of the beach does simple mains of seafood and chicken for around $8CUC. Daily 10am–6pm.

Cayo Levisa

On the same stretch of north coast as Cayo Jutías, 50km northeast of Viñales, the lonely military outpost of Palma Rubia is the jumping-off point for **Cayo Levisa**, more developed for tourism than Cayo Jutías but still relatively unspoilt. This 3km-wide, densely wooded islet boasts some of the finest white sands and clearest waters in Pinar del Río, and unless you take advantage of its **diving centre**, there's blissfully little to do here.

The boat moors on a rickety wooden jetty, a two-minute walk from the only accommodation on the island, *Villa Cayo Levisa*, sprawled untidily along the gleaming white beach. Behind the beach, thick woodland reaches across the island to the opposite shore, forming a natural screen that encourages a sense of escape and privacy.

ARRIVAL AND DEPARTURE
CAYO LEVISA

By boat The only regular boat to the island leaves at around 10am every day from Palma Rubia, where you can safely leave your car. If you're staying at one of the cabins on the island there's no charge for the 20min crossing, otherwise it's a hefty $10CUC each way or $25CUC return, which includes lunch at the island's restaurant. The return journey is at 5pm. The boat moors on a rickety wooden jetty, a 2min walk from the forty

grey-brick and newer wooden cabins.

Getting to Palma Rubia From Viñales, take the valley road north, past the turning for the Valle Ancón, and follow it to the small town of La Palma, just under 30km from Viñales village. From La Palma take the road heading roughly north, towards the coast, and stay on it for 17km until you reach a left turn which heads directly to Palma Rubia.

ACTIVITIES

Watersports The hotel has kayaks ($4–5.50CUC/hr) and catamarans ($18CUC/hr) for rent.

Diving and snorkelling A dive centre within the small hotel complex rents out snorkels ($5CUC/hr) and diving gear ($8CUC/hr), and offers courses and dives around the

nearby coral reef, a short boat trip away. Diving starts at $28CUC per immersion for up to four dives, while diving courses range from a basic two-immersion course ($60CUC) to a full course lasting for a week or more ($365CUC).

Fishing trips The dive centre also offers fishing trips

($40–55CUC per person) and a day-trip to nearby Cayo Paraíso ($25CUC per person), a similarly unspoilt islet once favoured by Ernest Hemingway, where you can dive or snorkel.

ACCOMMODATION AND EATING

Hotel Cayo Levisa ☎ 48 77 3015, ⓦ hotelcayolevisa -cuba.com. The grey-brick and newer wooden cabins right on the beach are well equipped, with spacious interiors and large porches. Loungers and hammocks hung under wooden shades line a beachfront dotted with *uva caleta* trees in front of the hotel. An attractive open-sided hotel restaurant serves mediocre meals like fresh fish, shell fish and pasta for $8–15CUC. As the phone line to the cay can be unreliable you should contact the Cubanacán head office (see p.142) if you're booking a room here from Havana. **$91CUC**

Southwestern Pinar del Río

Heading southwest from Pinar del Río city on the Carretera Central, the only main road through this part of the region, the tourist centres become less developed and the towns more isolated, snoozy but likeable little places that hold scant reward for even the most enthusiastic explorer – twenty minutes in any one of them should suffice for the whole lot. The one place that demands a longer visit between Pinar del Río city and the **Península de Guanahacabibes** is the **Alejandro Robaina tobacco plantation**, just under 25km from the centre of the provincial capital. Of the numerous *vegas* (tobacco farms) in the area, this is the one best prepared for visitors and the most renowned.

After the small town of **Isabel Rubio**, 60km from the provincial capital, the landscape becomes increasingly monotonous and doesn't improve until the dense forest and crystalline waters of the peninsula move into view, well beyond the end of the Carretera Central at the fishing village of **La Fe**. On Cuba's virtually untouched western tip, **María La Gorda** is one of the best scuba-diving locations in the country.

GETTING AROUND   SOUTHWESTERN PINAR DEL RÍO

By public transport Getting around by public transport can be a real problem, though the unreliable and very slow train service and the occasional bus from the provincial capital do at least provide the possibility of getting to some of the beaches.

By car Even with a car the going can be tough, as the Carretera Central features very few signs, becomes increasingly potholed and hands over to minor roads just before the Península de Guanahacabibes, the highlight of this area.

Alejandro Robaina tobacco plantation

Mon–Sat 10am–5pm, but calling in advance is recommended • 40min tours $5CUC • ☎ 48 79 7470

As the Carretera Central heads southwest from the provincial capital, it cuts through the famed **Vuelta Abajo** region, one of the most fertile areas in the country and the source of the finest **tobacco** in the world. There are countless *vegas* (tobacco plantations) in this zone, but one, the **Alejandro Robaina**, has an edge over the rest. While most plantations produce tobacco for one or more of the state-owned cigar brands, such as Cohiba, Monte Cristo and so on, this is the only one to farm the crop exclusively for its own brand, named after the grandson of the original founder, who bought the plantation in 1845. The brand was established in 1997,

---

BEACHES AROUND LA FE

There are a couple of **beaches** in the La Fe vicinity, around the wide-open bay of Ensenada de Cortés, although the appeal lies more in their proximity to the provincial capital and their popularity with locals than in their negligible beauty. Around 15km beyond San Juan y Martínez on the Carretera Central there's a clearly signposted turn-off for **Boca de Galafre**. Five kilometres past the turning for Boca de Galafre, a side road leads down 8km to a more substantial beach, **Playa Bailén**, the most popular seaside resort along the southern coastline.

2

then only the third brand to have been created since the Revolution in 1959. The owners have gone further than any other *vega* in their efforts to attract tourists, offering engaging guided tours of the plantation, product sampling opportunities and even the chance to meet members of the Robaina family, though Alejandro himself died in April 2010, aged 91. Visits here remain an unofficial tourist attraction, with the enterprising owners, not the state, running the short tours. Though this adds to the sense of authenticity, it also means the plantation is difficult to find, with no road signs pointing the way nor any mention of the place in tourist literature or on maps. To get there by car, take a left turn, marked by a small collection of huts and a solitary bungalow, off the Carretera Central 18km from Pinar del Río. Follow this almost ruler-straight sideroad for 4km until you reach another left turn, just before a concrete roadside plaque that reads "CCS Viet-Nam Heróico". This dusty track leads to the plantation.

The best time of year to visit is between October and January during the tobacco growing season. The **tour** with Carlos Forteza (who speaks English, French and Italian) takes in the various stages of tobacco production, starting with a visit to plots of land covered by cheesecloth under which the seeds are planted. Next you're taken to one of the *casas de secado*, the drying barns, where the leaves are strung up in bundles and the fermentation process takes place. There's a table here where cigar rolling is demonstrated, although no cigars are actually produced for sale on the farm.

Península de Guanahacabibes

Though a challenge to reach independently, the forest-covered **Península de Guanahacabibes** has become a popular destination for organized excursions and in this respect is easier than ever to get to. The journey is certainly not without its rewards,

TOBACCO

Tobacco is one of the most intrinsic elements of Cuban culture. Not as vital to the economy as sugar (Cuba's most widely grown crop), tobacco farming and cigar smoking are nonetheless more closely linked with the history and spirit of this Caribbean country. When Columbus arrived, the indigenous islanders had long been cultivating tobacco and smoking it in pipes that they inhaled through their nostrils rather than their mouth. When the leaf was first taken back to Europe it received a lukewarm reaction, but by the nineteenth century it had become one of the most profitable Spanish exports from its Caribbean territories. As early as the sixteenth century Cuban peasants had became tobacco farmers, known as *vegueros*, during an era in which sugar and cattle-ranching were the dominant forces in the economy.

As it became more profitable to grow tobacco, so the big landowners, most of them involved in the sugar industry, began to squeeze the *vegueros* off the land, forcing them either out of business altogether or into tenant farming. Many took their trade to the most remote parts of the country, out of reach of big business, and established small settlements from which many communities in places like Pinar del Río and northern Oriente now trace their roots. There nevertheless remained a conflict of interest which, to some extent, came to represent not just sugar versus tobacco but *criollos* versus *Peninsulares*. The tensions that would eventually lead to the Cuban Wars of Independence first emerged between **criollo**, or Cuban-born, tobacco growers and the Spanish ruling elite, the **Peninsulares**, who sought to control the industry through trade restrictions and price laws. Thus the tobacco trade has long been associated in Cuba with political activism. Today, when you visit a cigar factory and see the workers being read to from a newspaper or novel, you're witnessing the continuation of a tradition that began in the nineteenth century as a way of keeping the workers politically informed.

For an even broader perspective on the tobacco industry it's worth attending the annual **Festival del Habano**, which takes place principally in Havana and the Vuelta Abajo region (see p.48).

especially for scuba divers, who can enjoy some of the best **dive sites** in Cuba. One of the largest national forest-parks in the country, the **Parque Nacional Guanahacabibes** covers most of the peninsula, the whole of which was declared a UNESCO Biosphere Reserve in 1987. Some of Cuba's most beautiful and unspoilt coastline can be found here around the **Bahía de Corrientes**, the bay nestling inside this hook of land. It was on the peninsula that the Cuban Amerindians sought their last refuge, having been driven from the rest of the island by the Spanish colonists. Guanahacabibes is still relatively untouched by tourism and the only two hotel resorts are the low-key **María La Gorda** and **Villa Cabo San Antonio**. This is also an important area for wildlife; birdlife is particularly rich between November and March, during the migration season, while May to September is the best time for seeing turtles.

2

Make sure you bring enough cash to cover all your costs on a trip to this area, as you cannot withdraw money or use credit cards for accommodation or restaurants. The only way into the peninsula is along a potholed road through a thick forest that begins where the Carretera Central ends, at the tiny fishing village of **La Fe**, 15km beyond the turning for Laguna Grande.

La Bajada meteorological station

Daily 9am–4pm • $1CUC • ☎ 48 75 1007

From La Fe, the road twists and turns south and then west through the dense vegetation of the national park for some 30km until it reaches the broad, open bay, the Bahía de Corrientes, around which most of the peninsula's main attractions are based. The first of these, **La Bajada**, is a scrappy clearing on the edge of the forest just a few metres before the road hits the bay. The biggest and most obvious draw is the 23m-high sphere-topped tower of the **meteorological station**, which holds scant appeal for visitors, though for a small fee you can scale the tower's metal spiral staircase and enjoy 360-degree **views** across the treetops and over to the bay.

María La Gorda

$5CUC per person for non-guests to enter the Villa María La Gorda resort and use its beach • ☎ 48 77 8131, ✉ comercial@mlagorda.co.cu

Turn left after La Bajada to get to the Península de Guanahacabibes' most popular spot, **María La Gorda**, where there is an international dive centre and a small hotel complex on a fine white-sand beach. The relaxing drive here follows the shoreline of the bay, with dense forest on one side and an open expanse of brilliant, placid blue-green water on the other. Along the way are a few slightly scrappy but likeable little beaches, which you can make your own if you want complete privacy, but it's best to wait, as there's usually plenty of room on the much larger beach belonging to the resort at the end of the road. The white-sand **beach** is expansive enough for guests and non-guests (who can use the beach for free) to spread out without feeling too crowded. The sense of idyll is marred only slightly by the presence of a hard frill of rock which fringes the sand at the water's edge; and the fact that as the beach is rarely swept, a small amount of debris usually accumulates.

You should bring enough cash to cover all your costs here, as there are no banks, ATMs or places to change money, and the restaurants don't accept credit cards (though the little shop does).

ARRIVAL AND DEPARTURE	**MARÍA LA GORDA**
By pre-booked transfer The easiest way to visit María La Gorda is to book a transfer with one of the national travel agents based in Pinar del Río city or Viñales village.	Havanatur, for example, charges $20CUC for a return trip from its office in Pinar del Río (☎ 48 79 8494) and $25CUC for the trip from the Viñales branch (☎ 48 79 6262).

GETTING AROUND	
By car or scooter Cars and scooters can be rented from the Vía office (☎ 48 75 7693) near the dive centre; jeeps	cost $55CUC a day.

2

TOURS AND TRAILS AROUND PARQUE NACIONAL GUANAHACABIBES

Among the small cluster of buildings at La Bajada is the **Estación Ecológica Guanahacabibes** (☎48 75 0366, ✉aylen04@yahoo.es), a small lodge over the road from the meteorological station where you can arrange various trips around the peninsula. Access to the trails and indeed to any part of the peninsula beyond the road and resorts is forbidden without a guide, so if you want to explore you'll have to go on a tour. The centre employs six guides, two of whom speak English and all of whom are experts on the local flora and fauna. With no fixed days or times for excursions (the guides work on an ad hoc basis) it's vital to **ring in advance** to make arrangements. To get the most out of any of the three excursions, the staff at the centre generally advise start times of between 8.30am and 10am, when you are likely to see more birdlife and the day is not at its hottest.

There are currently three **organized tours** on offer, two hikes along the official Cueva Las Perlas and Del Bosque al Mar trails, and one that takes in the entire area by car or jeep. The centre is happy to tailor day-trips to your own specifications and can make them as long or short as you like. **Costs** are not fixed, but if you stick to the trips outlined below expect to pay between $4CUC and $10CUC per person. You'll need to present your passport or some form of ID before you can embark on any of the excursions here. Long sleeves and insect repellent are always a good idea, particularly in May and June when the mosquitoes are out in force.

THE TOURS

Del Bosque al Mar This is the shortest trail (around 2hr) and takes in both coastline and forested areas, beginning about 1500m from the Estación Ecológica. The route skirts small lagoons harbouring aquatic birds, while the floral highlight is orchids.

Cueva Las Perlas This 1.5km, 3hr trek through the semi-deciduous forest offers the chance to observe local birdlife such as the Cuban tody, the bee hummingbird and the red-legged thrush. At the end of the trail is the Cueva Las Perlas itself, an explorable cave sinking back over half a kilometre with various galleries and chambers, and shafts of light pouring through holes in the roof.

Safari tour The most expensive and comprehensive tour, this 50km, 5hr excursion includes the Cabo de San Antonio at the far western reaches of the peninsula. You will need your own vehicle, as the centre has no transport of its own; you can rent jeeps (though not cars, as the going is tough) from Vía in María La Gorda (see p.183). The tour follows the coast, with stops to observe wildlife and the changes in the landscape – from rocky-floored, semi-deciduous forest to marshy jungle and palm-fringed beaches, to jagged seaside cliffs. Animals you might see include iguanas, deer, jutias and boars.

ACTIVITIES

Watersports Snorkelling masks, snorkels and fins are available to rent at the dive centre for $7CUC a day.

Ball games There's a small soccer pitch and a sandy volleyball court which you can use for free; there's a $1CUC charge for renting a ball.

Board games You can rent board games ($2CUC) or use the hotel's oversized outdoor chess set for free.

ACCOMMODATION AND EATING

As the **food** at the hotel buffet is quite poor, it's worth bringing some of your own **supplies** if you intend to stay longer than one night – there is only a tiny grocery store here, and the nearest supermarket is at least 50km away.

El Carajuelo ☎48 77 8131. With a wooden-walled interior and shady front porch, this also serves as the *Villa María La Gorda* bar. You can get decent pizzas for around $6CUC and pricier chicken; when available, fresh fish simply served with lemon is the best option. Daily noon–3pm & 7.30–10pm.

Las Gorgonias ☎48 77 8131. Located at the top of the beach, with serene views out to sea, the buffet restaurant of the *Villa María La Gorda* serves $5CUC breakfasts and $15CUC dinners – each meal a very mediocre, all-you-can-eat feed. Take repellent to fend off the sandflies. Daily 8–10am, 1–3pm & 7–10pm.

Villa María La Gorda María La Gorda ☎48 77 8131, ⓦvillamarialagorda.com. Used as a base for divers as much as a beach hotel, and pleasant enough if somewhat basic for the price, with two distinct sets of accommodation.

Along the top of the beach, close to the water's edge, the most attractive options are the wood-panelled bungalows and two-storey concrete apartment blocks; a sea view costs $5CUC extra a night but is definitely worth considering. Hidden away from the beach in their own little wooden gangway-linked complex on the edge of the forest, the newer log cabins can be quite dark inside and are prey to legions of insects, so bring repellent. A buffet breakfast is included, and you can add a buffet dinner for a few CUC more. **$61CUC**

Cabo de San Antonio

From La Bajada, the right-hand turn-off from the main road through the peninsula (away from María La Gorda) is the fairly potholed road to the **Cabo de San Antonio**, the cape at the westernmost tip of the peninsula. There are several pleasant little beaches along the way, and at the extreme tip of the cape is a lighthouse, the **Faro Roncali**, built in 1849 (closed to visitors). Several kilometres beyond the lighthouse, past some more beautifully secluded beaches, are the last two stops on this 60km-stretch of coastal road, the picturesque and isolated white-sand beaches of **Las Tumbas** and neighbouring **Los Morros de Piedra**.

ACCOMMODATION AND EATING	**CABO DE SAN ANTONIO**

Marina cafeteria (no phone). The modest but well-kept cafeteria facing the marina is the only source of food hereabouts, with a small selection of sandwiches, soft drinks and ice cream for $4–5CUC. For a proper meal you'll have to travel the 77km to María La Gorda. Daily 9am–6pm.

Villa Cabo de San Antonio Los Morros de Piedra ☎ 48 75 7655. This eight-cabin, sixteen-room resort, with a simple, reconstructed marina, has been built with complete respect for the local environment. Located about 80m from the shore, the eight neat and comfortable wooden cabins, each with two rooms, have solar-powered air conditioning, and nothing has been built above the height of the trees. **$76CUC**

DIVING AND BOAT TRIPS AT MARÍA LA GORDA

The pristine waters around María La Gorda are widely regarded as among the best for **diving** in the whole of Cuba, protected by the bay and spectacularly calm and clear, averaging 25m in depth. Diving here is enhanced by a quick drop in water depth, with a large number of the fifty-odd dive sites only ten to twenty minutes by boat from the shore, while the spectacular variety of fish life here includes barracuda, moray eels, several species of rays, lobsters, whale sharks and more. Among the specific **dive sites** of note are Ancla del Pirata, featuring an two-ton eighteenth-century anchor covered in coral; colourful Paraiso Perdito, which reaches depths of 33m and is particularly abundant in coral and fish life; and Yemayá, a 2m-high cave at 32m deep, which ascends almost 20m through a long, gently curving, mysterious tunnel.

The two yachts belonging to the resort's diving club, **Centro Internacional de Buceo María La Gorda** (daily 8.30am–5.30pm; ring *Villa María La Gorda* on ☎ 48 77 8131, ask for the Centro de Buceo), depart for the dive sites twice a day. You need to be at the club at least thirty minutes before departure time to arrange equipment and pay for your diving. A single dive costs $35CUC but there are a number of more economical packages, starting with three dives at $100.80CUC, six dives $150CUC and eight dives $192CUC.

You will need to add an extra $7.50 for equipment rental, unless you bring your own. The club caters to both first-timers and advanced divers, with a short **initiation course** involving some theory and a single immersion ($45CUC). Also on offer are four- to five-day ACUC Open Water courses ($365CUC) and a number of other specialist courses such as "Stress and Rescue" ($200CUC).

Several **boat trips** are offered at the marina too. You can opt for an all-day excursion ($68CUC per person; 4-person minimum) which includes a visit to a beach, two dives, snorkelling and lunch on board; or the "Romantic Sunset" cruise (3hr; $24CUC per person), which is aimed at couples and includes an on-board dinner. The club also runs **fishing trips** for a minimum of four people (from $50CUC per person for 1hr).

Varadero, Matanzas and Mayabeque

VARADERO

Varadero, Matanzas and Mayabeque

The beach resort of Varadero is Cuban tourism at its most developed. Occupying the Península de Hicacos, reaching out from the northern coastline of the province of Matanzas into the warm currents of the Atlantic, almost the entire 25km length of this finger of land is fringed by sand white and fine enough to fulfil even the most jaded beach addict's expectations. Varadero is not, however, the complete package. Though the beach is stunning and the luxury hotels provide optimum accommodation, the poor nightlife, entertainment and restaurant options outside the hotels keep Varadero from being a truly world-class resort.

3

Roughly 30km west along the coastline from the peninsula is the provincial capital, also named **Matanzas**, while to the east, and somewhat closer, is the bayside town of **Cárdenas**. These once grand colonial towns now live largely in Varadero's shadow, relegated to day-trip destinations for holidaymakers. Many of their historic buildings are in considerable disrepair but they do still make a refreshing contrast to their more cultureless and one-dimensional neighbour. Equally, the Matanzas city surrounds hold three of the most captivating natural phenomena in the province: the subterranean cave network of the **Cuevas de Bellamar**; the broad, slinking **Río Canímar**, host to some great boat trips; and the enchanting tropical landscapes of the **Yumurí Valley**. Matanzas is also an important hub of agriculture: the traditional heart of the country's sugar industry, the centre of the province is covered in endless sugar-cane fields, while huge citrus orchards also shape the landscape. The Carretera Central cuts a scenic through-route, bisecting provincial towns like Colón and Jovellanos and passing within a few kilometres of the once wealthy village of **San Miguel de los Baños**, now a slightly surreal but intriguing testament to a bygone era.

On the southern side of the province, the **Península de Zapata**'s sweeping tracts of coastal marshlands and wooded interior can be explored with guides, who help protect this encouragingly unspoiled national park and Biosphere Reserve. There are a couple of very modest beaches here but the area is better suited to hiking, birdwatching and scuba diving than sunbathing. It is also the site of one of the most infamous acts in Cuban–US history – the Bay of Pigs invasion.

Most tourists bypass **Mayabeque** on the journey between Havana and Varadero. However, this predominantly rural province to the west of Matanzas, dotted with small uneventful towns, does feature some pretty coastline at the resort of **Playa Jibacoa** and a hilly retreat for the adventurous in the **Escaleras de Jaruco**.

Highlights

❶ Varadero beach Walk or run for miles on the golden sands of Cuba's most famous beach, then cool down in the shallow turquoise water. **See p.192**

❷ Mansión Xanadú Sleep, eat or drink in opulent style at one of Varadero's top spots. **See p.196**

❸ Classic American car ride Coast around Varadero or travel from Matanzas in a 1950s classic. **See p.197 and p.215**

❹ Hershey train It may be slow and unreliable, but this dinky electric train passes through some beautiful scenery. **See p.214**

❺ Cuevas de Bellamar Descend over 50m underground into these awesome underground caves and along 750m of atmospheric passageways. **See p.218**

❻ Río Canímar boat trip Enjoy the Cuban countryside on a fun-packed cruise up this broad, tree-lined river. **See p.219**

❼ Loma de Jacán Climb the hillside staircase outside San Miguel de los Baños to admire the forgotten village and fir-covered valley below. **See p.222**

❽ Diving at the Península de Zapata The flooded caves and coral reef here offer the best dive sites in the province. **See p.232**

HIGHLIGHTS ARE MARKED ON THE MAP ON PP.190–191

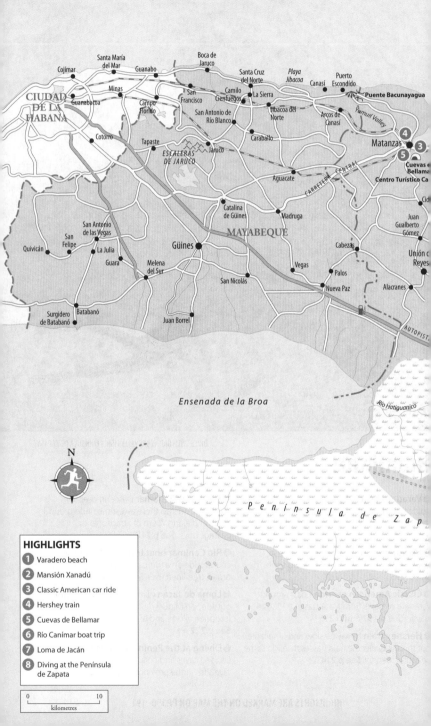

HIGHLIGHTS

1. Varadero beach
2. Mansión Xanadú
3. Classic American car ride
4. Hershey train
5. Cuevas de Bellamar
6. Río Canímar boat trip
7. Loma de Jacán
8. Diving at the Península de Zapata

0   10
kilometres

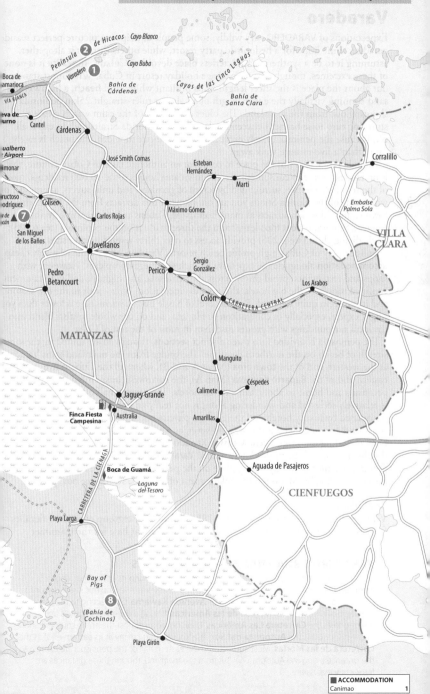

Península de Hicacos
Varadero
Cayo Blanco
Cayo Buba
Boca de Camarioca
VÍA BLANCA
Nueva de Bufno
Cantel
Cárdenas
Bahía de Cárdenas
Cayos de las Cinco Leguas
Bahía de Santa Clara
Corralillo
ualberto Airport
José Smith Comas
Esteban Hernández
Marti
imonar
ructoso odríguez
Coliseo
Máximo Gómez
Embalse Palma Sola
a de cán
Carlos Rojas
VILLA CLARA
San Miguel de los Baños
Jovellanos
Pedro Betancourt
Perico
Sergio González
Colón
CARRETERA CENTRAL
Los Arabos
MATANZAS
Manguito
Céspedes
Calimete
Jaguey Grande
Australia
Amarillas
Finca Fiesta Campesina
Aguada de Pasajeros
Boca de Guamá
CIENFUEGOS
Laguna del Tesoro
CARRETERA DE LA CIENAGA
Playa Larga
Bay of Pigs
(Bahía de Cochinos)
Playa Girón

ACCOMMODATION
Canimao   1

Varadero

Expectations of **VARADERO** vary wildly: some people anticipate a picture-perfect seaside paradise; some hope for a hedonistic party resort; while others dismiss it altogether, assuming it to be a synthetic, characterless place devoid of Cubans. In reality it is none of these extremes, though it is *the* package holiday resort in Cuba. What most stands out about the place is the sheer length of its brilliant white-sand **beach**, a highway of sand running virtually the entire length of an almost ruler-straight 25km peninsula shooting out from the mainland. The blues and greens of the calm waters create a stunning turquoise barrier between the land and the Florida Straits and, to cap it all off, because the peninsula rarely exceeds half a kilometre in width, the beach is rarely more than a five-minute walk away.

Though Varadero is not the place to come for an authentic taste of Cuban culture, this is no faceless shrine to consumerism – the town area houses some 10,000 residents, most of them in faded homes surrounded by scraps of grassland and unlit streets, a reminder of which side of the Florida Straits you are on. None of this detracts from the beach, the town section of which attracts as many holidaying Cubans as foreigners in July and August. Numerous **boat trips** leave from the three marinas on the peninsula (see p.203), while diving clubs (see p.206) provide access to over thirty rewarding **dive sites**.

Unline many of Cuba's high profile beach resorts, Varadero offers some relatively cheap **accommodation** alongside the expensive all-inclusive mega-complexes. However, with shops and restaurants spread thinly across the peninsula, and nightlife and entertainment confined mostly to the big hotels, there is a distinct lack of buzz – visit in the low season and it can seem quite deserted. But the level of hassle from *jineteros* here is lower than you might expect, especially in comparison to Havana, and on the whole tourists blend into the local surroundings with greater ease than in most of the rest of Cuba.

The peninsula is divided into three distinct **sections**, though all are united by the same stretch of beach on the northern coastline. The bridge from the mainland joins Varadero at the western end of the **town area** (Maps A and B), where all the Cubans live, and the eastern end of the **Reparto Kawama** (Map A), the narrowest, least visited section of the peninsula and home to about half a dozen hotels. The **eastern** half of the resort (Map C) is relatively secluded and wandering about is not really an option, as the landscape is dominated by luxury hotels and there are no pavements or footpaths. It's worth catching the tourist bus or a taxi out this way, however, as a number of the local highlights are here, including the magnificent **Mansión Xanadú**, the Varadero golf course, a dolphinarium, and the misleadingly named **Varahicacos Ecological Reserve**. The most dramatic changes currently taking place on the peninsula are on the hook of land at its eastern extreme, based around the enlargement of **Marina Gaviota** (see box, p.197).

Brief history

Varadero began life as a town as late as 1887, founded by a group of wealthy families from nearby Cárdenas intent on establishing a permanent base for their summer

---

VARADERO'S ROAD NAMES AND ADDRESSES

The principal street in Varadero town, and the only one running its entire 5km length, is **Avenida Primera**, shown on street signs and in addresses as Ave. 1ra. This street runs into Reparto Kawama, where it is also known as **Avenida Kawama**. Connecting to the other end of Avenida Primera is the **Avenida de las Américas**, linking a dozen or so hotels and also referred to as the **Carretera Las Américas**. Running along almost the entire southern shore of the peninsula is the **Autopista del Sur**, also known (particularly at its eastern end) as the **Carretera de las Morlas**. Most addresses in the eastern half of the peninsula are expressed as the distance along the Autopista del Sur from the mainland, though these distances are frequently inaccurate.

holidays. The archetypal old Varadero residence, built in the early decades of the twentieth century, was one modelled on the kinds of houses then typical of the southern US: two- or three-floor wooden constructions surrounded by broad verandas, with sloping terracotta-tile roofs, as exemplified by the Museo Varadero building (see below).

By the time of the Revolution at the end of the 1950s, Varadero had become one of the most renowned **beach resorts** in the Caribbean, attracting wealthy Americans and considered to be a thoroughly modern and hedonistic vacationland. Standards slipped, however, after power was seized by Fidel Castro and his rebels, who tended to frown on tourism. It wasn't until the government's attitude on this issue came full circle in the early 1990s that serious investment began to pour back into Varadero. Since then, over twenty new hotels have been built, most of them all-inclusive **mega-resorts** occupying the previously undeveloped land in the eastern section of the peninsula.

La Casa de Al

Ave. Kawama • Daily 10am–10pm • Free

The only notable sight outside the hotels in Reparto Kawama is the grand **Casa de Al**, the former holiday home of Al Capone. Now a restaurant (see p.201), this attractive, sprawling grey-stone villa with its broad arches, wooden balconies and terracotta-tile roof is one of the most distinct remaining hallmarks of Varadero's pre-1959 exclusivity. Have a meal or a drink here and you can take a look at the photos, spread around the interior, of some of the notorious gangsters that lived and did business in Cuba prior to the Revolution.

Museo Varadero

Calle 57 • Daily 10am–6pm • $1CUC • ☎ 45 61 3189

Housed in a classic 1920s wooden residence close to the beach, the **Museo Varadero** details the history of the peninsula via a small collection of disparately connected exhibits. Downstairs, the history display features one room of antique furniture and another packed with unrelated odds and ends, including some Amerindian burial site remains and a cauldron used by rebel troops in Cárdenas during the Second War of Independence. Upstairs is a poorly presented set of stuffed animals, representing a small cross section of Cuba's fauna, some sports memorabilia, including a few early twentieth-century photographs of the straight-faced aristocratic members of El Club Náutico de Varadero, and a room for temporary art exhibitions.

Parque Josone

Ave. 1ra e/ 56 y 60 • Daily 10am–11pm, pool closes 5pm • Free; rowing boats $0.50CUC/hr per person, pedal boats $5CUC/hr per boat, pool and ping-pong tables $4CUC/hr, swimming pool $2CUC

The underused **Parque Josone**, sometimes referred to as Retiro Josone, is the most tranquil and picturesque spot in central Varadero. The landscaping is simple, with no intricately designed gardens – just sweeping, well-kept lawns dotted with trees and a small lake where, perhaps unexpectedly, several ostriches are stranded on a palm-tree-studded island in the middle. Other animals in the park include ducks, geese, peacocks and, most bizarrely, two camels. There are rowing boats and pedal boats for hire, a couple of outdoor cafés, four restaurants (see pp.201–202), an intermittently operational crazy-golf course and, towards the back, the all-but-forgotten Complejo La Estrella, a star-shaped pavilion that holds a bar, pool and ping-pong tables. At the southern edge of the park, where it borders the Autopista del Sur, is a swimming pool.

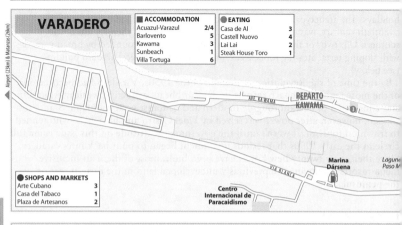

VARADERO

■ ACCOMMODATION	
Acuazul-Varazul	2/4
Barlovento	5
Kawama	3
Sunbeach	1
Villa Tortuga	6

● EATING	
Casa de Al	3
Castell Nuovo	4
Lai Lai	2
Steak House Toro	1

● SHOPS AND MARKETS	
Arte Cubano	3
Casa del Tabaco	1
Plaza de Artesanos	2

Airport (23km) & Matanzas (26km)

REPARTO KAWAMA

AVE. KAWAMA

VIA BLANCA

Marina Dársena

Centro Internacional de Paracaidismo

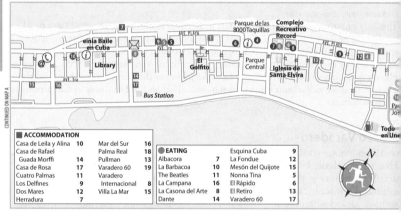

3

CONTINUED ON MAP A

Parque de las 8000 Taquillas

Complejo Recreativo Record

AVE. PLAYA

AVE. 1ra

AVE. PLAYA

einía Baile en Cuba

Library

AVE. 3ra

El Golfito

Parque Central

Iglesia de Santa Elvira

Bus Station

■ ACCOMMODATION			
Casa de Leila y Alina	10	Mar del Sur	16
Casa de Rafael		Palma Real	18
Guada Morffi	14	Pullman	13
Casa de Rosa	17	Varadero 60	19
Cuatro Palmas	11	Varadero	
Los Delfines	9	Internacional	8
Dos Mares	12	Villa La Mar	15
Herradura	7		

● EATING			
Albacora	7	Esquina Cuba	9
La Barbacoa	10	La Fondue	12
The Beatles	11	Mesón del Quijote	15
La Campana	16	Nonna Tina	5
La Casona del Arte	8	El Rápido	6
Dante	14	El Retiro	13
		Varadero 60	17

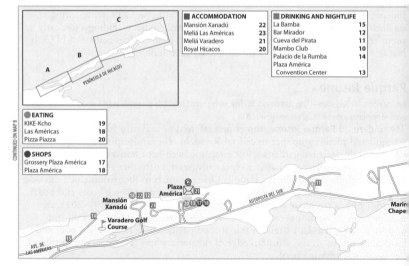

CONTINUED ON MAP B

■ ACCOMMODATION	
Mansión Xanadú	22
Meliá Las Américas	23
Meliá Varadero	21
Royal Hicacos	20

■ DRINKING AND NIGHTLIFE	
La Bamba	15
Bar Mirador	12
Cueva del Pirata	11
Mambo Club	10
Palacio de la Rumba	14
Plaza América Convention Center	13

● EATING	
KIKE-Kcho	19
Las Américas	18
Pizza Piazza	20

● SHOPS	
Grossery Plaza América	17
Plaza América	18

C

B

A

PENÍNSULA DE HICACOS

Plaza América

Mansión Xanadú

Varadero Golf Course

AVE. DE LAS AMÉRICAS

AUTOPISTA DEL SUR

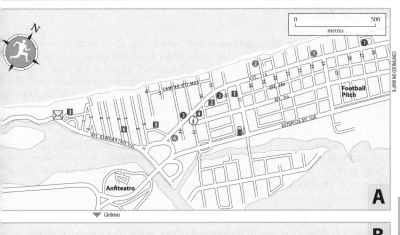

A

Cárdenas

3

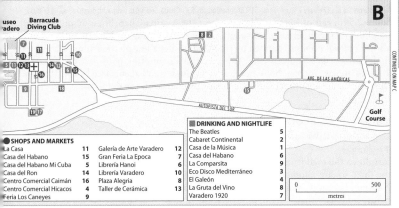

B

● SHOPS AND MARKETS

La Casa	11	Galería de Arte Varadero	12
Casa del Habano	15	Gran Feria La Epoca	7
Casa del Habano Mi Cuba	5	Librería Hanoi	6
Casa del Ron	14	Librería Varadero	10
Centro Comercial Caimán	16	Plaza Alegria	8
Centro Comercial Hicacos	4	Taller de Cerámica	13
Feria Los Caneyes	9		

■ DRINKING AND NIGHTLIFE

The Beatles	5
Cabaret Continental	2
Casa de la Música	1
Casa del Habano	6
La Comparsita	9
Eco Disco Mediterráneo	3
El Galeón	4
La Gruta del Vino	8
Varadero 1920	7

C

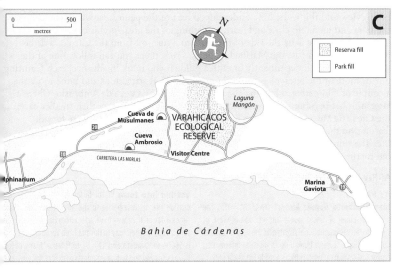

Reserva fill

Park fill

Bahía de Cárdenas

Mansión Xanadú

Autopista Sur Km 8 • ☎ 45 66 7388

The first tangible visitor attraction east of town, about 2km from central Varadero, is the **Mansión Xanadú**, located next door to the *Meliá Las Américas* hotel and now a small hotel itself. Sometimes referred to as the Mansión Dupont, it was built between 1926 and 1929 by the American millionaire Irenée Dupont at a cost of over $600,000, a vast sum for that era. At the same time, Dupont bought up large tracts of land on the peninsula for hotel development and effectively kick-started Varadero as a major holiday destination. The mansion has hardly changed since the Dupont family fled the island in 1959, and stands testament to the wealth and decadence of the pre-revolutionary years in Varadero. These days, to appreciate the splendidly furnished four-storey interior, its large rooms full of marble and mahogany, you either have to be a hotel guest, eat at the *Las Américas* restaurant (see p.201) or sip a cocktail and admire the views of the coast and golf course from the dignified top-floor bar (see p.202).

3

Dolphinarium

Autopista del Sur Km 12 • Daily 9.30am–5pm • $15CUC, photography $5CUC extra, $60CUC to swim with dolphins • ☎ 45 66 8031

Some 2.5km east of Mansión Xanadu, near the Marina Chapelín, is an outdoor **dolphinarium** with several shows daily. The verdant setting of the Laguna Los Taínos – a small natural pool surrounded by trees and bushes a few metres from the southern shoreline – makes a novel change from the usual swimming-pool-style design of these kinds of arenas. You can book in advance through travel agents (see box, p.199) and this is generally recommended if you want to swim with the dolphins.

Varahicacos Ecological Reserve

Autopista del Sur Km 17 • Visitor centre daily 8am–5pm • Trails $2–5CUC per route or $12CUC for all three • ☎ 45 61 3594, Ⓦ varahicacos.cu

Just down the road from the dolphinarium, at the eastern extreme of the peninsula, is the three-square-kilometre **Varahicacos Ecological Reserve**, also called the Parque Natural Hicacos. Given its billing as "the other Varadero", this is not quite the secluded nature sanctuary that you might expect; the undramatic, completely flat landscape is all but surrounded by enormous hotel complexes. Nevertheless, the hotels are generally not in view and this is the only undeveloped part of the peninsula, where you can view the flora and fauna up close and learn something of the area's prehistory.

The **visitor centre** is by the side of the road, at a turn-off from the Carretera de las Morlas about 1km past the Marina Chapelín. From there you can follow one of the three trails, either independently or with a guide if you book in advance, each featuring one or more of the reserve's ecological or archeological attractions and none more than a couple of kilometres in length. The first of these is the **Cueva de Ambrosio**, where a large number of Siboney cave paintings have been discovered. Another, smaller cave, the **Cueva de Musulmanes**, where human bones over 2500 years old were found, features on the longest trail which also offers insights into the local wildlife and plant life. The third and shortest route, **El Patriarca**, takes in an impressive five-hundred-year-old cactus.

ARRIVAL AND DEPARTURE
VARADERO

BY PLANE

Juan Gualberto Gómez Airport (☎ 45 24 7015) The single terminal of this modest airport, 25km west of Varadero, serves international flights and the very occasional domestic flight. It has a bureau de change, an information centre and several car rental offices outside in the car park.

Getting into town Víazul buses (see p.30) stop just outside the main entrance to the airport terminal three times a day on their way to Varadero from Havana, and four times a day on their way to Havana from Varadero; the fare is $6CUC to Varadero and $10CUC to Havana. Many hotels have buses waiting to pick up guests with reservations, and

It may be worth talking to the driver or tour guide to see if there are any spare seats. There are always plenty of taxis, which will take you to the centre of Varadero for $25–30CUC ($100CUC to Havana).

Airlines Aerocaribbean, Ave. 1ra esq. 23 (☎ 45 61 1470); Air Canada, Juan Gualberto Gómez Airport (☎ 45 61 3016); Cubana, Ave. 1ra e/ 54 y 55 (☎ 45 61 1823).

BY VIAZUL BUS

Terminal de Omnibus All interprovincial buses arrive and depart from this small terminal at Calle 36 esq. Autopista del Sur (☎ 45 61 4886), 150m from Avenida 1ra and with several hotels and *casas particulares* within a few blocks distance. If you need transport, the best option is Víazul's *continuidad* service; buses leave soon after every Víazul arrival and cost $3CUC to any hotel in Varadero. Alternatively, there are often taxis waiting out front; if not, call Taxi OK (☎ 45 61 4444). Most hotels in the town area are within a $5CUC taxi ride.

Bus tickets To book tickets you should either visit one of the local travel agents or information offices (see p.198) at least a day in advance, or purchase tickets from the Víazul ticket office at the bus station (daily 7am–9.30pm) no more than an hour before the time of departure.

Destinations Boca de Guamá (1 daily; 1hr 20min); Cárdenas (2 daily; 25min); Cienfuegos (2 daily; 4hr 45min & 2hr 35min); Havana (4 daily; 2hr 45min); Juan Gualberto Gómez Airport (4 daily; 30min); Matanzas (4 daily; 50min); Playa Girón (1 daily; 2hr 10min); Playa Larga (1 daily; 1hr 40min); Santa Clara (2 daily; 3hr 25min); Trinidad (2 daily; 5hr 50min & 4hr); Santiago de Cuba (1 daily; 15hr).

BY CAR

The road you'll need to take when driving to Varadero, either from the airport or Havana, is the Vía Blanca, 6km north of the airport, which leads right to the bridge providing the only road link between the peninsula and the mainland. There's a $2CUC charge at a tollgate a few kilometres before the bridge.

GETTING AROUND

BY TOURIST BUS

Varadero Beach Tour This double-decker bus is the cheapest way of getting around the peninsula. A hop-on, hop-off service, which goes as far as the Varahicacos Ecological Reserve and the few hotels just beyond it, it operates between 9am and 7pm, and costs $5CUC to ride all day (children under 6 travel free). There are 45 officially designated stops, and at most of these a timetable is posted; although they're worth checking for an estimate you shouldn't take these schedules too seriously, as buses are infrequent and you could end up waiting for up to an hour.

Matanzas Bus Tour Operating between Varadero and Matanzas, this costs $10CUC to ride all day, but as it only operates when there's sufficient demand, it's only reliable in peak season (Jan–March & July–Aug). When it does operate it usually runs between 9am and 7pm, with the last bus leaving Varadero at 3.30pm.

Turitren This theme-park-style tourist bus looks more like a toy train, but is only sporadically in use. It makes frequent stops along Avenida Primera between the *Superclubs Puntarena* hotel in Reparto Kawama and the Plaza América shopping mall east of the town; it also makes regular stops at and around Parque Josone. The fare is $2CUC, and it usually operates between 9am and 6pm.

BY TAXI

Regular taxis There's a constant stream of taxis along Avenida Primera, as well as a rank outside the *Cuatro Palmas* hotel between Calle 60 and Calle 62. Alternatively, ring Cubataxi (☎ 45 61 4444).

Scooter-taxis Two-seater scooter-taxis encased in yellow spheres, *cocotaxis* cost more or less the same as a normal taxi. There are ranks at Calle 15 esq. Ave. 1ra and outside the *Cuatro Palmas* hotel at Ave. 1ra e/ 60 y 64.

Gran Car For a ride in a classic American car, contact Gran Car (☎ 45 66 2454) or pick one up at Calle 16 next to the craft market there; rates are $30CUC per hour.

HORSE-DRAWN TRANSPORT

Horse-drawn carriages For a tour of the town or

MARINA GAVIOTA

At the furthest extreme of Varadero, the **Marina Gaviota** is currently undergoing a huge expansion, set to make it the largest marina in the Caribbean. In anticipation of the flood of American yachts and travellers expected to visit Cuba's north coast if and when Washington repeals its economic blockade, this huge project is set to transform the eastern end of the peninsula. With work well underway, the marina is already close to increasing its number of berths from 35 to 1200, while a fancy new port-side restaurant, *Kike Kcho* (see p.202), has been doing business for several years. The huge complex will eventually feature a hotel, a square and waterfront promenades, apartments, shops and restaurants, but for now it stands out as much as anything as one of the country's largest building sites.

beyond you can pick up a horse and carriage outside Parque Josone, among other places. Charges are $10CUC for the "whole city", which usually means as far as the *Meliá Varadero* hotel, or $5CUC for "half the city", usually just the town area.

Coches Hicacos Less touristy, and frequently used by locals, Coches Hicacos are horse-drawn carts closer to a local bus service than a taxi. They operate up and down Avenida Primera; Cubans pay $5CUP, but for tourists the price is a question of negotiation. They congregate at Ave. 1ra esq. 54 but you should be able to hail one anywhere you see them.

BY CAR, SCOOTER OR BICYCLE

Car rental Cubacar and Havanautos at Ave. 1ra esq. 31 (☎ 45 66 8196) and at Calle 20 e/ Ave. 1ra y Ave. 2da (☎ 45 61 1808; 24hr); Rex at Calle 36, opposite the bus station (☎ 45 66 2121).

Scooter rental Palmares Moto Club has rental points up and down the peninsula at various hotels and roadside locations such as at Ave. 1ra esq. 17 (daily 9am–6pm), and charges $13CUC/2hr or $25CUC/day.

Bike rental Bikes can be rented for around $5CUC per day from hotels *Solymar* on the Ave. de las Américas and *Tortuga* at Calle 7 y Ave. Kawana.

INFORMATION

Infotur The national tourist information provider can supply maps, book you accommodation, bus tickets and organized excursions, advise on public transport and almost anything you need to know about visiting the area.

There are two offices in Varadero: the more centrally located one is at Centro Comercial Hicacos, Ave. 1ra e/ 44 y 46 (daily 9am–5pm; ☎ 45 66 7044); the other is at Ave. 1ra esq. 13 (daily 8.30am–4.30pm; ☎ 45 66 2961).

ACCOMMODATION

As Cuba's tourism capital, Varadero has no shortage of **places to stay** – and, since the legalization of *casas particulares* in 2011, finally has a range of options for all budgets. All the cheaper **hotels** are located in the town area, and as the food in a lot of them is pretty poor, you're better off in the **casa particulares** here, which will also certainly be cheaper and often more comfortable, too. For the real luxury head for the east of the peninsula, beyond the town, home to all the newest hotels, the mega-complexes and the ultra **all-inclusives**, the highest grade of luxury hotel. Booking ahead is particularly worthwhile for the all-inclusive hotels, preferably via a discount website, since the rack rates appearing in this guide for these places can be four or five times higher than pre-booked prices. There is no **camping** on the peninsula.

HOTELS

REPARTO KAWAMA

Kawama Calle 1 y Ave. Kawama ☎ 45 61 4416, ⓦ gran -caribe.com. Large, landscaped all-inclusive complex, bordered by 300m of beach, which loses some character away from the main building, a stylish neo-colonial terraced structure built in 1930 as a gentlemen's club. Choose from private or shared houses, or apartments, though they could all do with some sprucing up. There's a fantastically chic restaurant and cosy basement cabaret. **$132CUC**

Villa Tortuga Calle 7 y Ave. Kawama ☎ 45 61 4747, ⓦ gran-caribe.com. This attractive complex is more enclosed than the others in Reparto Kawama, with pastel-coloured modern villas and two-storey apartment blocks, all set on a good patch of beach. Amenities include three restaurants, a pool, a gym, tennis courts and volleyball. **$128CUC**

THE TOWN

Acuazul-Varazul Ave. 1ra e/ 13 y 14 ☎ 45 66 7132, ⓦ islazul.cu. This twin hotel complex, consisting of two bulky, uninspired buildings within a block of one another, is disguised slightly by an upbeat blue and yellow paint job. Rooms are spacious and inoffensive, all with small balconies and many with great views. Only one of the buildings has a pool, albeit a small one, but guests in either can use it. There are also rooms in separate houses dotted around the local neighbourhood. **$76CUC**

Barlovento Ave. 1ra e/ 9 y 11 ☎ 45 66 7140, ⓔ reserva@barlovento.gca.tur.cu, ⓦ hotelesc.es. A stylish and sophisticated complex with a harmonious feel, featuring a superb lobby with a fountain and a captivating pool area enveloped by palm trees. Though a little dated, rooms are clean and come with sufficient mod cons, and there are tennis and basketball courts on site. **$190CUC**

Cuatro Palmas Ave. 1ra e/ 60 y 64 ☎ 45 66 7040, ⓦ mercurehotel.com. An artistically and thoughtfully designed complex in the heart of Varadero's shopping and dining centre, featuring a variety of accommodation buildings and slightly cheaper rooms neighbouring Parque Josone. There's a good choice of restaurants, a nice pool and watersports facilities. **$170CUC**

Los Delfines Ave. 1ra e/ 38 y 39 ☎ 45 66 7720, ⓦ islazul.cu. This is the most tasteful and attractive of the cheaper-than-average landscaped-garden hotels in this part of town, incorporating several accommodation blocks, linked together by outdoor corridors cutting across grassy lawns and a pool right down to the beach. **$120CUC**

TOURS AND EXCURSIONS FROM VARADERO

Public transport from Varadero to the rest of Matanzas is limited, and unless you rent a car, **organized excursions** provide the only convenient way of visiting some of the most memorable landscapes and natural spectacles in the province. This is especially true of the **Yumurí Valley**, which is bypassed by both local buses and long-distance coaches; the Jeep Safari Yumurí tour (see p.219) costs from around $45CUC. An organized excursion is also an excellent way to visit the **Cuevas de Bellamar**, from around $12CUC (see p.218); **Río Canímar**, from around $51CUC (see p.219); the **Península de Zapata**, from around $59CUC (see p.224) and **Matanzas city**, from around $45CUC (see p.210). Excursions to all of these places can be booked for very similar if not identical prices through any of the **national travel agents** operating in Varadero, from the agents' *buros de turismo*, found in the larger hotel lobbies, and through Infotur information offices (see p.198).

Contact the agents for activities within Varadero too, including the dolphinarium (see p.196), for which the cost of transportation, the show and a swim with the dolphins is $89CUC.

TRAVEL AGENTS

Cubatur Ave. 1ra esq. 33 ☎ 45 61 4405, ext.224.
Havanatur Ave. 3ra e/ 33 y 34 ☎ 45 66 7027.
Cubanacán Calle 24 y playa ☎ 45 66 7061.

Gaviota Tours Calle 56 y playa ☎ 45 61 1844.
Cubamar Hotel Varazul, 2do. piso, Ave. 1ra e/ 13 y 14 ☎ 45 66 8855.

3

★ **Dos Mares** Calle 53 esq. Ave. 1ra ☎ 45 61 2702, ⊕ islazul.cu. Atypically for Varadero, this agreeable little hotel feels more like those found in provincial colonial towns. What it lacks in facilities it makes up for with plenty of character and a pleasant intimacy, especially in the sunken bar. Rooms are quite small and simple. **$48CUC**
Herradura Ave. Playa e/ 35 y 36 ☎ 45 61 3703, ⊕ islazul.cu. This likeable, medium-sized hotel with a sea-view terrace and waves practically lapping on its walls is the cheapest beachfront option. Rooms are grouped in pairs, with shared lounges and sea-facing balconies. Appealingly simple and straightforward, but the food is below par. **$52CUC**
Mar del Sur Calle 30 e/ Ave. 3ra y Autopista del Sur ☎ 45 61 2246, ⊕ islazul.cu. Large, slightly run-down family-oriented complex with basic rooms, spread along both sides of the road; it's made up of uninspired box-shaped buildings, but pleasant gardens soften the edges, and there's a children's playground, a basketball court and a pool. One of the cheapest all-inclusives but you may not want to spend all your time here. **$78CUC**
Palma Real Ave. 3ra e/ 62 y 64 ☎ 45 61 4555, ⊕ gran-caribe.com. A successful conversion of a 1970s apartment-block hotel with the grounds extended way out from the original site to incorporate additional restaurant and accommodation buildings and two large swimming pools, one with a swim-up bar. Family-oriented, with unimpressive rooms but loads of outdoor space and a full programme of kid-friendly entertainment. **$188CUC**
Pullman Ave. 1ra e/ 49 y 50 ☎ 45 61 2702, ⊕ islazul.cu. One of the smallest, most subdued hotels in Varadero, with sixteen rooms around an attractive garden in the shadow

of a castle-like turret. It has a very relaxing atmosphere and is ideal if you want to avoid the hullabaloo laid on as "entertainment" at most of the other hotels on the peninsula. **$48CUC**
Sunbeach Calle 17 e/ Ave. 1ra y Ave. 3ra ☎ 45 61 3446, ⊕ gran-caribe.com. Though it comprises two huge, unsightly high-rise blocks, *Sunbeach* is one of the better-equipped hotels in this part of town, with a buffet restaurant, a pizzeria, several bars, a games room, a rooftop disco, a terraced pool and decent-sized rooms. Prices are fifty percent cheaper in low season. **$130CUC**
Villa La March Ave. 3ra e/ 28 y 29 ☎ 45 61 3910, ⊕ islazul.cu. Sociable but unsophisticated, this dated concrete complex is popular with Cubans and is among the cheapest hotels in Varadero. It's on the wrong side of the peninsula and backs onto the main road, but has a pool and large gardens. **$78CUC**

EASTERN VARADERO

★ **Mansión Xanadú** Autopista del Sur Km 7 ☎ 45 66 7388, ⊕ varaderogolfclub.com. Housed in the splendidly opulent Dupont Mansion, this is the most unique hotel in Varadero. The eight refined rooms, six of which face the sea, have been individually furnished – two with colonial American originals – and there is a delightful wine cellar and one of the peninsula's best restaurants, *Las Américas*. Aimed at golfers, room prices include golfing packages for the Varadero Golf Course, whose clubhouse is next door. **$240CUC**
★ **Meliá Las Américas** Autopista del Sur Km 7 ☎ 45 66 7600, ⊕ meliacuba.com. One of the most imaginatively designed hotels on the peninsula, with paths weaving down from the huge circular main building

3

FISHING AROUND VARADERO

There are plenty of better locations around Cuba to go **saltwater fishing** than off the coast of Varadero, but this is one of the easiest places to charter a boat, and sailing out to the surrounding cays is a great way for the casual enthusiast to combine a spot of fishing with a relaxing day-trip. You have to get well away from the beach to have even a chance of a half-decent catch, which could be wahoo, barracuda, grouper, snapper or tuna among others, and some fishing trips actually take place on the other side of the province, off the Península de Zapata (see box, p.229). Tailor-made excursions and fishing packages are available at the three **marinas** (see box, p.203), which will supply any necessary fishing equipment; the *buros de turismo* in most hotel lobbies can also usually also help with arrangements.

Marina Chapelín and **Marina Gaviota** offer various types of **fishing trips**, with packages (including an on-board open bar) starting at $290CUC for around five hours for one to four people, plus $30CUC for non-fishing passengers. **Marina Dársena** runs fishing trips around northern Varadero, which can be comparatively good value, with prices per boat for a day-trip starting at $240CUC; again boats take up to four passengers.

through intricately landscaped gardens to the beach – even the pool drops down a level while it twists itself around the pathways and pond. Rooms are tastefully furnished, and there are five restaurants, plus special deals for golfers who want to use the course over the road. Over-18s only. **$416CUC**

Meliá Varadero Autopista del Sur Km 7 ☎ 45 66 7013, ⓦ meliacuba.com. Sophisticated, star-shaped all-inclusive whose seven points meet spectacularly around an indoor rainforest where ivy cascades down the circular walls from high above. There's a swimming pool with a bar in the centre, and the small collection of varied restaurants and bars includes a large thatched-roof hall looking over the sea from a low cliff. **$460CUC**

★ **Royal Hicacos** Carretera Las Morlas Km 15 ☎ 45 66 8844, ⓦ sandalshicacos.com. The fabulous rooms here, all of them suites, have split-level designs, living-room areas, king-size beds and all the amenities you could want. Highlights include a two-man cave built into the side of the stunning pool, a fully equipped spa, a squash court and some great drinking and dining areas with waterways woven around them. Over-18s only. **$386CUC**

Varadero Internacional Ave. de las Américas Km 1 ☎ 45 66 7038, ⓦ gran-caribe.com. Not the most luxurious but probably the most individual all-inclusive in Varadero, and certainly the one with the most historical heritage. Opened in 1950, it has maintained much of its original character and oozes retro chic inside. It's also on an excellent section of beach and has the best cabaret in town. **$170CUC**

CASAS PARTICULARES
THE TOWN

Casa de Leila y Alina Calle 57 no.6 e/ Ave. 1ra y playa ☎ 45 66 9241, ✉ ciro@cargodex.tdc.cu. One of the best located *casas* in Varadero, on the grass-lined path to the museum and beach and a stone's throw from Parque Josone. Guests rent a separate, spacious and well-equipped apartment building around the back of a handsome bungalow, both of which share a garden patio area featuring an inviting outdoor lounge. **$40CUC**

Casa de Rafael Guada Morffi Calle 36 no.117 (alto) e/ Ave. 1ra y Autopista del Sur, ☎ 45 61 2925, ✉ rafaelguada@yahoo.es. A small but inviting first-floor apartment within a compact two-floor house near the bus station, consisting of a spruce kitchen-diner and a tightly packed little bedroom with a bunk bed and a single bed, plus a safety deposit box and internet access. **$35CUC**

Casa de Rosa Calle 36 no.119 e/ Ave. 1ra y Autopista del Sur ☎ 45 61 2016, ✉ ochidiaz@yahoo.es. The friendly landlady rents out one large room with a large bathroom in a bungalow with a garden and a patio wrapped around three of its sides. About a minute's walk from the bus station. **$35CUC**

★ **Varadero 60** Calle 60 esq. Ave. 3ra ☎ 45 61 3986, ✉ luisernestovar@yahoo.com. Great option where the two comfortable double rooms have their own garden patio, one room more like an apartment, with a fantastic spanking new bathroom. The owners also run an excellent paladar, and with a music venue round the corner, this is a great place for a lively stay. **$30–45CUC**

EATING

Following the long-awaited legalization of **paladars** in Varadero in 2010, eating out options have taken a leap forward and there's now a broader selection of places offering good quality Cuban cuisine. The food in the **state restaurants** remains mediocre, however, and there's still very little variety for such a large resort, with the few "international cuisine" options mostly rehashing Cuban staples and raising questions about their chef's geography. If you're staying at an upmarket all-inclusive, you'll almost certainly eat better non-Cuban food there than outside; non-guests can buy a

day-pass to some of these hotels (usually $30–70CUC), which covers use of their facilities and restaurants. To check out a few places before making your choice, head for Parque Josone, home to four state restaurants, or the few blocks between there and the top of town.

PALADARS

La Casona del Arte Calle 47 no.6 e/ Ave. 1ra y Ave. Playa ☎45 61 2237. The speciality at this interesting upstairs paladar in a classic Varadero wooden house is the love-it-or-hate-it fish and shrimp with cheese ($8CUC), while the eclectic menu also features two chop suey dishes ($2.50CUC). Eat out on the veranda or in the gloomier room indoors, which is brightened up by a mishmash of paintings. Daily noon–10.30pm.

Nonna Tina Calle 38 no.5 e/ Ave. 1ra y Ave. Playa ☎45 61 2450. A paladar specializing in Italian cuisine: the thin-crust pizzas are quite authentic, but the pasta options are limited by a disproportionate number of spaghetti dishes. A touch of surrealism is added by the guinea pig and rabbit enclosure over a fence from the tables on the front porch. Mains $3–10 CUC. Daily noon–11pm.

★ Varadero 60 Calle 60 esq. Ave. 3ra ☎45 61 3986. The most impressive and professional paladar in Varadero, where the owner Luis' collection of 1960s memorabilia, most notably a wonderful set of old posters and adverts, creates a memorable setting, as do the patio dining area and the shiny Buick '58 usually parked on the drive. Try the usually excellent lobster ($17.95CUC) or mix it up by choosing the Tesoros del March ($14.95CUC), a shrimp, fish and lobster medley. Daily noon–midnight.

STATE RESTAURANTS

Albacora Calle 59 ☎45 61 3650. One of the best beachside restaurants, where you can enjoy good fresh food including lobster ($10–15CUC), squid ($6.50CUC), pork ($5CUC), chicken ($5CUC) and beef fillet ($9.95CUC). Set under a protective canopy of low, twisting branches on a large terrace, this is a laidback place – except when there's a group playing music on the built-in stage. Daily 10.30am–9.30pm.

★ Las Américas Mansión Xanadú, Autopista Sur Km 7 ☎45 66 7750. One of the classiest and most expensive restaurants on the peninsula, with seating in the library, down in the wine cellar or out on the terrace overlooking the garden. The lobster is reliably good quality but starts at $35CUC, while most alternatives, such as honey-roast duck and grilled salmon with bacon, are priced around the $20CUC mark. Wander down to the garden perched above the waves or up to the rooftop bar (see p.202) for the perfect post-meal drink. Cash only. Daily 7–10.30pm.

La Barbacoa Ave. 1ra esq. 64 ☎45 66 7795. A steakhouse and barbecue grill tucked into the top corner of town, shielded from the road by a screen of trees. Topping the menu are the deservedly expensive tenderloin and sirloin steaks, but there's also $10CUC-lobster and the usual

chicken, pork and fish dishes. Daily noon–11pm.

The Beatles Ave. 1ra e/ 58 y 59 ☎45 66 7329. This monument to The Beatles is the most unlikely restaurant in town, a somewhat sterile place in the day, though the pictures of the Fab Four scattered all over the walls and the TV screen playing footage of their concerts may draw you inside where you can order meatballs ($1.50CUC), various skewered meats ($4.50–10CUC) and ubiquitous Cuban dishes. At night the place comes alive with shows by tribute bands out on the patio (see p.204). Daily noon–10.30pm.

La Campana Parque Josone ☎45 66 7224. The tasty *ropa vieja*, or shredded beef, is available with or without jerk seasoning (both $10.50CUC), and the pork slices ($10.50CUC) are also good at this rustic stone-and-wood hunting lodge with a large fireplace and animal heads adorning the walls of its cosy interior. There's also outdoor dining on the veranda. Daily noon–10.30pm.

Casa de Al Ave. Kawama ☎45 66 8018. The gangster-themed menu – Filet Mignon Lucky Luciano ($15CUC) or Al Pacino Salad ($4CUC), for example – is just a gimmicky version of the usual Cuban staples, but the setting in a refined two-storey stone mansion, once a holiday home of Al Capone, is one of the best on the peninsula, with views up the beach and tables on a cool, tiled terrace surrounded by low arches. Daily 10am–10pm.

Castell Nuovo Ave. 1ra no.503 esq. Calle 11 ☎45 66 7786. Popular despite being low on charm (thanks in part to its affordable prices, which start at $3.95CUC for a Napolitana pizza), *Castell Nuovo* offers reasonable Italian cuisine and a good selection of seafood. Daily noon–10.30pm.

Dante Parque Josone ☎45 66 7224. Hit-and-miss Italian food including very unsubtle pasta sauces – some rich and tasty, like the bolognese, some odd-tasting, like the carbonara – and slightly safer pizzas. Better in daylight hours, when you can enjoy the placid views across the lake and the pleasant veranda jutting out over the water. Main dishes $5–12CUC. Daily noon–10.30pm.

Esquina Cuba Ave. 1ra y 36 ☎45 61 4019. Sliced pork ($6.50CUC), shredded beef ($5CUC) and equally well-priced fish dishes are served on a wide open veranda under a thatched roof, where the bordering plants do just enough to separate the place from a sense of the road. A white-and-pink Oldsmobile makes up the bulk of the interior decoration. Daily noon–11pm.

La Fondue Ave. 1ra y 62 ☎45 66 7747. This supposedly French–Swiss restaurant, with its quaint homely interior, has been straying further and further over the years from the improvised fondue-based dishes on which it was founded. You can still order beef fillet fondue ($10CUC), but the likes of grilled shrimps ($9CUC) and breaded pork cutlet

3

3

($4.50CUC) now characterize the menu as much as anything else. Daily noon–11pm.

KIKE-Kcho Marina Gaviota, Autopista del Sur y final ☎ 45 66 4115. With a reputation for some of the best lobster in the country, which you can pick direct from nets in the sea, this splendid yet inconsistent seafood restaurant, hovering over the sea, can usually justify its relatively high prices, but occasionally disappoints with poor levels of service. Daily noon–11pm.

Lai Lai Ave. 1ra y 18 ☎ 45 66 7793. Not for the faint-hearted, the pseudo-Chinese food here, like shrimps in teriyaki sauce ($8CUC), or the four types of chop suey ($7–18CUC), is fairly crude. Less exclusive than its grand exterior suggests, with two private, cosier rooms upstairs (suitable for groups of four or more) that are worth booking in advance. Daily noon–11pm.

Mesón del Quijote Ave. de las Américas ☎ 45 66 7796. The speciality here is paella ($5–10CUC), but the lobster is more reliable, with all three sizes equally good value ($11–20CUC) and the food in general presented with minimal garnish, relying instead on simple flavours. Perched atop a small hill, the dining experience is better before dark, when the views negate the bare interior of dark benches and tables, wine racks and wall-to-wall windows lined with wax-covered bottles. Daily noon–10.30pm.

Pizza Piazza Plaza América, Autopista del Sur Km 7 ☎ 45 66 8585. A decent selection of American-style pizzas alongside mediocre pasta dishes. Choose a small ($5CUC), medium ($8CUC) or large ($11CUC) base and add the toppings ($0.75–1.75CUC) of your choice, or plump for the usual classics. The best seats are on a balcony that looks down to the sea. Daily noon–9pm.

El Rápido Calle 47 e/ Ave. 1ra y Ave. Playa ☎ 45 61 3326. A large branch of the national fast-food chain where pizzas, sandwiches and hot dogs are served with no sense of urgency. 24hr.

El Retiro Parque Josone ☎ 45 66 7316. This lobster specialist is Parque Josone's one option for fine dining, with decor that's restrained rather than refined. Other options besides lobster ($21CUC) include the seafood platter ($19CUC) but there are less expensive fish, shrimp and chicken dishes. Daily noon–10.30pm.

Steak House Toro Ave. 1ra esq. 25 ☎ 45 66 7145. Sunk just below street level and sticking firmly to the steakhouse script, with a meat-fest menu, a bull's head and a wagon-wheel on the wall. The headline dishes include reliable 10oz tenderloin steaks ($18CUC) and 12oz sirloins ($15CUC), though there are non-meat alternatives such as grilled lobster ($18CUC). Daily noon–11pm.

DRINKING

Finding a straightforward **bar** in Varadero is much harder than it should be. There is no area where you can easily bar-hop your way through the night, with most places in isolated pockets around the town. Only a tiny percentage of bars are designed simply for drinking and socializing, a formula abandoned all too often for karaoke or, in the hotels, live PA entertainment. **Cafés** are equally sparse and are found almost exclusively along Avenida Primera, though some of the places calling themselves bars could also pass as cafés, given that most of them serve snacks and a few offer table service.

BARS AND CAFÉS

★ **Bar Mirador Mansión Xanadú** Autopista Sur Km 7 ☎ 45 66 7388. A sophisticated place with an ornate wooden ceiling supported by black pillars. The location at the top of this splendid mansion affords fabulous views along the coastline. Daily 10am–11.45pm.

Casa del Habano Ave. 1ra e/ 63 y 64 ☎ 45 66 7843. The dinky, stylish, balconied café upstairs from an excellent cigar shop makes a good place for a quiet drink. Daily 9am–9pm.

El Galeón Hotel Dos Mares, Calle 53 esq. Ave. 1ra ☎ 45 61 2702. One of the few proper bars in the town, just a straight-up, laidback place to get a drink, set just below street level with a stylish varnished-wood finish and a slight Mediterranean feel. Daily 10am–11pm.

La Gruta del Vino Parque Josone ☎ 45 66 7224. This novel little bar and eatery, sinking back into a tiny cave on the far side of the lake in Parque Josone, has a wide selection of wine and a patio out front where you can sip your drinks near the water's edge. Daily 3.30–10.30pm.

Varadero 1920 Parque Josone ☎ 45 66 7224. An open-air café propped above the banks of the park lake, and one of the most laidback spots for a drink in Varadero. Daily 9am–9pm.

NIGHTLIFE, LIVE MUSIC AND ENTERTAINMENT

With so many of the hotels providing their own entertainment programmes, and surprisingly few places to go for **live music**, nightlife in Varadero falls way short of the standards you might expect for such a large resort. Note that some clubs and cabarets do not allow shorts or sleeveless tops to be worn.

CLUBS

Clubs Most hotels offer something more akin to a school disco than a nightclub, and a karaoke night is never far off, but there are a few hotel nightclubs that have become destinations in their own right. In the Cuban tradition, the music at these venues is sometimes performed by live

BOAT TRIPS AND THE MARINAS

With entertainment options a little thin on the ground in Varadero, it's no surprise that **boat trips** to the islets and reefs around the peninsula are so numerous and popular. The family of cays beyond the eastern tip of the peninsula – cayos Blanco, Piedras and Romero, among others – make up most of the stopping-off points; they're bordered by small coral reefs and offer the best opportunities for snorkelling.

Most of the trips can be booked through any one of the principal travel agents (see p.199) and include the transfer from your hotel to the point of departure in the price; children under 12 are usually charged half-price rates. Note that some of the prices below depend upon a minimum number of people booking the same trip.

Marina Chapelín, at Autopista del Sur Km 12 (☎45 66 7550 & 66 7565), has its own information kiosk at Ave. 1ra y 59 (daily 8am–5pm) from where you can book any of the various "seafaris" to Cayo Blanco ($39–109CUC) or the popular 2hr Boat Adventure ($88CUC), an excursion on ski-bikes or speedboats to a cay where you can see crocodiles, iguanas and other creatures.

Marina Gaviota Varadero, at the eastern end of Autopista del Sur (☎45 66 7755 & 66 7756), and currently undergoing expansion (see p.197). Most of the catamaran excursions to Cayo Blanco include snorkeling, lunch and some beach time, whilst one option includes swimming with dolphins ($85CUC).

Marina Dársena, 1km from the Varadero bridge at Vía Blanca (☎45 66 8060 ext. 661), is predominantly a docking station rather than a boat-trip departure point, with 112 berths, though it does organize fishing trips (see box, p.202).

3

---

bands, thus blurring the lines between club nights and live music shows, but they will almost always feature a DJ at some stage in proceedings and often for the whole night. Expect the same mix of reggaeton, salsa, Latin- and Euro-dance and pop at all of them.

La Bamba Hotel Tuxpán, Ave. de las Américas ☎45 66 7560. One of the largest and best-known hotel nightclubs, which caters predominantly to its own guests but does sometimes attract the crowds with its standard music policy of pop, salsa and reggaeton. Entry $5CUC. Daily 11pm–3am.

Mambo Club Carretera Las Morlas Km 14 ☎45 66 8565. Beyond the Marina Chapelín and attached to the *Aguas Azules* hotel, this is one of the largest clubs in Varadero where a combination of live bands and DJs spinning salsa and generic dance music usually manage to cook up quite a storm with the encouraging mix of Cuban and foreign punters. Entry $10CUC. Tues–Sun 11pm–5am.

Palacio de la Rumba Ave. de las Américas ☎45 66 8210. Often referred to simply as *La Rumba* and as lively a night as anywhere in Varadero, this is also one of the area's biggest and best-designed venues. It's just beyond the *Bella Costa* hotel. Entry $10CUC. Daily 11pm–3am.

DANCE SHOWS AND CABARETS

Cabarets The most popular alternative to clubs are the cabarets, with their displays of kitsch glamour, over-sentimental crooners and semi-naked dancers. The most famous Cuban cabaret, the *Tropicana*, has a branch just a short drive away in Matanzas, near the Río Canímar (see

p.219), which knocks the socks off anything on the peninsula for sheer scale.

Cabaret Continental Varadero Internacional, Ave. de las Américas ☎45 66 7038. Varadero's best and most famous cabaret. A significant part of the attraction is the building interior, a memorable preservation of 1950s kitsch and the perfect setting for the flamboyance of the cabaret. This venue also puts on DJ nights, with reggaeton usually dominating the playlist, and there's always a disco after the show. $25CUC or $40CUC with dinner. Tues–Sun 10pm–3.30am.

La Comparsita Centro Cultural Artex, Calle 60 e/ Ave. 2da y Ave. 3ra ☎45 66 7415. This relatively professional stage venue attracts a lively mix of locals and tourists. Though performances are often in the cabaret spirit they don't always get the full treatment, so some nights you might get the wailing vocalist but without the dancing girls, and other nights something more subdued altogether. Live music and dance are, however, a mainstay. $5CUC for bar, $10CUC for performances including unlimited drinks. Daily 10.30pm–3am.

Cueva del Pirata Ave. del Sur ☎45 66 7751. The show and the disco that follows take place in a cave next to the entrance of *Allegro Varadero*, which makes for a different atmosphere. The performers dress as pirates for a slight twist on the usual dress code. $10CUC. Mon–Sat 11pm–3am.

Eco Disco Mediterráneo Calle 54 e/ Ave. 1ra y Ave. Playa. Although this is one of Varadero's least glamorous and glitzy cabarets, set in the courtyard of a modest restaurant and bar complex, you'll find more local flavour

3

VARADERO BAILA

Every year, usually in the second week of July, Varadero hosts the **International Festival of Salsa**, also known as **Varadero Baila**, a week-long programme of concerts, dance shows and classes organized by the national "cultural tourism" agency Paradiso (⊛ paradiso.cu) and Baila en Cuba (⊛ bailaencuba.com). Dancers of all abilities as well as complete beginners can enrol on the festival's five-day dance courses, while the programme of concerts and events are spread around a half-dozen or so venues including the Academia Baile en Cuba (see box opposite) and a number of the nightclubs. Prices start at $175CUC for a set of classes and entry to a limited number of concerts. To make enquiries in person go to the Paradiso office at Calle 26 e/ Ave. 1ra y Ave. 2da (☎ 45 61 4758).

---

here than at any of the hotel shows. If you want to mix it up with the Cubans, head here. Shows are usually followed by a disco. $5–10CUC. Tues–Sat 10pm–3am.

LIVE MUSIC VENUES

The Beatles Ave. 1ra e/ 58 y 59 ☎ 45 66 7329. Most nights, the patio of this novelty restaurant is the stage for tribute bands playing homages not just to the Beatles but other rock and pop gods from Led Zeppelin and Pink Floyd to AC/DC and Guns N' Roses. The musicians are pretty accomplished and there's usually an enthusiastic crowd. Free entry. Daily 10pm–12.30am.

★ **Casa de la Música** Ave. Playa no.4206 e/ 42 y 43 ☎ 45 66 7568 ext. 111. Varadero's top venue for reliably high-quality live music, this converted cinema usually has comedy shows earlier in the week and, from Thurs to Sun,

concerts covering a broad variety of mostly Cuban styles, from traditional son and bolero to modern salsa and jazz. Usually $10CUC, more when top national bands perform. It's advisable to book advance tickets in July & Aug (box office Tues–Sun 8.30am–12.30pm). Over 18s only. Tues–Sun 10.30pm–3am.

★ **Plaza América Convention Center** Autopista del Sur Km 7 ☎ 45 66 8181. The best live music show in Varadero features various incarnations of the Buena Vista Social Club performing in the Salón Plenario of the convention centre adjoining Varadero's largest shopping mall. Shows usually feature a selection of some of the best-known songs from the world famous albums that reignited a global appetite for traditional Cuban music. Entry $22CUC. Wed 10–11.30pm.

SPORTS AND RECREATION

There are no **spectator sport** venues in Varadero – the nearest baseball stadium is in the city of Matanzas – but there are a number of participatory activities, not all of which are the sole domain of hotel guests.

LEISURE COMPLEXES

Complejo Recreativo Record Ave. Playa esq. 46 ☎ 45 61 4880. Features a pool hall ($3CUC per game), a snack bar and a bowling alley ($2CUC per person, per game). Daily 9am–2am.

Todo en Uno Calle 54 esq. Autopista del Sur ☎ 45 66 8290. A small amusement park featuring bumper cars, a carousel and a diminutive roller coaster (all $1CUC per ride) as well as a small videogames arcade, pool tables ($4CUC/hr), numerous fast-food outlets, a couple of shops and a four-lane bowling alley. Park Mon–Thurs 11am–11pm, Fri–Sun 11am–11.30pm; bowling alley 24hr.

WATERSPORTS

Essentials For watersports equipment you're largely dependent on the hotels, many of which have their own watersports clubs. Snorkelling is barely worth bothering with near the beach as there's little to see, but there are plenty of boat trips (see p.203) with snorkelling at the nearby cays. You can also go scuba diving (see box, p.206) or fishing (see box, p.200).

Barracuda Scuba Diving Centre Ave. 1ra e/ 58 y 59 ☎ 45 66 7072. Varadero's only non-hotel watersports club rents out aqua bikes ($5CUC/hr), catamarans ($12CUC/hr), kayaks ($3–5CUC/hr) and other bits and pieces of equipment plus sun chairs ($2CUC/day) and parasols ($3CUC/day. Daily 8am–5pm.

GOLF AND MINI-GOLF

El Golfito Ave. 1ra e/ 41 y 42 ☎ 45 61 4887. Mini-golf at a small roadside café for just $0.50CUC a game. 24hr.

Varadero Golf Club ☎ 45 66 7388, ⊛ varaderogolfclub .com. One of only two courses in Cuba, with eighteen holes in a narrow 3.5km strip alongside the Autopista del Sur; the caddy house and golf shop right next to the *Mansión Xanadú* hotel. Green fees are $48CUC for nine holes or $70CUC for all eighteen, to go with compulsory golf-cart rental ($30CUC); you can rent a set of clubs for $50CUC. There are also classes (from $30CUC/50min), and you can buy packages of rounds at a discount: five rounds, for example, will cost you $345CUC with green fees and golf cart included.

VARADERO DANCE CLASSES

Many of Varadero's larger hotels provide **salsa classes** as part of their entertainment package, and you can also take classes covering all Cuban dance styles at the excellent new **Academia Baile en Cuba,** Ave. 1ra e/ 34 y 35 (daily 8am–6pm), which opened in 2012 and offers anything from a two-hour class ($15CUC) to week-long courses tailored to your preferences. You book through the local branch of Paradiso (Calle 26 e/ Ave. 1ra y Ave. 2da, ☎45 61 4758, 61 4759 and 61 2506), the national "cultural tourism" agency that runs the centre.

TENNIS

La Raqueta Dorada Ave. 1ra e/ 37 y 38. An outdoor synthetic-surface court that's free to use, though you need your own racquet and balls. Daily 9am–noon & 2–6pm.

SKYDIVING AND ULTRALIGHT FLIGHTS

Centro Internacional de Paracaidismo Vía Blanca ☎45 66 7256, ✉skygators@cubairsports.itgo.com. Some 1.5km from Varadero bridge, this centre offers skydiving over Varadero for $160CUC, which includes the transfer from your hotel, a class and the drop itself, in tandem with the instructor. Flights, in old Russian biplanes or helicopters, are an experience in themselves, with stunning perspectives over the peninsula. Jumps usually take place at altitudes between 2500 and 3000m with freefall of around thirty seconds before the parachute opens. Ultralight flights can also be arranged and cost between $30CUC and $300CUC. The availability of aircraft is not guaranteed and the centre sometimes closes for months at a time. Bookings are taken directly or through Cubanacán or Cubatur (see p.199).

SHOPPING

Aside from the half-dozen or so **arts and crafts** markets along Avenida Primera, and the cigar shops in the town and the hotels, Varadero's shops are generally worth a quick browse only if you're passing. Note that market opening times vary and sometimes close an hour or two earlier than stated below in low season. Self-caterers have their work cut out, with no big **supermarkets** in the town or any fresh food markets on the entire peninsula. There are a few small convenience stores along Avenida Primera and in some of the hotels but the pickings are slim.

SUPERMARKETS

Grossery Plaza América Autopista del Sur Km 7 ☎45 66 7869. Inside the Plaza América mall, this is Varadero's largest and best supermarket, with a fresh meat counter and lots of packet-food but very little fresh vegetables or fruit. Daily 10am–8.30pm.

ARTS AND CRAFTS

Feria Los Caneyes Ave. 1ra e/ 51 y 52. Around thirty stalls with a good selection of jewellery and hand-carved wooden ornaments, plus all the other usual Cuban commercial arts and crafts. Daily 9am–7pm.

Galería de Arte Varadero Ave. 1ra e/ 59 y 60 ☎45 66 8260. A more highbrow option than most arts and crafts vendors, with framed paintings, lithographs, jewellery and screen prints starting at around $5CUC and going into the hundreds. Daily 9am–7pm.

Gran Feria La Epoca Ave. 1ra esq. 47. This smallish market is one of the better places in town for a broad selection of handmade products, from jewellery to ornamental drums and painted wall plaques. Daily 9am–7pm.

Plaza Alegria Ave. 1ra e/ 47 y 48. This indoor market with over thirty stalls is one of Varadero's best places to buy handmade jewellery. You'll also find plenty of paintings as well as the usual selection of carved wooden figures and statuettes, T-shirts and leather goods. Daily 9am–7pm.

Plaza de Artesanos Ave. 1ra e/ 15 y 16. Varadero's best and biggest craft market, with over one hundred stalls around a little roadside square selling all the trademark Cuban crafts, textiles and gift items: wooden statuettes, lace shawls, coral necklaces, cigar boxes and Che T-shirts as well as bags and ceramics. Daily 8am–6pm.

Taller de Cerámica Ave. 1ra e/ esq. 60 ☎45 66 7829. You can watch pottery being made in the busy workshop here, then buy a piece in the little shop where everything for sale is a good-quality original and not the usual tourist tat. Daily 8.30am–7pm.

CIGARS AND RUM

Casa del Habano Ave. 1ra e/ 63 y 64 ☎45 66 7843. Varadero's outstanding cigar store, with an impressive selection of all the major brands as well as all sorts of smoking paraphernalia, a smokers' lounge, a separate section selling rum and coffee, and an upstairs bar (see p.202). Daily 9am–9pm.

Casa del Habano Mi Cuba Ave. 1ra esq. 39 ☎45 61 4719. The choice of cigars here is only average but the options for where you smoke them are a cut above: choose between the upstairs smokers' lounge, the leather

3

SCUBA DIVING IN VARADERO

There are far superior dive sites around Cuba than the ones off the Varadero coast, but with several **diving clubs** on the peninsula this is one of the best-served areas for diving . The clubs below can offer diving equipment and instruction, and can arrange excursions to elsewhere in the province, commonly to the Península de Zapata in southern Matanzas (see p.232). Most of the local dive sites are on the coral reefs around the offshore cays to the east of Varadero, such as **Cayo Blanco** and **Cayo Piedras**, where there are various wrecks, and also at **Playa Coral**, with a coral reef just 30m from the shore along the coast towards Matanzas. As well as the standard coral reef visits, clubs usually offer night- and cave-dives, the latter often in the **Cueva de Saturno** to the west of Varadero, not far off the Vía Blanca (see p.209). The **prices** for diving are the same at three of the four clubs listed below; the Marina Gaviota Varadero is slightly cheaper. Basic packages are $50CUC for a single-tank dive or $70CUC with two tanks, reduced slightly if you supply your own equipment. **Multiple dive packages** include six for $170CUC and ten for $258CUC. The Acua Diving Centre on Avenida Kawama had closed at the time of writing but may reopen.

DIVING CLUBS

Barracuda Scuba Diving Centre Ave. 1ra e/ 58 y 59 ☎45 66 7072. Operating in partnership with the Marina Chapelín (see p.203), this club offers a comprehensive programme of diving including ACUC courses for advanced divers and instructors. It's also the best organized for first-time divers, with beginners' classes starting at $70CUC for a theory class, a lesson in the club's own swimming pool and then a sea dive.

Marina Gaviota Scuba Diving Centre Autopista del Sur y final ☎45 66 7755 & 7756. A well-equipped and very professionally run dive club. A single dive costs $50CUC, two dives $50CUC, five $130CUC and ten $230CUC. Night dives ($50CUC) and various ACUC courses are also offered.

three-piece suite downstairs or a bar with a leafy outdoor terrace. Daily 9am–9pm.

★ **Casa del Ron** Ave. 1ra e/ 62 y 63 ☎45 66 8393. As well as stocking the best selection of rum in Varadero, this is one of the peninsula's most novel shops. A captivating model of an early twentieth-century Cuban rum factory occupies almost the whole front room, while in the back there's a 1920s-era bar set up solely for try-before-you-buy purposes. Daily 9am–9pm.

Casa del Tabaco Ave. 1ra esq. 27 ☎45 66 7872. A small *tabaquería* where you can also sometimes watch cigars being made on a table out the front. Daily 9am–9pm.

BOOKS AND MUSIC

Arte Cubano Ave. 1ra esq. 12 ☎45 66 8172. A packed gift shop with one of the better selections of CDs in Varadero. Daily 9am–8pm.

La Casa Ave. 1ra esq. 59 ☎45 61 4584. A two-floor ranch-style building with too much space for its selection of books, mostly on revolutionary and political themes, Cuban wildlife and photography. Also stocks CDs, Cuban film posters and other pictures. Daily 9am–8pm.

DIRECTORY

Banks and money Banks include Banco Financiero Internacional, Ave. 1ra e/ 32 y 33, entrance on Ave. Playa (Mon–Fri 9am–7pm), and Ave. Kawama, near the *Hotel Kawama* (Mon–Fri 9am–12.30pm & 1.30–3pm); and Banco de Crédito y Comercio, Ave. 1ra esq. 36 (Mon–Fri

Librería Hanoí Ave. 1ra esq. 44 ☎45 61 2694. The cramped premises house a limited selection of mostly Cuban political literature and fiction which nevertheless constitute the biggest selection of new books in Varadero. Daily 9am–8.30pm.

SHOPPING CENTRES AND MALLS

Centro Comercial Caimán Ave. 1ra e/ 61 y 62 ☎45 66 8214. Half a dozen shops gathered around a pleasant outdoor space and selling toys, clothes, shoes, rum, perfume and groceries. Daily 9am–9pm.

Centro Comercial Hicacos Parque de las 8000 Taquillas, Ave. 1ra e/ 44 y 46 ☎45 66 8166. The largest shopping complex in the town area, with around a dozen fairly basic shops, though there is a decent cigar place and one of the few photography shops around. Daily 10am–10pm.

Plaza América Autopista del Sur Km 9 ☎45 66 8181. The slickest shopping centre in Varadero, with restaurants, clothing and jewellery boutiques, arts, crafts, T-shirts and souvenirs, a large cigar shop, a small bookshop, the area's best CD retailer and the largest supermarket on the peninsula. Daily 9am–9pm.

9am–3pm & Sat 9–11am). The CADECA *casas de cambio* are at the Centro Comercial Hicacos (daily 9am–7pm) and Ave. 1ra esq. 59 (Mon–Sat 8am–5pm, Sun 8am–noon). There are ATMs at the Banco de Crédito y Comercio and at Plaza América. For financial emergencies, including loss of credit cards or insurance matters, go to Asistur, Edificio Marbella, apto.6, Ave. 1ra no.4201 e/ 42 y 43 (☎45 66 7277).

Consulates Canadian Consulate, Calle 13 no.422 e/ Camino del March y Ave. 1ra (☎45 66 7395 & 61 2078). All other consulates and embassies are in Havana (see p.58).

Immigration and visas The Immigration office, for visa extensions and passport matters, is at Calle 39 esq. Ave. 1ra (Mon–Fri 9am–4pm; ☎45 61 3494). Tourist cards can also be extended through some hotels and information centres.

Internet The ETECSA Centro de Llamadas at Ave. 1ra y 30 (8.30am–7pm; $6CUC/hr) has internet facilities. The Sala de Telecomunicaciones (daily 8.30am–7pm; $6CUC/30min) at the Plaza América shopping mall has telephone booths and a couple of PCs for painfully slow internet use.

Left luggage Terminal de Omnibus, Calle 36 esq. Autopista del Sur ($1CUC per item).

Library Biblioteca José Smith Comas, Calle 33 e/ Ave. 1ra y Ave. 3ra ☎45 61 2358 (Mon–Fri 8am–7pm, Sat 9am–5pm). A selection of English literature, including a surprisingly good stock of Penguins.

Medical Clínica Internacional de Varadero at Ave. 1ra y 61 (☎45 66 7710), which includes the best-stocked pharmacy in Varadero, is open 24hr. At the other end of town is another reasonable pharmacy at Ave. Kawama e/ 2 y 3 (daily 9am–7pm). The nearest major hospital is in Matanzas (see p.218). For an ambulance call ☎45 61 2950.

Police ☎106. Police station at Calle 39 esq. Ave. 1ra.

Post office Branches Ave. 1ra e/ 36 y 37 and the Plaza América shopping mall (both Mon–Sat 8am–6pm). Many hotels also have their own post office service.

Telephone The ETECSA Centro de Llamadas is at Ave. 1ra y 30 (24hr). There are also ETECSA phone cabins at Ave. 1ra esq. 15, Ave. 1ra e/ 46 y 47 and Ave. Kawama e/ 5 y 6. For mobile phone products and services go to Cubacel at Ave. 1ra esq. 42 (Mon–Sat 8.30am–4pm).

Cárdenas

Ten kilometres southeast of Varadero and home to much of the peninsula's workforce, **CÁRDENAS** offers a taste of Cuban life away from the tourist spotlight, with a much stronger sense of history and a town centre dotted with crumbling colonial and neo-colonial buildings. Though it's on the coast, Cárdenas doesn't feel like a seaside town since most of its shoreline, hugging the **Bay of Cárdenas**, is an industrial zone. Few visitors are tempted to spend more than a day here, and the town is quite run down, its battered roads full of potholes, but the one or two excellent *casas particulares* are enough in themselves to merit an overnight stay. The **Catedral de la Inmaculada Concepción** is Cárdenas' most distinguished historic building; its creditable museums, including the **Museo a la Batalla de Ideas**, with its fantastic views of the town, are on or right next to the Parque José Antonio Echeverría, the most inviting square in the city, though far less lively than **Plaza Malacoff**, the bustling market square.

Brief history

Founded in 1828 and known as the **Ciudad Bandera** (Flag City), it was here in 1850 that what became the national flag was first raised by the Venezuelan General Narciso López and his troops, who had disembarked at Cárdenas in a US-backed attempt to spark a revolt against Spanish rule and clear the way for annexation. The attempt failed, but the flag's design was later adopted by the independence movement. The town's more recent claim to fame is as the birthplace of **Elian González**, the young boy who came to symbolize the ideological conflict between the US and Cuba during a 1999 custody battle of unusual geopolitical significance. The government wasted no time in setting up a **museum** here to commemorate their perceived triumph when Elian was returned to his home town.

ORIENTATION

Cárdenas revolves around **Avenida Céspedes**, running right down the centre of town towards the dilapidated port. Anything running parallel with it is also an avenue, while the calles run perpendicular to it, with **Calle 13** crossing Avenida Céspedes bang in the centre of town. However, locals refer to the old street names which the numbers replaced.

Parque Colón

Ave. Céspedes e/ 8 y 9

Cárdenas's main square, run-down **Parque Colón** is bisected by the city's main street and is conducive to neither a sit-down nor a stroll around. The only reason to stop here is to gawp at the noble but withered **Catedral de la Inmaculada Concepción**, the grandest building in the city, dating from 1846. Resembling twin lighthouses, two stone towers flank the body of the building and a dome pokes its head above the treetops. Unfortunately, the cathedral is almost always closed. In front of it is an elevated **statue** of a romantic-looking Columbus with a globe at his feet. Sculpted in 1862, it's said to be the oldest statue of the explorer in the whole of the Americas.

Parque José Antonio Echeverría

Two blocks from Avenida Céspedes, southeast along Calle 12, is plain but tranquil **Parque José Antonio Echeverría**, the archetypal town square that Parque Colón fails to be, dotted with trees and benches and enclosed by buildings on all sides. The real reason to visit, though, is for the three surrounding museums.

Museo Oscar María de Rojas

Calle 13 e/ Ave. 4 y Ave. 6 • Tues & Fri 8.30am–6pm, Wed, Thurs & Sat 9am–6pm, Sun 9am–1pm • $5CUC • ☎ 45 52 2417

Founded in 1900 and one of the oldest museums in the country, the **Museo Oscar María de Rojas**, occupying the entire southwestern side of Parque José Antonio Echeverría, brings together a jamboree of coins, medals, bugs, butterflies and weapons along with other seemingly random collections across its thirteen rooms. By far the most engaging and substantial sections are the two rooms of pre-Columbian Cuban and Latin American artefacts. Among the archeological finds displayed are human skeletal remains found on the island, dating back almost 5800 years, a bizarre shrunken head from southern Ecuador, examples of Mayan art and some stone idols from Mexico.

Museo José Antonio Echeverría

Ave. 4 e/ 12 y 13 • Tues–Sat 9am–6pm, Sun 9am–noon • $1CUC • ☎ 45 52 4145

On the northwestern side of Parque José Antonio Echeverría is the relatively illuminating **Museo José Antonio Echeverría**, set in the birthplace of the 1950s anti-Batista student leader and activist, a statue of whom stands casually, hand in pocket, in the square outside. Considered one of the martyrs of the Revolution, Echeverría and several of his comrades were shot and killed by Batista's police during an attack on the Presidential Palace in Havana on March 13, 1957. The museum charts his life growing up in Cárdenas and his protest years in Havana, as well as examining the wider role of the Federation of University Students (FEU) in Cuba, of which Echeverría became president in 1954. You can see his parents' pink 1954 Chrysler Windsor Deluxe parked in the courtyard.

Museo a la Batalla de Ideas

Ave. 6 esq. 12 • Tues–Sat 9am–noon & 1–5pm, Sun 9am–noon • $2CUC; guided tour $2CUC; rooftop viewing platform $1CUC • ☎ 45 52 7599.

Touching the corner of the Parque José Antonio Echeverría, the propagandist **Museo a la Batalla de Ideas** is set in a cheery yellow fortress of a building which is actually a nineteenth-century fire station. As much a symbol of victory as a museum, it was opened in June 2001 to mark the triumph claimed by Fidel Castro over the US when **Elian González**, the 6-year-old boy who came to personify the political and theoretical conflict between the US and Cuba, was repatriated from Florida. The whole Elian episode is charted in photographs with poster boards decrying US interference in

Cuban affairs. There are also insights into the national education system, like the Cuban classroom motto "*Seremos como el Che*" ("We will be like Che"). Be sure to venture upstairs to the rooftop **viewing platform** looking over the whole city and beyond – well worth the extra charge. A member of staff is often on hand to point out the various sights, including an otherwise rarely seen perspective, on the distant horizon, of the Varadero peninsula.

Plaza Malacoff
Calle 12 e/ Ave. 3 y 5

Since its foundation in 1859, curious-looking **Plaza Malacoff** has hosted the stalls and booths that make up the city's main **food market**. The centre of this old market square is occupied by a 15m-high, cross-shaped building consisting of four two-storey hallways and a large iron-and-zinc dome in the centre, which gives it the appearance of a run-down Islamic temple. While the square has seen better days, it is still full of life and perhaps the best place in Cárdenas to find some genuine local flavour.

3

ARRIVAL AND DEPARTURE
CÁRDENAS

By train Trains pull in at the station on Ave. 8 y Calle 5 (☎45 52 1362), a few blocks from the city centre.
Destinations Colón (2 daily; 1hr 30min); Jovellanos (runs according to availability of fuel; 1hr).
By bus The interprovincial bus terminal is at Ave. Céspedes esq. Calle 22 (☎45 52 1214) and serves mainly Astro buses. The cheapest way to get here from Varadero is to catch the Víazul coach destined for Trinidad, which passes through Cárdenas ($6CUC), and stops either at the terminal or drops off passengers on Avenida Céspedes. Local buses navigating this part of the province operate from the smaller terminal on Calle 13 esq. Ave. 13 (☎45

52 4958). There is a steady stream of workers' buses between Cárdenas and Varadero, and though these don't officially seat tourists most drivers will accept $1CUC to let you on board. They leave from Calle 13 between Avenida 1 and 3, a block away from Avenida Cespedes.
Destinations (Víazul) Cienfuegos (2 daily; 4hr 20min & 2hr 10min); Jagüey Grande, near Península de Zapata (2 daily; 1hr 10min); Santa Clara (1 daily; 2hr 35min); Trinidad (2 daily; 5hr 25min & 3hr 35min).
By car or scooter Arriving by car or scooter couldn't be easier as the main road from Varadero cuts directly into the centre of town.

ACCOMMODATION

Hostal Angelo's Ave. 14 no.656 e/ 14 y 15 ☎45 52 2451, ✉estangel01@yahoo.es. The impressive and extensive outdoor space here provides an oasis of leafy luxury amid the grime of central Cárdenas. Not only is there a small bathing pool but also a separate jacuzzi, a lovely tree and shrub-lined dining area and a simple concrete bar. Extrovert owner Angelo, with 25 years of work experience in Varadero hotels, provides three neat rooms, one with a theatrical ornate bathroom. **$30CUC**

Hostal El Parque Ave. 4 no.609 e/ 13 y 14 ☎45 52 1926, ✦hostalcubacardenas.com. A block from the Parque José Antonio Echeverría, the two comfy rooms here come well equipped, there's a dinky roof terrace full of plants overlooking the street and a lovely little patio area covered by a thatched palm-leaf canopy. The family is immersed in Afro–Cuban religious music and practices and invite guests to participate. **$30CUC**

CUEVA DE SATURNO
Just by the road connecting Juan Gualberto Gómez Airport to the Vía Blanca, a few hundred metres south from the Vía Blanca itself, is the **Cueva de Saturno** (daily 9.30am–5.20pm; $5CUC, snorkel equipment $1CUC; ☎45 25 3833), a flooded cave where you can snorkel and scuba dive. Modest in comparison to the Cuevas de Bellamar (see p.218) nearer Matanzas, the cave isn't worth going out of your way for unless you intend to dive – in which case you'll need to pre-book a visit with one of Varadero's dive clubs (see p.206) – but it does make a good stopoff between Varadero and Matanzas. You can walk down through the impressive gaping mouth of the cave to the pool at the bottom and take a swim or have a snorkel. A snack bar has been built near the steps down into the cave, mostly to serve the organized visits that regularly come here from Matanzas and Varadero.

EATING, DRINKING AND NIGHTLIFE

Café Espriu Parque José Antonio Echeverría, Calle 12 e/ Ave. 4 y Ave. 6 ☎ 45 52 3273. Small and simple place, where the smoked pork loin, shrimps in tomato sauce and several other meat and seafood dishes all cost less than $4CUC. Daily 9.30am–10pm.

D'Alonso Ave. Céspedes e/ 15 y 16 ☎ 45 52 3494. One of the few paladars in Cuba serving Japanese food, though Cuban dishes are available too. The indoor seating is clustered around the two teppanyaki grills from which the mains ($2.15–5.75CUC) are served. There's also sushi ($2.75CUC) and tempura ($1.60–2.80CUC). Daily noon–late.

Las Palmas Ave. Céspedes no.528 esq. Calle 16 ☎ 45 52 3762. The city's standout nightlife venue is the large courtyard of this pseudo-oriental Spanish villa, packed out at the weekends with a young crowd here to see popular music and dance routines performed by local talent. Entry $3CUP. Usually Wed–Sun evenings.

Studio 55 Parque José Antonio Echeverría, Calle 12 e/ Ave. 4 y Ave. 6 (no phone). This cosy little semi-outdoor café-bar centred around a handsome palm tree offers the most pleasant eating and drinking environment in the city, and serves serving decent *comida criolla*. Mon–Thurs & Sun 11am–11pm, Fri & Sat 11am–2am.

Matanzas

One of the closest and easiest day-trip destinations from Varadero is **MATANZAS**, the biggest and most interesting city in the province of the same name and just 25km west along the coast from the beach resort. Clustered on the hillsides around a large bay and endowed with several of its own beaches, albeit small and scrappy ones, the city's setting is perhaps its greatest asset, though as with much else about the place, this remains largely unexploited. This is slowly changing, however, as Matanzas is finally being dragged out of the doldrums via investment in the previously neglected city centre, where many of the most prominent buildings are undergoing renovations. For now, though, the city itself remains less appealing than the attractions on its outskirts and nearby, and one or two nights here usually suffices.

The best place to get your bearings – but also where you're most likely to be pestered by *jineteros* – is the more central of Matanzas' two main plazas, the **Parque de la Libertad**, home to the fantastically well-preserved **Museo Farmacéutico Matanzas**. Though the other main square, the **Plaza de la Vigía**, is less inviting, its worth visiting for the **Museo Provincial** and the stately, still functioning **Teatro Sauto**. Beyond the plazas and the main street, **Calle 85** (known to locals as Medio), the slightly claustrophobic city centre quickly becomes a series of similar-looking streets plagued by drainage problems, and tangible focal points are few and far between until you reach **Monserrate** on the edge of town, and the lovely views of the bay and city it provides.

Parque de la Libertad

A traditional Spanish-style plaza, the **Parque de la Libertad** is a welcome open space amid the city's claustrophobic streets. The mostly colonial and neo-colonial buildings around the square, many of them under renovation, allow for only a passing perusal, such as the provincial government headquarters from 1853, which occupies the entire east side, and the old *casino* building, a traditional Spanish social club, built in 1835 and now housing a library.

STREET NAMES

As with elsewhere in Cuba, streets in Matanzas are known by both **names** and **numbers**. Most Cuban maps and the signs on the streets themselves use the numbers but almost all locals refer to the older names. In this guide we show the old names in brackets.

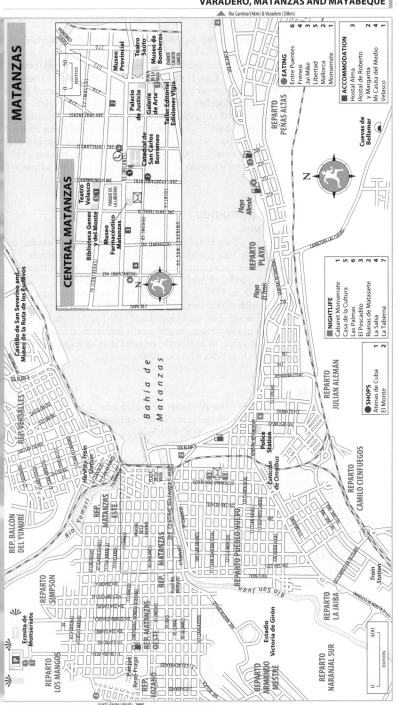

Río Canímar (4km) & Varadero (30km)

MATANZAS

CENTRAL MATANZAS

0   50
metres

Teatro Sauto

Museo Provincial

Museo de Bomberos

Palacio de Justicia

Galería de Arte

Taller Editorial Ediciones Vigía

Catedral de San Carlos Borromeo

Teatro Velasco

PARQUE DE LA LIBERTAD

Biblioteca Gener y del Monte

Museo Farmacéutico Matanzas

0   400
metres

Castillo de San Severino and Museo de la Ruta de los Esclavos

Bahía de Matanzas

REP. VERSALLES

Hershey Train Station

REP. BALCÓN DEL YUMURÍ

Río Yumurí

REP. MATANZAS ESTE

Ermita de Monserrate

REPARTO SIMPSON

REPARTO LOS MANGOS

Parque René Fraga

REP. LOZANO

REP. MATANZAS OESTE

REP. MATANZAS

Plaza del Mercado

Estadio Victoria de Girón

REPARTO ARMANDO MESTRE

REPARTO NARANJAL SUR

Yumurí Valley (2km)

Police Station

REPARTO JULIAN ALEMÁN

REPARTO PUEBLO NUEVO

Estación de Omnibus

REPARTO CAMILO CIENFUEGOS

Río San Juan

Train Station

REPARTO LA JAIBA

Playa Allende

Playa El Tenis

REPARTO PLAYA

Cuevas de Bellamar

REPARTO PEÑAS ALTAS

CARRETERA LAS CUEVAS

N

● EATING
Entre Puentes	6
Frenesí	4
Jai Mike	3
Libertad	5
Mallorca	2
Monserrate	1

■ ACCOMMODATION
Hostal Alma	3
Hostal de Roberto y Margarita	2
Mi Casita del Medio	4
Velasco	1

■ NIGHTLIFE
Cabaret Monserrate	1
Casa de la Cultura	5
Las Palmas	6
El Pescadito	3
Ruinas de Matasiete	4
La Salsa	2
La Taberna	7

● SHOPS
Atenas de Cuba	1
El Monte	2

3

Museo Farmacéutico Matanzas

Calle 83 (Milanés) e/ 288 (Ayuntamiento) y 290 (Santa Teresa) • Mon–Sat 10am–5pm, Sun 10am–2pm • $2CUC, or $3CUC including guided tour, photos permitted • ☎ 45 24 3479

One of the few essential places to visit in the city, the **Museo Farmacéutico Matanzas** was founded in 1882 by two doctors, Juan Fermín de Figueroa and Ernesto Triolet, and functioned as a pharmacy right up until May 1964, when it was converted into a museum. The hundreds of French porcelain jars lining the shelves and cabinets, along with the many medicine bottles (and even the medicines still inside them) are originals, making it hard to believe business ever stopped. Many of the concoctions were made in the laboratory at the back of the building, using formulae listed in one of the 55 recipe books kept in the compact but comprehensive **library**. You can't fail to spot the fabulous old cash till, which looks as though it should have been driven by a steam engine.

Catedral de San Carlos Borromeo

Calle 282 (Ayuntamiento) e/ 83 (Milanés) y 85 (Medio)

A block east towards the bay from Parque de la Libertad is the often-closed **Catedral de San Carlos Borromeo**, whose heavy frame, with its detailed Neoclassical exterior, is squeezed in between the two busiest streets in the city centre. One of the first buildings in Matanzas, it was founded in 1693 and originally made of wood which, unsurprisingly, didn't last. Rebuilt in 1755, it has not survived the last two and a half centuries entirely intact. The patchwork interior reveals the neglect which so much of the city's historic architecture has suffered, the chipped and faded paintwork contrasting with sporadic areas of restoration, mostly on the high arches. There is still much left of historic and artistic value, including the original altar, though the more modern-style paintings are slightly at odds with everything else.

Plaza de la Vigía

Two blocks from Catedral de San Carlos Borromeo and right next to the river, humble **Plaza de la Vigía** struggles for space with the heavy traffic running along one side. Little more than a road junction, the plaza features a swashbuckling statue of a rebel from the Wars of Independence on a concrete island in the centre.

Museo de Bomberos

Plaza de la Vigía • Tues–Fri 9am–noon & 1–4pm, Sat 9–11am • Free

Flanking the bay side of Plaza de la Vigía is an ornate but austere Neoclassical fire station, which also houses the simple **Museo de Bomberos**. It's worth peering inside to see the old fire engines, including one from 1888, still in perfect working order, alongside displays of uniforms and photographs.

Taller Editorial Ediciones Vigía

Plaza de la Vigía • Mon–Fri 8.30am–5pm • Free • ☎ 45 24 4845

In the corner of Plaza de la Vigía nearest the river, the **Taller Editorial Ediciones Vigía** may not look like much at first sight, but its humble interior belies its unique purpose. The home of a publishing cooperative founded in 1985, this intriguing little workshop produces books as works of art and craft. Dotted about the two floors are small cases containing the finished articles, each a one-off and most of them heavily illustrated. Upstairs are paintings and drawings and, most strikingly, a huge **mural** of Matanzas made entirely of paper. Though the books are for sale (prices by negotiation) there is little sense of commercialism here and while you're unlikely to spend much time inside, the friendly staff, sense of creativity and the books themselves make a visit here memorable.

Teatro Sauto

Plaza de la Vigía • ☏ 45 24 2721

Facing the ceremonious-looking pink Palacio de Justicia, the august **Teatro Sauto** is one of the city's best-preserved historic monuments and its most prestigious cultural institution. You can tour the theatre outside performance times, normally by joining an organized excursion from Varadero, but it's worth asking inside for an impromptu tour if you can find a member of staff in the reception area. Grand but lacking in decorative detail, the dignified Neoclassical exterior belies the more elaborate **interior**, whose main hall features a painted ceiling depicting the muses of Greek mythology, which leads into an Italianate three-tier auditorium.

Museo Provincial

Calle 83 (Milanés) esq. 272 (Magdalena) • Tues–Sat 9.30am–noon & 1–5pm, Sun 8.30am–noon • $2CUC • ☏ 45 24 3295

Just north of the Teatro Sauto, the orderly collection at the **Museo Provincial** charts the political and social history of the province. Its chronological layout – a rarity in Cuban history museums – helps to create a succinct overview of the last two hundred years in Matanzas. There are early plans and pictures of the city, including a fantastic, large-scale drawing dating from 1848; displays depicting the living and working conditions of slaves on the sugar plantations and in the mills (see box below) include a large wooden *cepo* and the leg clamps employed in the punishment of slaves.

Monserrate

Perched just above and beyond the residential neighbourhood in the northwestern corner of the city is **Monserrate**, a hilltop area of cafés and eateries centred on a recently renovated church. It's a peaceful spot where you can enjoy some of the best views in town, with the city and bay on one side and a fantastic perspective on the magnificent Yumurí Valley on the other. Seated on a large flat platform at the top of a steep slope is a humble and diminutive church, known as the **Ermita de Monserrate**. Built between 1872 and 1875 by colonists from Catalonia and the Balearic Islands, it was restored in

---

SUGAR AND SLAVERY

The **sugar industry** in Cuba, and indeed all over the Caribbean, was up until the end of the nineteenth century inextricably linked to the slave trade and **slavery** itself. It's been estimated that at least a third of the slaves in Cuba during the nineteenth century worked on sugar plantations, playing a vital role in Cuba's biggest industry and accounting for the largest single investment made by most plantation owners. **Working conditions** for slaves were even worse on the massive sugar estates than on the smaller tobacco or coffee plantations. Death from overwork was not uncommon as, unlike tobacco and coffee, levels of production were directly linked to the intensity of the labour, and plantation owners demanded the maximum possible output from their workforce. The six months of harvest were by far the most gruelling period of the year, when plantation slaves often slept for no more than four hours a day, rising as early as 2am. They were divided into gangs and those sent to cut cane in the fields might be working there for sixteen hours before they could take a significant break. A small proportion would work in the mill grinding the cane and boiling the sugar-cane juice. Accidents in the mills were frequent and punishments were harsh; it was not unknown for slaves to be left in the stocks – which took various forms but usually involved the head, hands and feet locked into the same flat wooden board – for days at a time.

Slaves were most often housed in communal **barrack buildings**, which replaced the collections of huts used in the eighteenth century, subdivided into cramped cells, with the men, who made up about two-thirds of the slave workforce, separated from the women. This was considered a more effective method of containment as there were fewer doors through which it was possible to escape.

2006. Set back from the church are several snack bars and cliff-edge cafés, with great views of the valley, and the more down-at-heel *Restaurante Monserrate* (see p.217) and *Cabaret Monserrate* (see p.217).

Parque René Fraga

On the western edge of the city centre is the **Parque René Fraga**, a concrete-dominated city park with a baseball diamond, basketball court and a dusty running track. Lively in the evenings, the park is not particularly picturesque but there are great views of the bay and it's a nice escape from the narrow streets of the centre.

The beaches

With one of the best beaches in Cuba just 25km up the road, few visitors bother with the rag-tag beaches in Matanzas. Some of them, however, do offer the chance of some secluded sunbathing, and if you're staying in the city for a couple of days you could do worse than to seek one of them out. By far the largest and most popular is **Playa El Tenis**, hemmed in by a busy viaduct and complemented by a bar and restaurant. Much smaller and more private is **Playa Allende**, hidden away below a steep slope just off General Betancourt. With overhanging trees and a sense of enclosure there is a more attractive look and feel here than at Playa El Tenis but there are no amenities and a lot less sand.

Versalles

About three blocks north from the Plaza de la Vigía, over the Puente de la Concordia, which spans the Río Yumurí, is the almost exclusively residential **Versalles** district. Few visitors to the city choose to explore this area and those who do are usually heading for the **Hershey train terminal** (see box below) or, in an industrial zone on the north face of the bay, the **Castillo de San Severino** fort and its **Museo de la Ruta de los Esclavos**.

THE HERSHEY TRAIN

In 1916 **Milton Hershey**, founder of US chocolate manufacturer Hersheys, established a sugar mill halfway between Matanzas and Havana. Built to process sugar cane for the company's chocolate factory in Pennsylvania, the renowned businessman and philanthropist also commissioned 135km of railway line to transport workers and goods to and from the mill and the workers' village he erected around it. Today the Hershey train line transports the only **electric trains** left in Cuba, which pass through the Yumurí Valley and within sight of the Atlantic coastline on their three-hour journey between the two termini, Casablanca in Havana and the Matanzas station in Versalles.

Calling at dozens of stations along the way, including the one in Camilo Cienfuegos (the post-1959 name for the tiny town of Hershey), a **ride on the Hershey train** is to experience Cuban public transport at its most idiosyncratic. Services are scheduled to leave four times a day, but there is never any guarantee of this, with reasons for delays and cancellations ranging from power failures to cattle on the line. The current tram-like interurban train cars were imported from Spain in the 1990s, though they date back to the 1940s. Rarely exceeding speeds of 40km/hr, the journey unfolds at the perfect speed for taking in the marvellous landscapes along the way, the best of them in the Yumurí Valley with its mosaic of cultivated fields, open countryside, patchwork forests and snaking rivers. Stations are more like bus stops, and some platforms are little more than a metre or two long, leaving some passengers having to literally jump off the train. To buy a **ticket**, arrive at the station an hour before the scheduled departure time. It costs $2.80CUC to travel the full length of the line between Matanzas and Havana. Full timetables are given in Chapter 1 (see p.116).

Castillo de San Severino

Tues–Sat 9am–noon & 1–4pm, Sun 9am–noon • $2CUC, $3CUC with a guide • ☎ 45 28 3259

Constructed in 1734, the **Castillo de San Severino** fort is based around a wide open central square and surrounded by a now-empty moat. With imposing, thick stone walls and broad ramparts, where three cannon still stand, this was the principal structure in the local colonial defence system, once guarding Matanzas from pirates intent on plundering the substantial wealth of the city. It functioned as a prison in the latter part of the nineteenth century but stood derelict thereafter, though hearsay has it that right up until the late 1970s political prisoners of the revolutionary regime were locked up inside. It now houses the **Museo de la Ruta de los Esclavos**. The limited displays on slavery and the slave trade reflect the fort's one-time use as a storage unit for slaves unloaded from boats on the coast below, many of them destined for nearby sugar plantations.

ARRIVAL AND DEPARTURE

MATANZAS

3

BY TRAIN

Mainline trains National network trains pull in at the nondescript station (☎ 45 29 2409) on the southern outskirts of the city, from where nothing of any convenience is within walking distance. Arrivals usually attract a few private taxis, which charge between $2CUC and $4CUC for the trip into town, but bicitaxis and horse-drawn carriages are more likely to be waiting; the latter charge around $1CUC to take you at least as far as the Plaza del Mercado; bicitaxis are usually a couple of CUCs more.

Destinations Havana (1 daily; 1hr 30min); Sancti Spíritus (3 weekly; 6hr); Santa Clara (5 weekly; 2hr 30min); Santiago (3 weekly; 12hr).

Hershey Line The other train service into the city is on the picturesque but leisurely Hershey line (see box opposite), running between Matanzas and Havana. The station (☎ 45 24 4805) is in the Versalles neighbourhood, north of the Río Yumurí, and you will most likely have to walk to the centre, which should take around 15min.

Destinations Havana Casablanca (3 daily; 4hr); Mena, Yumurí Valley (3 daily; 10min).

BY BUS

Víazul buses Interprovincial buses arrive at the Estación

de Omnibus (☎ 45 29 1473), at the junction between Calle 272, Calle 171 and General Betancourt.

Getting into town There are usually private taxis and bicitaxis waiting in the car park; the standard fare into town is $3CUC. If you have more patience and less money you could wait for the #12 bus to pass (approx every 45min; $1CUP) which will take you to the Parque de la Libertad. Walking isn't out of the question either – you should be able to get to the Parque de la Libertad within twenty minutes.

Destinations Havana (4 daily; 2hr); Varadero (4 daily; 45min).

BY CAR

If you drive to Matanzas from Varadero, be ready for the $2CUC charge at the Matanzas–Varadero tollgate on the Vía Blanca. Parking in the city can be a bit of a problem with no official car parks, though there are designated spaces at Plaza de la Vigía, where there's usually an unofficial attendant who will watch over the vehicle for a tip. This is also the best place to leave your car overnight, though if you're staying in a *casa particular* the chances are your hosts will make sure a safe spot is found for it.

FROM MATANZAS TO VARADERO, CUBAN STYLE

The going rate for a prearranged private taxi to Varadero is $25CUC, and most *casa particular* owners should be able to fix you up with a driver for this price. However, there are a number of cheaper – if less convenient – ways to get to the peninsula from here. **Taxis colectivos**, or *almendrones* (see p.31) as they are more colloquially known, bus mostly Cubans from Matanzas to Varadero and Santa Marta, the tiny town on the mainland side of the bridge over to the peninsula, for $1CUC, or around $24CUP. Unless you can convincingly disguise yourself as a Cuban you are unlikely to get away with this fare, but if you're prepared to negotiate with a driver you should be able to strike a deal for between $10CUC and $15CUC. *Almendrones*, which are invariably classic 1950s American cars, gather at the bus station; the junction where Calle 282 and Calle 83 cross, outside the cathedral; and the junction just over the train tracks where the road from the Plaza de la Vigía meets the Vía Blanca. Alternatively you can try flagging one down on General Betancourt or the Vía Blanca itself.

GETTING AROUND

By local bus Omnibus Yumurí runs a small number of buses in and around the city. By far the most useful is the #12, which leaves from outside the Museo Farmacéutico on the Parque de la Libertad roughly every 45min, between 9am and 8pm daily, linking the city centre with the Cuevas de Bellamar and Monserrate via the bus station and the Plaza del Mercado. The main central hub for local buses, including the #16 to the Río Canímar and the *Tropicana* cabaret, is on Calle 83 outside the cathedral.

By tourist bus Operating between Varadero and Matanzas, the Matanzas Bus Tour is a useful option, though

it's unreliable during low season (April–June & Sept–Dec), when it sometimes stops running altogether. In high season (Jan–March & July–Aug) it usually passes through the Parque de la Libertad four times a day on the way up to Monserrate, and also heads over the Río Canímar to and from Varadero. Tickets ($10CUC; children under 6 free) are bought on the bus itself and are valid for the whole day, allowing you to hop on and off, and go all the way to Varadero and back.

By taxi Try Cubataxi (☎45 24 4350), though they are only sporadically available.

INFORMATION , TRAVEL AGENCIES AND TOURS

Tourist information The best sources of local information are *casa particular* owners; the nearest thing to an official information office is the Havanatur travel agency (see below).

Travel agents Travel agents in Matanzas do not generally expect to be dealing with foreign nationals, and the only place you can book Víazul bus tickets for interprovincial

buses is at the bus station. You can book excursions leaving from Varadero from the new Havanatur office.

Havanatur The office is at Calle 85 (Medio) e/ 280 y 282 (Mon–Fri 8.30am–4pm; ☎45 25 3856).

Cubamar Medio e/ 290 y 292 (Mon–Sat 8.30am–4.30pm; ☎45 24 3951).

ACCOMMODATION

Hostal Alma Calle 83 (Milanés) no.29008 altos e/ 290 (Santa Teresa) y 292 (Zaragoza) ☎45 29 0857, ✉hostalalma63@gmail.com. Artistically decorated with vases, paintings, plants and other adornments, this house has plenty going for it. It's half a block from the main square. And has a large and attractive central terracotta terrace where you can sit or sunbathe, as well as a roof terrace with marvellous views across the city and three excellent rooms, one a quadruple. **$25CUC**

Hostal de Roberto y Margarita Calle 79 (Contreras) no.27608 e/ 280 (Matanzas) y 272 ☎45 24 2577, ✉roberto.margarita2000@gmail.com. One of the largest houses renting rooms in the centre of the city, this nineteenth-century residence has two airy rooms, both triples, and a garage. Almost everything here seems to be on a big scale, including the bedroom furniture and the open-air central patio. **$25CUC**

Mi Casita del Medio Calle 85 no.29215 e/ 292

(Zaragoza) y 294 (Manzaneda) ☎45 24 2703, ✉raisjo@yahoo.es. You won't find a more welcoming place to stay than at this *casa*, where owner Raisa and her two sons offer not only uncontrived friendliness but plenty of local knowledge and know-how, and fantastic meals. There are two large rooms and a spacious central courtyard. **$25CUC**

Velasco Contreras e/ 288 (Ayuntamiento) y 290 (Santa Teresa), Parque de la Libertad ☎45 25 3880 & 25 3884. Dating from 1902, this is the only hotel in Matanzas for non-Cubans, and one of the city's most stylish buildings thanks to lengthy restorations. It's saturated in early twentieth century elegance, from the refined, breezy lobby and its saloon bar to the pillared interior balcony hallways looking down on the central patio restaurant. Some of the standard rooms are a bit pokey and lack natural light – book a suite or ask to view a room before checking in. **$58CUC**

EATING

Entre Puentes Calle 294 (Manzaneda) e/ 83 (Milanés) y 85 (Medio) ☎45 28 2553. Hearty portions of value-for-money Cuban grub in a largely characterless first-floor paladar that's best approached as a chance to fill up and escape the heat at lunch time. You can have your pork a dozen different ways ($2.45–5.45CUC) or pick one of the chicken or seafood options, such as prawns in butter and garlic ($3.35CUC). Daily except Thurs noon–11pm.

Frenesi Calle 127 e/ 212 y 214 ☎45 28 1529. The

owners describe their food as fusion and the menu here is certainly a mix, albeit a strange one. Nevertheless, the chicken tempura, seafood *escabeche*, fish gratin and barbecued pork (all around $5CUC) cooked on the charcoal grill make for a refreshing eating out experience, and the cliff-edge terrace is one of the best restaurant locations in town. Daily noon–9.30pm, closed Thurs.

Jai Mike Calle 127 e/ 208 y 210 ☎52 70 3221 & ☎52 84 3705. Hidden away on a quiet street between General

Betancourt and the shoreline, this popular and atmospheric paladar serves up large pizzas ($3–7CUC), good lasagnes ($4–5.75CUC) and a set of acceptable spaghetti dishes ($3–4CUC). A thatched roof and bamboo walls provide the homespun setting. Daily noon–1pm.

Libertad Calle 79 (Contreras) e/ 288 (Ayuntamiento) y 290 (Santa Teresa), Parque de la Libertad ☎ 45 25 3880. Set in the elegant surroundings of the beautifully restored *Hotel Velasco*, the unusually short menu and the comprehensive wine and spirit list here raise expectations, but the food is a bit of a mixed bag. Nevertheless, it's the best state-run restaurant in the city – starters like Serrano ham salad are competently prepared but the mains are only average, with tropical lobster ($20CUC) and garlic shrimp ($12CUC) as likely to be served with hash browns and token salads as

anything complimentary. Daily 7.30–10am, noon–3pm, 7–10pm.

★ **Mallorca** Calle 334 no.7705 e/ 77 y 79 ☎ 45 28 3282. Among the best and most ambitious of the city's new spate of paladars. The extensive menu does feature the usual Cuban suspects but also tries to break the mould with tasty starters such as stuffed piquillo peppers ($4CUC) and mains like chicken breast filled with spinach ($4.50CUC). The back-street venue, in the west of the city, and the moody night time lighting add to the sense of exclusivity. Wed–Sun 12.30–9.30pm.

Monserrate End of Calle 306 (Domingo Mujica), Monserrate ☎ 45 24 4222. Standard Creole cooking in the best-located restaurant in the city, in an open-sided building with great views of the bay. Prices are in national pesos, making it good value. Daily noon–10.45pm.

DRINKING, NIGHTLIFE AND ENTERTAINMENT

Having earned the moniker the "Athens of Cuba" for the many renowned artists and intellectuals it has produced, particularly during the nineteenth century, present-day Matanzas lags behind its reputation. The city centre is remarkably lifeless at night, especially during the week, though locals come out every evening to shoot the breeze at Parque de la Libertad. Outside the centre, there are some small, low-key venues as well as the **Tropicana cabaret** (see p.220), just a short bus or taxi ride beyond the city limits and the most spectacular night-time venue in the province.

BARS, CLUBS AND LIVE MUSIC VENUES

Cabaret Monserrate End of Calle 306 (Domingo Mujica), Monserrate ☎ 45 24 2620. It can sometimes get a bit rowdy at this outdoor hilltop nightclub and live music venue, but it is undoubtedly the most memorably located nightspot in Matanzas, with great views from the seating area down into the city. Entry $1CUC. Thurs–Sun 9pm–2am.

Casa de la Cultura Calle 272 no.11916 esq. 121 (Mercedes) ☎ 45 29 2709. Rarely visited by foreigners, this is more a local community centre than anything else, and sometimes stages live music and dance or a disco at weekends. Performances usually Fri & Sat 9pm, Sun 8pm.

Las Palmas Calle 254 (Levante) e/ General Betancourt y Calle 137 (Pilar) ☎ 45 25 3255. Live and recorded music of all sorts and mid-week comedy shows performed under the stars, in the palm-studded, weather beaten courtyard of a large mansion. The music-and-light shows put on most weekends are among the city's most popular locals' night out. No shorts or sleeveless tops. Entry $1–2CUC. Thurs–Sat 8.30pm–2am, Sun 5–10pm.

El Pescadito Calle 272 e/ 115 y 117 ☎ 45 29 2258. This unpretentious venue, which stages small-scale cabarets, is a local favourite. $5CUC includes bottle of rum. Wed–Sun 9pm–2am.

Ruinas de Matasiete Vía Blanca ☎ 45 25 3387. The ruins of a colonial sugar warehouse have been

half-heartedly converted into this open-air restaurant, bar and music venue, stranded out by the main road to Varadero but still one of the more reliable spots for Saturday night live music and dancing shows ($2CUC). Restaurant and bar daily 10am–10pm, shows Sat 9.30pm–3am.

La Salsa Vía Blanca ☎ 45 25 3330. One of the most popular venues among young Matanceros, this semi-outdoor, slightly ramshackle discoteca between a busy road and the rocky shore hosts nights of pop, reggaeton and salsa. The best way to get here is by car, but there is a bus stop about half a kilometre away served by the #16 and #17. Fri–Sun 10pm–2am.

La Taberna Plaza de la Vigía (no phone). Cheesy but fun, this basement bar and nightclub has a weekly programme which includes live comedy, karaoke and small-scale live music performances. Entry $2CUC/$40CUP after 9pm. Fri–Sun 2pm–2am.

THEATRES

Teatro Sauto Plaza de la Vigía ☎ 45 24 2721. A reminder of Matanzas' past glory in the arts, the centrepiece of the city's contemporary cultural life stages dance, live music and comedy acts. National theatre groups and ballet companies sometimes grace the stage, though local productions are just as prevalent. Monthly programmes are sometimes posted at the entrance. Tickets for foreign nationals are usually $5–10CUC.

SHOPPING

Self-caterers would do well to visit the **Plaza del Mercado** next to the river at the Puente Sanchez Figueras. As well as a source of fruit, vegetables and meat, it's a good place for national peso-priced snacks; Saturdays are particularly lively.

Atenas de Cuba Calle 286 esq. 83 ☎ 45 28 4778. Department store with one of the better stocked supermarkets, though stock is still very limited.

El Monte Calle 85 (Medio) e/ 284 y 288 ☎ 45 28 7427. The city's best outlet for books and CDs; there's some craftwork here too, including ceramics.

DIRECTORY

Banks and money For foreign currency and credit card transactions, go to Banco Financiero Internacional at Medio esq. 2 de Mayo (Mon–Fri 8.30am–4.30pm) or Banco de Crédito y Comercio Calle 85 e/ 288 y 282 (Mon–Fri 8am–4.30pm); the latter has an ATM. The CADECA *casa de cambio* is at Calle 85 (Medio) e/ 280 y 282.

Baseball Estadio Victoria de Girón, at the southern end of San Carlos (☎ 45 24 3881), has weekly national-league baseball games from October to April. It's a 20min walk from Parque de la Libertad.

Hospital The relatively new and well-equipped hospital Comandante Faustino Pérez Hernández is located on the Carretera Central, 1km from the city (☎ 52 25 3426 & ☎ 52 25 3427, ✉ hospital@atenas.inf.cu).

Internet and telephone There is an ETECSA Telepunto in Matanzas at Calle 282 esq. Milanes (daily 8.30am–7pm), with several phone cabins and internet terminals.

Left luggage At the interprovincial bus station ($2CUC per day).

Post office The main branch is at Medio e/ 288 y 290.

Around Matanzas

The sights around Matanzas are more appealing than the city itself, and are the best justification for spending a few days in the area. The highlights are the **Cuevas de Bellamar**, also a popular day-trip from Varadero, while the **Yumurí Valley** offers a fantastic showcase of Cuban plant life in a sublime and peaceful landscape. The **Río Canímar** offers some excellent boat trips and organized excursions, while the hotel here is home to the prodigious **Tropicana** cabaret.

Local buses and the Matanzas Bus Tour (see p.216) will get you to all these places except the Yumurí Valley, which you can visit by catching the Hershey train (see p.214) or by taking a taxi or rental car.

Cuevas de Bellamar

Guided tours (minimum ten people) daily at 9.30am, 10.30am, 11.30am, 12.30pm, 1.15pm, 2.15pm, 3.15pm & 4.15pm; 45min–1hr • $5CUC, photos $5CUC • ☎ 45 25 3538 • The #12 bus from the Parque de la Libertad in Matanzas goes right to the caves; a private taxi from Matanzas bus station costs $6–8CUC • Varadero travel agents (see box, p.199) offer tours from around $12CUC

Just beyond the southeastern outskirts of Matanzas, the **Cuevas de Bellamar** is the most awe-inspiring natural wonder in the province. The cave system attracts coach-loads of tourists and is very visitor-friendly, allowing anyone who can scale a few sets of steps to descend 50m under the ground along 750m of underground corridors and caverns. The entrance is located within a small complex called Finca La Alcancía, hosting shops, two restaurants and a children's playground.

The caves were first happened upon in 1861 – although there's some dispute over whether credit should go to a slave working in a limestone pit or a shepherd looking for his lost sheep. **Tours** are conducted in various languages, including English, and start with a bang as a large staircase leads down into the first, huge gallery, where a gargantuan stalactite known as *El Manto de Colón* takes centre stage. From here the damp, occasionally muddy and moodily lit trail undulates gently through the rock, passing along narrow passageways. Every so often the cave widens out into larger but still tightly enclosed galleries and chambers lined with lichen and crystal formations.

The Yumurí Valley

Hidden behind the hills that skirt the northern edges of Matanzas, the **Yumurí Valley** is the provincial capital's giant back garden, stretching westwards from the city into Havana province. Out of sight until you reach the edge of the valley itself, it's the most beautiful landscape in the province, and it comes as quite a surprise to find it so close to the grimy city streets. There's a new vista around every corner, as rolling pastures merge into fields of palm trees, and small forests are interrupted by plots of banana, maize, tobacco and other crops.

The valley has remained relatively untouched by tourism, with its tiny villages few and far between, and though it draws much of its appeal from being so unspoilt, this also means that there's no obvious way to explore it independently. Several minor roads allow you to cut through its centre, but the best way to get here on public transport is to catch the Hershey train from Matanzas (see p.214) and get off at Mena, the first stop on the line and just ten minutes from the city. From the station you can wander in any direction and you'll soon chance upon an idyllic scene.

For a more structured approach, book the Jeep Safari Yumurí (see p.199), an organized excursion from Varadero to **Rancho Gaviota**, the only tourist-oriented stop in the valley, where you can eat a hearty Cuban meal and go horseriding. For the most breathtaking views of the valley, however, make your way to the **Puente Bacunayagua**, 20km northwest along the Vía Blanca from Matanzas. At 112m high, this is the tallest bridge in Cuba, spanning the border between Havana and Matanzas province. Up the hill from here is the viewpoint, **Mirador de Bacunayagua**, where a snack bar looks out to the coastline and from where a trail leads down to the sea, a thirty-minute walk away by the side of a river.

ARRIVAL AND DEPARTURE   **THE YUMURÍ VALLEY**

By train From the station in Matanzas, the Hershey has three daily services to Mena.

By car If you're driving from Matanzas, head for the Parque René Fraga, from where the road heading west out of town will take you directly into the valley.

Río Canímar

Snaking its way around fields and woodlands on its journey to the coast, the **Río Canímar** meets the Bay of Matanzas 4km east of the city. With thick, jungle-like vegetation clasping its banks and swaying bends twisting out of sight, a trip up the Canímar is an easily accessible way to delve a little deeper inland and is one of the most rewarding ways of experiencing the Cuban countryside around these parts. A short stay at the *Hotel Canimao*, which overlooks the river, combines well with one of the **boat trips** that

---

RÍO CANÍMAR CRUISES AND TOURS

Two of the most popular excursions from Varadero involve a **Río Canímar river cruise**. Cruises leave from the Centro Turístico Canímar (☏45 26 1516), a tourist centre at the foot of the Puente Antonio Guiteras, the bridge that carries the Vía Blanca road over the river. The centre features a snack bar and rents out rowing boats ($2CUC/hr), pedal boats ($5CUC/hr) and kayaks ($3CUC/hr). Depending on demand, the cruise boat leaves daily at 12.30 and travels 12km upstream to a wooded grove. Visitors arriving independently pay $25CUC which includes lunch at the grove, a chance to swim in the river and to explore beyond the riverbanks on horseback, though the highlight is traversing the river itself. Most visitors, however, are on organized excursions from Varadero, booked through the travel agents on the peninsula (see p.199) at a cost of $51CUC. Exclusive to visitors arriving via the Varadero travel agents are the fun-packed **Jeep Safaris** that include the river in a larger tour of the area for $73CUC. Tours can be booked through any agent in Varadero, but are administered by Cubamar (🖰cubamarviajes.cu).

leave from below the Puente Antonio Guiteras, the impressive bridge spanning the river near its mouth and the focal point for the area. Next to the hotel is the **Tropicana**, sister venue of the internationally renowned Havana cabaret and one of the most prestigious entertainment centres in the country; while the **Museo El Morrillo** by the mouth of the river offers a rather more sedate diversion.

Museo El Morrillo

Tues–Sun 9am–4pm • $1CUC, plus $1CUC for guided tour • ☎ 45 28 6675

Directly opposite the turning for the *Hotel Canimao*, a road slopes down to an isolated, simple two-storey building known as the **Castillo del Morrillo**, an eighteenth-century Spanish fortification near the mouth of the river and alongside a scrappy little beach. With its terracotta-tiled roof, beige paintwork and wooden shuttered windows, the so-called fort looks more like a large and very plain house, and only the two cannon facing out to sea suggest that it was once used to defend Matanzas from pirates and other invaders. Nowadays it's the home of the **Museo El Morrillo**, exhibiting a threadbare collection of pre-Columbian and colonial-era artefacts, including tools and broken ceramics, as well as some more interesting bits and pieces commemorating the life and death of **Antonio Guiteras Holmes**, a political activist in 1930s Cuba. With his companion Carlos Aponte and a small group of revolutionaries, Guiteras plotted to overthrow the Mendieta regime, and chose the Castillo del Morrillo as a hideout from where they would depart by boat to Mexico to plan their insurrection. Intercepted by military troops before they could leave, they were shot down on May 8, 1935, at this very spot. The rowing boat that transported the corpses of Guiteras and Aponte is on show, as well as the tomb containing their remains.

ARRIVAL AND DEPARTURE

RÍO CANÍMAR

By bus Buses #16 and #17 run daily between the city and the Puente Antonio Guiteras every hour or so. You can pick up either bus outside the cathedral on Calle 83; get off at the end of the route just over the bridge.

By car To drive here, simply follow the Vía Blanca from either Varadero or Matanzas and take the turn-off next to the bridge.
By organized tour There are plenty of organized excursions to the river from Varadero (see box, p.199).

ACCOMMODATION AND EATING

Hotel Canimao ☎ 45 26 1014, ✉ comercial @canimao.islazul.tur.cu. This hotel sits high above Río Canímar, which coils itself halfway around the foot of the steep, tree-lined slopes dropping down from the borders of the grounds, which feature a swimming pool and afford views of the river. Rooms are somewhat less picturesque, with only basic facilities, but this is not somewhere to spend time inside other than for meals

and perhaps the weekend discos in the cabaret building. **$33CUC**

El Marino ☎ 45 26 1014. At the entrance to the road leading up to *Hotel Canimao*, and less sophisticated than its bow-tied waiters would suggest, but still offering a good choice of food, with a menu of fish, shrimp and lobster. Most main dishes are priced between $6CUC and $15CUC. Daily noon–10pm.

NIGHTLIFE AND ENTERTAINMENT

Sala de Fiesta La Cumbre ☎ 45 25 3387. Right next to the *Tropicana* and part of the same complex, this cheesy nightclub, where karaoke and music videos are part of the entertainment, is incredibly popular with young locals at weekends. Entry $1–2CUC. Tues–Sun 10pm–2am.

Tropicana ☎ 45 26 5380 (switchboard), ☎ 45 26 5555 (reservations). Set in a spectacular outdoor auditorium, the 1.5hr shows here are everything you'd expect from such a renowned outfit, with lasers shot into the night sky, troops of glittering dancers and a stream of histrionic

singers working through back-to-back sets of ballads, ear busters and routines covering classic Cuban musical styles, from romantic bolero to energetic salsa and the more traditional son. There's also an after-show disco. Ticket prices ($40–70CUC) depend on whether you have a meal (for which you have to book in advance), how close your table is to the stage, and whether you opt for transfers to and from your hotel; only one complimentary drink is included in the cheapest entrance price. Thurs–Sat 8.30pm–2.30am, showtime 10pm.

San Miguel de los Baños

The provincial interior of Matanzas, wedged between the two touristic poles of Varadero and the Península de Zapata, is dominated by agriculture, with islands of banana and vegetable crops dotting the seas of sugar-cane fields. There are a few small towns in this sparsely populated territory – a couple of the larger ones, **Colón** and **Jovellanos**, are on the Carretera Central, the main road bisecting the northern half of the province. Away from the highway the smaller, more picturesque hamlet of **SAN MIGUEL DE LOS BAÑOS** is one of the province's lesser-known treats, off the official tourist track and accessible only by car, hidden away in its own cosy valley 25km southwest of Cárdenas. A cross between an alpine village and a Wild West ghost town, this once opulent settlement has lost most of its wealth, with the wood-panelled ranch-style houses and villas on the hillside among the few reminders of what San Miguel de los Baños once was. These faded signs of success are part of the enchantment of a place that made its fortune during the first half of the twentieth century through the popularity of its health spa and hotel, the **Balneario San Miguel de los Baños**, still one of the focal points for visits here, along with the public **swimming pool** and the **Loma de Jacán**.

Balneario San Miguel de los Baños

Located near the centre of the village, the turreted, mansion-like **Balneario San Miguel de los Baños** had its heyday in the 1930s but is now completely derelict, though you can still wander through its entrancingly overgrown gardens. At the rear of the building and spread around the garden, the red-brick wells and Romanesque baths built to accommodate the sulphurous springs that were discovered here in the mid-nineteenth century are still more or less intact, though the pools of water slushing around in them are no longer fit for human consumption. The three **wells** are themselves only about 3m deep; each was supplied from a different source and the supposed healing properties of the waters differed accordingly. With the stone benches encircling the centre of the garden and the wall of shade provided by the old trees, this is a pleasant spot for a picnic, the silence broken only by the sound of running water.

The swimming pool

Five minutes' walk from the Balneario San Miguel de los Baños through the centre of the village is a magnificently set outdoor public **swimming pool**, raised up on a small mound of land. There's no entrance fee (or set opening hours), so even if there's no water in the pool – which is quite possible given its sporadic maintenance – it's still worth stopping by just for the view of the fir-covered and palm-dotted hills enclosing the village. There are a few tables and chairs overlooking the water and a poorly stocked outdoor bar selling mostly rum for national pesos, but it's enough to just take a seat and digest the captivating scenery.

Loma de Jacán

From the swimming pool in San Miguel de los Baños village you should be able to see the route to the foot of the **Loma de Jacán**, the highest peak among the small set of hills in the north of Matanzas province, yet one of the easiest to climb, thanks to a large set of concrete steps leading up it. A short drive from the northern edge of town up a steep and potholed road takes you to the bottom of this giant staircase. The 448 steps up to the peak are marked by murals depicting the **Stations of the Cross**, and at the top is a shrine, whose concrete dome houses a spooky representation of the Crucifixion, the untouched overgrowth and the airy atmosphere contributing to the mood of contemplation. For years the shrine has

A HISTORY OF SUGAR IN CUBA

Despite the old Cuban saying "*sin azúcar no hay país*" ("without sugar there's no country"), the crop is not actually native to the island, having been introduced by colonial pioneer Diego Velázquez in 1511. Furthermore, though its humid tropical climate and fertile soil makes the island ideal for sugar cane cultivation, **sugar production** got off to a slow start here. Initially produced almost entirely for local consumption, decades of declining population in Cuba meant the market for sugar was initially very small. In 1595, as Europe was beginning to develop its sweet tooth, King Philip II of Spain authorized the construction of sugar refineries on the island but for the next century and a half, the industry remained relatively stagnant. Impeded by the **Spanish** failure to take notice of new techniques in sugar production developed by the English and French elsewhere in the Caribbean, the lack of a substantial and regular supply of slaves, and by stifling regulations imposed by the Spanish Crown forcing Cuba to trade sugar only with Spain, sugar production on the island initially developed slowly.

THE ENGLISH ARRIVE

In 1762, however, the **English** took control of Havana and during their short occupation opened up trade channels with the rest of the world, simultaneously introducing the industry to the technological advances Spain had failed to embrace. Subsequently, the number of slaves imported to Cuba almost doubled in the last two decades of the eighteenth century. In 1791 a slave-led revolution in Santo Domingo, the dominant force in world sugar at that time, all but wiped out its sugar industry, causing prices and the demand for Cuban sugar to rise, just as the global demand was also rising. By the end of the eighteenth century Cuba had become one of the world's three biggest sugar producers.

SLAVERY AND THE WARS OF INDEPENDENCE

Technological advances throughout the nineteenth century, including the mechanization of the refining process and the establishment of railways, saw Cuba's share of the world market more than double and the crop become the primary focus of the economy. With hundreds of thousands of **slaves** being shipped into Cuba during this period, the island's racial mix came to resemble something like it is today. Equally significant, the economic and structural imbalances between east and west, which were to influence the outbreak of the Ten Years' War in 1868 and its successor in 1895, emerged as a result of the concentration of more and larger sugar mills in the west, closer to Havana. These **Wars of Independence** (see pp.456–457) weakened the Cuban sugar industry to the point of vulnerability, thus clearing the way for a foreign takeover.

THE TWENTIETH CENTURY

Cuba began the twentieth century under indirect US control, and the **Americans** built huge factories known as *centrales,* able to process cane for a large number of different plantations. By 1959 there were 161 mills on the island, over half of them under foreign ownership, a fact that had not escaped the notice of Fidel Castro and his nationalist revolutionary followers. It was no surprise then that one of the first acts of the revolutionary government was, in 1960, to **nationalize** the entire sugar industry. Over the following decades Cuban economic policy fluctuated between attempts at diversification and greater dependency than ever on the *zafra* – the sugar harvest, influenced by artificially high prices paid by the Soviet Union for Cuban sugar. This dependency reached a disastrous peak when, in 1970, Castro zealously declared a target of ten million tons for the national annual sugar harvest, which has never been met.

THE INDUSTRY TODAY

Since the mid-1990s there has been a sharp decline in the productivity of sugar. In 2002 a government plan to make production more efficient meant almost half of Cuba's sugar mills were closed while the output of those that remained would, in theory, increase. While this plan patently failed, with Cuba's share of global sugar production currently at around one percent, there have been recent developments in the industry: in 2012, the Brazilian firm Odebrecht became the first foreign company to administer a Cuban sugar mill since the Revolution. Whether this will provide a boost to the industry is yet to be properly measured.

attracted local pilgrims who leave flowers and coins at its base, though the real attraction here is the all-encompassing **view** of the valley and beyond.

ARRIVAL AND DEPARTURE   SAN MIGUEL DE LOS BAÑO!

By car San Miguel de los Baños is easy to miss. To drive here, head east on the Carretera Central from Matanzas and

take a right turn just before entering the small town o Coliseo; the village is 8km from the turn-off.

Península de Zapata

The whole southern section of Matanzas province is taken up by the **Península de Zapata**, also known as the Ciénaga de Zapata, a large, flat national park and UNESCO-declared Biosphere Reserve covered by vast tracts of open swampland and contrastingly dense forests. The largest but least populated of all Cuba's municipalities, the peninsula is predominantly wild, unspoilt and a rich habitat for Cuban animal life, including boar mongoose, iguana and crocodile. It's also a birdwatcher's paradise, on the migratory routes between the Americas and home to endemic species such as the Zapata rail and Cuban pygmy owl. Despite its beaches and over 30km of accessible Caribbean coastline Península de Zapata holds little appeal as a sun-and-sand holiday destination, but it is an excellent area for **diving**, with crystal clear waters, coral reefs within swimming distance of the shore and a small network of flooded caves known as *cenotes*.

As one of the most popular day-trips from Havana and Varadero, the peninsula has built up a set of conveniently packaged diversions, though these are best combined with the more active business of birdwatching, fishing, diving or trekking, for which you'll need to hire a **guide** and, in some cases, rent a car – entrance is restricted to most of the protected wildlife zones, which are widespread and not accessible on foot. Of the ready-made attractions, the **Finca Fiesta Campesina**, just off the Autopista Nacional, is a somewhat contrived but nonetheless delightful cross between a farm and a tiny zoo. Further in, about halfway down to the coast, **Boca de Guamá** draws the largest number of bus parties with its **crocodile farm**, restaurants and pottery workshop. This is the point of departure for the boat trip to **Guamá**, a convincingly reconstructed **Taíno Indian village** on the edge of a huge lake. Further south on the **Bay of Pigs**, scene of the infamous 1961 **invasion**, the beaches of **Playa Girón** and **Playa Larga** are nowhere near as spectacular as their northern counterpart, but offer far superior scuba diving to the offerings near Varadero. The invasion itself is commemorated in a museum at Playa Girón and along the roadside in a series of grave-like **monuments**, each representing a Cuban casualty of the conflict.

KILLING CASTRO

Even before the dramatic failure of the military offensive at the Bay of Pigs, the US had been planning less overt methods for removing Fidel Castro from power. Fabián Escalante, the former head of Cuban State Security, claims that between 1959 and 1963 over six hundred **plots** were hatched to kill the Cuban president, which became more devious and ludicrous as the US grew increasingly desperate to take out the communist leader. In 1960, during a visit which Castro was making to the UN, it was planned that he be given a **cigar** which would explode in his face, while back in Cuba, in 1963, Rolando Cubela, who had been a commander in the rebel army, was given a **syringe** disguised as a pen to be used in an assassination attempt. The Mafia also took a stab at killing Castro with their **poison pill plot**, but got no further than their CIA counterparts. Some of the more outlandish schemes included poisoning a diving suit, poisoning a cigar, leaving an explosive shell on a beach frequented by Castro and spraying LSD in a television studio in the hope of inducing an attack of uncontrollable laughter.

ARRIVAL AND GETTING AROUND

BY BUS

Víazul buses Víazul runs a bus service which stops at the Entronque de Jagüey, Boca de Guamá, Playa Larga and Playa Girón on the way between Varadero and Cienfuegos and Trinidad.

Destinations (Viazul) Cienfuegos (1 daily; 1hr 50min); Trinidad (1 daily; 3hr); Varadero (1 daily; 1hr 40min).

Tourist buses Most of the peninsula is also covered by the twice-daily Guamá Bus Tour, a hop-on, hop-off tourist bus service that travels between Boca de Guamá and Playa Girón twice daily in both directions. The morning service leaves the *Hotel Playa Girón* at 9am, arrives at Boca de Guamá at 10am and heads back the other way at 10.30. In the afternoon it's 2pm from the *Hotel Playa Girón*, turning back at Boca de Guamá at 3.30pm. The cost is $3CUC to ride all day.

BY CAR

Driving to the peninsula If arriving by car from Havana or elsewhere in Matanzas province, your point of entry is the Entronque de Jagüey, the main entry to the park at a junction on the southern outskirts of the small town of Jagüey Grande. This is where the Autopista Nacional, which

runs more or less along the entire northern border of th peninsula, meets the Carretera de la Ciénaga, the onl reliable road leading south into the park. This junction i marked by the *La Finquita* snack bar and information centr (see below). Travelling from Cienfuegos, you'll arrive a Playa Girón (see p.232).

Driving around the peninsula The Carretera de l Ciénaga offers very few opportunities for wrong turn: cutting more or less straight down from the Autopist Nacional to the top of the Bay of Pigs. Almost all the lan west of this road (well over half the peninsula) is officiall protected territory and open only to those with a guide i tow (see box, 229).

CAR, SCOOTER AND BIKE RENTAL

Both Havanautos (☎ 45 98 4123) and Cubacar (☎ 45 9 4126) rent out cars, starting at around $50CUC per day for week, from Playa Girón, where you can also hire bicycles The car rental offices are opposite the museum and th cheapest cars cost between $30CUC and $40CUC a day Both of the beachfront hotels (see p.230 and p.232) ren out scooters (around $15CUC/3hr).

INFORMATION

Tourist information The best source of information is *La Finquita* (daily 8am–8pm; ☎ 45 91 3224, ✉ comercial @peninsula.co.cu), a snack bar/information centre by the side of the *autopista* at the junction with the main road into Zapata. It's run by Cubanacán (✆ cubanacan.cu), the travel agent and tour operator responsible for all the hotels and organized excursions on the peninsula, which also has *buros de turismo* in the lobbies of the *Playa Larga* (☎ 45 98

7294) and *Playa Girón* (☎ 45 98 4110) hotels.

Park information For information and arrangement relating to trekking, birdwatching or fishing, your firs point of contact should be Cubanacán, though you can als make enquiries at the Office of the Parque Naciona Cienaga de Zapata (daily, daylight hours; ☎ 45 98 7249 located in a signposted bungalow just before the fork in th main road at Playa Larga.

Finca Fiesta Campesina

Carretera de la Ciénaga • Daily 9am–5pm • Free; horseriding $1CUC

The pretty little **Finca Fiesta Campesina** is a kind of showcase of the Cuban countryside presenting an idealized picture of rural life and serving as a light-hearted introduction to traditional food, drink, crafts and native animals. You can watch cigars being made by hand, sample a Cuban coffee or raw-tasting *guarapo* (pure sugar-cane juice), or play spin-the-guinea-pig, a cruel but comical gambling game. Dotted around the landscaped gardens are small cages and enclosures containing various species of **local wildlife**, all of which can be found living wild on the peninsula, including a crocodile. Some of the most fascinating creatures are the *manjuarí*, eerie-looking stick-like fish, survivors of the Jurassic period. You can also ride horses or even ride the ranch's own bull, and there's an on-site restaurant.

ACCOMMODATION

★ **Batey Don Pedro** ☎ 45 91 2825, ✉ carpeta @donpedro.co.cu. Next door to Finca Fiesta Campesina, this immaculately kept little cabin complex is the peninsula's best bargain, consisting of ten spacious wooden cabins,

simply and thoughtfully furnished and connected by ston pathways running through cropped lawns. There are ceilin fans instead of a/c, but this is in keeping with the overa homespun appeal of this rural retreat. **$24CUC**

Museo de la Comandancia

Mon–Sat 8am–5pm, Sun 8am–noon • $1CUC • ☎ 45 91 2504

Less than 1km south of the Finca Fiesta Campesina is the pocket-sized village of **Australia**, where a right turn onto the Carretera de la Ciénaga takes you into the peninsula proper. Continuing straight on about 100m past the turning, however, brings you to **Central Australia**. This is not, as you might expect, the heart of the village, but a sugar refinery used by Fidel Castro in 1961 as a base of operations during the Bay of Pigs invasion. Despite its name, the **Museo de la Comandancia**, in the building which Castro and his men occupied, is less a tribute to its purpose in the famous Cuban victory over the US and more a survey of the whole area's broader history. Although the collection is a bit dated, there are some interesting photographs and documentation of life in Australia and the nearby town of Jagüey Grande in the early twentieth century.

Boca de Guamá

Eighteen kilometres down the Carretera de la Ciénaga from the Autopista Nacional, **Boca de Guamá** is a heavily visited and commercially packaged tour-group attraction, sandwiched between the road and a canal connecting to a huge lake. Its headline attraction is a crocodile farm, but there is also a pottery workshop, a replica Taíno village and a couple of restaurants and souvenir shops; and though the whole place has a rather contrived feel it is relatively slick for a Cuban operation and makes for an easy-going visit.

Criadero de Cocodrilos

Boca de Guamá • Daily 9am–5pm • $5CUC • ☎ 45 91 5562, ext. 112

Boca, as it's referred to locally, is most famous for the **Criadero de Cocodrilos**, a crocodile-breeding farm and show-pen that forms the centrepiece of the complex. Established in 1962, the farm was set up as a conservation project in the interests of saving the then-endangered Cuban crocodile (*cocodrilo rhombifer*) and American crocodile (*cocodrilo acutus*) from extinction. The farm itself is not set up for visitors but the **show-pen**, consisting of a small swamp with some snaking paths twisting around it contains a few crocs, which are left more or less alone; you may even have trouble spotting one. For a more dramatic encounter it's best to visit during one of the twice-weekly feeding times, though unfortunately there is no regular timetable. To get an idea of when the next **feeding session** is scheduled, call the office. On a tour round the swamp you can witness a mock capture of an exhausted-looking baby crocodile and are then invited to eat one at the *Croco Bar*.

Taller de Cerámica Celia Sánchez

Boca de Guamá • Mon–Sat 7am–4.30pm • Free, but tip welcome

Set in an open-fronted building, the mildly engaging **Taller de Cerámica Celia Sánchez** is a pottery workshop and warehouse-cum-production line where you can witness the ceramics production process, which includes setting the moulds and baking them in the large furnaces behind the stocks of finished pottery stored around the building. As well as the tacky ornamental pieces, there are replicas of Taíno cooking pots and the like, most of which get distributed to craft shops around the country.

EATING   BOCA DE GUAMÁ

El Colibri (no phone). You can dine on crocodile meat here ($15CUC) or opt for the alternatives, a reasonable choice of more familiar, moderately priced Cuban dishes. If you arrive after 5pm, food can sometimes still be ordered from the bar. Daily 9.30am–5pm.

Guamá

Boats daily 9am–5pm • Round-trip including guide $12CUC

Boca is the departure point for boats travelling to **GUAMÁ**, a replica Taíno village and hotel set on a network of small islands on the far side of the **Laguna de Tesoro**, the largest natural lake in Cuba. Boats depart several times daily along the perfectly straight, tree-lined canal connecting to the lake, into which a Taíno tribe, hundreds of years ago, threw its treasure to prevent the Spanish seizing it – hence its name, **Treasure Lagoon**. The complex, complete with lesser known Taíno constructions like a disco and swimming pool, may be a little contrived but is no worse for it, captivatingly linked together by a series of bridges and pathways. The first of the neatly spaced islets, where you'll be dropped off, is occupied by life-sized statues of Amerindians in photogenic poses, each representing an aspect of Taíno culture. Cross the footbridge to reach the diminutive **museum** detailing Taíno life and featuring a few genuine artefacts. If the hour or so allotted here for tours isn't enough, you could stay the night at Villa Guamá (see below). Note that the boats from Boca to the village leave according to demand, and take a minimum of four passengers.

ACCOMMODATION   GUAMÁ

Villa Guamá Laguna del Tesoro ☎ 45 95 9100, ✉ recepcion@hotelguama.co.cu. A novel and striking hotel complex of attractive wooden cabins, modestly equipped with TVs and showers. Dotted around a network of islets on the edge of the lake the location is enchanting but you'll feel a little stranded here if you stay more than a night, unless you love birdwatching – otherwise be prepared for a lot of swimming, sun bathing and mosquito swatting. **$58CUC**

NATURE TRAILS, BIRDWATCHING AND FISHING ON THE PENÍNSULA DE ZAPATA

Besides managing most of the attractions on the peninsula, Cubanacán (w cubanacan.cu) also organizes less touristy trips into the heart of the **Parque Nacional Cienaga de Zapata nature reserve**, offering tailor-made packages which can be spread over a number of days or weeks, or ready-made day-trips to specific areas of natural interest. They can supply specialist guides, some of whom speak English, for **diving** (see box, p.232), **fishing** and **birdwatching**. The marshes and rivers of Zapata are great areas for **fly-fishing**; however, very little equipment is available locally and you should bring your own kit (plus your passport, needed to obtain a fishing licence).

The three excursions described below are to UNESCO-protected parts of the peninsula that can only be visited with a guide, and which together provide a varied experience of what the area has to offer. The best place to **arrange a trip** is at *La Finquita*, at the entrance to the peninsula (see p.226), though the *buros de turismo* in the hotels can also sometimes help. Alternatively, go directly to the Office of the Parque Nacional Cienaga de Zapata (☎45 98 7249), where the guides are based. You will need your own car for these excursions, as Cubanacán cannot always supply transport. Havanautos and Cubacar have a rental office at Playa Girón.

THE RÍO HATIGUANICO

Hidden away in the woods on the northwestern edge of Zapata is the base camp for trips in small motor boats on the peninsula's widest river, the **Hatiguanico**. A tree-lined canal connects the camp to the river, and the whole route is abundant in birdlife, including Zapata sparrows and Cuban green woodpeckers. Before reaching the widest part of the river, the canal flows into a narrow, twisting corridor of water where you're brushed by leaning branches. After, the river opens out into an Amazonian-style waterscape and curves gracefully through the densely packed woodland. Trips last between one and two hours, cost $19CUC per person and usually include a packed lunch, a short hike into the woods, and a swim in one of the river alcoves. Fishing is also an option here; $125CUC per person pays for a total of up to eight hours with a guide on a small two-man boat; tarpon, snapper and snook are among the fish in these waters.

SANTO TOMÁS

Thirty kilometres west from the small village just before Playa Larga, along a dirt road through dense forest, **Santo Tomás** sits at the heart of the reserve. Beyond the scattered huts which make up the tiny community here is a small, 2m-wide tributary of the Hatiguanico. In winter it's dry enough to walk but during the wet season groups of four to six are punted quietly a few hundred metres down the hidden little waterway, brushing past the overhanging reeds. This is real swampland and will suit the dedicated birdwatcher who doesn't mind getting dirty looking out for, among many others, the three endemic species in this part of the peninsula: the Zapata wren, Zapata sparrow and Zapata rail. Trips cost $10CUC per person and vary considerably in length, depending on your preferences.

LAS SALINAS

In stark contrast to the dense woodlands of Santo Tomás, the open saltwater wetlands around **Las Salinas** are the best place on the peninsula for observing migratory and aquatic birds. From observation towers dotted along a track that cuts through the shallow waters you can see huge flocks of flamingos in the distance and solitary blue herons gliding over the shallow water, while blue-wing duck and many other species pop in and out of view from behind the scattered islets. Trips to Las Salinas cost $10CUC per person and usually last several hours but can go on longer if you arrange it with your guides. Las Salinas is also a great fly-fishing spot, home to bonefish, permit and barracuda among others. Fishing trips, on flat-bottomed non-motorized two-man boats, cost around $175CUC per angler for eight hours of fishing. Since this is a protected area, no more than six anglers per week are permitted to fish here.

Bay of Pigs

The Carretera de la Ciénaga splits at the point where it reaches the **Bay of Pigs**, the Bahía de Cochinos. The main road leads down the east side of the bay where virtually all the worthwhile distractions are along the seafront, including the hotel and beach resorts of **Playa Larga** and **Playa Girón**, based around the only sandy sections of the otherwise rocky shore. On the western side of the bay, in the protected **nature reserve** that occupies the most untouched part of this national park (and which you can only visit with a guide), are **Las Salinas** and **Santo Tomás**, two of the peninsula's best areas fo birdwatching (see box, p.229).

Playa Larga

Taking the main coastal road southeast from the junction at the top of the Bay of Pigs will bring you immediately to **Playa Larga**, a resort area right on the beach with little to offer other than the facilities of the hotel complex itself. The beach is about 100m long, with traces of seaweed on the shore and the grass encroaching onto the sand from behind. Nearby **diving** points can be explored by arrangement with the *Hotel Playa Larga*'s own Club Octopus diving centre (see box, p.232), on a jut of land at the opposite end of the beach, beyond the large car park just before the hotel.

3

ACCOMMODATION AND EATING   PLAYA LARGA

La Casa del Buzo Caletón ☎ 45 98 7396. This large house with three guest bedrooms is one of the best places to stay on the peninsula if you're here for the diving. Owner Osnedy, a qualified diving instructor, can rent out diving equipment at below-average prices and take you out on dives. **$25CUC**

★ **Casa Frank** Calle 3ra no.8 e/ 2da y 4ta, Entronque de Playa Larga ☎ 45 98 7189, ✉ vegasfrank22 @yahoo.es. A small network of staircases, terraces and balconies characterize this large house, with two of the three well-kept guest rooms on the huge mid-level terrace where meals are served. A level up from here there are views over to the bay and a rooftop swimming pool. The owners offer a taxi service and can arrange horse riding. **$25CUC**

Casa de Josefa Pita Caletón ☎ 45 98 7133. Backing onto the seafront, this is one of the more presentable houses among a grouping of shacks off an inlet at the top of the bay. The bedroom, with two double beds, en-suite bathroom and a/c, looks out onto the water, just 5m away, and you're usually given the run of the house as the owners like to stay out of the way. **$25CUC**

Fernando Pálpite ☎ 52 25 8023 & ☎ 58 21 1799 Backyard patio paladar in Pálpite, a village 4km inland o the Carretera de la Ciénaga, where for $10CUC per perso the owner-chefs offer platters of seafood and succulen meat, from pork and venison to lobster and crocodile, alon with the side orders of your choosing, allowing you to feas until full. Daily noon–9pm.

Hotel Playa Larga ☎ 45 98 7294, ✉ recepcio @hplargac.co.cu. With the look and feel of a sprawlin 1970s holiday camp, this tired out old place is nevertheles on the best swathe of beach on the peninsula and i reasonably well equipped. Stretching for a few hundre metres along the coastline, it has a swimming pool, tenni court and even a small soccer pitch, but the restaurant i poor. **$72CUC**

Villa Morena Barrio Mario López ☎ 45 98 7131. Tw pleasant a/c double rooms, one a twin in a house full o sculpted wooden furniture; the lower rates make up for it back-street location. Driving down to the bay on th Carretera de la Ciénaga, 50m beyond the sign announcin Playa Larga, a right-hand turn leads down to a dirt trac where another right turn leads up to the house. **$20CUC**

Cueva de los Peces

Daily 9am–5pm • Free

Midway between Playa Larga and Playa Girón, the **Cueva de los Peces**, also known as E **Cenote**, is a flooded cave full of tropical fish and one of the most relaxing spots on the peninsula (though do bring mosquito spray). At the bottom of a short track leading down from the road, the glassy-smooth natural **saltwater pool** emerges, oasis-like, against the backdrop of almost impenetrable woodlands. Enclosed by the scrub and about the size of a municipal swimming pool, it's the kind of place you'd want to keep secret if it hadn't already been discovered. Despite the pool's proximity to the road it's perfectly tranquil and you're free to dive in and swim with the numerous species of fish

THE BAY OF PIGS

The triumph of the Cuban revolution was initially treated with caution rather than hostility by the US government, but tensions between the two countries developed quickly. As Castro's reforms became more radical, the US tried harder to thwart the process and in particular refused to accept the terms of the **agrarian reform law**, which dispossessed a number of American landowners. Castro attacked the US in his speeches, became increasingly friendly with the Soviet Union and in the latter half of 1960 expropriated all US property in Cuba. The Americans responded by cancelling Cuba's **sugar quota** and secretly authorizing the CIA to organize the training of Cuban exiles, who had fled the country following the rebel triumph, for a future invasion of the island.

On April 15, 1961, US planes disguised with Cuban markings and piloted by exiles bombed Cuban airfields but caused more panic than actual damage, although seven people were killed. The intention had been to incapacitate the small Cuban air force so that the invading troops would be free from aerial bombardment, but Castro had cannily moved most of the Cuban bombers away from the airfields and camouflaged them. Two days later **Brigade 2506**, as the exile invasion force was known, landed at Playa Girón, in the **Bay of Pigs**. The brigade had been led to believe that the air attacks had been successful and were not prepared for what was in store. As soon as Castro learned the precise location of the invasion he moved his base of operations to the sugar refinery of Central Australia and ordered both his air force and land militias to repel the advancing invaders.

The unexpected aerial attacks caused much damage and confusion; two freighters were destroyed and the rest of the fleet fled, leaving 1300 troops trapped on Playa Larga and Playa Girón. During the night of April 17–18 the Cuban government forces, which had been reinforced with armoured cars and tanks, renewed attacks on the brigade. The battle continued into the next day as the brigade became increasingly outnumbered by the advancing revolutionary army. Several B-26 bombers, two manned by US pilots, flew over to the Bay of Pigs from Nicaragua the next morning in an attempt to weaken the Cuban army and clear the way for the landing of supplies needed by the stranded brigade. Most of the bombers were shot down and the supplies never arrived. Castro's army was victorious, having captured 1180 prisoners who were eventually traded for medical and other supplies from the US. Other ways would have to be found to topple the Cuban leader (see box, p.224).

3

many of which were introduced after the natural population died out. The pool leads to a flooded **cave system** of mostly unexplored underwater halls and corridors, more than 70m deep and ideal for scuba diving, which can be arranged through any of the dive centres in the area (see box, p.232), including the one at the entrance here.

EATING   CUEVA DE LOS PECES

Cueva de los Peces restaurant. Right on the edge of the pool in thick woodland, this simple, rustic restaurant is one of the best in the area, serving set meals for $12CUC.

Choose between squid, shrimp, fish, pork, chicken, crocodile or, for $15CUC, lobster, with all side orders included. Daily 10.30am–5pm.

Punta Perdíz

Daily 9am–5pm, restaurant daily 10.30am–4.30pm • $15CUC, includes open bar and buffet restaurant • Snorkelling equipment $3CUC/hr, kayaks $2–3CUC/hr, pedal boats $4CUC/hr, diving $25–100CUC

Southeast along the coast road, some 10km from Playa Girón, **Punta Perdíz** is a slice of sunbaked rocky coastline packaged up for visitors, where the entrance fee includes a buffet lunch, an open bar, use of the sun loungers and wooden sun shelters and, of course, access to the sea, where you can go snorkelling and diving. There is no beach here, just a large scrap of grassy land jutting out into the sea along a craggy shore, but it's a pleasant spot and features a recently built **watersports** and **dive club** building, where you can rent equipment and arrange diving packages. It's a short swim from the shore to a reef wall that drops down as far as 300m in places.

3

SCUBA DIVING AND SNORKELLING OFF THE PENÍNSULA DE ZAPATA

The Península de Zapata is one of the top spots in Cuba for **scuba diving** and **snorkelling**, with waters here generally calmer than those around Varadero, coral reefs close to the shore, some fantastic 30–40m coral walls and in-shore flooded caves. Scorpion fish, moray eels, groupers and barracuda are resident here, while the coral life is extremely healthy, with an abundance of brightly coloured sponges, some giant gorgonians and a proliferation of sea fans. At least ten good **dive sites** are spread along the eastern coast of the bay and beyond, right down to the more exposed waters around *Hotel Playa Girón*. Most of the coral walls are no more than 40m offshore, so to get to them you just swim from thr shore. The principal **cave dive** on the peninsula is at El Cenote, known in tourist literature as the Cueva de los Peces (see p.230), a limestone sinkhole linked to the sea through an underground channel and home to numerous tropical fish. There are a number of other flooded sinkholes around the peninsula and more excellent snorkelling and diving at Caleta Buena (see opposite) and Punta Perdiz (see p.231).

The dive clubs in Varadero (see p.206) organize some of the diving that goes on around these waters, but on the peninsula itself you should report to either **Club Octopus** (❶ 45 98 3224) at Playa Larga or the **Internacional Diving Center** (❶ 45 98 4118) at Playa Girón. There are also small diving and snorkelling clubs at Caleta Buena, Punta Perdiz and Cuevas de los Peces. Charges at all clubs are $25CUC for a single open-water dive, $40CUC for a cave dive or $45CUC for a night dive, with resort-based initiation classes for $70CUC. A package of five dives costs $100CUC.

Playa Girón

Following the coastal road southeast, it's roughly 10km from Punta Perdíz to **Playa Girón**, the place most synonymous with the Bay of Pigs invasion (see box, p.231) in April 1961 – Cubans actually refer to the invasion attempt as Girón. The **beach** here is more exposed than Playa Larga, and though it's blessed with the same transparent green waters, there is an unsightly 300m-long concrete wave breaker that creates a huge pool of calm seawater but ruins the view out to sea. Although the hotel complex hogs the seafront here, non-guests are free to use the facilities as well as wander down through the grounds to the beach.

Museo Girón

Daily 8am–5pm • $2CUC, guided visit $3CUC, photos $1CUC • ❶ 45 98 4122

Besides the beach, the other reason for stopping here is the **Museo Girón**, a two-room museum right next to the hotel, documenting the events prior to and during the US-backed invasion. Outside the building is one of the fighter planes used to attack the advancing American ships. Inside, the era is successfully evoked through depictions of pre-Revolution life, along with dramatic photographs of US sabotage and terrorism in Cuba leading up to the Bay of Pigs invasion. The second room goes on to document the battle itself, with papers outlining Castro's instructions and some incredible photography taken in the heat of battle.

ACCOMMODATION

PLAYA GIRÓN

Hostal Aida y Miguel ❶ 45 98 4251. Right on the junction where the hotel road meets the village, and just a few hundred metres from the beach. Both rooms have two beds (one has two doubles), en-suite bathroom and minibar. Owners Aida and Miguel, who both worked in the local hotel restaurant, rent out mountain bikes to guests ($10–12CUC for whole stay). **$25CUC**

Hotel Playa Girón ❶ 45 98 4110, ✉ recepcion @hpgiron.co.cu. With its uninspiring family-sized

bungalows spread out over a large site right on the beach, this tatty hotel complex is long past its best. There is a pool and tennis court, but it works best as a base for diving, as it's the closest of any hotel on the peninsula to the area's dive sites, and has its own diving club and its location. **$60CUC**

K.S. Abella Carretera a Cienfuegos ❶ 45 98 4383, ✉ ricardoabellamercy@yahoo.com. The English-speaking chef who owns this neatly kept house in the Playa Girón village offers great breakfasts and dinners. The two guest rooms, just off a lovely little backyard patio, have a connecting lounge and bathroom, making this a great option for groups of four or a family. $20–25CUC

DIRECTORY

Car rental There is a Cubacar/Havanautos car rental office (daily 8am–5pm; ☎45 98 4123) opposite the Museo Girón.

Money and exchange There's a CADECA *casa de cambio* (Mon–Fri 9–11.30am & noon–4.30pm, Sat 9–11.30am) opposite the Museo Girón.

Caleta Buena

Daily 10am–6pm • $15CUC, includes drinks and buffet lunch • Snorkel equipment $3CUC/hr; rowing boats $3CUC/hr; diving initiation $10CUC, single dive $25CUC

Eight kilometres further down the coastal road from Playa Girón, the last stop along this side of the bay is **Caleta Buena**, a pay-to-enter coastal park on a rocky but very picturesque stretch of coastline and one of the best places on the peninsula for snorkelling. Based around the calm waters of a large sheltered inlet with flat rocky platforms jutting out into the sea but no beach as such, the unspoilt serenity here befits this most secluded of Zapata's coastal havens. It's a perfect place for lazing about on the waterfront, with red-tile-roof shelters on wooden stilts providing protection from the midday sun. The best way to spend time here is to go snorkelling or diving and take advantage of the fact that you needn't go more than 150m out from the shore to enjoy a coral-coated sea bed. The site is equipped with its own **diving centre** and diving initiation courses are available, though these should be arranged in advance through Cubanacán. There is also a **volleyball** net and **rowing boats** for rent.

Mayabeque

Sandwiched in between Havana and Matanzas, **Mayabeque** is one of the two new provinces created in 2010 and previously one half of the province known as La Habana. Its main draws are the relatively secluded beach resorts of **Jibacoa** and low-key **Canasi**, along the northern coast, easily reachable from Matanzas if you have your own transport but really quite tricky to get to if you don't. Marooned inland and nearer to Havana than Matanzas, the **Escaleras de Jaruco** are even harder to reach, though this isolation is part of the charm of these beautiful forested hills.

Canasí

Around 25km west of Matanzas city along the Vía Blanca, high upon a cliff-like precipice overlooking the narrow Arroyo Bermejo estuary, the tiny hamlet of **CANASÍ** doubles as the informal weekend campsite for a hippie-chic crowd of young Habaneros. In the summer, scores of revellers descend every Friday to pitch tents in the tranquil woodland around the cliff's edge, spending the weekend swimming and snorkelling in the clear Atlantic waters, exploring the woods and nearby caves, singing folk songs and generally communing with nature. It's a refreshingly uncontrived experience with a peace-festival kind of atmosphere. There are no facilities, so you'll have to bring everything with you (most importantly fresh water), but don't worry too much if you don't have a tent, as the summer nights are warm enough to bed down beneath the stars.

ARRIVAL AND DEPARTURE   CANASÍ

By train The Hershey train (see box, p.214) connects Canasí to Havana and Matanzas. The road down to the water's edge is badly signposted, but look for a left turn off the Vía Blanca (a 5min walk from the station) and take the dirt track to the estuary mouth, where the fishermen who live in the waterside cottages will row you across the shallow waters to the site for about $2CUC a head, though the hardy can wade.

> ## DIVING IN MAYABEQUE
>
> The best **diving** opportunities along the Mayabeque coastline are at Puerto Escondido, 12km east along the Vía Blanca from Playa Jibacoa, where the nautical centre (☏78 66 2524) arranges boat trips and fishing as well as diving. This is a relatively small outfit but it does run a ten-man dive boat used to visit the five coral reefs that provide all the centre's dive sites. Prices can be negotiated, especially if you intend several dives, but a single dive usually costs $30CUC, two dives $40CUC.

Playa Jibacoa

Eight kilometres west of Canasí, tucked behind a barricade of white cliffs, is **Playa Jibacoa**, a stretch of coastline basking in relative anonymity. Approaching from Matanzas on the Vía Blanca road, the first turning before the bridge over the Río Jibacoa leads down onto the coastal road that runs the length of this laidback resort area. Predominantly the domain of Cuban holidaymakers, the beach is unspectacular but pleasantly protected by swathes of twisting trees and bushes, with an appealing sense of privacy. There are modest coral reefs offshore and basic snorkelling equipment can be rented at the *campismos* (see below).

ARRIVAL AND DEPARTURE
PLAYA JIBACOA

By train The Hershey train (see box p.214) connects Jibacoa to Havana and Matanzas.

ACCOMMODATION

The only top class international-standard hotel in these parts, the *Superclub Breezes Jibacoa* caters almost exclusively to tourists on pre-booked packages. More suitable for the casual visitor are the *campismo* sites along the shoreline, though some are a little run down. While those listed below are used to accepting foreign guests, others are for Cubans only or closed in winter.

Villa Loma ☏47 28 3316. Among the more developed *campismos* in Playa Jibacoa, this complex sits up on a small hill at the Havana end of this stretch of coastline, overlooking one of the widest sections of beach. The twelve-house site is simple, rather than basic, with a charming little restaurant, a pool and a fantastic bar in a stone watchtower. $30CUC

Villa Los Cocos Playa Jibacoa ☏47 29 5231. This excellent-value *campismo* has a pool, video room, small library and restaurant serving no-frills food. The concrete chalets, with rudimentary showers and only the most basic of facilities, are on the grassy slopes leading down to the beach. $16CUC

Villas Jibacoa ☏47 29 5213. Spread around an attractive site, this hotel has simple rooms, sweeping lawns, two restaurants, tennis courts, several modest bars and a pool, all on a great stretch of beach. It's currently branded as the *Cameleon Villas Jibacoa*. $100CUC

Escaleras de Jaruco

Around 25km east of Havana, 20km inland from the Playas del Este (see p.144), the **Escaleras de Jaruco**, a small crop of hills west of **Jaruco**, the nearest town of any significant size, makes for a stimulating detour on the way to or from Mayabeque's beaches. Covered in a kind of subtropical rainforest, this steep-sided mini-mountain range erupts from the surrounding flatlands. The Carretera Tapaste cuts through the area like a mountain pass, leading past the fantastically located *El Arabe* **restaurant** which, despite its erratic opening hours, provides a focus of sorts for the area. In its pre-Revolution heyday, it was undoubtedly a classic, with its splendid Arabic-style interior, balcony terrace with views to the coastline and domed tower, but it's now as low on food as it is on staff, and there's no guarantee it will even be open when you turn up; call ahead on ☏47 87 3828.

ARRIVAL AND DEPARTURE

ESCALERAS DE JARUCO

By train If you're prepared to do a bit of walking, you can catch the Hershey train (see p.214) and jump off at Jaruco station.

By car The best way to find the Escaleras de Jaruco is to first head for Jaruco, roughly 25km from the Vía Blanca. There are lonely roads inland from any of the beach resorts east of Havana, but the most straightforward route is to leave the Vía Blanca at the small coastal town of Santa Cruz del Norte, which the Vía Blanca passes through around 30km east of the Playas del Este. From Santa Cruz del Norte, the only road leading inland will take you through several small towns en route, first La Sierra, then Camilo Cienfuegos and San Antonio de Río Blanco, each only several kilometres apart, before arriving at the sloping roads of Jaruco.

3

SE ASIGNA AL COMANDANTE
ERNESTO GUEVARA LA MI.
SION DE CONDUCIR DESDE
LA SIERRA MAESTRA HASTA
LA PROVINCIA DE LAS VILLAS
UNA COLUMNA REBELDE

Cienfuegos and Villa Clara

CHE GUEVARA MONUMENT, SANTA CLARA

Cienfuegos and Villa Clara

From the outsider's viewpoint, the principal cities and resorts in the neighbouring provinces of Cienfuegos and Villa Clara have lower profiles than those in neighbouring Matanzas and Sancti Spíritus, offering a slightly less diluted taste of Cuban life than the likes of Varadero and Trinidad. With chimney stacks, large factories and power plants gathered around the Bahía de Jagua, the huge bay that's also the location of the pretty provincial capital of Cienfuegos city, Cienfuegos may be one of the country's most industrialized zones, but there's little sense of this for the visitor. In fact, the province's subdued feel and attractive, gentle landscapes – particularly in its southern reaches, lined with 60km of picturesque Caribbean coastline – could not contrast more with these mostly hidden clusters of industry. Cienfuegos city is within easy day-trip distance of the province's other popular destinations, including the memorable botanical gardens and the nearby beach at Rancho Luna, a modest, small-scale coastal resort suitable for a few days of lounging.

Villa Clara, sitting on top of Cienfuegos along its northern border, offers its own contrasts. Its historically rich towns and, particularly, its culturally diverse capital, Santa Clara, provide the focal points for most independent travellers, while on its northern coast, the postcard-perfect northern cays of **Cayo Las Brujas**, **Cayo Ensenachos** and **Cayo Santa María** make up Cuba's fastest expanding beach resort, attracting ever increasing numbers of package tourists. Though most of the tourist marketing for **Santa Clara** focuses on its connections to Che Guevara, there is much more to the city than the numerous homages to the revolutionary hero. More lively and dynamic a city than Cienfuegos, Santa Clara enjoys excellent theatrical and musical events and supports a broader spectrum of subcultures than most provincial Cuban cities, including a subversive heavy metal scene and a significant gay population.

Most of Villa Clara's other highlights are grouped fairly close together in the northeast of the province, where the main draw is **Remedios**, a tranquil, welcoming little town steeped in history and a short drive from the northern cays. On the other side of the province, **Embalse Hanabanilla** provides relatively straightforward access into the green slopes of the **Sierra del Escambray**. Like Remedios, the reservoir is a magnet for tourists looking for a more low-key experience: less developed than other nature-based resorts in Cuba, it's nonetheless equipped with facilities for fishing, hiking and simple boat trips.

PARQUE VIDAL, SANTA CLARA

Highlights

❶ Casas particulares on La Punta Stay at one of the exclusive *casas particulares* on this splendid little peninsula. **See p.249**

❷ Cienfuegos paladars La Punta's Finca del Mar and El Lagarto are two of the best paladars outside of Havana, serving great, simple food in unforgettable surroundings. **See p.250**

❸ Jardín Botánico de Cienfuegos Lose yourself amid bamboo cathedrals and countless varieties of palm trees. **See p.252**

❹ The Jagua ferry Enjoy the laidback pace of local life on the slow chug across the bay from Cienfuegos, taking in city views and the distant mountains. **See p.254**

❺ Parque El Nicho Walk to the picturesque El Nicho waterfalls and pools in the Sierra del Escambray. **See p.254**

❻ Parque Vidal The main square in Santa Clara is among the most vibrant in Cuba. **See p.258**

❼ El Mejunje A vibrant, unusual music and arts venue with an entertainingly diverse programme and a welcoming vibe. **See p.266**

❽ The northern cays The drive to these remote, beach-blessed islets – along a 50km-long causeway skimming above clear waters – is justification enough to visit. **See p.272**

HIGHLIGHTS ARE MARKED ON THE MAP ON PP.240–241

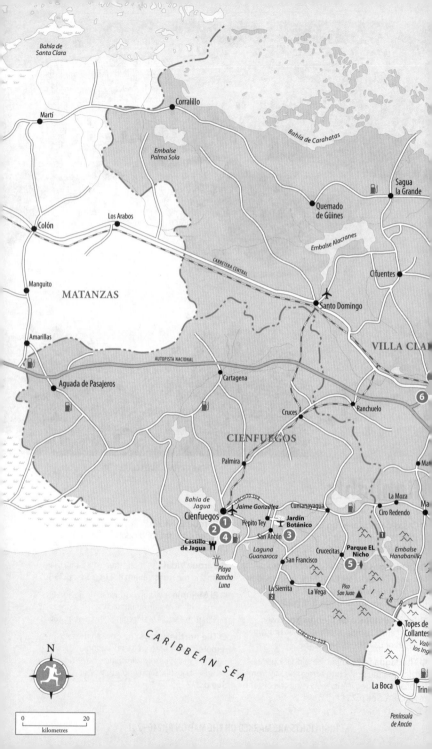

Bahía de
Santa Clara

Martí

Corralillo

Bahía de Carahatas

Embalse
Palma Sola

Sagua
la Grande

Quemado
de Güines

Colón

Los Arabos

CARRETERA CENTRAL

Embalse Alacranes

Cifuentes

Manguito

MATANZAS

Santo Domingo

Amarillas

VILLA CLA

AUTOPISTA NACIONAL

Aguada de Pasajeros

Cartagena

Cruces

Ranchuelo

6

CIENFUEGOS

Palmira

Ma

La Moza

Bahía de
Jagua

CIRCUITO SUR

Jaime González

Cumanayagua

Ciro Redendo

Cienfuegos

1

Pepito Tey

Jardín
Botánico

2

4

San Antón

3

La Vega

Castillo
de Jagua

Laguna
Guanaroca

Crucecitas

Parque EL
Nicho

Embalse
Hanabanilla

San Francisco

5

Playa
Rancho
Luna

La Sierrita

2

La Vega

Pico
San Juan

SIERRA

Topes de
Collantes

CARIBBEAN SEA

La Boca

Trin

N

La Boca

Península
de Ancón

0   20
kilometres

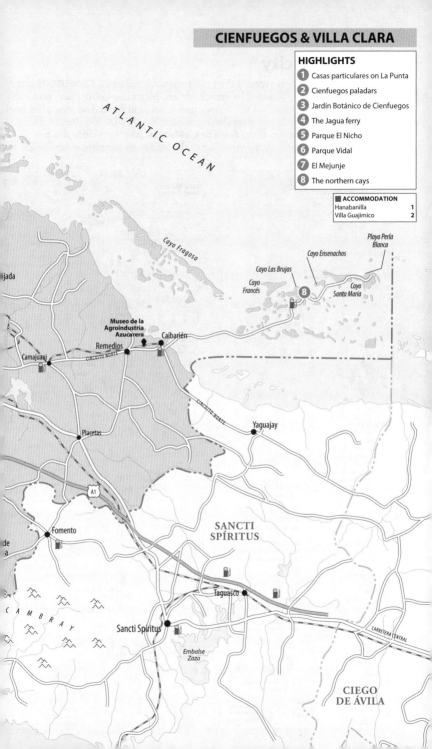

CIENFUEGOS & VILLA CLARA

HIGHLIGHTS

1. Casas particulares on La Punta
2. Cienfuegos paladars
3. Jardín Botánico de Cienfuegos
4. The Jagua ferry
5. Parque El Nicho
6. Parque Vidal
7. El Mejunje
8. The northern cays

■ ACCOMMODATION

Hanabanilla	1
Villa Guajimico	2

ATLANTIC OCEAN

Cayo Fragoso

Playa Perla Blanca

Cayo Ensenachos

Cayo Las Brujas

Cayo Francés

Cayo Santa María

8

jada

Museo de la Agroindustria Azucarera

Caibarién

Remedios

Camajuaní

CIRCUITO NORTE

Placetas

CIRCUITO NORTE

Yaguajay

A1

Fomento

SANCTI SPÍRITUS

Taguasco

CAMBRAY

Sancti Spíritus

Embalse Zaza

CARRETERA CENTRAL

CIEGO DE ÁVILA

Cienfuegos city

Established in 1819, more recently than most major Cuban cities, **CIENFUEGOS** is the only city in the country founded by French settlers. It's an easy-going place, noticeably cleaner and more spacious than the average provincial capital and deserving of its label as the "Pearl of the South". Its most alluring feature is its bayside location on the **Bahía de Jagua**, also known as the **Bahía de Cienfuegos**, which provides pleasant offshore breezes and some sleepy views across the usually undisturbed water. To get

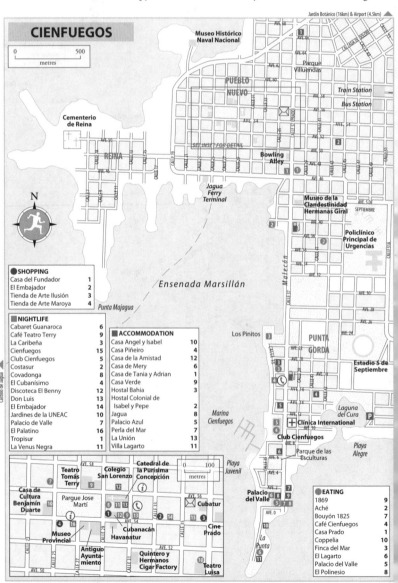

Jardín Botánico (16km) & Airport (4.5km)

CIENFUEGOS

0 — 500 metres

SHOPPING

Casa del Fundador	1
El Embajador	2
Tienda de Arte Ilusión	3
Tienda de Arte Maroya	4

NIGHTLIFE

Cabaret Guanaroca	6
Café Teatro Terry	9
La Caribeña	3
Cienfuegos	15
Club Cienfuegos	5
Costasur	2
Covadonga	8
El Cubanísimo	4
Discoteca El Benny	12
Don Luis	13
El Embajador	14
Jardines de la UNEAC	10
Palacio de Valle	7
El Palatino	16
Tropisur	1
La Venus Negra	11

ACCOMMODATION

Casa Angel y Isabel	10
Casa Piñeiro	4
Casa de la Amistad	12
Casa de Mery	6
Casa de Tania y Adrian	1
Casa Verde	9
Hostal Bahia	3
Hostal Colonial de Isabel y Pepe	2
Jagua	8
Palacio Azul	5
Perla del Mar	7
La Unión	13
Villa Lagarto	11

EATING

1869	9
Aché	2
Bouyón 1825	7
Café Cienfuegos	4
Casa Prado	1
Coppelia	10
Finca del Mar	3
El Lagarto	6
Palacio del Valle	5
El Polinesio	8

the best perspectives of the city and its surroundings you should catch the **Jagua ferry** (see p.246) to the old Spanish fortress at the mouth of the bay, a wonderfully unhurried journey. As a base for seeing what the rest of the province has to offer, Cienfuegos is ideal, with several easy day-trip destinations – beaches, botanical gardens and the old fortress – within a 25km radius.

Most visitors don't stray beyond two quite distinct districts, the relatively built-up northern borough of **Pueblo Nuevo**, the city's cultural and shopping centre, and **Punta Gorda**, a more modern, laidback, open-plan neighbourhood where you'll find a marina, a couple of scrappy little beaches and one of the most distinctive buildings in Cienfuegos, the **Palacio de Valle**. The two are linked together by the principal city street, **Calle 37**, the promenade section of which is known as **Prado**.

Pueblo Nuevo

The undisputed focal point of Pueblo Nuevo is the **Parque José Martí**, the city's main square, where the illustrious nineteenth-century **Teatro Tomás Terry** and the more modest **cathedral** head the list of prestigious buildings occupying its borders. None of the area's museums are particularly engaging, but the **Museo Provincial** has the broadest interest, and though the contents of the **Museo Histórico Naval Nacional** are a bit sketchy, its location in an old naval barracks on a small peninsula help make it worthwhile. The area's liveliest street is the pedestrianized section of **Avenida 54**, linking Parque José Martí with Prado and lined with shops, a couple of bars and some cheap, fairly poor restaurants. Round the corner from here, on Calle 29, is a daily arts and crafts **market** and, a block over on Calle 31, the diminutive **Quintero y Hermanos cigar factory**, rarely open to visitors but an emblem of the city.

Parque José Martí

With a statue of José Martí at the midway point of its central promenade, a traditional bandstand and neatly kept little gardens nestling in the shade of royal palm trees, the **Parque José Martí** perfectly encapsulates the city's graceful character and its tidy and pretty appearance. Though lacking in good bars and restaurants, this colourful and sometimes lively square is the heart of the city, surrounded by grand buildings occupying central roles in the political, cultural and religious life of Cienfuegos. In the northeastern corner is the **Colegio San Lorenzo**, the most classically Greco-Roman structure on the square, home to a school. Opposite is the dome-topped, Neoclassical provincial government headquarters, the **Antiguo Ayuntamiento**, built in 1929 with four columns flanking its grand entrance.

Teatro Tomás Terry

Ave. 56 e/ 27 y 29 • Daily 9am–6pm • $2CUC including guided tour; photos $5CUC, video cameras $50CUC • ☎ 43 51 3361

The **Teatro Tomás Terry** has stood proudly on the northern edge of the Parque José Martí since its foundation in 1890. Music, dance and theatre productions are still staged here, but the glorious **interior** is a show in itself, its original splendour still almost completely intact and well worth the daytime entrance fee. In the decorative lobby, featuring the original nineteenth-century ticket booths, is a statue of the theatre's namesake – a millionaire patron of the city, whose family part-funded the building's construction. The predominantly wooden, semicircular, 950-seat **auditorium** was fashioned on a traditional Italian design, with three tiers of balconies, a dreamy Baroque-style fresco on the ceiling and a gold-framed stage sloping towards the front row to allow the audience an improved view. For details of performances (see p.251), either call or check the noticeboard at the entrance; and note that guided tours aren't available if rehearsals are taking place.

Catedral de la Purísima Concepción

Calle 29 esq. Ave. 56 • Mon–Fri 7am–3pm, Sat 7am–noon & 2–4pm, Sun 7am–noon; Mass daily 7.15am, plus Sun 10am • ☎ 43 52 5297

Across from the school on the Parque José Martí's northeastern corner, the fetching altars and stained glass of the **Catedral de la Purísima Concepción** merit a look inside. Built in 1833, it had the bell tower added thirteen years later, and in 1903 cathedral status was granted. It retains much of its original spirit as a local church and receives as many resident worshippers as it does tourists. The only sign of ostentation among the elegant simplicity is at the main altar where a statue of the Virgin Mary, with snakes at her feet, shelters under an ornately decorated blue-and-gold half-dome.

Museo Provincial

Ave. 54 esq. 27 • Daily 10am–6pm • $2CUC; guide $1CUC; photos $1CUC • ☎ 43 51 9722

On the southern side of the square is the **Museo Provincial**, housed in a blue balconied building founded in 1892 and originally a Spanish *casino*, a kind of social centre for Spanish immigrants. Its two floors contain a hotchpotch of colonial-era furniture, relics from pre-Columbian Cuban culture, firearms used in the Wars of Independence and all sorts of other random bits and pieces, roughly glued together by rather dry display boards recounting local manifestations of national politics and history.

Museo Histórico Naval Nacional

Ave. 60 y Calle 21 • ☎ 43 51 6617 • Tues–Sat 10am–6pm, Sun 10am–1pm • $2CUC

A few blocks northwest of Parque José Martí, in a pleasant grassy setting on a small jut of land sticking out into the bay known as Cayo Loco, the **Museo Histórico Naval Nacional** houses a sketchy collection of items related to sea travel and naval warfare, alongside an eclectic set of displays painting a more general picture of local political, social and natural history. A whole section is devoted to the 1957 **September 5 uprising**, in which local revolutionaries instigated an insurrectional coup at the naval barracks, now the museum's buildings and grounds. They held the city for only a few hours before the dictator General Batista sent in some two thousand soldiers and crushed the rebellion, in a battle that ended with a shoot-out at the Colegio San Lorenzo on Parque José Martí. As well as various humdrum military possessions, the displays include the bloodstained shirt of one of the rebel marines and a neat little model of the naval base.

Punta Gorda

The southern part of the city, **Punta Gorda**, has a distinctly different flavour to the rest of Cienfuegos, and it's here that the city's relatively recent founding is most keenly felt.

ACTIVITIES IN CIENFUEGOS

As well as the mini-theme park at Club Cienfuegos, there are several other possibilities for activities in and around the city.

Arcade games and leisure centres There's a bowling alley ($1CUC) and small games arcade featuring pool ($2CUC/hr) and air hockey tables ($0.50CUC/game) at Prado e/ Ave. 48 y Ave. 50 (Mon–Fri 6pm–midnight, Sat & Sun 2pm–2am).

Boat tours and diving From Marina Cienfuegos (☎ 43 55 1699, ✉ comercial@marlin.cfg.tur.cu), next to Club Cienfuegos at Calle 35 e/ Ave. 6 y Ave. 8, you can arrange boat tours of the bay ($12CUC per person), as well as diving in conjunction with the

Centro de Buceo Rancho Luna (see box, p.256).

Swimming pools The swimming pool at the *La Unión* hotel is available to non-guests (daily 9am–5pm). The $10CUC fee includes $7CUC of credit for food and drinks. Likewise, the *Hotel Jagua* pool (daily 10am–6pm) costs $10CUC, including $8CUC food and drink credit. There's also a pool at Club Cienfuegos (see opposite).

Tennis Club Cienfuegos has two synthetic courts (daily 10am–6pm; $5CUC/hr).

Open streets and spacious bungalows – unmistakeably influenced by the United States of the 1940s and 1950s – project an image of affluence and suburban harmony. This image is perhaps more misleading today than it would have been in the 1950s, but you'll still find the most comfortable homes in Cienfuegos here, many of them with rooms for rent to visitors; there are also some gorgeous boutique hotels.

Other than the magnificent **Palacio de Valle**, Punta Gorda has no museums and few historic monuments, but other possibilities include the **Club Cienfuegos** leisure complex and boat trips from the marina. Of the scrappy beaches, the best are **Playa Juvenil**, next to the marina, a 50m wisp of sand with a few wooden parasols and a little refreshments kiosk; and **Playa Alegre**, six blocks east along Avenida 16 from Calle 37 and three blocks south from there. Before swimming at any beach in Cienfuegos, however, bear in mind that the city's waste water is emptied directly into the bay.

As much as anything, Punta Gorda is the best area in the city to spend time outside, whether taking an evening stroll down Calle 37, a drink at one of several open-air bars and music venues, sitting on the wall of the **Malecón** – the bayside promenade – and shooting the breeze or relaxing in the bayside park at La Punta, the pretty peninsula at Punta Gorda's southern tip.

Club Cienfuegos

Calle 37 e/ Ave. 8 y Ave. 12 • **Club** Daily 10am–1am • $1CUC 10am–7pm, $3–5CUC 7pm–1am • **Swimming pool** Daily 10am–6pm • $8CUC, including $5CUC food and drink credit • ☎ 43 52 6510

Club Cienfuegos, a gleaming white, palatial three-storey mansion dating back to 1918, looks as if it might house a prestigious museum or a distinguished embassy. In fact it's a small commercial and leisure complex featuring two restaurants, a 25m swimming pool, tennis courts, a shop, a few indoor games including pool tables and a very low-key **amusement park** with a minute go-kart track, bumper cars, pool tables and a couple of other activities. It also has its own marina, from where you can charter a boat, while the large, first-floor terrace overlooking the marina hosts a programme of night-time entertainment (see p.251).

Palacio de Valle

Calle 37 esq. Ave. 0 • Daily 10am–10pm • Free

One of the most popular targets for visitors to Punta Gorda is the striking **Palacio de Valle**. With its mismatched twin turrets, chiselled arches and carved windows, it looks like a cross between a medieval fortress, an Indian temple and a Moorish palace. The interior is just as fancy, with tiled mosaic floors, lavishly decorated walls and ceilings, a marble staircase, and painstakingly detailed arches and adornments scattered throughout. Built as a private home between 1913 and 1917, its decidedly Islamic-influenced interior is a curiosity for a city founded by Frenchmen. An Italian architect, Alfredo Collí, was responsible for the overall design, but structural contributions were made by a team of artisans, who included Frenchmen, Cubans, Italians and Arabs. Nowadays, its principal function is as a restaurant, but if you're not eating there's nothing to stop you wandering around its many rooms or up the spiral staircase to the **rooftop bar** (see p.251), the best spot for a drink in Cienfuegos. The views are better than you might expect given the building's unremarkable height.

La Punta

South of the Palacio de Valle, the land narrows to a 200m peninsula known as **La Punta**, home to the city's most opulent residences. Colourful wooden and concrete mansions and maisonettes, most of them now classy *casas particulares*, line the quiet road which leads down to the pretty little **park** right at the tip of the peninsula, almost completely surrounded by water. A great place to chill out during the week, the park springs into life at the weekends when the town's teenagers converge to listen to music, drink rum, flirt and cool down in the murky water.

4

Cementerio Tomás Acea

Avenida 5 de Septiembre • Daily 6am–5pm • Free

Some 2.5km from Calle 37, or a five-minute taxi ride from the centre, is the picturesque **Cementerio Tomás Acea**, the city's largest cemetery and the nearest thing in Cienfuegos to a landscaped metropolitan park. Completed in 1926, the overly grand Parthenon-styled entrance building, at the end of a long driveway with gardens on either side, leads into the gentle slopes of the cemetery **grounds**. Rolling, sweeping lawns are punctuated by the odd tree and, from the highest point, there are pleasant views of the distant bay. There are some interesting **tombs** to look out for, the most striking being the monument to the Martyrs of September 5, 1957 (see p.244). There's sometimes a guide on hand offering informal tours, with a tip the only payment expected.

ARRIVAL AND DEPARTURE
CIENFUEGOS

BY PLANE

International arrivals There are no scheduled domestic flights to or from the Jaime González Airport (☏43 55 1328), just over 5km from Pueblo Nuevo on the eastern outskirts of the city, and only very occasional international flights from Miami and Canada. Taxis provide the only transport to and from the city; the fare to Pueblo Nuevo should be around $5CUC.

BY BUS

Víazul buses All Víazul buses pull in at the Terminal de Omnibus on Calle 49 e/ 56 y 58 (☏43 51 5720), from where it's a 15min walk or a $2CUC taxi ride into the town centre; a taxi to Punta Gorda, out of reach on foot for most people, will cost around $4CUC. On departure, when catching a bus from the station, be prepared for the $0.50CUC charge per piece of luggage.

Destinations Havana (3 daily; 4hr); Playa Girón (1 daily; 1hr 30min); Playa Larga (1 daily; 2hr); Santa Clara (2 daily; 1hr 20min); Trinidad (4 daily; 1hr 30min); Varadero (3 daily; 4hr 45min & 2hr 35min).

Conectando Cuba buses This bus service (see p.30), run by Cubanacán and Transtur, has several drop off and pick up points in the city, including outside hotels *La Unión* and *Jagua*. To buy tickets, go to the local branch of Cubanacán (see p.248).

Destinations Havana (1 daily; 4hr); Pinar del Río (1 daily; 8hr); Trinidad (1 daily; 1hr 30min); Varadero (1 daily; 3hr 30min); Viñales (1 daily; 6hr 30min).

Local buses For visitors, the only useful intermunicipal bus service leaves from the Terminal de Omnibus for Playa Rancho Luna seven times daily; journey time is about 40min.

BY TRAIN

The train station is over the road from the bus station at Calle 49 e/ 58 y 60 (☏43 52 5495), though as services to or from anywhere are painfully slow, very few foreign visitors arrive or depart by train. From the station, it's a 15min walk or a $2CUC taxi ride into the town centre; a taxi to Punta Gorda costs around $4CUC.

Destinations Havana (every other day; 10hr); Santa Clara (1 daily; 2hr 30min).

BY CAR

Arriving by car from Trinidad, you'll enter Cienfuegos on Ave. 5 de Septiembre, which connects up with the city grid four blocks east of Calle 37, the main street and the road on which you'll arrive if you've driven from Havana or Varadero. The most convenient and secure place to park is in the *La Unión* hotel car park ($2CUC/day), opposite the hotel on Calle 31.

BY FERRY

Small tugboat-like ferries to and from Castillo de Jagua (3 daily; 1h; $1CUC each way) use the tiny ferry terminal at Ave. 46, at the foot of Calle 25, in Pueblo Nuevo, from where you can walk to Parque José Martí.

GETTING AROUND

You can **walk** around Pueblo Nuevo, but you'll probably want to use some kind of **transport** if you intend to explore the 3km length of Punta Gorda. Apart from the service down to the beach at Playa Rancho Luna (see p.253), local bus routes are useless for most visitors.

By horse-drawn carriage There are horse-drawn carriages operating up and down Calle 37 all day; there are no fixed stops, so you flag one down anywhere on the road. Cubans usually pay a set fare of one national peso, but non-

Cubans are as likely to be asked for a convertible peso.
By taxi Cubataxi (☏43 51 9145) has cars hanging around the *Jagua* hotel car park in Punta Gorda and outside the *La Unión* hotel in Pueblo Nuevo.

Car rental Havanautos/Cubacar are at Calle 37 e/ 16 y 18 (daily 8am–8pm; ☎ 43 55 1211), and opposite the *Hotel Unión* at Calle 31 e/ 54 y 56 (Mon–Fri 8am–8pm, Sat 8am–5pm; ☎ 43 55 1645).

Scooter rental Scooter rental is available from Motoclub at Ave. 18 esq. 37 (daily 9am–5pm; $13CUC/2hr, $25CUC/day).

INFORMATION AND TRAVEL AGENCIES

INFORMATION

Tourist information The local branch of Infotur is up the staircase leading directly from the street at Ave. 56 no.3117 (altos) e/ 31 y 33 (daily 9am–5pm; ☎ 43 51 4653).

Cultural information Representatives of the Casa de las Américas, one of Cuba's premier cultural institutions, sit at a desk on the terrace outside the Tienda de Arte Maroya on Parque Martí (see p.252), and provide advice on cultural events and places, including museums, music, theatre and visual arts.

Websites The best source for film, theatre performances and live music listings is the excellent state-sponsored ⓦ www.azurina.cult.cu.

TRAVEL AGENCIES

As well as offering tours from Cienfuegos (see box below), the travel agencies below can sell you Víazul bus tickets and book hotel rooms around the country. Cultural tours specialist Paradiso also arranges dance classes.

Cubanacán Ave. 54 no.2903 e/ 29 y 31 (Mon–Sat 8.30am–5pm; ☎ 43 55 1680).

Cubatur Prado no.5399 e/ Ave. 54 y Ave. 56 (Mon–Fri 9am–noon & 1–6pm, Sat 9am–noon; ☎ 43 55 1242).

Havanatur Ave. 54 no.2906 e/ 29 y 31 (Mon–Fri 8am–5pm, Sat 8am–noon; ☎ 43 55 1393).

Paradiso Ave. 54 e/ 33 y 35 (Mon–Sat 9am–5pm; ☎ 43 52 6673).

ACCOMMODATION

Cienfuegos has a great selection of **hotels**, all run by the Cuban Gran Caribe chain. The *Jagua*, *Casa Verde* and *Perla del Mar* form a small network, allowing guests at any to use the facilities at all. There are a large number of equally impressive and much cheaper **casas particulares**, many between the bus station and Parque José Martí as well as along the length of Calle 37, with some particularly comfortable options in Punta Gorda. For the most luxurious houses, head to the tranquil surroundings of **La Punta**, the southern tip of Punta Gorda, a bit of a hike from the centre but worth it if you want a touch of exclusivity and don't mind paying a little extra.

HOTELS

Casa Verde Calle 37 e/ Ave. 0 y Ave. 2 ☎ 43 55 1003 ext. 890, ⓦ gran-caribe.com. A fabulous conversion of a magnificent 1920s house right on the waterfront. With only eight rooms and an elegant Victorian-style interior there's both a sense of intimacy and exclusivity, and there's a restaurant, bar and natural pool on site. **$150CUC**

Jagua Calle 37 no.1 e/ Ave. 0 y Ave. 2 ☎ 43 55 1003, ⓦ gran-caribe.com. The interior of this boxy hotel is more graceful than the exterior, but it's nevertheless a relatively forgettable place. It does have a picturesque location at the foot of Punta Gorda, surrounded by gardens, with views into town and across the bay, and all the amenities you'd expect from a large hotel, including

two restaurants, a shop, a games room and a swimming pool. **$130CUC**

Palacio Azul Calle 37 e/ Ave. 12 y Ave. 14 ☎ 43 55 5828, ⓦ gran-caribe.com. Guests of this stately, attractive sky-blue mansion on the edge of the bay have free access to the pool at *La Unión* in town. All seven rooms are large (some are huge) and well equipped, and a few have views of the bay. Its location next to Club Cienfuegos means that nights here can be a bit noisy. The restaurant serves breakfast only. **$135CUC**

Perla del Mar Calle 37 e/ 0 y 2 ☎ 43 55 1003 ext.862/890, ⓦ gran-caribe.com. Opened in 2012, this nine-room boutique hotel, set in a converted 1950s bayside villa, has a lovely, graceful feel about it. Most of the

---

TOURS FROM CIENFUEGOS

The city's travel agencies (see above) can organize tours of Cienfuegos and excursions around the province and beyond. Prices don't vary much between the agencies.

City tour Includes pick up from hotel and takes in Parque José Martí, the Prado and Malecón, the Palacio de Valle and lunch. $21CUC each for two people; $10CUC each for six or more.

Paseo por la Bahía A tour of the bay by boat offering great perspectives on the city and reaching right down to the Castillo de Jagua (p.254). $12CUC, $16CUC with open bar.

Jardín Botánico A trip to the splendid botanical gardens (see p.252). $18CUC each for two people; $10 each for six or more.

El Nicho A guided trek (including lunch) around Parque El Nicho in the Sierra del Escambray (see p.254). $30CUC.

communal spaces – including a dining and sun-lounge area and two outdoor jacuzzis on the patio – face out over the water. **$150CUC**

La Unión Calle 31 esq. 54 ☎ 43 55 1020, ⊛ gran-caribe .com. This charming, stylish and comfortable hotel, occupying a Neoclassical building from 1869, has patios done in glorious Spanish tiles, a sauna, a gym, a hot tub, an art gallery and a small swimming pool. The 49 rooms are equipped with satellite TV and spotless bathrooms, and there's a roof-terrace bar overlooking the bay. **$143CUC**

CASAS PARTICULARES

Casa Angel y Isabel Calle 35 no.24 e/ 0 y Litoral ☎ 43 51 1519, ✉ angeleisabel@yahoo.es. Magnificent neo-colonial house on the water's edge, complete with a colonnaded porch and turrets on the roof. The three well-appointed double rooms are in a separate modern block at the back, where there's also a jetty, waterside patio and roof terrace. **$35CUC**

Casa Piñeiro Calle 41 no.1402 e/ 14 y 16 ☎ 43 51 3808, ⊛ casapineiro.com. The owner of this airy bungalow, surrounded by leafy lawns, is an excellent chef and an enthusiastic economist, full of local knowledge and well-connected around the city. Both bedrooms have a/c, en-suite bathroom and TV. Top-notch meals are served on the copious, covered patio, where's there's a well-stocked bar and a charcoal oven. **$30CUC**

★ **Casa de la Amistad** Ave. 56 no.2927 e/ 29 y 31 ☎ 43 51 6143, ✉ casamistad@correodecuba.cu. This first-floor flat, full of colonial character, is run by a gregarious elderly couple who are as impressively professional as they are personable. Armando will gladly talk revolutionary politics for hours while Leonor excels at playing the host, whether cooking up her house speciality of chicken in cola, or arranging excursions to the beaches and beyond. The two rooms for rent are comfortable and airy, with no a/c but good fans; a spiral staircase leads to a roof terrace with great views. **$30CUC**

Casa de Mery Ave. 6 no.3509 e/ 35 y 37 ☎ 43 51 8880, ✉ canto@jagua.cfg.sld.cu. A top-notch, bright and orderly place run with care and attention by talkative Mery.

The spacious and well-equipped guest rooms, in their own independent block out the back, are gathered around an intimate, leafy patio from where steps lead to a great little roof terrace with views of the bay. **$25CUC**

Casa de Tania y Adrian Ave. 66 no.3705 e/ 37 y 39 ☎ 43 51 1886, ✉ taniacabrera40@yahoo.com. There are two completely independent upstairs apartments for rent here, each with two double bedrooms, reception room, balcony, fully equipped kitchens with bar and well-appointed bathrooms. Meals are taken up on the impressive roof terrace where there are good views, another fully-stocked bar and even a little portable bathing pool. $50CUC whole apartment; $25CUC per room.

★ **Hostal Bahia** Ave. 20 esq. 35 no.3502 (altos) ☎ 43 52 6598, ✉ ag.reservas@gmail.com. Guest rooms sit alongside a bay-facing first-floor balcony, in an elegant house just over a quiet road from the water's edge. The fantastic location is matched by the graceful, arty and comfortable interior, and the rooms feature a/c, safety deposit boxes, TVs and fridges bursting with drinks. **$35CUC**

★ **Hostal Colonial de Isabel y Pepe** Ave. 52 no.4318 e/ 43 y 45 ☎ 43 51 8276, ✉ hostalcolonialisapepe @gmail.com. Within five blocks of the bus station and run by a warm and talkative couple, this *casa* is akin to a boutique hotel. Three of the five large guest rooms, each with its own fridge and bathroom, are in a fantastically elegant neo-colonial main house and are equipped with pristine antique furniture. The other two are in an adjoining house featuring one of the city's most impressive roof terraces, lined with park benches and street lamps. Guests dine on a covered ground-level patio. **$30CUC**

★ **Villa Lagarto** Calle 35 no.4B e/ 0 y Litoral ☎ 43 51 9966, ⊛ villalagartocuba.com. Bordering La Punta's small park, this sensational place has its own tiny pier and one of the best restaurants in the city. There are six high-standard rooms in total, three along an upstairs veranda which leads onto a wonderful treetop walkway suspended over the fantastically verdant back-garden terrace, where there's a small saltwater swimming pool. Rooms benefit from the fresh breezes blowing in across the bay. **$40CUC**

EATING

There are plenty of places to eat out in Cienfuegos, though with a few excellent exceptions these fall into two rather prosaic types. A large proportion of the burgeoning number of **paladars** offer value for money if you want functional food, but have little to distinguish between them in terms of quality or variety, with huge menus featuring slight variations on traditional Cuban dishes plus a few token pizzas and pastas. Most of the **state-run restaurants** offer a poorer version of the same on shorter menus, and many charge in national pesos and are suitable only for the shoestringiest of budgets. As is the case elsewhere, if you're staying in a *casa particular* you'll eat better there than in most of the state restaurants. For **fast food**, head for Prado or the Malecón.

STATE RESTAURANTS AND CAFÉS

1869 La Unión hotel, Calle 31 esq. 54 ☎ 43 55 1020. The likes of mixed-meat kebabs ($15CUC), grilled beef steak in

red wine ($14CUC) and garlic shrimps ($15CUC) make the choice and quality of main dishes at this half-way elegant hotel restaurant a cut above anything else in Pueblo Nuevo.

Though the cooking is nothing to get worked up about, it's way above the local average. Daily 7–9.45am, noon–2.45pm & 7–9.45pm.

Café Cienfuegos Club Cienfuegos, Calle 37 e/ Ave. 8 y Ave. 12 ☎ 43 51 2891 ext. 112. This polished first-floor restaurant, with a classic saloon bar, is particularly appealing during daylight hours, when you can enjoy views of Punta Gorda and the bay from the tables on the small balcony. Avoid the one or two non-Cuban dishes, like the tomato-flavoured rice masquerading as vegetarian *paella*, and go for the numerous simple seafood dishes ($5–10CUC). Daily noon–3pm & 6–10.30pm.

Coppelia Prado esq. Ave. 52 ☎ 43 51 7408. The local branch of the Cuban ice-cream chain, where the national-peso prices mean you can gorge on the stuff for loose change. Tues–Sun 11am–11pm.

Palacio del Valle Calle 37 esq. Ave. 0 ☎ 43 55 1226. A wide choice of seafood – such as succulent butterfly lobster ($25CUC) and simple grilled fish ($12CUC) – with some meat alternatives. The excellent pianist and elegant arched interior provide a sense of occasion and outshine the food, which is nevertheless just above average. Daily noon–9.30pm.

El Polinesio Calle 29 e/ Ave. 54 y Ave. 56, Parque José Martí ☎ 43 51 5723. One of the city's more atmospheric restaurants, dimly lit and hidden from the street in the belly of an old building, engendering an oddly clandestine feel. The no-frills beef, chicken and pork dishes are priced in national pesos at between $15CUP and $40CUP per main. Daily noon–3pm & 6–10pm.

PALADARS

Aché Ave. 38 no.4106 e/ 41 y 43 ☎ 43 52 6173. One of the city's longest-established paladars, *Aché* serves wholesome, well-prepared Cuban-style chicken, fish and pork, as well as some excellent seafood, in the roof-covered countrified backyard of a pretty bungalow surrounded by gardens. Main dishes are $7CUC. Mon–Fri noon–10pm.

Bouyón 1825 Calle 25 no.5605 e/ 56 y 58 ☎ 43 51 7376. The wall of photos of bygone Cienfuegos, an open kitchen, music videos of Cuban greats and the building itself (a colonial house near the central city square) provide more atmosphere and character than in most comparable paladars nearby, though you'll eat better in many of the *casas particulares*. Avoid the pasta and stick to Cuban basics like smoked pork loin ($8CUC) or grilled shrimps ($9CUC). Daily noon–10pm.

Casa Prado Prado no.4626 e/ 46 y 48 ☎ 52 62 3858. Vast portions of pretty authentic tasting paella ($4.50) are among the house specialities here, and rightly so when compared against the perfectly decent but standard-issue Cuban-style pork, beef and chicken options ($2.50–15CUC) which are nonetheless good value. Daily 11.30am–10.30pm.

★ **Finca del Mar** Calle 35 e/ 18 y 20 ☎ 43 52 6598. This outstanding, beautifully constructed, delightfully laid out paladar busts out of the Cuban culinary straightjacket. Its fantastic starters work just as well as tapas and can make a meal in themselves: the stuffed piquillo peppers ($6CUC) are delicious, the caprese salad ($6CUC) spot on, and the sausage selection ($6CUC) top quality. Mains, like the shrimps ($9CUC), are more typically Cuban but are fresh and perfectly prepared, with minimum fuss but maximum care. Daily noon–midnight.

★ **El Lagarto** Calle 35 no.4B e/ Ave. 0 y Litoral, La Punta ☎ 43 51 9966. Knocking most of the competition out of the game thanks to its flavoursome food and atmospheric setting, this paladar is really special. Tables are spread around a backyard terrace woven into an enchanting bayside grove, filled every evening by the irresistible smell of whatever meat is slow-cooking in the outdoor charcoal oven. There are no menus, just a daily-changing choice of top quality meat and seafood with delicious soups and sides. Average cost of a three-course meal $15–18CUC. Daily 8am–10pm.

DRINKING AND NIGHTLIFE

Cienfuegos has several **non-tourist bars** offering cheap rum and plenty of undiluted local flavour. However, the tourist places, including some of the hotel ones, are not to be sniffed at, as they offer by far the best selection of drinks and some character of their own. Some bars double up as **cafés**. During the week, the city's **nightlife** is subdued, especially outside July and August, with venues often relatively empty. At the weekends, however, **Punta Gorda** really comes alive, with locals out in force – particularly around the *malecón* – and reggaeton and salsa echoing through the streets. On Saturdays from around 8pm, some brilliant local musicians grace the bandstand in the square, attracting an older but buoyant and sociable crowd.

BARS

Cienfuegos Ave. 54 e/ 35 y 37 ☎ 43 55 0289. This is no more than a few tables huddled around a dinky street-facing bar counter, but there are always a few locals here and it's a good place to get chatting to strangers. Daily noon–10pm.

Covadonga Calle 37 e/ 0 y 2 ☎ 43 51 6949. It's all about the location here, on a breezy waterside platform terrace

looking out over the bay. Mojitos and Cuba Libres go for $1CUC. Avoid the restaurant and its low-grade food. Daily 10am–11pm.

Don Luis Calle 31 e/ 54 y 56 (no phone). A tiny but atmospheric saloon opposite the *Unión* hotel, where you can prop up the bar and sip cheap rum with the locals. Mon–Fri 9am–midnight, Sat & Sun noon–midnight.

★ **El Embajador** Ave. 54 esq. 33 ☎ 43 55 2144. This cigar shop is ideal for a good-quality coffee or rum during the afternoon, accompanied by the aroma of tobacco. There's a stylishly simple but inviting little bar at the back and a more comfortable upstairs gallery, with easy chairs around a coffee table. Mon–Sat 9am–6pm.

★ **Palacio de Valle** Calle 37 esq. Ave. 0 ☎ 43 55 1226. The views over the bay and the city from the rooftop bar make this hands-down the best place in Cienfuegos for a laidback drink. Daily 10am–10pm.

El Palatino Ave. 54 esq. Calle 27, Parque José Martí T43 55 1244. A pleasant bar on the main square with one of the town's better selections of drinks; it's a popular spot with tour groups. Daily 9am–10pm.

La Venus Negra Hotel Unión, Calle 31 esq. 54. The fourth-floor rooftop patio bar in this excellent hotel has fabulous 360-degree views of the city and is a great place to hide out and chill. There's a pool table here too. Daily noon–midnight.

CABARETS, CLUBS AND LIVE MUSIC VENUES

Cabaret Guanaroca Hotel Jagua, Calle 37 no.1 e/ Ave. 0 y Ave. 2 ☎ 43 55 1003. Cheesy hotel disco where reggaeton and salsa are played nightly. Entry $5CUC, includes $4CUC drinks credit. Daily 10pm–late.

Café Teatro Terry Ave. 56 e/ 27 y 29, Parque José Martí ☎ 43 51 0770. Squeezed down the side of the theatre, this is a bijou courtyard under a roof of exuberant hanging vines and flowers where mostly traditional music genres like trova and son are performed on a cramped stage. Entry $2CUC. Sun–Fri 10.30pm–1am, Sat 3pm & 10.30pm.

La Caribeña Calle 37 esq. Ave. 22 (no phone). A huge concrete outdoor dancefloor and performance area set in gardens protruding into the bay from the end of the *malecón*. Local salsa bands attract big crowds here. Entry $2CUC. Fri–Sun 9.30pm–2am.

Club Cienfuegos Calle 37 e/ Ave. 8 y Ave. 12 ☎ 43 51 2891. The city's glossiest music venue, on a wide terrace looking over the marina where you can enjoy waiter service at your table. DJ nights and live music, from Cuban styles to local rock and reggaeton acts. There's a basement bar, too. Entry $3CUC Mon–Fri & Sun, or $5CUC Sat, including $2CUC food and drink credit. Mon–Fri & Sun 10pm–1am, Sat 10pm–2am.

Costasur Ave. 40 e/ 35 y bahía ☎ 43 52 5808. One of the most popular nights out with locals of all ages, this large-scale, open-air cabaret-style music venue has a great location, with the waters of the bay literally lapping at its edges. There are rumba, salsa and techno-lite nights, among others. Loud, flamboyant and good fun. Entry $1–5CUC. Wed–Fri 9.30pm–2am, Sat & Sun 9.30pm–3am.

El Cubanísimo Calle 35 e/ Ave. 16 y Ave. 18 ☎ 43 55 1255. Over the road from the edge of the bay, this atmospherically enclosed open-air venue hosts anything from comedy nights and karaoke to live singers and bands, and attracts a good mix of locals and tourists. Entry $1–2CUC. Tues–Sun 9am–2am, shows at 11pm.

Discoteca El Benny Ave. 54 e/ 29 y 31 ☎ 43 55 1105. Unusually slick and polished for a Cuban nightclub, especially one in the provinces, with a music policy dominated by pop, salsa and reggaeton. Don't expect any action before 11pm. Entry $3CUC. Daily 10pm–3am.

★ **Jardines de la UNEAC** Calle 25 e/ Ave. 54 y Ave. 56, Parque José Martí ☎ 43 51 6117. One of the city's most congenial and intimate live music venues, This leafy, enchanting open-air patio has a bar and is a great place to enjoy some local bands and soloists playing Cuban musical styles such as bolero, trova and son. There are no fixed performance times but there's usually something on in the afternoons and evenings; check the noticeboard posted at the gate. Usually free. Thurs–Sun.

TropiSur Calle 37 e/ 46 y 48 ☎ 43 52 5488. The city's most prestigious cabaret venue, with extravagant shows in a large outdoor space and the crowds that flock here at weekends to get lively. Reggaeton concerts are sometimes staged here too. No shorts or vests. Entry $2–10CUC. Shows Fri–Sun 10am–2pm.

ENTERTAINMENT

Teatro Tomás Terry Parque José Martí ☎ 43 51 3361, ⊕ teatroterry.azurina.cult.cu. Plays, concerts, dance, kids' shows and live comedy. Performances usually start at 9pm Mon–Sat, while on Sun there's only a matinee performance, usually at 5pm. A monthly programme is posted on the noticeboards out front. Tickets cost $5CUC–10CUC; shorts and sleeveless tops are not permitted.

Cine-Teatro Luisa Prado esq. Ave. 50 ☎ 43 51 5339. Originally opened as a theatre in 1911 this classic old cinema was remodelled in the 1940s and continues to show films throughout the week. Tickets are $1CUP.

CIENFUEGOS BASEBALL

The local **baseball** team, nicknamed the **Elefantes de Cienfuegos**, has had some rare success recently and currently plays in the top tier of the national league. Games (usually Tues–Sun) take place in the 30,000-capacity Estadio 5 de Septiembre, at Ave. 20 y 47 (☎ 43 51 3644). Tickets ($1–3CUC for non-Cubans) are sold on the door.

SHOPPING

There's a daily **street market** on the pedestrianized section of Calle 29 selling arts and crafts aimed squarely at the tourist market.

Casa del Fundador Calle 29 esq. Ave. 54, Parque José Martí ☎ 43 55 2134. Aimed squarely at tourists, though the quality of goods here is pretty decent and includes a good selection of cigars, some CDs, T-shirts, maps and souvenirs. Mon–Sat 9am–7pm, Sun 9am–1pm.
El Embajador Ave. 54 esq. 33 ☎ 43 55 2144. Cigars and rum in an inviting shop with its own little bar and lounge. Mon–Sat 9am–6pm.

Ilusión Ave. 54 e/ 35 y 37. A better-than-average selection of T-shirts, bags, wood carvings, paintings, housewares, shoes and ornamentation. Mon–Sat 9am–5pm, Sun 9am–noon.
Maroya Ave. 54 no.2506 e/ 25 y 27, Parque José Martí ☎ 43 55 1208. The best place in the city by far for arts and crafts with a wide variety of stock, from photography and painting to sculpture and textiles. Mon–Sat 9am–6.30pm, Sun 9am–1pm.

DIRECTORY

Internet and telephones ETECSA Telepunto, Calle 31 e/ 54 y 56 (daily 8.30am–7pm), has several internet terminals ($6CUC/hr) and six phone booths. There are several ETECSA *minipunto* phone cabins dotted around town, including one at Calle 37 e/ Ave. 16 y Ave. 18, and sets of public phones in the street on the pedestrianized section of Ave. 54.
Laundry El Lavatín launderette, Ave. 56 e/ 41 y 43 (Mon–Sat 8am–7pm, Sun 8am–noon).
Medical care The best-stocked pharmacy is in the Clínica Internacional at Ave. 10 no.3705 e/ 37 y 39 (24hr; ☎ 43 55 1622), in Punta Gorda. This is also the best place for foreign nationals to come to see a nurse or doctor, or to call for an ambulance. There's also a small but well-stocked convertible-peso pharmacy in the *La Unión* hotel

(Mon–Fri 8am–4.30pm, Sat 8am–noon).
Money and exchange The bank best prepared to deal with foreign currency is the Banco Financiero Internacional, at Ave. 54 esq. 29 (Mon–Fri 8.30am–3.30pm). The CADECA *casa de cambio* is at Ave. 56 no.3314 e/ 33 y 35 (Mon–Sat 8am–4pm, Sun 8am–1pm).
Police Call ☎ 116.
Postal services The main branch of the post office is at Calle 35 esq. Ave. 56 (Mon–Sat 8am–6pm, Sun 8am–noon). There's a DHL office, which sells stamps, at Ave. 54 e/ 35 y 37 (Mon–Fri 9am–noon, 1–5pm, Sat 9am–noon).
Visas To extend tourist visas, visit the Department of Immigration at Ave. 46 esq. 29 (Mon–Thurs 8am–3pm; ☎ 43 55 1283).

Around Cienfuegos city

There are several manageable **day-** or **half-day** trips from Cienfuegos city that offer some satisfyingly uncontrived but still visitor-friendly diversions. Chief among them is the exuberant **Jardín Botánico**, compact enough to tour in a couple of hours but with a sufficient variety of species to keep you there all day. A little closer to the city, toward the coast, the focus at the wilder **Laguna Guanaroca** nature reserve is birds rather than plants.

Near to the mouth of the Bahía de Jagua, **Playa Rancho Luna** has a pleasant beach and is the most obvious alternative to the city for a longer stay in the province. Further along, this coastline forms the eastern bank of the narrow channel that links the sea to the bay. On the western bank is the **Castillo de Jagua**, a plain but atmospheric eighteenth-century Spanish fortress. Though accessible from Playa Rancho Luna via a ferry across the narrow channel, it's well worth taking the boat to the fortress from Cienfuegos and enjoying the full serenity of the bay. Further afield are the forested peaks of the **Sierra del Escambray** mountains, where you can do some gentle trekking or explore the beautiful set of waterfalls at **Parque El Nicho**.

Jardín Botánico de Cienfuegos

Circuito Sur, near Pepito Tey • Daily 8am–6pm, last entry at around 4.30pm • $2.50CUC, including guide • ☎ 43 54 5115 • There is no publi transport to the gardens; to drive there from Calle 37 in Cienfuegos, head east on Avenida 64 (aka Calzada de Dolores), and continue east on Circuito Sur. Round-trip taxi fares are around $20CUC

About 15km east of the Cienfuegos city limits, the **Jardín Botánico de Cienfuegos** has one of the most complete collections of tropical plants in the country. The 11-acre site is home to over two thousand different species, divided up into various different groups, most of them merging seamlessly into one another so that in places this feels more like a natural forest than an artificially created garden. A road runs down through the grounds to a café and a little shop selling maps of the park. This is where the only indoor areas are found, a cactus house and another greenhouse full of tropical plants.

Guides are essential if you want to know what you're looking at, but though it can be difficult to find your way around, there's a definite appeal to just wandering around on your own, following the roughly marked tracks through the varied terrain and past a series of (usually dry) pools and waterways. Highlights include the amphitheatre of **bamboo** and the vast array of **palm trees**, totalling some 325 different species.

Laguna Guanaroca

Carretera a Rancho Luna • Daily 8am–3pm • Refugio de Fauna Guanaroca-Gavilanes ☎ 43 54 8117 • Excursion from Cienfuegos $10CUC

Some 12km from Cienfuegos and 5km from Playa Rancho Luna, on the way to the south coast beaches, is the **Laguna de Guanaroca**. Joined to the Bahía de Cienfuegos by a narrow channel, the lake is the site of the **Refugio de Fauna Guanaroca-Gavilanes** nature reserve; the signposted entrance is marked by a small roadside building. Guided tours – which you should arrange in advance through one of the travel agents in Cienfuegos (see p.248) – last between two and three hours and allow visitors to learn about the rich variety of birds that make their home here, and provide some insights into the plant life. **Lookout towers** have been erected to help you spot the reserve's many bird species, including the tocororo, cartacuba, zunzún hummingbirds, pink flamingos and pelicans.

Playa Rancho Luna

Less than 20km south of Cienfuegos city is the province's most developed section of coastline, centred on an uspoilt but unspectacular 1km-stretch of beach called **Playa Rancho Luna**. Peppered with broad-branched trees sinking into warm, slightly murky waters, the beach is flanked by craggy headlands, and though several hundred metres of it fall within the grounds of the *Rancho Luna* hotel, it's all open to the public; the section closest to the headland occupied by the much smaller *Faro Luna* hotel is a favoured spot for locals at weekends and in the summer months.

A longer stretch of rocky coastline sits between the beach and the channel linking the sea to the Cienfuegos bay, and it's 6km along the coast from Playa Rancho Luna to the departure point for ferries to the Castillo de Jagua (see p.254) and back to the city. This coastline is also a good place for **scuba diving**, with a dive centre at the *Rancho Luna* and *Faro Luna* hotels (see box, p.256).

Dolphinarium

Carretera a Pasacaballos Km 18 • Mon–Tues & Thurs–Sun 9am–4pm, shows 10am & 2pm • $10CUC adults; swimming with dolphins $45CUC; photos $10CUC • ☎ 43 54 8120

A couple of hundred metres along the coast from the *Faro Luna* hotel is an attractive **dolphinarium** set in natural surroundings. The stands of the small seaside arena have been built on the edge of an inlet surrounded by trees and bushes, where submerged fences prevent the animals from escaping. There are two excellent daily shows (some with sea lions as well as dolphins) featuring all kinds of tricks, audience participation and the chance for an unforgettable swim with the dolphins.

ARRIVAL AND DEPARTURE	**PLAYA RANCHO LUNA**
By bus Though the timetable is unreliable, and the service is sporadically suspended, buses in theory leave the main station in Cienfuegos for the beach eight times a day at	5.20am, 8am, 10am, 11.25am, 1pm, 3.30pm, 5.30pm and 10.15pm, and cost $0.85CUP each way. Buses are most likely to run in July and August.

By ferry Ferries leave and depart three times daily from both sides of the channel linking the bay to the sea; catch the ferry either from below the *Pasacaballo* hotel or just below the Castillo de Jagua; the fare to the city is $1CUC.

ACCOMMODATION

Spread out along 4km of mostly rocky, tree-lined shores that reach round to the mouth of the Jagua Bay, Rancho Luna's three **hotels** are the main focus of the area. Two of them, the *Rancho Luna* and *Faro Luna*, are part of the Gran Caribe chain and share one another's facilities, though they are 1km apart. There are also a few **casas particulares** along the coastal road between the *Faro Luna* and *Pasacaballo* hotels.

Faro Luna Carretera a Pasacaballos Km 18 ☎43 54 8030, ⊕gran-caribe.com. Small and quite subdued, this is Rancho Playa Luna's best hotel option for couples. The neatly kept grounds roost just above the rocky water's edge, 300m from the beach, and there's a diminutive pool and scooter rental facilities. $90CUC

Finca Los Colorados Carretera a Pasacaballos Km 20 ☎43 54 8044, ✉jorge@casapineiro.com. Over the road from a lighthouse, this attractive old ranch house has two double rooms for rent, featuring stylishly rustic furniture and sturdy iron beds; there's also a fabulously leafy patio garden where meals are sometimes served. $25CUC

Pasacaballo Carretera a Pasacaballos Km 23 ☎43 59 2100, ✉reserva@pasacaballos.cfg.tur.cu. This 1970s hulk of a hotel looms above the channel linking the bay to the sea. Its brutalist architecture has been softened by a colourful paintjob but it's still a little at odds with its picturesque surroundings. There's a huge swimming pool but not a lot of beach round here. $38CUC

Rancho Luna Carretera a Rancho Luna Km 17.5 ☎43 54 8012, ⊕gran-caribe.com. This large, all-inclusive family hotel has by far the best section of beach and features a buffet and Italian restaurants, a beach grill, games room, mini-golf, tennis courts and swimming pool. $110CUC

Castillo de Jagua

Daily 8am–4pm • $1CUC

Half the fun of a visit to the seventeenth-century Spanish fortress at the mouth of the Jagua Bay, known as the **Castillo de Jagua**, is getting there. The **ferry** from Cienfuegos (see box below) docks just below the fortress, on the opposite side of the channel to Playa Rancho Luna, from where a dusty track leads up to the cannon guarding the castle drawbridge. Inside, a small **museum** details the history of the fort, which was originally built to defend against pirate attacks. There's also a couple of tables in a sunken courtyard where you can get something to eat and drink; and steps winding up to the top of the single turret from where there are modest views. It's also worth taking a peek at the cramped and dingy **prison cell** and the **chapel** on the courtyard level.

Parque El Nicho

Daily 8.30am–6.30pm • $5CUC

Near the eastern border of the province, in the lush green Sierra del Escambray mountains 5km from the hamlet of Crucecitas and around 60km from Cienfuegos city

THE CASTILLO DE JAGUA FERRY

A rusty old vessel looking vaguely like a tugboat, the passenger **ferry** between Cienfuegos and the Castillo de Jagua chugs across the placid waters of the bay at a pace slow enough to allow a relaxed contemplation of the surroundings, including the tiny, barely inhabited cays where the ferry makes a brief call to pick up passengers. The deck is lined with benches but the metal roof is the best place to sit, allowing unobscured views in all directions.

Sailing from a wharf next to the junction between Calle 25 and Avenida 46, the ferry departs Cienfuegos two to three times a day, currently 8am, 1pm and sometimes at 5.30pm, and from the fortress at 6.30am, 10am and 3pm; journey time is a little less than an hour, and the fare is $1CUC.

DIVING AND SNORKELLING IN CIENFUEGOS PROVINCE

With over thirty dive sites along the coral reef that stretches the length of the local coastline, southern Cienfuegos is a good place to go **diving**. There are two principal dive centres in the province, one at Playa Rancho Luna and the other at the pretty *Villa Guajimico*, just off Carretera de Cienfuegos and exactly halfway along the coastal road between Trinidad and Cienfuegos. You can also rent **snorkelling gear** from the Faro Luna centre ($2CUC/day).

DIVE CENTRES

Centro de Buceo Villa Guajimico, Carretera de Cienfuegos Km 42 ☎43 54 0947, ✉guajimico @enet.cu, 🌐cubamarviajes.cu. There are around twenty offshore dive sites close by to this club, including the wreck of *La Arabela*. A single dive costs $40CUC and there are two daily departures. The club is ACUC, CMAS and ESA certified, and there's a comfortable and well-run *campismo* tailored to divers on site (☎43 54 0946, 🌐campismopopular.cu; $36CUC).
Centro de Buceo Rancho Luna ☎43 54 8087, ✉buceo@nautica.cfg.tur.cu, 🌐nauticamarlin.com.

This dive club operates out of both the sister *Rancho Luna* and *Faro Luna* hotels at Playa Rancho Luna. All dives take place within a couple of hundred metres of the shore, where a varied stretch of coral is punctuated by a number of wrecked ships. Among the sheer vertical walls and numerous caves and tunnels, you can usually see big fish such as nurse sharks, barracuda and tarpon. A single dive costs $30CUC, two dives cost $55CUC; ACUC, SNSI and RSTC certificated diving courses start at $60CUC for a single-immersion resort dive.

by road, **Parque El Nicho** is a natural park with trails cutting through it, culminating at a delightful set of waterfalls and natural pools. This is one of the five smaller hiking areas, which can only loosely be considered parks, that make up the Gran Parque Natural Topes de Collantes nature reserve, which is usually visited from Trinidad (see p.298). The entrance to the park, marked by a stone gateway, leads into an official trail, the **Reino de las Aguas**, which cuts through the dense woodlands and crosses over rivers and streams, taking in numerous waterfalls, mountain vistas and abundant birdlife before arriving at the **El Nicho waterfalls**. More becalming and enchanting than spectacular, the waterfalls drop from over 15m at their highest, and there are several pools ideal for bathing, all of them fed by cascading water. There is also a restaurant within the park, lunch at which is included in organized excursions to the area.

ARRIVAL AND TOURS

By car Driving here independently from Cienfuegos is much easier now than it was a few years ago, as much of the road between the park and the city has been resurfaced. Turn off the main road at Crucecitas, from where it's 5km to the start of the trails to the waterfalls.
Tours If you don't have your own car, organized day-trips

from Cienfuegos are the best way to get here, since there is no public transport. Havanatur (☎43 55 1393) and Cubanacán (☎43 55 1680) both offer day-trips for $30CUC per person; it's worth booking well in advance, as minimum of six people is usually required.

Santa Clara

One of the largest and liveliest cities in Cuba, the provincial capital of **SANTA CLARA**, landlocked near the centre of Villa Clara province, has long been a place of pilgrimage for **Che Guevara** worshippers, with two large monuments and a museum commemorating the man, his life and his part in the rebel victory. Home to a large student population and the country's third-biggest university, and with only two tourist hotels in the centre, there's a strong sense here that the city is getting on with its own business despite receiving coachloads of visitors, and Santa Clara remains an idiosyncratically Cuban place. Its social life revolves around the vibrant central square, **Parque Vidal**, just a block away from the main shopping street, part-pedestrianized **Independencia**. The plaza is definitely one of Santa Clara's highlights, though there are

SANTA CLARA

■ ACCOMMODATION
Alba Hostal	9
América	7
Aparthostal Eva y Ernesto	4
Los Caneyes	13
Casa de Consuelo	3
Ramos y Nelson Turiño	2
Casa de Héctor Martínez	11
Casa Mercy	12
El Castillito	5
Hostal Adelaida y Rolando	10
Hostal D'Cordero	8
Hostal Florida Center	1
Santa Clara Libre	
Villa La Granjita	

● SHOPS AND MARKETS
Agromercado	2
Buen Viaje	6
La Campana	3
Fondo de Bienes Culturales	5
Licorama Centro	4
Mil Ilusión	1
La Veguita	

● EATING
El Alba	2
Casa del Gobernador	5
Coppelia	6
Florida Center	1
SaboreArte	3
Sabor Latino	4
Santa Rosalía	
Los Tainos	8

■ DRINKING AND NIGHTLIFE
El Bosque	11
Café Literario	5
Casa de la Ciudad	6
Casa de la Cultura	7
Casa Mercy	10
Club Boulevard	1
La Cuevita de Ultra	2
El Dorado	3
La Marquesina	4
El Mejunje	9
Vista a la Ciudad	8

Sancti Spíritus (85km)

Monumento a la Toma del Tren Blindado

Estadio Sandino

Río Cubanicay

Cubanacán

Cine Camilo Cienfuegos

Iglesia de Buen Viaje

Palacio Provincial

Parque Vidal

Cubatur

Havanatur

Fábrica de Tabacos

Museo de Artes Decorativas

Teatro La Caridad

Río Bélico

Train Station

Parque de los Mártires

Parque del Carmen

Iglesia de Carmen

Cine Cubanacán

Casa de la Ciudad

Galería Provincial de Arte

Iglesia Santa Clara de Asís

Museo Provincial

Terminal de Autos de Alquiler

Terminal de Ómnibus Intermunicipal

Zoo

Terminal de Ómnibus Nacionales

Complejo Monumental Ernesto Che Guevara

PLAZA DE LA REVOLUCIÓN

N

0   100
metres

🚂 (1.3m) & 🏨 (1.5m)

4

several other places worth visiting. On the square itself, the **Museo de Artes Decorativas** offers accurate reconstructions of colonial aristocratic living conditions, while within walking distance is one of two famous national Che Guevara memorial sites, the **Monumento a la Toma del Tren Blindado**. A derailed train here marks one of the most dramatic events of the Battle of Santa Clara, a decisive event in the revolutionary war of the late 1950s, while on the other side of town the **Complejo Monumental Ernesto Che Guevara** is a eulogy to the man himself and is much more substantial.

Parque Vidal

Declared a national monument in 1996, **Parque Vidal** is the geographical, social and cultural nucleus of Santa Clara. A spacious, traditional, pedestrianized and always crowded town square, it exudes a vivacious atmosphere. Weekends are particularly animated, with live music performances on the central bandstand in the evenings, and on the porch of the ornate Casa de la Cultura (see p.266). The square's attractive core, a paved circular **promenade** laced with towering palms and shrub-peppered lawns, is traversed by shoppers and workers throughout the day and, in the evenings, fills up with young and old alike, when music is often piped through speakers in the lampposts.

Biblioteca José Martí

Parque Vidal • Mon–Fri 8am–6pm, Sat 8am–4pm • ☎ 42 20 6222

Parque Vidal is elegantly framed by a mixture of predominantly colonial and neo-colonial buildings, the grandest of which is the **Palacio Provincial** on the northeastern side, once the seat of the local government and now home to the **Biblioteca José Martí**. Built between 1904 and 1912, its wide facade, featuring two bold porticoes, stands out as the square's most classical piece of architecture. There are occasional musical performances in the fabulous concert room – check the board at the entrance for details.

Museo de Artes Decorativas

Parque Vidal • Mon, Wed & Thurs 9am–6pm, Fri & Sat 1–10pm, Sun 6–10pm • $2CUC, photos $5CUC • ☎ 42 20 5368

On the northwest side of Parque Vidal is the **Museo de Artes Decorativas**, featuring furniture and objets d'art spanning four centuries of style, from Renaissance to Art Deco. Each of the eleven rooms is opulently furnished, with most of the exhibits collected from houses around Santa Clara; some of them appear as they might have been when the building – older than most of its neighbours but of no particular architectural merit in itself – was home to a string of aristocratic families during the colonial period. In addition to the **front room**, with its marvellous crystal chandelier, there is a **dining room** with a fully laid table, a **bedroom** with an ostentatiously designed wardrobe and individual pieces like the stunning seventeenth-century bureau with ivory detailing.

Teatro La Caridad

Parque Vidal • Guided tours Tues–Sun 8am–5pm; $1CUC, photos $1CUC • ☎ 42 20 5548

A few doors down from the Museo de Artes Decorativas, on the same northwestern side of Parque Vidal, is the **Teatro La Caridad**, with a fabulous, ornate interior that's sold short by its relatively sober exterior. It was built in 1885 with money donated b

Marta Abreu Estévez, a civic-minded nineteenth-century native of Santa Clara with an inherited fortune; a bronze statue of her stands on the opposite side of the square. As part of Estévez's wider quest to help the poor and contribute to the city's civil, cultural and academic institutions, a portion of the box office receipts was set aside to improve living conditions for the impoverished, thus spawning the theatre's name ("Charity"). Restored for a second time in the early 1980s, and then a third in 2009, it's in fantastic condition, with a semicircular three-tiered balcony enveloping the central seating area and a stunning painted ceiling. You can get closer to it during a performance (see p.266) or the twenty-minute **guided tour** in English, which takes you up into the balcony.

Galería Provincial de Arte

Máximo Gómez no.3 e/ Martha Abreu y Barreras • Tues–Thurs 9am–5pm, Fri & Sat 2–10pm, Sun 6–10pm • Free • ☎ 43 20 7715

Just off the Parque Vidal, round the corner from the theatre, is the **Galería Provincial de Arte**, hosting temporary exhibitions showcasing the work of predominantly Cuban artists. It's always worth a peak inside as the exhibitions vary enormously, from photography and painting to sculpture and installation art, and from young local artists to nationally famous painters.

Casa de la Ciudad

Boulevard esq. J.B. Zayas • Closed for renovations, but usually open for guided visits daily 8am–5pm • $1CUC, photos $5CUC • ☎ 43 20 5593

A couple of blocks west of Parque Vidal, the grand family house that holds the **Casa de la Ciudad** was built in the late 1840s by a wealthy Barcelona-born businessman, and retains a strong sense of its former glory with some of the original floor tiles in the largest rooms, porticoed doorways, stained-glass windows and a central courtyard where concerts are sometimes held (see p.265). The museum was closed for major renovations in 2012, but prior to the refit its motley collection comprised paintings, antique furniture, musical instruments, photographs and other paraphernalia relating to the people, buildings and legends of the city and province, all spread over eight rooms.

Fábrica de Tabacos Constantino Pérez Carrodegua

Maceo esq. Berenguer • 45min guided tours Mon–Fri 9–11am & 1–3pm • $4CUC • ☎ 42 20 2211

Just north of Parque Vidal, the **Fábrica de Tabacos Constantino Pérez Carrodegua** cigar factory employs more than four hundred people and produces some thirty million cigars annually for several dozen brands, including Romeo y Julieta, Partagás, Punch and Montecristo, all of which are on sale in La Veguita across the road (see p.266). **Guided tours** of the factory are very engaging and take in the whole production process, from rolling, sorting, boxing and packaging; to arrange one, it's a good idea to ring in advance or, more reliably, contact Havanatur (see p.263), which regularly organizes visits.

Monumento a la Toma del Tren Blindado

Carretera de Camajuani • Train wagons open Mon–Sat 9am–5pm • $1CUC, photos $1CUC • ☎ 42 20 2758

A block behind the Parque Vidal, Independencia runs toward the river and the **Monumento a la Toma del Tren Blindado**, which honours one of the city's most historic events. The derailed wagons of an armoured train that make up most of the site have lain here since they were toppled from the tracks to the north during the **Battle of Santa Clara**, in 1958. That clash – between the dictator Fulgencio Batista's forces and a small detachment of about three hundred rebels, led by Che Guevara – was to be one of the last military encounters of the Revolutionary War. By December 1958, over ten thousand government troops had been sent by Batista to the centre of the island to prevent the rebels from advancing further west towards Havana, and one of the principal components of this defensive manoeuvre was an **armoured train**. However, Guevara, with only a fraction of his total number of troops, took the upper hand when using a bulldozer to raise the rails, they crashed the armoured train and ambushed the 408 officers and soldiers within, who soon surrendered. The train was later used by the rebels as a base for further attacks.

Few visitors leave Santa Clara without a snapshot of the derailed train, but the monument lacks a sense of gravitas, the drama of what happened here undermined partly by the traffic passing just yards from the derailed wagons, which are strewn at the side of the road. That said, some sense of this historic event and its repercussions are evoked by the **exhibits** displayed inside four of the five wagons, including photos taken at the time, guns and uniforms, and, looking over the scene atop a large concrete star, the bulldozer that did the damage.

Complejo Monumental Ernesto Che Guevara

On the southwestern outskirts of the city, about 1km from Parque Vidal, the **Complejo Monumental Ernesto Che Guevara** marks the final resting place of Che Guevara's body and pays tribute to Santa Clara's adopted son and hero, who led the Cuban rebels to victory against General Batista's dictatorship here in 1958, in one of the decisive battles of the Revolution (see box opposite).

The large thundering **monument** is in classic Cuban revolutionary style: big, bold and made of concrete. Atop the grey-tiled steps of a hulking grandstand are four bulky monoliths; towering down from the tallest one is a burly-looking **statue of Guevara**, on the move and dressed in his usual military garb, rifle in hand. Next to the statue in a huge, somewhat jumbled mural, with Guevara's march from the Sierra Maestra to Santa Clara and the decisive victory over Batista's troops depicted in cement. Spreading out before the monument, the **Plaza de la Revolución**, like its counterpart in Havana, is little more than an open space, though there are two huge posterboards on the far side with revolutionary slogans inspired by Che.

To the rear of the complex is a memorial cemetery in honour of the casualties of Guevara's rebel column which he led from the Sierra Maestra to Santa Clara, known as **Column 8**.

Museo and Memorial al Che

Tues–Sun 9.30am–4.30pm • Free

Underneath the monument, accessed from the rear, the surprisingly small **Museo and Memorial al Che** occupies a single U-shaped room, and provides a succinct overview of Che's life. **Photographs** line the walls, and it's these that tend to hold the most interest, with depictions of Che from his early childhood all the way through to his life as a rebel soldier in the Sierra Maestra and a Cuban statesman in the early years of the Revolution. There are some particularly interesting exhibits relating to the earlier phase of his life, including photos taken by Che himself during his travels around Latin America. Less engaging items include the various guns that he used during his times in combat, but even if you ignore all these there is just about enough here to paint a picture of his life.

Opposite the museum entrance is the **mausoleum**, a softly lit chamber where the mood of reverence and respect is quite affecting. Resembling a kind of tomb with an eternally flickering flame, this is the resting place of Che's remains, as well as those of a number of the Peruvians, Bolivians and Cubans who died with him in Bolivia, each of whom is commemorated by a simple stone portrait set into the wall.

ERNESTO "CHE" GUEVARA

No one embodies the romanticism of the Cuban Revolution more than **Ernesto "Che" Guevara**, the handsome, brave and principled guerrilla who fought alongside Fidel Castro in the Sierra Maestra during the revolutionary war of 1956–59. Referred to in Cuba today simply as "El Che", he is probably the most universally liked and respected of the Revolution's heroes, his early death allowing him to remain untarnished by the souring of attitudes over time, and his willingness to fight so energetically for his principles viewed as evidence of his indefatigable spirit.

THE EARLY YEARS

Born to middle-class, strongly left-wing parents in Rosario, Argentina, on June 14, 1928, the young Ernesto Guevara – later nicknamed "Che", a popular term of affectionate address in Argentina – suffered from severe asthma attacks as a child. Despite this life-long affliction, he became a keen soccer and rugby player while at the University of Buenos Aires, where, in 1948, he began studying medicine.

Before he graduated in 1953, finishing a six-year course in half the time, Che had taken time out from his studies and made an epic journey around South America on a motorbike (which he chronicled later in *The Motorcycle Diaries*), with his doctor friend Alberto Granado. These travels, which he continued after graduation, were instrumental in the formation of Guevara's political character, instilling in him a strong sense of Latin American identity and opening his eyes to the widespread suffering and social injustice throughout the continent. He was in Guatemala in 1954 when the government was overthrown by a US-backed right-wing military coup, and had to escape to Mexico.

GUEVARA AND CASTRO'S REVOLT

It was there, in November 1955, that Guevara met the exiled Fidel Castro and, learning of his intentions to return to Cuba and ignite a popular revolution, decided to join Castro's small rebel army, the **M-26-7 Movement**. The Argentine was among the 82 who set sail for Cuba in the yacht *Granma* on November 24, 1956, and, following the disastrous landing, one of the few who made it safely into the Sierra Maestra. As both a guerrilla and a doctor, Guevara played a vital role for the rebels as they set about drumming up support for their cause among the local peasants while fighting Batista's troops. His most prominent role in the conflict, however, came in 1958 when he led a rebel column west to the then province of Las Villas, where he was to cut all means of communication between the two ends of the island and thus cement Castro's control over the east. This he did in great style, exemplified in his manoeuvres during the **Battle of Santa Clara** (see p.259).

EL HOMBRE NUEVO

Guevara insisted on enduring the same harsh conditions as the other rebels and refused to grant himself any comforts that his higher status might have allowed. It was this spirit of sacrifice and brotherhood that he brought to the philosophies which he developed and instituted after the triumph of the Revolution in 1959, during his role as Minister for Industry. The cornerstone of his vision was the concept of **El Hombre Nuevo** – the New Man – which became his most enduring contribution to Cuban communist theory. Guevara believed that in order to build communism a new man must be created, and the key to this was to alter the popular consciousness. The emphasis was on motivation: new attitudes would have to be instilled in people, devoid of selfish sentiment and with a goal of moral rather than material reward, gained through the pursuit of the aims of the Revolution.

GUEVARA'S FINAL YEARS

Despite working out these abstract theories, Guevara remained at heart a man of action and, after serving four years as a roaming ambassador for Cuba to the rest of the world, he left for Africa to play a more direct role in the spread of communism, becoming involved in a revolutionary conflict in the Congo. In 1966 he travelled to Bolivia where he once again fought as a guerrilla against the Bolivian army. There, on October 8, 1967, Guevara was captured and shot. The exact location of his burial was kept secret until 1995, when it was revealed by a Bolivian general. Two years later, in 1997, his body was exhumed and transported to Santa Clara, where it now lies in the mausoleum of the Complejo Monumental Ernesto Che Guevara.

Loma del Capiro

To get to the hill, take the fifth right turn off the Carretera de Camajuaní after the Monumento a la Toma del Tren Blindado, at the Cupet-Cimex gas station, onto Ana Pegudo, then the second left onto Felix Huergo from where the route is clearly signposted • Taxis from the centre cost around $3CUC

On the northeastern outskirts of Santa Clara, a couple of kilometres and a good 45-minute walk from the centre, is the surprisingly inconspicuous **Loma del Capiro**, a large mound rising abruptly from the comparatively flat surroundings, providing splendid views over the city and the flatlands to the north and east. This is a peaceful, unspoilt spot for a picnic, where you're more likely to encounter a few kids flying kites than other tourists. There's a small car park near the summit from where a concrete staircase climbs gently 150m up to the top, which is capped by a steel monument commemorating the capture of the hill by Che Guevara in 1958, during the Battle of Santa Clara.

ARRIVAL AND DEPARTURE

BY PLANE

Aeropuerto Abel Santamaría Just off the the Carretera Maleza at Km 11 (☎42 22 7525) Santa Clara's airport has no scheduled domestic flights, but does handle charter flights from the UK, Canada, Argentina, France and Italy. There's no public transport to the city; an official taxi to the centre will cost around $12CUC.

By Viazul bus The Terminal de Omnibus Nacionales (Víazul ☎42 22 2524, general information ☎42 29 2114), where Víazul services arrive and depart, is in the western limits of the city on the corner of Carretera Central and Oquendo. A taxi to the Parque Vidal will cost $3CUC.

Destinations Bayamo (4 daily; 8hr 30min); Caibarién (1 daily; 1hr 10min); Camagüey (4 daily; 4hr 20min); Ciego de Avila (4 daily; 2hr 30min); Cienfuegos (2 daily; 1hr 20min); Havana (3 daily; 3hr 45min); Holguín (3 daily; 8hr); Remedios (1 daily; 55min); Sancti Spíritus (4 daily; 1hr 30min); Santiago (4 daily; 11hr); Trinidad (1 daily; 3hr); Varadero (2 daily; 3hr 30min).

By local bus Buses serving provincial destinations, such as Remedios, depart from and arrive at the Terminal de Omnibus Intermunicipal on the Carretera Central e/ Pichardo y Amparo.

Destinations Caibarién (1 daily; 1hr 50min); Remedios (3 daily; 1hr 30min).

By taxi colectivo Santa Clara has its own *almendrón* station, the Terminal de Autos de Alquiler, directly opposite the Terminal de Omnibus Intermunicipal, where privately run long-distance taxis (see p.31) load up with passengers. Destinations are entirely dependent on demand, but there are usually cars heading for Remedios and Caibarién.

By train The train station (☎42 20 2895) is at Parque de los Mártires at the northern end of Luis Estévez. You can walk to Parque Vidal in 15min, or you can jump in one of the horse-drawn carriages or taxis that wait outside ($1–2CUC). Very few train services run on daily schedules and services or whole routes are often suspended. The most reliable long-distance service, the Especial, stopping at Santa Clara between Havana and Santiago, currently runs once every three days. It's advisable to book your train ticket at least a day in advance.

Destinations Bayamo (2 weekly; 12hr); Caibarién (1 daily; 2hr); Camagüey (8 weekly; 7hr); Cienfuegos (1 daily; 3hr); Havana (11 weekly; 4–6hr); Matanzas (9 weekly; 3hr 30min); Santiago (6 weekly; 12hr).

By car Arriving by car, you'll most likely enter the city on the Carretera Central; from the east, turn off the Carretera Central at Colón, and from the west at Rafael Tristá, both one-way streets which lead right to the Parque Vidal.

GETTING AROUND

Getting around the centre can be done on foot, but you may want to find some transport to the Complejo Monumental Ernesto Che Guevara and the Loma del Capiro.

By bicitaxi *Bicitaxis* congregate around the Parque Vidal, particularly on the corner of Máximo Gómez and Marta Abreu. All prices are by negotiation.

By horse-drawn carriage Horse-drawn carriages operate up and down Marta Abreu, Cuba, Colón and a number of other streets emanating out from Parque Vidal. For journeys toward the two bus stations and the Memorial al Che, catch one on Marta Abreu; going in the opposite direction head for Rafael Tristá. Carriages on Cuba, Colón, Máximo Gómez and Luis Estevez head to and from the southeast and the northwest of the city.

Cubans usually pay $1CUP, but the very few foreigners who actually use this form of public transport tend to get charged $1–2CUC.

By taxi To get to either of the two hotels on the edge of the city you'll need to ring for a taxi (☎42 20 7647).

Car rental Rex (☎42 22 2244) and Havanautos/Cubacar (☎42 21 8177) are both at Marta Abreu e/ Alemán y J.B. Zayas.

Scooter rental Motoclub at Marta Abreu e/ Alemán y J.B. Zayas (daily 8am–5pm; ☎42 21 8177; $13CUC/2hr, $25CUC/24hr).

INFORMATION, TRAVEL AGENCIES AND TOURS

INFORMATION

Infotur This local branch of the national tourist information provider, at Cuba no.66 e/ Eduardo Machado y Maestra Nicolasa (Mon–Sat 8.30–noon & 1–5pm; ☎ 42 20 1352), supplies maps, can book accommodation, bus tickets and excursions, and offers internet access ($3CUC/30min).

TRAVEL AGENCIES AND TOURS

The travel agents listed below can sell you Víazul bus tickets and organize day-trips to Embalse Hanabanilla, Remedios and the northern cays. They usually require a minimum number of customers, effectively meaning that excursions don't often run in low season (April–June & Sept–Nov). City tours are more reliable, visiting all the major attractions by minibus for around $10CUC per person, usually with a minimum of three people.

Cubanacán Colón no.101 esq. Maestra Nicolasa (Mon–Fri 8.30am–5.30pm & Sat 8.30am–12.30pm; ☎ 42 20 5189).

Cubatur Marta Abreu no.10 e/ Máximo Gómez y Enrique Villuendas (Mon–Fri 8.30am–5pm, Sat 8.30am–noon; ☎ 42 20 8980).

Havanatur Máximo Gómez no.13 e/ Boulevard y Barreras (Mon–Fri 8am–noon & 1–4pm, Sat 8am–noon; ☎ 42 20 4001).

Paradiso Independencia no.314 e/ Plácido y Luís Estévez (Mon–Fri 8.30am–5pm, Sat 8.30am–noon; ☎42 20 1374).

ACCOMMODATION

There's a reasonable variety of accommodation in Santa Clara, including a great selection of **casas particulares** clustered around the centre, and along Maceo and Colón. As in most major Cuban cities, tourists arriving at the bus station are met by an enthusiastic crowd of accommodation **touts** (see p.37).

HOTELS

América Mujica no.9 e/ Colón y Maceo ☎ 42 20 1585, ✉ recepcion@americavc.co.cu. The newest hotel in town, opened in 2012, is a simple little affair, worthy of its three stars, with small, understated but colourful rooms and perfectly pleasant communal areas. There are neat little Art Deco touches throughout, and it has the only city-centre swimming pool. **$94CUC**

Los Caneyes Ave. de los Eucaliptos y Circunvalación ☎ 42 21 8140, ✉ comercial@caneyes.vcl.tur.cu. This neatly laid-out complex, on the edge of a small wood and tucked away in the low grassy hills just beyond the city's southwestern outskirts, features Amerindian-style huts, thoughtfully furnished and with good facilities. There's a restaurant, small pool and a hot tub. It's a $3CUC taxi ride from Parque Vidal. **$86CUC**

Santa Clara Libre Parque Vidal no.6 e/ Rafael Tristá y Padre Chao ☎ 42 20 7548, ✉ hscl.jcarpeta@islazulvc.tur.cu. A lime-green, eleven-storey Santa Clara landmark, with superb views from its rooftop bar and tenth-floor restaurant and an unbeatable central location, but a cramped and worn interior. Some rooms are a little dim and confined, though many have good views. Cheap but not cheerful. **$32CUC**

Villa La Granjita Carretera de Maleza Km 2 ☎ 42 21 8190, ✉ reservas@granjita.vcl.tur.cu. Sizeable and simply furnished rooms in concrete cabins, scattered throughout a spacious, natural site with its own woodlands, full of palms and pines, and a stream; there's a restaurant, a pool and a hot tub as well. Five kilometres from Parque Vidal. **$78CUC**

CASAS PARTICULARES

Alba Hostal Eduardo Machado (San Cristóbal) no.7 e/ Cuba y Colón ☎ 42 29 4108, ✉ wilfredo.alba@yahoo.com. Impressive and elegant, the definite crowd pleaser here is the splendid narrow patio spilling over with potted plants. Opening onto the patio, the two guest rooms maintain these high standards, and are decked out in colonial style, with an original eighteenth-century bed in one of them. **$25CUC**

★ **Aparthostal Eva y Ernesto** J.B. Zayas no.253a e/ Berenguer (San Mateo) y Padre Tuduri ☎ 42 20 4076, ✉ nestyhostal@yahoo.es. There's an air of understated sophistication about this cushy first-floor apartment, with its orderly open-plan kitchen/living room with bar stools, comfy couch and coffee table. Neat and dinky balconies back and front and a delightfully intimate terrace with park benches complete the picture. Rented as a two-bed apartment, with its own entrance (perfect for groups), or available as two separate one-bedroom apartments. **$25CUC**

Casa de Consuelo Ramos y Nelson Turiño Independencia no.265, apto. 1 e/ Pedro Estévez (Unión) y Miguel Gutiérrez (San Isidro) ☎ 42 20 2064, ✉ marielatram@yahoo.es. An unexpectedly cavernous, somewhat tired-looking ground-floor apartment with a piano and a claim to having housed Che Guevara in the early 1960s. The large, tree-filled garden patio, with benches shaded underneath a leafy canopy, brightens things up. The spacious double rooms each have a bathroom, a fridge and a/c. **$25CUC**

Casa de Héctor Martínez Rolando Pardo (Buen Viaje) no.8 e/ Maceo y Parque Vidal ☎ 42 21 7463. Given the relatively plain exterior, it's a surprise to find a beautiful patio resplendent with plantlife at the heart of this smart house dating from 1902, just 40m from the Parque Vidal. The two guest rooms are furnished in colonial style, and the place has an easy-going feel. **$25CUC**

★ **Casa Mercy** Eduardo Machado (San Cristóbal) no.4 e/ Cuba y Colón ☎42 21 6941, ✉casamercy@gmail.com. Guests have the run of the first floor where, beyond the two clean, spacious quadruple rooms with bathrooms, there are two cosy terraces. The charming and unendingly helpful hosts, who speak English, Italian and French, provide laundry and internet services and plenty of local info, as well as making an impressive list of cocktails and excellent meals (including vegetarian food). **$25CUC**

El Castillito Céspedes no.65A e/ Maceo y Pedro Estévez (Unión) ☎42 29 2671. One cosy, light and airy room with TV, DVD, safety-deposit box, fridge and a/c in a peaceful house with three terraces, one of which serves as a pleasant dining area. The man in charge, easy-going José, offers free pick-ups from the bus station if you book in advance. **$25CUC**

Hostal Adelaida y Rolando Maceo no.355a e/ Serafín García (Nazareno) y E.P. Morales (Síndico) ☎42 20 6725, ✉rolandosacerio@gmail.com. Two comfortable double rooms, both with a/c and bathroom and one with its own little lounge attached, in a simple, spick-and-span house with a first-floor terrace. You'll be made to feel very welcome by the warm and friendly hosts, Adelaida and Rolando, who speak good English and have a small library of books on Cuban history. **$25CUC**

Hostal D'Cordero Rolando Pardo (Buen Viaje) no.16 e/ Parque Vidal y Maceo ☎42 20 6456, ✉o_cordero2003@yahoo.com. Lavishly furnished with antiques and collectable original Cuban paintings, this museum of a house is very clean, has a lovely upstairs terrace where meals are served, and is less than a block from the main square. The two large bedrooms have a/c, TV, fridge, grand double beds and en-suite bathrooms. **$25CUC**

★ **Hostal Florida Center** Maestra Nicolasa (Candelaria) no.56 e/ Colón y Maceo ☎42 20 8161 ✉angel.floridacenter@yahoo.com. Based around a fantastic, rainforest-like courtyard, this large, authentic colonial residence crammed with nineteenth-century furnishings has two superbly distinguished rooms for rent, one with a fantastic Art Deco bed and wardrobe, the other with colonial-era beds. Both have TV, minibar, a/c and a spotless private bathroom. Breakfast and dinner are served on tables that nestle among the fronds and ferns. English, French and Italian are spoken. **$25CUC**

4 EATING

Unlike many Cuban cities, Santa Clara's **eating** scene hasn't improved that much since private enterprise laws were loosened up, and though there are certainly many more **paladars** than before, many remain quite poor. Most of the city's **state restaurants** still fail to combine good food with an agreeable atmosphere (or vice versa) and in many cases lack both. On the whole you're better off at one of the paladars, but if you're staying in a *casa particular*, you'll do as well (or better) to eat there.

STATE RESTAURANTS AND CAFÉS

Coppelia Colón e/ Eduardo Machado (San Cristóbal) y Domingo Mujica ☎42 22 2288. The Santa Clara branch of the national ice-cream chain is set in a monstrous, airy building just off the Parque Vidal. Wed–Fri noon–10pm, Sat & Sun 10am–4.30pm & 5–11.30pm.

Casa del Gobernador Independencia esq. J.B.Zayas ☎42 20 2273. Slightly doughy but generously topped pizzas ($3–4.50CUC) or unimaginative but perfectly decent, inexpensive Cuban-style meat and fish dishes like smoked pork ($2.60CUC), served on the downstairs patio, the balcony above it or the formal air-conditioned dining room of this recently restored colonial mansion. Tues–Sun 11am–5pm & 7–11pm.

Santa Rosalia Máximo Gómez e/ Independencia y Parque Vidal ☎42 20 1438. One of the newest and best state restaurants in the city, in a splendid nineteenth-century mansion that was once a school for impoverished children, with a lovely central courtyard. A broad choice of good quality meat and seafood dishes, including rabbit ($5.40–9.80CUC), lamb ($5.50–6.50CUC) and pork ($3.50–6.80CUC) options. Daily 11am–11am.

Los Tainos Ave. de los Eucaliptos y Circunvalación ☎42 21 8140. The all-you-can-eat buffet ($12CUC) at the *Los Caneyes* hotel restaurant, in a Taíno-style circular lodge, serves up some of the best-quality food in the city and usually includes plenty of vegetables, a decent pasta and a salad counter. Evening meals are accompanied by live music. Daily 7.30–10am, noon–3.30pm & 7–10pm.

PALADARS

El Alba Rolando Pardo (Buen Viaje) no.26 e/ Parque Vidal y Maceo (no phone). Top notch, excellent value Cuban home cooking at this packed little paladar right in the centre. The food, though the usual meat and seafood, is cooked to an unusually high standard for a Santa Clara restaurant, and comes in huge portions. Expect to pay around $6CUC for a meal. Tues–Sun noon–4pm & 6–10pm.

★ **Florida Center** Maestra Nicolasa (Candelaria) no.56 e/ Colón y Maceo ☎42 20 8161. The verdant central patio of one of the city's best *casas particulares* is now home to one of its best paladars, too. There's no fixed menu, so listen carefully when the staff tell you what's on offer; lobster, fish, pork and chicken usually feature. Food is freshly sourced and always cooked expertly to your taste, though always along Cuban culinary lines. Main courses generally $8–$15CUC. Daily noon–11pm.

SaboreArte Maceo no.7 e/ Independencia y Céspedes ☎42 22 3969. A very congenial spot for a meal, where inexpensive Cuban food like the traditional Ajiaco Campesino stew ($1CUC), seafood salad ($4.20CUC) and grilled red snapper ($4.85CUC) are served up from the open kitchen in a large, plant-strewn, partially covered patio sitting snugly between buildings and hidden away from the street. Daily 10am–11pm.

Sabor Latino Esquerra no.157 e/ Julio Jover (San Vicente) y Berenguer (San Mateo) ☎42 22 4279. The longest-standing paladar in the city serves humongous portions of pork fricassee ($12CUC), roast chicken ($12CUC), paella ($15CUC) and rock lobster ($18CUC), as well as several other main dishes, with copious side orders. Service is attentive and the decor attractively restrained. Daily noon–midnight.

DRINKING

Drinking venues in Santa Clara are generally down-at-heel joints or soulless cafés, with only a few exceptions. Boulevard is lined with snack bars and grubby cafés open until late, some of which have simple bar counters providing a space for quick-refill-drinkers, but most with a strictly limited selection of drinks.

BARS AND CAFÉS

Café Literario Rafael Tristá esq. Colón, Parque Vidal (no phone). A simple little coffee place on the main square and a popular meeting place for many of the city's artists and writers, with regular talks, readings and live music. Daily 9am–9pm.

Casa Mercy Eduardo Machado (San Cristóbal) no.4 e/ Cuba y Colón ☎42 21 6941. Not exactly a bar ,but the hosts at this excellent *casa particular* run what they call a "cocktail service". Sit on one of their two upstairs terraces and choose from their excellent cocktail menu at $2–3CUC a pop. Usually daily 6–10pm.

La Cuevita de Ultra Boulevard e/ Lorda y Luis Estévez (no phone.) Behind a smoked-glass door, this grotto-like bar has an off-beat atmosphere and a slight underworld feel. It's not the cleanest place in town, but has plenty of character. Mon–Fri & Sun 9am–9pm, Sat 9am–2am.

La Marquesina Parque Vidal esq. Máximo Gómez ☎42 22 4848. In the corner of the theatre building, serving beer, rum, soft drinks and a couple of cocktails, this is the busiest bar after dark, when there's live music almost every night. Daily 10am–1am.

Vista a la Ciudad Piso 11, Parque Vidal ☎42 20 7548 ext.1100. The roof-terrace bar of the *Hotel Santa Clara Libre* has the best possible views right across the city, though they disappear behind walls once you sit down. There are a few cheap cocktails, plus beers, whiskies and soft drinks. Daily 2pm–2am.

NIGHTLIFE AND ENTERTAINMENT

Santa Clara's **nightlife** focuses predominantly on Boulevard and lively **Parque Vidal**, where there are plenty of people buzzing around until the early hours of the morning at weekends,. You could conceivably spend the whole night hanging out here, but there are several venues within a few blocks that can provide something different, from club nights to cabaret or theatre.

NIGHTCLUBS

Club Boulevard Independencia 225 e/ Maceo y Pedro Estévez (Unión) ☎42 21 6236. The only place in town that can call itself a true nightclub, albeit a very small one, and slightly more sophisticated and image-conscious than other spots. Entry $1–2CUC. Daily 10pm–2am.

El Dorado Luis Estévez e/ Independencia y Céspedes ☎42 21 5215. A cross between a school disco and an underground jazz club, this usually buzzing "piano bar" attracting predominantly local couples is full of 1980s cheesiness, but it's still authentic contemporary Cuban nightlife. You may have to tap on the door to get in. Entry 1CUC Mon–Thurs, $5CUC Fri–Sun. Daily 9.30pm–1am.

LIVE MUSIC VENUES

El Bosque Calle 1 esq. Carretera Central ☎42 20 4444. Offering cabaret and comedy, matinées of live son, feeling and trova and nights full of salsa and reggaeton, supplied by either live bands or DJs, this is the most upmarket and professional show in town. It's next to the bridge over the Río Cubanicay. Entry $2CUP. Usually Wed–Sun 9pm–1am, matinées Mon & Tues 6–9pm.

Casa de la Ciudad Boulevard esq. J.B. Zayas ☎42 20 5593. Monthly programmes of traditional Cuban music, such as trova, bolero and son, performed on the attractive central patio of this impressive colonial residence. Entry $3CUC. Performances Sat & Sun 1pm, 5pm and 9pm.

SANTA CLARA'S FESTIVALS

Santa Clara's busy cultural calendar, the fullest in the region, includes a seven-day **theatre festival** at *El Mejunje* (see p.266) during the last week of January; the **Festival Nacional de la Danza** in April and, in November, a five-day city-wide film festival, the **Festival de Invierno**, and the **Ciudad Metal** heavy metal event.

BASEBALL IN SANTA CLARA

The **Villa Clara Naranjas**, the local national-league team whose distinctive orange uniform is their chief trademark, are traditionally among the top four teams in the league and have consistently qualified for the playoffs over the last decade. They play their games at the **Estadio Augusto César Sandino** (☎42 22 2855), a relatively intimate ballpark, founded in 1966, with a capacity of just 18,000; the entrance is on Calle 2. Games take place Tues–Sun, usually at 1pm during the regular season (currently November to March); playoffs finish in May. Tickets are $1–2CUP, though there is a separate section, well located for views, for CUC-paying visitors which costs $3CUC. Enquire at the travel agents in town (see p.263) about excursions to see a game.

Casa de la Cultura Parque Vidal ☎ 42 21 7181. There is a fairly diverse monthly programme (posted in the foyer) at this cultural community centre, including local musicians performing traditional Cuban music, often trova, danzón or rumba. Entrance free. Performances often spill onto the park outside. Usually Fri 9pm, Sat 4pm & 9pm, Sun 4pm.

★ **El Mejunje** Marta Abreu no.12 e/ J.B. Zayas y Rafael Lubián ☎42 28 2572. The city's most varied programme of live shows, dance and music, attracting a bohemian crowd and popular with both the gay community and the Santa Clara rock contingent. The main area is a rough-and-ready brick-walled open-air courtyard, but there's also an indoor performance area, a café and a gallery. The entertainment ranges from live rock, rap, jazz and traditional Cuban music to drag shows and small-scale theatrical productions, and at the weekends there's either a disco or a transvestite show. The week's programme is posted on a board just inside or on the door. Entry $1–2CUC. Mon–Fri 5pm–late, Sat & Sun 10am–late.

THEATRE

Teatro La Caridad Parque Vidal ☎42 20 5548. The venue for most of the high-profile cultural events, including plays, orchestral performances and ballet. Past performers here have included Alicia Alonso and the Cuban National Ballet as well as Chucho Valdés, one of the greatest Cuban pianists of all time. Ticket prices vary, but rarely exceed $10CUC. Shows generally Wed, Fri & Sat from 8.30pm, Sun from 5pm.

CINEMAS

Cine Camilo Cienfuegos Santa Clara Libre hotel, Parque Vidal no.6 e/ Rafael Tristá y Padre Chao ☎42 20 3005. As well as its own regular schedule of films, the cinema's noticeboard is a useful resource for films showing throughout the city, at both cinemas and salas de video.

Cine Cubanacán Boulevard no.60 e/ Villuendas y J.B Zayas ☎42 20 5366. The home of one of the country's most renowned cinema clubs, and a good place to catch both blockbusters and independent Latin American films.

SHOPPING

Agromercado Buen Viaje. A farmers' market at the northeastern end of Rolando Pardo (Buen Viaje), with a wide variety of fresh fruit, vegetables and meat for sale; prices are in national pesos. Mon–Fri 9am–6pm, Sat 8am–5pm, Sun 8am–noon.

La Campana Colón esq. Eduardo Machado ☎42 21 1920. This casa comisionista, the Cuban version of a pawnbrokers, sells old and new stuff, but the secondhand jewellery, watches, glassware, crockery and other assorted paraphernalia mean this is one of the more novel shops in town for a browse. Mon–Wed & Fri–Sun 9am–4pm, Thurs 9am–6pm.

Fondo Cubano de Bienes Culturales Luís Estévez e/ Parque Vidal y Boulevard ☎42 20 8480. The best variety and quality of arts and crafts for sale in the city and the place to come for leather bags, ornaments and paintings and prints.

Mon–Fri 8.30am–1pm & 1.30–7pm, Sat 8.30am–1pm.

Licorama Centro Cuba e/ Parque Vidal y Eduardo Machado ☎42 20 3308. A great place to pick up inexpensive Cuban rum. You won't find any Havana Club here – instead there are lesser-known brands like Yayabo Cienfuegos and Cubay at an average of $80CUP a bottle. Daily 10am–10pm.

Mi Ilusión Colón e/ Eduardo Machado (San Cristóbal) y Parque Vidal ☎42 21 4397. A half-decent selection of arts, crafts and traditional Cuban instruments. Mon–Sat 9am–5pm, Sun 9am–noon.

La Veguita Maceo no.176 e/ Berenguer (San Mateo) y Julio Jover (san vicente) ☎42 20 8952. This excellent little cigar shop sells rum, coffee and a good selection of habanos. Mon–Sat 9am–5pm.

DIRECTORY

Internet The following places charge about $6CUC/hr: Telepunto, Marta Abreu no.51 esq. Enrique Villuendas (daily 8.30am–7pm); InfoInternet, Marta Abreu no.57 e/

Parque Vidal y Enrique Villuendas (Mon–Sat 8am–5pm); Infotur, Cuba no.66 e/ Eduardo Machado y Maestra Nicolasa (Mon–Sat 8.30–noon, 1–5pm).

Medical care The Clínico Quirúrgíco Arnaldo Milián Castro at Cicunvalación y 26 de Julio, Reparto Escambray, in the southeast of the city, is the most comprehensively equipped hospital in the province (switchboard ☎ 42 27 2016, information ☎ 42 27 0070, ambulance ☎ 104).

Money and exchange The best two banks for foreign currency transactions are the Banco Financiero Internacional, Cuba e/ Rafael Tristá y Eduardo Machado (San Cristóbal) (Mon–Fri 8.30am–3.30pm) and the Banco de Crédito y Comercio, Parque Vidal esq. Rafael Tristá y Cuba (Mon–Fri 8am–3pm). To change convertible pesos to national pesos, go to the CADECA *casa de cambio*, Rafael Tristá esq. Cuba (Mon–Sat 8am–8pm, Sun 9am–6pm), where there's also an ATM.

Pharmacy The best-stocked pharmacy is at Colón no.106 e/ Ave. 9 de Abril (San Miguel) y Maestra Nicolasa (Candelaria) (Mon–Fri 8.30–4.30, Sat 8.30–noon).

Police In an emergency call ☎ 116. The central police station is at Colón no.222 e/ Serafín Garcia (Nazareno) y E.P.

Morales (Síndico) (☎ 42 21 2623).

Post The main post office is at Colón no.10 e/ Parque Vidal y Eduardo Machado (San Cristóbal) (Mon–Sat 8am–10pm); DHL is at Cuba no.7 e/ Rafael Tristá y Eduardo Machado (San Cristóbal) (Mon–Fri 8am–6pm, Sat 8–11am).

Swimming pools The only easy-to-access swimming pool in the centre of Santa Clara is at the *Hotel America*. Non-guests can use it for a cost of $5CUC (daily 10am–6pm), which includes $3CUC credit for food and drinks.

Telephones There are seven public phones of several kinds on Enrique Villuendas e/ Marta Abreu y Padre Chao. For mobile phones visit Cubacel at Barreras no.4 e/ Máximo Gómez y Enrique Villuendas.

Visas To extend your tourist card go to the Department of Immigration office near the Estadio Sandino at Reparto Sandino no.9 e/ Carretera Central y Avenida Sandino (Mon & Wed 8am–7pm, Tues & Fri 8am–5pm, Thurs & Sat 8am–noon; ☎ 42 21 3626).

Remedios

4

Just over 40km northeast of Santa Clara and less than 10km from the coast, the town of **REMEDIOS** sits unobtrusively near the beach resort on the northern cays, and remains comparatively unexploited. The faded paintwork and terracotta roofs of the generally modest, still-lived-in colonial buildings, as well as the noticeable absence of modern constructions around the centre, reflect a town that lived on the periphery of modern Cuba until relatively recently. Remedios has now established its place on the visitor map, and is commonly used by tourists as a base for or a stopoff on the way to the nearby beach resort on the cays. On (or within shouting distance) of the central **Plaza Martí**, the town's modest sights provide no more than a few hours of sightseeing, but its superb and reasonably priced hotels, appealing and abundant *casas particulares* and friendly atmosphere make it well worth a stopover. This sleepy place does, however, explode into live every Christmas when **Las Parrandas**, the festival for which the town is best known among Cubans, takes place (see box, p.270).

Brief history

One of the oldest towns in Cuba, founded shortly after the establishment of the seven *villas* (see p.452), Remedios has a history rivalling that of Trinidad and Santa Clara, going back as far as the 1520s. Today's provincial capital was, in fact, founded by citizens of Remedios who, following a series of pirate attacks towards the end of the sixteenth century, transplanted the settlement further inland. The local populace was far from united in its desire to desert Remedios, however, and in an attempt to force the issue, those who wanted to leave burnt the town to the ground. Rebuilt from the ashes, by 1696 the town had its own civic council and went on to produce not only one of Cuba's most renowned composers, Alejandro García Caturla, but also a Spanish president, Dámaso Berenguer Fuste, who governed Spain in the 1930s.

Iglesia de San Juan Bautista

Plaza Martí • Mon–Sat 9–11am • Free

By far the most stunning sight in Remedios is the main altar of the **Iglesia de San Juan Bautista**, the town's principal church, occupying the southern face of the Plaza

REMEDIOS

N

Museo de las
Parrandas
Remedianas

CADECA
Casa de
Cambio

Fondo Cubano de
Bienes Culturales

BALMASEDA

PLAZA
MARTÍ

Iglesia del
Buen Viaje

Museo de la Música
Alejandro García Caturla

Iglesia de
San Juan
Bautista

Teatro Rubén
Martínez Villena

Museo de
Historia Local

Santa Clara (49km) & Bus station (300m)

■ ACCOMMODATION	
Barcelona	3
Hostal La Casona Cueto	1
Hostal El Chalet	6
Hostal La Estancia	5
Hostal Haydee y Juan K	4
Mascotte	2

● EATING	
Las Arcadas	2
La Paloma	1

■ DRINKING AND NIGHTLIFE	
Casa de la Cultura	5
Driver's Bar	4
El Guije	3
Las Leyendas	2
El Louvre	1

0   100
metres

Martí (entry is sometimes via the back door). A church has stood on this site since the sixteenth century, but the current building dates to the late eighteenth century. Once inside, the magnificence of the illustriously detailed main **altar**, made from gilded wood, comes as quite a shock given the simple and rather withered exterior. It was commissioned by a Cuban millionaire named **Eutimio Falla Bonet**, who funded the restoration of the church between 1944 and 1954 following his discovery that he had family roots in Remedios. Bonet's revamp, which also featured the installation of a set of golden altars lining the walls, collected from around Cuba and beyond, have transformed the place into a kind of religious trophy cabinet.

Museo de la Música Alejandro García Caturla

Camilo Cienfuegos no.5, Plaza Martí • Mon–Sat 9am–noon, Sun 9am–1pm • $0.50CUC • ☎ 42 39 6851

On the eastern side of Plaza Martí is the simple **Museo de la Música Alejandro García Caturla**. A lawyer with a passion for music, especially the piano and violin, Caturla lived and worked in the building for the last twenty years of his life. He is most famous for his boundary-breaking compositions from the 1920s and 1930s which combined traditional symphonic styles with African rhythms. In December 1940, he was murdered by a man whom he was due to prosecute the following day. Caturla's study has been preserved and there are various engaging photographs and less engaging documents. There's also a small concert room where you can sometimes catch live musical performances.

Museo de las Parrandas Remedianas

Máximo Gómez no.71 e/ Andrés del Río y Alejandro del Río • Tues–Sat 9am–noon, Sun 9am–1pm • $1CUC • ☎ 42 39 5448

The **Museo de las Parrandas Remedianas** is, for most of the year, the nearest you'll get to experiencing **Las Parrandas**, the annual Christmas Eve festival for which Remedios is renowned (see box, p.270). The scene is portrayed downstairs with a scale model of the main square and two opposing floats, which form the centrepieces of the event. Upstairs, photographs dating back to 1899 provide a more vivid picture of what goes on, showing some of the spectacular floats, known as **carrozas**, and the stationary **trabajos de plaza**, which have graced the event over the years. There are also examples of the torches, instruments, colourful costumes and flags which form an integral part of the raucous celebrations.

Museo de Historia Local

Maceo no.56 e/ Ave. General Carrillo y Fe del Valle • Mon 8am–noon, Tues–Sat 8am–noon & 1–5pm • $1CUC • ☎ 42 39 6792

A few minutes' walk from the Plaza Martí and slightly deeper into the local neighbourhood, the **Museo de Historia Local** charts the history of Remedios and surrounding region, providing insights into the local role in the Wars of Independence and the Revolution. There are also some fine examples of nineteenth-century Cuban Baroque furniture – easier to appreciate than many of the other displays, which skim the surface of themes like geology and wildlife.

ARRIVAL AND DEPARTURE REMEDIOS

By bus Local and interprovincial Víazul buses arrive at and depart from the Terminal de Omnibus (☎ 42 39 5290), on the western outskirts of town at Avenida Céspedes e/ Pi y Margall y Ave. de los Mártires, from where it's an eight-block walk along Pi y Margall or a five-minute *bicitaxi* ride to Plaza Martí.

Local bus destinations Caibarién (3 daily; 25min); Santa Clara (3 daily; 2hr).

Víazul bus destinations Caibarién (1 daily; 10min); Ciego de Avila (1 daily; 2hr 35min); Cienfuegos (1 daily; 2hr); Morón (1 daily; 2hr); Santa Clara (1 daily; 55min); Trinidad (1 daily; 4hr).

By private taxi A taxi between Remedios and Santa Clara takes about 50min and costs around $25CUC.

By taxi colectivo Cubans normally pay around $20CUP for the journey between Remedios and Santa Clara, but non-Cubans will usually be asked for convertible pesos and have to negotiate a price with the driver. In Remedios look for them near the bus station or opposite the hospital on the road to Santa Clara.

INFORMATION

Tourist information Head for the local branch of Infotur, the national tourist information provider, at Pi y Margall esq. Brigadier González (Mon–Fri 8.30am–noon, 1–5pm; ☎ 42 39 7227).

Services The only place in town to exchange foreign currency is the CADECA *casa de cambio* at Máximo Gómez e/ Balmaseda y Alejandro del Río (Mon–Sat 8am–5pm, Sun 8am–noon). There's a post office at José Antonio Peña esq. Antonio Romero (Mon–Sat 8am–6pm).

ACCOMMODATION

HOTELS

Barcelona José Antonio Peña e/ La Pastora y Antonio Maceo ☎ 42 39 5144, Ereservas@mascotte.vcl.cyt.cu. A meticulous restoration has converted this three-storey building from 1926 into a delightful, cheery 24-room hotel. The sunny pastels of the graceful, loungey lobby and the bright central patio make this the most restful place in town. $70CUC

Mascotte Máximo Gómez no.114, Plaza Martí ☎ 42 39 5144, 5145 & 5467, ⊕ hotelescubanacan.com. A loveable little hotel with courteous staff and a charmingly elegant yet simple, tasteful interior. Booking is advisable as

there are only ten rooms, all well furnished and most of them located around an open-air balcony overlooking the delightful patio bar. $50CUC

CASAS PARTICULARES

★ **Hostal El Chalet** Brigadier González no.29 e/ Independencia y José Antonio Peña ☎ 42 39 6538. Luxurious by local standards, this spacious, modern house has a patio garden and parking for two cars. Bathed in a lovely natural light, the two double rooms, one more like a mini apartment with its own comfortable reception area, are located up on a roof terrace, affording views over the treetops to the church on the main square and providing a sense of privacy. **$25CUC**

Hostal La Casona Cueto Alejandro del Río no.72 esq. E. Morales ☎42 39 5350, ✉luisenrique@capiro.vcl.sld .cu. This cavernous late nineteenth-century house just behind the Plaza Martí has two simple double rooms, a capacious and very leafy central courtyard and an impressive interior full of colonial antiques. **$25CUC**

Hostal La Estancia Camilo Cienfuegos no.34 e/ Ave. General Carrillo y José Antonio Peña ☎42 39 5582, 🌐laestanciahostal.com. A grand old nineteenth-century residence retaining many of its original features, most

strikingly in the cavernous reception room which is full of antiques, including an ornate grand piano. The three huge guest rooms, all en suite, are based around a large courtyard featuring a small pool and a jungle of plants. **$25CUC**

Hostal Haydee y Juan K José Antonio Peña no.73 e/ Maceo y La Pastora ☎42 39 5082, ✉haydejk@enet.cu. A neat and compact house, run by a friendly couple. Two of the three spruce and decorous rooms, both with a/c and en-suite bathroom, are based around a gorgeous central patio, while the spacious third is up on a lovely roof terrace. Juan loves to talk politics, so this is a good option for anyone with an interest in the Revolution. **$25CUC**

EATING

There are several national-peso charging state restaurants around the centre, but they're not worth bothering with unless your priority is to eat cheap regardless of quality and flavour. You're better off at the hotels, *casas particulares* or one of the small number of **paladars**.

Las Arcadas Máximo Gómez no.114, Plaza Martí ☎42 39 5144. The *Hotel Mascotte* restaurant is one of the most reliable places to eat in town, with reasonably priced Cuban seafood and meat dishes. The half-dignified dining room

with simple little ceramic craftworks dotted around is as formal as it gets in Remedios, but it's still very laid back. Daily 7.30–10.30am, noon–3pm & 7–10pm.

La Paloma Balmaseda no.4 e/ Máximo Gómez y

LAS PARRANDAS

Once a year, on the night of December 24, usually sedate Remedios erupts into organized anarchy during **Las Parrandas**, a 200-year-old tradition which originated in the town and has spread throughout the province and beyond. Since the end of the nineteenth century there have been annual *parrandas* in neighbouring towns like Camajuani, Zulueta and Caibarién, but the one in Remedios remains the biggest and the best. In the days building up to the main event the streets around the plaza fill up with market stalls and the town becomes overrun with visitors. For the festival itself, Remedios divides into northern and southern halves, with the frontier running through the centre of Plaza Martí: north is the **San Salvador** neighbourhood, whose emblem is an eagle on a blue background, and south is the **Carmen** neighbourhood, represented by a rooster on a red background. The opposing sides mark their territory with huge static constructions (which look like floats but are in fact stationary), known as **trabajos de plaza**, whose extravagant designs change annually, each one built to be more spectacular than the last. The celebrations kick off around 4pm, when the whole town gathers in the plaza to drink, dance, shout and sing. *Artilleros*, the fireworks experts, set off hundreds of eardrum-popping **firecrackers** until the square is shrouded in an acrid pall of black smoke and people can hardly see. Following that, the revellers form huge, pulsing **congas** and traipse around the square for hours, cheering their own team and chanting insulting songs at their rivals. The neighbourhoods' avian symbols appear on a sea of waving banners, flags, staffs, placards and bandanas tied around their citizens' necks.

As night falls, the two large floats, the **carrozas**, which along with the *trabajos de plaza* form the focus of the celebrations, do a ceremonial round of the plaza. Built to represent their respective halves of Remedios, the floats are fantastical creations with multicoloured decorations and flashing lights forming intricate patterns. Constructed by the town's resident population of *parrandas* fanatics, who devote the majority of their free time throughout the year to designing and creating them, the floats are judged by the rest of the town on looks and originality. As everyone makes up their minds, a massive **fireworks display** illuminates the sky and further heightens the tension. Finally, in the early morning hours, the church bell is ceremoniously rung and the **winner** announced. The president of the winning neighbourhood is then triumphantly paraded around on his jubilant team's shoulders before everyone heads home to recover, enjoy Christmas and start planning the next year's festivities.

Ramiro Capablanca ☎ 42 39 5490. This elegant *casa particular* also houses a paladar, specializing in seafood, where you can enjoy good-value lobster ($12CUC), shrimps ($12CUC) and seafood medleys ($15CUC); prices include plentiful sides and a dessert. Daily 8am–10pm.

DRINKING, NIGHTLIFE AND ENTERTAINMENT

Casa de la Cultura José Antonio Peña no.67 e/ La Pastora y Antonio Maceo ☎ 42 39 5581. This local community cultural centre posts a weekly programme on its porch which usually includes live and recorded music on Friday and Saturday nights at 9pm and during the day at weekends.

Driver's Bar José Antonio Peña esq. Camilo Cienfuegos ☎ 42 39 5175. A sociable mix of locals, foreigners and flies, added to the images of 1950s advertising on the wall, provide this bar with a distinct mix of workaday and novelty character. Beer, rum, soft drinks and sandwiches. 24hr.

El Guije Maceo esq. Independencia ☎ 42 36 3305. This open-air venue with a bar and dance floor set within high walls has karaoke, live music and participatory salsa on its weekly schedule. Tues–Thurs 6pm–midnight, Fri–Sun 6pm–2am.

Las Leyendas Máximo Gómez no.124, Plaza Martí ☎ 42 39 6264. A pleasant patio with a bar and stage hosting small-scale cabarets and live music. Entry $0.50–1CUC. Wed–Sun 10am–2am.

El Louvre Máximo Gómez no.122 e/ Independencia y Pi y Margall, Plaza Martí ☎ 42 39 5639. Often the first port of call for visitors, thanks to its location on the plaza, this is by far the smartest, most stylish bar in Remedios (though there isn't much competition), and has the best choice of drinks too. Mon–Fri 8am–midnight, Sat & Sun 8am–1am.

Caibarién

From Remedios it's about 8km east to the run-down but pleasant port of **CAIBARIÉN**, where you'll find the closest *casas particulares* to the cays – the town is a convenient base from which to explore the cays without having to pay for a package holiday or shell out for an all-inclusive.

Caibarién's streets are lined by rows of wooden sugar warehouses, painted in a faded rainbow of colours, which testify to this sleepy backwater's nineteenth-century heyday. Largely unaffected by tourism and enjoying a leisurely speed of life, Caibarién provides a marked contrast to the development on the cays. The town in itself is unlikely to hold you for long. There's a small beach next to the only hotel where non-Cubans can stay, a quiet central square, **Parque de la Libertad**, and a seafront promenade, the *malecón*. West of town, on the road to Remedios, the **Museo de la Agroindustria Azucarera** is worth a half-hour stopoff.

Museo de la Agroindustria Azucarera

Mon–Sat 9am–4.30pm • $3CUC, $9CUC including steam train • ☎ 42 36 3636

On the road from Remedios, 1.5km east of Caibarién, a large sign marks the turn-off for the **Museo de la Agroindustria Azucarera** (sometimes known as the **Museo de Vapor**), dedicated to the Cuban sugar industry. The museum is set in the spacious, dilapidated grounds of the old Marcelo Salado sugar refinery, founded in 1891 and still much as it was when it finally ground to a halt in 1999, as part of a wave of closures affecting the most inefficient branches of the industry.

Though it's a little disjointed and the layout a bit messy, the museum's functioning steam trains and the real-life setting make it an engaging place to visit. At its core is a dormant, metal-roofed factory floor where much of the machinery used in the **sugar production** process is on display in the setting in which it was once used; there are also reconstructed scenes depicting sugar production during the age of slavery. The nearby train shed holds six fabulous working **steam trains**, built in the US between 1904 and 1920 by the famous Baldwin Locomotive Works. A seventh engine is on display with its shell removed, revealing all the working parts. In a separate, smaller building are pictures of Cuba's earliest steam engines and information on their history. It's well worth paying the higher entrance fee to ride the train to Remedios and back – but ring in advance if you want a guarantee of this, as trains sometimes only leave for pre-booked tours.

ARRIVAL AND GETTING AROUND | CAIBARIÉN

By train There is a train line between Caibarién and Santa Clara but the service is not currently operating, though it could be reinstated at any time. The train station is three blocks west of Parque de la Libertad.

By Víazul bus Víazul buses between Ciego de Avila and Trinidad stop at Caibarién's train station, from where it's a three-block walk to the centre.

Víazul destinations Ciego de Avila (1 daily; 2hr 25min); Cienfuegos (1 daily; 2hr 10min); Morón (1 daily; 1hr 50min); Remedios (1 daily; 10min); Santa Clara (1 daily;

1 hr 5min); Trinidad (1 daily; 4hr 10min).

By local bus Services from Remedios and Santa Clara stop just outside Caibarién's train station. From here, it's a short walk along Calle 8 into town.

Destinations Remedios (3 daily; 25min); Santa Clara (3 daily; 2hr).

By taxi A taxi from Caibarién (☎ 42 39 5555) to the cays or Santa Clara will cost $30–35CUC.

By car Cubacar has an office in town at Ave. 11 e/ 6 y 8 (☎ 42 35 1970).

INFORMATION AND TOURS

Havanatur Staff at the Havanatur office on the square (Mon–Fri 8.30am–noon & 1.30–4.30pm, Sat 8.30am–noon; ☎ 42 35 1171) will happily recommend places to eat

and stay in town, as well as transport information for journeys to the cays, Remedios and Santa Clara, including the organized excursions that the agency runs.

ACCOMMODATION

Brisas del Mar Playa Caibarien, Reparto Mar Azul ☎ 42 35 1699, ✉ recepcion@brisas.co.cu. Located beyond the *malecón*, from where the coastal road runs along the edge of a small natural harbour full of fishing boats onto a small peninsula. The rooms face out to sea; guests have use of a pool just over the road. $29CUC

Pension de Eladio Ave. 35 no.1016b e/ 10 y 12 ☎ 42 36 4253. Half a block from the seafront near the *malecón*, this upstairs flat has two pleasant and adequately equipped

rooms. There are views of the town from the roof terrace and rocking chairs on the balcony. $25CUC

Villa Virginia Ciudad Pesquera no.73 ☎ 42 36 3303, ✉ virginiaspension@gmail.com. A *casa particular* 1.5km west of the centre along the seafront. The friendly hosts offer good food and two decent, slightly dark double rooms with air-conditioned, tiled bathrooms and shared TV and fridge. $25CUC

EATING

Cafetería Piropo Malecón e/ 4 y 5 (no phone). Opposite the *malecón* wall, this is a fast-food joint serving inexpensive hot dogs, fried chicken and sandwiches. Daily 10am–6pm.

Cafetería Villa Blanca Ave. 9 esq. 18 ☎ 42 36 3305. Reasonably priced seafood, chicken and steaks are served

in a small garden four blocks from the square. Daily 9am–midnight.

La Ruina Calle 6 esq. 11 ☎ 42 36 3686. Light meals including fried chicken, fish and pork dishes for no more than $4CUC each. Daily noon–10pm.

The northern cays

The **northern cays** form one of Cuba's newest major tourist resorts, set on a network of small islets leading up to the much larger **Cayo Santa María**, almost 15km in length. The drive down the 48km **causeway** from just outside Caibarién to the islands is quite spectacular, and is half the fun of a visit. The dark, deeper waters nearer the land give way to shallow turquoise around the cays, then become almost clear as the network of islets increases in number and complexity. The sea is dotted with mangrove colonies, while herons and cormorants swoop overhead and the occasional iguana basks in the sun on the hot tarmac. The solid rock causeway is broken up by around fifty small **bridges**, which allow the currents to flow through and provide drivers with distance markers; development on the cays begins just after bridge 36. Only one of the islands, **Cayo Las Brujas**, is suitable for day-trippers; the others are mostly the exclusive domain of hotel guests, though you can pay for a day pass (usually around $95CUC), which entitles you to full use of all the facilities.

Cayo Las Brujas

The nearest cay to the mainland to have been developed for visitors, **Cayo Las Brujas** is home to the only marina in the area as well as the least exclusive hotel and beach, making it both more affordable and accessible than Cayo Ensenachos and Cayo Santa María, the only other cays where hotels have been built.

As you arrive via the causeway, there are two left-hand turns in succession, 1km apart. The first, at the pocket-sized airport terminal, cuts down to the only marina on the cays (see box, p.274) and the hotel *Villa Las Brujas*, at one end of the beach, **Playa La Salina**. Only guests of the hotel, or anyone paying for a day-pass (see p.274), can access the beach this way and will be asked to present their passport at the car park; everyone else must take the second left-hand turn, after the airport terminal and beyond the only **petrol station** on the cays, which leads down to the same beach, though the slightly scrappier end of it.

Note that credit cards cannot be used on the cay.

Playa La Salina

Day-passes for the *Villa Las Brujas* section $15CUC, includes $12CUC credit for the restaurant (valid 9am–5pm)

Two kilometres in length, this narrow, sandy **Playa La Salina**, barely 5m wide in places, divides the blue-green waters on one side from the sea of green scrub that covers most of the cay on the other. Dotted with palm-thatch umbrellas, the beach arches round enough to form a bay, which helps to keep the water placid and usually more or less waveless. Sitting snugly at one end, on the craggy platform that it shares with the hotel cabins is *Restaurant El Farallón* (see p.274). At the other end are a few palm-leaf parasols plus a short jetty to jump off, but no amenities other than toilets.

4

Cayo Santa María

From Cayo Las Brujas, the causeway passes a dolphinarium (see box, p.274) and the next significant cay, **Cayo Ensenachos**, where the beach is the exclusive domain of guests at the *Iberostar Ensenachos*. Several bridges beyond Ensenachos, about 15km from Cayo Las Brujas, the causeway concludes at **Cayo Santa María**, home to the remaining nine hotels built on the cays, all of them slung along a stunning 15km beach which Fidel Castro is said to have described as superior to Varadero.

Among the few places open to non-hotel guests on Cayo Santa Maria are the two shopping villages, at opposite ends of the cay: **Pueblo Las Dunas** in the west, in between the *Meliá Cayo Santa María* and the *Meliá Las Dunas* hotels; and the larger **Pueblo La Estrella**, in the far east, between the *HUSA Cayo Santa María* and the *Memories Paraiso Beach Resort* hotels. Unsurprisingly, they're very artificial places, both consisting of mock-colonial buildings housing shops, bars, restaurants, discos and bowling alleys.

Playa Perla Blanca

At the far eastern end of Cayo Santa María, the splendid **Playa Perla Blanca** is one of the most untouched yet still accessible beaches in the whole of the northern cays. It's a bit of a trek – at the end of a dusty track that takes over from the asphalt road, 52km from the mainland in all, but there are several kilometres of beach and the sand is as fine as it gets in Cuba. As there are no facilities here it's worth stocking up on supplies at Pueblo Las Dunas or La Estrella (see above) before making the trip here.

ARRIVAL AND GETTING AROUND

THE NORTHERN CAYS

By plane The small airport (☎ 42 35 0009) on Cayo Las Brujas has three flights a week between Havana and Cayo Coco.

By tourist bus Once on the cays you can make use of the Panoramic Bus Tour, an open-top hop-on, hop-off bus

service running roughly 9am–9pm daily and calling in at all the hotels on its trip round the resort. It costs $1CUC per trip.

By car From Caibarién, a road out of town runs roughly parallel with the coastline for 4km to the bridge that leads

---

ACTIVITIES ON THE NORTHERN CAYS

Marina Gaviota Las Brujas (☎42 35 0013), next to the *Villa Las Brujas* hotel on Cayo Las Brujas, offers **snorkelling** ($35CUC/hr per person) and a full-day snorkelling excursion with lunch ($100CUC per person; min 10 people). **Diving** costs $45CUC for a single immersion and $65CUC for two, while **fishing trips** for the likes of tarpon, marlin and snapper start at $260CUC for four hours, with capacity for four people fishing and equipment included. **Catamaran cruises** cost between $57CUC and $99CUC.

Just off the causeway, about 800m from the southern edge of Cayo Ensenacho, is the largest **dolphinarium** (☎42 35 0013) in Latin America, consisting of six separate pools covering over three thousand square metres. Entrance is $3CUC; shows (twice daily) are $30CUC; interaction with dolphins on a submerged platform is $60CUC for 30min.

---

to the 24-hour checkpoint which marks the start of the causeway linking the mainland to the cays. To pass the checkpoint, you'll need to produce your passport and pay $2CUC per vehicle; keep the receipt as you will need to show it, and pay another $2CUC, on your return.

By taxi Taxis from Caibarién to the cays ($25CUC each way)

can be organized through Transgaviota, which has an office in the town (☎42 35 1353) and another in the *Sol Cayo Santa María* hotel on Cayo Santa Maria.

Bike, car and scooter rental All of the all-inclusive hotels have car, scooter and bicycle rental.

ACCOMMODATION AND EATING

There are currently eleven **hotels** on the cays but only *Villa Las Brujas* is accustomed to regularly receiving guests on spec. However, if you're prepared to pay rack rates upwards of $170CUC a night (and over $400CUC per night for some), there's nothing to stop you turning up unannounced at one of the **all-inclusive hotels**, though you'll save a lot of money by booking a package holiday in advance. The Spanish hotel chain Meliá (☲meliacuba.com) has the longest established presence on the cays and runs four of the hotels, while Iberostar (☲iberostar.com), HUSA (☲husa.es), Royalton (☲royaltonresorts.com) and the Cuban chain Gaviota (☲gaviota-grupo.com) account for the other seven. All hotels have evening entertainment in the form of live music or cabaret. If you just want to take advantage of the hotels' facilities, you can also buy a **day-pass**, which will cost $70–100CUC and covers all food and drink.

Villa Las Brujas Cayo Las Brujas ☎42 35 0024 & 35 0025, ✉reservas@villa.lasbrujas.co.cu. The only hotel on the cays not based on all-inclusive package tourism, this is a simple, picturesque and peaceful little complex, with two lines of comfortable wooden cabins on a natural platform along the rocky shore, connected by a boardwalk. Most rooms have sea-facing balconies and all have a/c and cable TV. The restaurant, *El Farallón* (daily 7am–10pm), serves good quality grilled chicken ($6CUC), mixed seafood grills ($19CUC) and the like. No credit cards. **$84CUC**

Embalse Hanabanilla

Closer to Trinidad but actually easier to access from Santa Clara, 50km away, **Embalse Hanabanilla**, a 36-square-kilometre reservoir, twists, turns and stretches around the hills in a valley on the northern edges of the Sierra del Escambray. On arrival, views of the reservoir reveal no more than a small section as it slinks out of sight behind the steep slopes which make up most of its borders, some of them covered in thick forest and others grassy and peppered with palm trees. Along with its unforgettable setting, the reservoir's claim to fame is as host to the largest population of largemouth bass in the world, and is one of the prime locations for freshwater **fishing** in Cuba. The bass in here reach record sizes, many weighing in at over 7kg, which attracts a growing number of enthusiasts from abroad. Peak season for fishing is from November until the end of March

Whether on a day-trip from Santa Clara or a longer stay, almost all visits are channelled through the *Hanabanilla* hotel (see opposite). On the whole, the banks of the reservoir are difficult to access, though the various **boat excursions** offered by the hotel offer a way round this (see box opposite).

EMBALSE HANABANILLA ACTIVITIES

The *Hanabanilla* hotel (☎42 20 8461, Ecarpeta@hanabanilla.co.cu) offers various tours around the surrounding countryside and on the lake and, between 7am and 3pm daily, rents out kayaks ($1CUC/hr) and rowing boats ($1CUC/hr). **Boat trips** include an excursion to the **Río Negro restaurant** – an assemblage of covered platforms, perched on a forested slope and resembling an elaborate Tarzan camp –cost $18.50CUC per person including lunch if you go by speedboat (max 3 people), or $7.50CUC if you go in a larger, slower boat (max 12 people) which depart daily, usually between 10am and 11am. The same prices apply to the trip to the **Casa del Campesino**, a traditional rural house in a clearing in the woods, where you can sample and buy the cigars manufactured here or the locally grown coffee or honey; and a waterfall where you can bathe, following the 1.5km walk from the edge of the reservoir to get there.

The hotel also arranges **fishing**, starting at $50CUC per person for four hours of fishing with a guide, though as no equipment is supplied you'll need to bring your own.

ARRIVAL AND DEPARTURE

Tours There is no public transport to the reservoir, though you can book an organized excursion through one of the travel agents in Santa Clara (see p.263).
By taxi A taxi from Santa Clara will cost around $30CUC.

EMBALSE HANABANILLA

By car To drive to the reservoir from Santa Clara, take a right turn at the crossroads in the centre of the small town of Manicaragua, then take the left turn marked by the faded sign for the lake about 15km beyond this.

ACCOMMODATION

Hanabanilla ☎42 20 8461 & 0630, ✉carpeta@hana banilla.co.cu. Set in a large, unsubtle, blocky building right on the edge of Embalse Hanabanilla near its northern tip –

the location takes the ugly edge off the hotel, just as the view from the lake-facing rooms makes up for their small size and basic furnishings. There's a pool and a restaurant. **$38CUC**

4

Trinidad and Sancti Spíritus

TRINIDAD

5

Trinidad and Sancti Spíritus

The vast majority of visitors to Sancti Spíritus province head directly for the attractive and colourful sixteenth-century town of Trinidad, one of the country's most perfectly preserved and restored colonial settlements. Situated close to both beach and mountains, in the southwestern corner of Sancti Spíritus and just 13km from the provincial border with Cienfuegos, Trinidad is justifiably the single most-visited destination in central Cuba, and has been declared a World Heritage Site by UNESCO. But despite this protected status, Trinidad is far from being a lifeless architectural showpiece. One of the most touristy places in the country, the town is well set up to receive visitors, with a fantastic selection of *casas particulares*, two memorable hotels right in the centre, a burgeoning set of very good paladars and some popular, lively music venues.

There are several more hotels on the Península de Ancón, 15km south of Trinidad and with one of the best beaches on mainland Cuba's less spectacularly sandy south coast. In the opposite direction, the mountain resort of Topes de Collantes makes an excellent base for hiking around the steep, lavishly forested slopes of the Sierra del Escambray. A few kilometres northeast of Trinidad is the beautiful **Valle de los Ingenios**, home to the sugar estates that made Trinidad's colonial elite so wealthy. Further east, the provincial capital of Sancti Spíritus, though larger than its more famous neighbour, attracts fewer visitors. For some, this is the source of the city's appeal: comparatively free of tour groups, it boasts a long history of its own and a subdued pace of life.

Trinidad

Plenty of other Cuban towns are filled with beautiful old buildings, but there is a completeness about **TRINIDAD**'s cobbled, traffic-free centre and its jumble of pastel-coloured mansions and houses, with their red-tiled rooftops and shuttered porticoes, that puts it in a league of its own. Its pedestrianized colonial district has a distinct village feel, where people walk at a subdued pace over the uneven ground and neighbours chat from their doorsteps. With tourism continuously on the rise, however, you're as likely to see a foreign face as a local one on walks around the centre.

In general, if you're walking on cobblestones you're in the UNESCO-protected part of the city, the old town, at the heart of which is beautiful **Plaza Mayor**. All of Trinidad's prominent **museums**, including the stand-out **Museo Romántico**, are either on the square or within a few blocks of it, so you can enjoy a full day of sightseeing without walking too far. That said, wandering around the old town's jumble of steep streets, shadowed by colonial houses and enlivened here and there by arts and crafts

CASA DE LA MÚSICA, TRINIDAD

Highlights

❶ The Trinidad towers Scale the winding wooden staircases in the towers at the Museo de la Lucha Contra Bandidos and the Museo de Historia Municipal for the best views of Trinidad, framed by coastline and mountains. **See p.284**

❷ Horseriding Take a ride to the outskirts of Trinidad, in the foothills of the Escambray mountains, and enjoy the beauty of the area from the saddle. **See p.287**

❸ Casa de la Música The standout live music venue in Trinidad, offering big-band salsa and traditional Cuban music most nights. **See p.290**

❹ Vintage shopping in Trinidad Pick out a gem from the memorabilia and antiques on sale in the shops and homes of private sellers. **See p.291**

❺ Playa Ancón One of the biggest and best beaches on the southern coast of Cuba. **See p.294**

❻ Steam train to Manaca-Iznaga Enjoy an hour-long ride from Trinidad in a charming old wooden carriage. **See p.296**

❼ Trekking at Topes de Collantes This beautiful national park in the steep, forested slopes of the Sierra del Escambray has some excellent hiking trails. **See p.298**

HIGHLIGHTS ARE MARKED ON THE MAP ON P.280

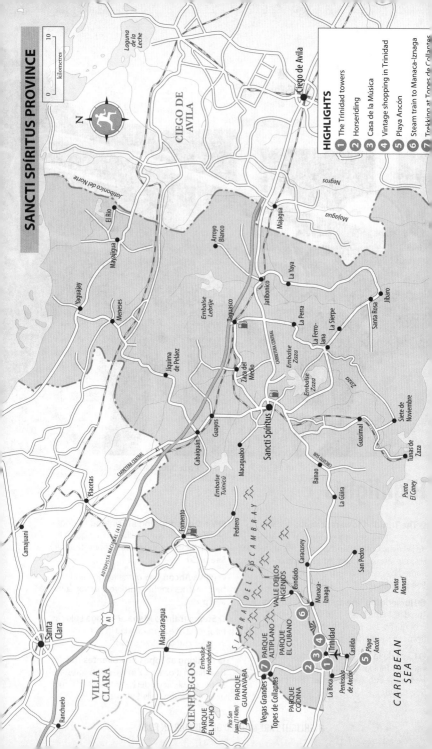

SANCTI SPÍRITUS PROVINCE

0 10
kilometres

N

CIEGO DE ÁVILA

VILLA CLARA

CIENFUEGOS

CARIBBEAN SEA

Laguna de la Leche

Ciego de Ávila

Jatibónico del Norte

El Río

Mayajigua

Yaguajay

Meneses

Negros

Majagua

Arroyo Blanco

La Yaya

Jatibónico

Jíquima de Peláez

Embalse Lebrije

Taguasco

La Perra

La Sierpe

La Ferro-lana

Santa Rosa

Jíbaro

Zaza del Medio

Embalse Zaza

Embalse Zaza

Zaza

Siete de Noviembre

Tunas de Zaza

Guasimal

Punta El Caney

Sancti Spíritus

Guayos

Cabaiguán

Macaguabo

Banao

La Güira

San Pedro

Punta Manatí

CARRETERA CENTRAL

Embalse Tuinicú

Fomento

Pedrero

Caracusey

Condado

Manaca-Iznaga

Placetas

Camajuaní

AUTOPISTA NACIONAL (A1)

Santa Clara

A1

Ranchuelo

Manicaragua

Embalse Hanabanilla

PARQUE EL NICHO

PARQUE GUANAYARA

Pico San Juan (1140m)

PARQUE CODINA

Vegas Grandes

Topes de Collantes

PARQUE ALTIPLANO

PARQUE EL CUBANO

SIERRA DEL ESCAMBRAY

VALLE DE LOS INGENIOS

La Boca

Península de Ancón

Trinidad

Casilda

Playa Ancón

CIRCUITO SUR

markets, is one of Trinidad's highlights and at least as stimulating as visiting the museums. North of the Plaza Mayor you soon reach the northern limits of the city, where some of the streets are little more than mud tracks. One of these leads to the top of the **Loma de la Vigía**, an easily climbable hill overlooking Trinidad, marked at its base by a ruined church, the **Ermita de la Popa**.

Heading downhill from Plaza Mayor will lead you south, out of the historic centre towards **Parque Céspedes**, the centre of town for locals and a sociable hub of activity. Beyond this square and the historic centre there are very few specific sights; you'll get far more out of a visit if you take advantage of the nearby valley (see p.296), beach (see p.293) and mountains (see p.297).

Brief history

A Spanish settlement was first established in Trinidad in 1514, but interest in the area was short-lived. The **gold** mined in the area soon ran out and news spread of the riches to be found in Central America, contributing to a flow of emigration that left the town all but empty by the mid-1540s. It wasn't until the 1580s that the Spanish population rose again and local **agriculture** began to take off. By the 1750s the region possessed over a hundred tobacco plantations and at least as many farms and sugar mills, as well as a population of almost six thousand.

The mid-eighteenth century marked the start of the **sugar boom** (see p.454), a roughly hundred-year period during which Trinidad became one of the country's most prosperous cities. Thousands of **African slaves** were imported to cope with the increasing demands of the sugar industry. Trinidad's prosperity peaked when the economic tide began to turn in the 1830s and 1840s. Slave revolts, the exhaustion of cultivable land and the rising challenge of European sugar beet sent the town into a downward spiral, accelerated by the **Wars of Independence** (see pp.456–457). In the early twentieth century local land fell increasingly into foreign – and especially US – hands, and unemployment shot up. Trinidad's fortunes turned again in the 1950s as tourism increased, encouraging the construction of a small airport and the *Hotel Las Cuevas*, both still standing today. This brief period of prosperity was cut short by the **revolutionary war** that ended in January 1959.

TRINIDAD'S STREET NAMES

The confusion arising from old and new **street names** encountered in many Cuban towns is particularly acute in Trinidad. Most names were changed after the Revolution, but some new maps and tourist literature are reverting to the old names in the interests of the town's historical heritage, and locals usually use the old names. Many street signs now display both names, but the addresses appearing in this book are the post-Revolution versions.

Old name	New name	Old name	New name
Alameda	Jesús Menéndez	**Las Guasimas**	Julio A. Mella
Amargura	Juan Manuel Márquez	**Lirio Blanco**	Abel Santamaría
Angarilla	Fidel Claro	**Media Luna**	Ernesto Valdés Muñoz
Boca	Piro Guinart	**Olvido**	Santiago Escobar
Carmen	Frank País	**Peña**	Francisco Gómez Toro
Coco	Francisco Pettersen	**Real**	Rubén Martínez Villena
Cristo	F.H. Echerrí	**Rosario**	Francisco Javier
Desengaño	Simón Bolívar		Zerquera
Gloria	Gustavo Izquierdo	**San Antonio**	Isidoro Armenteros
Gracia	Francisco Cadahía	**San Procopio**	General Lino Pérez
Gutiérrez	Maceo or Antonio	**Santa Ana**	José Mendoza
	Maceo	**Santo Domingo**	Camilo Cienfuegos
Jesús María	Martí or José Martí	**Vigía**	Eliope Paz

5

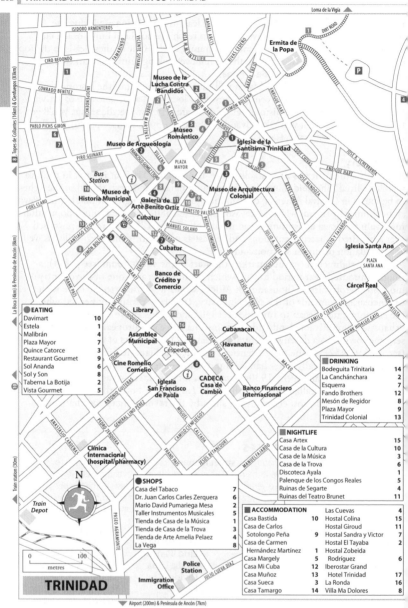

Loma de la Vigía

Ermita de la Popa

Museo de la Lucha Contra Bandidos

Museo Romántico

Museo de Arqueología

Iglesia de la Santísima Trinidad

Plaza Mayor

Bus Station

Museo de Historia Municipal

Galería de Arte Benito Ortiz

Museo de Arquitectura Colonial

Cubatur

Cubatur

Iglesia Santa Ana

Banco de Crédito y Comercio

Plaza Santa Ana

Cárcel Real

Library

Cubanacan

Asamblea Municipal

Parque Céspedes

Havanatur

Cine Romelio Cornelio

CADECA Casa de Cambio

Iglesia San Francisco de Paula

Banco Financiero Internacional

Clínica Internacional (hospital/pharmacy)

N

Train Depot

0   100
metres

TRINIDAD

Police Station

Immigration Office

Airport (200m) & Península de Ancón (7km)

Topes de Collantes (16km) & Cienfuegos (83km)

La Boca (4km) & Península de Ancón (8km)

Train station (30m)

EATING	
Davimart	10
Estela	1
Malibrán	4
Plaza Mayor	7
Quince Catorce	3
Restaurant Gourmet	9
Sol Ananda	6
Sol y Son	8
Taberna La Botija	2
Vista Gourmet	5

DRINKING	
Bodeguita Trinitaria	14
La Canchánchara	2
Esquerra	7
Fando Brothers	12
Mesón de Regidor	8
Plaza Mayor	9
Trinidad Colonial	13

NIGHTLIFE	
Casa Artex	15
Casa de la Cultura	10
Casa de la Música	3
Casa de la Trova	6
Discoteca Ayala	5
Palenque de los Congos Reales	5
Ruinas de Segarte	4
Ruinas del Teatro Brunet	11

SHOPS	
Casa del Tabaco	7
Dr. Juan Carlos Carles Zerquera	6
Mario David Pumariega Mesa	2
Taller Instrumentos Musicales	5
Tienda de Casa de la Música	1
Tienda de Casa de la Trova	3
Tienda de Arte Amelia Pelaez	4
La Vega	8

ACCOMMODATION			
Casa Bastida	10	Las Cuevas	4
Casa de Carlos		Hostal Colina	15
Sotolongo Peña	9	Hostal Giroud	11
Casa de Carmen		Hostal Sandra y Victor	7
Hernández Martínez	1	Hostal El Tayaba	2
Casa Margely	5	Hostal Zobeida	
Casa Mi Cuba	12	Rodríguez	6
Casa Muñoz	13	Iberostar Grand	
Casa Sueca	3	Hotel Trinidad	17
Casa Tamargo	14	La Ronda	16
		Villa Ma Dolores	8

It was in the Sierra del Escambray around Trinidad that, for five years following the rebel triumph, US-backed **counter-revolutionaries** fought in a guerrilla conflict during which significant numbers of local men were killed. Celebrating its 500th anniversary in 2014, Trinidad began the rise to its current prominence after its historic centre and the nearby Valle de los Ingenios were declared World Heritage Sites by UNESCO in 1988.

Plaza Mayor

The beautiful **Plaza Mayor** is the heart of Trinidad's colonial old town. Comprising four simple fenced-in gardens, each with a palm tree or two and dotted with various statuettes and other ornamental touches, it's surrounded by painted colonial mansions, which are adorned with arches and balconies and home to and an art gallery. Plaza Mayor is a focal point for tourists rather than locals, but this vibrant, compact little square is a captivating place nevertheless.

Museo Romántico

Fernando Echerrí esq. Simón Bolívar, Plaza Mayor • Mon–Sat 9am–5pm, Sun 9am–1pm • $2CUC, photos $1CUC • ☎ 41 99 4363

The fabulous **Museo Romántico** is an essential part of Trinidad's delve into the past. With one of the country's finest and most valuable collections of colonial **furniture** packed into its fourteen rooms, there is no better place to go for a picture of aristocratic lifestyle and tastes in eighteenth- and nineteenth-century Cuba. Dating from 1808, the house itself – built for the very wealthy Brunet family – is a magnificent example of elegant nineteenth-century domestic Cuban architecture. Though the museum's contents have been gathered together from various buildings all over town, there is a wonderful consistency and completeness to the collection, befitting the perfectly preserved and restored rooms.

Iglesia de la Santísima Trinidad

Francisco Javier Zerquera no.456 esq. F.H. Echerrí, Plaza Mayor • Mon–Sat 10.30am–1pm • Free • ☎ 41 99 3668

Looking down on Plaza Mayor is the city's main church, **Iglesia de la Santísima Trinidad**, also known as the Parroquial Mayor. Though there has been a church on this site since 1620, the structure now standing was officially finished in 1892. Among the pictures and paintings inside are a disproportionate number of impressively crafted **altars**, especially the neo-Gothic structure in the central nave, with its mass of pointed spires. Most of them were created by Amadeo Fiogere. A Dominican friar assigned to the church in 1912, he set about livening up the interior, drawing on his own personal fortune to donate many of the images on display today.

Museo de Arquitectura Colonial

Ripalda e/ F.H. Echerrí y Rubén Martínez Villena, Plaza Mayor • Mon–Sat Sun 9am–5pm, plus alternate Sundays • $1CUC • ☎ 41 99 3208

The **Museo de Arquitectura Colonial** exhibits the components that make up a typical colonial-era house in Trinidad, but the small collection of fixtures and fittings won't keep you for long. The former residence of the Sánchez-Iznaga family – local aristocrats who made their fortune from sugar – the building was constructed in 1738 and then extended to its current size in 1785. Don't leave before taking a look at the quirky-looking US-made Art Nouveau shower, dating from 1912. It's in a block out the back, off a courtyard vibrantly bedecked with plants.

Galería de Arte Benito Ortiz

Rubén Martínez Villena e/ Simón Bolívar y Ripalda, Plaza Mayor • Mon–Sat 9am–4pm • Free • Shop ☎ 41 99 6626

It won't take long to look round the **Galería de Arte Benito Ortiz**, whose displays comprise mostly temporary exhibitions of lacework, ceramics, sculpture and paintings – often with a quite original slant – and some soulless artwork for sale. Most of the exhibitions are housed in the six rooms upstairs, where you can also catch a perfectly framed view of the plaza through the open shutters of this colonial residence, built between 1800 and 1809.

Museo de Arqueología

Simón Bolívar esq. Rubén Martínez Villena, Plaza Mayor • Tues–Sun 9am–5pm • $1CUC • ☎ 41 99 3420

Set in another eighteenth century house, the **Museo de Arqueología** holds a modest collection of pre-Columbian and colonial-era artefacts which vaguely chart the

5

development of tools and other man-made objects, from the Palaeolithic era of prehistory through the Mesolithic and Neolithic eras and up to the colonial period. Among the fragments of ceramics and primitive stone tools is a 2000-year-old **skeleton**, the bits and pieces buried with it providing insights into ancient burial rituals.

Museo de Historia Municipal

Simón Bolívar no.423 e/ Francisco Gómez Toro y Gustavo Izquierdo • Mon–Sat 9am–5pm • $2CUC

The first part of the **Museo de Historia Municipal** contains various superb examples of nineteenth-century furniture that reflect the wealth and taste of one of Trinidad's sugar industry families, the **Canteros**. Born in this colonial residence in 1815, Justo German Cantero was the owner of the Buena Vista sugar mill; his portrait, along with that of his wife, can be found in the most well-rounded part of the museum, the first three rooms, full of well-presented colonial exhibits; from here on the collection moves abruptly into a rundown of the area's history. Though there are some interesting objects scattered about, like a gramophone from the early twentieth century, the museum never really gets going and runs out of exhibits too quickly. Don't leave, however, without heading upstairs, where a spiral staircase leads up into a **tower** providing some great **views**, including a classic snapshot of the plaza.

Museo de la Lucha Contra Bandidos

Fernando Echerrí esq. Piro Guinart • Daily 9am–5pm • $1CUC • ☎ 41 99 4121

A block northwest of Plaza Mayor, the building housing the **Museo de la Lucha Contra Bandidos** is also host to Trinidad's trademark dome-topped yellow-and-white-trimmed **belltower**. The tower is part of the eighteenth-century church and convent, the Iglesia and Convento de San Francisco de Asís, which previously stood on this site. Even if the museum's contents don't appeal to you, it's well worth paying the entrance fee to climb up the rickety wooden staircase to the top of the **tower**, which has a panoramic **view** over the city and across to the hills and coastline.

The **museum displays** are mostly themed around the post-1959 fight against counter-revolutionary groups – the **bandidos**, or bandits – that fought Castro's army during the years immediately following his seizure of power. Much of the fighting took place in the nearby Sierra del Escambray. Most striking, in the central courtyard, is a military truck and a motorboat mounted with machine gun stands, examples of the hardware employed by and against the *bandidos.*

Ermita de la Popa

Looking down on the colonial centre, beyond the end of Simón Bolívar, in a more run down part of town, a dirt track leads steeply up to a dilapidated church, the **Ermita de Nuestra Señora de la Candelaria de la Popa del Barco**, marking the last line of buildings before the town dissolves into the countryside. Known locally as La Popa, there's nothing to see of the church itself but a ruined framework, but it's worth making the easy fifteen-minute walk up the hill to the rear of the church, the **Loma de la Vigía**, for the views at the top.

At the summit the lush landscape of the Valle de los Ingenios (see p.296) on the other side of the hill is revealed, as well as views back across the town and down to the coast. Just beyond the ruined church you can easily cut across to the *Las Cuevas* hotel complex, on the adjoining hillside, where non-guests can use the hillside **swimming pool** and other facilities (see p.287).

5

Parque Céspedes

Plaza Mayor may be the city centre for sightseers, but as far as the town's population is concerned, **Parque Céspedes** is Trinidad's main square. South of the cobbled streets that define the protected part of the town, at about the mid-point of Martí, Parque Céspedes may not have Plaza Mayor's enchanting surroundings but it's got a charm of its own and is markedly more lively, particularly in the evenings. Schoolchildren run out onto the square in the afternoon, while older locals head here at the end of the day to chat on the benches lining the three walkways. In the square's centre, a distinctive dome-shaped leafy canopy provides plenty of shade, while flower-frilled bushes encase the simple gardens, which are marked in each corner by a handsome royal palm. The stately yellow-columned entrance of the **Asamblea Municipal** building, the town council headquarters, occupies the square's entire northwestern side. Set back from the southwestern edge of the square, next to the school, are a cinema and a modest tiled-roof church.

Cárcel Real

Daily 10am–midnight • Free • ☎ 41 99 6423

To the east of Trinidad, in a relatively subdued neighbourhood where visitors are more conspicuous than elsewhere, the rather neglected **Plaza Santa Ana** is surrounded by houses, the derelict shell of the Iglesia Santa Ana church and the **Cárcel Real**, a former prison now converted into a tourist complex. Coach-loads of tour groups stop here for the souvenir shops, bar and restaurant around the Cárcel Real's courtyard but, disappointingly, very little is made of its history as a military jail.

ARRIVAL AND DEPARTURE   TRINIDAD

By plane Just a few hundred metres out of town on Paseo Agramonte is Trinidad's tiny and rarely used airport (☎ 41 99 6393), serving chartered flights only. From here it's a 1.5km walk into town; the alternative is to take a taxi for a few convertible pesos.

By bus Víazul buses navigate slowly into Trinidad's bus station (☎ 41 99 4448) at Piro Guinart e/ Maceo e Izquierdo, within easy walking distance of a large number of *casas particulares*. Be ready for the scrum that usually forms as locals tout their houses to passengers descending from the bus. Transtur buses drop off and pick up at the city hotels. There's more advice on the different bus services in Basics (see p.30).

Viazul destinations Cienfuegos (5 daily; 1hr 30min); Havana (3 daily; 6hr); Playa Girón (1 daily; 3hr 30min); Playa Larga (1 daily; 4hr); Sancti Spíritus (1 daily; 1hr 30min);

Santa Clara (1 daily; 3hr); Varadero (2 daily; 5hr 30min).

Transtur destinations: Cienfuegos (2 daily; 1hr 30min); Havana (1 daily; 6hr); Pinar del Río (1 daily; 10hr); Viñales (1 daily; 9hr).

By car Arriving on the coastal road by car from Cienfuegos and the west will bring you into town on Piro Guinart, which leads directly up to the two main roads cutting through the centre of the city, Martí and Maceo. From Sancti Spíritus and points east, the Circuito Sur takes cars closer to the Las Cuevas hotel, but a left turn at Lino Pérez will take you into *casa particular* territory.

By train On the southwestern edge of town, at the foot of General Lino Pérez, the train station (☎ 41 99 3348) serves only local destinations, most of them in the Valle de los Ingenios.

Destinations Manaca Iznaga (2 daily; 30min).

GETTING AROUND

Trinidad is small enough to get around on foot or bicycle, though walking is the best way to tackle its steep, cobblestoned streets. If you want to make trips to the mountains or valley, you'll need to use motorized transport. The beach is within cycling distance but most people use the Trinibus (see p.294).

By bicitaxi *Bicitaxis* are available for areas where the streets are not cobbled. They congregate outside the *Las Begonias* café at Maceo esq. Simón Bolívar.

By bicycle Ruinas del Teatro Brunet, Maceo e/ Francisco Javier Zerquera y Simón Bolívar (8.30am–6.30pm; ☎ 41 99 8416; $4CUC/day), offers bike rental.

By car Cubacar is at the Cupet-Cimex gas station on the road to the airport (daily 9am–noon & 1–5.20pm; ☎ 41 99 6301), and in the Cubatur office at Simón Bolívar no.352 e/ Maceo y Izquierdo (daily 8am–8pm; ☎ 41 99 6368).

By scooter Rent scooters at Vía on Frank País e/ Simón Bolívar y Fidel Claro (☎ 41 99 6388) or through the

Havanatur or Cubanacan travel agents (see p.292), Maceo e/ Francisco Javier Zerquera y Simón Bolívar, which charge $5CUC/hr or $30CUC per day.

By taxi There are usually plenty of private taxis waiting on Piro Guinart near the bus station. A day-trip to the mountains or the valley can be negotiated for $20–30CUC

depending on the car and the driver, while a trip to the beach should cost half that. Alternatively, to rent a car with driver, call Ariel Gónzales Valera (mobile ☎ 53 59 2761) or visit him at Maceo no.759 e/ Ciro Redondo e Isidoro Armentero. For metered state taxis, call Cubataxi (☎ 41 99 8080).

INFORMATION

Infotur The local branch of the national tourist information provider is less than a block from the bus station at Gustavo Izquierdo e/ Piro Guinart y Simón Bolívar (☎ 41 99 8258; Mon–Fri 8am–6.30pm, Sat & Sun

8.30am–4.30pm). You can book excursions and Víazul bus tickets here, pick up maps and leaflets and get visitor advice on just about anything.

ACCOMMODATION

Trinidad has several **hotels** and one of the best selections of **casas particulares** in the country: some 400 are spread throughout the city, and there's at least one on almost every block in the centre. As in other Cuban tourist hotspots, groups of locals greet Víazul bus arrivals with pictureboards of their houses. Some are perfectly legitimate, but be aware of **touts** who, if you say you've already booked a place, claim that it is full or has closed down – it's always a scam. If you do book ahead, it's sometimes worth asking your hosts to meet you at the bus station with your name on a sign.

HOTELS

Las Cuevas Finca Santa Ana ☎ 41 99 6133, ✉ reservas @cuevas.co.cu. A large, spacious complex of simple but sufficiently equipped concrete cabins, superbly located on a hillside overlooking the town and the coast. It's only a 20min walk from the Plaza Mayor but perfectly secluded. There's access to the cave network over which the site was built, nightly music and dance shows, a tennis court and a pool. **$106CUC**

★ **Iberostar Grand Hotel Trinidad** José Martí no.262 e/ Lino Pérez y Colón ☎ 41 99 6073, ✉ recepcion@iberostar.trinidad.co.cu. This fabulously plush hotel on Parque Céspedes is full of understated luxury, with just one or two ostentatious touches. There's a

delightfully reposeful central patio dotted with plants and a fountain, a cushy yet dignified smokers' lounge, a large buffet restaurant and forty fantastically furnished rooms, most with either a balcony or a terrace. **$300CUC**

La Ronda Martí no.45 e/ Lino Pérez y Colón ☎ 41 99 8538, ✉ comercial@cuevas.co.cu. The comfortable, tastefully furnished rooms are set around a delightful central courtyard at this marvellous boutique hotel, reopened in 2012 after years of restoration. The nineteenth-century building has a rooftop bar, brilliant for sunset drinks, and the staff have a reputation for good service. **$170CUC**

Villa Ma Dolores Carretera de Cienfuegos Km 1.5 ☎ 41 99 6394, ✉ comercial@dolores.co.cu. Outside town, on

---

ACTIVITIES IN TRINIDAD

Travel agents and local individuals offer recreational **horseriding**, usually around the foothills and parkland of the Sierra del Escambray, especially in Parque El Cubano (see p.298). Local man Julio Muñoz (☎ 41 99 3673, ⊕ diana.trinidadphoto.com) offers excursions by horseback to the Valle de los Ingenios ($25CUC; 4–5hr) and runs a project promoting the humane treatment of horses. You can visit him at Martí no.401 e/ Fidel Claro y Santiago Escobar, where he keeps his own horse. The two best travel agents to consult for horseriding are Trinidad Travels and Ecotur (see p.292); the latter offers a trip to nearby Parque El Palmito for $20CUC, which includes transport to the park.

Salsa and other Cuban **dance lessons** are offered by state and privately run enterprises alike. Enquire at the *Casa de la Música* (see p.290), the Paradiso travel agency (see p.292) or Trinidad Travels (see p.292). Costs average at $10CUC per hour.

Local jack-of-all-trades Julio Muñoz (see above) also runs a really worthwhile set of **photography workshops** (☎ 41 99 3673, ⊕ photo.trinidadphoto.com) catering to beginners as well as more advanced photographers. Prices start at $25CUC for a half-day tour of Trinidad designed to provide photo opportunities that most visitors would otherwise miss, and rise to $80CUC for a two- to three-day course in photography as well as a tour.

Finally, The hillside **swimming pool** at the *Hotel Las Cuevas* is open to non-guests for a fee of $6CUC, which includes $5CUC credit for food and drink.

5

the scenic banks of the moss-green Guaurabo River and popular with tour groups, the plain cabins here come with TVs, fridges and kitchenettes. Activities include horseriding and Cuban country-music evenings. There's a swimming pool, restaurant and bar. See Around Trinidad map (p.293) for location. **$76CUC**

CASAS PARTICULARES

⭐ **Casa Bastida** Maceo no.537 e/ Simón Bolívar y Piro Guinart ☎41 99 6686, ✉juliobastida@gmail.com. Two lovely en-suite rooms, one a very spacious triple with a streetside balcony, in a house full of artistic and antique touches, run by a down-to-earth, personable couple. There are two levels of attractive roof terraces, one with outstanding views, and a delightful bamboo-roof patio out the back, full of plants, where excellent meals are served. **$25CUC**

Casa de Carlos Sotolongo Peña Rubén Martínez Villena no.33 e/ Simón Bolívar y Francisco Javier Zerquera ☎41 99 4169, ✉galinkapuig@gmail.com. Built in 1825, and occupied by sixth-generation Trinitarios, this spacious house right on the Plaza Mayor has a large colonial-era room inside as well as a modern one in an extension at the back. Both rooms have en-suite bathrooms and look onto a large courtyard. **$25CUC**

Casa de Carmen Hernández Martínez Maceo no.718 e/ Conrado Benítez y Ciro Redondo ☎52 51 2081 (mobile). There are two double a/c bedrooms at this basic bungalow, and the pleasant owners are prepared to rent out the whole house (complete with kitchen and backyard patio) if you want total self-sufficiency. It's on a bumpy track in a more run-down part of town, only a few blocks from the bus station. **$20CUC**

Casa Margely Piro Guinart no.360a e/ F.H. Echerrí y Juan Manuel Márquez ☎41 99 6525. Peace and tranquillity reign in the private guest section of this house, tucked away behind a pretty garden gate at the rear of a central patio, where there's an open-air, roof-covered dining room in addition to two double rooms off a plant-lined passageway. The house itself, built in 1796, is a graceful display of colonial opulence. **$30CUC**

Casa Mi Cuba Simón Bolívar no.309 e/ Maceo y Martí ☎41 99 6686, ✉juliobastida@gmail.com. This lovely house has been beautifully renovated and refurbished by the astute owner who lives round the corner; you can rent the whole thing, or just one of its two bedrooms. A delightfully inviting, balustraded roof terrace, a cosy little patio and a well-equipped kitchen help to make this one of the most agreeable places to stay in the city if you want complete independence. Room **$25CUC**; whole apartment **$50CUC**

⭐ **Casa Muñoz** Martí no.401 e/ Fidel Claro y Stgo Escobar ☎41 99 3673, ⊕casa.trinidadphoto.com. There's so much to admire and appreciate at this huge house, built in 1800, and it's not just the antique cabinets,

armchairs, tables and clocks. The four large, high-spec guest rooms, one an impressive two-floor suite ideal for families, feature comfortable new colonial-style mahogany beds, hair dryers in the en-suite bathrooms and have even had 220-volt, three-pin plug sockets fitted specifically for British guests. English-speaking Julio, the proprietor, runs photography workshops, horseriding excursions and has a highly engaging photo gallery. There are two terraces, a patio and space for parking. **$30CUC**

Casa Sueca Juan Manuel Márquez no.70a e/ Piro Guinart y Ciro Redondo ☎41 99 8060, ✉casasueca tdad@yahoo.es. Two cavernous, simply styled rooms, one with three double beds and one with two, in a beautiful tranquil colonial-era house at the top of town. Communal areas include an intimate central split-level patio. It's run by a mother and her English-speaking daughter, both accomplished cooks, who help to create a warm family atmosphere. **$30CUC**

Casa Tamargo Francisco Javier Zerquera no.266 e/ Martí y Maceo ☎41 99 6669, ✉felixmatilde@yahoo .com. A very professionally and proudly run *casa particular*. A smart dining room opens up onto one of the prettiest patios in the city, full of hanging plants and shrubs, around which the rooms are based. There's also a lovely roof terrace with a swinging chair and sun loungers. **$30CUC**

⭐ **Hostal Colina** Maceo no.374 e/ Lino Pérez y Colón ☎41 99 2319, ✉zulenaa@yahoo.com.es. A highly impressive *casa particular* with an immaculate split-level central patio with a hotel-standard bar, and countless plants creating a park-like feel. The perfectly restored section of the house from 1820 is authentically furnished and decorated, and contrasts nicely with the rest of the otherwise modern mini-complex. All three of the fantastic pastel bedrooms are en suite. **$30CUC**

Hostal Giroud Francisco Javier Zerquera no.403 esq Ernesto Valdes Muñoz ☎41 99 3818, ✉anibal782002 @yahoo.es. Plain and simple furnishings characterize the three guest rooms at this eighteenth-century house in the heart of the old town. A connecting door between two rooms and an adjoining outdoor dining room for the exclusive use of guests make this a good option for parties of four. The other room is up on a roof terrace. Rosa, the host, is a great source of local history. **$25CUC**

Hostal El Tayaba Juan Manuel Márquez no.70 e/ Piro Guinart y Ciro Redondo ☎41 99 4197, ✉eltayaba @yahoo.es. Three beautifully appointed rooms in a *casa particular par excellence*. The house is dotted with decorative colonial curios and there's an enclosed central patio perfect for leisurely breakfasts. A rooftop terrace with views over the nearby church is an added bonus, as are the helpful and bubbly young hosts, Iris and Yoel, who are always upbeat and friendly. **$30CUC**

Hostal Sandra y Victor Maceo no.613a e/ Pablo Pichs Girón y Piro Guinart ☎41 99 6444, w hostalsandra.com. Two large bedrooms, each with two double beds and its own bathroom, in a fabulously airy and clean modern house. The upstairs is exclusively for guests; there's a balcony at the front and a wide-open terrace at the back, plus two communal rooms indoors. The food is excellent. 30CUC

★ **Hostal Zobeida Rodríguez** Maceo no.619 e/ Piro Guinart y Pablo Pichs Girón ☎ 41 99 4162,

e zobeidarguez@yahoo.es. One of the best-appointed, most pristine homes in the city, the comfortable, modern and thoughtfully designed interior is luxurious by Cuban standards. Two of the guest rooms are in their own independent block upstairs, another faces onto a little patio downstairs and there are two more on the way in a custom-built block out the back. Excellent showers, and views to the coast from the roof terrace. $30CUC

EATING

The explosion of **paladars** in Trinidad in the last few years has provided the city with a really good choice of worthwhile eating-out options and relegated most of the state restaurants to the second division. There's a concentration of paladars in the old town, half a dozen within a block or two of Plaza Mayor, and others worth venturing out of the centre for.

STATE RESTAURANTS

Plaza Mayor Rubén Martínez Villena no.15 esq. Francisco Javier Zerquera ☎ 41 99 6470. A good-value daytime buffet ($8CUC) offering pasta and a way-above-average selection of vegetables and salad alongside the trays of meat and fish. The attractive terraces around the crumbling brick arches of this restored colonial mansion provide one of the nicest outdoor dining spots in the city. Daily noon–11pm, buffet noon–2.30pm.

★ **Restaurant Gourmet** Grand Hotel Trinidad, Martí no.262 e/ Lino Pérez y Colón ☎ 41 99 6073. Luxuries (at least by local standards) such as smoked salmon, beef carpaccio and – unheard of in most Cuban restaurants – a selection of cheeses can be enjoyed in this hotel's grand dining room. Main dishes include candied tenderloin steak in red wine and pork fillet with vegetable risotto. Set-menu three-course lunches are $20CUC and buffet dinners are $35CUC. Daily 7–10am, 12.30–3pm & 7–10pm.

PALADARS

★ **Davimart** Anastasio Cárdenas no.518 esq. Simon Bolívar ☎ 41 99 3153. Though inauspiciously located way from the touristy centre, this paladar serves the best lobster ($18CUC) in Trinidad, and is one of the top choices in town. The sociable owner-chef, working from the open kitchen facing the inviting patio dining area, takes great pride in the presentation and quality of his food, creating fantastic soups, sides and salads, plus signature dishes like lamb in red wine sauce ($13CUC), garlic shrimp ($15CUC) and sumptuous chocolate desserts. Bookings advised. Mon–Sat 6pm–midnight.

★ **Estela** Simón Bolívar no.557 e/ Juan Manuel Márquez y José Mendoza ☎ 41 99 4329. The house speciality *cordero a la cubana* ($10CUC), a tangy shredded lamb dish, as well as the other fish, pork and tortilla mains ($8–10CUC) represent the best in Cuban home-cooking, with a feast of extras like bean salads, yucca and avocado. The two-tier backyard patio surrounded by high walls and trees makes this an enchanting place for a meal. Mon–Sat

2–10.30pm.

Malibrán Simón Bolívar no.507 e/ F.H. Echerri y Juan Manuel Marquez ☎ 53 53 0190 (mobile). A good choice for lovers of shellfish, with crab enchilado ($6CUC), lobster rings ($14CUC) and white wine shrimp ($10CUC) among the dozen or so shellfish options, as well as plenty of meat alternatives. The front-room walls of this striking, cavernous old house are decorated with vinyl records, there's a working vintage jukebox in the corner and the proprietor – a troubadour with a butter-smooth voice – serenades diners every night. Daily 9am–11pm.

Quince Catorce Simón Bolívar no.515 e/ F.H. Echerri y Juan Manuel Marquez ☎ 41 99 4255. Brimming with antique furniture and features, its tables beautifully and strikingly set with vintage china, cutlery, candelabras and cut crystal glassware, this self-styled restaurant-museum is an unusual option. With a captivating central patio, the option of rooftop dining, a live band and dancers thrown into the mix, the food takes second place to the experience, but the lobster ($12–14CUC) is fresh and well cooked and the fish, shrimp, pork or chicken alternatives (mostly $10CUC) are not bad either. Daily noon–4pm & 6.30pm–late.

Sol Ananda Rubén Martínez Villena no.45 esq. Simón Bolívar ☎ 41 99 8281. Just off the Plaza Mayor in a superbly striking building, laid out like a decorative arts museum, this is a really good go at doing something different, offering dishes from an eclectic set of countries around the world on a hit-and-miss menu. Some of it works, like the decent salad selection ($5–9CUC), the vegetable tempura ($6.75CUC) or the *tamboril de vegetales* ($8.50CUC); and some of it doesn't – avoid the spicy lamb and potato stew ($9.75CUC). Daily noon–11pm.

Sol y Son Simón Bolívar no.283 e/ Frank País y Martí ☎ 41 99 8281. A long-standing paladar where huge portions of fairly priced mains like grilled pork in rum ($6.75CUC) and fish in fruit sauce ($7.50CUC) are fine but unremarkable, though with over two dozen main dishes, they appear to have overstretched themselves somewhat. Nonetheless the beautiful, romantically lit courtyard,

5

brimming with plantlife, is a great spot for a meal. Daily 7pm–late.

Taberna La Botija Juan Manuel Márquez no.71B esq. Piro Guinart ☏ 52 83 0147. The pizzas here aren't award-winning but they are among the best in Trinidad, and from around $3.50CUC you can't go too far wrong. There's pasta, sandwiches and classic Cuban cooking too, served in a rustic, stone-walled old house, marked by earthy tones, picnic benches and an easy-going atmosphere. Daily 24hrs.

★ **Vista Gourmet** Galdós e/ Ernesto Valdes Muñoz y Callejón de Gallegos ☏ 41 99 6700. Up on the roof of a house high up in the old town, the excellent location matches the way-above-average cuisine at this fantastic paladar. Pay $16.95CUC for a buffet starter, featuring salads, pates, pastas and soups, a main course such as roast suckling pig, octopus or chicken with olive puree and honey, and a buffet dessert. As romantic a spot as any in the city. Daily noon–11pm.

DRINKING AND NIGHTLIFE

Though most of Trinidad lies relatively dormant at night, there's a small concentration of live music venues just beyond the Plaza Mayor. Parque Céspedes provides the other focal point, especially at weekends when there are often open-air disco and live music geared to the large crowd of young locals who provide the atmosphere and numbers. Most of the bars are in the restaurants, paladars and hotels, with only a few places existing solely as a place to go for a **drink**. Many **live music** venues also double up as bars, and you can usually get a drink whether or not a band is playing. Opening times at most bars are variable.

BARS

Bodeguita Trinitaria Colón no.91 e/ Martí y Maceo ☏ 41 99 2477. If you fancy some Cuban flavour untainted by any attempt to cater to tourists, visit this slightly run-down restaurant-cum-bar, popular with local drinkers. Daily 7am–10pm.

★ **La Canchánchara** Rubén Martínez Villena e/ Piro Guinart y Ciro Redondo ☏ 41 99 6231. One of the best bars for live music, with a band here most days and nights. A long shady courtyard, lined with squat little benches, provides a sociable and laidback environment. The house special is a cocktail of rum, honey, lemon, water and ice. Daily 9am–9pm.

Esquerra Francisco Javier Zerquera no.464 esq. F.H. Echerrí ☏ 41 99 3434. Opposite the *Casa de la Música* steps, at night the simple little patio bar at this restaurant provides a pleasant spot for a sit-down and drink while remaining in the thick of the action. During the day it works well as a convenient stop-off on a tour of the old town. Daily 11am–midnight.

Fando Brothers Maceo esq. F.J. Zerquera (no phone). The restaurant bar here stands out for its long opening hours, its popularity with both foreigners and Cubans and its location, away from the nightly hubbub of the old town music venues but still very central. Among the best places in town for sociable late-night drinks. Daily 24hrs.

Mesón del Regidor Simón Bolívar no.424 e/ Ernesto Valdés Muñoz y Rubén Martínez Villena ☏ 41 99 6573. This simple bar attached to a rustic restaurant near the Plaza Mayor makes for a convenient place to cool off with a *mojito*. Daily 10am–10pm.

Plaza Mayor Rubén Martínez Villena no.15 esq. Francisco Javier Zerquera ☏ 41 99 6470. The terrace bar tucked into a corner of the *Plaza Mayor* restaurant is a very pleasant and subdued spot for a lazy outdoor drink. Daily noon–10pm.

Trinidad Colonial Maceo no.402 esq. Colón ☏ 41 99 6473. With one of the only authentic colonial-style bar counters in Trinidad, this restaurant-bar is one of the best spots in town for straight-up drinking. A spiral staircase leads up to a roof terrace offering great views. Daily 11am–10pm.

CLUBS AND LIVE MUSIC VENUES

Casa Artex Lino Pérez e/ Francisco Cadahía y Martí ☏ 41 99 6486. One of Trinidad's less reliable music venues, in an old colonial mansion near Parque Céspedes. Puts on Cuban dance and music shows in its spacious central courtyard; when there's no live music, it functions as a bar and pumps out modern salsa and reggaeton. Entry $1CUC. Mon–Sat 10am–2am & Sun 10am–midnight.

Casa de la Cultura Francisco Javier Zerquera no.406 esq. Ernesto Valdes Muñoz ☏ 41 99 4308. Not a live music venue as such, but it's worth dropping by to check out the weekly programme usually posted outside this community arts centre. A live trova performance or something similar usually features at some point. Performances are as likely to be in the day as at night. Free.

★ **Casa de la Música** Francisco Javier Zerquera no. ☏ 41 99 6622. Drawing the largest crowds in town, this is Trinidad's busiest, most animated spot for big-band salsa and guaranteed dancing. Performances usually take place at the *Bar Escalinata*, halfway up the broad flight of steps leading up to the venue itself, leaving the walled-in terrace at the top, officially the main concert area, comparatively underused, though there is sometimes a disco here from 11.30pm. Local and national Cuban groups play most nights, starting at around 9pm. Free or $1CUC for the venue itself. Daily 10am–2am.

5

★ **Casa de la Trova** F.H. Echerrí no.29 e/ Patricio Lumumba y Jesús Menéndez, Plazuela Segarte ☎ 41 99 5445. Of similar renown to the Casa de la Música, this tightly packed little place, with its intimate covered terrace bar, is more likely to stage guitar soloists and traditional trova and son groups than the large salsa outfits that play at its neighbour. Expect to see several groups in one night. Entry $1CUC after dark. Daily 9am–2am.

Discoteca Ayala Loma de la Vigía ☎ 41 99 6133. The only nightclub in Trinidad is buried in a hillside cave network making a night here an exceptional experience – whether or not the reggaeton, house, salsa and pop floats your boat. Quieter in low season than elsewhere in town. Entry $3CUC. Mon–Fri 10.30pm–3am, Sun 5pm–2am.

Palenque de los Congos Reales F.H. Echerrí no.33 e/ Francisco Javier Zerquera y Patricio Lumumba ☎ 41 99 4512. A walled-in, open-air venue under a canopy of branches where energetic rumba and other Afro-Cuban dance shows and musical performances are staged. There are several different shows and groups every day, the first

usually starting around 2pm, the last at 11pm. $1CUC. Daily 10am–midnight.

Ruinas de Segarte Jesús Menéndez e/ Galdos y Juan Manuel Márquez, Plazuela Segarte (no phone). Outdoor, cosy and atmospheric little enclosure in the old town which tends to attract people whether or not there is live music (there generally is). Expect traditional Cuban sounds. Free. Daily 8.30am–midnight.

Ruinas del Teatro Brunet Maceo e/ Francisco Javier Zerquera y Simón Bolívar ☎ 41 99 8416. Cabaret-style song-and-dance performances are the mainstay on the weekly schedule here, though live traditional Cuban music features too, all in an enchanting courtyard under the ruined arches of Trinidad's first theatre. Shows most nights, starting around 9.30pm. Free. Daily 10am–midnight.

CINEMA

Cine Romelio Cornelio Antonio Guiteras, Parque Céspedes ☎ 41 99 3458. The principal local cinema shows the widest variety of films in the city. Closed Mon.

SHOPPING

Trinidad is a great place to buy **textiles**, with a wide selection in the street markets of the old town. There are various kinds of **arts and crafts** shops, with a particular concentration of them on the old-town stretch of Francisco Javier Zerquera. This is also one of the best places outside Havana to pick up **vintage memorabilia** and **antiques**, thanks largely to some local collectors-cum-entrepreneurs (see box below).

Casa del Tabaco Maceo esq. Francisco Javier Zerquera ☎ 41 99 6256. The best-stocked cigar shop in the city sells rum and coffee too. Daily 9am–6pm.

Tienda de Arte Amelia Pelaez Simón Bolívar esq. Ernesto Valdés Muñoz ☎ 41 99 3590. Among the town's shops (as opposed to its markets), this place sells the largest selection of handmade crafts, paintings, jewellery

and more touristy bits and pieces. Mon–Sat 9am–6pm, Sun 9am–noon.

Tienda de Casa de la Música Francisco Javier Zerquera no.3 ☎ 41 99 6622. One of Trinidad's best options for Cuban music, with a wide selection on CD. You can listen before you buy. Daily 10am–6pm.

Tienda de Casa de la Trova F.H. Echerrí no.29 e/ Patricio Lumumba y Jesús Menéndez, Plazuela Segarte

---

TRINIDAD TREASURE

Trinidad is bursting with **vintage** and **antique** furniture, ornaments, housewares and art but it's only relatively recently that there has been an open market for any of it. Now, with laws governing private businesses loosened, local collectors are cashing in on the demand for this hitherto hidden memorabilia, providing a great opportunity for visitors to find something unique to take home. Not everyone selling this stuff does so from a shop, so it's always worth asking around in the search for local traders. Prices are always by negotiation. The sellers below have two of the best collections in the city.

Mario David Pumariega Mesa Piro Guinart no.252 e/ Francisco Gómez Toro y Rubén Martínez Villena ☎ 41 99 3162. Mayito, as he is known, runs the only antique shop in town. Its small rooms are spilling over with glassware, plates, bowls and other kitchen items, tea sets, clocks, paintings and all sorts of bric-a-brac. Daily 10am–6pm.

Dr Juan Carlos Carles Zerquera Simón Bolívar

no.306 e/ Maceo y Martí ☎ 41 99 4099. Juan Carlos has been collecting antiques for years and has amassed a staggering collection, filling several rooms in his own house and another that he uses to display his wares. You'll find anything from badges and brooches, candelabras and vases to paintings and furniture, figurines and clocks. There are no set opening hours; call the owner before visiting.

5

🕿 41 99 6445. By local standards this is a well-stocked music shop, attached to a live music venue, selling contemporary and traditional Cuban music on CD. Daily 9am–5pm.

La Vega Lino Pérez esq. Martí 🕿 41 99 6149. An excellent little cigar store with a good stock of rum too, facing the main square, Parque Cespedes. Daily 9am–7pm.

DIRECTORY

Banks and exchange Banco Financiero Internacional (Mon–Fri 8.30am–3.30pm) at Camilo Cienfuegos esq. Martí, and Banco de Crédito y Comercio (Mon–Fri 8am–3pm & Sat 8–11am) at Martí no.264 e/ Colón y Francisco Javier Zerquera. You can change travellers' cheques and withdraw money with Visa or Mastercard at both, and the latter has an ATM. The CADECA *casas de cambio* is at Martí no.166 e/ Lino Pérez y Camilo Cienfuegos (Mon–Sat 8.30am–8pm, Sun 1–8pm) and Maceo e/ Camilo Cienfuegos y Lino Pérez (Mon–Sat 8.30–noon & 12.30–8pm, Sun 9am–noon & 12.30–6pm).

Immigration For tourist cards and visa issues go to the Immigration Office (Tues & Thurs 9am–noon; 🕿 41 99 6650), near the police station on Julio Cuevas Díaz.

Internet and telephone *Las Begonias* café at Maceo esq. Simón Bolívar has a bank of computers with internet connections (daily 7am–10pm; $6CUC/hr), or try the ETECSA Telepunto centre on Lino Pérez no.274 at Parque Céspedes e/ Martí y Miguel Calzada (daily 8.30am–7pm; $6CUC/hr), where international calls can also be made.

Medical Clínica Internacional at Lino Pérez no.103 esq. Anastasio Cárdenas (🕿 41 99 6492), which has a 24h pharmacy, should cover most medical needs. For an ambulance call 🕿 41 99 2362. Serious cases may be referred to the Clínico Quirúrgico Camilo Cienfuego (🕿 41 32 4017), the provincial hospital in Sancti Spíritus.

Police Call 🕿 116 in emergencies. The main station is at Julio Cuevas Díaz e/ Pedro Zerquera y Anastasio Cárdenas (🕿 41 99 6330), to the south of town.

Post office The only branch providing international services is at Maceo no.418–420 e/ Colón y Francisco Javier Zerquera (Mon–Sat 8am–8pm).

TOURS FROM TRINIDAD

Trinidad's **state travel agents**, particularly Cubatur, are well used to offering general information and advice on sightseeing in town, but their principal purpose is to book hotel accommodation and sell organized excursions (see below); you can also use them to book a taxi or a rental car or buy Víazul bus tickets. It's a good idea to consult them before making a trip to Topes de Collantes, itself geared towards organized visits, and to a lesser extent the Valle de los Ingenios. The town also has an excellent independent agent, Trinidad Travels; run by three locals, it offers more flexibility than the state-run outfits.

TOUR OPTIONS

The state travel agents offer more or less the same sets of tours for the same prices. The most popular organized excursions in Topes de Collantes are to **Parque Guanayara** by truck or jeep ($55CUC) and the hike to the **Salto del Caburní** ($29CUC). There are several variations on trips to the **Valle de los Ingenios** ($10–20CUC) but they all involve a stop at Manaca-Iznaga. An organized excursion by catamaran to **Cayo Blanco** ($45CUC per person) is the only way to visit this offshore cay, around 5km south of the Península de Ancón. Ecotur is one of the best agents for organized **trekking**, including an exclusive trip to the Alturas de Banao ecological reserve, in the hills between Trinidad and the provincial capital. Most excursions include a lunch and there is normally a minimum of at least three people required.

Trinidad Travels offers a range of hiking, walking and horseback tours and all sorts of other activities at competitive prices; get in touch for prices and to work out a tour that suits you.

TRAVEL AGENTS

Cubanacan Lino Pérez no.366 e/ Maceo y Francisco Cadahía 🕿 41 99 4753. Daily 8.30am–12.30pm & 1.30–5.30pm.

Cubatur Maceo esq. Francisco Javier Zerquera 🕿 41 99 6314, and Simón Bolívar no.352 e/ Maceo y Izquierdo 🕿 41 99 6368. Daily 8am–8pm.

Ecotur Ruinas del Teatro Brunet, Maceo e/ Francisco Javier Zerquera y Simón Bolívar 🕿 41 99 8416. Mon–Fri 8am–noon & 2–6pm, Sat & Sun 9am–noon.

Havanatur Lino Pérez no.368 e/ Maceo y Francisco Cadahía 🕿 41 99 6317. Mon–Fri 8am–noon & 1–5pm, Sat 8am–noon.

Paradiso Foyer of Casa Artex at Lino Pérez e/ Francisco Cadahía y Martí 🕿 41 99 6486. Mon–Fri 8am–noon & 2–6pm, Sat & Sun 9am–noon.

Trinidad Travels Maceo no.613a e/ Pablo Pisch Girón y Piro Guinart 🕿 41 99 6444, 🌐 trinidadtravels .com. Daily 9am–6pm.

Península de Ancón

A narrow 8km finger of land curling like a twisted root out into the placid waters of the Caribbean, set against a backdrop of rugged green mountains, the **Península de Ancón** enjoys a truly fantastic setting. Covered predominantly in low-lying scrub, the peninsula itself is unspoilt yet unenchanting once you get away from the coastline, but it does boast several enticing **beaches**, including Playa Ancón, and an idyllic stretch of mostly undisturbed seashore.

The 7km journey from Trinidad is a glorious ride along the coast, with the turquoise blue of the Caribbean just a few metres away and the lofty mountains of the Sierra del Escambray rarely out of sight.

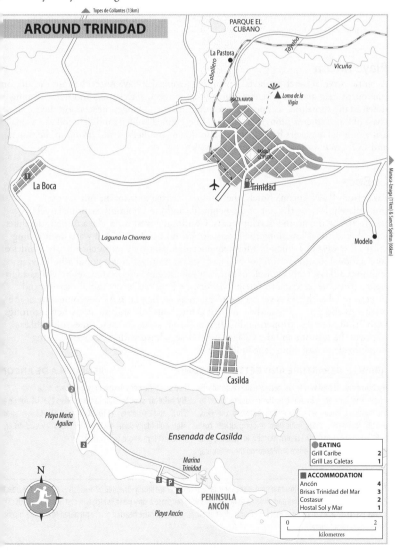

AROUND TRINIDAD

Topes de Collantes (13km)

PARQUE EL CUBANO

La Pastora

Vicuña

Loma de la Vigía

PLAZA MAYOR

PARQUE CÉSPEDES

La Boca

Trinidad

Laguna la Chorrera

Modelo

Manaca-Iznaga (11km) & Sancti Spíritus (66km)

Casilda

Playa María Aguilar

Ensenada de Casilda

Marina Trinidad

PENÍNSULA ANCÓN

Playa Ancón

N

● EATING	
Grill Caribe	2
Grill Las Caletas	1

■ ACCOMMODATION	
Ancón	4
Brisas Trinidad del Mar	3
Costasur	2
Hostal Sol y Mar	1

0   2

kilometres

5

DIVING, SNORKELLING AND FISHING AROUND THE PENÍNSULA DE ANCÓN

Marina Trinidad (daily 9am–5pm; ☎41 99 6205), opposite *Hotel Ancón*, offers **diving** excursions at a cost of $35CUC for a single dive or $64CUC for two dives. Dive trips leave at 9am and 11am daily. Diving courses, including beginners classes for $60CUC, are also available. **Fishing excursions** include deep-sea fishing ($400CUC/6hr), trolling for big-game ($300CUC/4hr) and bottom fishing ($280CUC/6hr). These trips are aimed at groups of four to six anglers, but if you're prepared to pay the whole cost yourself you can go with fewer people.

One of the most popular **snorkelling excursions** is to **Cayo Blanco**, a narrow islet 8km from the peninsula with its own coral reef, where the waters teem with parrotfish, trumpetfish and moray eels. Trips last six hours, cost $50CUC per person and usually include a lobster lunch. The area is known for its easy diving with good visibility, minimal currents and an abundance of vertical coral walls. You'll need your passport for any trip leaving from the marina.

Playa Ancón

A gentle curve of beach at the far end of the peninsula, **Playa Ancón** has put the area on the tourist map and has an encouragingly natural feel, with shrubs and trees creeping down to the shoreline. As one of one of the largest and longest beaches on the south coast of Cuba, there's more than enough fine-grained golden sand here to keep a small army of holidaymakers happy. There's also decent **snorkelling** and **diving** in the waters and reefs around these shores (see box above).

La Boca

Away from Playa Ancón's hotels, the signs of package tourism die out almost immediately, leaving the rest of the peninsula and the adjoining coastline largely unaffected by the nearby developments. Continuing west from Playa Ancón, the quiet coastal road runs 7km along the mostly rocky shore to **LA BOCA**, a waterfront fishing village due west of Trinidad. It has remained comparatively untouched by the hordes of international tourists settling upon Playa Ancón nearby, but is a popular holidaying spot for Cubans, with a couple of tatty, nationals-only hotel complexes as well as a few *casas particulares* catering to foreign visitors. La Boca has its own small, scruffy and rather stony beach and is very tranquil for most of the year but does come alive at the weekends and gets particularly animated throughout July and August, when it throngs with Trinitarios, day-trippers and Cuban holidaymakers. At these times music blasts out over the seafront and the village's main drag is lined with snack stalls serving home-made pizzas, sandwiches and soda.

ARRIVAL, DEPARTURE AND GETTING AROUND · PENÍNSULA DE ANCÓN

By Trinibus The best way to get between the Península de Ancón and Trinidad is by Trinibus, the nickname given to the tourist minibus service running between the two, usually four times a day from 9am to 6pm; tickets cost $2CUC and are valid for the return journey. In Trinidad, pick it up outside the Cubatur office on Maceo; on the peninsula,

hop on at the *Hotel Ancón*, or flag it down in La Boca..

By bike or scooter You can hire bikes ($3CUC for up to 7hr) and scooters ($10CUC/2hr, $20CUC/day) from Motoclub (daily 9am–4pm) at the *Brisas Trinidad del Mar* hotel in Playa Ancón (see p.296).

ACCOMMODATION

The three **hotels** on the peninsula aimed at the international market are family-oriented all-inclusives right on the beach, each with watersports facilities and all open to non-guests who purchase a **day pass**, which will cost around $30CUC. The **casas particulares** in La Boca make a great budget alternative base for the beach if you're prepared to use the Trinibus (see above) to get there.

Ancón Playa Ancón ☎41 99 6123, ⊛hoteles cubanacan.com. With its Soviet-influenced architecture, this is the peninsula's oldest and most dated hotel. Some of the rooms are quite tired, but it has been given a colourful face-lift, has a welcoming atmosphere and is on the most sociable section of beach. Facilities – including numerous snack bars, a large swimming pool, two tennis courts, a basketball hoop, volleyball net and pool tables – help make it a lively place to stay. **$140CUC**

Brisas Trinidad del Mar Playa Ancón ☎41 99 6500, ⊛hotelescubanacan.com. The newest and most luxurious option here has smart if unremarkable rooms and basic food but memorable outdoor areas, featuring a lookout tower with views over the peninsula, a twisting pool divided by bridges and a delightful little square, surrounded by accommodation blocks, modelled on the Plaza Mayor in Trinidad. **$156CUC**

Costasur Playa María Aguilar ☎41 99 6174, ⊛hotelescubanacan.com. This small hotel complex has a basic pool and its own private section of beach – inferior to Playa Ancón, and 1km along the coast, but still very pleasant and with some good snorkelling. The best rooms here are in attractive and roomy bungalows right on the seafront, each featuring a lounge, bedroom and bathroom. **$132CUC**

Hostal Sol y Mar Ave. del Mar no.87, La Boca ☎52 64 5530 (mobile). Facing the seafront on the main drag in the village, this is one of La Boca's best *casas*. Guests have their own little living room while bedrooms look onto the spacious, florid garden at the side of this pretty house. The food here is excellent and the owner, Joaquín, very personable. **$30CUC**

EATING

Grill Caribe ☎41 99 6241. An outdoor restaurant on a platform above a tiny strip of beach, serving freshly caught seafood like shrimp in hot sauce ($10CUC) and lobster ($12.50CUC). Ideally, you should aim to stop by at sunset when the atmosphere is tantalizingly calm. Daily 11am–10pm.

Grill Las Caletas (no phone). Simple, mid-priced seafood at an equally simple, no-frills roadside grill. Daily 11am–9pm.

Valle de los Ingenios

The **VALLE DE LOS INGENIOS**, a sprawling, open valley bordered by the eastern slopes of the Sierra del Escambray, was once one of Cuba's most productive agricultural areas. In its heyday it was crammed with dozens of the sugar estates and refineries on which Trinidad built its wealth during the eighteenth and nineteenth centuries. Today just one refinery remains, but the valley's prestigious past can be partly appreciated at **Manaca-Iznaga**, one of the old colonial estates, best reached on the **steam train** from Trinidad, whose engines, dating from the early twentieth century, pull rickety wooden carriages on an hour-long ride to the estate through rich layers of rural countryside, rattling and puffing through thick bush and small forests, then open, lush grazing land and maize fields, with green hills and low mountains forming the backdrop.

Manaca-Iznaga estate

Tower daily 9am–4pm • $2CUC

The tiny train station at **Manaca-Iznaga** is two minutes' walk from the old house and tower, the main attractions at this former estate. Most people can't resist heading straight for the 45m **tower**, built by one of the most successful sugar planters in Cuba, Alejo María del Carmen e Iznaga. You can climb the precarious wooden staircase to one of the tower's seven levels for views of the entire valley, a patchwork of sugar-cane fields, wooded countryside and farmland dotted with palm trees and the odd house. This lofty perspective over the surrounding area would have been used by plantation overseers for surveillance of their slaves working in the fields below. The huge bell that once hung in the tower, used to ring out the start and finish of the working day, now sits near the front of the **Casa Hacienda**, the colonial mansion where the Iznaga family would have stayed, though they spent more of their time at their residences in Trinidad and Sancti Spíritus. The building's main function is as a gift shop, bar and **restaurant**, the latter occupying a terrace overlooking a small garden. Over the road are the scattered dwellings of the old slave barracks, now converted into family homes.

By steam train The steam train to Manaca-Iznaga is extremely unreliable as it is constantly breaking down. When it does operate, it leaves Trinidad at 9.30am, and returns from Manaca-Iznaga around 1.30pm. Tickets ($10CUC) can be bought in advance from Infotur or the state travel agents in Trinidad (see p.292), or at the station in Trinidad from 8.30am on the day.

By local train Though less of a novelty, commuter trains are more reliable than the steam service, and at a fraction of the

cost they are worth considering. Two daily services currently leave Trinidad in the early hours of the morning; the fare to Manaca-Iznaga is a mere $0.40CUP, and journey time is 30min. The official line on these local trains is that passenger safety cannot be guaranteed and therefore their use by tourists is frowned upon, but you are unlikely to be stopped.

By car To drive to Manaca-Iznaga, follow the main road to Sancti Spíritus, the Circuito Sur, from the east of Trinidad for around 12km.

Sierra del Escambray

Rising up to the northwest of Trinidad are the steep, pine-coated slopes of the Guamuhaya mountains, more popularly known as the **Sierra del Escambray**. This area is home to some of the most spectacular scenery in Cuba, though its highest peak – the Pico San Juan – is a modest 1140m high. A large proportion of this mountain range sits within the borders of the neighbouring provinces of Cienfuegos and Villa Clara but the heart of the visitor park and hiking area, the **Gran Parque Natural Topes de Collantes**, is in Sancti Spíritus province.

Topes de Collantes

The mountain resort of **Topes de Collantes** is a kind of hotel village, its unsubtle architecture completely out of keeping with the beauty of its surroundings – as is the road clumsily blasted down the middle of the resort. Though there are a couple of likeable museums around the village, and one or two modest venues for eating and drinking, the main reason to make the trip up here is to use the resort as a base for **hiking** along designated **trails**, which you can follow as part of an organized excursion from Trinidad (see p.292) or independently by first visiting the park's information centre (see box, p.298).

This mountainous area has its own **microclimate** and is always a couple of degrees cooler than Trinidad. It's also far more likely to rain here than down by the coast, and as the heavens open almost every afternoon for much of the year, it's a good idea to get up here early if you're visiting on a day-trip.

Museo de Arte Cubano Contemporaneo

Daily 8am–8pm • $3CUC

During the 1980s the hotels of Topes de Collantes were filled with hundreds of artworks by Cuban artists of national renown. Scores of these are now installed in the rooms of the engaging **Museo de Arte Cubano Contemporaneo**, opened in 2008 on the main road through Topes de Collantes, 350m before the information centre on the approach from Trinidad. In all there are some sixty paintings by artists such as Rubén Torres Llorca, Zaida del Río and Tomás Sánchez, as well as some sculptures and prints. The pretty museum building, with its colourful stained-glass windows, dates from 1944, and was owned by a Cuban senator before the Revolution and its subsequent appropriation by the State.

Casa del Café

Daily 7am–7pm • Free

A neatly packaged shop, café and small museum near the *Hotel Los Helechos*, the **Casa del Café** is a simple homage to coffee, which has been grown on the slopes of these mountains for centuries. Tools used in local coffee production are on display, including an industrial-size nineteenth-century grinder outside. You can buy packets of coffee in the shop, or just sip a brew on the veranda.

5

HIKING AT GRAN PARQUE NATURAL TOPES DE COLLANTES

If you want to go **hiking** around Topes de Collantes, the best way to do so is to book an **organized excursion** in Trinidad (see box, p.292). If you arrive **independently** you won't be permitted access to all areas of this protected park, but at the Centro de Información (daily 8am–6pm; ☎42 54 0117, ✉comercial@topescom.co.cu), the park's **information centre** – marked by a huge sundial at the heart of the resort – you can get advice on the trails you can visit without a guide.

The Centro de Información is also where you pay if you want to follow any of the **official trails**, each of them located within smaller parks highlighted below. There are no clearly defined borders between these parks, which have been designated as separate entities primarily for marketing purposes (note that Parque el Nicho, over the border in the province of Cienfuegos and characterized by a network of countless waterfalls, is covered in Chapter 4). Typically, trails here are well marked and shady, cutting through dense woodlands, smothered in every kind of vegetation – from needle-straight conifers to bushy fern and grassy matted floors – opening out here and there for breathtaking views of the landscape.

Charges for the trails are $7–9CUC per person if you visit independently. The English-speaking staff at the centre can advise you on the various trails and parks, but if you want a guide to accompany you, you will need to have booked an organized excursion in advance. Several of the parks have their own restaurants, catering predominantly to groups.

As to **what to bring**, you may need sturdy hiking boots if it's pouring with rain (which it often is up here); otherwise trainers should be adequate. The air is a few degrees cooler than in the city or on the beach, so you may need more than just a T-shirt.

PARQUE ALTIPLANO

As well as being the location of all the local hotels, **Parque Altiplano** also contains the area's most popular target for hikers, the fantastically situated 62m-high **Caburní waterfall**, surrounded by pines and eucalyptus trees at the end of a 2.5-km trek down steep inclines and through dense forest. Independent access is at the northernmost point of Topes de Collantes. There are several other relatively easy trails within this park, including the **Vegas Grandes**, which also finishes at a waterfall.

PARQUE GUANAYARA

Fifteen kilometres north of the hotels, **Parque Guanayara** is host to one of the area's most scenic hiking routes. The gentler hike here follows the Guanayara River for a couple of kilometres up to the **Salto El Rocío,** a beautiful waterfall, and the **Poza del Venado**, a natural pool; along the way it incorporates some memorable views of Pico San Juan.

PARQUE CODINA

The focal point of **Parque Codina** is **Hacienda Codina**, an old Spanish coffee-growing ranch where you can eat and drink. From the ranch there are easily manageable walks, some no more than 1km, into the forest. Several trails lead to **La Batata**, a subterranean river at the foot of a lush green valley where you can bathe in the cool waters of the cave. You access this area independently from the southwestern corner of Topes de Collantes.

PARQUE EL CUBANO

Just 5km from Trinidad, **Parque El Cubano** is the most popular location for **horseriding**. The route here, which can also be followed on foot, takes in a *campesino* house and the remains of a colonial sugar ranch, as well as rivers, brooks and waterfalls.

ARRIVAL AND DEPARTURE   TOPES DE COLLANTES

By taxi Given the lack of public transport and the dangerous roads, a taxi is the best way of getting here unless you are on an organized excursion; the round-trip fare from Trinidad shouldn't cost more than $25CUC. There are no taxis actually based at Topes de Collantes,

so you should arrange for your driver to wait for you at the resort.

By car The turnoff for the dangerously winding road into the mountains is about 3km west of Trinidad along the road to Cienfuegos; Topes de Collantes is 14km along.

ACCOMMODATION

Los Helechos ☏ 42 54 0330, ⓦ gaviota-grupo.com. Rooms here have balconies and are pleasantly light and airy. There's a disco and a restaurant in a separate, marginally more run-down building, as well as a bowling alley and a large indoor pool. **$42CUC**

Kurhotel ☏ 42 54 0180, ⓦ gaviota-grupo.com. The only reason to opt for this massive eyesore of an hotel is for the views from its eighth-floor rooms or to make use of its fitness and therapy centre, which includes outdoor squash and tennis courts, a basic gymnasium but no longer a pool.

Many Cubans staying here are on programmes of physical therapy. **$45CUC**

Villa Caburní ☏ 42 54 0231, ⓦ gaviota-grupo.com. The best of the Topes de Collantes hotels is at the start of the trail to the eponymous waterfall, featuring dinky bungalows, each with its own little lawn and parking space, spread around a grassy area like a model 1950s American village. Most have two double rooms, bathroom and kitchenette, and all have wonderful views of the mountains. **$39CUC**

EATING

Several of the Topes de Collantes parks feature their own **restaurants**, all more geared to groups on organized excursions than impromptu visits from independent hikers. It's a good idea to ask at the information office to find out which of the restaurants are expecting visitors, as those that are not may not open at all.

Casa La Gallega Parque Guanayara (no phone). There's not normally a great deal of choice at this ranch building surrounded by lush greenery, and if no tour groups are expected there may be nothing at all, but whatever the main dish of the day is (most likely roast chicken), it'll be good, hearty Cuban country food with plenty of extras. Daily, lunch only.

El Lagarto Verde Vegas Grandes ☏ 42 54 1325. Some 2km south of the Topes de Collantes resort on the road to Trinidad, and set just back from the road over a footbridge, this excellent paladar offers set meals ($10CUC), often of

pork and always accompanied by rice, beans and all sorts of fruit and vegetables grown in the surrounding area, and served up on a wooden veranda surrounded by thick vegetation. Call ahead as hours can vary. Usually open daily 12–8pm.

Mi Retiro (no phone). The most accessible of the hiking-trail restaurants, 3km south of the Topes de Collantes resort on the road to Trinidad; choose from roast pork ($5.95CUC), ham steak ($4.40CUC) or omelettes ($2–2.75CUC), served on a veranda on top of a small hill in a scenic valley. Daily 10am–8pm.

Sancti Spíritus

The provincial capital, also called **SANCTI SPÍRITUS**, sits in the dead centre of the island, 30km inland and around 70km east of Trinidad by road. It's a good place to stop for the night if you're making the journey between Havana and Santiago – few visitors stay for more than a night or two, but as one of Cuba's original seven *villas* founded by Diego Velázquez in the early 1500s, it has plenty of historic character and holds some appeal as one of the country's least touristy original cities. There's less to do and see here than in neighbouring provincial capitals, but if you keep it short you should also be able to keep it relatively sweet in Sancti Spíritus.

Plaza Serafín Sánchez

The logical place to begin exploring is the central square, **Plaza Serafín Sánchez**, from where all the museums, and most of the best restaurants and music venues are a short walk away. Though its one of the more pleasant and lively spaces in the centre of town, the square lacks the laidback, sociable feel characteristic of other Cuban town squares. Nevertheless, it does attract an enthusiastic young crowd on weekend nights and though it's disturbed by the traffic passing through on all sides during the day, there are plenty of rickety metal seats around the simple bandstand for a sit-down in the shade. On the corner of Máximo Gómez and Solano is the provincial library, the majestic **Biblioteca Provincial Rubén Martínez Villena**, built between 1927 and 1929, and resembling a colonial theatre with its balustraded

5

balconies, Corinthian columns and arched entrance. Connecting to the southeast corner of the square is the main shopping street, the pedestrianized section of Independencia known as **Boulevard**. The square's southwestern corner is occupied by the eminently missable Museo de Historia Natural.

Museo Provincial

Máximo Gómez no.3, Plaza Serafín Sánchez • Mon–Thurs & Sat 9am–5pm, Sun 8am–noon • $1CUC • ☎ 41 32 7435

The **Museo Provincial** showcases a hotchpotch of historical objects dating mostly from the nineteenth and twentieth centuries. The photos of Castro and his band of merry men entering Sancti Spíritus on January 6, 1959, on their victory march to Havana, are as engaging as anything else on display.

Iglesia Parroquial Mayor

Agramonte Oeste no.58 • Tues–Fri 9–11am & 2–4pm • Free • ☎ 41 32 4855

Sancti Spíritus's main church, and its oldest building, **Iglesia Parroquial Mayor** was built in 1680. With the dramatic exception of an unusual blue-and-gold arch spanning the top section of the nave, the interior is underwhelmingly simple.

Museo de Arte Colonial

Plácido no.74 esq. Ave. Jesús Menéndez • Tues–Sat 9.30am–5pm, Sun 8am–noon • $2CUC, photos $1CUC • ☎ 41 32 5455

One block east of the river is the **Museo de Arte Colonial**, easily the best museum in Sancti Spíritus, with a collection of precious colonial furniture and household objects, though it has not yet fully recovered its former glory following severe storm damage in 2008.

Puente Yayabo

On the other side of Jesús Menéndez from the Museo de Arte Colonial, an area of cobblestone streets extends down to the river. Walk down A. Rodríguez to the *Quinta Santa Elena* restaurant and bar (see p.304) for a good view of the fairy-tale **Puente Yayabo**, the five-arch humpbacked stone bridge, built in 1825 and among the oldest of its kind in Cuba.

Galería Oscar F. Morera

Céspedes no.26 e/ Cervantes y E. Valdés Muñoz • Tues–Sat 8.30am–noon & 1–5pm, Sun 8.30am–noon • Free • ☎ 41 32 3117

The **Galería Oscar F. Morera** showcases the work of the city's first well-known painter, who died in 1946. Morera's amateurish still-lifes and landscapes, hung around several

---

FISHING AND HUNTING AT EMBALSE ZAZA

Ten kilometres or so east of Sancti Spíritus is Cuba's largest artificial lake, the **Embalse Zaza**, only worth a visit if you're intent on hunting or fishing. There's no public transport to the reservoir, but a taxi from Sancti Spíritus (☎41 32 8533) usually costs $8–10CUC one way. Most activities revolve around the hulking *Hotel Zaza* (☎41 32 7015, ✉recepcion.hzaza@islazulssp .tur.co.cu; $33CUC), sited on the network of inlets at the lake's northern edge. The 1970s Soviet-style building is run down, the rooms rudimentary and the feel of the place somewhere between tranquil and deserted. The **hunting** here is mostly for duck, quail and pigeon while **fishing** offers an abundance of giant bass. Most guests engaged in these activities are on pre-packaged holidays but you can arrange ad-hoc fishing trips starting at $30CUC for four hours through the hotel.

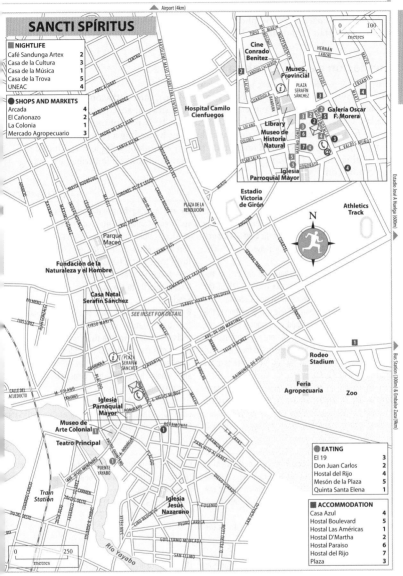

▲ Airport (4km)

SANCTI SPÍRITUS

5

■ **NIGHTLIFE**
Café Sandunga Artex	2
Casa de la Cultura	3
Casa de la Música	1
Casa de la Trova	5
UNEAC	4

● **SHOPS AND MARKETS**
Arcada	4
El Cañonazo	2
La Colonia	1
Mercado Agropecuario	3

● **EATING**
El 19	3
Don Juan Carlos	2
Hostal del Rijo	4
Mesón de la Plaza	5
Quinta Santa Elena	1

■ **ACCOMMODATION**
Casa Azul	4
Hostal Boulevard	5
Hostal Las Américas	1
Hostal D'Martha	2
Hostal Paraiso	6
Hostal del Rijo	7
Plaza	3

small rooms, include various Sancti Spíritus scenes, but you'll probably find more value in the two rooms dedicated to temporary exhibitions, usually displaying the work of contemporary local artists.

Casa Natal Serafín Sánchez

Céspedes no.112 e/ Comandante Fajardo y Frank País • Tues–Sat 8.30am–5pm, Sun 8am–noon • $0.50CUC • ☎ 41 32 7791

The **Casa Natal Serafín Sánchez** commemorates one of the city's heroes of the two Wars of Independence, killed in combat on November 18, 1896. Consisting mostly of

5

Sánchez's personal effects and photographs of him and his family, along with a colourful portrait of the man on his horse, it's a bit bare and not terribly interesting.

Fundación de la Naturaleza y el Hombre

Parque Antonio Maceo • Mon & Sat 9am–noon, Tues–Fri 9am–4pm • $1CUC

On the southern side of a pretty little Parque Maceo, the **Fundación de la Naturaleza y el Hombre** is a unique little museum that tells the story of an expedition organized by the late Cuban writer Antonio Nuñez Jiménez. In 1987 he replicated the journey made by the first colonizers of Cuba, the Guanahatabey, by leading a team down the Amazon in five 13m-long canoes, each one carved from the trunk of a single tree. One of the monolithic canoes and some yellowing photographs of Amazonian tribes are among the exhibits on display.

ARRIVAL AND DEPARTURE   SANCTI SPÍRITUS

By plane The city's tiny national airport (☎ 41 36 1590) is in the northern reaches of Sancti Spíritus, conveniently close to the two best places to stay on the Carretera Central, *Rancho Hatuey* and *Los Laureles*. Otherwise, it's a $3–4CUC taxi ride to the centre.

By bus If you arrive by bus, you'll be dropped at the Terminal Provincial de Omnibus (☎ 41 32 4142), at the intersection of the Carretera Central and Circunvalación, the outer ring road. The only reliable way of getting to the centre is by taxi, which should cost around $3CUC. The arrival of a Víazul bus usually prompts a few private taxi drivers to come looking for business, but as there is no taxi rank as such, you may have to ring for a state taxi; try Cubataxi (☎ 41 32 2133).

Víazul destinations Camaguey (6 daily; 3hr 5min); Ciego de Ávila (6 daily; 1hr 15min); Havana (5 daily; 5hr); Santa Clara (4 daily; 1hr 30min); Santiago de Cuba (5 daily; 10hr); Trinidad (1 daily; 1hr 30min); Varadero (1 daily; 3hr 30min).

By car Arriving from either the west or the east, you'll enter Sancti Spíritus on the Carretera Central, which cuts along the eastern edge of the city, becoming Bartolomé Masó as it enters Sancti Spíritus proper. To get to the centre, turn southwest off Bartolomé Masó onto Avenida de los Mártires, an attractive boulevard leading directly to the main square, the Plaza Serafín Sánchez.

By train It's a 500m walk to the central plaza from the train station (☎41 32 7914) on Avenida Jesús Menéndez, over the river from the city centre; if you want a taxi you'll need to call for one (see below). Train services are constantly subject to severe disruption and whole lines can be suspended for months (see p.31).

Destinations Cienfuegos (3 weekly; 6hr); Havana (every other day; 11hr); Matanzas (every other day; 9hr); Santa Clara (every other day; 3hr 30min).

GETTING AROUND

By horse-drawn carriage The city's bus system is too inefficient to be worth using; for journeys outside the centre, you're better off flagging down one of the horse-drawn carriages which operate up and down Bartolomé Masó.

Car rental Cubacar (☎ 41 32 8533) has a booth on the northern side of Plaza Serafín Sánchez and an office in the *Los Laureles* hotel. Vía (☎ 41 33 6697) is opposite the Iglesia Parroquial Mayor.

Taxis Cubataxi (☎ 41 32 2133); Taxi OK at the *Villa Rancho Hatuey* hotel (☎ 41 32 8315).

INFORMATION AND TRAVEL AGENTS

Tourist information As Infotur does not have a branch in Sancti Spíritus, your best bet for information is Cubatur at Máximo Gómez no.7 esq. Guardiola, Plaza Serafín Sánchez (Mon–Sat 10am–5pm; ☎ 41 32 8518). Staff can help with hotel reservations, sell Víazul bus tickets and offer general visitor advice.

ACCOMMODATION

Of the four **hotels** in Sancti Spíritus, the two in the centre are by far the most comfortable and attractive. The other two are on the main highway that runs through the city, the Carretera Central, and if you stay at either of them you'll want to have your own transport or be prepared to pay for taxis to visit the centre, as they're both 4km from the main square. There are plenty of *casas particulares*, both on the Carretera Central, and a high proportion located on or within a few blocks of Plaza Serafín Sánchez in the centre. All the tourist hotels in town are run by the Islazul chain (🖳 islazul.cu).

HOTELS

★ **Hostal del Rijo** Honorato del Castillo no.12 ☎41 32 8588, @ aloja.rijo@islazulssp.tur.co.cu. Exquisite little hotel in a fine colonial mansion built in 1818, whose careful renovation highlights original features such as the crumbly terracotta-and-wood staircase. The spacious rooms, arranged around a charming patio, strike a perfect balance between comfort and stylish simplicity, with stained-wood furnishings, marble washbasins, iron-base lamps, minibar and satellite TV. $100CUC

Los Laureles Carretera Central Km 383 ☎41 36 1016, @ mgarcia@islazulssp.tur.co.cu. A sociable roadside complex of concrete bungalows and close-cropped lawns with a swimming pool, a restaurant serving Cuban staples and pizza, and occasional entertainment in the form of an open-air cabaret and karaoke. Rooms are large and cheery, with cable TV. $44CUC

Plaza Independencia esq. Ave. de los Mártires, Plaza Serafín Sánchez ☎41 32 7102, @ aloja.rijo@islazulssp .tur.co.cu. Neat and compact hotel on the main square with a plain reception area and a quirky central patio café. The rooms are reasonably equipped, although slightly poky – ask for one of the four larger ones. $75CUC

Villa Rancho Hatuey Carretera Central Km 384 ☎41 36 1315, @ reserva.vrhatuey@islazulssp.tur.co.cu. This picturesque complex, set back some 400m from the road, is mostly used by tour groups stopping over for a night or two. The grassy site is larger than it needs to be, leaving the box-like villas a little stranded, but there's a nice pool area and a relaxing sense of space. Has a regular schedule of traditional Cuban music concerts. $60CUC

CASAS PARTICULARES

Casa Azul Maceo no.4 (sur) e/ Ave. de los Mártires y Doll ☎41 32 4336, @ omaidacasaazul@yahoo.es. Two inviting, well-equipped double rooms in a modern, homely apartment. One has a pair of fetching hand-crafted, colonial-style mahogany beds and the other (up on the roof garden) has a double and a single bed and plenty of natural light. Both come with TV and fridge. $25CUC

Hostal Boulevard Independencia no.17 (altos) e/ Ave. de los Mártires y E Valdes Muñoz ☎41 32 6745 or ☎53 80 8373 (mobile). This huge and impressive first-floor establishment effectively has two one-bedroom apartments for rent. Both have lounges and are smartly and comfortably furnished, but the larger of the two also has a dining room with balcony. They can be rented completely separately or as one big unit with a connecting door. $25CUC

Hostal Las Américas Bartolomé Masó no.157 (sur) e/ Cuba y Cuartel ☎41 32 2984, @ hostallasamericas @yahoo.es4. This 1950s house is the best option for those who like their home comforts. Each of the four cool, airy rooms has its own bathroom, TV, safety deposit box, fridge and mosquito-proof windows, plus you can feast on the bananas and mangoes that grow in the back garden. Parking is available and the bus station is a five-minute walk away. $25CUC

Hostal D'Martha Plácido no.69 e/ Calderón y Tirso Marín ☎41 32 3556, @ martharodriguezssp@gmail .com. Martha takes her role as host very seriously, insisting that the freshly furnished rooms are cleaned daily, offering a bilingual menu for meals and always keeping her relatively small house, with its modern interior, spick and span. There's a neat little dining area just outside the two rooms, and the split-level terraces on the roof, with views of the city and the Escambray mountains, provide the space missing indoors. $25CUC

Hostal Paraíso Máximo Gómez sur no.11 e/ Honorato y Parque Serafín Sánchez ☎41 33 4658, @ hectorluisparaiso64@gmail.com. At the heart of this elegant 1830-built residence is a lovely patio full of large potted plants; at the back are two of the four guest rooms, one of which opens onto a much smaller, cosier patio; and upstairs is a terrace where the other two rooms, are located. The en-suite rooms have a/c, TV and safety deposit boxes. $25CUC

EATING

Sancti Spíritus has plenty of fairly poor but very cheap national-peso **restaurants** and a couple of convertible-peso joints apart from the hotels. Similarly, most of the **paladars** cater to an almost exclusively Cuban clientele and are below the standards set in more touristy cities, though many are still good value as they also tend to charge in national pesos, also accepting the equivalent in convertibles.

STATE RESTAURANTS

Hostal del Rijo Honorato del Castillo no.12 ☎41 32 8588. The hotel restaurant serves decent fish and meat dishes, such as shrimp casserole ($7.50CUC) and slices of pork in fruit sauce ($7.15CUC) on the attractive central patio, where there's a fountain and views over to the pretty little plaza out front. Daily 7–10am, noon–3pm & 7–10.30pm.

Mesón de la Plaza Máximo Gómez no.34 ☎41 32 8546. This rustic tavern-restaurant with earthenware plates, heavy wooden tables and wrought-iron lamps hanging from the ceiling rafters offers an eclectic menu that includes beef stewed with corn ($6CUC), *ropa vieja* with raisins and red wine ($4.70CUC) and an excellent, rich chickpea stew ($2CUC) among the specials. Unusually, it also serves two types of sangria. Daily 9am–10.45pm.

5

Quinta Santa Elena Padre Quintero s/n e/ Llano y Manolico Día ☎ 41 32 8167. The flavourful house special – slices of fried beef marinated in a garlic sauce ($6CUC) – sits alongside half a dozen chicken and pork mains ($5–6.25CUC), while shrimp is offered grilled, fried with garlic or in tomato sauce ($9CUC). The dining room is in a handsome colonial building but the best tables are on the large terrace shaded by trees, overlooking the Puente Yayabo and the river. Daily 10am–11pm.

PALADARS

El 19 Máximo Gómez no.9 e/ Honorato y Parque Serafín Sánchez ☎ 41 33 1919. This simple streetside dining room

with minimal decor is the most conveniently located paladar in the city, knocking out mixed meat grills ($7.25CUC) and paella ($7.50CUC) to a reasonable standard. Daily 6.30am–10pm.

Don Juan Carlos Independencia no.9c, 2nd floor, e/ Ernesto Valdés Muñoz y Cervantes ☎ 52 47 3686 (mobile). Popular with locals, the food here is well judged compared to the efforts of many of its competitors, with sensible portion sizes, well-dressed salads and quality cuts of meat. Pork and seafood feature heavily and main dishes are a snip at between $50 and $120CUP. Several flights of stairs lead to the forgettable interior. Wed–Sun noon–2pm & 7–11pm.

NIGHTLIFE, DRINKING AND ENTERTAINMENT

The focal point for a lot of the city's weekend nightlife is the Plaza Serafín Sánchez, where some locals hang out all evening and others pass through on their way to the nearby **music venues**. The music venues are the best spots for an evening **drink** but the restaurants *Mesón de la Plaza* and *Quinta Santa Elena* (see above) also have bars, and at the latter there is live music some weekends.

CLUBS AND LIVE MUSIC VENUES

Café Sandunga Cervantes e/ Máximo Gómez y Independencia, Plaza Serafín Sánchez ☎ 41 32 8051. Sometimes referred to as *Café Artex*, the discos and karaoke nights here attract the city's up-for-it young crowd and are the most raucous entertainment available in the centre. Entry $1–1.50CUC. Wed–Fri 10pm–1.30am, Sat 10pm–2am, Sun 10pm–1.30am.

Casa de la Cultura Cervantes esq. Máximo Gómez, Plaza Serafín Sánchez ☎ 41 32 3772. Home to occasional bolero nights, and worth checking out for other low-key musical performances; however there's no regular programme of events. Free.

Casa de la Música Padre Quintero no.32 ☎ 41 32 4963. Hosts live salsa music and cabaret-style entertainment on Friday, Saturday and Sunday nights in an open-air setting with a stage and a terrace that overlooks the river. $1CUC. Fri–Sun 9pm–late.

Casa de la Trova Máximo Gómez sur no.26 e/ Solano y Honorato ☎ 41 32 8048. The most reliable venue for live music in the city, especially for traditional styles with a monthly programme of bolero, trova and son nights. The patio bar is also one of the best places in town for a drink. Entry $1CUC. Mon–Fri 9pm–midnight, Sat 9pm–1am, Sun 10am–2pm.

UNEAC Independencia no.10 e/ Plaza Serafín Sánchez y Honorato ☎ 41 32 6375. The local branch of this national artists' and writers' organization hosts small-scale live

music most Saturdays, with matinee and evening concerts, and caters to all tastes, from traditional bolero to rock. There's an inviting patio and a bar. Performance times are usually 4pm and 9pm. Free.

CINEMA AND THEATRE

Cine Conrado Benítez Máximo Gómez no.13, Plaza Serafín Sánchez ☎ 41 32 5327. There are two cinemas on the main square but this one is more likely to actually be showing films. There are sometimes other cultural events here too, including comedy and musical performance, advertised on the posterboard inside.

Teatro Principal Jesús Menéndez esq. Padre Quintero ☎ 41 32 5755. One of the oldest theatres in Cuba, founded in 1839 and now reopened after a lengthy restoration, stages shows for children and infrequent music and dance performances. Check the poster board out front for performance details. Prices from $5CUP.

SPECTATOR SPORTS

Baseball National-league baseball games are played at the Estadio José A. Huelga (☎ 41 32 2504), just beyond Circunvalación on Ave. de los Mártires.

Rodeo The main local event to draw in the crowds is the rodeo, held once or twice a month at the weekend, in the Feria Agropecuaria (☎ 41 32 3112) on Bartolomé Masó to the east of the centre; entrance is $1CUP.

SHOPPING

Arcada Independencia no.55 e/ E Valdes Muñoz y Agramonte ☎ 41 32 7106. This is the local branch of the Fondo Cubano de Bienes Culturales, and stocks the usual mixture of quality arts and crafts alongside made-for-

tourists tat. Mon–Sat 9am–6pm, Sun 9am–noon.

El Cañonazo Independencia no.6 e/ Plaza Serafín Sánchez y Honorato ☎ 41 32 5742. A Cuban-style pawn shop where you can find old watches, vintage cameras,

glassware, candelabras, ceramics and various other bric-a-brac. Mon–Sat 8am–9pm, Sun 8am–noon.
La Colonia Agramonte esq. Independencia ☎41 32 8225. The city's principal department store features one of the better supermarkets. Mon–Sat 9am–6pm, Sun 8am–noon.

Mercado Agropecuario Entrances on Boulevard and Céspedes e/ Cervantes and E. Valdes Muñoz ☎41 32 1049. The central fresh-food market has meat, vegetables and fruit for sale. Mon–Sat 7am–5.30pm, Sun 7am–noon.

DIRECTORY

Banks and exchange For cash, try the Banco Financiero Internacional, at Independencia no.2 e/ Plaza Serafín Sánchez y Honorato (Mon–Fri 8.30am–3.30pm). The CADECA *casa de cambio* is at Independencia no.31 e/ Plaza Serafín Sánchez y E. Valdes Muñoz (Mon–Sat 8.30am–4pm, Sun 8.30–11.30am).

Immigration and legal Consultoría Jurídica Internacional at Independencia no.39 e/ Plaza Serafín Sánchez y E Valdes Muñoz (Mon–Fri 8.30am–12.30pm & 1.30–5.30pm; ☎41 32 8448).

Internet and telephones Telepunto is at Independencia no.14 e/ Plaza Serafín Sánchez y Honorato (daily 8.30am–7pm).
Medical The main hospital is the Clínico Quirúrgico Camilo Cienfuegos (☎41 32 4017), halfway down Bartolomé Masó. For an ambulance call ☎41 32 4462.
Pharmacy The best-stocked pharmacy is in the *Los Laureles* hotel at Carretera Central Km 383 (☎41 32 7016).
Police Emergency number ☎106 or 115.
Post office Independencia no.8 e/ Plaza Serafín Sánchez y Honorato (Mon–Sat 8am–8pm, Sun 8am–noon). Also offers DHL and EMS services.

Ciego de Ávila and Camagüey

FLAMINGOS ON THE NORTHERN CAYS

Ciego de Ávila and Camagüey

Spanning the trunk of the island some 450km east of Havana, the low-lying provinces of Ciego de Ávila and Camagüey form the agricultural heart of Cuba. The westernmost of the two, sleepy Ciego de Ávila, is sparsely populated, with only two medium-sized towns that are often bypassed by visitors keen to reach the province's star attraction: the line of cays stretching west from Cayo Coco to Cayo Guillermo, home to some flamboyant birdlife and the country's most dazzling beaches, with one of the Caribbean's biggest barrier reefs creating a superb offshore diving zone. Further north, smaller but more appealing Morón attracts a few day-trippers and is a good base from which to visit the cays without shelling out for an all-inclusive hotel. The town is close to the nearby lakes, Laguna de la Leche and Laguna la Redonda, the nucleus of a hunting and fishing centre popular with enthusiasts from Europe and Canada.

Livelier than its neighbour, **Camagüey** is the country's largest province, largely made up of low-lying farmland dappled with a rural villages. Its main draws are the northern beaches and the provincial capital of **Camagüey city**, one of the original seven *villas* founded by Diego Velázquez in 1515. Nurtured by sugar wealth that dates to the late sixteenth century, Camagüey has grown into a large and stalwart city with many of the architectural hallmarks of a Spanish colonial town, and is deservedly beginning to compete as a tourist centre. While the government pushes the plush northern beach resort of **Santa Lucía** as the province's chief attraction, its least spoilt beach is just west of the resort at **Cayo Sabinal**.

Ciego de Ávila city

CIEGO DE ÁVILA is more like the suburb of a larger town than an urban centre in its own right. A friendly though pedestrian place set in the plains of the province, it is surprisingly young for a provincial capital – only established in 1849 – and its youth is its sole newsworthy feature. With no tourist attractions, and precious little nightlife, Ciego de Ávila is often bypassed by visitors en route to the northern cays, but the town is not without charm and an afternoon here, on your way to the showier parts of the province, will reveal Cuba at its most modest and unaffected. Refreshingly, Ciego de Ávila also has much less of a problem with hustlers and *jineteros* than bigger towns.

PLAYA PILAR

Highlights

❶ **Laguna la Redonda** This idyllic lake is perfect for an afternoon of bass fishing or simply messing around in boats. **See p.318**

❷ **Loma de Cunagua** The lone high ground in an area of unremittingly flat farmland, this 364m hill is a favourite with birdwatchers. **See p.319**

❸ **Boquerón campsite** Hidden in the depths of the Ciego de Ávila countryside, this rustic retreat is hard to reach independently but is well worth the hassle. **See p.320**

❹ **Diving the coral reefs** Two of the longest coral reefs in the world can be found on opposite sides of Ciego de Ávila, at the northern cays and the Jardines de la Reina. **See p.325 and p.328**

❺ **Playa Pilar** A gorgeous beach on Cayo Guillermo's western tip, named after Ernest Hemingway's yacht. **See p.327**

❻ **Hotel Colón** Almost a museum in itself, this beautiful 1927 hotel in the heart of Camagüey has been artfully renovated, preserving its eclectic mix of styles. **See p.337**

❼ **Cayo Sabinal** Cayo Sabinal's isolated white sands, woodland and wildlife make for the perfect island retreat. **See p.342**

HIGHLIGHTS ARE MARKED ON THE MAP ON PP.310–311

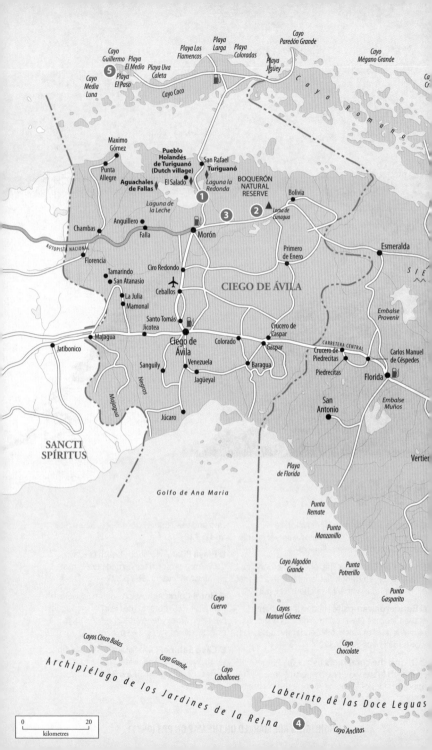

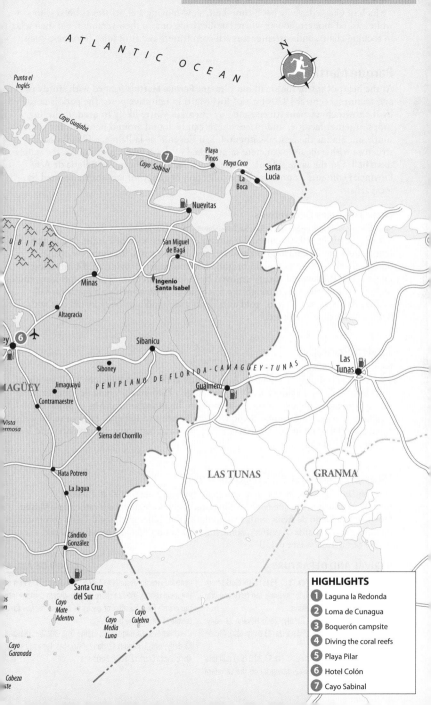

ATLANTIC OCEAN

N

Punta el Inglés

Cayo Guajaba

Cayo Sabinal 7

Playa Pinos

Playa Coco

Santa Lucia

La Boca

Nuevitas

San Miguel de Bagá

Ingenio Santa Isabel

CUBITAS

Minas

Altagracia

6

Sibanicu

ey 7

Siboney

MAGÜEY

Jimaguayú

PENIPLANO DE FLORIDA-CAMAGÜEY-TUNAS

Las Tunas

Guáimaro

Contramaestre

Vista ermosa

Sierra del Chorrillo

Hata Potrero

LAS TUNAS

GRANMA

La Jagua

Cándido González

os n

Santa Cruz del Sur

Cayo Mate Adentro

Cayo Media Luna

Cayo Culebra

Cayo Garanada

Cabeza ste

HIGHLIGHTS

1 Laguna la Redonda
2 Loma de Cunagua
3 Boquerón campsite
4 Diving the coral reefs
5 Playa Pilar
6 Hotel Colón
7 Cayo Sabinal

Much of Ciego de Ávila has a close-knit, slow-moving feel, its streets lined with whitewashed modern houses where families hang out on their verandas, old men relax in rocking chairs, and entrepreneurs sell corn fritters and fruit juice from peso stalls.

Parque Martí

At the heart of town, the small but pleasant **Parque Martí** is fringed with sturdy trees and features a central 1920s bust of José Martí in reflective pose. The park is bordered by the town's four main streets, and any essentials you're likely to need, including shops, internet facilities and places to eat, can be found around here. On the park's south side stands the central **cathedral**, San Eugenio de la Palma, a bland modern structure with a gigantic concrete saint tacked to the outside; next door is the stately **town hall**. On the same side of the square, on Independencia, the **Galería de Arte Provincial** contains a rather anodyne collection of glossy oil landscapes painted by local artists.

Museo de Artes Decorativos
Parque Martí • Mon–Thurs 9am–5pm, Sat 1–9pm, Sun 8am–12noon • $1CUC • ☏ 33 20 1661

Set in a beautiful 1920s colonial building on the east side of Parque Martí, the **Museo de Artes Decorativos** is the jewel in Ciego's crown. Though few of the beautiful exhibits are of Cuban origin, as a whole they provide an illuminating insight into the level of luxury enjoyed by colonial Creoles. Spanish-speaking guides are on hand to talk you through the finer pieces, which include a fabulous tall-necked Art Nouveau vase in gold and claret glass, and a nursery kitted out with white pajilla cane furniture.

Teatro Principal
Joaquín Agüero esq. Honorato del Castillo • ☏ 33 22 2086

The prettiest building in Ciego de Ávila's centre is the **Teatro Principal**, built between 1924 and 1927 by wealthy society widow Angela Hernández Viuda de Jiménez in an attempt to make the town more cosmopolitan. In an architectural fit of pique the building manages to combine Baroque, Renaissance and Imperial exterior styles with an equally elaborate interior. There is no official tour, but you're free to enter and look around in the daytime.

Museo Provincial de Ciego de Ávila
Honorato del Castillo esq. Máximo Gómez • Tues–Sat 8am–noon & 1–5pm, Sun 8am–noon • $1CUC • ☏ 33 20 4488

One block north of Parque Martí is the attractively housed though rather dull **Museo Provincial de Ciego de Ávila**, with a room devoted to relics from local Taíno communities including some shards of pottery, some information on Afro-Cuba religions and a scale model of La Trocha (see p.330).

ARRIVAL AND DEPARTURE   CIEGO DE ÁVILA

By train The train station (☏ 33 22 3313) is six blocks from the centre on Avenida Iriondo; *bicitaxis* can ferry you into town if you're not up to walking.
Destinations Camagüey (1 daily; 2hr); Havana (3 daily; 7hr); Holguín (1 daily; 5hr); Matanzas (3 daily; 6hr); Morón (3 daily; 1hr).
By bus Buses operated by Víazul (☏ 33 20 3197) pull into the Terminal de Omnibus Interprovincial on the Carretera

Central Extremo Oeste (☏ 33 22 5109), about 3km east of the town centre. You can share a horse-drawn carriage into the centre for a handful of pesos or catch a *bicitaxi* for a couple of convertible pesos.
Destinations Camagüey (2 daily; 1hr 30min); Havana (2 daily; 6hr); Holguín (2 daily; 6hr); Las Tunas (2 daily; 4hr); Santa Clara (2 daily; 3hr).

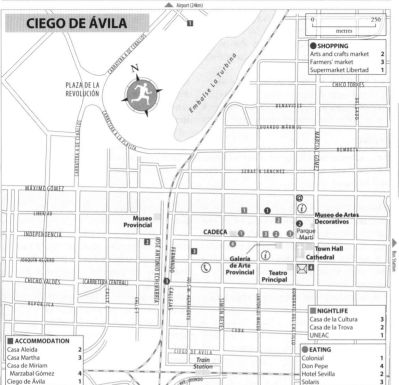

GETTING AROUND

Car rental Micar has an office at Fernando Callejas esq. Libertad (☎33 26 6157) and at the *Hotel Santiago-Habana*, Honorato del Castillo esq. Carretera Central (☎33 26 6169). Rex is based at the *Ciego de Ávila* hotel (☎33 21 3456; see p.314).

By taxi Taxis are available from Cubataxi (☎33 26 6666) or Taxis Ávila (☎33 22 3582).

INFORMATION, TRAVEL AGENCIES AND TOURS

Infotur The office at Calle Honorato del Castillo, Edificio 12 Planta (Mon–Fri 8am–noon & 1–6pm, Sat 8am–noon; ☎33 20 9109, ⓦinfotur.cu) has general information on the area, and can arrange diving excursions and day-trips to Cayo Coco.

Havanatur As well as selling maps, the office at Libertad no.54 e/ Maceo y Honorato del Castillo (Mon–Sat 8am–noon & 1–6pm; ☎33 26 6342) has information on trips to local sights and to Cayo Coco and other attractions in the province.

ACCOMMODATION

The better of the two **state hotels** – all things being relative – is the *Ciego de Ávila* on the outskirts of town, though a **casa particular** is a much better choice, and most owners will also be able to arrange transport to the cays.

Casa Aleida Independencia no.259 e/ José Antonio Echevarría y Calle 1 ☎33 20 0162. Two sizeable double rooms, each en suite and with a/c, in a welcoming house just beyond the railway tracks. There's a spacious living room with an attractively tiled floor and carved wooden furniture and a shady patio with rocking chairs. Meals available. **$20CUC**

★**Casa Martha** José M. Agramonte no.19 e/ Independencia y Joaquín Agüero ☎33 20 1327. This warm, cosy, centrally located house, run by a friendly young couple, is tastefully decorated in a different style to the Cuban norm, with crazy paving detail on the stone walls. There are two double bedrooms with TVs and spotless bathrooms, and a comfortable roof terrace with tables and chairs. **$20CUC**

Casa de Miriam Marzabal Gómez Marcial Gómez no.58 e/ Joaquín Agüero y Chicho Valdés ☎33 20 3295. This pleasant house, around a 10min walk from the centre, has two decent-sized rooms, both with

TV and a/c. The sun-filled patio is an added bonus. **$20CUC**

Ciego de Ávila Carretera a Ceballos Km 1.5 ☎33 22 8013. The town's largest hotel is reasonably attractive, has friendly staff and is liveliest at weekends, when the pool is crowded with townsfolk. There's a passable, hairdresser, disco and bar, though the restaurant is best avoided. It's 2km from the centre of town – *bicitaxis* wait outside to ferry you back and forth. **$20CUC**

EATING

State restaurants are thin on the ground in Ciego de Ávila, and are popular at weekends; you'll have to call early in the morning to reserve a table in the evening. Alternatively, you can snack well at the **peso stalls** along and around Independencia.

Colonial Independencia no.110 e/ Maceo y Simón Reyes ☎33 22 3595. A Spanish restaurant hung with bullfight posters, and with some outdoor seating in a dainty courtyard complete with a well. The menu makes a change from the usual Cuban fare, and includes a hearty broth, *fabada* (bean stew) and tortilla. A main course with drinks costs about $8CUC, and there are three daily seating times. Reservations advised. Daily 6pm, 8pm and 10pm.

Don Pepe Independencia no.303 e/ Maceo y Simón Reyes ☎33 22 3713. An atmospheric little eatery, with walls adorned with are caricatures of local characters, some of whom regularly prop up the bar. It serves good pork dishes with rice and peas for pesos, and the unique Don Pepe cocktail (a house speciality made from rum and orange with a sprig of mint), and has live music and dancing most nights. Reservations advised.

Daily noon–midnight.

Hotel Sevilla Calle Independencia 57 e/ Honorato del Castillo y Antonio Maceo ☎33 22 5603. This pleasant hotel restaurant serves tasty chicken and pork, and has a small cabaret bar on the third floor. Evening reservations recommended. Daily noon–2pm & 7pm–midnight.

Solaris Doce Plantas, 12th floor, Honorato del Castillo e/ Libertad y Independencia ☎33 22 2156. Standard meat-based dishes for mid-range prices, served in an original setting on the top floor of Parque Martí's tallest building. To get there, walk under the building through the alley next to the telephone office; turn left at the back and the lift there will whisk you skywards. A dress code – no sandals, men must wear a formal shirt – is strictly enforced. Tues–Sun noon–midnight.

NIGHTLIFE AND ENTERTAINMENT

Ciego de Ávila has a couple of options for **live music**, and on Saturday nights the town rouses itself from its habitual torpor for the weekly Fiesta Ávileña, when the younger population gather near the centre to dance to booming sound systems and feast on huge joints of pork roasting on sidewalk barbecues. Some of the town's restaurants (see above) also offer live music followed by dancing later in the evening.

Casa de la Cultura Independencia no.76 e/ Maceo y Honorato del Castillo. This rather elegant colonial building serves as a catch-all arts venue and hosts a range of bands encompassing everything from bolero to Mexican country music plays. There's an open-air patio on the first floor which can get lively later in the evening when recorded music follows the live acts and people spill out to drink, dance and try out a range of inventive pick-up lines. Fri–Sun 9pm–late.

★ **Casa de la Trova** Libertad no.130 e/ Maceo y

Simón Reyes. Ciego de Ávila's best bet for a night out – the bar sometimes serves locally brewed beer and always has good Cuban rum and a wide choice of cocktails, while local music groups play traditional bolero, son and guaracha to an older crowd when there's a full house. Closed Mon.

UNEAC Libertad no.105 e/ Maceo y Simón Reyes. The pale tiled floors and high ceilings of this rather romantic building suit the regular bolero and choral concerts that are held here. Tues–Sun 8am–midnight.

DIRECTORY

Banks You can change travellers' cheques and get cash advances on credit and debit cards at the Banco Financiero Internacional on Honorato del Castillo, at the edge of the

square (Mon–Fri 8am–3pm, last working day of month 8am–noon), and at the CADECA *casa de cambio*, at Independencia no.118 e/ Maceo y Simón Reyes (Mon–Sat

8.30am–6pm, Sun 8.30am–12.30pm), where you can also buy national pesos.

Internet The ETECSA centre on Honorato de Castillo y Maceo (daily 9am–9pm) charges $5CUC for 30min.

Markets Facing the park on Honorato del Castillo is a small arts and crafts market where a clutch of stalls selling homespun jewellery and the like is worth a swift browse. West of here, parallel to the tracks on Chicho Valdes and Fernando Callejas, a vibrant farmers' market (Tues–Sun 8am–4.30pm) sells fresh produce.

Medical There is a 24 hour surgery on República no.52 esq. A. Delgado (☎ 33 22 2611). For an ambulance call ☎ 185.

Pharmacy There's a 24hr pharmacy at Independencia no.163.

Police Call ☎ 116.

Post office You can buy peso stamps and use DHL and EMS services at the main 24hr post office on Máximo Gómez esq. Carretera Central.

Shopping Supermarket Libertad at Libertad no.68 e/ Maceo y Honorato del Castillo is the best place for picnic supplies and rum.

Telephones ETECSA has an international call centre opposite the square in the Doce Plantas building (daily 9.15am–9.15pm) and a phone cabin on Independencia e/ Simón Reyes y José M. Agramonte, where you can buy phonecards. There is also a centre on Honorato de Castillo y Maceo (daily 9am–9pm).

6

Morón

Lying 36km north of Ciego de Ávila on the road to the cays, picturesque **MORÓN** is surrounded by flat farming countryside replete with glistening palm trees, banks of sugar cane and citrus trees. Fanning out from a cosy downtown nucleus, its few gaily painted colonial buildings and proximity to Cayo Guillermo and Cayo Coco ensure its popularity with day-trippers from the cays, and it's certainly the best place to stay if you want to visit the cays but can't afford a luxury hotel. For now, though, the area's main tourist revenue comes from hunting and fishing, as enthusiasts from around the world converge on **Laguna de la Leche** and **Laguna la Redonda**, both 15km north of town, where several species of fish and flocks of migrating ducks are sitting targets.

The train station

Morón is bisected by train tracks that aren't separated from the road by any barriers – it's quite common to see trains impatiently honking horns as bicycles bearing two or three passengers lazily roll over the rails – and slice through the town's main street, **Martí** (its southern reaches also known as Avenida Tarafa). At the mouth of the tracks, roughly in the centre of town, is the **train station**. Built in the 1920s and one of the oldest in Cuba, it remains largely unchanged, and inside, amid the elegant archways and fine wrought-iron awnings, you can still buy tickets at the original booths and check destinations on a hand-painted blackboard, while high above the rows of worn wooden benches and the original stained-glass *vitrales*, birds nest under the eaves.

THE COCK OF MORÓN

The first thing to strike you about clean, compact Morón is the shining **bronze cockerel**, perched at the foot of a clock tower on an oval green in front of the *Hotel Morón*, just inside the southern entrance to the town. In the sixteenth century, the townsfolk of Spanish Morón found themselves the victims of a corrupt judiciary that continually levied high taxes and confiscated their land without explanation. Having suffered these oppressive conditions for several years, the people set upon and expelled the main offender, an official nicknamed **"the cock of Morón"**. The incident was quickly immortalized in an Andalucían ballad that proclaimed that "the cock of the walk has been left plucked and crowing" (a saying still used throughout Cuba today to mean that somebody has had their plans scuppered). The current statue dates from 1981.

Museo de Arqueología e Historia

Martí no. 374 • Tues–Sat 9am–noon & 1.30–5pm, Sun 9–noon • $1CUC • ☎ 33 504501

From Morón's train station, a five-minute walk north along Martí will take you to the **Museo de Arqueología e Historia**, housed in one of the town's eye-catching colonial buildings, this one fronted by simple columns and wide steps. The collection comprises an assortment of small pre-Columbian Cuban artefacts, mainly fragments of clay bowls and shards of bone necklace. By far the most impressive exhibit is the *Idolillo de Barro*, a clay idol of a fierce snarling head, found outside the city in 1947.

6

Galería del Arte

Martí no.151 • Tues–Sat 8am–noon & 1–5.30pm, Sun 8am–noon

North of the archeological museum, the **Galería del Arte** exhibits and sells an array of locally painted landscapes, colourful abstracts, lovingly executed sculptures of female nudes and mawkish religious figures. If you're planning to buy a sculpture in the area, this is the place to do it as they're a lot cheaper here than at the resorts.

ARRIVAL AND DEPARTURE   MORÓN

By train Three daily trains from Ciego de Ávila call at the elegant station in the centre of town.
Destinations Camagüey (1 daily; 3hr); Ciego de Ávila (5 daily; 1hr); Júcaro (1 daily; 40min); Santa Clara (1 daily; 4hr).
By bus Víazul buses use the bus station (☎ 33 50 3774) at Calle Marti no.12 e/ Felipe Poey y Carlos Manuel de Céspedes. Municipal buses arrive and depart from

outside the train station.
Víazul destinations Trinidad (1 daily; 5hr 30min)
Municipal bus destinations Ciego de Ávila (2 daily; 1hr)
By colectivo and camion You can usually find *colectivos* and *camiones* to Ciego de Ávila and Camagüey outside the train station; fares are usually $10–15CUC and $15CUC respectively.

INFORMATION AND TOURS

Cubatur The office at Marti no 169 e/ Libertad y Agramonte (☎ 33 50 5513) sells maps and has some

information about local excursions.

ACCOMMODATION

Morón's growing clutch of very reasonable **casas particulares** are your best choice for an overnight stay. They will all be able to help sort out taxis to and from the cays, and some will even provide a packed picnic lunch.

★ **Alojamiento Maite Valor Morales** Luz Caballero no. 40B e/ Libertad y Agramonte ☎ 33 50 4181, ✉ yio@moron.cav.sld.cu or ✉ maite68@enet .cu. Three rooms to rent in a lovingly run household. One is ideal for larger families as it sleeps up to five, while the other sleeps three, and each has a/c, private bathroom with hot and cold water, fridge, TV, 110/220 voltage and security box. A recently completed third room has space for five people, a private bathroom, sitting room, kitchen and terrace. There's a fabulous sun terrace with views over the city, a garden and parking ($2CUC a night). The highly professional Maite also serves tasty meals, speaks English and Italian and is a font of information on the area. **$25CUC**
Casa Belkys Calle Cristóbal Colon no.37 e/ Carretera de Patria y Línea del Ferrocarril ☎ 33 50 5763. One attractive double room with its own bathroom in a house with a sunny terrace and a garage a few metres from the train station. **$25CUC**

Casa de Idolka Maria Gonzalez Rizo Luz Caballero no.49D (altos) Libertad y Agramonte ☎ 33 50 4181, ✉ yio@moron.cav.sld.cu or ✉ maite69@enet.cu. Situated opposite the Balinga children's playground close to the centre of town, this house has one a/c double room with private bathroom, 110/220 voltage, TV and fridge. There's a well-stocked bar and a sun terrace with views over the city. Car parking ($2CUC) is available and English is spoken. **$25CUC**
La Casona de Morón Cristóbal Colon no.41 Carretera de Patria y Ferrocarril ☎ 33 50 4563. Recently remodelled, and set in a pretty sunshine-yellow villa with bags of personality, this friendly boutique-style hotel is more akin to the *hostales* of Habana Vieja than a provincial hotel, both in size and high levels of service. It caters to the hunting and fishing crowd, offering tours of the local sporting grounds and the chance to cook your spoils yourself on the open grill by the tiny swimming pool. **$35CUC**

Juan C. Peréz Oquendo Belgica Silva Castillo no.189 e/ San José y Serafín Sánchez ☎ 33 50 3823. Very friendly owners and two comfortable en-suite double rooms with a/c, a short walk from the centre of town. **$25CUC**

Onaida Ruíz Fumero Calle 5 no.46 e/ 6 y 8 ☎ 33 50 3409. Pleasant a/c rooms, one double and one triple, in a house on a quiet residential street. Parking and meals are available. **$25CUC**

EATING

Alondra Martí no.298 e/ Serafín Sánchez y Calleja (no phone). Slick, shiny glass-and-tile ice-cream parlour, charging around $1CUC for a very kitsch candy-coated sundae complete with spangly cocktail stick. Daily 10am–11pm.

Doña Neli Serafín Sánchez no.86 e/ Narciso López y Martí (no phone). A bakery serving an excellent selection of fresh breads, flaky pastries and cakes coated in meringue. Arrive early in the morning to avoid being stuck with the bullet-like bread rolls. Daily 8am–8pm.

Las Fuentes Martí no.169 e/ Libertad y Agramonte ☎ 33 50 5758. Creamy soups and pastas enliven the standard selection of chicken and pork dishes in this warm, rustic-style restaurant where you eat to the sound of water trickling down the eponymous fountains, surrounded by exuberant ferns. Main courses are around $5CUC. Daily 11am–1pm.

★ **Restaurant Maite la Qbana** Luz Caballero no.40B e/ Libertad y Agramonte ☎ 33 50 4181. The proprietor of the town's best *casa particular* has expanded her enterprise to include a paladar, and the delicious and inventive home-cooked meals make this one of the best places to eat in the province. House specialities include dressed crab, fresh lobster, paella and soups, with mains costing $5–12CUC. Dinner reservations recommended; it opens for lunch on request only. Daily 7–10am & 6–11pm.

DRINKING AND ENTERTAINMENT

Morón is a town of modest means, where the locals' idea of a good night's **entertainment** is to cluster around a neighbour's television (or even peer through their window) to catch up with the latest soap opera. Your options, all rather tame, are to enjoy a gentle promenade around the star-lit streets, catch a film or, if you're driving, to head out in the early evening to one of the restaurants on the banks of Laguna de la Leche and Laguna la Redonda (see p.318).

BARS AND LIVE MUSIC VENUES

Casa de la Cultura Calle Martí (no phone). There's live music to be had most nights here with a concert held on the last Saturday of each month. Daily 7pm–late.

Casa de la Trova Libertad e/ Narciso López y Martí ☎ 33 50 4158. A small but pleasantly unassuming local watering hole and an authentic Cuban experience, where the town's minstrels serenade drinkers with traditional *guajiras* and son amid basic decor that's remained unchanged for years. Closed Tues. Mon & Wed–Sun 7–11pm.

CINEMA

Apolo Martí e/ Carlos Manuel de Céspedes y Resedad. A roster of contemporary Cuban and north American films play throughout the day and evening.

DIRECTORY

Money CADECA *casa de cambio*, Calle Martí no.346 e/ González Arena y Serafín Sánchez (Mon–Sat 8.30am–5.30pm, Sun 8.30am–noon; ☎ 33 50 2246), handles all types of foreign currency transactions and sells pesos.

Phones The ETECSA telecommunications centre (daily 8am–9.45pm) in the same building as the post office.

Post office Housed in the blue-and-white 1920s period building, the post office is at Colonial Española, Calle Martí (Mon–Sat 8am–5pm).

Taxis The private taxis waiting under the trees in front of the station are useful for forays into the countryside and to the cays. Prices are negotiable depending on how hard you're prepared to bargain. State taxis include Cubataxi (☎ 33 50 3290) on Avenida Tarafa.

Around Morón

Set in lush countryside dappled by lakes and low hills, the area surrounding Morón offers a welcome contrast to the unrelentingly flat land to the south, and holds a few surprises well worth venturing beyond the town limits to explore. Ten kilometres north of town, the large **Laguna de la Leche** is fringed by reeds and woodland that hide the **Aguachales de Falla** game reserve, while 7km further northeast the tranquil **Laguna la Redonda** is an idyllic spot for drifting about in a

6

boat. Just north of the lakes is the peninsula **La Isla de Turiguanó**, home to the mock-Dutch village **Pueblo Holandés de Turiguanó**, its faux-timbered, red-roofed houses looking completely out of place beneath tropical palms. Towards the east, rising from the plains like the shell of a tortoise, is the gently rounded **Loma de Cunagua**, its dense tangle of woodland full of bright parakeets and parrots, and a favourite spot for day-trekkers and birdwatchers. West from Morón, in an area straddled by the tiny villages of Chambas and Florencia, is the **Boquerón reserve campsite**, where horseriding, river-swimming and rock-climbing are an irresistible draw for nature enthusiasts.

GETTING AROUND   **AROUND MORÓN**

By taxi Unless you're driving, the only way to get around the Morón area is to negotiate a day rate with one of the Moronero taxi drivers (see p.316). The bigger your group, the more they'll want to charge you, but for two people you should count on $25–30CUC per day.

Laguna de la Leche

Ecotur in Cayo Coco offers boat rental, which costs $5CUC per person for 20min • ☎ 33 30 8163 • A private taxi from Morón should be $5–10CUC one-way, or $12–15CUC return. If driving, take Martí north out of Morón, turn left and head for the cays; the turning for the lake is signposted

With a circumference of 66km, **Laguna de la Leche** (Milk Lake) is the largest lake in Cuba and, decked out with palm trees and a pint-sized lighthouse, looks like a tiny seafront. The opacity of its water comes from gypsum and limestone deposits beneath the surface, but despite the evocative name it looks nothing like Cleopatra's bath: rather, the lake fans out from a cloudy centre to disperse into smudgy pools of green and blue around the edges. The lake's wooded north and west shores, soupy with rushes and overhung branches, are great for exploring but are accessible only by **boat**; rental can be arranged through Ecotur.

Aguachales de Falla hunting reserve

Hunting expeditions are arranged through Ecotur ☎ 33 30 8163 • Four excursions including guide, permit and transfer from Morón cost $550CUC; gun hire is $10CUC, and a box of cartridges $15CUC

Laguna de la Leche's peaceful calm is only mildly disturbed by the distant gunshots of eager sportsmen firing at the hapless ducks, white-crowned pigeons and doves that swoop through the **Aguachales de Falla hunting reserve** on the western shore. The government's promotion of blood sports here may seem at odds with the ecotourism touted on the northern cays just a few kilometres north, but firearms are entrenched in Cuban culture and familiarity with them is seen as an essential skill in a country still intermittently defending its sovereignty. As the popular motto goes, "Every Cuban should know how to shoot and shoot well".

EATING AND DRINKING   **LAGUNA DE LA LECHE**

La Atarraya Perched on a jetty overlooking Laguna de la Leche, this expansive open-sided bar and restaurant serves fresh fish caught in the lake. With views right across the water, it's also a beautiful spot to soak up the sunset over a *mojito*. Tues–Sun 12.30–2pm & 4–6pm.

Laguna la Redonda

Boats and guides can be hired at the the lakeside *La Redonda* restaurant, both costing $5CUC/45min, and arrange a fishing excursion at $70CUC/4hr; equipment is not included • There's no public transport to Laguna la Redonda, but a taxi from Morón should charge $15–20CUC for the round trip

Some 7km north of Laguna de la Leche and reached by a canalside turning off the main road to the cays, **Laguna la Redonda** (Circle Lake) is the smaller of the region's two lakes, measuring only 3km at its widest point, and has five mangrove canals that radiate out from the central body of water like the spokes on a bicycle wheel. Quieter and altogether more intimate than Laguna de la Leche, it's perfect for an idle afternoon's boating or trout fishing, or for just drifting over to the uncharted territory on the far side of the lake and wandering through the undergrowth.

EATING

LAGUNA LA REDONDA

La Redonda ☎ 33 30 2489. This serene restaurant overhanging the lake serves freshly caught tilapia and carp as well as pasta, steaks, chicken and omelettes. Daily 9am–8pm.

San Fernando Carretera Ciego de Ávila Rotonda (no phone). This pleasant villa off the lakeside road has been converted into an upmarket restaurant serving good Cuban cuisine (and dire spaghetti); mains are $7–10CUC. It has an attractive outside bar which should be avoided on Saturday nights when a tawdry cabaret show takes over. Daily 9am–8pm.

Loma de Cunagua

Daily 9am–4pm • $5CUC • There's no public transport; the return taxi fare from Morón to Loma de Cunagua is $15–20CUC

The lone high ground in an area of unremittingly flat farmland that stretches all the way to the coast, the **Loma de Cunagua**, 18km from Morón and 364m high, can be seen for miles around. Just past the foot of the hill is a gate where you pay the entrance fee; from here, a gravelly road weaves its way up through the dense tangle of spindly trees clinging precariously to the steep slopes. A favourite with **birdwatchers**, the hill's forests, crisscrossed by a network of trails, are home to dazzlingly coloured parrots, as well as the *tojosa* (a small endemic dove), the *zunzún* (Cuban emerald hummingbird) and the *tocororo*, which was chosen as the country's national bird because of its startling red, white and blue plumage, the same colour scheme as the Cuban flag. If you're lucky, you might also catch a glimpse of an enormous Cuban tree rat, known locally as *jutía*. Take the dirt track up to the summit, which offers panoramic views over the surrounding countryside and out to sea.

Boquerón natural reserve

The undulating terrain around the tiny towns of **Florencia** and **Chambas**, 30km west of Morón, is prime farming country, pocketed with dazzling green-gold sugarcane fields, corrals of slow-moving cattle and tobacco meadows. Florencia's name – given for its resemblance to the Italian town – is an indication of its arcadian beauty, set in an area of simple tourist pleasures built around nature. The best spot to base yourself is the **Boquerón natural reserve**, 5km west of Florencia. Veiled behind the folds of the Jatibonico Sierra (the rugged tail of the Sierra de Meneses chain, which

---

HORSERIDING AROUND BOQUERÓN

The glorious countryside around Boquerón can be explored on guided **horserides** through the coconut groves and banana fields, run daily by Cubatur (☎ 33 50 5513) in Morón. Popular options include a trek past local farms to a **rodeo show** ($20CUC), where local cowboys wow the crowd with demonstrations of their animal-handling prowess; the day culminates with a pig roast. During the tobacco harvest the tour also includes a bus trip to a tobacco-curing house near Florencia.

You can also ride to the shores of the **Liberación de Florencia** lake ($30CUC), to the east of Florencia, from where you're whisked by motorboat for lunch at the restaurant on an island in the middle of the lake. Keep a lookout for the majestic *ceiba* tree near the lake. Identifiable by its gigantic size and webbed roots overlaying the tree base, it's accorded magical powers by followers of the Afro-Cuban Santería religion.

steals into the province from Sancti Spíritus to the west) and framed by a halo of royal palms, the campsite here (see below) occupies a hidden paradise of banana groves, fruit trees and flitting hummingbirds. The nearby Jatibonico River twists through the hills and makes an excellent spot for shady swimming, while a phalanx of skinny horses waits to take you cross-country trekking (see box, p.319), and the ponderous crags pocked with caves jutting out above the site are ripe for mountaineering.

ARRIVAL AND DEPARTURE
BOQUERÓN NATURAL RESERVE

By taxi A taxi from Morón will cost around $20CUC.
By train Chambas and Florencia are served by a train from Morón three times a week.

By organized tour Trips to the area can be arranged through Havanatur in Ciego de Ávila (☎ 33 26 6339).

ACCOMMODATION

Campismo Boquerón Boquerón natural reserve ☎ 78 33 2523. Some 5km west of Florencia, tucked away down a series of twisted lanes that occasionally degenerate into waterlogged dirt tracks, this isn't the easiest place to reach independently, but it really is worth the hassle. As well as tent pitches, there are triangular huts with four basic but clean single bunks (bring your own sheets). Meals are available, but you're better off bringing provisions and cooking on the communal barbecue. Bookings are through Cubamar in Havana; priority booking is given to Cubans in the very busy summer season. Huts $15CUC

The northern cays

Christened "The King's Garden" by Diego Velázquez in 1514 in honour of King Ferdinand of Spain, the **northern cays**, lying 30km off Ciego de Ávila's coast and hemmed in by 400km of coral reef, are indisputably the dazzling jewels in the province's crown: a rich tangle of mangroves, mahogany trees and lagoons iced by sugar sands and thick with pink flamingos, and a top **diving** location with an infrastructure to match.

Despite their auspicious naming in the sixteenth century, the numerous islets spanning the coastline from Ciego de Ávila to Camagüey remained uninhabited and relatively unexplored until as recently as the late 1980s. Until then, they had only been visited by colonial-era pirates and corsairs seeking a bolthole to stash their spoils; Ernest Hemingway, who sailed around them in the 1930s and 1940s; and former dictator Fulgencio Batista, who had a secret hideaway on tiny Cayo Media Luna, a mere pinprick on the map and now a favourite haunt for sunbathers and snorkellers.

The exclusivity of the northern cays was breached in 1988 by the construction of a 29km stone **causeway** (or *pedraplén*) across the Bahía de los Perros, connecting the Isla de Turiguanó peninsula to Cayo Coco. The delighted state began to create a tourist haven destined to be as sumptuous as Varadero, and so far two of the islands – **Cayo Coco** and smaller **Cayo Guillermo** – have been primed for luxury tourism, with a string of all-inclusive hotels planted along their northern shores. The causeway has had a negative environmental impact on the cays, however, disrupting the natural flow of water and impoverishing conditions for local wildlife. The two cays are themselves connected by another causeway, with an offshoot running east to the breakaway **Cayo Paredón Grande**, uninhabited but providing another beach option should you exhaust those on the main islets.

ARRIVAL AND DEPARTURE
THE NORTHERN CAYS

Essentials All road traffic enters the cays along the causeway; there's a booth at the entrance where passports are checked and a $2CUC toll is levied.

By car or motorbike As there are no organized tours or public buses to the cays, getting there independently can be a bit of a mission. Your most flexible option is to rent a car in Ciego de Ávila; try Micar, Fernando Callejas esq. Libertad (☎ 33 26 6157) and at *Hotel Santiago-Habana* (☎ 33 26 6169; see p.313), or Rex at the *Ciego de Ávila* hotel (☎ 33 21 3456; see p.314). You can also rent a motorbike from a couple of hotels in Morón: *Hotel Morón* (☎ 33 50 2230) and *La Casona* (☎ 33 50 4563; see p.316).

By taxi From Morón, a private taxi will take you, wait and bring you back to Cayo Coco for $30–50CUC, and to Cayo Guillermo and Cayo Paredón for $40–70CUC

depending on how hard you're prepared to haggle. A metered state taxi will charge around $100CUC one-way.

By plane Jardínes del Rey airport (☎ 33 30 8228), on the east of Cayo Coco, has flights from Havana (3 weekly; 2hr), as well as some international services from Europe. From here hotel representatives whisk passengers off to their accommodation; if you haven't booked accommodation with your flight, you should be able to hitch a lift to a hotel of your choice.

6

GETTING AROUND

By moped, jeep and sand-buggy Zipping around the near-empty roads on a moped is the best way to get around. All the hotels have desks offering moped

($5CUC/hr), jeep and sand-buggy rental (both around $12CUC/hr).

By taxi You can book taxis from all the hotel desks.

INFORMATION

Tourist information There's no tourist office, but each hotel has a PR officer who can provide general information and supply maps of the cays which give a good impression of the islands but are distinctly lacking in specifics.

Banks The BFI bank (Mon–Fri 9am–3pm), by the Cupet

Garage mini-complex in the centre of Cayo Coco, gives cash advances on cards and cashes travellers' cheques.

Internet access Most of the hotels have on-site internet access, with rates of $3–5CUC/30min.

Cayo Coco

With 22km of creamy-white sands and cerulean waters, **CAYO COCO** easily fulfils its tourist-blurb claim of offering a holiday in paradise. The islet is 32km wide from east to west, with a hill like a camel's hump rising from the middle. The best beaches are clustered on the north coast, dominated by the all-inclusive hotels whose tendrils are gradually spreading along the rest of the northern coastline. Cayo Coco's big three beaches, home to the all-inclusives, hog the narrow easternmost peninsula jutting out of the cay's north coast. Non-guests can use the hotels' facilities once they've stumped up for a **day pass**, which covers all meals and drinks and will cost $35–60CUC. **Playa Las Coloradas** and **Playa Larga** (of which **Playa Las Conchas** is a continuation) are boisterous beaches with activities laid on by the hotels, but if you'd prefer peace and quiet to volleyball and aerobics sessions, you'll still find a few pockets of tranquillity, like **Playa Los Flamencos**.

Away from the beach strip, dirt roads allow easy access into the lush wooded **interior**, where hidden delights include hummingbirds, pelicans, some gorgeous lagoons and **Sitio La Güira**, a re-creation of an old Cuban peasant village. Heading toward the extreme south, the land becomes marshier but still navigable on foot. This area is a haven for herons and the **white ibis** or *coco* that give the cay its name, and a number of animals live here, too – it's not uncommon to see wild boars rooting out of the undergrowth and wild bulls lumbering across the road. Also keep an eye out for the colony of **iguanas** that originally floated here on coconut husks from other islands.

Playa Las Coloradas

Spanning the extreme northeastern tip of the island and home to the *Sol Club Cayo Coco*, *Meliá Cayo Coco* and *Iberostar Cayo Coco* all-inclusives, **Playa Las Coloradas**, though filled with crowds of beach chairs, is exceptionally picturesque, with fine sand and calm waters. It's a good place for **watersports**, busy with cruising catamarans and pedalos, though these are only accessible to hotel guests or those with day-passes. It does have an independent restaurant, however (see p.325).

6

Playa Larga and Playa Las Conchas

Three kilometres west of Las Coloradas, and divided by name only, **Playa Larga** and **Playa Las Conchas** form a continuous strip of silvery sand lapped by shallow crystal waters, and are arguably the best beaches on the island, although very crowded during the organized activities laid on by the *Tryp Cayo Coco* hotel. Non-guests are welcome to use the beaches during the day – access is through the hotel – though to use any of its facilities you'll have to pay for a day pass. Access is restricted at night.

Playa Prohibida

Hidden behind a sand dune 1km east of Playa Larga off the coast road is **Playa Prohibida**. Strewn with seaweed, the beach here has no facilities at all, but it's usually deserted and a high dune seeded with wild grasses makes for a pleasing backdrop.

Playa Los Flamencos

For solitude, head west from Playa Larga along the coastal dirt road to **Playa Los Flamencos**. Demarcated by a stout stucco flamingo, the beach offers 3km of clean golden sands and clear waters where tangerine-coloured starfish float through the shallows, as well as good **snorkelling** out to sea. It gets busy in the daytime, but wandering away from the lively, expensive **bar** (see p.325) should guarantee some privacy.

Centro de Talasoterapia Acuavida

Daily 9am–7pm • Individual treatments from $30CUC; five-day programmes from $260CUC; use of outdoor and indoor pools $17CUC/3hr; all prices include transfer from hotels • ☎ 33 30 2157, ⓦ servimedcuba.com

Perched on a rocky outcrop to the east of Playa Larga, the stylish and tastefully designed **Centro de Talasoterapia Acuavida** is the cays' only independent spa, with treatment rooms leading off a central atrium that's set around a fountain and planted with trees alive with hummingbirds. Facilities include four hot pools, a swimming pool, gym and various water massage chambers. The tranquil **outdoor seawater pool** has an unmarred view over the cobalt waters, while there's a smaller indoor pool for swimming lengths. Other treatments include chocolate wraps, algae treatments, aromatherapy, water therapy and massage.

Sitio La Güira

Daily 9am–11pm • Free • Horseriding $5CUC/hr; prices for guided walks are negotiable • ☎ 33 30 1208

In the centre of Cayo Coco, 6km from the north coast, is **Sitio La Güira**, a mocked-up early twentieth-century peasant community built to impart some idea of traditional Cuban farming culture to visitors who might never venture further

---

COCKFIGHTING

Cockfighting has been the sport of Cuban farmers since the eighteenth century, with sizeable sums of money changing hands on bets, and thefts of prized specimens and allegations of rooster nobbling common. There is a particular breed of rooster indigenous to Cuba that exercises considerable cunning in defeating its opponent, parrying attacks and throwing false moves, and the bloodlines of these birds are protected and nurtured as carefully as those of any racehorse.

Since the **ban on gambling** introduced by the Revolution, this rather cruel practice has been pushed underground – although the sport itself is still legal. Nowadays cockfighting is a clandestine affair, taking place on smallholdings deep in the country at the break of dawn, when the fowl are in vicious ill-humour and at their fighting best. Unlike the shows laid on for tourists, where the cocks are eventually separated, the spurred cocks here will slug it out to the death.

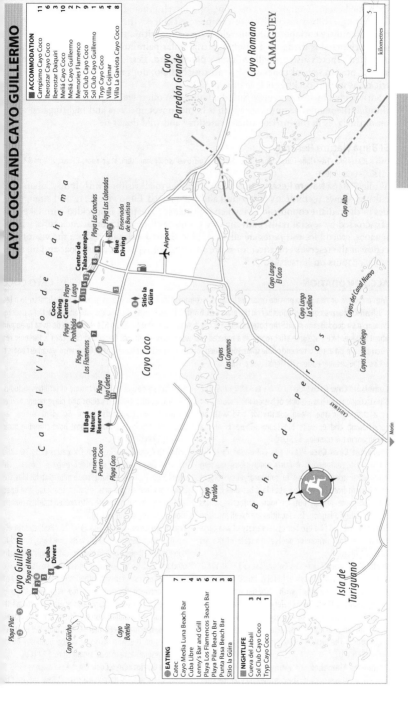

CAYO COCO AND CAYO GUILLERMO

ACCOMMODATION

Campismo Cayo Coco	11
Iberostar Cayo Coco	6
Iberostar Daiquiri	3
Meliá Cayo Coco	10
Meliá Cayo Guillermo	2
Memories Flamenco	7
Sol Club Cayo Coco	9
Sol Club Cayo Guillermo	1
Tryp Cayo Coco	5
Villa Cojímar	4
Villa La Gaviota Cayo Coco	8

EATING

Catec.	7
Cayo Media Luna Beach Bar	1
Cuba Libre	4
Lenny's Bar and Grill	5
Playa Los Flamencos Beach Bar	6
Playa Pilar Beach Bar	2
Punta Rasa Beach Bar	3
Sitio la Güira	8

NIGHTLIFE

Cueva del Jabalí	3
Sol Club Cayo Coco	2
Tryp Cayo Coco	1

6

than the beach. Though it's something of a novelty theme park, a number of interesting exhibits rescue it from complete tackiness. The main features are a typical **country cottage** made entirely from palms with a thatched roof, a **ranch** where charcoal is made, and a **bohío**, a triangular palm hut in which tobacco leaves are dried. There's also a small children's **playground**. Less appealing are the animal shows, put on several times a day, featuring buffalo, dogs and bulls performing tricks, as well as cockfights (see box, p.322).

Surrounded by lush greenery, Sitio La Güira also offers **walking** and **riding tours** through the mangrove outback, which is home to woodpeckers and nightingales, and on to the lakes in the interior where waterfowl and wild ducks nest.

El Bagá Nature Reserve

Daily 8.30am–5pm • Free • Indo-Cuban cultural shows $10CUC • Guided walks daily 9am, 10am, 11am, noon, 1.30pm, 2.30pm & 3.30pm • $18CUC • ☎ 33 30 1063

While **El Bagá Nature Reserve** tries to be all things to all visitors, with Indo-Cuban cultural shows, a children's fairground and a re-created Taíno village, its real strength lies in the radiant **countryside** in which it's situated. The park is speckled with lakes and crisscrossed by several trails, enlivened by various well-tended animal enclosures where iguanas, crocodiles and *jutías* are all on display. **Guided walks** leave from the visitors' centre at the reserve's entrance; for more adventurous types, there are boat and bike trips, or tours on horseback.

ACCOMMODATION   **CAYO COCO**

With no towns or villages to provide *casas particulares*, accommodation on Cayo Coco is almost totally limited to a few plush **all-inclusives** grouped together on the main beach strips. If you haven't pre-booked into one as part of a package holiday, it's a good idea to phone the hotels directly or check with Havanatur (☎ 33 26 6342) in Ciego de Ávila to enquire about cheaper rates, as some offer rooms at a reduced cost when they're not full. *Campismo Cayo Coco* is the only real alternative, right at the other end of the scale; you'll need your own transport if staying here. Otherwise, your best bet is to seek out the cheaper options in Morón (see p.316).

Campismo Cayo Coco Sitio La Güira ☎ 33 30 1208. The Sitio La Güira ranch has a couple of basic double rooms, set in a clearing in the island countryside and with air conditioning and en-suite bathrooms. There is also a restaurant in the complex. **$25CUC**

Iberostar Cayo Coco Playa Las Coloradas ☎ 33 30 1470, ⓦ iberostar.com. A fairly anonymous, modern hotel with accommodation in mustard-yellow blocks that benefit from big windows but lack balconies; there are also some pricier, but far more attractive, villas spread around a lagoon. The facilities are excellent, with international and Chinese buffets, a variety of à la carte restaurants, four swimming pools and a state-of-the-art gym. **$270CUC**

Meliá Cayo Coco Playa Las Coloradas ☎ 33 30 1180, ⓦ solmelia.com. This opulent hotel is aimed squarely at the couples' market, with special deals for honeymooners. The de luxe chalet-style accommodation is set around a natural lagoon, and there's a large pool and a full range of amenities, including sauna, gym and watersports. The lack of a disco makes it peaceful and quiet. **$200CUC**

Memories Flamenco Los Flamencos ☎ 33 30 4100, ⓦ memoriesresorts.com. The newest hotel on the strip,

with an airy design and a multitude of facilities including five restaurants, children's clubs and playgrounds and an ebullient entertainments team. Standard rooms are tasteful if a little anonymous; some have stunning ocean views. **$170CUC**

Sol Club Cayo Coco Playa Las Coloradas ☎ 33 30 1280, ⓦ melia.com. Painted in bright tropical colours, this popular family-oriented hotel has a mini-club for kids, free non-motorized watersports, a buffet, snack bar and beach grill, and a lively atmosphere with excited children running around causing mayhem. **$180CUC**

Tryp Cayo Coco Playa Larga ☎ 33 30 1300, ⓦ solmelia .com. Though beginning to show its grey hairs, this 1990 hotel is nonetheless a solid choice, with brightly painted blocks dotted around expansive grounds. Guests can eat at the range of restaurants in either of two sections and are ferried between the two by a toy-train bus. Although reminiscent of a theme park, and equipped with all the usual mod cons including nursery, fitness centre and beach activities, it actually feels more Cuban than the other all inclusives on the strip, as some of the buildings bear passing resemblance to local architecture. **$271CUC**

Villa La GaviotaCayo Coco Playa Las Conchas ☎ 33 33 2180, ⓔ carpeta@villagaviota.co.cu. While this isn't the

BOAT TRIPS, DIVING AND EXCURSIONS FROM THE CAYS

While many head to the cays to bask in the Caribbean sun, there are many opportunities for those up for more energetic pastimes. **Diving** is a prime activity here, as is exploring on **foot** or **horseback** through the lush interior that spreads south of the hotel strip. Further pursuits include **fishing** expeditions and **boat trips**.

DIVING

The Atlantic Ocean on the northeast coast of the Cayo Coco holds one of the world's longest coral reefs, with shoals of angel fish, butterfly fish, nurse sharks and surgeon fish weaving through forests of colourful sponges, and alarmingly large barracudas bucking below the water line. There are at least five excellent **dive sites** spread between Cayo Paredón and Cayo La Jaula (east of Cayo Coco), where you can reach depths of 35m, and all the hotels organize dive trips and give free induction classes to guests. The Coco Diving Centre (☎ 33 30 1323, ⓦ amazing-coco-diving.designxworld.com), just west of the *Tryp Cayo Coco* on Playa Larga, offers single for $40CUC, including all equipment and transport to the dive site, as well as four-day SNSI open-water courses at $310CUC. An alternative dive school is the Cuban–Italian-owned Blue Diving (☎ 33 30 8180), on Playa Las Coloradas in front of the *Meliá Cayo Coco*, which has single dives for $40CUC, including equipment, and charges $365CUC for the SNSI open-water course.

BOAT TRIPS AND FISHING

Coco Diving Centre runs **"seafari"** trips in a pleasure yacht that cruises around the coast and to the cay's celebrated flamingo community, and **catamaran excursions** for offshore swimming and snorkelling (both $43CUC per person for half a day, including lunch and an open bar). It also offers **fishing expeditions** around Cayo Media Luna, where the plentiful billfish, snapper and bass make rich pickings; four hours at sea costs $290CUC for up to six people including all the tackle and an open bar.

Jungle Tours (☎ 33 30 1515), based on Cayo Guillermo but with representatives in all the hotels, offers the chance to captain your own two-person **motorboat** ($41CUC/2hr) on tours into the narrow canals between the dense mangrove thickets that fringe the cays, while Cubatur (desks are in all the hotels) organizes glass-bottomed boat trips and a range of snorkelling excursions. Independent operator In Cloud 9 (☎ 72 06 9062, ⓦ incloud9.com) can also arrange tailor-made fishing trips in the area.

EXCURSIONS

Though you can strike off on your own – ask at the hotels' PR desks about hiring horses or arranging horse-drawn carriage tours – **Cubatur** organizes land-based day-trips to various locations throughout the cays as well as day-trips to Morón. For those who have always wanted to gallop through the shallows on a tropical beach, Catec (☎ 33 30 1404, or ask at the hotels) offers **horse-trekking** ($10CUC/2hr) on Playa Piedra, during the day and at sunset.

---

ashest all-inclusive on the cay, it still has its good points, ke two-storey blocks laid out in spacious surroundings vith sea views, and a jetty leading down to a small private

beach with golden sand. An on-site fitness centre provides a sauna and massages, though these are not included in the price. **$150CUC**

ATING AND DRINKING

each bar Playa Los Flamencos (no phone). The basic ut reasonably well-prepared mains here include lobster, hicken and pork (around $6CUC), while sides include fried reen bananas and rice. Daily 9am–7pm.

atec Playa Las Coloradas (no phone). Open-sided each bar serving lobster for $15CUC; washed down with n ice cold Cristal, it's the perfect way to end a day on the each. Daily 9am–7pm.

enny's Bar and Grill Playa Prohibida (no phone). This

tiny thatched beach bar serves tasty barbecue chicken, fish and lobster, as well as soft drinks and beers. Daily 9am–7pm.

Sitio la Güira ☎ 33 30 1208. A ranch restaurant in the midst of the theme park, serving moderately priced spaghetti and steaks ($6CUC) and expensive seafood ($15CUC), and holding a daily *Guateque*, "a farm party with animation activities and lessons on typical dances". Daily 9am–10pm.

NIGHTLIFE AND ENTERTAINMENT

If you've paid for a day-pass at one of the all-inclusive hotels, you can have dinner and go on to the **hotel disco** afterwards for no extra charge; otherwise, the hotel places change an entrance fee for non-guests.

Cueva del Jabalí (no phone). For a different kind of nightlife, try this glittery, loud cabaret followed by a disco, all staged in a natural cave 5km inland from the hotel strip which takes its name from the wild boar evicted to make way for the venue. Entry $25CUC including drinks and transfers. Tues–Sat 9pm–late.

Sol Club Cayo Coco Playa Las Coloradas ☎ 33 30 1280 With live salsa bands playing at top volume, glitter balls and a dancefloor of illuminated tiles, the disco here is raucous, glitzy and lots of fun without being too tacky. Free to guests of all Solmelía-owned hotels, otherwise $5CUC including open bar. Tues & Thurs midnight–2am.

Cayo Guillermo

Bordered by pearl-white sand melting into opal waters, sleepy **CAYO GUILLERMO**, west of Cayo Coco and joined to it by a 15km causeway, is a quieter, more serene retreat than its neighbour: a place to fish, dive and relax. The cays' colony of twelve thousand **flamingos** (celebrated in all Cuban tourist literature) gather here to feed, and although they are wary of passing traffic, you can usually glimpse them swaying in the shallows and feeding on the sandbanks as you cross the causeway. As the presence of the birds testifies, the waters around Cayo Guillermo are home to an abundance of sea life including a wealth of fish, notably marlin, and the marina here offers a range of deep-sea fishing expeditions.

At only thirteen square kilometres the cay is tiny, but its 4km of deserted **beaches** seem infinite nonetheless. **Development** on Cayo Guillermo has been steadily growing, and although still considerably quieter than its rowdier neighbour, it's no longer the peaceful haven it once was. However, all the hotels are fairly close together on **Playa El Medio** and **Playa El Paso**, while the rest of the cay's stunning **beaches** remain largely untouched – with so much space, you'll never have a problem finding solitude. It's quite a trek from the mainland if you're not staying overnight, but arriving early and spending a day lounging on the sands and exploring the beautiful offshore coral reef definitely merits the effort. **Day-passes** to enter any of the all-inclusive hotels (which cover all meals and drinks) will set you back $40–50CUC, though there are plenty of other places to access the beach if that's all you want.

Playa El Medio and Playa El Paso

The two main beaches on Guillermo are **Playa El Medio** and **Playa El Paso** on the north coast, where all the hotels are located. Popular with package-tour holidaymakers, both are suitably idyllic with shallow swimming areas and lengthy swathes of sand. El Medio

DIVING AND DEEP-SEA FISHING AROUND CAYO MEDIA LUNA

The shallow waters around **Cayo Media Luna** make it a popular destination for snorkellers, while deeper offshore, the kaleidoscopic **coral reef** is rich with sponges, anemone, fish and corals. Marlin, tuna, barracuda and sailfish are the potential haul for anglers.

Two daily **dive trips** to the best sites around Cayo Media Luna are organized by the Green Moray International Dive Centre (☎ 33 30 1680) beside the *Melía Cayo Guillermo* hotel. Prices start at $50CUC for a single dive including equipment, and reduce with the more you book. Some divers have complained about lax safety checks here, however– something to bear in mind if you are a novice.

For **deep-sea fishing** excursions ($90CUC per person for half day) and all-day yacht "seafaris" ($35CUC per person), with time set aside for offshore swimming and snorkelling, head to the Cayo Guillermo Fishing Club at Marina Puerto Sol (☎ 33 30 1737), which is back on Cayo Guillermo at Playa El Paso.

also has towering **sand dunes** celebrated as the highest in the Caribbean, and on low tides sandbars allow you to wade far out to sea.

Playa Pilar

On the western tip of Cayo Guillermo, gorgeous **Playa Pilar** is named after Ernest Hemingway's yacht, *Pilar*, and was the author's favourite hideaway in Cuba. With limpid clear shallows and squeaky-clean beaches, Playa Pilar is without doubt the top beach choice on Guillermo, if not in the entire cays; however, there are no facilities here other than a small beach bar (see p.328).

6

Cayo Media Luna
Return boat-trip from Playa Pilar $25CUC

From Playa Pilar, speedboats ferry sunbathers and snorkellers the short distance to **Cayo Media Luna**, a tiny crescent cay just across the water, with nothing other than a small, simple café. Add a few more convertible pesos to the cost of the boat trip over and you can stop off to go snorkelling at a nearby reef.

ACCOMMODATION   CAYO GUILLERMO

Iberostar Daiquiri Playa El Paso ☎33 30 1650, Ⓦiberostar.com. Despite the palatial reception area, this hotel lacks the charm of its neighbours. Rooms are pleasant enough, strung along corridors in rather austere blocks done out in earthy tones and topped with crenellations, and there are four restaurants as well as a nightly show and disco. **$270CUC**

★ **Meliá Cayo Guillermo** Playa El Paso ☎33 30 1680, Ⓦsolmelia.com. Popular with divers on account of the nearby scuba centre, this swish hotel is the smartest on the strip following a refit in 2011. Rooms are attractive and the range of restaurants includes Italian, international and an outdoor grill. There's a high-tech gym, beauty salon and tennis courts, and a long rickety wooden pier on the beach that's perfect for sunset strolls. **$190CUC**

Sol Club Cayo Guillermo Playa El Medio ☎33 30 1760, Ⓦsolmelia.com. Small, friendly, painted in pretty pastels and patronized largely by couples and honeymooners, this hotel has a very Spanish feel with its immaculately tiled reception area full of tinkling fountains. The appealing, sunny rooms have wooden furniture, balconies and all the standard facilities. **$271CUC**

Villa Cojímar Playa El Paso ☎33 30 1712, Ⓦgran-caribe.com. Set apart from the others, this calm and quiet hotel has snazzy blue-and-yellow bungalows spread around spacious, manicured gardens, as well as a large free-form pool, four restaurants and ample sports facilities. It's noticeably less expensive than the other hotels here, and the website offers good discounted deals. **$153CUC**

EATING, DRINKING AND ENTERTAINMENT

Cayo Media Luna beach bar A few hundred metres out to sea, the wooden bar here mirrors the one on Playa Pilar, with the same expensive menu of barbecued fish and lobster. Daily 11am–dusk.

ERNEST HEMINGWAY'S SUBMARINE HUNT

The affection that **Ernest Hemingway** had for Cuba sprang from his love of **fishing**, and numerous photographs of him brandishing dripping marlin and swordfish testify to his success around the clear waters of the northern cays. He came to know the waters well and, when the United States entered World War II, Hemingway, already having seen action in World War I and the Spanish Civil War, was more than ready to do his bit.

With the full support of the US ambassador to Cuba, Spruille Braden, he began to spy on Nazi sympathizers living in Cuba. He gathered enough information to have his 12m fishing boat **Pilar** commissioned and equipped by the Chief of Naval Intelligence for Central America as a kind of Q-ship (an armed and disguised merchant ship used as a decoy or to destroy submarines). His search-and-destroy missions for Nazi submarines off the cays continued until 1944 and he was commended by the ambassador, although according to some critics – notably his wife Martha Gellhorn – the whole thing was mainly a ruse for Hemingway to obtain rationed petrol for his fishing trips. Although he never engaged in combat with submarines, Hemingway's boys' own fantasies found their way into print in the novel *Islands in the Stream*.

6

Cuba Libre Playa El Paso This tiny beach bar between the *Iberostar Daiquiri* and *Meliá Cayo Guillermo* hotels serves fresh fish, lobster, fried chicken and drinks. Mains are around $7CUC. Daily 11am–dusk.

Playa Pilar beach bar Excellent but pricey barbecued fish and lobster, served up in a simple wooden lean-to with skinny cats twirling around your ankles as you eat. Opening times fluctuate depending on the whims of the chef, but you are usually guaranteed service around lunchtime. Daily 11am–dusk.

Punta Rasa beach bar Halfway along the unpaved road to Playa Pilar, a turning to the right leads to the small wooden pavilion on the beach of the same name, which offers cheap chicken and costly seafood as well as beer, cocktails and soft drinks. Every night the tables are pushed back to make space for post-dinner dancing. Daily, 24 hours.

Cayo Paredón Grande

Some 12km to the northeast of Cayo Coco and connected to it by a small causeway starting around 6km east of Playa Las Coloradas, **Cayo Paredón Grande** is a thumbnail of a cay. With a couple of clean, pleasant beaches on the northern coastline, it makes an ideal retreat if you can get there, particularly as the view over the sea as you cross the causeway is glorious. The islet's focal point is the elegant nineteenth-century **lighthouse** (no entry) on the rocky headland of the northern tip, built by Chinese immigrant workers to guide ships through the coral-filled waters. If you visit Paredón Grande on a day-trip, take provisions with you as there are no facilities. The causeway leads through the uninhabited **Cayo Romano**, which is technically in Camagüey province though usually treated as an extension of the major cays.

Archipiélago de los Jardines de la Reina

Back on the mainland, the area below Ciego de Ávila is made up of agricultural farming areas and small one-street towns like **Venezuela** and **Silveira**, each a clutch of humble concrete houses (built since the Revolution to house workers who previously lived in shacks), a central grocery store and a doctor. The only reason for heading south of the provincial capital, however, is for the outstanding diving and fishing at the **Archipiélago de los Jardines de la Reina**, a cluster of over six hundred tiny virgin cays some 80km from the mainland. The jumping-off point for trips to the cays is the barren fishing village of **Júcaro**, 32km south of Ciego de Ávila. It's a miserable collection of wooden shacks and half-finished cement constructions set around the

---

DIVING AT THE JARDINES DE LA REINA

The diving at **Jardines de la Reina** is considered by many to be among the best in the world. More than eighty **dive sites** around the archipelago boast caves, canyons, and wall, spur and groove **coral** formations. The real draw, though, is the phenomenal abundance of **fish**, including many large species. Spectacular **feeding shows** are staged by Avalon staff, who attract scores of sharks with scraps of fish. Also abundant are monster-sized goliath groupers, barracudas, cubera snappers and tarpons; with luck, you may see eagle rays, hammerhead sharks, lemon sharks, nurse sharks and turtles.

All diving, fishing and accommodation is organized by the Italian specialist **tour operator** Avalon, which has been granted exclusive operating rights in this area and caters for no more than seven hundred divers per year. Accommodation is provided aboard *La Tortuga*, an air-conditioned, seven-cabin floating **hotel**, or on one of five impressive yachts. More information and booking is available directly from Avalon (☎78 26 6879, ⓦcubandivingcenters .com & ⓦcubanfishingcenters.com), or, more reliably, you can also book with Avalon through the UK operator **Scuba Place** (☎44 7644 8252), whose local office is on the seafront in Júcaro opposite the square (☎33 98 1004). Prices start at around $1500CUC for a stay of six nights on board, including full board, fifteen dives and transfers to and from Havana.

6

LA TROCHA FORTIFICATIONS

Driving north to south on the road running from Júcaro to Morón via Ciego de Ávila, you'll pass the remnants of an old Spanish **garrison** which at one time divided the province from north to south. The tumbledown, stubby structures are the remains of a fortification line known as **La Trocha**, built between April 1871 and 1873. Increasingly worried by the Mambises (the rebel army fighting for independence) and their plans to move west through the island, the Spanish General Blas Villate de la Hera planned a 67km-long row of fortifications to block the advance. The forts were made of concrete with solid walls of stone, brick and wood and built at intervals of 3–4km. Each was manned by a single sentry, who had to enter by a removable wooden staircase, and each had two cannon. It was supposedly an impassable chain of defence, but the ineffectiveness of the whole idea was immediately apparent in 1874 when the Cuban General Manuel Suárez triumphantly breezed through with his cavalry. Most of the forts are in a poor state of repair today, though the odd one still gives an impression of its original appearance. Plans to restore them have been under way for some time.

derelict-looking Parque Martí and a malodorous fishing port. Don't let this deter you, however, as the real beauty round these parts is hidden underwater. As the whole area was declared a National Marine Park in 1996, protected from commercial fishing and with public access strictly controlled, the only way to get out to the cays is on a fishing or diving trip, usually for a minimum of six days, with the Italian specialist tour operator Avalon (see box, p.328). The cays themselves, all completely deserted, are mostly covered in scrub with one of the only significant beaches at **Cayo Caguamas**, in the waters of Camagüey, where you can see iguanas and turtles, the latter venturing out onto the sand in the moonlight.

Camagüey city

Nestled 30km from the north coast in the heart of Camagüey, the provincial capital of **CAMAGÜEY** is aptly called the city of legends, its winding streets and wizened buildings weaving an atmosphere of intrigue. On first view it is a bewildering place to negotiate, with a seemingly incomprehensible labyrinth of roads that were laid out in a futile attempt to confuse marauding pirates (see box, p.332). It is this maze-like layout, highly unusual for the Americas, which won the historic centre of Camagüey UNESCO World Heritage status in 2008. So long as you're not in a hurry to get anywhere, the odd wrong turn needn't matter too much, and an aimless wander along the narrow cobbled streets overhung by delicate balustrades and Rococo balconies is the best way to explore, as you round corners onto handsome parks and happen upon crumbling churches.

Despite its quaint appearance, Camagüey is by no means a sleepy colonial town. There are regular free concerts in the Plaza de los Trabajadores and in summer alfresco cinema screenings, and townsfolk pull out all the stops for the annual June **carnival**, the highlight of the Camagüeyan calendar. Unfortunately Camagüey suffers from more of a **jinetero** problem (see p.57) than other provincial towns. Most of the attention is easy enough to deal with, with a firm "no gracias", but there have been reports of bag snatching, particularly at night and around the Casino Campestre.

Sprinkled with churches and colonial squares, Camagüey will take a couple of days to explore fully, although those breezing through can do the main sights in a half-day or so. Most are in easy walking distance of the main shopping drag, **Calle Maceo**, including a cluster of churches and the **Casa Natal de Ignacio Agramonte**, birthplace of the city's most revered son, a martyr of the struggle for independence. South of

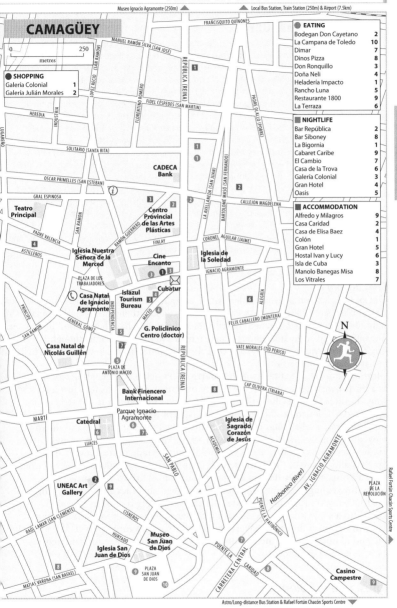

CAMAGÜEY

Museo Ignacio Agramonte (250m) ▲   ▲ Local Bus Station, Train Station (250m) & Airport (7.5km)

FRANCISQUITO QUIÑONES

MANUEL RAMÓN SILVA (SAN JOSÉ)

REPÚBLICA (REINA)

PADRE OLALLO (POBRE)

● **SHOPPING**
Galería Colonial	1
Galería Julián Morales	2

HEREDIA

LÓPEZ RECIO (SAN RAMÓN)

FLORENTINO ROMERO

FIDEL CÉSPEDES (SAN MARTÍN)

INDUSTRIA

SOLITARIO (SANTA RITA)

CADECA Bank

OSCAR PRIMELLES (SAN ESTEBAN)

GRAL ESPINOSA

LA AVELLANEDA (SAN JUAN)

BARTOLOMÉ MASÓ (SAN FERNANDO)

CALLEJÓN MAGDELENA

Teatro Principal

PADRE VALENCIA

SAN RAMÓN

RAMÓN GUERRERO

FINLAY

Centro Próvincial de las Artes Plásticas

ASTILLEROS

Iglesia Nuestra Señora de la Merced

Cine Encanto

Iglesia de la Soledad

CORONEL AGUILAR (JAIME)

PLAZA DE LOS TRABAJADORES

IGNACIO AGRAMONTE

Casa Natal de Ignacio Agramonte

Islazul Tourism Bureau

Cubatur

MACEO

ALEGRÍA

PRÍNCIPE

GENERAL GÓMEZ

SAN RAMÓN

INDEPENDENCIA

G. Policlínico Centro (doctor)

FÉLIX CABALLERO (MONTERA)

Casa Natal de Nicolás Guillén

REPÚBLICA (REINA)

VATE MORALES (TÍO PERICO)

PLAZA DE ANTONIO MACEO

Bank Finencero Internacional

CAP OLIVERA (TRIANA)

MARTÍ

Parque Ignacio Agramonte

Catedral

LUACES

Iglesia de Sagrado Corazón de Jesús

ACADEMIA

SAN PABLO

Haníbonico (River)

UNEAC Art Gallery

CISNEROS

AV. IGNACIO AGRAMONTE

PLAZA DE LA REVOLUCIÓN

RAÚL LAMAR (SAN CLEMENTE)

HURTADO

Museo San Juan de Dios

PUENTE LA HATIBÓNICO

Iglesia San Juan de Dios

PLAZA SAN JUAN DE DIOS

PUENTE LA CARIDAD

CARRETERA CENTRAL

Casino Campestre

MATÍAS VARONA (SAN RAFAEL)

Rafael Fortún Chacón Sports Centre

Astro/Long-distance Bus Station & Rafael Fortún Chacón Sports Centre ▼

● **EATING**
Bodegan Don Cayetano	2
La Campana de Toledo	10
Dimar	7
Dinos Pizza	8
Don Ronquillo	3
Doña Neli	4
Heladería Impacto	1
Rancho Luna	5
Restaurante 1800	9
La Terraza	6

■ **NIGHTLIFE**
Bar República	2
Bar Siboney	8
La Bigornia	1
Cabaret Caribe	9
El Cambio	7
Casa de la Trova	6
Galería Colonial	3
Gran Hotel	4
Oasis	5

■ **ACCOMMODATION**
Alfredo y Milagros	9
Casa Caridad	2
Casa de Elisa Baez	4
Colón	1
Gran Hotel	5
Hostal Ivan y Lucy	6
Isla de Cuba	3
Manolo Banegas Misa	8
Los Vitrales	7

6

here, past the Plaza de Antonio Maceo, is the congenial **Parque Agramonte**, Camagüey's main park, home to the city's **cathedral** and close to the more picturesque **Sagrado Corazón de Jesús**. Further south again is the **Plaza de San Juan de Dios** which, blessed with the **Iglesia San Juan de Dios** and **Museo de San Juan de Dios**, is Camagüey's most attractive colonial square. Although the northern end of town has fewer sights, it's still worth venturing up for a breeze around the quietly impressive **Museo Ignacio Agramonte**.

6

PIRATES IN CAMAGÜEY

Although not the only Cuban city to suffer constant attacks from **pirates**, irresistibly wealthy Camagüey was one consistently plagued, with buccaneers regularly rampaging through the city before retiring to the northern cays or the Isla de la Juventud to hide their spoils. To confound pirates, the centre of Camagüey was built as a web of narrow and twisted streets rather than the usual colonial city plan, with roads laid out in a regular grid pattern; however, the design did not deter the invaders, who left many legends in their wake. The first pirate to arrive was the singularly unpleasant Frenchman **Jacques de Sores** in 1555, who roamed the farms on the north coast stealing cows, cheese and women. (These last he would abandon violated in Cayo Coco to the mercy of the elements.) In 1668, English buccaneer **Henry Morgan** – the terror of the Caribbean seas – and his men managed to occupy the city for several days before making off with a hefty booty of gold and jewels belonging to the Spanish bourgeoisie. With a dashing show of irreverence, he is also reputed to have locked the town elders into the Catedral de Santa Iglesia to starve them into revealing the whereabouts of their riches. Struggling to reassert itself eleven years later, in 1679 the city fell prey to the wiles of another Frenchman, **François de Granmont**. Nicknamed *El Caballero* (the gentleman), he sacked the city and captured fourteen women. After nearly a month of occupying the town he marched to the coast and released all the women unharmed, thus earning his nickname.

Brief history

One of Cuba's seven original settlements, Camagüey was established between 1514 and 1515 on the site of a sizeable Amerindian village, and although the original inhabitants were swiftly eradicated, traces of burial sites and ceramics have been found in the area. The only legacy of the indigenous people remains in the city's name, thought to originate from the word *camagua*, a wild shrub common to the lowlands that's believed to have magical properties.

Initially known as **Santa María del Puerto del Príncipe**, the fledgling city started life as a port town on the north coast, where present-day Nuevitas lies. Just a year later, when farmers from Seville arrived in 1516, it was moved to the fertile lands of present-day Caonao on the northwestern edge of the province, until, according to some sources, a rebel band of Amerindians forced the settlers out, and the town moved once more, to its present site, in 1528. Straddling the Tínima and Hatibonico rivers, so as to be in the middle of the trade route between Sancti Spíritus and Bayamo, the newly settled town began to consolidate itself. During the 1600s its economy developed around sugar plantations and cattle farms, generating enough income to build distinguished churches and civil buildings in the following century. Despite intermittent ransacking by pirates, Puerto Príncipe grew into a sophisticated and elegant city, one its townsfolk fought hard to win from the Spanish during the Wars of Independence. Eventually, in 1903, following the end of Spanish rule, the city dropped its lengthy moniker and adopted the name by which it is now known.

Iglesia de la Soledad

Maceo esq. Ignacio Agramonte • Daily 8am–noon • Free

The town is centred on the two streets of **Maceo** and **República**, home to the most picturesque hotels as well as the hard currency shops and peso markets. Presiding over the intersection of the two streets is the **Iglesia de la Soledad**, tiered like a wedding cake and with a lofty tower that can be seen from all over the city. Although the exterior is in disrepair, the **interior**, its domed roof painted with Baroque frescoes, merits a look. There has been a church on this site since 1697 (the original was built from wood and guano), though the present structure dates from 1758. Like others in the town, the church has its very own creation myth. Apparently one rainy morning an animal carrier's cart became stuck in the mud in the road in front of the site. Everyone gathered around to push the wagon free and in the process a box bounced off the back and smashed open to reveal a statue of the Virgin. As the cart-driver could lay no claim to it, it was taken as a sign that the Virgin wanted a chapel built on this spot.

Centro Provincial de las Artes Plásticas

República no.289 • Daily 10am–6pm • Free

About halfway along República, the **Centro Provincial de las Artes Plásticas** stages a mixed bag of temporary exhibitions that are well worth dipping into – if only for the cool, airy space. The works featured are predominantly paintings by artists from Camagüey as well as other provinces, and are of a generally high standard, affording an insight into visual arts in Cuba away from the tourist trail.

Iglesia Nuestra Señora de la Merced

Plaza de los Trabajadores • Mon 3.30–6pm, Tues–Sat 9.30–11.30am & 3.30–6pm • Free

One block west of Maceo is the **Plaza de los Trabajadores**, a disappointingly modern polygon of tarmac beautified by a border of attractive colonial buildings and the **Iglesia Nuestra Señora de la Merced**, Camagüey's most impressive building. A slick of paint has taken the edge off its whimsical appeal, though the romance of its whispered origins endures undiminished. The story goes that one day in the seventeenth century, when the plaza was still said to be submerged beneath a lake, the townsfolk heard shouts and screams from the thickets on the banks. Terrified to approach, they kept watch from a distance over several days until, to their amazement, a shimmering white church emerged from the water. Beckoning from the portal was a priest with a cross clasped in his hand: the Merced church had arrived. A more prosaic history tells that the church was built as a convent in 1747, and the rooms to the left of the chapel, set around a cool and attractive central patio, still serve as such today.

The church which adjoins the convent and chapel is a confection of styles following several rebuilds and extensions. Inside, the richly ornate neo-Gothic altar imported from Spain contrasts with the delicate eighteenth-century Baroque balconies swooping above. The most intriguing item is the **Santo Sepulcro**, an ornate silver coffin, thickly coated with intertwined hand-beaten bells and flowers, made in 1762 from 25,000 molten silver coins by Mexican silversmith Juan de Benítez, and commissioned by an ill-fated merchant (see box below).

THE STORY OF EL SANTO SEPULCRO

In eighteenth-century Puerto Príncipe (as Camagüey was then known), a wealthy merchant named **Manuel de Agüero** employed a widowed housekeeper, **Señora Moya**. Master and servant each had a son of the same age, and it seemed natural for the boys to play and grow up together. Agüero paid for both to go to Havana to study at the university, and they seemed assured of bright futures. Tragedy struck when both young men met and fell in love with the same woman, and in a fit of pique Moya challenged Agüero to a **duel** and killed him.

Distraught, Agüero Senior promptly banished the murderous boy and his mother from his sight, lest his remaining sons avenge their brother's death. However, his woes were not over, as his wife, sick with a broken heart, wasted away and died soon after. Torn apart by grief, Agüero decided to become a friar, and, with his surviving sons' approval, poured their inheritance into jewels and treasures for the church. The most splendid of all his tributes was the **Santo Sepulcro**, the silver coffin that he commissioned in readiness of his own death. Long seen as a hero who rose above personal disaster to overcome bitterness, his is a puzzling tale of uneasy colonial values.

6

The crypt

Guided tours daily 8.30am–5pm – ask at the convent • Free

Hidden beneath the church, accessible by a tiny flight of stairs behind the main altar, is a fascinatingly macabre little **crypt**. Formerly an underground cemetery that ran all the way to López Recio, 500m away, much of it was bricked up following a fire and only a claustrophobic sliver remains. Among the musty **relics**, several life-sized statues gleam in the half-light, while embedded in the walls are the skeletal remains of a woman and her child: look carefully and you may see cockroaches skittering across the bones. There's no charge but contributions towards the upkeep of the church are much appreciated.

Casa Natal de Ignacio Agramonte

Plaza de los Trabajadores • Tues–Sat 10am–6pm, Sun 8am–noon • $2CUC

On the south side of Plaza de los Trabajadores is the **Casa Natal de Ignacio Agramonte**, an attractive colonial house with dark-wood balustrades. Birthplace of the local hero of the first War of Independence, Ignacio Agramonte, it was converted after his death into a market and then later, adding insult to injury, into a bar. It opened as a museum in 1973. All Agramonte's possessions were confiscated when he took up arms against the Spanish colonial powers and, although never returned to him while he was alive, they now form part of the displays here. The standard of life enjoyed by wealthy sugar plantation owners like the Agramontes is well highlighted by their impressive furniture, including a well-crafted piano and oversized *tinajones* out in the central patio. Free piano recitals are held every Saturday night at 8.30pm.

Casa Natal de Nicolás Guillén

Calle Hermanos Agüero 58 Cisneros y Príncipe • Mon–Fri 8am–noon & 1–4.30pm, Sat 8am–noon • $1CUC

One block south of Plaza de los Trabajadores is the **Casa Natal de Nicolás Guillén**. An Afro-Cuban born in 1902, Guillén was one of Cuba's foremost poets and is renowned throughout Latin America, particularly for his eloquent pieces on the condition of black people in Cuba, whose profile he raised and cause he championed in his writing. A founding member of the National Union of Writers and Artists (UNEAC), an organization responsible for much of the promotion of the arts in Cuba, and recipient of the Lenin Peace Prize, he died in 1989. The small house has relics of his life, but nothing really gives much of an insight into his days there. There are, however, many of his poems in poster form on the walls, and a good selection of photographs to peruse.

IGNACIO AGRAMONTE – DAREDEVIL OF THE WARS OF INDEPENDENCE

The son of wealthy Camagüeyan cattle farmers, **Ignacio Agramonte** (1841–73) studied law in Havana and then in Spain before returning in 1868 to become a revolutionary leader in the first War of Independence against Spain. Back in his homeland, he incited the men of Camagüey to take up arms against the Spanish, taking the town at the end of that year and forming a small unorthodox republic with some of the local farm owners. He was known as the **Daredevil of the Wars of Independence** for his often misguided valour – on one occasion, when one of his fighters was captured by the Spanish, he dashed off to rescue his unfortunate compatriot from the 120-strong enemy column, armed only with a machete and 34 of his most trusted men – and actually lived to tell the tale. Killed aged 32 on the battlefields of Jimaguayú, Agramonte's youth as well as his passion for his province guaranteed him a revered place as one of the local martyrs of the Wars of Independence.

TINAJONES

Tucked beneath the trees in Parque Agramonte are the large bulbous clay jars known as **tinajones**. Seen throughout Camagüey, they were originally storage jars used to transport wine, oil and grain and were introduced by the Spanish as the solution to the city's water shortage, placed beneath gutters so that they could fill with water. Slightly tapered at one end, they were half-buried in earth, keeping the water cool and fresh. They soon came to be produced in the town, and every house had one outside; inevitably, they became a status symbol, and a family's wealth could be assessed by the style and quantity of their *tinajones*. They also came in handy during the Wars of Independence when soldiers escaping the Spanish would hide in them. Indeed, so proud are the Camagüeyans of their *tinajones* that a local saying has it that all who drink the water from one fall in love and never leave town.

6

Parque Ignacio Agramonte

A few blocks south of the Casa Natal de Nicolás Guillén is the bijou **Plaza de Antonio Maceo**, from where it's one block south through narrow streets to **Parque Ignacio Agramonte**. Filled with shady tamarind trees, *tinajones* and marble benches, this small square is the town's social centre. Each corner is pegged by a **royal palm** to symbolize the deaths of four independence fighters – leader Joaquín Agüero, Tomás Betancourt y Zayas, Fernando de Zayas and Miguel Benavides – shot for treason here by the Spanish in the early struggles for independence. The men were immediately hailed as martyrs and the townsfolk planted the palms as a secret tribute, the Spanish authorities ignorant of their significance. Dominating the *parque*'s south side is the large but rather unremarkable **Catedral de Santa Iglesia**.

Iglesia de Nuestra Señora del Carmen

Plaza del Carmen • Tues–Sat 8am–noon & 3–5pm, services Sun 11am & 6pm • Free

Ten minutes' walk west of Parque Ignacio Agramonte is Camagüey's only twin-towered church, the **Iglesia de Nuestra Señora del Carmen**, completed in 1825. The simple interior is enlivened by bright panels of stained glass in red, blue and green, while the cupola ceiling painting of various saints is worth a look. Outside the church, the photogenic **Plaza del Carmen** is peppered with amusing life-sized statues of local people – several of their real life counterparts attempt to capitalize on their bronze incarnations by asking for money in return for a posed photograph.

Iglesia de Sagrado Corazón de Jesús

Plaza de la Juventud • Daily 9am–noon • Free

A ten-minute walk along Luaces from Parque Agramonte is one of the city's only twentieth-century churches, the **Iglesia de Sagrado Corazón de Jesús**. Built in 1920, it is quaint rather than awesome, but nevertheless worth a look if you are passing. After passing through the forbidding mahogany doorway, you'll find yourself under a neo-Gothic crossed roof; lining the walls are four wooden altars skilfully painted in trompe l'oeil to look like marble, typical of the era. Birds nest behind the marble main altar, while light trickling through cracked stained glass gives this rather faded church a pleasing air of serenity.

Plaza de San Juan de Dios

Six blocks south of the Sagrado Corazón is the eighteenth-century **Plaza de San Juan de Dios**, the city's most photogenic square. A neat cobbled plaza with red-tiled pavements and little traffic, it's bordered with well-kept lemon-yellow and dusty-pink buildings, their windows hemmed with twists of sky-blue balustrades. A stall selling artisans' products can be found in the square most days.

Iglesia San Juan de Dios

Plaza de San Juan de Dios • Daily 8am–noon • Free

On the northern corner of Plaza de San Juan de Diosis is the **Iglesia San Juan de Dios**, built in 1728. A single squat bell tower rises like a turret from a simple symmetrical facade saved from austerity by soft hues of green and cream. The dark interior is richly Baroque, typical of Cuban colonial style, with rows of chocolatey wood pews and a gilded altar. Note the original brick floor, the only one remaining in any church in Camagüey.

Museo de San Juan de Dios

Plaza de San Juan de Dios • Tues–Sat 9am–5pm, Sun 9am–1pm • $1CUC, including Spanish-speaking guide

Fitted snugly to the side of the Iglesia San Juan de Dios is the old **Hospital de San Juan de Dios**. It was to this hospital that the body of Ignacio Agramonte was brought after he was slain on the battlefield; the Spanish hid his body from the Cubans without allowing them to pay their last respects and burned him as an example to other would-be dissidents. It now houses the **Museo de San Juan de Dios**, with some early maps and photographs of the town in bygone years. The display only takes up a small corner of the hospital, and the real pleasure lies in looking around the well-preserved building, admiring the original heavy wood staircase, cracked *vitrales*, courtyard filled with *tinajones* and palms, and the view over the church tower from the second floor.

Casino Campestre

East of Plaza de San Juan de Dios is the main road through the town, Avenida Ignacio Agramonte, which runs parallel to the murky Río Hatibonico. On the other side of this is the vast **Casino Campestre**, the biggest city park in Cuba. Spliced by the Hatibonico and Juan del Toro rivers and dappled by royal palms, it has a beer tent, children's area and a bandstand, while among the shady trees are monuments to local martyr Salvador Cisneros Betancourt and former mayor Manuel Ramón Silva.

Rafael Fortún Chacón Sports Centre

Daily 6am–7pm • ☎ 32 28 8893

To the east of the Casino Campestre is the huge concrete **Rafael Fortún Chacón Sports Centre**. Named after Camagüey's 100m athletics champion of the 1950s, it boasts a swimming pool and large arena with activities as varied as tae kwon do, basketball and trampolining, as well as a beauty centre offering mud wraps, honey treatments and the chance to bake in the sauna for a nominal fee. Amateur sports competitions, including judo and basketball, and salsa concerts are often held here: ask for details at reception.

Museo Ignacio Agramonte

Avenida de los Mártires • Tues–Thurs & Sat 10am–5.45pm, Sun 8am–2pm • $2CUC plus $1CUC photos

While the north end of Camagüey has few sights, it's worth making the effort to check out the **Museo Ignacio Agramonte**, at the top end of República. Also known as the Museo Provincial, it has an elegant Art Deco exterior, the unassuming white facade masking its sleek lines and geometric lettering. While there's nothing within to suggest a connection with its namesake, the museum's engaging array of exhibits includes some quality nineteenth-century **furniture**, most notably a *tinajero* washstand with a stone basin inset and some fine Sèvres china. Most impressive is the **fine art collection**, which includes a Victor Manuel García original, *Muchacha*, and a good example of the Cuban vanguard movement, which introduced modern art to the country between 1920 and 1960.

ARRIVAL AND DEPARTURE CAMAGÜEY CITY

By plane Daily flights from Havana arrive at the Ignacio Agramonte airport (☎ 32 26 1010), 7km northeast of the city, from where you can catch a bus (5 daily) or taxi (around $4CUC) into town.

Destinations Havana: (9 weekly; 1hr 35min).

Airlines Cubana, República no.400 esq. Correa (Mon–Fri 8am–4pm, Sat 8.30–11.00am; ☎ 32 29 2156).

By train Trains from Havana and the neighbouring provinces arrive at the frenetic train station (☎ 32 29 2633) on the northern edge of town, next door to the local bus station. A ride to the centre in a *bicitaxi* should cost $10–15CUP, a taxi $4CUC. For those who feel up to negotiating the imbroglio of town planning, it's a fifteen-minute walk along Van Horne to República, the straight road leading directly into the centre.

Destinations Bayamo (1 daily; 6hr); Ciego de Ávila (1 daily; 2hr); Havana (3 daily; 8hr); Holguín (1 daily; 3hr); Matanzas (3 daily; 6hr); Morón (1 daily; 3hr); Santiago de Cuba (1 daily; 6hr); Las Tunas (1 daily; 2hr).

By bus Víazul buses (call ☎ 32 27 0396 Mon–Fri 10am–6pm, Sat 10am–2pm for reservations) pull in at the bus station on the Carretera Central, 3km south of the town centre; an unmetered taxi or horse-drawn carriage into town from here should cost $6–10CUC.

Destinations Ciego de Ávila (2 daily; 1hr 30min); Havana (2 daily; 8hr); Santa Clara (2 daily; 4 hr); Sancti Spíritus (2 daily; 2hr 30min); Santiago de Cuba (3 daily; 6hr); Trinidad (1 daily; 5hr).

GETTING AROUND

By car Car rental is available from Cubacar in *Hotel Plaza* (Mon–Sat 8am–4pm; ☎ 32 28 2413) and Havanautos at Independencia no.210 (Mon–Sat 9am–5pm; ☎ 32 29 6270).

By bicitax You can flag these down anywhere in the city, and they usually cost no more than $5-6CUC for any journey within the centre.

By taxi Call Cubacar (☎ 32 29 2550) or Transtur (☎ 32 27 1015).

INFORMATION AND TOURS

Cubanacán One of the best sources of information in town, with offices at the *Hotel Plaza* (Mon–Sat 9am–5pm; ☎ 32 29 7374) and at no.1 Calle Van Horne e/ Avellaneda y República (Mon–Fri 9am–noon & 1–5pm, Sat 9am–noon; ☎ 32 28 3551) that also sell maps, phonecards and flight, bus and train tickets, and organize day-trips around the province, including the Jardines de la Reina.

Cubatur The office at Ignacio Agramonte no.421 (Mon–Fri 9am–noon; ☎ 32 25 4785, ✉ cubatur@cmg

.colombus.cu) can just about cobble together a hotel reservation in Santa Lucía but little else, though staff can assist with extending tourist visas. More useful is the Paradiso desk in the Cubatur office, which sells tickets for the Cabaret Caribe.

Islazul The tourism bureau at no.448 Ignacio Agramonte e/ López Recio y Independencia (Mon–Fri 1–5pm, Sat 8am–noon; ☎ 32 29 8947) sells maps, and has a car rental and taxi desk.

ACCOMMODATION

In comparison to the towns in Ciego de Ávila, Camagüey has a decent variety of reasonably priced **hotels**, most of them charming hideaways rather than fancy tourist palaces. There are also a number of excellent, centrally located **casas particulares** to choose from. Be aware that some touts in Camagüey are particularly aggressive and will stoop to underhand tricks to guide you to a house that will pay them commission. A problem particular to Camagüey is *jineteros* (see box, p.37), who offer to park your car safely, often pretending to be affiliated with the house in which you're staying, and then use the car for their own purposes.

HOTELS

★ **Colón** República no.472 e/ San José y San Martín ☎ 32 25 4878, ✉ reservas@hcolon.camaguey.cu. This beautiful hotel in the heart of the city is almost a museum piece. Built in 1927, it has been artfully renovated, preserving its Baroque balconies, exquisite tiling, cracked marble staircase and corridors bathed in greenish light. The comfortable rooms, furnished with reproduction 1920s furniture, are small and lack natural light, but this is more

than compensated for by the building's class and character; the best rooms are arranged around a pretty patio housing a bar and a veranda where breakfast is served. **$60CUC**

Gran Hotel Maceo no.67 e/ Ignacio Agramonte y General Gómez ☎ 32 29 2093. Graciously faded eighteenth-century building that became a hotel in the 1930s, with well-maintained rooms; the best have balconies overlooking the busy street below, though others are a little pokey. The small pool (with regular synchronized

6

swimming displays for guests), elegant marble dining room with panoramic views, and a dark and sultry piano bar are nice additions. **$78CUC**

★ **Isla de Cuba** San Esteban no.453 e/ Lopez Recio y Popular ☎32 29 2248. With a clean, airy and pleasant feel, this hotel set one block back from República offers the cheapest accommodation in town. Breakfast included. **$15CUC**

CASAS PARTICULARES

Alfredo y Milagros Cisneros no.124 esq. Raúl Lamar ☎32 29 7436, ✉allan.carnot@gmail.com. Very professionally run outfit, with English and French spoken. Both of the rooms are well appointed, with fridges, fans, a/c, private bathrooms and desks, and there are extensive menus for meals and cocktails. The owners' son, a trained masseur, offers a massage service. A pretty patio tiled in pink and green marble and a tropical fish tank complete the picture. Garage parking available. **$35CUC**

Casa Caridad Oscar Primelles no.310a e/ Bartolomé Masó y Padre Olallo ☎32 29 1554, ✉caridadgarciavalera@gmail.com. Three rooms – with private bathrooms, a/c and fully stocked minibar-style fridges – arranged along a sunny passageway. The best feature of the spacious house is a pretty garden complete with a large *tinajon* under a flowery bower. Garage parking available. **$25CUC**

★ **Casa de Elisa Baez** Astillero no.24 e/ San Ramón y Lugareño ☎32 29 2054. One double room and huge, tasty home-cooked meals in a comfortable, clean and very friendly spot close to the centre. One of the best-value houses in town. **$20CUC**

★ **Hostal Ivan y Lucy** Alegría no.23 e/ Ignacio Agramonte y Montera ☎32 28 3701. A roomy, spotlessly clean house run by a charming family. The two big bedrooms have private bathrooms and minibars, while the beautiful garden boasts a fountain, caged songbirds, rocking chairs, its very own bar and a pond filled with carp and terrapins. An upper terrace and huge breakfasts help make this an exceptional choice. **$25CUC**

Manolo Banegas Misa Independencia no.251 (altos) esq. Plaza Maceo ☎32 29 4606. This fabulous apartment overlooking Plaza Maceo is decorated with antique furniture, colourful floor tiles and chandeliers. The four large double rooms have wrought-iron and brass bedsteads and their own bathroom (two are en suite), and there's a balcony from where you can watch life go by on the square below. *Jineteros* often attempt to direct guests to a similarly numbered house on another street; call ahead and make sure that you enter the door marked "Manolo", which is next door to the El Mercado shop. **$25CUC**

Los Vitrales Avalleneda no.3 e/ General Gómez y Martí ☎32 29 5866, ✉requejobarreto@gmail.com. This beautiful former convent is chock-full of antiquities and stained-glass panels, from which it takes its name. The three bedrooms are big, with a/c, fridge and minibar. The hosts are friendly (Rafael, an architect, is extremely knowledgeable about Camagüey) and the food is excellent. Parking available and English and Italian spoken. **$25CUC**

EATING

For a provincial capital, Camagüey has a good selection of **restaurants**, and there are a couple of good local specialities that will come as a welcome break after the gastronomic wastelands of other parts of the island. At carnival time, look out for steaming pots of a meat and vegetable broth called *ajiaco*, cooked in the street over wood fires. All the neighbours pile out of the houses and chuck in their own ingredients while an elected chef stirs the concoction to perfection. You can also sample this delicacy in local eateries throughout the year. Camagüey also boasts a couple of excellent **paladars**; as with elsewhere in Cuba, watch out for overcharging and always ask for a menu where the prices are clearly stated.

Bodegan Don Cayetano República no.79 e/ Callejón de la Soledad y Callejón Magdelena. Immense wooden doors, tiled floor and dark-stained wooden beams all give this atmospheric restaurant a taverna feel in keeping with the tapas menu. Chorizo, prawns, tuna and *frituras* (corn fritters) are all tasty and good value, from $2CUC upwards. There's a pleasant cobbled outdoor area as well. Watch for overcharging in the form of items added to your bill. Daily noon–midnight.

La Campana de Toledo Plaza de San Juan de Dios. This state restaurant is set in a leafy courtyard inside a pretty blue-and-yellow building with a red-brick roof and a quaint tradition of tolling the bell when anyone enters or leaves. It serves the usual quasi-international and Cuban cuisine, but the tranquil setting makes it a top choice for a

mellow, moderately priced meal. Dishes from $7CUC. Daily noon–midnight.

Dimar Carretera Central e/ Puente Caballero Rojo y Puente La Caridad el Casino. Despite the cheap takeaway facade, the food at this seafood restaurant (including prawn cocktail, stir-fried vegetables and fish pan-fried in lemon) is very good, and at $2.95–12CUC (the latter for lobster) great value for money. Daily 24hr.

Dinos Pizza Humbolt San Joaquín y Ave. Libertad. Decent pizzas and spaghetti dishes ($4–8CUC) at this bustling café, which has a takeaway outlet at the side. Daily noon–midnight.

Don Ronquillo Galería Colonial, Ignacio Agramonte no.406 e/ República y López Recio. Cuban cuisine cooked to a quasi-gourmet standard, with high prices (mains

$8–12CUC) to match, in a shaded patio at the back of the Galería Colonial. Daily noon–midnight.

Doña Neli Maceo e/ Ignacio Agramonte y General Gómez. This bakery, directly opposite the *Gran Hotel*, serves freshly baked bread, biscuits, delicious pastries and other sticky treats. Daily 10am–8pm.

Heladería Impacto República no.366 e/ Santa Rita y Oscar Primelles. Extravagant sundaes with sauces and foamy whipped cream from $0.70CUC to $2.20CUC, served in a spotlessly clean ice-cream parlour. Daily 11am–7pm.

Rancho Luna no.2 Plaza Maceo. For an authentic Cuban experience, join the queue at this spick-and-span peso restaurant and enjoy a veritable smorgasbord of pork dishes for the equivalent of $2–4CUC. Wait to be seated and bossed about by gloriously irreverent waitresses. Daily noon–10pm.

★ **Restaurante 1800** Plaza San Juan del Dios. It's rare to find a buffet outside the all-inclusives and even more unusual to find one with such excellent starters as in this atmospheric paladar. Sit in the pretty courtyard and you can watch the chef prepare your food on the outdoor grill to the strains of a local band. Specialities include a succulent grilled fish, *malanga* fritters and home-made ice cream. The well-stocked wine cellar is an unexpected treat. Daily noon–midnight.

★ **La Terraza** Santa Rosa no.8 e/ San Martín y Santa Rita ☎32 29 8705. Also known as *Papito Rizo*, this atmospheric, wood-panelled paladar is identifiable by a string of lights over the door. The ample menu is excellent. Alongside pork and chicken stalwarts there are real treats including roast leg of lamb for $2.85CUC, plus sides of pumpkin in garlic sauce and yucca fried with garlic (both $1CUC each). The range of omelettes is also good fodder for vegetarians. Daily noon–midnight.

DRINKING, NIGHTLIFE AND ENTERTAINMENT

BARS, CLUBS AND LIVE MUSIC VENUES

Bar República República no.293 e/ San Esteban y Finlay (no phone). Pleasant little local bar where you can get an ice-cold Tinima beer for a handful of Cuban pesos. Daily noon–midnight.

Bar Siboney San Rafael esq. Lugareño (no phone). Much cleaner, lighter and friendlier than most – and less intimidating for lone women – this excellent rum bar sells a couple of local specialities including Timina beer. Daily noon–midnight.

La Bigornia República no.394 esq. Correa ☎32 28 4784. There's a good mix of Cubans and tourists at this airy open-sided jazz bar and café, which has an attractive brick-tiled floor. Live jazz on Saturday evenings from 10pm. Mon–Fri & Sun 10am–10pm, Sat 10am–6pm & 8.30pm–1am.

Cabaret Caribe Alturas del Casino ☎32 29 8112. This cabaret-cum-club is a dark and sultry space with a music show or on Tuesdays a comedy show at 11pm. Tuesday and Saturday are considered the best nights; on Saturday the cabaret is followed by a banging reggaeton and salsa disco. It's worth booking a ticket in advance ($5CUC) from the Paradiso office within the Cubatur office (see p.337).

Tues–Sun 8pm–late.

El Cambio Parque Agramonte (no phone). A friendly rum bar opening onto the park, with an old-fashioned though silent jukebox. A great place to slowly sip an afternoon away. Daily 24hr.

Casa de la Trova Salvador Cisneros no.171 e/ Martí y Cristo ☎32 29 1357. A good place to catch live music all day long. The fun really kicks off at the weekends, when excellent local bands play in the palm-tree-fringed courtyard and get audiences (a good mix of locals and visitors) on their feet and dancing. Entry $3CUC, of which $2CUC can be spent on drinks. Mon–Sat noon–7pm & 9pm–1am, Sun 11am–6pm & 9pm–2am.

Galería Colonial Ignacio Agramonte no.406 e/ República y López Recio ☎32 28 5239. Attracting tourists and Cubans alike, the *Galería* hosts slick cabaret shows on weekend nights, featuring a mix of professional dancers, international singers and touring Cuban bands. Attractions earlier in the week range from stand-up comedians to fashion shows but most often a raucous disco. $1CUC. Daily 10pm–2am.

Gran Hotel Maceo no.67 e/ Ignacio Agramonte y

CARNIVAL TIME

Camagüey is particularly vibrant during its week-long **carnival** in late June, when an exuberant parade takes place on the main streets and musicians dressed in multicoloured, frilled costumes twirl huge batons adorned with silver glitz, bang drums and clap cymbals while others dance, swig beer and quarrel with the parade officials. Floats with disco lights, bouncing speakers and unsmiling girls in home-made costumes dancing energetically bring up the rear, while running in between the different trucks are **diablitos**, men disguised head to foot in raffia, who dart into the crowd with the seemingly sole purpose of terrorizing the assembled children. Stalls selling gut-rot beer in vast paper cups (hang on to your empties – cup supplies often run out) and roast suckling pig provide refreshment.

General Gómez ☎ 32 29 2093. Though all the big hotels have their own bars, the only one worth lingering in is this dark, atmospheric piano bar, which sometimes has live music. Daily noon–2am.

Oasis Independencia esq. General Gómez (no phone). An attractive, open-sided street-corner bar where vaguely chilled beer is served with a smile. Daily 24hr.

THEATRE AND CINEMA

Cinema Cine Casablanca Ignacio Agramonte e/ República y López Recio ☎ 32 29 2244. This cinema shows a selection of Cuban, Spanish and North American films. In summer there are free outdoor screenings on a nearby wall.

SHOPPING

Galería Colonial Ignacio Agramonte no.406 e/ República y López Recio ☎ 32 28 5239. Designed as a sort of one-stop shop for visitors to the city, with a smart cigar shop that sells all the major brands and has a smoking room, furnished with big squashy chairs, where you can watch TV and sample one of your purchases. Another separate outlet specializes in coffee and rum. Daily 10am–10pm.

DIRECTORY

Banks and money You can draw cash advances on credit cards, change travellers' cheques and buy pesos at the CADECA *casa de cambio*, República no.353 e/ Oscar Primelles y Santa Rita (Mon–Sat 8am–6pm, Sun 8am–1pm), or El Banco Financiero Internacional, at Independencia no.221 on Plaza Maceo (Mon–Fri 8.30am–3.30pm), where there's usually less of a queue.

Internet and telephone ETECSA Telepunto República, at no.453 esq. San Martí y San José (daily 8.30am–7.30pm), has internet access ($6CUC/hr), phones and sells both local

Teatro Principal Padre Valencia no.64 ☎ 32 29 3048. Regular theatre and ballet performances, the latter from the excellent Camagüey Ballet Company, which are usually thoroughly entertaining. Tickets are around $5CUC.

GAMES AND SPORTS

Sala Recreativa Oxio Club República no.278 e/ San Esteban y Finlay ☎ 32 28 7384. This games and sports arcade is likely to appal die-hard Cuba traditionalists but delight bored teenagers. Big and brash, it sports a bowling alley ($2CUC a lane), a pleasant but smallish outdoor pool ($8CUC including $7CUC worth of snacks and drink), a billiards table ($3CUC/hr) and various noisy arcade games. Daily 10am–6pm.

Galería Julián Morales Cisneros no.159 e/ Cristo y Rosa La Bayamesa ☎ 32 29 1508. Part of the Union of Writers and Artists, this gallery has a range of excellent contemporary painting and sculpture as well as photographs by some of most established artists in the province – and the country. Exhibitions change regularly and are sensitively curated by the critic Pavel Alejandro Barrios Sosa. Mon–Sat 9am–5pm.

and international phonecards.

Medical The 24hr Policlínico Centro is on República no.211 e/ Grl. Gómez y Castellano (☎ 32 29 7810). For an ambulance call ☎ 32 28 1248.

Pharmacy There's a convertible-peso pharmacy at Ignacio Agramonte no.449, near the post office (Mon–Sat 9am–5pm).

Police Call ☎ 116 in an emergency.

Post office The main post office is at Ignacio Agramonte no.461 (daily 7am–10pm).

Camagüey's north coast

Cut off from the mainland by the Bahía de Nuevitas, 10km north of Nuevitas town, are Camagüey's north-coast **beaches**. The remote resorts of **Santa Lucía**, and **Cayo Sabinal** to the west, make perfect retreats for those seeking sun and sea holidays. While Santa Lucía derives an infrastructure of sorts from the knot of all-inclusive hotels arrayed along the beachfront, Cayo Sabinal is castaway country – with only the most basic accommodation, it virtually guarantees solitude. Those wishing to explore completely virgin territory should head for **Cayo Romano** in the far western reaches of the province.

Santa Lucía

Hemmed in by salt flats on the northern coast, 128km from Camagüey, **SANTA LUCÍA** is one of Cuba's smaller beach resorts. Much more low-key than the hectic resorts on the northern cays, it's perfect if you want to park yourself on the sand for a fortnight,

DIVING AT SANTA LUCÍA

The optimistically named **Shark's Friends Diving Centre** (☎ 32 36 5182, ⓦ thescubadiving place.co.uk), on the stretch of beach nearest to *Hotel Brisas Santa Lucia*, runs two daytime **dive trips**, at 9am and 1pm ($40CUC per dive including equipment), and night dives, when the sea glitters with starry phosphorescence ($40CUC). It also offers ACUC (American Canadian Underwater Certification) and SNSI registered courses (around $300CUC), excursions to fish for sea bream, barracuda, reef sharks and snapper starting at $200CUC for a half-day, and trips to Cayo Sabinal.

As part of their dives at La Mortera ($78CUC), instructors from the same company hand-feed the female **bull sharks** which use this underwater channel as part of their breeding ground. Organizers assert that this practice has actually protected the shark population from local fishermen, who have now stopped catching them in return for a share in the profits from the dives. However, shark conservationists have expressed serious concerns both for the safety of divers – bull sharks are among the four species most likely to attack humans – and over potential upset to the ecological balance, which can be disturbed by such feeding. Although the organizers assert that the pregnant sharks are at their most benign, non-fatal attacks have been reported; as a consequence, you should think carefully before embarking on such a potentially dangerous dive.

6

soak up some rays and indulge in a few watersports, but those looking for a more well-rounded destination may find it lacking. The road up here from Camagüey passes through the idyllic pastoral countryside that typifies this region, with lush grazing meadows, cowboys herding their cattle and meandering goats impeding the traffic, the air thick with clouds of multicoloured butterflies. Less appealing are the clouds of mosquitoes that descend at sunset. Now that laws have been relaxed and Cubans are easily able to stay in the hotels (if they have the funds), the resort has a less contrived feel. The downside is that there has been an influx of escorts staying in the hotels and *jineteros* on the beach.

The **resort**, such as it is, consists of little more than a beach strip lined by a few hotels, set well back from the coastal road, while the surrounding vicinity is restricted by marshland. The **town**, which you pass en route to the hotel strip, has nothing to offer tourists, and you will quickly get the impression that you're out in the middle of nowhere with nothing to see or do away from the sun and sea.

The beaches

The **beaches** are wide expanses of soft, fine sand bordered by turquoise waters, if a little sullied by seaweed drifting in from the barrier reef. There are five excellent **dive sites** catered to by a competent dive centre (see box above). As with many resorts in Cuba, the scene revolves around the all-inclusive hotels, most of them set in attractive properties and all with friendly staff. Non-guests are free to access the beaches.

ARRIVAL AND DEPARTURE   SANTA LUCÍA

By taxi If you're not driving to Santa Lucía, you can catch an unmetered taxi ($35CUC) from outside the train station in Camagüey.

On an organized transfer Cubatur (see p.337) can organize transfers from Camagüey and day-trips for groups of ten or more people, both costing $20CUC per person.

ACCOMMODATION

The Santa Lucía beach scene revolves around its four rather tired looking all-inclusive hotels, which between them carve up almost the entire beach strip. Residency at one entitles you to use the beaches (though not the facilities) of the others. All hotels offer a range of watersports, including windsurfing, snorkelling and catamarans. There's no legal accommodation outside the hotels but there are plenty of people offering rooms in Santa Lucía village. Cubanacán (☎ 32 29 4905) and Cubatur (☎ 32 25 4785) in Camagüey are often able to offer discounts on the rates quoted by the hotels; check with them before setting out.

6

Brisas Santa Lucia ☎32 33 6317. A friendly and unpretentious family-oriented hotel with excellent rooms, a pool with a swim-up bar, a gym, billiards, darts, archery, watersports and activities for children. **$148CUC**

Club Amigo Caracol ☎32 36 5158, @hoteles cubanacan.com. The emphasis here is on activity, with beach volleyball, table tennis, windsurfing, catamarans, kayaks, mountain biking and tennis offered. The cabin-style layout gives the hotel a more personalized and less institutional feel than the others. **$101CUC**

Gran Club Santa Lucia ☎32 33 6109, @aloja@clubst .stl.cyt.cu. This part-Italian-owned complex enjoys a spacious layout of bungalows and two-storey apartment blocks. With palatial rooms, ample shops, a good pool, a gym, three restaurants and a pier-end bar that's perfect for sunset-watching, this is far and away the best hotel on the strip. **$104CUC**

EATING, DRINKING AND ENTERTAINMENT

Outside of the hotel restaurants, there's little in the way of independent **eating** and **drinking** in the area. Evening entertainment is also limited to the hotels, with an endless diet of jovial staff roping drunken guests into bawdy Benny Hill-type pantomimes.

La Jungla Gran Club Santa Lucia (no phone). The resort's only disco: swanky, soulless and given to playing uninspiring mainstream Cuban and international disco music at deafening volumes. There's air hockey and billiards, too. Non-guests are welcome; entry is $5CUC with open bar. Daily 11pm–3am.

Luna Mar Near the beach between the *Gran Club Santa Lucia* and *Club Amigo Caracol* hotels, this is a relatively authentic Italian restaurant that provides a welcome respite from the hotel eateries and offers pizzas, pastas and lobster. Mains around $6CUC. Daily 11am–11pm.

Playa Coco

Eight kilometres west from Santa Lucía's main beach drag, idyllic **Playa Coco** offers a change of scene. The local claim that it's a beach to rival the best in Cuba is stretching it a bit, but the wide arc of fine white sand and quieter atmosphere certainly makes a welcome break from Santa Lucía. On the way there, you pass salt flats swarming with flamingos and the egrets (*cocos*) that give the beach its name.

ARRIVAL AND DEPARTURE   PLAYA COCO

By minibus A minibus picks up from the Santa Lucía hotels at 10am and drops you back at 3pm.

By horse-drawn carriage You can hire one of the horse-drawn carriages that wait outside the Santa Lucía hotels for around $5CUC one-way.

ACCOMMODATION AND EATING

There's not official **accommodation** here, but in La Boca, a fishing community that's basically just a string of wooden shacks at the entrance to Playa Coco, some locals run unregistered *casas particulares* for around $15CUC.

La Bocana (no phone). Chicken, fish, lobster and spaghetti are served up for reasonable prices at this wooden hut at the far end of the beach with tables on the sand where curious crabs dance around your feet but never come too close. Daily, 24hr.

Bucanero (no phone). At the Santa Lucía end of the beach, this is the smarter of Playa Coco's two restaurants, with a more formal dining room and nautical decor. There's a massive range of sumptuous seafood dishes as well as brochettes and the house speciality, roast beef. A meal will set you back $10–15CUC with drinks. Daily 11am–midnight.

Cayo Sabinal and around

Twenty-five kilometres west along the north coast from Santa Lucía, **Cayo Sabinal** could not be more different – a deserted white-sand beach cay that's so paradisiacal it's almost eerie. The reason it's yet to be discovered by the masses is its geographical isolation, hidden away at the end of a 7km stretch of notoriously bumpy dirt-track road, part of which forms a causeway across the bay, flanked by foaming salt marshes; there's no public transport, and very little general traffic makes it this far.

All the **beaches** are on the north side, accessible by signposted turnings off the single main road, itself bordered by thick vegetation. The longest beach is pearl-white **Playa Los Pinos**, where the sea is a clear, calm turquoise and wild deer and horses roam through the woodland that backs onto the sand. Occasionally a group of holidaymakers arrives by boat from Santa Lucía, but otherwise it's a top choice for a couple of days' total tranquillity. Just 2km further west, smaller **Playa Brava** has similar soft white sands. **Playa Bonita**, another 3km west, has a lengthy stretch of coral reef perfect for snorkelling, as well as 3km of pure white sand.

6

ARRIVAL AND DEPARTURE

CAYO SABINAL

By car Peppered with rocks and cavernous potholes, the road is sometimes impassable without a 4WD, especially during the rainy season, so check conditions before you set off.

By taxi A taxi from Camagüey will set you back $45–60CUC one-way.

Cayo Romano

Towards the western end of Camagüey's Atlantic coastline, **Cayo Romano** is an undeveloped 90km-long mass of fragmented cays covered with marshes and woodland. With no accommodation or restaurants, it is an archetypal untamed wilderness worth exploring if you have the time and your own transport. A causeway runs from Playa Jigüey on the north coast into the centre of the cay, although you can also reach the western tip from Cayo Coco. The only feasible way to get here is if you are driving yourself.

Northern Oriente

RÍO DE MIEL, BARACOA

Northern Oriente

Traditionally, the whole of the country east of Camagüey is known simply as the "Oriente", a region that in many ways represents the soul of Cuba, awash with historic sites, propaganda billboards and political passions. Running the length of the area's north coast, the three provinces that make up the northern Oriente – Las Tunas, Holguín and Guantánamo – form a landscape of panoramic pine-scented and palm-studded mountains, all fringed by flatlands where lonely railroads thrust through the vast swathes of sugarcane. Home to some of the country's most striking peaks and beaches from the flat-topped El Yunque to the stunning protected coves at Guardalavaca, Maguana and Saetía, the Northern Oriente also boasts some of Cuba's quirkiest towns – namely Baracoa, Gibara and Banes.

7

The smallest and most westerly of the three provinces is **Las Tunas**, often overlooked by visitors, though its unassuming and friendly provincial capital, **Victoria de las Tunas**, is not without charm. Nearby, the picturesque coastal town of **Puerto Padre** has a couple of congenial beaches close by.

By contrast, larger and livelier **Holguín** province has a variety of attractions. Chequered with parks, the busy and crowded provincial capital, **San Isidoro de Holguín**, manages to be modern and cosmopolitan whilst retaining the feel of its colonial past, with several handsome old buildings, museums and antique churches. The once mighty nineteenth-century port of **Gibara**, presiding over the north coast, also has vestiges of its former glory visible in a few fine buildings and an old fort, while the gently undulating hills around town are honeycombed with underground caves that are perfect for independent exploration. Holguín's biggest attraction is the popular **Guardalavaca** beach resort, while the province's ancient historical pedigree can be seen in the remnants of pre-Columbian Taíno culture in and around the little village of **Banes**. Further east, the exclusive beach resort of **Cayo Saetía** is a paradise of white sands and glistening seas, an idyllic place to relax. Inland, where rugged terrain dominates the landscape, the cool pine forests, waterfalls and lakes of **Mayarí** are unmatched for isolated serenity, while the sugar-farm country further south is home to Fidel Castro's prosaic birthplace at **Birán**.

Of the three provinces, the best known is undoubtedly **Guantánamo**, with the notorious US naval base at **Caimanera**. Although Guantánamo town is largely unspectacular, it forms a useful jumping-off point for the seaside settlement of **Baracoa**, one of Cuba's most beautiful and enjoyable destinations. Sealed off from the rest of the island by a truly awe-inspiring range of rainforested mountains – which are fantastic for trekking – Baracoa's small-town charm is immensely welcoming.

GIBARA

Highlights

❶ Gibara This picture-perfect coastal town is the ideal base for trips to the geologically rich Cavernas de Panadernos, one of the region's treasures. **See p.358**

❷ Playa Guardalavaca With over 1.5km of sugar-like sand, this beach is the crown jewel of Northern Oriente's coastline. **See p.362**

❸ Cayo Saetía White sands and coral reef against a backdrop of savannah wilds – complete with roaming ostrich and zebra – make for a fantastic juxtaposition. **See p.367**

❹ Villa Pinares de Mayarí Waterfalls, lakes and pine forests create an idyllic haven of calm at

this hotel, cupped by mountains and the centre of the ultimate nature retreat. **See p.369**

❺ Baracoa This vibrant small town set on Cuba's southeastern tip is surrounded by some of the country's most breathtaking mountains, rainforest and countryside. **See p.373**

❻ Guantánamo's musical heritage Search for Haitian heritage and the musical tradition of changüí in Guantánamo. **See p.370**

❼ El Yunque The easily scaled El Yunque is as famous for its mention in the 1492 log of Christopher Columbus as its rare orchids and ferns. **See p.382**

HIGHLIGHTS ARE MARKED ON THE MAP ON PP.348–349

Victoria de las Tunas

VICTORIA DE LAS TUNAS seems to have been built to a traditional Cuban recipe for a quiet town: take one central plaza, a small main hotel, a Revolution square and a thriving market, add a pinch of culture and bake in the sun for two hundred years. The result is a pleasant but slow-moving town where the faster pace of life elsewhere in the world seems but a rumour. The town's hub is **Parque Vicente García**, a small but comfortable central plaza hemmed by trees and cacti, which holds a number of attractions.

Museo Provincial Mayor General Vicente García

Parque Vicente García • Tues–Sat 9am–5pm, Sun 8am–noon • $1CUC • ☎ 31 34 8201.

On the east side of Parque Vicente García, the **Museo Provincial Mayor General Vicente García** is housed in a distinguished duck-blue-and-white colonial building adorned with an elegant clock face. The city history detailed within includes a worthy – though brief – record of **slavery**, as well as two rooms featuring art and clocks.

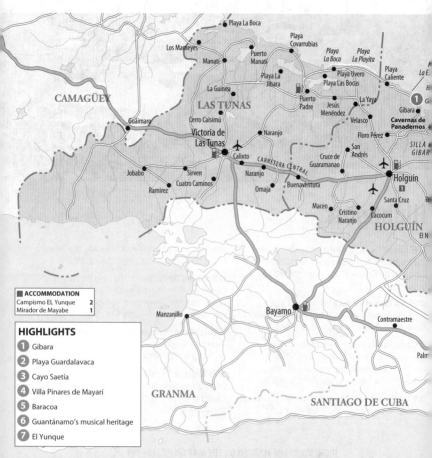

ACCOMMODATION

Campismo EL Yunque	2
Mirador de Mayabe	1

HIGHLIGHTS

1. Gibara
2. Playa Guardalavaca
3. Cayo Saetía
4. Villa Pinares de Mayarí
5. Baracoa
6. Guantánamo's musical heritage
7. El Yunque

Plaza Martiana de las Tunas

Opposite the southeastern corner of Parque Vicente García is the **Plaza Martiana de las Tunas**, a modern art monument to José Martí made up of six white man-sized spikes, one embossed with a bust of Martí by Cuba's most famous sculptor, Rita Longa. The whole plaza forms an ingenious gigantic sundial that illuminates the bust each May 19 to commemorate the hero's death in 1895.

Museo Memorial Mártires de Barbados

Lucas Ortíz no.344 • Tues–Sun 11am–7pm • Free

The most arresting museum in Las Tunas is the small but poignant **Museo Memorial Mártires de Barbados**, just west of Parque Vicente García. It commemorates the horrific **plane crash** on October 6, 1976, that wiped out the national junior fencing team. When it was later revealed that an anti-Castro terrorist linked to the CIA had planted the bomb, the incident was popularly seen as a direct attack on Cuban revolutionary youth and achievement. The museum itself is located in the tiny former home of one of the three team members from Las Tunas, and has some affecting **memorabilia** like photographs of weeping crowds in Havana and the victims' fencing trophies.

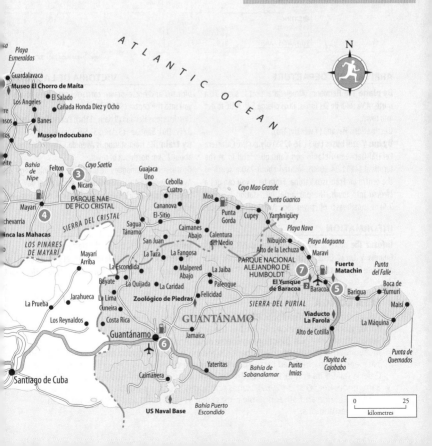

ACCOMMODATION
Casa de Esperanza Fresco — 1
Hotel Cadillac — 2

EATING
La Bodeguita — 2
La Romana — 1
Taberna Don Juan — 3

Bus Station (750m) & Market (1km)

ARRIVAL AND DEPARTURE

VICTORIA DE LAS TUNAS

By plane The Hermanos Almejeira airport is some 3km north of Victoria de las Tunas. Taxis charge $2–3CUC to get into town.

Destinations Havana (4 weekly; 1hr).

By bus Víazul buses (☎ 31 36 4295) plying the Carretera Central between Holguín and Camagüey pull in at the terminal (☎ 31 34 3060), located about 250m south of the centre on Francisco Varona. From here you can get a *bicitaxi* into town. The provincial bus station is about 2.5km northeast of town on Avenida Cienfuegos;

bicitaxis and horse-drawn carriages wait here to whisk you into the centre ($2CUC).

Destinations Havana (9 daily; 11hr); Puerto Padre (several daily; 1hr); Santiago (5 daily; 3–5hr 30min).

By train The train station is Avenida Camilo Cienfuegos, about 2.5km northeast of town.

Destinations Camagüey (daily; 12hr 45min); Ciego de Ávila (2 weekly; 4hr); Guantánamo (every other day; 6hr); Havana (daily; 12hr); Holguín (daily; 1hr 40min); Santiago (daily; 8hr).

INFORMATION

Infotur The office at Francisco Varona no.298 e/ Angel Guardia y Lucas Ortiz (Mon–Fri 8.15am–4.15pm, plus alternate Saturdays 8.15am–4.15pm; ☎ 31 37 2717) offers

limited information, though the staff are helpful.

Services CADECA *casa de cambio* is at Angel Guardia e/ Francisco Varona y Francisco Vega (Mon–Sat

---

RITA LONGA

Cuba's most famous sculptor, **Rita Longa**, considered Las Tunas her second home and two of her works adorn the city. As well as the José Martí monument in Plaza Martiana de las Tunas, there's the non-functioning *Fuente de las Antillas* fountain, across the street from the Museo Memorial Mártires de Barbados, a reclining female body in the shape of Cuba, which has been much emulated by the island's contemporary artists. East of the centre, the small Galería Taller Rita Longa, Lucas Ortíz e/ Villalón (Tues–Sun 8am–noon & 1.30–4pm, Sun 8am–noon; free; ☎ 31 34 2969), stages temporary sculpture exhibitions and displays works by Longa and other notable artists such as Flora Fong and Sergio Martínez in rotating exhibitions.

FESTIVALS IN VICTORIA DE LAS TUNAS

There's not much nightlife or entertainment to speak of in Las Tunas except during the summer, when the annual **El Cucalambé music festival** is held over three days in June. Based in the grounds of the otherwise unremarkable *Hotel El Cornito* (❶31 34 5015), about 7km out of town, the festival features live folk and salsa in a lively atmosphere awash with beer and food stalls. Other events include **rodeos**, which take place in August and December at *Hotel El Cornito*, while fireworks and parades are held every September 26 to commemorate Major General Vicente García. The city also celebrates its carnival and *semana de la cultura* in September with music, poetry and art events.

3.30am–4pm, Sun 8.30–11.30am). Telepunto, Francisco Vegas no.237 e/ Lucas Ortiz y Vincente García (daily

8.30am–7pm), has internet access ($6CUC/hr), phones and phonecards.

ACCOMMODATION

Casa de Esperanza Fresco Avenida Frank País no.62 e/ Villalón y R López ❶31 34 5630. Run by the gregarious Esperanza, this is a comfortable, quiet room with en-suite bathroom and its own independent entrance. Off-street parking available. **$25CUC**

Hotel Cadillac Angel Guardia s/n ❶31 37 2791,

❷jose.daniel@hoteltu.co.cu. This Art Deco-style hotel is a welcome addition to the Las Tunas accommodation scene. The eight rooms are furnished in chocolate and cream fabrics and come with TVs, fridges and a/c. The 24hr bar is the city's social hotspot. **$70CUC**

EATING AND DRINKING

La Bodeguita Francisco Varona no.303 e/ Vicente García y Lucas Ortiz (no phone). The main convertible-peso state option in town, this inexpensive central restaurant has mediocre fried chicken, pasta dishes and fish and shellfish. Daily noon–3pm & 7–11pm.

La Romana Francisco Varona no.331 e/ Lucas Ortiz and L Cruz ❶31 34 7755. This Italian-run paladar makes a very welcome addition to the Las Tunas' dining scene, and is by far the best place to eat in town. Owner Franco,

from Rome, uses Authentic Italian parmesan and pecorino to rustle up pasta and pesto, carbonara, a delicious lasagne and hearty salads. Mains $3.50–4.50CUC. Daily noon–11pm.

Taberna Don Juan Francisco Varona no.225 (no phone). Near Parque Vicente García, overlooking the main road and Plaza Martiana, and offering decent *comida criolla* and excellent local beer, priced in national pesos. Daily noon–midnight.

Puerto Padre

Although Las Tunas has just 70km of coastline – a small stretch compared with neighbouring provinces – there are still some pleasant spots. The attractive little seaside town of **Puerto Padre**, 56km northeast of Las Tunas, is a worthwhile diversion on the coastal road through the province. Here, a clutch of colonial buildings, including a church with a handsome spire, spreads along a spacious boulevard that heads down to a *malecón*.

Fuerte de la Loma

Tues–Sat 9.30am–4.30pm, Sun 8.30am–11.30am • $1CUC

Puerto Padre's chief attraction is a small, crumbling and quietly impressive stone fort, **Fuerte de la Loma**, on the town's main boulevard. Built by the Spanish in 1875, with a circular tower on two of its four corners linking its once solid walls, it offers pleasant views of the coast from its batteries.

ARRIVAL AND DEPARTURE   PUERTO PADRE

By bus Services from Las Tunas (departing from the Avenida Cienfuegos terminal) arrive in the town centre daily.

By taxi A taxi to Puerto Padre will cost $40–50CUC from Las Tunas.

San Isidoro de Holguín

Nestled in a valley surrounded by hills, 72km east of Las Tunas, the provincial capital of **SAN ISIDORO DE HOLGUÍN** – or Holguín for short – is a thriving industrial town balancing quieter backstreets with a busier central district of handsome colonial buildings, bicycles and horn-blasting cars. Despite having the bustling air of a large metropolis, Holguín's centre is compact enough to explore on foot and has a couple of fine eighteenth-century **churches** and some small-scale **museums** which will keep you quietly absorbed for a day. The city is also spotted with numerous elegant **plazas**; these open spaces, ideal for people-watching, are central to the Holguín lifestyle, and in the evenings it seems that the whole city turns out just to sit, chat and watch their children play in one or other of them.

Brief history

The area around Holguín was once densely populated by indigenous Taíno, but the Spanish had wiped them out by 1545, after **Captain García Holguín**, early colonizer and veteran of the conquest of Mexico, established his cattle ranch around La Loma de la Cruz. Although a small settlement remained after his death, a town wasn't fully established here for 150 years, and it was only officially named on April 4, 1720 – San Isidoro's Day – with a commemorative Mass held in the cathedral.

Being an inland town with no port, Holguín was destined to be overshadowed in importance by coastal Gibara. In spite of its rather grand blueprint, laid out in accordance with Spanish colonial city planning laws, it developed slowly. But by the nineteenth century an economy based on sugar production and fruit-growing, as well as a little tobacco cultivation, was established and the town grew accordingly. As with other parts of Oriente, Holguín province saw plenty of action during the **Wars of Independence**. Shortly after the start of the Ten Years' War, on October 30, 1868, the city was captured by General Julio Grave de Peralta's force of Mambises, who lost Holguín to the Spanish on December 6. The tides turned again four years later on December 19, 1872, when the city was recaptured by General Máximo Gómez and Holguín-born General Calixto García. After independence, the province was largely dominated by US corporations and Holguín chugged along much the same as it always had. Since the Revolution, however, it has become more of an **industrial city**, with several factories and engineering plants, and was designated provincial capital when the province was created in 1975.

Parque Calixto García

Most of Holguín's sights spread out from the central **Parque Calixto García**, an expanse of ornamental pink and green marble. In the park's centre, a square marble column is topped by a statue of war hero **Calixto García** leaning upon his sword. A bushy rim of trees lines the park's outer edge and the benches beneath are packed with old men relaxing in the shade, the more garrulous of whom will gladly fill you in on the entire history of the province.

Museo Provincial de Holguín

Calle Frexes e/ Maceo y Libertad • Tues–Sat 8am–noon & 12.30–4.30pm, Sun 8am–noon • $1CUC, photos $5CUC

Presiding over the northeastern side of Parque Calixto García is the **Museo Provincial de Holguín**, where a number of worthwhile exhibits are displayed in one of the town's most impressive buildings. The handsome ochre edifice was built between 1860 and 1868 as both the private house and business premises of Francisco Roldán y Rodríguez, a wealthy Spanish merchant. He never managed to move in, however; while the great house awaited the finishing touches, the first War of Independence broke out and, with Rodríguez's

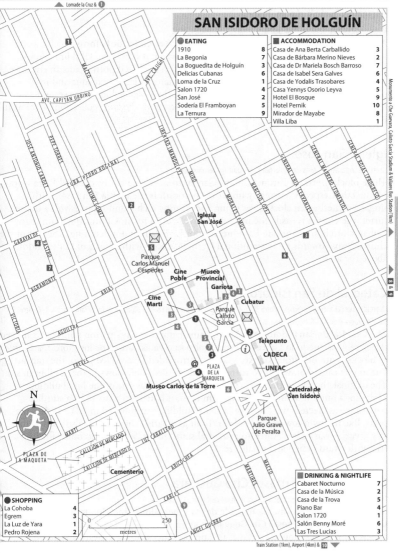

SAN ISIDORO DE HOLGUÍN

● EATING	
1910	8
La Begonia	7
La Boguedita de Holguín	3
Delicias Cubanas	6
Loma de la Cruz	1
Salon 1720	4
San José	2
Soderia El Framboyan	5
La Ternura	9

■ ACCOMMODATION	
Casa de Ana Berta Carballido	3
Casa de Bárbara Merino Nieves	2
Casa de Dr Mariela Bosch Barroso	7
Casa de Isabel Sera Galves	6
Casa de Yodalis Trasobares	4
Casa Yennys Osorio Leyva	5
Hotel El Bosque	9
Hotel Pernik	10
Mirador de Mayabe	8
Villa Liba	1

● SHOPPING	
La Cohoba	4
Egrem	3
La Luz de Yara	1
Pedro Rojena	2

■ DRINKING & NIGHTLIFE	
Cabaret Nocturno	7
Casa de la Música	2
Casa de la Trova	5
Piano Bar	4
Salon 1720	1
Salón Benny Moré	6
Las Tres Lucias	3

Train Station (1km), Airport (4km) & [10]

blessing, the Spanish army in Holguín hastily holed up here, capitalizing on its fortress-like proportions. The measure paid off and throughout the siege of the city the Mambises, unable to capture the building, had to content themselves with yelling "Parrots, parrots, climb out of your cage" at the yellow-and-red-clad Spanish soldiers as they peeked from the windows. The house has since been known as **La Periquera** or "the parrot cage".

The primary reason to come here is actually the building, as the historical miscellanea on display are rather sparse. The best section is the small set of **pre-Columbian artefacts** discovered in and around Holguín, including bone fragments of necklaces and pieces of clay pots. Most impressive is a polished, olive-coloured Taíno axe, known as the **Axe of Holguín**, which was discovered in 1860 in the hills surrounding the city. Carved with a grimacing, crowned male figure, it was most likely used for religious ceremonies.

Museo Carlos de la Torre

Maceo no.129 • Tues–Sat 9am–5pm, Sun 9am–noon • $1CUC, photos $5CUC

A block south of Parque Calixto García is the **Museo Carlos de la Torre**, chiefly worth visiting for the nineteenth-century building in which it's set. A fanciful lime, forest green, mustard and custard-yellow confection with a pillared portico and an entrance portal, it is exquisitely tiled in bright ceramic squares of lacquered aqua and rose, complementing the richly patterned floor inside. Exhibits include some second-rate **taxidermy**, though conchologists might be interested in the large collection of colourful **Baracoa polymita snails**.

Iglesia San José

Libertad e/ Agramonte y Arias • Irregular hours, but usually open mornings

Three blocks north of Parque Calixto García, fronting the shady, cobbled Plaza Carlos Manuel de Céspedes (currently under restoration), is the **Iglesia San José**. With a single weatherbeaten clocktower rising above stone arches and topped with a domed turret, the church is easily the most attractive spot in town. Contrasting with many Cuban churches, the ornate Baroque **interior** is vibrant and welcoming. The rest of the church leans towards more traditional Catholic decor, with effigies of saints huddled above the altars.

Catedral de San Isidoro

Libertad e/ Luz Caballero y Aricochea • Mon 5.30–6.45pm, Tues & Fri 7am–noon & 3–5.30pm, Wed–Thurs 7am–noon & 3–6.45pm, Sat–Sun 7am–noon & 7–8.45pm • Free

The **Catedral de San Isidoro de Holguín**, named after the city's patron saint, lords it over the stately Parque Julio Grave de Peralta (also known as Parque de los Flores), a couple of blocks south of Parque Calixto García. Surrounded by a walled patio, the stalwart but simple cathedral, with two turrets and a red-tiled roof, glows in the Caribbean sun. The original church on this site, completed in 1720, was one of the first buildings in Holguín; a humble affair built from palm trees, it lasted ten years until a sturdier structure was erected in 1730. The current building was finished in 1815 with some parts, like the twin towers, added later. Built as a parish church, and also used as the city crypt, it was only elevated to cathedral status in 1979, which accounts for its straightforward design and small size.

Monumento al Ernesto Che Guevara

Avenida de los Libertadores • Take a bicitaxi or taxi from the centre for $1–2CUC

Some 1.5kn east of town, via Avenida de los Libertadores, the **Monumento al Guerrillero Heróico Ernesto Che Guevara** is an impressive three-part sculpture with panels showing a silhouette of Guevara approaching, striding forward and receding. Executed in sombre stone, it's an eye-catching and accomplished piece of work, its triptych of images said to allude to, respectively, his revolutionary influence, presence and lasting legacy.

Loma de la Cruz

Metered taxis to the summit from downtown cost $3–4CUC

Rising above Holguín, the **Loma de la Cruz**, or Hill of the Cross, is the largest of the hills that form a natural border to the north of the city. A steep, 458-step **stairway** starts from the northern end of Maceo and heads up to the summit, where you'll find a faithful replica of the hefty wooden cross erected on May 3, 1790, by Friar Antonio de Algerías, following the Spanish tradition of the **Romería de la Cruz** (Pilgrimage of the

Cross). This custom commemorates the day that, according to legend, St Elena, mother of Constantine the Great, rediscovered the original cross of Christ's crucifixion. Every May 3, a Mass is held for the faithful – who until the construction of the staircase in 1950 had to toil up the hill the long way round – along with a low-key week-long **festival** in town, where locals gather nightly around beer stalls and food stands set up around the centre.

The hill was also used by the Spanish as a lookout during the Wars of Independence, and a bijou **fort** on the plateau set back from the cross remains as evidence. You can appreciate why they chose this point when you gaze down at the town's rigid grid below, and the panorama of lush green land on one side and dry countryside on the other, with parched and dusty hillocks visible in the distance. A small café takes advantage of the magnificent views, and there's also a restaurant up here (see p.357).

ARRIVAL AND DEPARTURE SAN ISIDORO DE HOLGUÍN

7

BY PLANE

Airport International (☎ 24 47 4525) and domestic flights (☎ 24 47 4583) land at the Aeropuerto Frank País about 14km south of town, from where metered taxis will run you to the centre for about $10CUC.

Airlines Cubana, Martí esq. Libertad (☎ 24 47 4630).
Destinations Havana (2–3 daily; 1hr 45min).

BY BUS OR COLECTIVO

Valiares Terminal de Omnibus Local buses and interprovincial *colectivos* pull into the Valiares terminal (☎ 24 48 1170), to the east of the centre in front of the Calixto García stadium car park on Avenida de los Libertadores.

Estación José María Víazul buses arrive at the Astro Estación José María, at Carretera Central e/ Independencia y 20 de Mayo, about 1km west from the centre;

horse-drawn carriages, *bicitaxis* and taxis ($3CUC) wait to ferry you into town.

Destinations Banes (daily; 2hr 30min); Gibara (1 daily; 1hr); Havana (4 daily; 12hr); Santa Clara (3 daily; 5hr); Santiago de Cuba (3 daily; 3hr 20min).

Conectando Cuba Daily services to and from Havana and Santiago (with stops at main cities) arrive and depart outside *Hotel Pernik*.

BY TRAIN

Terminal de Ferrocaril Vidal The terminal is at Pita no.3 e/ Libertad y Maceo (☎ 24 42 2331), 1km south of the town centre, and is served by taxis ($3CUC) and *bicitaxis*.

Destinations Guantánamo (every other day; 6hr); Havana (every other day; 14hr); Las Tunas (daily; 2hr 30min).

GETTING AROUND

Car rental Havanautos has a desk at the airport (daily 8am–8pm; ☎ 24 46 8412), and another at Edificio Pico de Cristal, Libertad esq. Martí (Mon–Sat 9am–5pm; ☎ 24 46 8559).

Scooter rental *Restaurante 1720*, Frexes no 290 esq. Miró

(daily 8am–5pm; ☎ 24 46 8150) rents out scooters for $25CUC per day.

By taxi Cubataxi is at Maceo no.79 e/ Garayalde y Cuba (☎ 24 47 3155).

INFORMATION, TRAVEL AGENCIES AND TOURS

Infotur The best port of call for tourist information is Infotur in the Edificio Pico Cristal, at Libertad esq. Martí (Mon–Fri 8am–noon & 12.30–4.30pm, plus every other Sat; ☎ 24 42 5013, @ infotur@holguin.infotur.cu), where you can book tours and pick up leaflets on local attractions.

Events information A listings board outside the Fondo Bienes Cultural Centre, at no.196 Frexes, details weekly cultural and arts events in Holguín.

Festivals Holguín's carnival takes place over the third weekend in August, while the Fiesta de la Cultura Iberoamericana in October celebrates the arrival of Christopher Columbus to Cuba with a host of

cultural events (@ casadeiberoamerica.cult.cu/fcia /index.php).

Cubatur With offices inside *Salon 1720*, Frexes 190 e/ Miró y Holguín (Mon–Fri 1–5pm; ☎ 24 42 1679) and *La Begonia*, Maceo 176 e/ Frexes y Martí (Mon–Sat 8am–noon), Cubatur is a full service tour operator, and runs buses to Guardalavaca, departing at 8am and returning at 5pm (July & Aug Sat & Sun; $5CUC return).

Gaviota Based at no.220 Frexes (usually Mon–Sat 8am–5pm; ☎ 24 42 1602), Gaviota organizes overnight excursions from Guardalavaca to Pinares de Mayarí and Salto El Guayabo ($71CUC per person).

ACCOMMODATION

While the three **state hotels** catering for tourists are sound options, they're all slightly out of town, which is a drag if you don't have your own transport. A more central option is any one of the numerous well-appointed **casas particulares**. Bear in mind that the taxi drivers who pick up from the bus station are fairly mercenary, and even if you direct them to your chosen *casa particular* they may still try to charge you a proprietor's commission – the more unscrupulous will attempt to drive you to a *casa particular* of their own choosing. To avoid any hassle, book in advance and ask the owners to come and collect you themselves.

HOTELS

Hotel El Bosque Ave Jorge Dimitrov Reparto Pedro Díaz Coello ☎ 24 48 1012, ✉ bosque@bosque.holguin .info.cu. Although not very modern, the self-contained blocks set in leafy grounds, with two or three rooms apiece, are well maintained. Some rooms have refrigerators, while two restaurants, a bar and a pool flesh out the attractive package. Located on the outskirts of town, 2km east of the centre. **$45CUC**

Hotel Pernik Ave. Jorge Dimitrov ☎ 24 48 1011, 🌐 islazul.cu. A bulky, imposing hotel near the Plaza de la Revolución, a good 30min walk from the town centre; taxis wait outside to ferry you in. It's a bit grim and overpriced, and with half-hearted service, but there are usually rooms available which are clean and good-sized, with satellite TV. The choice rooms are the five decorated by different contemporary artists. **$45CUC**

★ **Mirador de Mayabe** Alturas de Mayabe ☎ 24 42 2160. Some 8km south of town, this is Holguín's most picturesque hotel. The clean and comfortable rooms are grouped in tile-roofed, pale yellow chalets connected by flowerbeds tangled with verdant vines and creepers (rooms 11–17 are larger and newer). There's a lobby bar with panoramic views over the valley and swinging wooden love seats, two restaurants and an invitingly large pool from which to admire the amazing view of the plain below. Rates include breakfast. **$45CUC**

CASAS PARTICULARES

Casa de Ana Berta Carballido Aguilera 163 e/ Narciso López y G. Feria ☎ 24 46 5675, ✉ mariana6412@gmail .com. One double room in a bright, airy house, with a bathroom, fridge, pleasant patio and a private entrance. English, Portuguese and Italian spoken. **$20CUC**

★ **Casa de Bárbara Merino Nieves** Mártires no.31 e/ Agramonte y Garayalde ☎ 24 42 3805, ✉ rosellsoler @cristal.hlg.slc.cu. Two excellent double rooms, each with a/c and its own bathroom and TV; one has a small kitchen.

Use of a sunny terrace and very friendly and helpful owner make this one of the best *casas particulares* in town. **$25CUC**

Casa de Dr Mariela Bosch Barroso Rastro no.41 e/ Agramonte y Garayalde ☎ 24 45 2109, ✉ rfrutosrojas @gmail.com. One enormous self-contained apartment with a picturesque terrace, spacious living room and leafy garden kitchen. Ideal for a family, with one double bed and one single. **$25CUC**

Casa de Isabel Sera Galves Narciso López no.142 e/ Aguilera y Frexes ☎ 24 42 2529. Two sizeable double rooms with fridges in a handsome and grand colonial house, with a patio, a pretty garden shaded by coconut palms and a mini-Che museum. The disadvantage is that both rooms share a single bathroom, though each one does have a basin. **$25CUC**

Casa de Yodalis Trasobares Rastro no.37 e/ Agramonte y Garayalde ☎ 24 42 5229, ✉ trasobares @cristalhlg.sld.cu. Three pleasantly decorated a/c rooms: the one in the main house has its own lavishly tiled bathroom, while the others are on the second floor accessed by an independent entrance. There's a beautiful crazy-paved patio out the back where you can take home-cooked meals. **$20CUC**

Casa Yennys Osorio Leyva Mártires no 53 (altos) e/ Arias y Agramonte ☎ 05 53 55 7241 (mobile). A spacious top-floor room with an en-suite bathroom, fridge and sink and a terrace with sofas for admiring the cityscape and sunbathing. The super friendly owner Yennys is good fun and knows a lot about the city, its nightlife and its attractions. **$25CUC**

Villa Liba Maceo no.46 esq. 18 ☎ 24 42 3823. Two a/c rooms with TVs in an airy 1950s apartment near the Loma de la Cruz steps. Each simply furnished room has its own bathroom, plus there's a sun-trap patio for eating. Jorge, of Lebanese descent, cooks Lebanese and vegetarian food and his wife, Mariela, gives deeply relaxing massages and teaches yoga and Reiki. Garage parking available. **$25CUC**

EATING

CAFÉS

La Begonia Maceo 176 e/ Frexes y Martí ☎ 24 42 7354. Overlooking Parque Calixto García from beneath a canopy of begonias, this reasonably priced open-air café serves up unexciting but decent sandwiches ($3CUC), beers ($2CUC) and Nestlé ice cream (from $1.50CUC). Note that this is a popular hangout for *jineteros*. Daily 8am–2am.

Sodería El Framboyan Maceo e/ Frexes y Aguilera. With a mind-boggling list of sundaes and other delicious confections, this open-air ice-cream parlour offers a range of exotic flavours including orange-pineapple, almond, hazelnut and chocolate ripple alongside the standard strawberry and chocolate. Prices start at around $1CUC for a cone. Daily noon–7pm.

STATE RESTAURANTS

La Boguedita de Holguín Aguilera no.249 esq. Mártires. A pleasant, if dingy, national-peso restaurant specializing in grilled pork, with a bar area where *trovadores* play in the evenings. The cheap prices (the equivalent of $2–3CUC for mains) and friendly atmosphere more than compensate for the fact that most of the menu options are usually unavailable. Daily noon–10.45pm.

Loma de la Cruz La Loma de la Cruz. Good-value open-air restaurant at the top of the hill (to the left of the summit), featuring *comida criolla* dishes and *al dente* pasta for $2.50–8CUC. Friendly and unpretentious, with superb views over the city, this is a much better spot to pause for a drink than the nearby café. Daily noon–10.45pm.

Salon 1720 Frexes 190 e/ Miró y Holguín ☎ 24 46 8150. With splendid decor and attentive service, this is one of Holguín's better state dining experiences and, surprisingly, everything on the menu actually appears to be available. You can relax over a *mojito* in the rooftop bar beforehand and eat either in the smart dining rooms or in the central courtyard. Options include onion soup, beef medallions or lamb chops with tamarind sauce accompanied by perfect mashed potato and lightly cooked vegetables. Expect to pay $6–11CUC for a main course, $22CUC for lobster. Daily noon–10.30pm, bar closed Mon.

PALADARS

1910 Mártires no.143 e/ Aricochea y Cables, ☎ 24 42 3994, ⌨ 1910restaurantebar.com. A hugely popular paladar inside a columned colonial home. While the standard, national Cuban *criollo* menu has been stretched to include grilled octopus in garlic sauce and shrimps with caramelized pineapple, and the food is delicious and beautifully presented, the service is unacceptably slow (mains $90–200CUP). Daily noon–midnight.

Delicias Cubanas Dositeo Aguilera no.78 e/ Agramonte y Garayalde ☎ 24 46 4397. A little off the beaten track but frequented by those in the know, and insanely popular at weekends. It offers standard *comida criolla* fare, carefully cooked and in generous portions. Try its *ropa vieja*, or the slices of pork in Creole sauce. Rounds of *boniato* chips go down a treat, too. Mains $4–12CUC. Daily noon–midnight.

★**San José** Agramonte no.188 e/ Maceo y Libertad ☎ 24 42 4877. The most professional and best paladar in Holguín. Succulent fish and tender meats (such as roast lamb or smoked pork in pineapple sauce) are cooked to order from the small kitchen on display at the back of a narrow alfresco courtyard. There's air-conditioned cool in the interior dining room but it lacks the comfortable ambience of the outside space. Mains $5.20–9CUC. Daily 11am–11pm.

La Ternura José Antonio Cardet no.293 (altos) e/ Cables y Angel Guerra ☎ 24 42 1223. Small, cosy paladar serving chicken, lamb, fish and pork prepared in a variety of styles. It's also a good choice for veggies with an omelette menu. Mains $1–4CUC. Daily noon–midnight.

NIGHTLIFE AND ENTERTAINMENT

BARS, CLUBS AND LIVE MUSIC VENUES

Cabaret Nocturno Carretera Central Vía Las Tunas, Km 2 ☎ 24 42 9345. Saturday is the big night here, with young Holguineros descending to see the cabaret, hear the singers, compete in dancing competitions and dance to Fiesta Kaliente's techno sounds. It's a totally authentic night out as there are few foreigners. Entry $8CUC for visitors. Mon & Wed–Sun 9pm–2am.

★**Casa de la Música** Frexes esq. Libertad ☎ 24 42 9561. Slick nightspot with four busy *salons* hosting great salsa and jazz bands, and a 24hr open-air bar flanking the building on Libertad. Of the four *salons*, the darkly atmospheric Santa Palabra ($3CUC) has nightly live music and a Wed–Sat dance matinee ($10CUP), while the Terraza Bucanero ($1CUC, free before 8pm) is a lively beer-only rooftop bar, playing disco, up-tempo salsa and reggaeton. Santa Palabra daily 10pm–3am, plus Wed–Sat 4–7pm; Terraza Bucanero daily 2pm–1am.

Casa de la Trova Maceo no.174 e/ Frexes y Martí (no phone). A mixed crowd of cross-generational foreigners and Cubans fills the big wooden dancefloor for exuberant salsa and traditional trova sessions, with live bands playing daytimes and evenings ($1CUC). There's a $10CUC charge on Sundays 2–8pm. Daily 2–6pm & 9pm–2am.

Piano Bar Mártires esq. Frexes (no phone). Night owls in search of more mellow entertainment should head to this sultry late-night piano bar with an original 1950s counter. Free. Daily 8pm–4am.

Salon 1720 Calle Frexes 190 e/ Miró y Holguín ☎ 24 46 8150. The restaurant's well-stocked bar, on a romantic lantern-lit roof terrace, is the city's top choice for moonlight cocktails. Tues–Sun noon–12.30am.

Salón Benny Moré Luz Caballero esq. Maceo (no phone). A new Artex space with a large alfresco stage in the round surrounded by comfy plastic rattan sofas, and an eclectic lineup of live music. It's also a popular off-street bar during the afternoon. Entry $1CUC at night. Tues–Sun 1–6pm & 9pm–2am.

Las Tres Lucias Mártires e/ Frexes y Aguilera (no phone). Appealing little national-peso café with a cinematic theme. Film posters and black-and-white stills hang on the walls, and the name itself is a reference to the Humberto Solás film. Movies are shown on some evenings. Daily 7am–1am.

CINEMA, THEATRE AND ACTIVITIES

La Bolera Calle Habana e/ Maceo y Libertad ☎ 24 46 8812 ($1CUC per game). A 10min walk from the centre, this is a popular bowling alley that has clowns and magic

shows for kids on Sunday mornings. Daily 10am–1am.
Cine Martí Calle Frexes e/ Maceo y Libertad (no phone).
This small, intimate venue on Parque Calixto García screens
Cuban and international films. Tickets are $2CUP.
Estadio Calixto García ☎ 24 462014. Baseball games at
Holguín's staduim, 1km east of town, take place between
December and May; tickets are $3CUC. Mon & Sat 8.15pm,
Wed, Thurs & Fri 1pm.
Teatro Eddy Suñol Calle Martí e/ Maceo y Libertad
☎ 24 45 4930. On the north side of Parque Calixto García,
this recently restored chocolate-coloured Art Deco theatre
puts on plays, ballet and musical entertainment.

SHOPPING

La Cohoba Plaza de la Marqueta ☎ 24 46 8697. Offers a
fine selection of rum, cigars and coffee. Mon–Sat
9am–4.45pm, Sun 9am–noon.
Egrem Maceo esq. Martí on Parque Calixto García ☎ 24
45 3135. An official music shop selling CDs, guitars and
strings, maracas and other Cuban musical instruments.
Staff are friendly and helpful. Daily 8am–8pm.
La Luz de Yara Maceo esq. Frexes ☎ 24 46 8526. The
largest supermarket in town – which isn't saying much, but
drinks, biscuits and other snacks are available. Mon–Sat
8.30am–7.30pm, Sun 8.30am–1.30pm.
Pedro Rojena Libertad no.193, e/ Frexes y Martí (no
phome). Sells a selection of T-shirts, tapes, CDs, postcards,
stationery and socialist-themed books in English, French
and Spanish. More importantly, it has the *Guia de
Carreteras*, the indispensable Cuban road map book for
drivers. Mon–Fri 9am–4.45pm, Sat 9am–4.15pm, Sun
9am–noon.

DIRECTORY

Banks and exchange BFI, at Libertad e/ Aguilera y Frexes
(Mon–Fri 8am–3pm, last day of month 8am–noon), can
change travellers' cheques and give cash advances on credit
and debit cards. CADECA *casa de cambio* is at Libertad
no.205 e/ Martí e Luz Caballero (daily 7.30am–6pm).
Immigration You can extend standard tourist visas at the
immigration office, Fomento s/n esq. Peralejo, Reparto
Peralta (☎ 24 40 2321).
Internet and telephones Telepunto ETECSA (daily
8.30am–7.30pm), facing Parque Calixto García on Martí
esq. Maceo, sells phone cards. Internet is found half a block
a way in a small blue building at Martí s/n esq. Mártires
(daily 8.30am–12.30pm, 1–7pm; $6CUC/hr). Passport is
required.
Medical Hotel Pernik and Hotel El Bosque both have
medical services. Asistur is also at Hotel Pernik (Mon–Fri
8am–4.30pm; ☎ 24 47 1580). Call ☎ 104 for an
ambulance.
Police Call ☎ 106.
Post office The most central post office is at Libertad no.183
e/ Frexes y Martí (Mon–Fri 8am–8pm, Sat 8am–6pm, Sun
8am–noon), with a DHL service and payphones for
international calls. There is also a 24hr office at Maceo 114 e/
Aria y Agramonte on Parque Carlos Manuel Cespedes.

Gibara

Travelling 35km north from Holguín, through a set of mountains that locals compare to a
woman's breasts, you'll reach the pleasingly somnolent fishing port of **GIBARA**, which
spreads from a calm and sparkling bay into the surrounding rugged hillside. This
little-visited gem is just the place to spend a few hours – or even days – enjoying the
tranquil views, historical ambience, get-away-from-it-all atmosphere and lush scenery; the
tiny scoops of sand at **Playacita Ballado** and **Playa La Concha** are both good options for a
dip after meandering through the town. Gibara is also an ideal base from which to explore
the countryside and nearby pockets of interest such as the **Cavernas de Panadernos** caves.

In 2008, **Hurricane Ike** wreaked havoc upon Gibara; although repairs and rebuilding
are well under way, some sights are still closed, and **Hurricane Sandy**, which rattled
through eastern Cuba in October 2012, hasn't helped the recovery.

Brief history

Founded in 1827, Gibara became the main north-coast port in Oriente because of its
wide bay. During the nineteenth century the town enjoyed valuable **trade links** with
Spain, the rest of Europe and the US, and was considered important enough to justify
construction of a small fortification on the Los Caneyes hilltop, the ruins of which
remain. Though small, Gibara was a fashionable and wealthy town, home to several
aristocratic families and famed for its elegant edifices.

COLUMBUS AND GIBARA

The name "Gibara" comes from the word *giba*, or hump, and refers to the **Silla de Gibara**, a hill which, seen from the sea, looks like a horse's saddle. Gibarans swear this is the one **Christopher Columbus** mentioned in his log when approaching Cuban shores, but although he did first land in Holguín province, the hill he wrote about is generally taken to be El Yunque in Baracoa. The spot where Columbus first disembarked in Cuba on October 28, 1492, is **Playa Blanca**, about 20km east of Gibara, in the Bahía de Bariay; it's marked today by a small monument on the hillside near the pretty, pale-sand beach.

The glory days were not to last, however, and Gibara's importance began to slip away with the introduction of the **railway**, which could more easily transport freight around the country. The decrease in trade left the town floundering, and during the 1920s and 1930s many townsfolk moved elsewhere in search of work, leaving Gibara to shrink into today's pleasant village whose main industries are farming and fishing.

7

Plaza Calixto García

An enjoyable place for a wander, Gibara's streets fan out from the dainty **Plaza Calixto García**. Rimmed with large Inbondeiro African oak trees imported from Angola in the 1970s, the plaza is dominated by the **Iglesia de San Fulgencio**, a mid nineteenth-century church built in a medley of styles. In the centre of the square is the marble **Statue of Liberty**, erected to commemorate the rebel army's triumphant entrance into town on July 25, 1898, during the second War of Independence. Sculpted in Italy, the statue is smaller and less austere than her North American counterpart and bears the winsome face of Aurora Peréz Desdín, a local woman considered so captivating that the town supplied the sculptor with her photograph so that he might preserve her beauty forever. The aubergine-and-yellow building on the c/ Independencia side of the square is a **cigar factory**, where a peek inside reveals workers industriously rolling away.

Museo Historia Natural

Luz Caballero 21 e/ Independencia y Sartorio • Mon 1–5pm, Tues–Fri 8am–5pm, Sat 8am–noon & 1–5pm, Sun 9am–noon • $1CUC, guide $5CUC, photos $5CUC

Even the smallest Cuban town has a moth-eaten collection of stuffed animals, and Gibara is no exception, although its **Museo Historia Natural**, which borders Plaza Calixto García, is worth a peek, not least for its *pièce de résistance* of Cuban grotesque: a long-dead hermaphrodite chicken which was once both rooster and hen.

Museo de Artes Decorativas

Independencia no.19 • Mon–Wed 8am–noon & 1–5pm, Thurs–Sun same hours plus 8–10pm • $1CUC

Before it was closed thanks to damage wreaked by Hurricane Ike in 2008, Gibara's best museum was the **Museo de Artes Decorativas**, set in a sumptuous building built in the nineteenth century as the private residence of José Beola, a wealthy local merchant. When it eventually reopens, you should be able to admire the quietly splendid interior with its narrow staircase sweeping upstairs to the fine, though small, collection of paintings and colonial furniture. The delicately coloured stained-glass windows are original to the house and the biggest in the province.

Cavernas de Panadernos

On the outskirts of Gibara, about 2km from the centre, the town's most rewarding feature are the **Cavernas de Panadernos**, one of 29 caves in the area. Formed from glacial movement during the ice age, the caves have gradually flooded and drained to form a labyrinth of **mineral galleries**. The caves are home to a sizeable colony of **bats** that hover above you as you pass from gallery to gallery and whose presence adds to the generally eerie air.

In all, there are several galleries stretching 11km under the Gibara hillside, though you probably won't go the whole distance. There's much to be seen in the most accessible chambers, however, including red pictographs and the largest collection of red petroglyphs in Cuba. Heading further underground, you're rewarded with a magnificent lake glinting in the Tolkienesque gloom.

You can walk to the Cavernas de Panadernos from Gibara, but you'll need a **guide**, who will provide lanterns and helmets. Nature specialist José Corella knows the caves inside out and has buckets of information on them to boot. He works at the Oficina de Monumentos Technicos, at no.7 Calle Sartorio, next to the old theatre (☎24 84 5107, ✉gibara@baibrama.cult.cu); prices are negotiable.

7

ARRIVAL AND INFORMATION

GIBARA

By bus or truck Buses to Gibara leave the Valiares depot in Holguín around 7am daily and take an hour; you can catch a private *camión* truck from the same place for about $10CUP.

By taxi An unmetered taxi will cost $25–30CUC from Holguín to Gibara, depending on the number of passengers and how hard you bargain.

Services BPA, at Indpendencia no.26 (Mon–Sat 8am–3pm), offers cash withdrawals on Visa and MasterCard and exchange facilities.. The Post Office is at Independencia no.17, just off Parque Calixto García (Mon–Sat 8am–8pm).

ACCOMMODATION

Los Hermanos Calle Céspedes no.13 e/ Luz Caballero y J. Peralta ☎24 84 4542, ✉odalisgonzalezgurri@gmail .com. Three rooms set alongside a sunny courtyard in a very handsome colonial home. All rooms have their own bath but only one is in the old colonial section of the house. **$25CUC**

Hostal La Muralla Calle Joaquin Agüero no.77 ☎24 84 4848. Mariela Barciela runs an excellent and efficient *casa particular* with two comfortable and quiet rooms that open out onto the back patio, where meals are served and there's a communal TV. It's one and a half blocks from the main Calle Independencia. **$25CUC**

Hotel Encanto Ordoño J. Peralta e/ D Mármol y Independencia ☎24 84 4448, ✉direccion @hotelordono.co.cu. This enormous tangerine and papaya coloured building has been recently restored and reopened. Furnished in dusky blue, grey and chocolate fabrics, the super-smart rooms have TVs and plush bathrooms with rain showers. The suite is a feast, with a gloriously kitsch Cuban meringue cake imitation on the bedroom ceiling and a bathroom painted with a charming rural scene. There are two terraces with outstanding views. Rates include breakfast. Rooms **$74CUC**, suite **$104CUC**

La Terraza de Ileana Calle Donato Marmol no.51A ☎24 84 4977. One large room in a third-floor apartment with its own bathroom, kitchen with cooking facilities, sitting room and private terrace, plusa second bedroom off the main living room of the house with a tiny terrace and table. Bonuses include the shared back terrace with hill views, and a lovely host, Ileana Rámirez Ramos. **$25CUC**

EATING AND DRINKING

El Faro Parque de las Madres ☎24 84 4596. Also known as *La Concha*, this state restaurant is cavernous and a little unloved. Although there's not much to recommend in the rather substandard fried-chicken-and-fries fare (mains $2.25–5.65CUC), it does boast a sea view and a cracking sound system. Daily 10am–10pm.

Los Hermanos Calle Céspedes e/ Luz Caballero y Peralta ☎24 84 4542. A paladar doubling as a *casa particular*, with a couple of tables set around a sunny, attractive courtyard. Service and food are both excellent, with satisfying portions of *comida criolla* and some seafood, all served with imagination and flair for $9–13CUC. Daily lunch and dinner.

Paladar El Curujey J. Peralta no.48 e/ J. Mora y Céspedes ☎05 314 1785 (mobile). Professionally run by Dairon Teruca, this new paladar on the top terrace of a private home offers sea views and tasty seafood – lobster, crab and octopus for $7–10CUC, plus one of the best *flan de leches* in Cuba. Daily 11am–late.

NIGHTLIFE AND ENTERTAINMENT

Batería de Fernando VII bar Independencia Final. Set in the diminutive pale yellow fort next to La Concha beach, this bar has singing and dancing shows on and live music. Entry is $10CUP. Shows Mon, Wed & Fri 2pm, concerts

GIBARA'S FESTIVALS

Despite being off the tourist trail, Gibara is notable for its film festival, the biennial **Festival de Cine Pobre** (ⓦfestivalcinepobre.com), which celebrates low-budget fringe movies. Held in April , it's based at the town's cute Cine Jiba.

During Gibara's annual **Semana de la Cultura**, which takes place in mid-January, cultural, music and dance events enliven the town, while in late January, the three-day **Cine de la Cueva** festival sees the subterranean movie nights held in the Panadernos Caves.

Fri, Sat & Sun 10pm.

El Colonial Centro Cultural Luz Caballero no.23A e/ Sartorio y Independencia ⓣ24 84 4471. This leafy courtyard space spends most of its life as a bar but at weekends there's live music alongside the palm trees and fountain. Entry $10CUP. Daily 9am–7pm, shows Sat & Sun 5pm.

Cine Jiba Luz Caballero no.17 e/Sartorio y Independencia facing Parque Calixto García ⓣ24 84 4629. The town's cinema has a large screen and a *sala de video*, and shows a mixture of Cuban and international films.

Mirador del Gibara Los Caneyes (no phone). For the best view over the town, head up to this hilltop bar near the fort. A regular hangout for locals, it has a certain ramshackle charm. Daily 24hr.

Guardalavaca

Despite being the province's main tourist resort, **GUARDALAVACA**, on the north coast 72km northeast from Holguín, retains a charmingly homespun air. The area's name pays tribute to a buccaneer past – Guardalavaca meaning "keep the cow safe", which is thought to refer to the need to protect livestock and valuables from marauding pirates who once used the area as a refuge point. The lively **Playa Guardalavaca** and **Playa Las Brisas** have one plush hotel complex each (with a third and a nearby golf course in the planning); the two exclusive satellite resorts to the west, **Playa Esmeralda** and **Playa Pesquero** (which incorporates the nearby Playa Turquesa) are popular with those seeking luxury and solitude. Surrounded by hilly countryside and shining fields of sugar cane, the **town of Guardalavaca**, which backs onto its namesake resort, is little more than a clutch of houses, many now turned *casas particulares*.

Should you tire of sunning yourself on the beach, the surrounding area has enough sights to keep you busy for a few days, many of them reachable via tours organized by the hotels. About 6km south in the Maniabon hills, a fascinating Taíno burial ground incorporates the **Museo de Chorro de Maíta** and **Aldea Taína**, a re-creation of a Taíno village that really brings the lost culture to life. Close to Playa Esmeralda, at the Bahía

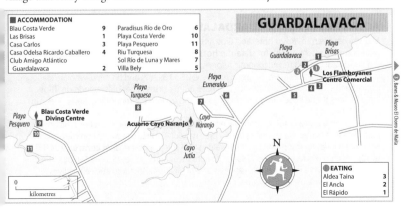

■ ACCOMMODATION			
Blau Costa Verde	9	Paradisus Río de Oro	6
Las Brisas	1	Playa Costa Verde	10
Casa Carlos	3	Playa Pesquero	11
Casa Odelsa Ricardo Caballero	4	Riu Turquesa	8
Club Amigo Atlántico		Sol Río de Luna y Mares	7
Guardalavaca	2	Villa Bely	5

GUARDALAVACA

Playa Guardalavaca
Playa Brisas
Los Flamboyanes Centro Comercial
Playa Esmeralda
Playa Turquesa
Blau Costa Verde Diving Centre
Playa Pesquero
Acuario Cayo Naranjo
Cayo Naranjo
Cayo Jutía

N

Banes & Museo El Chorro de Maíta

0		2
	kilometres	

● EATING	
Aldea Taina	3
El Ancla	2
El Rápido	1

de Naranjo, an offshore **aquarium** offers an entertaining day out, though one of the most rewarding pastimes in Guardalavaca is to **rent a bicycle or moped** and head off into the dazzling countryside to enjoy stunning views over hills and sea; you can also do this on **horseback** with a guide.

Playa Guardalavaca

Snorkelling equipment $10CUC/3hr • Club Amigo Atlántico day-pass $25CUC

A 1500m-long stretch of sugar-white sand dappled with light streaming through abundant foliage, **Playa Guardalavaca** is a delight. A shady boulevard of palms, tamarind and sea grape trees runs along the centre of the beach. One of the most refreshing aspects of Playa Guardalavaca is that the beach is well used by Cubans as well as tourists, giving it a certain vitality with a lack of hustle. Midway along, a **restaurant** serves simple snacks and drinks, and there are stands renting out **snorkelling equipment** so you can explore the coral reef offshore.

Playa Las Brisas

Las Brisas day-pass $30CUC

A chain of large natural boulders divides Playa Guardalavaca from the relatively small **Playa Las Brisas** to the east. The beach here fronts the *Las Brisas* hotel (see p.364), and non-guests are not permitted to access it via the hotel unless they purchase a day-pass. About midway between the two hotels on the opposite side of the road behind the beach, the **Los Flamboyanes Centro Comercial** comprises a few shops selling beach accessories, snacks and postcards, a Casa del Habano and an *El Rápido* fast-food outlet. A second mini-complex a few metres away has a more upmarket version of the same.

Playa Esmeralda

Paradisus del Oro day-pass around $150CUC; Sol Río de Luna y Mares day-pass $63CUC

Some 5km west from Guardalavaca along the Holguín road, picture-perfect **Playa Esmeralda** (also known as Estero Ciego) boasts clear blue water, powdery sand speckled with thatched sunshades and two luxury hotels (see p.365) hidden from view by thoughtfully planted bushes and shrubs. If you want unashamed hassle-free luxury, where the intrusion of local culture is kept to a bare minimum, this is the place for you. To access the beach, non-guests have to buy a day pass that covers facilities, meals and drinks.

ACTIVITIES IN PLAYA GUARDALAVACA

Midway between *Las Brisas* hotel and *Club Amigo Atlántico*, next to the Los Flamboyanes mini-complex, is a hire point for state-run **horseriding**, where rides cost $10/hr. However, thanks to Raúl Castro's new economic reforms, **private horseriding** is now available from Daniel Avila Hernández (daily 10–5pm; mobile ☎05 33 89287) and his crew, who are stationed opposite the *Las Brisas* hotel entrance and have eight horses in beautiful condition. Trips include rides to the beach, into the countryside and up into the mountains, and prices run from $8CUC/hr.

Playa Guardalavaca is also a good place to go **diving**; local marine attractions include parrotfish and barracuda as well as black coral. The *Sol Río de Luna y Mares* complex and the *Paradisus Río de Oro* resort on Playa Esmeralda share the Sea Lovers **dive centre** (☎24 43 0132), which offers regular dives ($35CUC), night dives and courses ($335–365CUC). The Blue World diving centre in front of the *Blau Costa Verde* on Playa Pesquero also offers dives ($35CUC) and various ACUC courses.

Playa Pesquero and Playa Turquesa

Hotel day-passes $48–65CUC

Fifteen kilometres west of Playa Guardalavaca, the three state-of-the-art hotels (see p.365) on Playa Pesquero and one on the exquisite Playa Turquesa, 3km away, represent Guardalavaca's most recent development. Lined with gnarled and twisted sea grape trees and thatch umbrellas providing much-needed shade, **Playa Pesquero** is a 1.2km-long horseshoe-shaped bay of sparkling sand. The quieter **Playa Turquesa** (also known as Playa Yuraguanal) is one of the most beautiful in the region. Bordered by mangrove forest at its eastern boundary, the shallow bay has a small coral reef a short swim offshore, while a strip of dense forest between *Riu Playa Turquesa* and the beach makes it feel like an undiscovered paradise.

There are no facilities outside of the hotels; both beaches can be accessed from the road, but you'll have to buy a day-pass if you want to use the hotel facilities.

Museo El Chorro de Maíta

7

Tues–Sat 9am–5pm, Sun 9am–1pm • $2CUC, photos $5CUC

Some 6km southeast of the Playa Guardalavaca hotel strip in the Maniabon hills, the fascinating **Museo El Chorro de Maíta** is a must-see for anyone interested in pre-Columbian history. A shallow pit in the middle of the museum holds 108 Taíno **skeletons** (mostly original, some reproductions) buried on this site between the 1490s and the 1540s, and uncovered in 1986. The most interesting aspect of the burial pit is that one of the skeletons was found to be a young male European buried in a Christian position with his arms folded across his chest. While no records exist to support this theory, it's thought that the European had been living in harmony with the Taíno community.

Cabinets around the walls of the museum display fragments of earthenware pots along with shell and ceramic jewellery, while arrows positioned in the grave indicate where these were found. The area around the museum has more indigenous remains than any other part of Cuba, with villagers still unearthing artefacts and remnants of jewellery today.

Aldea Taína

Daily 9am–4.30pm • $5CUC

Just across the road from the Museo de Chorro de Maíta is the **Aldea Taína**, an evocative reconstruction of a Taíno village, offering valuable insight into an extinguished culture and bringing to life many of the artefacts seen in museums around the country. The painstakingly authentic little settlement features **houses** made from royal palm trees populated by life-sized models of Taínos posed cooking and preparing food or attending to community rituals. Of particular note is the group inside one of the houses watching the **medicine man** attempt to cure a patient, and another group outside depicted in a **ceremonial dance**. The Taíno-themed restaurant (see p.366) is also pretty decent.

Acuario Cayo Naranjo

Daily 7am–4pm, marine show noon–1pm • Local hotels offer a package covering bus transfers, boat passage and dolphin and sea-lion show for $50CUC; a 20min swim with dolphins is $58CUC extra • ☎ 24 43 0132

Some 6km west of Guardalavaca beach, the **Acuario Cayo Naranjo** complex is built on stilts about 250m offshore in the shallows of the Bahía de Naranjo. Although calling itself an aquarium, it's really more of a tourist centre cum marine zoo, as its smattering of sea creatures in tanks are overshadowed by giddier attractions: yacht and speedboat "**seafari**" excursions around the bay, a saccharine **dolphin** and sea-lion show, and the chance to swim with a few of the dolphins themselves.

ARRIVAL AND INFORMATION

By plane Flights for visitors on package holidays land at Holguín's Aeropuerto Frank País, from where special buses ferry guests to the resorts.

By taxi or colectivo There's no public transport from Holguín to Guardalavaca, but a metered taxi will take you there for $30CUC ($40CUC from the airport) one-way. Alternatively, *colectivo* shared taxis also run this route and leave throughout the day until about 5pm, costing $10–15CUC per person (depending on how full the car is). State and private taxis from Gibara are $40CUC, and from Cayo Saetía $120CUC.

By tourist bus Cubatur in Holguín (see p.355) runs buses to Guardalavaca, departing at 8am and returning at 5pm

GUARDALAVACA

(July & Aug Sat & Sun; $5CUC return).

Tourist information Each hotel has its own excursions officer who arranges trips to the local sights (see box opposite) and can supply some information in the absence of formal tourist offices.

Services You can cash travellers' cheques at all the hotels and at the Banco Financiero Internacional (Mon–Fri 9am–3pm; last day of month 9am–noon), in the back section of the Centro Comercial Los Flamboyanes, where you can also get advances on credit cards. For medical matters, there's Clínica Internacional (24hr; ☎ 24 43 0312), part of the Islazul *cabaña* complex set behind the Guardalavaca beach. *Club Amigo-Atlantico* also has an on-site pharmacy.

GETTING AROUND

By car All the hotels have car rental desks, or you can visit Cubacar or Havanautos (both ☎ 24 43 0389), in adjacent offices next door to *Las Brisas* hotel in Playa Guardalavaca.

By moped You can rent mopeds ($13–25CUC/24hr) outside *Paradisus Ro de Oro* hotel at Playa Esmeralda, from *Club Amigo Atlántico* and *Las Brisas* hotels in Playa Guardalavaca, or the *Maritím* at Playa Pesquero (all open daily 9am–5pm).

By tourist bus The Guardalavaca Bus Tour is a hop-on-hop-off service that covers a wide loop travelling from Playa Guardalavaca west to Playa Pesquero and inland to the Chorro de Maíta museum. It runs from 9am to 5pm, and tickets cost $5CUC.

By bicycle All the local hotels offer bicycles free of charge, an excellent way to get around.

By horse-drawn carriage Carriage rides are available around the Guardalavaca beach area from $15CUC/hr.

ACCOMMODATION

As a prime resort, Guardalavaca's beachside accommodation consists of **all-inclusive hotels**, mostly at the top end of the price range; the exception are the excellent *Las Brisas* and the lacklustre *Club Amigo Atlántico*. It's worth checking with Gaviota and Cubatur tour operators in Holguín (see p.355) before booking directly with one of the all-inclusive hotels, as they offer discounted weekend promotional offers when occupancy is low. The many **casas particulares** in Guardalavaca town are a less expensive alternative.

PLAYA GUARDALAVACA

Club Amigo Atlántico Guardalavaca ☎ 24 43 0180, ✉ rpublic@clubamigo.gvc.tur.cu. Although quite old and dated, this free-form complex of guestrooms, pools, bars and restaurants is a friendly and unpretentious resort. Of the various accommodation options, the premium "Villa" section is easily the most appealing, with cool, airy pastel-painted houses with balconies and simple but attractive furnishings; the "Tropical" and "Standard" areas offer plain but decent rooms – some with a sea view – strung along shadowy corridors, while the best-avoided "Bungalow" section seems stuck in a 1970s time warp. Standard **$72CUC**; Tropical **$78CUC**; bungalow **$86CUC**; villa **$158CUC**

GUARDALAVACA MAIN ROAD

Casa Carlos Edificio 15, Apt 1, Av Guardalavaca ☎ 53 55 7265. A totally independent, smart and well-equipped one-bedroom apartment with large living room-diner and kitchen. **$35CUC**

Casa Odelsa Ricardo Caballero Av Guardalavaca, Edificio 11, Apto 2, 2nd floor ☎ 24 43 0485. One compact

room in a spotless apartment run by the friendly Odelsa and her husband, Luis. It has a/c, fridge, TV and DVD; the bathroom is just outside the room past the kitchen. Odelsa serves up breakfast, lunch and dinner. **$35CUC**

Villa Bely Carretera a Guardalavaca ☎ 05 26 14192 (mobile), ⊕ villabely.orgfree.com. This large, spacious house is set back off the main Guardalavaca road and is accessed by turning right just before the bridge when arriving in Guardalavaca. Owners Mircelia and Asbel offer a huge first-floor apartment with kitchen and dining area (although no cooking facilities) plus a terrace. Although further from the beach than those in the *edificios* on the main road, this is a quieter spot. **$30CUC**

PLAYA LAS BRISAS

Las Brisas ☎ 24 43 0218, ⊕ hotelescubancan.com. This plush resort has four restaurants, two snack bars, a beauty salon, massage parlour, kids' camp and watersports, as well as mercifully restrained variety-show-style entertainment. There's a choice between rooms and suites

EXCURSIONS FROM GUARDALAVACA

While you can get to most sites independently, it is usually easier to go on a tour. All excursions from Guardalavaca are organized by Cubatur (☎ 24 43 0171), Havanatur (☎ 24 43 0406), Viajes Cubanacán (☎ 24 43 0226) and Gaviota Tours (☎ 24 43 0907, ext 120) , all of which have representatives in each hotel and a central office behind the Centro Comercial Los Flamboyanes.

Cayo Saetía A day-trip by catamaran to one of the most unusual resorts in the country. Enjoy the white-sand beach and take a safari through the surrounding woodland and savannahs to see zebras, ostriches and the like roaming freely. $79CUC.

Havana You are flown to Havana for a one-night whistle-stop tour of La Habana Vieja and Vedado, with some free time for shopping. A night at Tropicana cabaret can be included. $356CUC, $422CUC with Tropicana.

Holguín A half-day jaunt to the provincial capital,

including a visit to a cigar factory to see cigars being handmade, a trip up the Loma de la Cruz hill, lunch and free time to explore the town centre. Although you could just as easily rent a car to get to Holguín, the tour is the only way to visit the cigar factory. $59CUC.

Santiago de Cuba A full day-trip to Cuba's second-biggest city. The bus ride there and back takes you through some of the region's most scenic countryside, and the trip includes visits to the Santa Ifigenia cemetery, the Castillo el Morro and a cigar factory. $69–99CUC.

within the hotel block or more privacy in newer bungalow-style rooms, although all are equally luxurious. **$228CUC**

PLAYA ESMERALDA

Paradisus Río de Oro ☎ 24 43 0090, ⓦ melia.com. One of the best hotels in Cuba, aimed at those seeking top-of-the-line Caribbean-style luxury. The attractive two-storey villas in muted colours are set among gardens brimming with fragrant tropical plant life. Rooms are attractive, with minibar, cable TV and large, smart bathrooms, including two with disabled access. The hotel boasts four excellent à la carte restaurants, including a Japanese one serving a range of sushi, as well as an airy buffet restaurant. Four beaches, three private, are within easy reach. There's a spa with a sauna as well. **$540CUC**

Sol Río de Luna y Mares ☎ 24 43 0060, ⓦ melia.com. This complex comprises two hotels joined together to operate as one. The more attractive "Luna" section offers spacious, light accommodation in three-storey blocks arranged around a central pool, while "Mares" features spacious rooms grouped in a single block. There are two buffet restaurants, four à la carte restaurants, four bars and two pools. Facilities include tennis, sauna, gym and various watersports equipment, although some of this could do with replacing. **$300CUC**

PLAYA PESQUERO AND PLAYA TURQUESA

Blau Costa Verde ☎ 24 433 510, ⓦ blau-hotels-cuba .com. A large, sinuous pool forms the centrepiece of this

hotel, comprised of two-storey hacienda-style blocks scattered around pleasant grounds. Rooms are expansive with huge beds, large bathrooms, attractive balconies and a decent array of mod cons. **$170CUC**

Playa Costa Verde ☎ 24 43 3520, ⓦ gaviota-grupo .com. Popular with scuba enthusiasts, with smart if slightly sterile rooms in small blocks. There's quite a sociable atmosphere, partly due to the range of entertainment, including outdoor jacuzzis, pool tables, table football, ping-pong and a disco. The beach is a few minutes' walk away over a wooden bridge spanning a mangrove lagoon. **$230CUC**

Playa Pesquero ☎ 24 433 530, ⓔ jefe.ventas @ppesquero.tur.cu. This huge complex, offering the ultimate in get-away-from-it-all luxury, is one of the biggest hotels in Cuba. With a large selection of restaurants, a vast swimming pool, its own mini shopping mall, sports facilities and activities for all ages, this is a good option for families. The cool, stylish rooms, furnished with natural materials, are set in two-storey blocks; each has its own balcony with flower-filled window boxes and wicker furniture. **$280CUC**

Riu Turquesa ☎ 24 43 3540, ⓦ riu.com. The only hotel on the exquisite Playa Turquesa, with extensive gardens in which the original forest habitat has been preserved. Attractions include elegant rooms, seven restaurants including Mexican and Mediterranean, and circular swimming pools arranged in a descending series and fed by a cascade of water. The proliferation of stairs may prove tiresome for anyone with mobility issues. **$200CUC**

EATING, DRINKING AND NIGHTLIFE

Most visitors to the area eat most meals at their hotel **restaurants**, but there are a couple of alternatives. Similarly, **bars** and **nightlife** are largely confined to the hotels, where entertainment teams host nightly stage shows in which they urge guests to take part in boisterous slapstick sketches and dances. If you've bought a day-pass to any of the all-inclusives, you can stay on for dinner and evening shenanigans.

7

Aldea Taína (no phone). Decorated with designs found on the walls of Taíno caves, the restaurant of the museum village (see p.363) serves Taíno foods including herb teas, sweet potato and cassava bread. The recommended dish is the *ajiaco*, a tasty potato, maize and meat stew for $10CUC. Daily 9am–4.30pm.

El Anda Playa Guardalavaca ☏ 24 43 0381. Some 100m west of *Club Amigo* along the beach, this wind-swept cabin-like state-run restaurant offers standard *comida criolla* and seafood (mains $6.45–25.90CUC) and is a good place for a drink after walking along the beach. Daily 11am–10pm.

El Rápido Los Flamboyanes complex (no phone). Close to the *Atlántico* complex, and serving pizzas, hot dogs and sandwiches. Daily, 24hr.

Banes

A mix of characterful wooden houses, dishevelled Art Deco beauties and rather more anonymous concrete buildings, the sleepy town of **BANES** lies 31km southeast of Guardalavaca. Refreshingly untouristy, it's known for its museum of pre-Columbian artefacts and for its association with the two titans of twentieth century Cuban history – Fidel Castro and Fulgencio Batista. Castro married his first wife in Banes, and Cuba's elected president-turned dictator was born here in 1901.

Iglesia de Nuestra Señora de la Caridad

The Art Deco-style **Iglesia de Nuestra Señora de la Caridad** sits on the edge of a central park with a neat domed bandstand. This is where, on October 10, 1948, **Fidel Castro** married his first wife, Mirta Diaz-Balart, sister of a university friend and daughter of the mayor of Banes. The couple divorced in 1954, the bride's conservative family allegedly disapproving of the young Castro, already known as a firebrand at the university. Although the church interior is fairly prosaic in itself, it's mildly interesting for the historical connection. To go inside, you'll need to ask at the priest's house next door, another handsome Art Deco building.

Museo Indocubano Bani

Avenida General Marreo no.305 • Tues–Sat 9am–5pm, Sun 8am–noon • $1CUC including guided tour in Spanish or English, photos $5CUC

Banes' most substantial attraction is the **Museo Indocubano Bani**, one of the few museums in Cuba exclusively devoted to **pre-Columbian Cuban history**. While many of the fragments and representational sketches of indigenous communities are similar to exhibits in larger museums in the country, it also has a unique gathering of **jewellery** gleaned from the Holguín region. Only a tiny selection of the 22,000 pieces owned by the museum are on display; these include the first skeleton found at Chorro de Maíta as well as its *pièce de résistance*, a tiny but stunning gold (replica) idol.

Casa de la Cultura

General Marreo no.327 • Daily 8am–10pm • Free • ☏ 24 80 2111

On the opposite side of General Marreo from the Museo Indocubano Bani, the elegant **Casa de la Cultura** is one of Banes's most outstanding buildings, with a black-and-white marble-tiled floor, pale pink and gold walls and a sunny courtyard at the back. As the town's theatre and music hall it has regular performances of traditional music and dance, and players are generally unfazed if you pass by to admire the building and catch snippets of their rehearsals during the daytime.

ARRIVAL AND DEPARTURE
BANES

By camiones and colectivo Services from Guardalavaca, Holguín, Mayarí and Santiago arrive at the bus station on Calle Los Angeles esq Tráfico.

By taxi Taxis from Guardalavaca cost around $30CUC.

By workers' bus Many travellers also use the workers' transport from Guardalavaca to Holguín but you'd need a bit of Spanish to negotiate this one.

By car The road from Banes to Mayarí (see p.368) is in an appalling state, but it is passable in a normal hire car if you drive carefully.

ACCOMMODATION, EATING AND DRINKING

Casa Las Delicias Augusto Blanca no.1107 e/ Bruno Meriño y Bayamo, Reparto Cardenas ☎ 24 80 2905. Jorge and Caridad offer a spotless, large room with its own bathroom, a small kitchen and a covered terrace. The friendly couple also runs a paladar (daily noon–midnight), in an additional private dining room with a bar, offering seafood as well as spaghetti and chicken dishes ($5–12CUC). **$25CUC**

Cafétería Las Palmas General Marreo no.730 ☎ 24 80 2803. A thatched restaurant and bar that dishes up indifferent pizza, spaghetti, sandwiches and the ubiquitous fried chicken ($2.80–4.85CUC). Restaurant daily 1–2pm and 6–11pm; bar daily 24hr.

El Latino Av Martí s/n ☎ 24 80 2298. Just down the road from the church, this is the smartest convertible peso establishment in town, serving up *comida criolla* and tortillas ($2.30–4.5CUC5) in air-conditioned surrounds. Daily 7am–11pm.

Cayo Saetía

7

Hidden away on the east side of the Bahía de Nipe near the village of Felton, and connected to the mainland by a drawbridge, picture-postcard, isolated **Cayo Saetía** is the most bizarre – and exclusive – resort in the country. A one-time private game reserve and beach catering to government party officials, it was opened up to the public during the 1990s, yet still retains its air of exclusivity. It's run by Gaviota, the army-owned tourist group, which may explain the vaguely military aura, notably in the ranks of jeeps and other vehicles stationed across the island. Oddly, Cayo Saetía's beauty is not diminished by the pale orange smog drifting across the bay from grimy **Nicaro**, a distinctly uneventful town wreathed in plumes of smoke from an electricity plant.

Cayo Saetía beach

Daily 9am–5pm • $10CUC

Cayo Saetía's northern coast offers scoops of practically deserted soft white **sand**, hemmed in by a buttery yellow rockface and sliding into the bay's sparkling turquoise green waters. Close to shore, the island's shelf makes for perfect **snorkelling**, with a wealth of brightly coloured sea life, while further out a coral reef offers even better pickings. If you want the beach to yourself, arrive early, as an invasion of tourists on catamaran trips from Playa Guardalavaca arrives from noon onwards. The beach is some 8km from the hotel.

Cayo Saetía safari park

Cayo Saetía's 42 square kilometres of woodland and savannahs (unique in Cuba) are home to the most exotic collection of animals in the country – a menagerie of imported zebra, antelope, deer, wild boar and even three ostriches, all freely galloping about. It's as close as Cuba gets to a **safari park** and guests are driven off-piste in a jeep safari through the lush grounds, to admire and photograph the creatures – just before sunset is the ideal time.

ARRIVAL AND ACTIVITIES   CAYO SAETÍA

By car Most people arrive in a hire car; from the main-road turn-off to Cayo Saetía, it's around 21km to the hotel, passing the small town of Felton. The road is mildly bumpy but a 4WD isn't necessary.

Taxis A metered taxi from Guardalavaca costs $120CUC one-way. Private taxis are not allowed to pass the drawbridge, but the guards there can arrange for onward transport (8km) to the hotel.

Activities Jeep safari tours ($9CUC/1–1.5hr) take you through the grounds and can be arranged from the hotel or at the beach restaurant. The latter also offers reasonably priced horseriding ($6CUC), snorkelling expeditions ($5CUC), day-trips around the cay by speedboat ($6CUC) and catamaran safaris ($15–40CUC). Pedalo and kayak usage is free for all visitors.

ACCOMMODATION AND EATING

Cayo Saetía ☎ 24 24 51 6900, ⊛ gaviota-grupo.com. Spread about a grassy compound on a knoll overlooking the sea is this twelve-room lodge, which offers eight comfortable double cabins, three superior rooms and one suite. Rooms are spacious and comfortable but spartan. The lodge's restaurant cooks up exotic meats such as antelope ($6–12CUC). Cabins $65CUC, superior rooms $90CUC, suite $100CUC

Parque Nacional La Mensura

Some 45km southwest of Cayo Saetía, the ground swells and erupts into the livid green Sierra de Cristal mountains in which lies the **Parque Nacional La Mensura**. High above the cloud line here, the beautiful **Pinares de Mayarí** pine forest here is a great place for some hiking or relaxation, or a stay at the *Villa Pinares de Mayarí* (see opposite). The forest is reached from the nondescript little town of **Mayarí**, 26km to the north, from where you head south towards the Carretera Pinares and take the right-hand track where the road forks, past tiny Las Coloradas; from Holguín, it's a 2.5-hour drive. Though passable in a rental car, the road is steep and poorly maintained so requires masterful driving, and during the wet season it's advisable to check in advance if it's passable.

The drive up the hill to the forest affords crisp views over the Bahía de Nipe and the terracotta nickel mines to the east, near Nicaro. This lofty region is also Cuba's main producer of **coffee**, with stretches of coffee plants visible along the way. At the top of the hill the sharp incline evens out into a plateau, where the lush green grass cool air form a scene that's more alpine than Caribbean.

Saltón de Guayabo

Viewpoint daily 8am–4pm • $5CUC including guided treks

You can take a dip in the wide and tranquil **La Presa lake** near the *Villa Pinares de Mayarí* hotel, but there's more exhilarating swimming to be had at the foot of the majestic **Saltón de Guayabo waterfall**, a definite must-see if you are in the area. If you drive for about ten minutes back down the hill towards Mayarí, a steep and narrow dirt track on the left will get you to a **viewpoint**, which provides a splendid vista over a misty and pine tree-covered mountainside, parted here by the two turbulent cascades that comprise the Saltón de Guayabo, thundering down to a pool below. At 104m, the larger of the two is the highest waterfall in Cuba. **Guided treks** (1–2hr) along the nature trail to the foot of the falls can also be arranged at the viewpoint.

> ### CASTRO AND BIRÁN
>
> A vast area of swaying cane and working plantations, the whole swathe of land southwest from Bahía de Nipe and west of the Pinares de Mayarí is given over to sugar. There's nothing here for the casual visitor, though true Castro devotees may wish to make a pilgrimage to the tiny community of **Birán**, 44km southwest of Mayarí, near which, at the **Finca Las Manacas** plantation, **Fidel Castro** was born on August 13, 1926. He spent part of his youth here, until he was sent to school in Santiago, and he still owns the farm. Home to the former school, post office, bar, butcher's, cock-fighting arena and a hotel, the tidy and well-maintained farm also holds the **Sitio Histórico de Birán museum** (Tues–Sun 9am–3pm, closed if raining; $10CUC, photos $5CUC), with a collection of photographs, clothes, Fidel's childhood bed and a 1918 Ford. Near the entrance are the well-tended graves of Fidel's father Angel Castro and mother Lina Ruz.
>
> Finding the *finca* is something of a challenge: from Holguín follow the road east to Cueto, then turn south onto the road to Loynaz Hechevarría; turn east at the sign to Birán and carry on a further 2km north.

ACCOMMODATION

Villa Pinares de Mayarí Pinares de Mayarí ☎ 24 50 3308, ✉ comercial@vpinares.co.cu. Comprising several huge chalet-style villas with quaint rooms richly inlaid with wood, this hotel makes a perfect base for exploring the nearby wilds and is decidedly picturesque in itself, with a

PARQUE NACIONAL LA MENSURA

small pool and a central dining room boasting a beamed ceiling, like some giant's cabin. The friendly staff are extremely accommodating, and guided walks are available into the pine-scented mountains. Call ahead as it sometimes closes in slow periods. $40CUC

Guantánamo town

Even though the provincial capital of **GUANTÁNAMO** is only on the tourist map because of its proximity to the US Guantánamo naval station, 22km southeast, the base plays a very small part in the everyday life of the town itself. For the most part, this is a slow-paced place marked by a few ornate buildings, attractive but largely featureless streets and an easy-going populace. Most visitors bypass it altogether, and those who don't tend to use it simply as a stepping-stone to the naval base and attractions further afield. However, it's worth visiting the **Casa del Changüí**, where changüí genre (a country music which predates son) is nurtured and performed, or taking in a performance by the **Tumba Francesa Pompadour**, an Afro–Haitian cultural and dance group.

Parque Martí

Guantánamo town fans out around the central **Parque Martí**, a small concrete square neatly bordered by intricately trimmed evergreens with hooped gateways. On its north side is the **Parroquía Santa Catalina de Riccis**, a pretty ochre church built in 1863, while one block north, the **Palacio de Salcines** is an eclectic neo-Rococo building with shuttered windows, cherubs over the door and, on its high spire, an outstretched figure with bugle in hand, which has become the symbol of the city. The art museum and gallery inside were closed indefinitely for renovation at the time of writing.

Museo Provincial

Martí no.804 • Mon–Fri 8am–4.30pm, Sat 8am–noon • $1CUC, guide $1CUC

One block behind Parque Martí is the humble **Museo Provincial**. Built on an old prison site, it displays some fearsome padlocks and bolts alongside archaeological remains and stuffed animals and birds. Much more interesting is the room devoted to the joint USSR and Cuban **space flight**, which sent the first Cuban (and, indeed, Latin American) astronaut – Arnaldo Tamayo Ménendez – into space in September 1980. A peek inside the actual capsule used in their descent back to earth is the museum's highlight.

GUANTANAMERA

Synonymous with the beleaguered history of the US naval base, Guantánamo province is an enduring legacy of the struggle between the US and Cuba. In name at least, it's one of the best-known places in Cuba: many a Cuban and a fair few visitors can sing the first bars of the immortal song **Guantanamera** – written by Joseito Fernández in the 1940s as a tribute to the women of Guantánamo. Made internationally famous by North American folk singer Pete Seeger during the 1970s, it has become something of a Cuban anthem and a firm – if somewhat hackneyed – favourite of tourist-bar troubadours the country over, a fitting fate for the song which includes words from José Martí's most famous work, *Versos Sencillos* ("simple verses").

Plaza del Mercado

Los Maceos esq. Prado

A couple of blocks northeast of Parque Martí, one of the most intriguing buildings in Guantánamo town is the quite fantastical agricultural marketplace, **Plaza del Mercado**, with its big pink dome and crown-like roof bearing statues of regal long-necked geese at each corner. It was designed by Guantánamo's most famous architect, Leticio Salcines, who along with the Palacio Salcines, designed three hundred buildings in the town. Closed for repairs at the time of writing, it's due to reopen in 2014.

Casa del Changüí

Serafín Sánchez e/ Narcisco López y Jesús del Sol • Performances Fri, Sat & Sun 8pm • $3CUC • ☎ 21 32 4178

The **Casa del Changüí** cultural and nightlife venue is a great place to catch live shows by changüí groups, with performances by the likes of Tumbao de Monte, Universales del Son, Morenos de Changui and Estrellas Campesinas in an alfresco courtyard decorated with colourful murals. Changüi emerged from the Guantánamo countryside as campesino music in the late nineteenth century, and is played by an ensemble that incorporates the Cuban *tres* – the only melodic instrument in the genre – the *marímbula* and a metal *guayo* as well as maracas and bongo drums.

Tumba Francesa Pompadour

Serafín Sánchez 715 e/ Narcisco López y Jesús del Sol • Performances Tues, Wed, Thurs & Fri 9.30am • $5CUC • ☎ 21 381 669

Formed following the migration of French landowners, slaves and free slaves from Haiti to Cuba after the 1791 Haitian Revolution, the **Tumba Francesa Pompadour** is an Afro–Cuban–Haitian society and dance group who perform traditional dances at their base here in Guantánamo town. Sundays are often booked out with large tourist groups but all visitors are welcome.

ARRIVAL AND DEPARTURE
GUANTÁNAMO TOWN

By plane Mariana Grajales Airport (☎ 21 355 912) is 12km southeast of town. Taxis into town cost $6–8CUC.
Destinations Havana (2 weekly; 2hr 10min).
By train The town's train station (☎ 21 32 55 18) is centrally located in a squat Art Deco folly on Pedro A. Pérez.
Destinations Havana (every other day; 16hr); Holguín (every other day; 6hr); Matanzas (every other day; 14hr); Santa Clara (every other day; 11hr 30min); Las Tunas (every other day; 5hr).
By bus Víazul services (☎ 21 32 57 80) arrive at the Astro

Terminal de Omnibus(☎ 21 32 5588) on Carretera Santiago, 2.5km out of town; you can walk or catch a *bicitaxi* into the centre, but as it's so remote you may want to organize a taxi or pickup in advance.
Destinations Baracoa (daily; 3hr 10min; Santiago de Cuba (daily; 1hr 30min).
By Conectando Cuba bus Services for Baracoa depart Guantánamo town on Tues, Thurs and Saturday at 9.30am $10CUC.

INFORMATION, TRAVEL AGENTS AND TOURS

Infotur The helpful office at Calle García s/n e/ E Giro y F Crombet (Mon–Sat 8.30am–5pm; ☎ 21 35 1993) offers a weekly events list, internet ($6CUC/hr), and can arrange permits to Caimanera (see p.372) with three working days' notice.
Islazul Based at Aguilera s/n e/ Calixto García y Maceo (Mon–Fri 10am–noon & 3–5pm; ☎ 21 32 7197), Islazul

can secure permits to visit Caimanera.
Havanatur at Aguilera s/n e/ Calixto García y Los Maceo (Mon–Sat 9am–noon & 2–4pm; ☎ 21 32 6365) offers the Guajira Guantanamera excursion ($56CUC per person, min four people) visiting the stone zoo, taking a train to Jamaica, touring a sugar mill and a city tour that includes a visit to the Tumba Francesa and Casa del Changüí.

ACCOMMODATION

Casa de Amelia Hernández Roger Sol no.664 e/ Paseo y N López ☎ 21 35 1766. A two-bedroom apartment with

an independent entrance in a friendly household close to the Casa del Changüí. Rates include breakfast. **$20CUC**

THE US AT GUANTÁNAMO

Described by Fidel Castro as the dagger in the side of Cuban sovereignty, the **US naval base at Guantánamo** is approximately 118 square kilometres of leased North American territory, armed to the teeth and planted on Cuba's southeastern coast.

The history of the naval base here dates back to Cuba's nominal victory in the Wars of Independence with Spain, whereupon the US government immediately began to erode Cuba's autonomy. Under the terms of the **1901 Platt Amendment**, the US ordered Cuba to sell or lease land necessary for a naval station, declaring without irony that it was "to enable the United States to maintain the independence of Cuba". Its primary aim, however, was to protect the nascent Panama Canal from any naval attacks. An annual rent was set at two thousand gold coins, and the base was born. In 1934 the Treaty of Reciprocity repealed the Platt Amendment but did not alter the conditions surrounding the lease; and as it's stipulated that the lease cannot be terminated without both parties' consent, it seems unlikely that Cuba will regain sovereignty of the land under its present regime. Famously, Fidel Castro has not cashed a single rent cheque from the US government, preferring to preserve them for posterity in a locked desk drawer.

GITMO DEVELOPS

Although the US quickly broke off all relations with the Cuban government after the Revolution, they were less speedy to give up their territory. Known as "**Gitmo**" by US servicemen, Guantánamo base is like an American theme park inside, with stateside cars zooming along perfectly paved roads bordered by shops and suburban houses. From the 1970s until the mid-1990s, such material riches gave the base an El Dorado lustre that lured many a dissident Cuban to brave the heavily mined perimeter or chance the choppy waters to reach this ersatz chunk of North America in the hope of gaining US citizenship as a political asylum seeker. US immigration policy was changed in 1994 and now Cubans who make it into the base usually find themselves making a swift exit back onto Cuban soil via the nearest gate.

CAMP DELTA AND THE WAR ON TERROR

The base's history took another twist in December 2001 with the decision of the Bush administration to detain Islamic militants captured as part of the "**War on Terror**". Prisoners were initially kept in the makeshift Camp X-Ray but in April 2002 were transferred to **Camp Delta**, a larger, permanent site, which comprises several detention camps, manned by six hundred soldiers as part of the Joint Task Force Guantánamo. Controversy immediately arose around the circumstances under which the men were held. Because they were classed as "**illegal combatants**" rather than prisoners of war, the US military felt they did not have to uphold the Geneva Convention and that the detainees could be held indefinitely without charge. Some 779 people (including a number of children) representing forty different nationalities have to date been held here, many without access to any court, legal counsel or family visits.

Since 2002, images of shackled detainees in orange jumpsuits – along with reports of numerous suicide attempts and persistent allegations of abuse and torture of prisoners – have provoked international condemnation, including the accusation that the detainees are being held unlawfully. While the majority of them have not been charged, those who have were tried in the **Guantánamo Military Commissions** to determine whether their crimes warrant further detention. No one has been convicted by a trial in a US court of law. To date, more than 570 prisoners have been released.

THE FUTURE OF THE BASE

A decision in June 2004 by the US Supreme Court ruled that the detainees should come under the jurisdiction of US courts and that the policy of holding prisoners indefinitely without the right to judicial review was unlawful. Rather than address these charges, the Bush administration passed the **Military Commissions Act 2006**, which overrode the main objections. In January 2009, as part of a broader aim to restore the international reputation of the US's justice system and foreign policies, President Obama suspended the Guantánamo Military Commissions and vowed that the detainee camp would be **closed** by January 2010. This promise remains unfulfilled.

Casa de Lissett Foster Lara Pedro A. Pérez 761 e/ Jesús del Sol y Prado ☎ 21 32 5970, ✉ lisset128 @gmail.com. Three clean and comfortable double rooms with a/c and private bathrooms in a large, airy, modern apartment with a roof terrace and balcony overlooking the street, a stone's throw from Parque Martí. $25CUC

Casa de Osmaida Carlos Manuel 811 e/ Prado y Aguilera ☎ 21 32 5193. One large spacious room with a kitchen and patio doors, and a smaller internal room in this helpful household, four blocks from Parque Martí. Parking available. $20CUC

Hotel Martí Calixto García esquina Aguilera 820 ☎ 21 32 9500. The only state-run accommodation in town, this new small, 21-room hotel with its smart wooden desks, TVs and comfortable beds is a good central option. Those wanting a bit of grandeur should opt for room 206, with its three balconies. The top-floor bar and terrace opens Fri, Sat and Sun from 8.30pm. Rates include breakfast. $56CUC

EATING

La Fuente (no phone). This kiosk next to the Casa del Chocolate, behind the church on Parque Martí sells chocolates, bonbons and delicious *turrones de coco* (coconut sweets) – in national pesos. Daily 8am–3pm & 4–11pm.

Sabor Melian Av Camilo Cienfuegos e/ Pedro A Pérez y Martí ☎ 21 32 4422. One of only three paladars in the city, this off-centre, friendly, candy-pink restaurant offers a large *criollo* menu in *moneda nacional* but with limited availability. Daily 11am–11pm.

Around Guantánamo

Many visitors come to the Guantánamo area just to see the US base (see box, p.371), but although you can get to the lookout point in **Caimanera** with a little groundwork, there really isn't a lot to see, as you cannot enter the base itself – or barely see it at all from Cuban territory. Venturing into the **countryside** around Guantánamo town is more rewarding, with bizarre contrasts between lush valleys and the weird desert scenery of sun-bleached barren trees. Just north of town is the offbeat **Zoológico de Piedras**, a "zoo" entirely populated by sculpted stone animals.

Caimanera

A taxi from town costs $25CUC, and you will need a guide and permit (see box below)

Bordered by salt flats that score the ground with deep cracks and lend a haunting wildness, **CAIMANERA**, 23km south of Guantánamo, takes its name from the giant caiman lizards that used to roam here, although today it's far more notable as the closest point in Cuba to the US naval base. Prior to the Revolution, Caimanera was the site of carousing between the naval-base officers and the townswomen: its main streets were lined with bars, and rampant prostitution, gambling and drugs were the order of the day. Little evidence of that remains in today's sleepy and parochial town.

The village is a **restricted area**, with the ground between it and the base one of the most heavily mined areas in the world, though the US removed their mines in 1999. This hasn't stopped many Cubans from braving it in the slim hope of reaching foreign soil and escaping to America. Visitors, meanwhile, have to have a **permit** to enter (see box below). The village is entered via a checkpoint at which guards scrutinize your

---

CAIMANERA PERMITS

To visit Caimanera for the day or stay at the hotel, you'll need a permit, available free from travel agencies in Guantánamo town (see p.370) or by emailing ✉ infogtmo@enetcu in advance. Unless staying at the hotel, visitors must also be accompanied by a guide, which will cost $10CUC and can also be arranged by the Guantánamo travel agencies. The permit is for a fixed date of entry so if, for any reason, you are late arriving to pick up your permit, you will have to apply for a further one.

passport and permit before waving you through; note that taking pictures en route is not permitted.

The **lookout** in the grounds of the *Caimanera* hotel has a view over the bay and mountains to the base – though even with binoculars you only see a sliver of it. Inside the hotel is a small **museum** (opened on demand), with a history of the base, a floor model and photos.

ACCOMMODATION AND EATING | **CAIMANERA**

Hotel Caimanera ☎ 21 49 9414. The most unusual hotel in Cuba, facing the watchtowers and the US naval base. The rooms and restaurant are adequate for a one-night stay, though think twice about a bay view, as the 24hr revolving searchlights are a tortuous experience. There's a pool to while away the hours once you've finished scoping out the base. Rates include breakfast. **$23CUC**

Zoológico de Piedras

Altos de Boquerón, Km 27 Carretera a Yateras • Daily 9am–6pm • $1CUC • Taxis from Guantánamo cost $20–25CUC

Roughly 20km north of Guantánamo, in the foothills of the Sierra Cristal and set in a private coffee farm, the whimsical and slightly surreal sculpture park known as the **Zoológico de Piedras** was created in 1977 by local artist Angel Iñigo Blanco, who carved the stone *in situ*. Cool and fresh, dotted with lime and breadfruit trees, hanging vines and coffee plants, the park centres on a path that weaves around the mountainside, with **stone animals** peeking out from the undergrowth at every turn. Slightly cartoonish in form, the creatures bear little relationship to their real-life counterparts: a giant tortoise towers over a hippo the size of a modest guinea pig. Needless to say, it's a hit with children.

Baracoa

In the eyes of many visitors, the countryside around **BARACOA** is quite simply the most beautiful in Cuba. Set on the coast at Cuba's southeast tip and protected by a deep curve of mountains, the town's isolation has so far managed to protect it from some of the more pernicious effects of tourism that have crept into other areas of the island. Self-contained and secluded, Baracoa vibrates with an energy that is surprising for such a small place, and has become a must on the traveller's circuit. It's also home to a uniquely mixed population, with many locals of Haitian and Jamaican origin – the result of late nineteenth- and early twentieth-century immigration.

Just wandering around is one of the town's greatest pleasures. The quaint central streets are lined with tiny, pastel-coloured colonial houses with wedding-cake trim, and modern development is confined to the outskirts and the **Malecón**, where new apartment blocks were built after the Revolution. All the sites of interest are within easy walking distance of one another, radiating out from the **Parque Independencia** on Antonio Maceo, where, under the shade of the wide laurel trees, generations of Baracoans gather around rickety tables to play chess and dominoes.

Brief history

Baracoa – Nuestra Señora de la Asunción de Baracoa – was the **first town** to be established in Cuba, founded by Diego de Velázquez in August 1511 on a spot christened Porto Santo in 1492 by Christopher Columbus who, as legend has it, planted a cross in the soil. The early conquistadors never quite succeeded in exterminating the indigenous population, and today Baracoa is the only place in Cuba where descendants of the **Taíno** can still be found. Their legacy is also present in the food and transport and several myths and legends habitually told to visitors.

Catedral de Nuestra Señora de la Asunción

Parque Independencia • Tues–Sat 8am–noon & 4–7pm, Sun 8am–noon • Mass at 9am

On the east side of Parque Independencia – opposite a bronze bust of Taíno hero Hatuey by Cuba's most famous sculptor, Rita Longa – stands the **Catedral Nuestra Señora de la Asunción**, built in 1807 on the site of a sixteenth-century church and fully restored between 2010 and 2012. This unobtrusive structure houses one of the most important religious relics in the whole of Latin America, the antique **La Cruz de la Parra**, supposedly the antique cross brought from Spain and planted in the sands of the harbour beach by Christopher Columbus. It's undeniably of the period, having been carbon-dated to around 30 years before the arrival of Columbus, but as the wood is also from the tree *Cocoloba Diversifolia*, indigenous to Cuba, the truth of the legend is doubtful. It was in front of this cross that the celebrated defender of the Indians, Fray Bartolomé de Las Casas, gave his first Mass in 1510. Originally 2m tall, the cross was gradually worn down by time and souvenir hunters to its present modest height of 1m, at which point it was encased in silver for its protection. It now stands in a glass case to the left of the main church door, on an ornate silver base donated by a French marquis at the beginning of the twentieth century.

Parque Martí

A block north of Parque Independencia towards the sea, **Parque Martí**, more a collection of benches and trees than a park, is the town's busiest square, crowded with shops and stalls selling snacks and drinks, notably *Prú*, the local speciality (see p.379).

Museo Arqueológico Cueva Paraíso

Loma Paraíso • Daily 8am–5pm • $3CUC ($2CUC if bought at Infotur), English- or Spanish-speaking guide $1CUC

A steep climb up the thickly forested Loma Paraíso brings you to Las Cuevas del Paraíso, a series of **caves** once used by the Taíno for ceremonies and funeral chambers that are now home to Baracoa's fascinating **Museo Arqueológico Cueva Paraíso**. Archeologists have unearthed a treasure-trove of pre-Columbian artefacts, in the caves themselves and the surrounding countryside, that pertain to the successive indigenous groups who made the region their home: the Guanahatabey occupied the area from about 3000 to 1000 BC, the Siboney from approximately 1000 BC until 1100 AD, and the Taíno who supplanted them until the arrival of the Spanish in the fifteenth century.

The most interesting exhibits are undoubtedly the **human remains** in the funerary chamber. The skeletons are displayed as they were found, in the traditional foetal position, and all the specimens' skulls are badly misshapen. It is thought likely that the Taíno tied heavy weights to babies' heads, flattening the forehead by pushing the bone

---

BARACOA'S FORTS

As a defence against marauding pirates in the eighteenth and nineteenth century, the Captain of Baracoa, one Pedro Oviedo, ordered the fortifications of three forts in Baracoa between 1739 and 1742. **Castillo Seburuco**, which overlooks the town and El Yunque from the northern hills, has been converted into a hotel (see p.379), while the Malecón is sealed by **La Punta**, now a restaurant (see p.380), a door in its western wall that leads down a flight of stairs to the tiny **Playa La Punta**, a good spot for a quiet dip (daily 9am–5pm). East of the centre, past the shops and the triangular Parque Maceo – complete with bust – is **Fuerte Matachín** (Mon–Sat 8am–noon & 2–6pm, Sun 8am–noon; $1CUC), a well-preserved structure with the original cannons ranged along its walls. The cool interior now houses the town **museum**, with a good collection of delicately striped *polymitas* snail shells, some Amerindian relics and a history of the town's most celebrated characters.

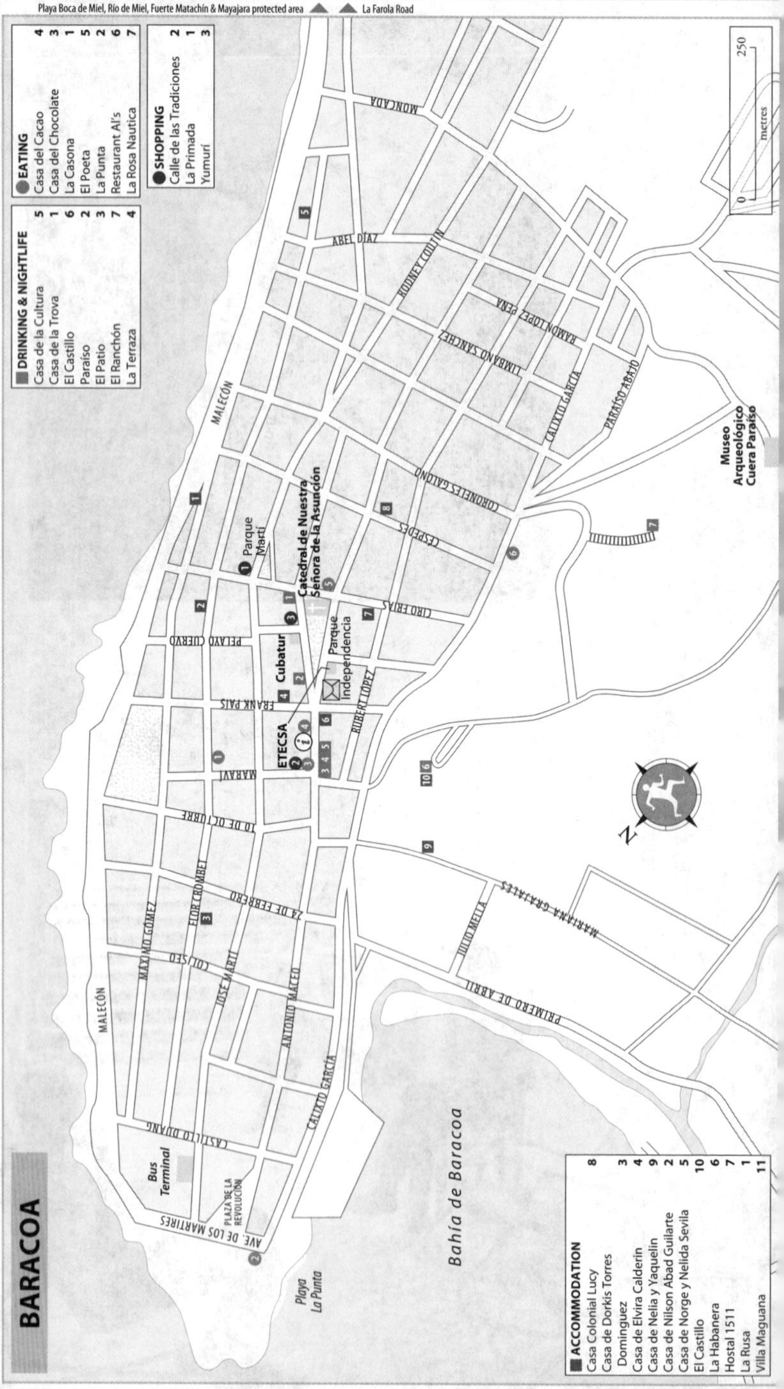

Playa Boca de Miel, Río de Miel, Fuerte Matachín & Mayajara protected area ▲ ▲ La Farola Road

BARACOA

DRINKING & NIGHTLIFE
Casa de la Cultura	5
Casa de la Trova	1
El Castillo	6
Paraíso	2
El Patio	3
El Ranchón	7
La Terraza	4

● EATING
Casa del Cacao	4
Casa del Chocolate	3
La Casona	1
La Punta	5
El Poeta	6
Restaurant Al's	2
La Rosa Nautica	7

● SHOPPING
Calle de las Tradiciones	2
La Primada	1
Yumurí	3

■ ACCOMMODATION
Casa Colonial Lucy	8
Casa de Dorkis Torres Domínguez	3
Casa de Elvira Calderín	4
Casa de Nelia y Yaquelin	9
Casa de Nilson Abad Guilarte	2
Casa de Norge y Nelida Sevila	5
El Castillo	10
La Habanera	6
Hostal 1511	7
La Rusa	1
Villa Maguana	11

MONCADA

ABEL DÍAZ

MALECÓN

Parque Martí

Catedral de Nuestra Señora de la Asunción

Parque Independencia

Cubatur

ETECSA

RODNEY COUTIN

RAMÓN LÓPEZ PEÑA

LIMBANO SÁNCHEZ

GALIXTO GARCÍA

PARASO ABAJO

CÉSPEDES

CIRO FRÍAS

RUBER LÓPEZ

CORONELES GALDÓN

Museo Arqueológico Cuera Paraíso

PELAYO CUERVO

FRANK PAÍS

MARAVÍ

10 DE OCTUBRE

24 DE FEBRERO

FLOR CROMBET

MÁXIMO GÓMEZ

COL/CSO

JOSÉ MARTÍ

ANTONIO MACEO

CELEDIO GARCÍA

CASTILLO DUANY

MALECÓN

AVE. DE LOS MÁRTIRES

PLAZA DE LA REVOLUCIÓN

PRIMERO DE ABRIL

MARIANA GRAJALES

Bus Terminal

Playa La Punta

Bahía de Baracoa

N

0   metres   250

down horizontally and extending the back of the skull. The malformed bodies were buried with *esferolitas*, small round stones used to indicate the person's age and social standing – the *esferolitas* found here indicate that this was the resting place for important and wealthy people.

The Malecón

A walk along the **Malecón**, a ragged collection of the backsides of houses and ugly apartment blocks, is something of a disappointment, not least because the area was ravaged by hurricanes in 2008. To the west is the town's **Plaza de la Revolución**, surely the smallest in Cuba, decorated only with one revolutionary poster.

Playa Boca de Miel

At the eastern end of the Malecón, accessed by the stone stairs to the right of an imposing stone statue of Christopher Columbus, is the main town beach, **Playa Boca de Miel**, a boisterous hangout mobbed in summer by vacationing schoolchildren. People walk their dogs along the multicoloured shingle near town, but the brilliant jade, grey and crimson of the stones fade into sand a little further along, making for a decent swimming spot. The best place for a paddle, however, lies beyond the clump of trees at the far eastern end of the beach, in the gentle **Río de Miel**, which has its own legend (see box, p.378).

Boca de Miel

Beyond the reaches of Playa Boca de Miel, there's an unaffected and intimate view of Baracoan life at the hamlet of **Boca de Miel**, comprising little more than a handful of simple, single-storey homes and, further on, the pale-sand beach at Playa Blanca. At the easternmost edge of Playa Boca de Miel, where the river reaches the sea, turn towards the river and follow the path down to the picturesque though rickety wooden bridge. Take the path to the left of the bridge and head up the hill. Here, there's a control post for the Mayajara protected area (see below) where you must pay $2CUC to visit **Playa Blanca** on the other side of a little grove of trees. The tiny hoop of coarse, blondish sand makes a good spot to relax for an afternoon, though you should be very mindful of the vigorous undertow if you go swimming. There are no facilities here, so be sure to take a supply of water; locals will offer to prepare you fried fish and water coconuts.

Mayajara protected area

Daily 8.30am–5.30pm • Guided walks $5–15CUC

Just outside Boca de Miel village, and accessed from the guardpost close to Playa Blanca, the **Mayajara protected area** is riddled with caves and petroglyphs, but best

---

LA FAROLA

Before the Revolution, Baracoa was only accessible by sea, but the opening of the **La Farola** road in 1965 changed all that, providing a direct link with Guantánamo 120km away, and allowing a flood of cars to pour into the previously little-visited town. Considered one of the triumphs of the Revolution, the road was actually started by Batista's regime, but was temporarily abandoned when he refused to pay a fair wage to the workers, and work was only resumed in the 1960s. Today, La Farola makes for an amazing trip through the knife-sharp peaks of the Cuchillas de Baracoa mountains. However the route should only be attempted in daylight, as the steep banks bordering the road in places, combined with a cracked and broken road surface, make it extremely dangerous in the dark. In 2013, work was due to start on repaving the coastal road to Moa; once this is complete, La Farola will be closed to fix the bridges that are sinking.

known for its incredible 500m-long **Balcón Arqueológico**, an extensive elevated limestone balcony accessed by ladders sturdy and rickety. The views through the palms to the ocean are outstanding.

ARRIVAL AND DEPARTURE

BARACOA

By plane The Aeropuerto Gustavo Rizo (☎ 21 64 5376) is near the *Porto Santo* hotel, on the west side of the bay 4km from the centre. Taxis into town cost $2–3CUC.

Airlines The Cubana office is at Martí no.181 (Mon, Wed, Fri 8am–noon & 12.30–4pm; ☎ 21 64 5374).
Destinations Havana (4 weekly; 2hr 30min).

By Víazul bus Demand for Víazul tickets to and from Baracoa always outstrips supply, especially in the summer, so make sure you book yours well in advance, preferably before you arrive. If you don't you could find yourself queuing early in the morning for a first-come-first-served distribution of remaining spaces and may end up waiting several days to leave. Víazul buses pull up at the Astro bus terminal (☎ 21 64 3880), west on the Malecón; it's a short walk down Maceo to the centre, or you can take a *bicitaxi* for $1–2CUC.
Destinations Guantánamo (1 daily; 3hr 10min); Santiago (1 daily; 4hr 45min).

By private bus Cubanacán's Conectando Cuba runs to Guantánamo ($10CUC) and Santiago ($15CUC) on Mon, Wed, Fri at noon from Parque Martí; tickets are sold at Infotur and Cubatur (see below). Gaviota Tours, inside *La Habanera* hotel (daily 8am–6pm; ☎ 21 64 4115) and at *Cafetería El Parque* (daily 8am–noon & 2–6pm; ☎ 21 64 5164), runs a new service to Holguín, departing at 8.30am on Sat ($30CUC). Cubatur (see below) has a bus to Holguín, departing on Tues and Sun at 7.30am ($30CUC), and to Guardalavaca, departing Fri at 7.30am ($35CUC).

By car Driving is an infinitely preferable manner of arrival, since half the pleasure of a visit to Baracoa is the view en route through the mountains on the La Farola road (see box, p.377). Note that the only gas station on the coastal road between Mayarí and Baracoa is at Moa.

By truck The private peso trucks that arrive from over the mountains via La Farola drop off on Maceo.

GETTING AROUND

On foot The best way to get around Baracoa is on foot, as most of the places you'll want to see are within easy reach of the centre. There's little point relying on public transport – buses are scarce and always jam-packed.

By bicitaxi or unmetered taxi If travelling further afield, you can catch a *bicitaxi* from anywhere in town, or an unmetered taxi from behind the church.

By metered taxi Call Cubataxi (☎ 21 64 3737).

By car and moped For car rental, try Cubacar, Martí no. 202 e/ Céspedes y Coroneles Galanao (Mon–Sat 8am–5pm; ☎ 21 64 5225). Víacar/Transgaviota is based at *Hotel Porto Santo* (Mon–Sat 8am–5pm; ☎ 21 64 5137), at the airport (Sun 9am–1pm & 2–6pm) and at *Cafetería El Parque Maceo* s/n esq. Rafael Trejo (Mon–Sat 9am–1pm & 2–6pm; ☎ 21 64 1671), from where you can also rent mopeds from $24CUC a day.

INFORMATION

Infotur The very helpful office at Maceo no.129A e/ Frank País y Maraví (Mon–Sat 8.30am–noon & 1–5pm; ☎ 21 64 1781) has general information about the area such as tours, hikes, museums and entertainment, and sells Conectando Cuba tickets.

Cubatur The office at Maceo no.147 (Mon–Sat 8am–noon & 2–6pm, Sun 8.30am–noon; ☎ 21 64 5306) is manned by

the extremely helpful Eric, who can book plane, Víazul and Conectando Cuba tickets.

Festivals The Semana de la Cultura is held in the last week of March, and the even bigger celebration of the Fiesta de las Aguas takes place between August 10/12 and 15.

THE RIVER OF HONEY

Many years ago, a Taíno maiden with honey-coloured hair used to bathe daily in the waters of the **Río de Miel**. One day a young sailor steered his ship down the river and spotted her. Captivated by her beauty, he instantly fell in love and for a while the happy couple frolicked daily in the river. However, as the day of the sailor's departure approached, the young girl became increasingly depressed and would sit in the river crying until her tears swelled its banks. Impressed by this demonstration of her love, the sailor decided to stay in Baracoa and marry her, from which grew the saying that if you swim in the Río de Miel, you will never leave Baracoa, or that if you do you will always return.

ACCOMMODATION

HOTELS

El Castillo Calixto García ☎ 21 64 5165. Perched high on a hill overlooking the town, this former military post is now an intimate, comfortable and very welcoming hotel. Glossy tiles and wood finishes give the rooms a unique charm, while the handsome pool patio with views over the bay is the best place in town to sip *mojitos*. Very popular and often fully booked, making a reservation essential. **$60CUC**

La Habanera Maceo 126 esq. Frank País ☎ 21 64 5273. Right in the centre of town, with a pretty pink exterior and an airy reception filled with comfy sofas. The ten rooms, arranged around a courtyard, are clean and comfortable with TV, a/c and private bathrooms. Guests can use *El Castillo's* pool. **$40CUC**

Hostal 1511 Ciro Frías ☎ 21 64 5700. A charming, small hotel which has been kitted out in brand new furniture. Its main attraction, however, is its lovely veranda. Rooms are comfortable, but standard ones don't have a view. Guests can use *El Castillo's* pool. **$40CUC**

La Rusa Máximo Gómez no.161 ☎ 21 64 3011. Named after its much-esteemed Russian former owner, Magdelana Robiskiai, who settled in Baracoa before the Revolution, this small and squat hotel sits on the Malecón. The rooms are modest but adequate and complemented by a friendly atmosphere. Guests can use *El Castillo's* pool. **$30CUC**

CASAS PARTICULARES AND HOSTALES

Casa Colonial Lucy Céspedes 29 e/ Maceo y Rubert López ☎ 21 64 3548, ✉ astrasol36@gmail.com. Two spacious, comfortable rooms, each with two double beds, a/c, fridge, private bathroom and an independent entrance. The attractive house, with seaview terrace, and its friendly owners (who offer excellent meals) make this a top choice. English, German and Italian spoken, and massage, salsa lessons and a private guide can be organized. **$30CUC**

Casa de Dorkis Torres Dominguez Flor Crombet no.58 (altos) e/ 24 de febrero y Coliseo ☎ 21 64 3451, ✉ dorkistd72@yahoo.es. Two modern, en-suite a/c rooms with minibar, fridge and sea view in a friendly

household. A terrace next to one of the bedrooms on which to eat the delicious home-cooked meals seals the deal. **$25CUC**

Casa de Elvira Calderín Frank País no.19 e/ Martí y Maceo ☎ 21 64 5869. This spacious, central property has three pleasant, airy rooms with a/c and private bathroom, and a courtyard out back. Meals are available and Elvira is building more rooms on the top terrace and a further open terrace for eating, yoga and dance. Massage and salsa classes offered. **$25CUC**

Casa de Nelia y Yaquelin Mariana Grajales no.11 and no 11 (altos) e/ Calixto García y Julio Mella ☎ 21 64 2412. Two smallish a/c rooms on the ground floor of a friendly house. Up top, off the terrace, Yaquelin and Adrián have also created a spacious, semi-independent apartment with two bedrooms, a large living room and use of kitchen. A huge sun terrace with uninterrupted views of El Yunque was under construction in 2013. Rooms **$25CUC**; apartment **$30CUC**

★ **Casa de Nilson** Flor Crombet no.143 e/ Ciro Frías y Pelayo Cuervo ☎ 21 64 3123. Fantastic, spacious apartment close to the centre of town, with two beds (one double, one single) and use of a kitchen. The attractive roof terrace with decorated wooden carvings of Cuban birds, *Paladar La Terraza*, where the amicable owners serve up traditional Baracoan meals, makes this one of the best choices in town. **$30CUC**

Casa de Norge y Nelida Sevila Flor Crombet no.265A e/ Glicerio Blanco y Abel Díaz ☎ 21 64 3218, ✉ cnorge@rocketmail.com. A royal blue house with a double room and dining room accessed by an independent entrance. There's a small balcony for sunning out back, and Norge is a charming host. **$20CUC**

Finca La Esperanza ☎ 01 5218 0735 (cell). On the banks of the beautiful River Toa, 4km from town, this rustic *hostal* is a delightful spot for those wanting to escape the city. There are sixteen beds across six rooms, with two shared bathrooms, and a bar and restaurant. Rates include breakfast. **$16CUC**

EATING AND DRINKING

After the monotonous cuisine in much of the rest of Cuba, **food** in Baracoa is ambrosial in comparison, drawing on a rich local heritage and the region's plentiful supply of coconuts. Tuna, red snapper and swordfish fried in coconut oil are all favourite dishes, and there is an abundance of lobster, as well as a few vegetarian specials. **Local specialities** include *cucurucho*, a deceptively filling concoction of coconut, orange, guava and lots of sugar sold in a palm-leaf wrap on the hillside roads leading into the town. Other treats for the sweet-toothed include locally produced chocolate and the soft drink *Prú*, a fermented blend of sugar and secret spices that's something of an acquired taste and is widely available from *oferta* stands.

STATE RESTAURANTS AND CAFÉS

Casa del Cacao Maceo no.129 ☎ 21 64 2125. Just along from the *Casa del Chocolate*, this new convertible peso café-cum-museum is a lot less dour than the national peso chocolate house, with displays of chocolate growing and

collecting instruments. Prices are higher (ask for the menu to avoid overcharging) although you can purchase fat, chocolately cakes from the window in *moneda nacional*. The bar out back stays open late for drinks and bonbons. Restaurant daily 7am–11pm, bar daily 11pm–late.

7

★ **Casa del Chocolate** Maceo no.121 ☎ 21 64 1553. This quaint little national-peso café sells chocolate-related dishes and drinks. What's on offer is the luck of the draw, though chocolate ice cream, a blancmange-style chocolate pudding and drinking chocolate crop up regularly. Prices rarely exceed the equivalent of $2CUC but you will need $CUP currency to pay. Knock on the door hard; it's usually open but is kept locked to preserve the ferocious a/c. Daily 7am–11pm.

La Punta Ave. de los Mártires, at the west end of the Malecón ☎ 21 64 1480. An elegant restaurant in the grounds of La Punta fort, cooled by sea breezes and serving traditional Cuban and Baracoan food, some spaghetti dishes and the house speciality of fish cooked with crab and shrimp ($8.95CUC). Mon–Thurs 10am–10pm, Fri–Sun 10am–midnight.

PALADARS

La Casona Martí no.114 esq. Maraví ☎ 21 64 1122. This brand new no-frills paladar in an emerald green colonial building is as unassuming as they come – they even ask what music you'd like to hear while you dine. The generous servings of fried chicken or platters of shrimps or octopus in tomato sauce or coconut milk come accompanied by soup, rice, salad and *chatinos* (fried plantain strips), and cost $7–8CUC. Daily 11am–midnight.

ENTERTAINMENT AND NIGHTLIFE

Casa de la Cultura Maceo no.124 e/ Frank País y Maraví ☎ 21 64 2364. A haven of jaded charm, with live music and dancing on the patio nightly, plus regular rumba shows. Things tend to get going around 9pm. Free. Daily 9pm–1am.

★ **Casa de la Trova** Victorino Rodríguez no.149B e/ Ciro Frias y Pelayo Cuevo (no phone). Concerts take place in this tiny room opposite Parque Independencia, after which the chairs are pushed back to the wall and exuberant dancers spill onto the pavement. A lively, unaffected atmosphere makes for one of the most vibrant and authentic nights out in town. Entry $1CUC. Daily 5pm–midnight.

El Castillo Calixto García ☎ 21 64 5165. Overlooking El Yunque and the Porto Santo bay, the poolside bar of this hotel is one of the most attractive options in town for twilight cocktails. Daily 1pm–midnight.

Paraíso Calle Maceo (no phone). On the one hand, there's nothing intrinsically Cuban about this popular disco-cum-karaoke club opposite the park, but watching

SHOPPING

Yumurí Maceo no.149 ☎ 21 64 2212. This small supermarket is useful for everyday supplies. Mon–Sat 8.30am–7.30pm, Sun 8.30am–3pm.

La Primada Martí opposite the park esq. Ciro Frías (no phone). Convertible-peso store selling food, clothes,

★ **El Poeta** Maceo no.159 esq. Ciro Frías ☎ 21 64 3017. A smorgasbord of local delicacies, deliciously cooked and beautifully served in gourds and cacao pods. The fish in a thick coating of coconut sauce is outstanding, and the coconut ice cream, served with cacao beans to suck on and a local banana delicacy, is delightful. Owner Pablo's presentation is no cover up for mediocre food; it's all moreish and delicious, and priced at $10–15CUC. Daily noon–midnight.

Restaurant Al's Calixto García no.158A e/ Céspedes y Coroneles Galano ☎ 05 29 03651 (mobile), ✉ choco .al.65@yahoo.es. Owner Al has great position with his high terrace overlooking the town and the sea, and he serves up barbecued food with panache. In addition to fish in coconut sauce, try octopus in its own ink or chicken fricassee ($6–15CUC). Daily noon–10pm.

La Rosa Nautica 1 de Abril no.185 (altos) ☎ 21 64 5764. On the road out of town towards the airport, this is Baracoa's only fine dining restaurant, and offers a somewhat mixed experience. While too far from town for most, it does boast an elegant setting and impeccable service, as well as a large surf and turf menu and a separate kebab menu ($5.50–15CUC). Opt for chorizo and pork and steer clear of the shrimps and beef; and note that the *brochette Alerón* comes with six huge kebabs – enough for two. Daily noon–midnight.

Baracoans belt out their favourite pop song or lord it over the dancefloor takes you to the heart of the country's determination to have fun. Entry $5CUC. Tues–Sun 10.30pm–2am, closed Tues & Wed in low season.

El Patio Maceo esq. Maraví (no phone). Nightly traditional music shows at 9pm draw a crowd, while the bar does a fine trade in expertly prepared *mojitos*. Entrance is free. Daily 9am–midnight.

El Ranchón Loma Paraíso ☎ 21 64 3268. Up on Paradise Hill behind Baracoa and reached by a stone staircase, this large, open-sided bar and club is popular with local youngsters as well as tourists. Disco music plays nightly and food is available. Entry $5CUC per couple. Daily 9pm–2am.

La Terraza Calle Maceo no.120 (no phone). This appealing rooftop terrace is a good spot for a quiet early-evening drink, while later in the evening it heats up as crowds of Baracoans and foreigners alike pile in for the comedy and traditional music and dance shows, followed by a disco. Entry $2CUC. Daily 8pm–2/3am.

toiletries and small electrics. Mon–Sat 8.30am–4.30pm, Sun 8.30am–noon.

Calle de las Tradiciones Calle Maraví y Maceo. An artisans' market operates here daily in this tiny plaza.

DIRECTORY

Banks and exchange Banco de Crédito y Comercio, José Martí no.166 (Mon–Fri 8am–3pm, Sat 8–11am), gives cash advances on MasterCard and Visa and changes travellers' cheques, as does the CADECA at José Martí no.241, which also converts $CUC to $CUP (Mon–Fri 8.15am–2pm, Sat 8.15–11.30am).

Internet and telephones You can get internet access ($6CUC/hr), buy phonecards and make calls at the ETECSA Centro de Llamadas (daily 8.30am–7.30pm) on Maceo, next door to the post office.

Medical Clínica Internacional, Martí 237, has a pharmacy (daily 8am–8pm; ☎ 21 64 1038). There's a 24hr national-peso pharmacy at Maceo no.132 (☎ 21 64 2271). The 24hr *policlínico* (medical practice) is on Martí no.427 (☎ 21 64 2162).

Police The police station is on Martí towards the *Malecón*, near the bus station (☎ 21 64 2479). In an emergency call ☎ 116.

Post office Maceo no.136 (Mon–Sat 8am–8pm).

Around Baracoa

Cradled by verdant mountains smothered in palm and cacao trees, and threaded with swimmable rivers, the Baracoan countryside has much to offer. **El Yunque**, the hallmark of Baracoa's landscape, can easily be climbed in a day, while if you have a car and a little time to spare you could take a drive east along the coast and seek out some quintessentially Cuban fishing villages, including **Boca de Yumurí**. Alternatively, just head for the **beach** – there are a couple of good options northwest of town.

7

TOURS AROUND BARACOA

With an abundance of verdant countryside, exploring the surrounding area is one of the pleasures of a visit to the Baracoa region. Without your own car, the only option is to take a **guided tour**, which can be arranged at the Cubatur office at Maceo no.147 (Mon–Sat 8am–noon & 2–6pm, Sun 8.30am–noon; ☎ 21 64 5306). The prices quoted below are for guide and transport only; note that some trips only run with a minimum number of people.

Boca de Yumurí Though its tranquil nature has been damaged somewhat by tourism, Boca de Yumurí still offers splendid views and swimming spots. This excursion includes a boat ride and a tour of the local cocoa plantation, which cannot be visited any other way. $22CUC per person.

Parque Nacional Alejandro de Humboldt These lush rainforests, curving and swelling into hills above coastline tangled with mangroves, cover some 700 square kilometres of land and sea and were deservedly designated a UNESCO biosphere and national park in 2001. Views are fantastic and access to secluded beaches and surrounding countryside easy. Guided tours take you through some of the most beautiful scenery on hillside hikes or boat trips around the coast. $24CUC, minimum four people.

Playa Duaba Only 6km outside of Baracoa, Playa Duaba is set on an estuary. The beach itself is a scrubby grey, but is pleasant enough for a swim. The tour includes a short guided walk, while lunch at the *Finca Duaba* is an optional extra. This tour is offered with the Río Toa tour as a full-day excursion for $20CUC per person.

Playa Maguana A daily bus leaves for the beach from outside the Cubatur office at 10am, returning at 4.30pm. You need to reserve at least half an hour before departure. $5CUC per person; minimum five people.

Río Toa Reached through some gently undulating rainforest filled with a cornucopia of cocoa trees, one of the country's longest rivers lies 10km northwest of Baracoa. Wide and deep, the Río Toa is one of the most pleasant places to swim in, although you should choose your spot carefully and watch out for a fairly brisk current. Return is by boat. $20CUC per person.

Saltadero A visit to the picturesque waterfall at Saltadero, 10km west of the town, makes for a relaxing day-trip. Secluded by a rugged rock face, the 35m waterfall cascades down into a natural swimming pool. The route down to the pool is fairly slippery, so wear shoes with some grip. $6CUC per person.

El Yunque Nestling in lush rainforest is the hallmark of Baracoa's landscape, El Yunque. The area is rich with banana and coconut trees, while the views are astounding. If you are striking out alone, start your climb at the *Campismo El Yunque*. Entrance and guided tour costs $16CUC per person and includes an obligatory guide.

El Yunque

The walk to the summit starts near *Campismo El Yunque*, 3km off the Moa road • Entrance is $13CUC, $10CUC if bought at Infotur • Guided excursions can be arranged by the Cubatur office

As square as a slab of butter, 575m **El Yunque**, 10km west of Baracoa and streaked in mist, seems to float above the other mountains in the Sagua Baracoa range. Christopher Columbus noted its conspicuousness: his journal entry of November 27, 1492, mentions a "high square mountain which seemed to be an island" seen on his approach to shore – no other mountain fits the description as well. El Yunque is the remnant of a huge plateau that dominated the region in its primordial past. Isolated for millions of years, its square summit has evolved unique species of ferns and palms, and much of the forest is still virgin, a haven for rare plants including orchids and bright red epiphytes. The energetic though not unduly strenuous **hike to the summit** should take about two hours.

ACCOMMODATION EL YUNQUE

7

Campismo El Yunque ☎ 21 64 5262, office at Calle Martí 225, Baracoa ☎ 21 64 2776. The boxy concrete cabins sleeping up to six here are scattered across a beautiful grove of palm trees near the River Duaba and starting point for climbing El Yunque. It's a perfect escape, but you'd need your own transport. Five cabins are reserved for tourists. Cabins **$14CUC**

Playa Maguana

Some 25km northwest of Baracoa along the road to Moa, **Playa Maguana** is an attractive, narrow beach with golden sand, some seaweed, plenty of shade and a reef for snorkelling. Partly bordered by with the spindly though leafy *Coco thrinas* palm, indigenous to the area, its popular with locals as well as visitors, and is less exclusive than many in Cuba. At the far end of the beach, *Villa Maguana* (see below) sits in its own private cove. Take care of valuables while swimming at Maguana, as there have been reports of bags being taken.

ACCOMMODATION AND EATING PLAYA MAGUANA

Playa Maguana now offers a handful of new **paladars**, on or just off the beach, while pop-up places also open during the summer months. Alternatively, beach fishermen often approach sunbathers and will offer to cook freshly caught fish with rice and banana, served with rum-laced milk coconuts, for $5–8CUC.

Beach bar (no phone). Set back from the water, Playa Maguana's beach bar sells drinks and some snacks like fried chicken and spaghetti for $3–6CUC. Daily 10am–6pm.
Paladar El Pulpo ☎ 05 22 78598 (mobile). One of several paladars on the beach; this one stays open all year

serving seafood ($5–6CUC) and a few plates of pasta. Daily 10am–6pm.
⭐ **Villa Maguana** Playa Maguana ☎ 21 64 1204 or 1205. The only beach accommodation in the area, this is a little idyll, with plenty of privacy and sixteen comfortable

---

THE POLYMITA SNAIL

Along the Boca de Yumurí beach you may spot the brightly coloured shells of the **polymita snail**. According to local Amerindian legend, there was once a man who wanted to give his beloved a gift. As he had nothing of his own to give, he set out to capture the colours of the universe: he took the green of the mountains, the red of the earth, the pink of the flowers, the white of the foam of the sea, the yellow of the sun and the black of the night sky. He then set all the colours into the shells of the snails and presented them to his love. Each snail is unique, ornately decorated in delicate stripes and consequently quite sought-after – the Duchess of Windsor in the 1950s, for instance, had a pair encrusted with gold studs and made into earrings. Such caprices have severely depleted the snails' numbers, and although locals still sell them, buying is not recommended, and a local campaign has started to raise awareness of the danger the sale of shells poses for the species – and it is now prohibited to buy them.

WALKS IN PARQUE NACIONAL ALEJANDRO DE HUMBOLDT

There are several **guided walks** on offer in the Humboldt national park that allow you to experience the peculiar plants and wildlife of the region. The **El Recreo** (3hr) and **Sendero Balcón de Iberia** (5hr) trails can be booked at the park gate or through travel agencies in Baracoa, and cost $10 per person, or $24CUC per person with transport from Baracoa included. Exclusive walks, which can only be booked in the National Park HQ in Baracoa at Calle Martí s/n, opposite the stadium bus stop (Mon–Fri 8am–noon & 2–5pm; no phone), include **Sendero El Copal** (4hr), **Sendero Riveras del Jiguaní** (5hr), which includes a boat ride, **Sendero Loma de Piedra** (6hr) and **Sendero Cascada La Jaragua** (5hr); all of these cost $18–32CUC per person including transport from Baracoa. A new **agroecoturismo route** involving living from the earth like a *campesino*, and making honey and local crafts, costs $10 per person. Another new option, the 22km, three-day **Ruta Humboldt**, was about to be launched at the time of writing, and costs $35CUC per person per day including food and transport.

double rooms, tastefully decorated and housed in a series of tall, smart, rustic cabins overlooking a little hoop of semi-private beach. There are two restaurants and a beach bar to boot. Well worth at least a night's stay. **$83CUC**

Boca de Yumurí

Thirty kilometres east of Baracoa, past the Bahía de Mata – a tranquil bay with a slim, shingled beach and a splendid view of the mountains – is the little fishing village of **BOCA DE YUMURÍ**, standing at the mouth of the eponymous river. Known as a place to find the highly prized *polyimita* snails (see box opposite), the rather bland, brown-sand beach is also lined with houses whose owners will offer to cook you inexpensive **meals** of fish, rice and bananas. The village has suffered somewhat from the more pernicious effects of tourism and it's more than likely that you'll be besieged with *jineteros* trying to steer you towards their restaurant of choice and flog you shells from your moment of arrival. Avoid all but the most insistent and head to the end of the beach and a wooden jetty from where you can catch a **raft taxi** ($2CUC) further upstream, where the river is clearer and better for swimming and banked by a high rock face.

Parque Nacional Alejandro de Humboldt

Park office • Daily 8am–4pm • $1CUC; boat trips $5CUC

Some 56km north out of Baracoa on the Moa road, with an office right on the *carretera* where you pay your entry fee, the **Parque Nacional Alejandro de Humboldt** stretches across more than 32,000 hectares of mountainous rainforest and sea. Its forests are home to the world's smallest bird, bat, frog and male scorpion, and the park also includes the stunning, discus-shaped **Taco Bay**, fringed by beautiful coconut palms and hemmed in by dense mangrove and frequented by an elusive cluster of manatees. The best time to spot these unusual mammals (also known as sea cows) is November to January via a two-hour boat trip across the bay to the mangroves.

ACCOMMODATION AND EATING PARQUE NACIONAL ALEJANDRO DE HUMBOLDT

Park dormitories @ sergiosg@gu.rimed.cu. The park runs a site next to Taco Bay, where the basic dormitories have ten bunk beds and two shared bathrooms with cold water. Simple food is offered at $2CUC per person. Beds **$8CUC**

Santiago de Cuba and Granma

PARQUE CÉSPEDES, SANTIAGO DE CUBA CITY

Santiago de Cuba and Granma

The southern part of Oriente – the island's easternmost third – is defined by the Sierra Maestra, Cuba's largest mountain range, which binds together the provinces of Santiago de Cuba and Granma. Rising directly from the shores of the Caribbean along the southern coast, the mountains make much of the region largely inaccessible – a quality appreciated by Fidel Castro and his rebels, who spent two years waging war here. At the eastern end of the sierra is the roiling, romantic city of Santiago de Cuba, capital of the eponymous province and with a rich colonial heritage that's evident throughout its historical core. Cuba's most important urban area outside Havana, the city draws visitors mainly for its music. Developed by the legions of bands that have grown up here, the regional scene is always strong, but it boils over in July when the Fiesta del Caribe and carnival drench the town in rumba beats, fabulous costumes and song.

8

Spread along the coastline around the city are the magnificent coastal fortification of **El Morro** and the **Gran Parque Natural Baconao**; inland, there's gentle **trekking** in the **Parque Nacional de la Gran Piedra** where one of the highest points in the province, Gran Piedra itself, offers far-reaching vistas. In the lush, cool mountains west of the city, the town of **El Cobre** features one of the country's most important churches, housing the much-revered relic of the Virgen de la Caridad del Cobre. Still further west, bordering Granma province, the heights of the **Sierra Maestra** vanish into cloudforests, and although access to the **Parque Nacional Turquino** – around Pico Turquino, Cuba's highest peak – can be restricted, you can still admire from afar.

Unlike Santiago de Cuba, which revolves around its main city, the province of **Granma** has no definite focus and is much more low-key than its neighbour. The small black-sand beach resort at **Marea del Portillo** on the south coast is a favourite for Canadian visitors, but the highlight of the province, missed out on by many, is the **Parque Nacional Desembarco del Granma**. Lying in wooded countryside at the foot of the Sierra Maestra, this idyllic park, home to an assortment of intriguing stone petroglyphs, can be easily explored from the beach of **Las Coloradas**. Further north, along the Gulf of Guacanayabo, the museum at **Parque Nacional La Demajagua**, formerly the sugar estate and home of Carlos Manuel de Céspedes, celebrates the War of Independence amid tranquil, park-like grounds.

Granma's two main towns are underrated and often ignored, but the fantastic Moorish architecture in the coastal town of **Manzanillo** is reason enough to drop by, while **Bayamo**, the provincial capital, with its quiet atmosphere and pleasant scenery, appeals to discerning visitors looking for an easy-going spot to stay.

CASA DE LA TROVA, SANTIAGO DE CUBA (P.408)

Highlights

❶ Museo Ambiente Histórico Cubano Stuffed full of colonial treasures from the sixteenth century onwards, Diego Velázquez's former residence is an unmissable treat. **See p.392**

❷ Santiago's summer festivals The city's musical *joie de vivre* is summed up in a cacophony of salsa, trova, conga and fabulous costumes at its double summertime fiesta bill. **See p.397**

❸ El Castillo del Morro San Pedro de la Roca An impressive seventeenth-century stone fortress, built on a cliff outside Santiago to ward off pirates. **See p.402**

❹ Hotel Casa Granda Presiding over Santiago's main park, the rooftop bar of this historic hotel

is a perfect spot to soak up the city's atmosphere. **See p.404**

❺ Santiago's Casa de la Trova An atmospheric music house thrumming with authentic Cuban sounds. **See p.408**

❻ Comandancia de La Plata A trek through verdant peaks of the Sierra Maestra to the rebels' mountain base brings the 1959 revolution to colourful life. **See p.419**

❼ Playa Las Coloradas The site where the *Granma* yacht deposited Fidel, Che and the other revolutionaries at the inception of the struggle is both a historic and scenic pleasure. **See p.422**

HIGHLIGHTS ARE MARKED ON THE MAP ON PP.388–389

Santiago de Cuba city

Beautiful, heady **SANTIAGO DE CUBA** is the crown jewel of Oriente. Nowhere outside Havana is there a city with such definite character or such determination to have a good time. Spanning out from the base of a deep-water bay and cradled by mountains, Santiago is credited with being the most Caribbean part of Cuba, a claim borne out by its laidback lifestyle and rich mix of inhabitants. It was here that the first slaves arrived from West Africa, and today Santiago boasts a larger percentage of black people than anywhere else in Cuba. Afro-Cuban **culture**, with its music, myths and rituals, has its roots here, with later additions brought by French coffee planters fleeing revolution in Haiti in the eighteenth century.

The leisurely pace of life doesn't make for a quiet city, however, with the higgledy-piggledy net of narrow streets around the colonial quarter ringing night and day with the beat of drums and the toot of horns. **Music** is a vital element of Santiaguero life, whether heard at the country's most famous **Casa de la Trova** and the city's various other venues, or at the impromptu gatherings that tend to reach a crescendo around **carnival** in July. As well as being the liveliest, the summer months are also the hottest – the mountains surrounding the city act as a windbreak and the lack of breeze means that Santiago is often several degrees hotter than Havana, and almost unbearably humid.

HIGHLIGHTS

1. Museo Ambiente Histórico Cubano
2. Santiago's summer festivals
3. El Castillo del Morro San Pedro de la Roca
4. Hotel Casa Granda
5. Santiago's Casa de la Trova
6. Comandancia de La Plata
7. Playa Las Coloradas

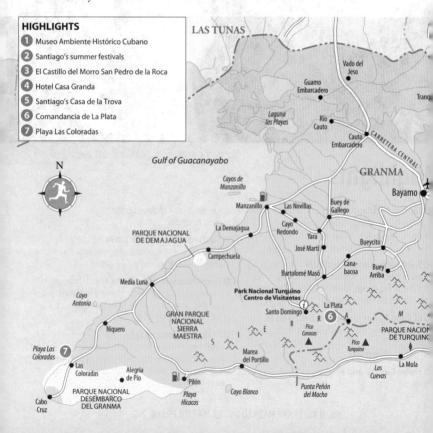

Although Santiago's music scene and carnival are good enough reasons to visit, there are a host of more concrete attractions. Diego Velázquez's sixteenth-century merchant house and the elegant governor's residence, both around **Parque Céspedes** in the colonial heart of town, and the commanding **El Morro** castle at the entrance to the bay, exemplify the city's prominent role in Cuban history. Additionally, the part played by townsfolk in the **revolutionary struggle**, detailed in several fascinating museums, makes Santiago an important stop on the Revolution trail.

One downside to a visit here is **street hustle** (see Basics, p.57) in the downtown area. Begging and being propositioned is an unbearable problem, especially in and around Parque Céspedes. The level and persistence of hassle is worse than in any other Cuban city – and women travelling on their own, in particular, need to grit their teeth.

Brief history

Established by **Diego Velázquez de Cuéllar** in 1515, the port of Santiago de Cuba was one of the original seven *villas* founded in Cuba. Velázquez, pleased to find so excellent a natural port near to reported sources of **gold** (which were quickly exhausted), named the port Santiago (St James) after the patron saint of Spain. With the construction of the central trading house shortly afterwards, the settlement became Cuba's capital.

After this auspicious start – boosted by the discovery of a rich vein of **copper** in the foothills in nearby El Cobre – the city's importance dwindled somewhat. Buffeted by

severe earthquakes and **pirate attacks**, Santiago developed more slowly than its western rival and in 1553 was effectively ousted as capital when the governor of Cuba, Gonzalo Pérez de Angulo, moved his office to Havana.

Sugar, coffee and slaves

Santiago's physical bounty led to a new boom in the eighteenth century, when Creoles from other areas of the country poured **sugar** wealth into the area by developing plantations. The cool mountain slopes around Santiago proved ideal for growing **coffee**, and French planters, accompanied by their slaves, emigrated here after the 1791 revolution in Haiti, bringing with them a cosmopolitan air and continental elegance, as well as a culturally complex slave culture.

Relations with Havana had always been frosty, especially as culturally distinct Santiago had fewer Spanish-born *Penínsulares*, who made up the ruling elite. This rivalry boiled over during the **Wars of Independence**, which were led by the people of Oriente. Much of the fighting between 1868 and 1898 took place around Santiago, led in part by the city's most celebrated son, **Antonio Maceo**.

The US takeover

The Cuban army had almost gained control of Santiago when, in 1898, the **United States** intervened. Eager to gain control of the imminent republic, it usurped victory from the Cubans by securing Santiago and subsequently forcing Spanish surrender after a dramatic battle on **Loma de San Juan**. The Cubans were not even signatories to the resultant Paris peace settlement between the US and Spain, and all residents of Santiago province were made subject to the protection and authority of the US. As an added insult, the rebel army that had fought for independence for thirty years was not even allowed to enter Santiago city.

The Revolution and Santiago today

Over the following decades, the American betrayal nourished local anger and resentment, and by the 1950s Santiago's citizens were playing a prime role in the civil uprisings against the US-backed president Fulgencio Batista. Assured of general support, **Fidel Castro** chose Santiago for his debut battle in 1953, when he and a small band of rebels attacked the **Moncada barracks**. Further support for their rebel army was later given by the M-26-7 underground movement that was spearheaded in Santiago by **Frank and Josue País**. It was in Santiago's courtrooms that Fidel Castro and the other rebels were subsequently tried and imprisoned.

When the victorious Castro swept down from the mountains, it was in Santiago that he chose to deliver his maiden speech, in the first week of January 1959. The city, which now carries the title "Hero City of the Republic of Cuba", is still seen – especially in Havana – as home to the most zealous revolutionaries, and support for the

---

HURRICANE SANDY

In October 2012, the category three **Hurricane Sandy** hit Santiago de Cuba province hard, tearing through the coastal Gran Parque Natural de Baconao before wreaking havoc on Santiago city. Some 200,000 homes were damaged and 15,000 people lost their homes entirely; many buildings lost roofs, and the city was also almost entirely denuded of its trees and greenery. Even more tragically, eleven people lost their lives – an unusual occurrence in Cuba, as the government's hurricane evacuation strategy is heralded the world over for its effectiveness, and fatalities are a rare event.

Immediately after the storm, the army was sent in to start on the **clear up** of the city. Six months on, though many families in the outskirts were still living in makeshift accommodation, the historic heart of Santiago was more or less back to normal, though many of the colonial-era buildings showed roof, tile and wall damage, and the lack of greenery remained noticeable.

SANTIAGO'S STREET NAMES

Many streets in Santiago have two names, one from before the Revolution and one from after. Theoretically, street signs show the post-revolutionary name, but as these signs are few and far between, and locals tend to use the original name in conversation, we follow suit in the text. Cuban maps, however, usually show both names, with the original in brackets; in our maps we've followed their example. The most important roads are listed below.

Old name	New name	Old name	New name
Calvario	Porfirio Valiente	Sagarra	San Francisco
Carnicería	Pío Rosado	San Basilio	Bartolomé Masó
Clarín	Padre Quiroga	San Félix	Hartmann
Enramada	José A. Saco	San Gerónimo	Echevarría
Máximo Gómez	San Germán	San Pedro	General Lacret
Reloj	Mayía Rodríguez		

Revolution is certainly stronger here than in the west. The rift between east and west still manifests itself today in various prejudices, with Habaneros viewing their eastern neighbours as troublemaking criminals, and considered as solipsistic and unfriendly by Santiagueros in return.

Parque Céspedes

Originally the Plaza de Armas, the first square laid out by the conquistadors, **Parque Céspedes** is the spiritual centre of Santiago. Sadly, it suffered significant damage in October 2012 when Hurricane Sandy uprooted all its fig trees and nearly all its plants, and it's now a shadeless spot where few brave the sun to sit on the wrought-iron benches. There's still a gentle ebb and flow of activity, however, as sightseers wander through between museum visits, musicians strum their instruments around the edges and impromptu performances by a brass and percussion band draw in a crowd. Unfortunately, the engaging nineteenth-century tradition of the evening promenade, which saw gentlemen perambulating the park in one direction, ladies in the other, coquettishly flirting as they passed, has been replaced in recent years by a less attractive influx of Western men on the prowl for *jineteras*, and local men severely hassling Western women.

The rooftop bar at the picturesque *Casa Granda* hotel, on the park's east side, provides a fantastic setting to admire the sunset as well as the surrounding sights, while the hotel's balcony bar, on the ground floor, is a great place to people-watch over a glass of fresh lemonade. Two doors down from the hotel is the old high-society **Club San Carlos**, housed in an exquisite nineteenth-century building, part of which holds an art gallery. On the south side, a small **monument** celebrates the park's namesake, Carlos Manuel de Céspedes, one of the first Cubans to take up arms against the Spanish, issuing the *Grito de Yara* (cry of Yara) and urging his slaves and his comrades to arm themselves (see box, p.416). Facing the cathedral on the park's north side is the brilliant-white **Ayuntamiento**, or town hall, whose balcony was the site of Fidel Castro's triumphant speech in January, 1959.

Catedral de Nuestra Señora de la Asunción

Parque Céspedes • Tues–Fri 8am–noon & 5–8pm, Sat 8am–noon & 4–5.30pm; Mass Tues–Fri 6.30pm, Sat 4.30pm, Sun 9am & 6.30pm

On the south side of Parque Céspedes is the handsome **Catedral de Nuestra Señora de la Asunción**. The first cathedral in Santiago was built on this site in 1522, but repeated run-ins with earthquakes and pirates – in 1606 English privateer Christopher Myngs even stole the church bells after blowing the roof off – made their mark, and Santiagueros started work on a second cathedral on the site in 1674, only to see the building demolished by an earthquake just three years later. A third cathedral was erected in 1690 but was wiped out by another earthquake in 1766.

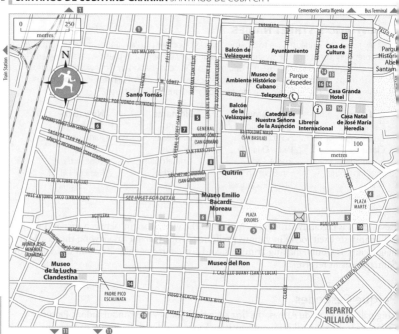

The present cathedral, completed in 1818, has fared better, having been built with a fortified roof and walls in order to withstand natural disasters. However, it has been shaken by quakes in 1852 and 1932, and lost much of its roof after Hurricane Sandy tunnelled into the city in October 2012, also toppling the two crosses that once capped its twin towers. The cathedral features a Baroque-style facade, its twin towers gleaming in the sunshine and its doorway topped by an imposing herald angel, statues of **Christopher Columbus** and **Bartolomé de las Casas**, defender of the Indians, erected in the 1920s, and four Neoclassical columns.

The interior

The **interior** is no less ornate, with an arched Rococo ceiling rising above the pews into a celestial blue dome painted with a cloud of cherubs. Facing the congregation is a modest marble altar framed by rich dark-wood choir stalls, while to the right a more ornate altar honours the Virgen de la Caridad, patron saint of Cuba. The prize piece, almost hidden on the left-hand side, is the tremendous **organ**, no longer used but still replete with tall gilded pipes. Lining the wall is a noteworthy frieze detailing the history of St James, the eponymous patron saint of Santiago.

Museo Ambiente Histórico Cubano

Parque Martí e/ Aguilera y Heredia • Mon–Thurs & Sat–Sun 9am–4.45pm, Fri 1–4.45pm • $2CUC, photos $5CUC

Built in 1515 for Diego Velázquez, the first *conquistador* of Cuba, the magnificent stone edifice on the west side of the park is the oldest residential building in Cuba. It now houses the **Museo Ambiente Histórico Cubano**, a wonderful collection of furniture, curios, weapons and fripperies which offers one of the country's best insights into colonial lifestyles, and is so large that it spills over into the house next door. There are also traditional music *peñas* and choral performances here on Monday, Wednesday, Thursday and Sunday mornings.

Estadio Guillermón Moncada, Plaza de la Revolución & Monumento Antonio Maceo

SANTIAGO DE CUBA

DRINKING & NIGHTLIFE

Artex	10	Coro Madrigalista	7
Barrita Ron Caney	1	Iris Jazz Club	5
El Baturro	6	Los Dos Abuelos	4
Casa del Caribe	3	Hotel Casa Granda	14
Casa de los Estudiantes	15	La Maqueta	17
Casa de la Música	12	de Santiago	
Casa de las Tradiciones	11	Pista Bailable	2
Casa de la Trova	16	Sala de Conciertos	9
Club 300	13	UNEAC	8

Cuartel Moncada

REPARTO VISTA ALEGRE

REPARTO VISTA

Museo de la Imagen

REPARTO SANTA BÁRBARA

ACCOMMODATION

Las Américas	4	Casa Granda	16
Casa Colonial Maruchi	5	Casa Yisel y Martin	14
Casa de Jorge Juan Manchon	1	La Confronta	3
Casa de Leonardo y Rosa	11	Gran Hotel	15
Casa de Mary	6	Islazul San Juan	9
Casa de Nolvis		Libertad	10
Rivaflecha Martínez	13	Meliá Santiago	
Casa de Noris y Pedro	8	de Cuba	2
Casa de Ylia Deas Díaz	7	San Basilio	12

EATING

La Arboleda Coppelia	6	El Morro	11
Cafetería La Isabelica	8	El Palenquito	4
Casa Micaela	1	Pan.Com	14
La Casona	2	Restaurant El Cayo	13
La Corona	10	Salon Tropical	7
La Fontana	3	La Taberna de Dolores	9
El Madrileño	5	El Zunzún	3
El Marino	12		

8

Cayo Granma, El Morro Castle (8km) & Airport (8km)

The first floor

Start your tour on the first floor, in the family's living quarters, where you'll find some unusual **sixteenth-century** pieces exhibited beneath stunning Mudéjar ceilings. All the windows have heavy wooden lattice balconies and shutters – intended to hide the women, keep the sun out and protect against attack – which lend the house a surprising coolness, as well as the look of an indomitable fortress. The house was strategically built facing west so that the first-floor windows looked out over the bay, and a **cannon** is still trained out of the bedroom window. The next two adjoining rooms represent the mid- and late **seventeenth century**; the burn damage outside the rooms was caused by a fire in 1990. The first room holds a chunky, carved mahogany chest, and a delicate Spanish ceramic inkwell that has survived intact through three centuries.

The final rooms on this floor take you into the **eighteenth century**, and the furnishings seem incongruously grand, set against the plain white walls and cool tiled floors of the house. Also in this room, cut into the inner wall, there's the **Poyo de la Ventana**, a latticed spy window overlooking the hallway, which allowed inhabitants to check on the movements of other people in the house.

Out in the cool upstairs **hallway** you can fully appreciate the cleverness of its design in its stark contrast with the dazzling, sunny central courtyard visible below, where there's an elegant central fountain and a huge *tinajón* water jar from Camagüey. Before you venture downstairs, walk to the end of the hallway to see the remains of the stone **furnace** that Velázquez built into the corner of the house so that he could smelt his own gold.

The ground floor

The rooms on the **ground floor**, where Velázquez had his offices, are now laid out with more extravagant eighteenth-century furniture and artefacts, though more impressive, perhaps, are the details of the house itself, such as the wide entrance made to accommodate a carriage and the expansive trading rooms with a stone central arch, marble flagged floor and window seats.

The annexe

The collection overflows into the **house next door**, which dates from the nineteenth century. Again, much of what's on display is imported from Europe and shows off the good life enjoyed by Santiago's bourgeoisie, but the most interesting items are native to Cuba, like the reclining *pajilla* smoking chair with an ornate ashtray attached to the arm, made for the proper enjoyment of a fine cigar.

Balcón de Velázquez

Corona esq. San Basilio • Daily 9am–9pm • Free; photos $1CUC, video $5CUC

West of Parque Céspedes, the **Balcón de Velázquez** fortification was built between 1539 and 1550 as a lookout point for incoming ships, and was originally equipped with a semicircle of cannons facing out over the bay. It was renovated in 1953, sadly without its most intriguing feature, a tunnel entered from beneath the circular platform in the centre of the patio and running for less than 1km down to the seafront. This was presumably used by the early townsfolk for making a swift exit when under siege. The modern covered entrance is lined with a history of Santiago (in Spanish) and honorary plaques to influential dignitaries, but the highlight here is the **view** over the ramshackle, red-tiled rooftops down towards the bay and the ring of mountains beyond.

El Tivolí

8

Occupying the hills about four blocks south of the Balcón de Velázquez is the **El Tivolí** neighbourhood, named by the French plantation owners who settled here at the end of the eighteenth century. With no real boundaries – it lies loosely between Avenida Trocha to the south and Calle Padre Pico in the north – there's not much to distinguish it from the rest of the old quarter, save for its intensely hilly narrow streets heading down towards the bay. The immigrant French made this the most fashionable area of town, and for a while its bars and music venues were *the* place for well-to-do Santiagueros to be seen. While the *Casa de las Tradiciones* (see p.407) is still a great, intimate venue, the area has definitely lost its former glory, though it is worth visiting the **Museo de la Lucha Clandestina** and climbing the **Padre Pico Escalinata**, a towering staircase of over fifty steps, built to accommodate the almost sheer hill that rises from the lower end of Calle Padre Pico.

Museo de la Lucha Clandestina

General Rabi 1 e/ Sta Rita y San Carlos • Tues–Sun 9am–5pm • $1CUC, photos $5CUC • English, Italian and Spanish guides available

Just west of Padre Pico, perched on the Loma del Intendente, the **Museo de la Lucha Clandestina** is a tribute to the pre-revolutionary struggle. Spread over two floors, it comprises a photographic and journalistic history of the final years of the Batista regime and is a must for anyone struggling to understand the intricacies of the events leading up to the Revolution.

The immaculate building is a reproduction of an eighteenth-century house built on the site as the residence of the quartermaster general under Spanish rule. In the 1950s it served as the Santiago police headquarters until burnt to the ground during an assault orchestrated by schoolteacher-cum-underground leader **Frank País** on November 30, 1956. The three-pronged attack also took in the customs house and the harbour headquarters, in an attempt to divert the authorities' attention from the arrival of Fidel Castro and other dissidents at Las Coloradas beach on the southwestern coast. The attack is well documented here, with part of the museum focusing on the lives of Frank País and his brother and co-collaborator Josue, both subsequently murdered by Batista's henchmen in 1957.

FROM TOP GIRL WITH CARNIVAL CROWN, SANTIAGO (P.397); CONGA PARADE DRUMMERS, SANTIAGO (P.397) >

The best exhibits are those that give an idea of the turbulent climate of fear, unrest and excitement that existed in the 1950s in the lead-up to the Revolution. Most memorable is a clutch of **Molotov cocktails** made from old-fashioned Pepsi Cola bottles, a hysterical newspaper cutting announcing Fidel Castro's death and another published by the rebels themselves refuting the claim.

Calle Heredia

A couple of blocks east of Parque Céspedes is the lively patch of **Calle Heredia**, where the catcalls of street vendors hawking hand-carved necklaces, wood sculptures and gimcrack souvenirs combine with the drums emanating from the Casa de la Trova music hall (see p.408) to create one of the liveliest areas in the city. Santiagueros often comment that you haven't really been to the city until you've been to Calle Heredia, and you could spend hours checking out the sights here – namely the mildly interesting **Casa Natal de José María Heredia** and the excellent **Museo del Carnaval** – and just drinking in the atmosphere and enjoying idiosyncrasies like the Librería La Escalera secondhand bookshop (see p.409).

Casa Natal de José María Heredia

Heredia no.260 • Tues–Sat 8am–8pm, Sun 8am–noon • $1CUC, photos $1CUC, guide $1CUC

The handsome colonial **Casa Natal de José María Heredia** is the birthplace of one of the greatest Latin American poets. His poetry combined romanticism and nationalism, and was forbidden in Cuba until the end of Spanish rule. While not the most dynamic museum in the world, it's worth a quick breeze through the spartan rooms to see the luxurious French *bateau* bed, the family photos and the various first editions. A good time to visit is on Tuesdays at 7pm, when local poets meet for (free) discussions and recitals on the sunny patio at the back of the house.

Museo del Carnaval

Heredia no.301 • Tues–Fri 9am–5.15pm, Sat 9am–10pm, Sun 9am–1pm • $1CUC, photos $5CUC • Dance recitals Mon–Sat 4–5pm and Sat 7–10pm

A must if you can't make it for the real thing in July, the **Museo del Carnaval** is a small but bright and colourful collection of psychedelic costumes, atmospheric photographs and carnival memorabilia. Beginning with scene-setting **photographs** of Santiago in the early twentieth century, showing roads laced with tram tracks and well-dressed people promenading through the parks, the exhibition moves on to newspaper cuttings and **costumes** belonging to the pre-revolutionary carnivals of the 1940s and 1950s. In a separate room are photographs of some of the musicians who have played at carnival accompanied by their **instruments**, displayed in glass cases. A final room shows off costumes made for post-Revolution carnivals, along with some of the immensely intricate prototypes of floats that are constructed in miniature months before the final models are made.

The flamboyant carnival atmosphere is brought to life with a free, open-air, hour-long **dance recital** called the *Tardes de Folklórico* (folklore afternoon), showcasing the dances and music of various *orishas* (deities).

Museo Emilio Bacardí Moreau

Aguilera esq. Pío Rosado • Mon 1–4.30pm, Tues–Sat 9am–4.30pm, Sun 9am–1pm • $2CUC including guide, photos $5CUC

Of all the museums in Santiago, by far the most essential is the stately **Museo Emilio Bacardí Moreau**. Its colonial antiquities, excellent collection of Cuban fine art and archeological curios make it one of the most comprehensive hoards in the country. Styled along the lines of a traditional European city museum, it was founded in 1899 by Emilio Bacardí Moreau, then mayor of Santiago and patriarch of the Bacardí rum

SANTIAGO'S CARNIVAL

The extravaganza that is **Santiago's carnival** has its origins in the festival of Santiago (St James), which is held annually on July 25. While the Spanish colonists venerated the saint, patron of Spain and Santiago city, their African slaves celebrated their own religions, predominantly Yoruba. A religious procession would wend its way around the town towards the cathedral, with the Spanish taking the lead and slaves bringing up the rear. Once the Spanish had entered the cathedral, the slaves took their own celebration onto the streets, with dancers, singers and musicians creating a ritual that had little to do with the solemn religion of the Spanish – the frenzied gaiety of the festival even earned it the rather derisive name **Los Mamarrachos** (The Mad Ones).

Music was a key element, and slaves of similar ethnic groups would form *comparsas* (carnival bands) to make music with home-made bells, drums and chants. Often accompanying the *comparsas* on the procession were *diablitos* (little devils), male dancers masked from head to toe in raffia costumes. This tradition is still upheld today and you can see the rather unnerving, jester-like figures running through the crowds and scaring children. Carnival's popularity grew, and in the seventeenth century the festival was gradually extended to cover July 24, the festival of Santa Cristina, and July 26, Santa Ana's day.

The festival underwent its biggest change in 1902 with the birth of the new republic, when politics and advertising began to muscle in on the action. It was during this era that the festival's name was changed to the more conventional **carnaval**, as the middle classes sought to distance the celebrations from their Afro-Cuban roots. With the introduction of the annually selected *Reina de Carnaval* (Carnival Queen) – usually a white, middle-class girl – and carnival floats sponsored by big-name companies like Hatuey beer and Bacardí, the celebration was transformed from marginal black community event to populist extravaganza. With sponsorship deals abundant, the **carrozas** (floats) flourished, using extravagant and grandiose designs.

Perhaps the most distinctive element of modern-day carnival in Santiago is the **conga parade** that takes place in each neighbourhood on the first day of the celebrations. Led by the *comparsas*, almost everyone in the neighbourhood, many still dressed in hair curlers and house slippers, leaves their houses as the performers lead them around the streets in a vigorous parade. The week before carnival starts, you can see the Conga de los Hoyos practising around town and visiting the seven other city conga groups every day from 3pm to 8pm.

CARNAVAL PRACTICALITIES

Carnaval takes place every year from around July 18 to July 27. The main parade is on the first day, and is followed by smaller parades on the second, third and fourth days. On the 25th, there's a general parade from 10pm in honour of the city's patron saint; the 26th sees a grand parade, and there's prize-giving on the 27th. The parades process down Ave. Garzón, where there are seats for viewing ($2CUP after 10pm); to buy a ticket, visit the temporary wooden booths near the seating stands earlier in the evening. Don't be corralled into the foreigners', section, where you'll be charged $5CUC.

8

dynasty (see box, p.398), to house his vast private collection of artefacts amassed over the previous decades.

The ground floor

The exhibits are arranged over three floors. The ground floor is devoted to the **Sala de Conquista y Colonización**, full of elaborate weaponry like sixteenth-century helmets, cannons and spurs, although copper cooking pots and the like add a suggestion of social history. Much more sinister here are the whips, heavy iron chains and the *Palo Mata Negro* (or Kill-the-Black stick), all used to whip and beat slaves. A separate room at the back houses the **Sala de Arqueología**, where a substantial selection of Egyptian artefacts includes some fine jade and bluestone eagle-head idols, as well an **Egyptian mummy**, thought to be a young woman from the Thebes dynasty and brought over from Luxor by Bacardí himself; her well-preserved casket is on display nearby, covered in hieroglyphs and pictures.

8

THE BACARDÍ DYNASTY

Don Facundo Bacardí Massó emigrated to Santiago de Cuba from Spanish Catalonia in 1829, and eventually established one of the largest spirits companies in the world. At the time, **rum** was a rasping drink favoured by pirates and slaves – hardly the type of tipple served to the Cuban aristocracy. However, Bacardí was swift to see the drink's potential and set to work refining it. He discovered that filtering the rum through charcoal removed impurities, while ageing it in oak barrels provided a depth that made it eminently more drinkable.

Buoyed by his successful discovery, Facundo and his brother Jos opened their first distillery on February 4, 1862. Company legend relates that when Don Facundo's wife Dona Amalia glimpsed the colony of fruit bats living in the building's rafters, she suggested they adopt the insignia of a **bat**, symbolizing good luck in Taíno folklore, as the company logo. This proved a shrewd marketing tool as many more illiterate Cubans could recognize the trademark bat than could read the name "Bacardí".

The company went from strength to strength, quickly becoming the major producer of quality rum, while the family's involvement in **Cuban politics** grew in tandem with their business interests, and they became instrumental in the push for independence and subsequent alliance with the US. Emilio Bacardí, Don Facundo's eldest son, was exiled from Cuba for anti-colonial activities but later returned as a Mambises liberation fighter in the rebel army during the Second War of Independence. The Bacardís' loyalty to the cause was rewarded in 1899 when American General Leonard Wood appointed Emilio Bacardí mayor of Santiago de Cuba. While Facundito – Facundo senior's younger son – ran the company and supervised research into further refining the rum, Emilio Bacardí concentrated on public life. The **Emilio Bacardí Moreau Municipal Museum** opened the year he became mayor. The old Santiago HQ, with the bat motifs imprinted in the columns, still stands two blocks west of Parque Céspedes at Aguilera 55–59. Testimony to the family bounty stands in the fabulous 1930 Art Deco **Edifico Bacardí** on Havana's San Juan de Dios, which combined a company headquarters with an elegant bar. During World War II, the company was led by Schueg's son-in-law José Pepin Bosch, who also founded Bacardí Imports in New York City. Also a political mover and shaker, he was appointed Cuba's Minister of the Treasury in 1949 during Carlos Prío's government.

The **Revolution**, with its core aim of redistributing the country's wealth to the benefit of the underprivileged peasant classes, completely altered the course of the Bacardí family's history. Enraged by the 1960 nationalization of its main distillery in Santiago, and later, of all its Cuban assets, the company shipped out of Cuba, relocating their headquarters to the Bahamas where sugar cane – and cheap labour – were in plentiful supply. Though no longer based in Cuba, the Bacardí family did not relinquish its desire to shape the country's destiny. Author Hernando Calvo Ospina, in his 2002 book *Bacardí, The Hidden War*, claims that Bacardí financed 1960s counter-revolutionary groups (including the attack on the Bay of Pigs), and helped found the ultra-right-wing Cuban American National Foundation (CANF). The Bacardís have denied most of these allegations but have made no secret of the fact that there is no love lost between them and the Cuban government.

The first floor

Centred on the history of the fight for **independence**, the first floor's exhibits include the printing press where Carlos Manuel de Céspedes's independence manifesto newspaper *El Cubano Libre* was produced. Representing the actual fighting is an assortment of the Mambises' ingenious bullet belts, cups, sandals and trousers, all handmade from natural products while on the warpath.

The second floor

The museum really comes into its own on the second floor, with an excellent display of **paintings** and **sculpture**, including some fascinating nineteenth-century portraits of colonial Cubans. A surprise is the delicately executed series of watercolours – including a rather camp cavalryman and an enigmatic picador – by the multitalented Emilio Bacardí himself.

The second floor also features a strong collection of **contemporary** painting and sculpture, with several of the country's most prominent artists represented. Highlights include the iridescent *Paisaje* by Víctor Manuel García, who died in the late 1960s, and the simple but powerful *Maternidad*, by Pedro Arrate, a perfect composition with a young mother kneeling on a bare wooden floor nursing her newborn child.

Museo del Ron

San Basilio no.358 esq. Carnicería • Mon–Sat 9am–5pm • $2CUC, includes Spanish-, English- or German-speaking guide

One block south of Calle Heredia, the restored **Museo del Ron** explores the history and production of Cuba's most popular liquor. The collection includes a number of antique machines used in the various stages of rum production, from the extraction of molasses from sugar cane to the ageing and bottling of the rum. Occupying the fine nineteenth-century home of Mariano Gómez, who was in charge of managing the Bacardí family's enormous wealth, the museum is replete with Carrara marble floors, glittering chandeliers and red-and-green *vitrales*. There is an on-site bar, but you get a free shot with admission.

Plaza Marte

Ten minutes' walk beyond the east end of Enramada is the lively **Plaza Marte**, where gaggles of game-playing schoolchildren, loudspeakers transmitting radio broadcasts, occasional live bands and plenty of benches make for an enjoyable place to spend some time – though it's pretty shadeless since Hurricane Sandy wiped out all but two of its palms. The tall column, a **monument** to local veterans of the Wars of Independence, has a particular significance – the plaza was formerly the execution ground for prisoners held by the Spanish. The Smurf-like cap at its summit is the *gorro frigio*, given to slaves in ancient Rome when they were granted their freedom, and a traditional symbol of Cuban independence.

8

Cuartel Moncada

Calle Trinidad esq. Moncada

Several blocks north from Plaza Marte and just off the Avenida de los Libertadores is the **Cuartel Moncada**. Scene of a bungled attack by Fidel Castro and his band of revolutionaries on July 26, 1953 (see box, p.400), the fort is a must-see, if only for the place it has in Cuban history. With a commanding view over the mountains, the ochre-and-white building, topped with a row of castellations, is still peppered with bullet holes from the attack. These were plastered over on Fulgencio Batista's orders, only to be hollowed out again rather obsessively by Fidel Castro when he came to power, with photographs used to make sure the positions were as authentic as possible.

Castro closed the barracks altogether in 1960, turning part of the building into a school, while the one-time parade grounds outside are now occasionally used for state speeches and music concerts.

Museo 26 de Julio

Mon 9am–12.30pm, Tues–Sat 9am–4.30pm, Sun 9am–12.30pm • $2CUC, photos $5CUC

Inside Cuartel Moncada, the **Museo 26 de Julio** boasts flashes of brilliance when it comes to telling the story of the attack, but is otherwise rather dry. Bypassing the pedantic history of the garrison, the museum gets properly under way with its coverage of the 1953 attack. A meticulous **scale model** details the barracks, the now-demolished hospital and the Palacio de Justicia, and gives the events a welcome clarity – the model is even marked with the positions where rebel bullets landed. The museum pulls no punches on the subject of the **atrocities** visited upon the captured rebels by the

THE ATTACK ON CUARTEL MONCADA

Summing up his goals with the words "a small engine is needed to help start the big engine", Fidel Castro decided in 1953 to lead an attack to capture the weapons his guerrilla organization needed and hopefully also spark a national uprising against the Batista regime. Santiago's **Cuartel Moncada** seemed perfect: not only was it the second largest in the country, but it was also based in Oriente, where support for the clandestine movement against the government was already strongest.

A three-pronged assault was planned, with the main body of men, led by Fidel Castro, attacking the barracks themselves, while Raúl Castro would attack the nearby Palace of Justice, overlooking the barracks, with ten men to form a covering crossfire. At the same time, Abel Santamaría, Castro's second-in-command, was to take the civil hospital opposite the Palace of Justice with 22 men; the two women, his sister Haydee Santamaría and his girlfriend Melba Hernández, were to treat the wounded.

The attack was an unqualified fiasco. At 5.30am on July 26, the rebels' motorcade of 26 cars set off for Santiago from the farm they had rented in Siboney. Somewhere between the farm and the city limits, several cars headed off in the wrong direction and never made it to the Cuartel Moncada. The remaining cars reached the barracks, calling on the sentries to make way for the general, a ruse which allowed the attackers to seize the sentries' weapons and force their way into the barracks.

Outside, things were going less well. Castro, who was in the second car, stopped after an unexpected encounter with patrolling soldiers and the subsequent gunfire alerted the troops throughout the barracks. Following their previous orders, once they saw that Castro's car had stopped, the men in the other cars streamed out to attack other buildings in the barracks before Castro had a chance to re-evaluate the situation. The rebels inside the first building found themselves cut off amid the general confusion, and as free-for-all gunfire ensued, the attackers were reduced to fleeing and cowering behind cars. Castro gave the order to withdraw, leaving behind two dead and one wounded.

By contrast, the unprotected Palace of Justice and hospital had been attacked successfully, but both groups were forced to withdraw or hide once their role was rendered useless.

THE AFTERMATH

The real bloodshed was yet to come, however, as within 48 hours of the attack somewhere between 55 and 70 of the original rebels had been captured, tortured and **executed** by Batista's officers after an extensive operation in which thousands were detained. The casualties included Abel Santamaría, whose eyes were gouged out, while his sister, Haydee, was forced to watch. The soldiers then attempted to pass the bodies off as casualties of the attack two days before. Thirty-two rebels survived to be brought to trial, including Fidel Castro himself. Others managed to escape altogether and returned to Havana. Although a disaster in military terms, the attack was a political triumph: the army's **brutality** towards the rebels sent many previously indifferent people into the arms of the clandestine movement and elevated Fidel Castro – previously seen as just a maverick young lawyer – to hero status throughout Cuba.

The rebels were tried in October, and despite efforts to prevent Castro appearing in court – an attempt was apparently made to poison him – he gave an erudite and impassioned speech in his own defence. A reprise of the speech was later published as a manifesto for revolution, known as "History will absolve me" (the last words of the speech). Although the declamation did little to help Castro at the time – he was sentenced to fifteen years' imprisonment – the whole episode set him on the path to leadership of the Revolution.

Regimental Intelligence Service, Batista's henchmen: a huge collage, blotted with crimson paint, has been created from photographs of the dead rebels lying in their own gore. Gruesome bloodstained uniforms and some sobering sketches of the type of weapons used are also on display.

Thankfully, the last room has a less oppressive theme, with **photographs** of the surviving rebels leaving the Isla de Pinos (now Isla de la Juventud), where they had been imprisoned following the attack, and in exile in Mexico. There's also a scale model of the celebrated yacht *Granma* that carried them back to Cuba. Have a look at the

guns used in the war, in particular the one in the final display cabinet, carved with the national flag and the inscription "*Vale más morir de pies a vivir de rodillas*" ("It's better to die on your feet than to live on your knees").

Parque Histórico Abel Santamaría

A couple of blocks west of the Cuartel Moncada, on the site of the Civil Hospital which Santamaría captured during the Moncada attack, **Parque Histórico Abel Santamaría** is less of a park and more like a small field of concrete centred on a monument to Abel Santamaría. Set above a onetime gushing fountain, a gigantic cube of concrete is carved with the faces of Santamaría and fellow martyr José Martí and the epigram "*Morir por la patria es vivir*" ("To die for your country is to live"). The giant grey monument is rather impressive and worth a look while you're in the area.

Monumento Antonio Maceo

Plaza de la Revolución • Museum Mon–Sat 9am–5pm, Sun 9am–1pm • \$1CUC

Two kilometres north of the centre, on Avenida de los Américas, by the busy junction with Avenida de los Libertadores, is the **Plaza de la Revolución**, an empty space backed by a park in which stands the gargantuan **Monumento Antonio Maceo**. The 16m steel effigy, on a wide plateau at the top of a jade marble staircase, shows Maceo, the "Bronze Titan" – so named because he was of mixed race – on his rearing horse, backed by a forest of gigantic steel machetes representing his rebellion and courage. On the other side of the marble plateau, wide steps lead down behind an eternal flame dedicated to the general, to the entirely missable **Museo Antonio Maceo**, housed in the plateau basement.

Cementerio Santa Ifigenia

Calzada Crombet • Daily 7am–6pm • \$1CUC • A private taxi from the centre will cost \$3–5CUC

Most visitors who trek out to the **Cementerio Santa Ifigenia**, about 3km northwest of Parque Céspedes, do so to visit **José Martí's mausoleum**, a grandiose affair of heavy white stone with the inevitable statue located near the cemetery entrance at the end of a private walkway where, every half an hour, there's a five-minute changing of the guard ceremony.

A relatively recent arrival at the cemetery is **Compay Segundo**, a native Santiaguero, legendary singer and guitarist, member of the Buena Vista Social Club and composer of the ubiquitous *Chan Chan*. Segundo, who died in 2003 at the age of 95, was buried with full military honours in recognition of his achievements during the Revolution, long before he became famous as a musician.

The burial site of **Frank and Josue País** is flanked by the flags of Cuba and the M-26–7 movement. A former schoolteacher and much-loved revolutionary, Frank País led the movement in the Oriente until his assassination, on Batista's orders, at the age of 22. Among other luminaries buried here are Carlos Manuel de Céspedes and Antonio Maceo's widow. Guides are available to show you around in return for a small tip.

Reparto Vista Alegre

East of town is the residential suburb of **Reparto Vista Alegre**, established at the beginning of the twentieth century as an exclusive neighbourhood for Santiago's middle classes. Today, its lingering air of wealth is confined to a few **restaurants** (see p.406) dotted around wide and regal Avenida Manduley, which are most people's reason for visiting, although a clutch of interesting museums also makes a trip up here worthwhile. Some of the handsome Neoclassical buildings lining the main road – best seen in springtime under a cloud of pink blossoms – are still private residences, while others are government offices and new government hostels. Although most of the buildings are a bit worn around the edges, they make for pleasant sightseeing, especially the madly ornate peach-coloured palace – one-time Bacardí family residence – that's now the headquarters of the children's youth movement Pionero.

Museo de la Imagen

Calle 8 no.106 • Mon–Fri 9am–5pm, Sat & Sun 2–10pm • $1CUC, photos $5CUC

The small and quirky **Museo de la Imagen** presents a brief history of photography told through antique Leicas, Polaroids and Kodaks, and some brilliant (and odd) one-off **photographs**, such as the one showing Fidel Castro, in Native American feathered headdress, accepting a peace pipe from the leader of the White Bird tribe.

Casa de las Religiones Populares

Calle 13 no.206 esq. 10 • Mon–Sat 9am–6pm • $2CUC including guide

Anyone interested in Cuba's idiosyncratic home-grown religions should head four blocks east of the Museo de la Imagen to the fascinating **Casa de las Religiones Populares**. The collection spans the different belief systems, including Santería and voodoo, which developed in different parts of the country, each local variation shaped by the traditions of the homelands of the African slaves and all influenced by the Catholicism of the Spanish settlers. It's striking to see how Christian iconography has been fused with some of the African culture-based paraphernalia, with the animal bones, dried leaves and rag dolls presented alongside church candles, crucifixes and images of the Virgin and Child.

Loma de San Juan

The **Loma de San Juan**, the hill where Teddy Roosevelt rode his army to victory against the Spanish, is about 250m south from Avenida Manduley, which runs through the centre of Reparto Vista Alegre. The neatly mowed lawns framing a bijou fountain, the dainty flowerbeds and the sweeping vista of mountain peaks beyond the city make it all look more suited to a tea party than a battle, but the numerous plaques and monuments erected by the North Americans to honour their soldiers are evidence enough. The sole monument to the Cuban sacrifice is squeezed into a corner; erected in 1934 by Emilio Bacardí to the unknown Mambí soldier, it's a tribute to all liberation soldiers whose deaths went unrecorded. The park would be a peaceful retreat were it not for the persistent attentions of the attendant crowd of hustlers.

El Castillo del Morro San Pedro de la Roca

Carretera del Morro Km 7.5 • Daily 8am–7pm • $4CUC, photos $5CUC • Taxis from Santiago cost $10–12CUC; a less reliable but much cheaper option are buses #11 and #12, which leave from Plaza de la Revolución

Just 8km south of the city is one of Santiago's most dramatic and popular sights, **El Castillo del Morro San Pedro de la Roca**, a fortress poised on the high cliffs that flank the entrance to the Bahía de Santiago de Cuba. Designed by the Italian military engineer Juan Bautista Antonelli (also responsible for the similar fortification in Havana) and named after Santiago's then-governor, it was built between 1633 and 1639 to ward off pirates. However, despite an indomitable appearance – including a heavy drawbridge spanning a deep moat, thick stone walls angled sharply to one another and, inside, expansive parade grounds stippled with cannons trained out to sea – it turned out to be nothing of the sort. In 1662 the English pirate Christopher Myngs captured El Morro after discovering, to his surprise, that it had been left unguarded. Ramps and steps cut precise angles through the heart of the fortress, which is spread over three levels, and it's only as you wander deeper into the labyrinth of rooms that you get a sense of how huge it is. Now home to the Museo de la Piratería, El Morro is also notable for its daily cannon firing ceremony, which takes place at dusk, but the real splendour here is the structure's magnificent scale, the sheer cliff-edge drop and its superb views out to sea.

Museo de Piratería

Daily 8am–7pm • Entry is included in the El Morro ticket

Inside El Castillo del Morro San Pedro de la Roca, the **Museo de Piratería** details the pirate raids on Santiago during the sixteenth century by the infamous Frenchman Jacques de Sores and Englishman Henry Morgan. Detailed explanations in Spanish are complemented by weapons used in the era, now rusted by the passing years.

Cayo Granma

Carretera al Castillo del Morro • Ferries to the island depart at half past each hour from 5am to 1am; the fare is $1CUC and journey time is about 15min

A half-day trip out to El Morro can easily take in the diminutive **Cayo Granma**, 2km offshore, where a peaceful rural village offers an excellent spot for a meal. You can work up an appetite by walking round the tiny island, which is home to 2000 people and takes just twenty minutes to circumnavigate. The village boasts some attractive wooden buildings trimmed with ornamental fretwork, the tiny hilltop church of San Rafael and a couple of **restaurants** (see p.406).

There's no sign for the actual ferry point, but it's roughly opposite the cay and there are usually a few people queuing; take the road to El Morro and look for the steps down to the ferry jetty.

ARRIVAL AND DEPARTURE

SANTIAGO DE CUBA

BY PLANE

Essentials International and domestic flights arrive at the Aeropuerto Internacional Antonio Maceo (☎22 69 1052), near the southern coast, 8km from the city. There are regular flights to Havana (2hr 15min). Metered and unmetered taxis wait outside and charge $7–15CUC to take you to the centre, though there's sometimes a bus that meets flights from Havana, charging around $5CUP for the same journey. You can arrange car rental at the Transtur desk at the airport (☎22 68 6161) or Rex (☎22 68 6444), or at travel agencies in town (see box, p.404).

Airlines Cubana, Enramada esq. San Pedro (Mon–Fri 8.15am–1pm; ☎22 65 1577); Aerocaribbean, San Pedro 601A e/ Heredia y San Basilio (Mon–Fri 9am–noon & 1–4.30pm, Sat 9am–noon; ☎22 68 7255, Eaerocaribbeanscu@enet.cu).

BY BUS

Víazul buses Taxi drivers and touts descend on tourists arriving at the Víazul bus terminal (☎22 62 8484) on Avenida de los Libertadores, 2km north of the town centre, like locusts on ears of corn; the journey to the centre is around $3CUC. You can book Víazul tickets to Holguín,

Havana and Baracoa (subject to limited availability), and domestic plane tickets, at the Infotur office (see below), as well as at the *Hotel Santiago de Cuba*.

Destinations Baracoa (1 daily; 4hr 20min); Bayamo (5 daily; 2hr 5min); Camagüey (7 daily; 5hr 15min); Ciego de Ávila (6 daily; 7hr 15min); Guantánamo (1 daily; 1hr 25min); Havana (5 daily; 15hr 30min); Holguín (5 daily; 3hr 25min); Las Tunas (5 daily; 4hr 40min); Sancti Spíritus (5 daily; 8hr 40min); Santa Clara (3 daily; 12hr).

Local buses Provincial buses pull in at the Intermunicipal bus terminal (☎22 62 4325), next door to the Astro terminal on Avenida de los Libertadores.

Tourist buses The Conectando Cuba tourist bus to Havana ($51CUC), stopping at a number of provincial cities, leaves from *Hotel Santiago* at 7am daily.

BY TRAIN

Essentials Trains arrive at the modern station (☎22 62 2836) near the port, on Paseo de Martí esq. Jesús Menéndez. From here, horse-drawn buggies and *bicitaxis* can take you to the centre for $2–3CUC, while a taxi will cost about $3CUC.

Destinations Bayamo (1 daily; 4hr 15min); Havana (1 daily; 12–14hr); Manzanillo (1 daily; 6hr).

GETTING AROUND

On foot Although a large city, Santiago is easy to negotiate on foot, as much of what you'll want to see is compactly fitted into the historic core around Parque Céspedes.

By taxi Taxis are the best way to reach outlying sights as

the buses are overcrowded and irregular. State-registered metered taxis and *coco* taxis wait on the cathedral side of Parque Céspedes or around Plaza Marte, and charge $0.50CUC per km with a $1CUC

8

surcharge. The unmetered taxis parked on San Pedro negotiate a rate for the whole journey – expect to pay about $3CUC to cross town. Touts skulk around the main streets but you'll strike a slightly cheaper deal if you negotiate with the drivers themselves. To call a state-registered taxi try Cubataxi (☎22 65 1038). For a private taxi, try the professional and reliable Tomas Rodríguez (☎22 64 1765, ☎5 293 6655 (mobile).

By car or moped Renting a car can be handy for out-of-the-way places, and the city itself is easy to drive around in. There are Transtur car rental offices at the airport (☎22 68 6161), at *Hotel Las Américas* (☎22 68 7160), and in the basement of *Hotel Casa Granda* (☎22 62 3884). Rex has an office in the car park behind *Hotel Santiago de Cuba* (☎22 68 7141), from where Transtur (☎22 64 4181) also rents out mopeds, starting at $14CUC for two hours.

INFORMATION

Tourist information The helpful staff at Infotur, Heredia no.701 esq. San Pedro (daily 8am–6pm; ☎22 68 6068), can book Víazul tickets to Holguín, Havana and Baracoa (subject to limited availability) and domestic plane tickets.
Maps Try the Librería Internacional (Mon–Sat 9am–5pm; ☎22 68 7147) on Parque Céspedes.
Cultural information Infotur usually has a weekly cultural calendar, while the Casa de la Cultura posts one at the Librería Renacimiento (Centro Información Cultural),

Enramadas 350 e/ Carnicería y San Felix (Mon–Fri 9am–5pm; ☎22 65 5708); look out also for its copy of elusive cultural mag, *Espectro*.
Listings information Santiago's weekly newspaper, the *Sierra Maestra* (ⓦsierramaestra.cu), is available from street vendors and occasionally from the bigger hotels, and has a brief listings section detailing cinema, theatre and other cultural activities.

ACCOMMODATION

Accommodation in Santiago is plentiful and varied. Except during carnival and the Fiesta del Caribe in July, when rooms are snapped up well in advance, you can usually turn up on spec, though making a reservation will save you having to trudge around looking, especially as the city's accommodation is spread over a wide area. There are a handful of **state hotels**, while **casa particulares** are abundant, many conveniently central and most offering reduced rates for stays longer than a couple of nights; those outside the centre are more likely to negotiate a lower price. **Touts** (see p.37) for *casas* are everywhere; avoid them and their $5CUC-a-night surcharge by booking directly.

HOTELS AND HOSTELS

Las Américas Ave. de Las Américas y General Cebreco ☎22 64 2011, ✉jcarpeta@hamerica.scu.tur.cu. While not the ritziest in town, this pleasantly low-key hotel combines a comfortable, friendly atmosphere and good facilities – including a taxi rank, car rental office and pool – with clean, bright and functional rooms equipped with cable TV and refrigerator. A short taxi ride from the main sights. Breakfast included. **$70 CUC**
Casa Granda Heredia no.201 e/ San Pedro y San Félix ☎22 65 3021, ✉reserva@cubanacan.tur.cu. An

attraction in itself on account of its beauty, the regal *Casa Granda* is a 1920s hotel overlooking Parque Céspedes. From the elegant, airy lobby to its two atmospheric bars, it has a stately, colonial air – it's a shame that the rooms are in such a shoddy state. **$112CUC**
La Confronta Ave. Manduley no.301 e/ 11 y 13 ☎22 64 9600. One of a number of new state-run hostels run by Compay Tiago, offering five basic, lacklustre rooms and a dining room and sitting room in houses that lack beauty or soul. Nonetheless, it's a good option for long stays, large groups or during high season and carnival if

TOURS FROM SANTIAGO

City tours and excursions throughout the province are available from Viajes Cubanacán, which has an office in the basement of the *Casa Granda* hotel (Mon–Sat 9am–5pm, Sun 9am–noon; ☎22 68 7482), and from Havanatur and Cubatur, which share offices in *Hotel Santiago de Cuba* (daily 8am–12.30pm & 1.30–5pm; ☎22 68 7040) and at Infotur on Parque Céspedes (daily 8am–6pm; ☎22 68 6068). All three charge similar prices, and reduce them slightly according to the number of people participating; the rates quoted here are based on the minimum number of people required.

Tour options include a leisurely excursion to the Gran Piedra (5hr; $31CUC with lunch; minimum 8 people), and a Santiago city tour covering El Castillo del Morro San Pedro de la Roca, Cayo Granma and El Cobre (6hr; $39CUC with lunch; minimum 8 people); the same excursion but with a longer city tour included is $62CUC with lunch, and lasts eight hours (this latter tour is good value and excellent for those short on time).

the city's *casas* sell out. Rates include breakfast. $17CUC

Gran Hotel Enramada esq. San Félix ☎ 22 65 3020, ✉ carpeta@granhotelsc.tur.cu. While this central and friendly hotel no longer merits the "grand" of its title, the vaguely colonial exterior and faded charm of the rooms are very appealing. Singles, doubles and triples all come with a/c, and many have a tiny balcony overlooking the busy shopping street. The huge triples are particularly good value. $42CUC

Islazul San Juan Carretera de Siboney, Km 1 ☎ 22 68 7200, ⊛islazul.cu. Close to historic Loma de San Juan, and boasting the most congenial location of all Santiago's hotels, set amid tropical trees and lush plants. The hotel itself is tasteful though a bit bland, with smart, attractive rooms and clean communal areas. An inviting pool area and friendly staff complete the pleasant atmosphere. $70CUC

Libertad Aguilera no.658 e/ Serafin Sánchez y Pérez Carbo ☎ 22 62 7710. This cosy, mid-range hotel offers unexciting but decent a/c rooms with cable TV; rooms at the back are quieter. $38CUC

Meliá Santiago de Cuba Ave. de las Américas y Calle M ☎ 22 68 7070, ⊛meliacuba.com. Santiago's biggest, brashest hotel caters for business types and seekers of luxury. The blocky red, white and blue exterior is ultramodern and fits well with the shiny green marble interior, while facilities include a beauty parlour, boutiques, a gym, conference rooms and the best pool in town, as well as bars and restaurants galore. The rooms are tastefully decorated, some with original paintings by local artists, and fully equipped with all mod cons. $140CUC

San Basilio San Basilio 403 e/ Calvario y Carnicería ☎ 22 65 1702, ✉ comercial@hsanbasilio.tur.cu. This gorgeous little hotel has eight tastefully furnished rooms, arranged around a bright, plant-filled patio, each with cable TV, fridge and a/c. Breakfast is included. $90CUC

CASAS PARTICULARES

★ **Casa Colonial Maruchi** San Félix no.357 e/ San Germán y Trinidad ☎ 22 62 0767, ✉ maruchib@yahoo .es. Three rooms (one with its own terrace) in a magnificent colonial house. Vintage brass beds, exposed brickwork and wooden beams add romance, while a well-tended patio filled with lush plants and a menagerie of birds and other pets is the perfect spot for the alfresco breakfast, included in the price. $25CUC

Casa de Jorge Juan Manchon Calle 6 no.204 e/ 7 y 9,

Vista Alegre ☎ 22 67 4827, ✉ amalia@fco.uo.edu.cu. A smart, airy and friendly Vista Alegre house offering two en-suite rooms featuring TVs, DVD players, wardrobes and fridges. $30CUC

Casa de Leonardo y Rosa Clarín no.9 e/ Aguilera y Heredia ☎ 22 62 3574, ✉ rosa-renta@yahoo.es. A mini-apartment with two beds, a bathroom, a fridge and a small patio in a wonderful eighteenth-century house featuring period ironwork, wooden walls, high ceilings and stained-glass windows. There are also two further rooms downstairs; one is much larger than the other with two double beds. $25CUC

Casa de Marcos y Victoria Calle G no.109 (altos) e/ 3ra y Avenida, Reparto Sueño, ☎ 22 66 3676, esalomonantonio70@yahoo.es. For families or those seeking solitude or independence, this smart new two-bedroom apartment is the ticket. There's a balcony, sun terrace and fully equipped kitchen. $30CUC

★ **Casa de Mary** San Germán no.165 e/ Rastro y Gallo ☎ 22 65 3720, ✉ elsacu10@gmail.com. Three nicely furnished, comfortable a/c rooms in an exceptionally friendly household, also known as *Casa Jardín*. An enchanting lantern-lit garden out back and a roof terrace decorated in potted plants with swings are a real bonus. A fourth room is being planned. $25CUC

Casa de Nolvis Rivaflecha Martínez San Basilio no.122 e/ Padre Pico y Teniente Rey ☎ 22 62 2972. Two clean, a/c rooms (with independent entrance) each with two beds and its own hot-water bathroom, in a sociable house with a lively communal area. Close to the Padre Pico steps, in a quiet area of town with off-road parking, it's a good option for those with a car. $25CUC

Casa de Noris y Pedro Pío Rosado no.413 e/ San Gerónimo y San Francisco ☎ 22 65 6716. This lovely colonial house set back from the road has two quiet a/c rooms each with its own bathroom and fridge, plus a patio and roof terrace to share. The friendly owners cook great meals and speak a little Italian. $25CUC

Casa de Ylia Deas Díaz San Félix no.362 e/ San Germán y Trinidad ☎ 22 65 4138. A pleasant house owned by a big welcoming family offering two spacious, high-ceilinged, comfortable rooms with a/c and large bathroom. $30CUC

Casa Yisel y Martin Santa Rita no.177 e/ Mariano Corona y General Feria ☎ 22 62 0522, ✉ martingisel78 @gmail.com. A top-notch house a few blocks south of the cathedral with a lovely, plant-filled dining terrace and two spacious en-suite rooms. $25CUC

EATING

You won't be stuck for places to eat in Santiago, with plenty of **restaurants** and **cafés** around the centre serving meals at affordable prices, and several new **paladars** in and around the centre and in Vista Alegre. On Saturday and Sunday nights, Avenida Garcón is also worth checking out, with food stalls offering – among other things – a whole roasted pig, with bands livening up the atmosphere.

Avoid drinking **unsterilized** or **unboiled water** in Santiago (remember that this includes ice cubes in drinks), especially during the summer months, when reports of parasites in the water supply are common.

STATE RESTAURANTS AND CAFÉS

La Arboleda Coppelia Ave. de los Libertadores esq. Garzón ☎ 22 66 1435. Freshly made ice cream at unbeatable $CUP prices in an outdoor café that looks like a mini-golf course. Very popular with locals, so arrive early before the best flavours of the day sell out; expect a long queue. Daily 9am–11.40pm.

Cafetería La Isabelica Calvario esq. Aguilera (no phone). Atmospheric little coffee shop with wooden fittings and whirling ceiling fans offering a variety of coffees; the most popular come with a shot of rum. Daily 7am–10.45pm.

La Casona Meliã Santiago de Cuba, Ave. de las Américas y Calle M ☎ 22 68 7070. If you can't stomach another piece of fried pork, head to *Hotel Santiago*, where thin-crust pizza, fresh salads and overcooked broccoli are part of an all-you-can-eat buffet ($20CUC a head, excluding drinks). Daily 7–10pm.

La Corona Félix Pena no.807 esq. San Carlos (no phone). Excellent bakery with an indoor café serving up a wide variety of breads and sweets, as well as pastries filled with custard or smothered in super-sticky meringue. Mon–Sat 9am–8pm.

La Fontana Meliã Santiago de Cuba, Ave. de las Américas y Calle M ☎ 22 68 7070. Although slightly expensive, the pasta and pizzas ($6–15CUC) at this open-air restaurant are authentic and carefully prepared, and portions are a decent size. Daily 7–10pm.

★ **El Morro** Castillo El Morro ☎ 22 69 1576. Perched next to the fortress in a lovely, breezy spot overlooking the bay, this relatively pricey restaurant boasts a generous array of choices and serves good-quality cuisine including soups, fish, seafood, chicken and pork dishes. Main combination menus start at $12CUC, though lobster will set you back $25CUC. Daily noon–4.30pm.

Pan.Com Aguilera e/ San Félix y San Pedro (no phone). Hamburgers, sandwiches, rolls and other half-decent snacks for $1–4CUC. Daily 9am–8pm.

Restaurant El Cayo Cayo Granma ☎ 22 69 0109. An attractive blue-and-white wooden restaurant building perched on the edge of Cayo Granma. It mostly serves tour groups, and offers fancy seafood, including lobster, paella and shrimp, with prices starting at $6CUC. Daily noon–4pm.

La Taberna de Dolores Aguilera no.468 esq. Reloj ☎ 22 62 3913. A lively restaurant, popular with older Cuban men who while away the afternoon with a bottle of rum on the sunny patio, and serving reasonable *comida criolla* for $5–8CUC. Musicians play in the evenings. Book to reserve a seat on the balcony overlooking the patio or street. Daily noon–4pm & 6–11pm.

El Zunzún Ave. Manduley no.159 esq. Calle 7 ☎ 22 64 1528. One of the classiest restaurants in town, with a series of private dining rooms perfect for an intimate dinner. Choose from an imaginative menu including pork in citrus sauce or seafood stir-fried in garlic butter and flaming rum. Main courses are $4–15CUC; there's an international wine list and injudicious use of reggaeton music. Daily noon–10pm.

PALADARS

Casa Mícaela San Felix no.260 e/ Habana y Maceo ☎ 22 62 0970. A small and friendly paladar just north of the downtown area, offering up hearty *comida criolla*, barbecued platters and shellfish. Mains $2.40–4.80CUC. Daily noon–11pm.

★ **El Madrileño** Calle 8 no.105 e/ 3 y 5 ☎ 22 64 4138. This is the best new paladar on the Santiago dining block. The pretty plant-filled patio provides a pleasant setting, and the menu includes lobster and tasty shellfish dishes such as large flamed shrimps in a whisky sauce. Try its signature Turquino Madrileño, an indulgent chocolate cake with ice cream. Mains $4–15CUC. Daily noon–11pm.

El Marino Cayo Granma ☎ 22 69 0181. The only paladar on Cayo Granma, serving up simple *comida criolla* dishes on an upstairs terrace overlooking the sea. Mains from $2CUC. Daily noon–10pm.

El Palenquito Ave. del Río no.28 e/ 6 y Carretera del Caney, Reparto Pastorita ☎ 22 64 5220. Smart tables in a garden filled with hummingbirds and hibiscus are one of the highlights of this out-of-town paladar, but the well-prepared *comida criolla*, shellfish and pasta (mains $2.50–16CUC) merit the trek out here too. Daily noon–midnight.

Salon Tropical Fernando Markane Reparto Santa Barbara e/ 9 y 11 ☎ 22 64 1161. A long-standing paladar with a pleasant terrace for pre-dinner drinks. Tasty though salty chicken fricassee, shish kebabs and grilled fish served with tamales are good choices here ($4–6CUC). Round the meal off with crème caramel and coffee. As this is really on the outskirts of town, you'll want to arrange a taxi there and back. Reservations are advised. Daily noon–midnight.

LIVE MUSIC AND DANCE IN SANTIAGO

Musical entertainment in Santiago is hard to beat, with several excellent live **trova venues** – all a giddy whirl of rum and high spirits, with soulful boleros, son and salsa banged out by wizened old men who share the tunes and the talent of the likes of Ibrahim Ferrer and Compay Segundo, if not their fame. You don't have to exert too much effort to enjoy the best of the town's music scene; the music often spills onto the streets at weekends and around carnival time, when bands set up just about everywhere. Sometimes the best way to organize your night out is to follow the beat you like the most. The best nights are often the cheapest, and it's rare to find a venue charging more than $5CUC.

Santiago has some fantastic **dance** and **folkloric groups**, too, offering mesmerizing performances. Ballet Folklórico Cutumba is an outstandingly brilliant *folklórico* group that practises and performs at the former Cine Galaxia, Calle Trocha esq. Santa Ursula (Tues–Fri 9am–1pm; ☎ 22 65 5173). Accompanied by some passionate percussive rhythms, Haitian folkloric group Tumba Francesa practise at Carnicería 268 on Tues and Thurs at 9pm.

DRINKING AND NIGHTLIFE

As much of the action in Santiago revolves around music, there are few places that cater specifically for **drinkers**, although the *Hotel Casa Granda* has two convivial bars (see below). Music played in **discos** tends to be as loud as the sound system will permit – sometimes louder – and anything goes, from Cuban and imported salsa, through reggaeton and rock to very cheesy house. They tend to draw a young, sometimes edgy and high-spirited crowd, including many of the *jinetero* and *jinetera* types who hang out in Parque Céspedes trying to win your attention. Taken in the right vein it can be amusing and even make you some friends, but if you're not interested in new friends, just be firm in saying you want to hang out alone.

8

BARS

El Baturro Aguilera esq. San Félix (no phone). This pub-style bar, decorated with Spanish bullfighting memorabilia, hosts live bands playing Santana covers and other crowd-pleasers (from 8/9pm) until 11.45pm. Serving cocktails and beers, this is a rough-and-ready venue which on some nights can feel a bit edgy. Daily 11am–midnight.

★ **Hotel Casa Granda** Heredia no.201 e/ San Pedro y San Félix ☎ 22 65 3021. Benefiting from a cool breeze, the hotel's balcony bar is the best central spot to soak up the local atmosphere by day, with comfortable seating that invites you to linger. Later on, you can retire to the open-air rooftop bar, which has views over the bay and the surrounding countryside and is the best place from which to watch the sun slide down behind the mountains. There's a $2CUC entry fee to the rooftop bar in the evenings. Balcony bar daily 11am–midnight; roof garden Mon–Thurs 9am–11pm, Fri 9am–1am.

La Maqueta de Santiago Corona no.704 e/ San Basilio y Santa Lucia (no phone). The little bar at the back of the *maqueta* (city model) is a tranquil retreat with cheap drinks – beer $1CUC – and wonderful views over the mountains and rooftops leading down to the bay. Mon 5–7pm, Tues–Sun 9am–9pm.

LIVE MUSIC VENUES AND CABARET

Artex Heredia no.304 e/ Calvario y Carnicería ☎ 22 65 4814. Bypass the inside bar (which smells of fried chicken) and head to the outside patio for live bolero, rumba, son and lively salsa. There's music at 11am, 1pm, 2–4pm and

after 8pm. It's a good place to warm up before heading on to *Casa de la Trova*, further down the same road. Entry fee varies. Daily 9am–midnight.

★ **Casa del Caribe** Calle 13 no.154 esq. 8, Reparto Vista Alegre ☎ 22 64 3609. This Afro-Cuban cultural and study centre hosts free traditional music performances and a Sunday rumba *peña*. Performances are either here on the patio, or at the patio of the nearby Casa de las Religiones (see p.402) just up the road. An informal atmosphere and enthusiastic performances make this worthy of the trip to the town outskirts. Performances Mon–Thurs & Sat 6pm, Fri 4pm, 6pm & 7pm, Sun 4pm.

Casa de la Música Corona no.564 e/ Aguilera y Enramadas ☎ 22 65 2227. Santiago's glitziest music venue, with the country's most popular bands regularly headlining. There's live music every night, with dancing and high-spirited *jineteras* much in evidence. Entry $3CUC, or $5CUC Wed & Sun. Daily 10pm–2.30am.

★ **Casa de las Tradiciones** Rabí no.154 e/ Princesa y San Fernando (no phone). A different trova band plays into the small hours every night in this tiny, atmospheric house where the walls have photographs and album sleeves. Entry $2CUC. Mon–Thurs 8pm–midnight, Fri–Sat 8pm–2am.

Casa de los Estudiantes Heredia e/ San Pedro y San Félix ☎ 226 2780. This appealing building with a long balcony hosts traditional music rehearsals. Bands play to a lively crowd – usually an even mix of Cubans and visitors – and there's a bar as well. It's an excellent place to drink, dance and socialize. Mon, Wed & Fri 7–10pm.

FIESTA DEL CARIBE

Taking place annually between July 3–9, the **Fiesta del Caribe**, or Fiesta del Fuego, brings academics, foreign participants and dance, music and cultural groups from across the Caribbean and Latin America to celebrate the culture and music of a designated Caribbean country or region each year. Organized by the city's Casa del Caribe, it's a highlight of Santiago's cultural calendar,with a finale celebrated via a city-wide conga and the burning of an effigy of the devil.

★ **Casa de la Trova** Heredia no.208 e/ San Pedro y San Félix ☎ 22 65 2689. A visit to the famous, pocket-sized *Casa de la Trova* is the highlight of a trip to Santiago, with musicians playing day and night to an audience packed into the tiny downstairs room or hanging in through the window. Upstairs is more expansive but just as atmospheric, and excellent bands play every evening. Although this venue attracts much tourist attention, it is still the top choice in town. Entry $1–10CUC depending on who's playing. Performances, 10am, 6pm & 10pm.

Coro Madrigalista Carnicería no.555 e/ Aguilera y Heredia ☎ 22 65 9439. This homely venue, which feels much like a village hall, is home to Santiago's oldest choir, whose repertoire includes classical, sacred and traditional Cuban music. You're welcome to pop in and listen to the free daily practice session, while the *peña* ($1CUC) features an assortment of local son and trova bands. Daily: rehearsals 9am–noon; peña from 8.30pm.

Los Dos Abuelos Pérez Carbó 5, Plaza Marte ☎ 22 62 3302. A variety of local groups play son and guaracha on this bar's pretty patio, shaded by fruit trees, at 10pm every night. There's an extensive range of rums and snacks available. Daily 9am–2am.

Irís Jazz Club Paraíso s/n e/ Enramadas y Aguilera no.617, Plaza Marte ☎ 22 62 7312. One of the city's newest hangouts, complete with bouncer at the door, this bar is a suitably moody venue for live jazz bands. Entrance $3CUC. Daily 9pm–2am.

Sala de Conciertos Esteban Salas Plaza Dolores ☎ 22 62 6167. Take a break from the salsa and son drums and refresh your soul with a choral or classical concert in a former church on the corner of Plaza Dolores. Performances are staged daily both evenings and daytimes; ask inside for performance details. The Coro Madrigalista sometimes perform here.

★ **Santiago Tropicana** Autopista Nacional Km 1.5 ☎ 22 64 2579. Not quite the Tropicana of the east, but a fun night out if you're with friends watching the costumed dancers perform a show. Tickets are $25CUC, with one drink included, or $37CUC with transport from central Santiago hotels included. You can make reservations at Infotur (see p.404) or tour agencies. Fri & Sat 10pm–1.30am.

UNEAC Heredia no.266 e/ San Felix y Carnecería ☎ 22 65 3465. Traditional and contemporary music *peñas* play here most nights. Check the door for the weekly programme. Boleros are sung at 6pm on Sat, and there's jazz at 6pm on Sun. Tues–Sat 6pm–midnight.

CLUBS

Club 300 Aguilera no.300 e/ San Pedro y San Félix ☎ 22 65 3532. A café by day, transformed into a disco by night, this slick and sultry little hideaway with leather seats serves cheap cocktails, quality rum and single malt whiskies. Entry is from $2CUC. Daily 11am–8pm & 10pm–3am.

Pista Bailable Teatro Heredia, Ave. de las Américas s/n ☎ 22 64 3190. Pumped-up salsa, son, bolero and merengue tunes get the crowd dancing at this unpretentious local club, with live music some nights. Entry $3CUC (includes drink).

THEATRES AND CINEMAS

Cine Rialto San Tomás 654 ☎ 22 62 3035. Near the cathedral, this is Santiago's most central cinema, with daily showings at 3pm, 5pm and 8pm.

Teatro Heredia Plaza de la Revolución ☎ 22 64 3190. The city's only large venue for plays, musicals and children's drama.

SHOPPING

Although Santiago is no shoppers' paradise, there are still several places to sniff out an authentic bargain or curiosity, while the town's art galleries occasionally have some worthy paintings and sculptures. Also good for a browse is Heredia's thriving **street market** (daily 9am–6pm), selling bone and shell jewellery, bootleg tapes, maracas and drums, as well as general souvenirs. The national-peso shops in Enramada, one street north of Parque Céspedes – still bedecked with original, though non-functioning, neon signs – hold some surprising treasures if you're prepared to trawl.

Barrita Ron Caney Ave. Jesús Menéndez s/n San Ricardo y San Antonio ☎ 22 62 5576. Rum aficionados will adore this shop/bar at the side of the eponymous factory which has friendly staff and a huge selection, including a wicked, silky-smooth fifteen-year-old Havana Club ($85CUC). There are tables and chairs where you can indulge in your purchases straight away. Mon–Sat 10am–4pm.

Galería Oriente San Pedro no.163 ☎ 22 65 7501. Some excellent revolutionary and carnival screen-printed posters for around $20CUC, and a few colourful surrealist oil paintings by local artists. Tues–Sun 9am–9pm.

Librería Internacional Parque Céspedes ☎ 22 68 7147. A bookshop in the former crypt of the cathedral, with a decent but expensive selection of novels, history and natural history books, some in English. Mon–Sat 9am–5pm.

Librería La Escalera Heredia no.265 e/ San Félix y Carnicería (no phone). An extraordinary little den filled with all manner of secondhand books, as well as the eccentric owner's display of business cards and liquor bottles from around the world; there's also a small selection of foreign-language titles available on an exchange basis ($1CUC). Daily 10am–10pm.

Quitrín 477 San Geronimo e/Calvario y Carnicería ☎ 22 62 2528. Although somewhat off the beaten track, it's worth the walk as all the exquisitely made cotton dresses, skirts and shirts, for men and women, are fashioned on site in this eighteenth-century house. If you can't find your size, ask about their bespoke service; the seamstresses can make up clothes within five or six days. The highlights include traditional *guayabera* shirts, dresses and sun tops with hand-worked lace insets and contemporary crochet work. Mon–Sat 9am–5pm.

DIRECTORY

Banks and exchange There are several banks near Parque Céspedes, including the Banco de Crédito y Comercio & ATM at Aguilera esq. San Pedro (Mon–Fri 8am–3pm, Sat 8–11am) and the Banco Popular de Ahorro at Aguilera no.458 e/ Reloj y Calvario (Mon–Sat 8am–7pm); you can change travellers' cheques and get an advance on a credit card at both, while the latter also has an ATM. The CADECA is at Aguilera 508 e/ Reloj y Rabí (Mon–Fri 8.15am–4pm, Sat 8.15am–noon).

Immigration You can renew visas at the immigration office, at Calle 13 no.6 e/ 4 y Carretera del Caney, Reparto Vista Alegre (Mon, Wed, Fri 8am–noon & 2–5pm; ☎ 22 64 1983).

Internet Try *Hotel Casa Granda* (open 24hr; $3CUC per 30min) or the ETECSA Centro de Multiservicios de Comunicaciones (daily 8.30am–7pm; $6CUC/hr) at Heredia esq. Félix Pena on Parque Céspedes.

Medical Call ☎ 185 for a public ambulance or, for a private ambulance, the Clínica Internacional (☎ 22 64 2589) at Ave. Raúl Pujol esq. Calle 10, which also offers general medical services to foreigners. The most central state hospital is the Hospital Provincial Clínico Quirúrgico Docente, at Ave. de los Libertadores (☎ 22 62 6571 to 9).

Policlínico Camilo Torres is a 24hr doctors' surgery at Heredia no.358 e/ Reloj y Calvario. There are pharmacies at Enramada no.402, *Hotel Santiago* and the Clínica Internacional. The latter also has a dental surgery.

Police The main station is at Corona y San Gerónimo. In an emergency call ☎ 106. The tourist support group Asistur offers 24hr assistance in emergency situations (☎ 78 67 1315); the local headquarters (Mon–Fri 8.30am–5pm; ☎ 22 68 6128) is in the offices beneath *Hotel Casa Granda*.

Post office The main post office is at Aguilera y Clarín. Stamps can also be bought from *Hotel Casa Granda* and *Hotel Santiago de Cuba*. The most central agent for DHL is at Aguilera no.310, esq. San Félix (Mon–Fri 8am–noon, 1–4pm, Sat 8am–11am).

Sports Baseball games are played at the Estadio Guillermon Moncada (☎ 22 64 2640) on Ave. las Américas from Dec to April.

Telephones The ETECSA Centro de Multiservicios de Comunicaciones (daily 8.30am–7pm) at Heredia esq. Félix Pena on Parque Céspedes sells phone cards and allows international calls. Phone cards are also available from *Hotel Casa Granda* and *Hotel Santiago de Cuba*, which both have international pay phones.

8

East of Santiago

Many of the attractions surrounding Santiago are east of the city, and you'll need at least a couple of days to do them justice. Cool and fresh, the mountains of the **Sierra de la Gran Piedra** make an excellent break from the harsh Santiago heat, and the giant **Gran Piedra** is an extraordinary lookout point. Nearby, there's the atmospheric, little-visited **Museo Isabelica**, set on one of several colonial coffee plantations in the mountains; and the formerly lovely **Jardín Botánico**, totally wrecked by Hurricane Sandy and closed to the public for the foreseeable future. Spanning the east coast is the **Gran Parque Natural Baconao**, not so much a park as a vast (and currently hurricane-raddled) collection of beaches and other tourist attractions, among them a vintage **car collection** and the **Comunidad Artística Verraco** – home, gallery and workplace for several local artists.

By car If you've got your own transport, head east out of the city towards the Loma de San Juan, then take the road south down Avenida Raúl Pujol, from where it runs straight towards the coast and the turn-off for the Sierra de la Gran Piedra.

Parque Nacional de la Gran Piedra

There's no public transport on the mountain road, but an unmetered taxi from Parque Céspedes in Santiago will charge $15–18CUC to take you to the foot of the Gran Piedra staircase

Just east of Santiago, the mountains of the **Parque Nacional de la Gran Piedra** are some of the most easily accessible peaks in the country. Eleven kilometres along the coastal road from town, a turn-off inland leads you up a steep, curving mountain road. As the route ascends, temperate vegetation such as fir and pine trees gradually replace the more tropical palms and vines of the lower levels.

La Gran Piedra

Daily 8am–5pm • $1CUC

Around 15km along the road into the Parque Nacional de la Gran Piedra, a purpose-built staircase leads up from the visitors' centre to **La Gran Piedra**, or "The Big Rock", sculpted by ancient geological movement from surrounding bedrock and now forming a convenient viewing plateau 1234m above Santiago de Cuba. It's an easy though still invigorating climb to the top, through woodland rich in animal and plant-life, including over two hundred species of fern, and is best made before noon, when you've a better chance of clear views. When the thick cloud that often hangs over the area melts away there's a panoramic view over the province and beyond to the sea.

Museo Isabelica

Daily 8am–4pm • $1CUC

Around 1km or so along the mountain road from La Gran Piedra, a left turn leads to the **Museo Isabelica**, set in the grounds of the Cafetal Isabelica, a coffee plantation established by an immigrant French grower who fled the Haitian slave revolution of 1791. Housed in a restored, small, two-storey estate house covered in red lichen and surrounded by ferns, the museum's collection contains original furniture. The main reason to come here, though, is the atmosphere, with the mountains' mist-shrouded hush broken only by birdsong and the tapping of sheep crossing the stone area used to dry coffee beans. You can explore the overgrown paths leading off round the house into the derelict plantation and inspect what is left of the disused mill – now just a stone wheel and a few wooden poles.

Gran Parque Natural Baconao

There's no public transport here; a taxi from Santiago will cost upwards of $60CUC for the trip out to Laguna Baconao

A mountainous stretch of countryside interspersed with several tourist attractions, the **Gran Parque Natural Baconao**, 25km southeast of Santiago, took a real beating from Hurricane Sandy in late 2012, and currently offers few incentives for travellers. Full recovery is likely to take some years, so do bear this in mind if you decide to visit, as private taxi transport here isn't cheap and you may be disappointed by what Sandy left behind.

Granjita Siboney

Carretera Siboney s/n km 13.5 • Daily 9am–5pm • $1CUC

Some 2km along the park road past the La Gran Piedra turn-off is the **Granjita Siboney**, the farm that Fidel Castro and his rebel group used as their base for the Moncada attack (see box, p.400). The pretty little red-and-white house, pockmarked by bullet holes (perhaps from target practice, as no fighting actually took place here), now holds a **museum** that largely reproduces information found in bigger collections in the city, with newspaper cuttings, guns and bloodstained uniforms presented in glass cabinets.

Playa Siboney

Just beyond the Granjita Siboney is **Playa Siboney**, 19km from Santiago and the closest beach to the city. Overlooked by a towering cliff, this brown-sand beach was devastated by Hurricane Sandy, with all its shade-giving palm trees uprooted and its beachside shacks and cabins blown away. Tourism is recovering here, though the scene is considerably less lively than it was, and some *casas particulares* and restaurants have survived the storm.

ACCOMMODATION AND EATING · PLAYA SIBONEY

Casa de Ovidio González Sabaldo Avenida Serrano Alto de Farmacia ☎ 22 39 9340. A *casa particular* with a sea view right in the village centre offering four rooms, just two minutes from the beach. Rooms are comfortable with fridges and a/c. $25CUC

Finca el Porvenir ☎ 22 62 9064. Five kilometres east of Playa Siboney on the coastal road, a signposted turn left (north) down a potholed track leads to this rustic countryside spot, which makes a pleasant stop for lunch. A stone staircase descends the hillside to the bar-restaurant, where tables are shaded by mango and palm trees, and sun loungers surround a swimming pool. The menu includes reasonably priced grilled fish, shrimp, pork and fried chicken ($3.50–15CUC). Daily 9am–7pm.

La Rueda ☎ 22 39 9325. Just behind the beach, this state restaurant offers inexpensive fried chicken, tasty fish and good lobster, as well as sandwiches and pizza (mains $4.90–7.30CUC). There's a pleasant top-terrace on which to eat, while the bar below is less appealing. Order ahead if you want to eat after 5pm. Restaurant daily 9am–5pm, bar daily 9am–late.

Valle de la Prehistoria

Carretera Baconao km 6.5 • Daily 8am–6pm • $1CUC

Five kilometres east from Playa Siboney along the coastal road, you'll come across one of the area's more unusual attractions, the **Valle de la Prehistoria**, populated by practically life-sized stone models of dinosaurs and Stone Age men. While essentially a bit kitsch, it's worth a look for those with kids.

Museo Nacional del Transporte

Carretera Baconao km 8.5 • Daily 8am–5pm • $1CUC, photos $1CUC, video $2CUC

About 4km east of the Valle de Prehistorica, the **Museo Nacional del Transporte** is one of Baconao's biggest attractions (though it's under repair following hurricane damage), with an excellent collection of vintage cars and a formidable display of 2500 toy cars. Outside in the car park sits a 1929 Ford Roadster belonging to Alina Ruz, Fidel Castro's mother; Benny Moré's ostentatious golden Cadillac; and the 1951 Chevrolet that Raúl Castro drove to the attack on the Moncada barracks (see box, p.400).

Playa Daiquirí

Close to the Museo Nacional del Transporte is the turning for **Playa Daiquirí**, the beach where the US army landed when they intervened in the War of Independence in 1898 and which gave its name to the famous cocktail. Home to a holiday camp for military personnel, the beach is closed to foreign visitors.

Comunidad Artística Verraco

Playa Verraco

Ten kilometres east from the Museo Nacional del Transporte on the main coast road, in an attractive clearing beneath tall trees next to the local Playa Verraco, the unique **Comunidad Artística Verraco** is a highlight of a trip out to Baconao. A small artists' community that's home to nine sculptors, painters and potters, you can tour the individual home-studios, and there's a small communal gallery where their work is on sale.

ACCOMMODATION	COMUNIDAD ARTÍSTICA VERRACO

Casa de Rosa y Enrique (Galería Aguilar) Carretera de Baconao Km 17.5, Comunidad Artística ☎ 58 22 7529 or 53 40 4465 (mobile). A spacious, quiet room within the | Comunidad Artística Verraco, in the lovely house of ceramic artists Oscar and Yordanka. It's the perfect getaway and you might even learn how to throw a few pots. **$25CUC**

Acuario Baconao

Carretera Baconao km 27.5 • Tues–Sun 9am–5pm • Dolphin shows 10.30am & 3pm • $7CUC, swimming with dolphins $39CUC

Some 8km east of the Comunidad Artística Verraco on the coast road, the **Acuario Baconao** suffered terribly from the ravages of Hurricane Sandy; damage to its hydraulic system led to the death of the entire marine collection, which included seven sharks. It may well take years for the aquarium to fully recover, but it was open to visitors at the time of writing. The dolphins and two sea lions survived, and still perform shows twice a day in a reasonably sized pool; there's also the chance to hop into the water with them.

Playa Cazonal

Club Amigo Carisol-Los Corales day-pass $25CUC; includes buffet meal and drinks • Diving $25CUC per dive • A bus runs to Santiago once a week on Sundays for hotel guests

Playa Cazonal, just under 1km east of Acuario Baconao, is the most appealing beach east of Santiago, though it's no secluded paradise despite being a long way from the city. Backed by a huge, congenial all-inclusive hotel, the small stretches of off-white sand compete with vast blankets of tiny shells and broken coral dotted by randomly spaced palms. Most people come for the snorkelling and diving on the nearby coral reef.

8

ACCOMMODATION	PLAYA CAZONAL

Club Amigo Carisol-Los Corales, Carretera Baconao, Km 54 ☎ 22 35 6115, ⓦ hotelescubanacan.com. All-inclusive hotel spread across a large swathe of beach in two separate buildings. The most pleasant section of beach | fronts the Los Corales building, which also houses the complex's only junior suites. Staff are pleasant and friendly and the dining area of the *Carisol*, in particular, is very attractive. A day pass costs $25CUC. **$130CUC**

Laguna Baconao

Tues–Sun 9am–4.30pm • Boat hire $2CUC; minimum five people • Sendero el Cimarron $2CUC

Roughly 3km from Playa Cazonal, **Laguna Baconao** is a serene spot from which to enjoy the unaffected beauty of the surrounding mountains. There are sad caged crocs and flamingos but you can take in a more natural scene by hiring a **boat** to row on the lake and a guide to walk the area's **trails**, such as the Sendero el Cimarron. Bizarrely, there are three dolphins living in the semi salt-water lake and lagoon's managers are waiting to see if they'll reproduce in this environment. Laguna Baconao marks the end of the line for travelling easy; a checkpoint here prevents cars travelling into Guantánamo province due to the US Naval Base.

West of Santiago

Although there are few sights to see west of Santiago, those that exist are interesting enough to warrant a visit if you have a spare day. The **Basilica de la Caridad del Cobre**, presiding over the town of El Cobre in the hills to the northwest, is one of the most important – and most visited – churches in the country. The **beaches** west of the city are mostly smaller than those on the eastern side, and correspondingly less developed and more intimate, the playgrounds of Cubans rather than foreign visitors. In contrast, the resort of **Chivirico** is dedicated to international tourism, with two large hotels dominating its fine-sand beach.

There is no reliable public transport west of the city, so you'll need to hire a taxi or take your own transport.

Basilica de la Caridad del Cobre

El Cobre • Daily 6.30am–6pm; Mass Tues–Sat 8am, Thurs 8pm, Sun 10am & 4.30pm

A lovely structure nestling in palm-studded forest 18km northwest of Santiago, the imposing cream-coloured, copper-domed **Basilica de la Caridad del Cobre** houses the icon of **Nuestra Señora de la Caridad**, Cuba's patron saint, and is one of the holiest sanctuaries in the country. Pleasingly symmetrical, with three towers capped in red domes, the present basilica was constructed in 1927, on the site of a previous shrine. Inside, the icon has pride of place high up in the altar, and during Mass looks down over the congregation; at other times she is rotated to face into an inner sanctum reached by stairs at the back of the church, where another altar is always garlanded with floral tributes left by worshippers.

Soon after her discovery, local mythology endowed the Virgin with the power to grant wishes and heal the sick, and a steady flow of believers visits the church to solicit her help. A downstairs chamber holds an eclectic display of the many **relics** left by grateful recipients of the Virgin's benevolence, including a rosette and team shirt from Olympic 800m gold medallist Ana Fidelia Quirot Moret, as well as college diplomas, countless photographs and, most bizarrely, an asthmatic's ventilator.

The western beaches

The drive along the coast west towards Chivirico and beyond, with the seemingly endless curve of vivid mountains on one side and a ribbon of sparkling shallow sea on the other, is one of the most fantastic in the country, though potholes and hurricane damage make it somewhat treacherous after dark. About 15km from the city, don't be put off by **Playa Mar Verde**, a small, rather grubby hoop of roadside shingle-sand with a café and restaurant; instead, carry on along the coastal road for another couple of kilometres to **Playa Bueycabón**. Here, an orderly lawn dotted with short palms stretches almost to the sea, and with its calm, shallow waters and narrow belt of sand it is altogether an excellent little spot to pass the day. There is a café here, but no other facilities.

Chivirico

Nearly 70km from Santiago, **CHIVIRICO** is a quiet coastal village and an interchange point for buses and trucks running between Pilón and Santiago. Other than that, the main action, such as it is, centres on a micro-resort of three hotels capitalizing on good brown-sand beaches and impressive mountain views. This is a better place to stay rather than visit on a day-trip, as the most appealing beach is now the domain of an all-inclusive resort which charges non-guests for the privilege of using it.

NUESTRA SEÑORA DE LA CARIDAD

Nuestra Señora de la Caridad, also known as La Virgen de la Caridad del Cobre (the Virgin of Charity), and just "Cachita", is so much more than just Cuba's patron saint: source of succour, icon and artists' muse, her presence is embedded in the cultural, religious and social life of Cubans of all colour and creed.

Legend relates that in 1612, a statue of the virgin was found floating in the Bahía de Nipe, off Cuba's northern coast, by three sailors (or salt workers depending on which storyline you adhere to) from El Cobre town on the verge of being shipwrecked. They claimed not only that the icon – a mother and child figurine – was completely dry when drawn from the water but also that the sea was instantly becalmed. Inscribed with the words *Yo soy la Virgen de la Caridad* ("I am the Virgin of Charity"), the icon became the most important image in Cuban Roman Catholicism, gaining significance by becoming the alter ego of **Ochún**, the Santería goddess of love, whose colour, yellow, mirrors the Virgin's golden robe. In 1916 the Virgen de la Caridad became the patron saint of Cuba, following a decree by Pope Benedict XV. Her saint's day is September 8, when an annual pilgrimage is held.

Access to **Playa Sevilla** (daily 9.30am–6pm; day pass $27CUC, inclusive of meals and drinks), the easternmost beach of the three, is controlled by the beachfront *Brisas Sierra Mar* hotel. Location of the *Motel Guáma*, the central **Playa Virginia** is narrower but free to enter. Tiny mangrove-coated cays lie not far offshore, though there can be dangerous undertow currents. Finally, **Playa Chivirico** is the private preserve of the attractive hilltop *Hotel Los Galeones*, the secondary outpost of *Brisas Sierra del Mar*.

ARRIVAL AND DEPARTURE CHIVIRICO

By taxi A private taxi from Santiago to Chivirico will cost $70CUC.

ACCOMMODATION

Brisas Sierra Mar Carretera a Chivirico km 60, Playa Sevilla ☎ 22 32 9110, ⊕ hotelescubanacan.com. A large, attractive all-inclusive hotel offering spacious, comfortable rooms and a full complement of watersports, including diving, plus five bars and several restaurants. Parts of the hotel sustain hurricane damage but repairs were well under way by early 2013. **§144CUC**

Motel Guáma Playa Sevilla Reservations through Villa Trópico, Santiago ☎ 22 64 6557. The strip's sole budget accommodation option with just eight rooms and a small bar and restaurant. **§25CUC**

Bayamo

On the northern edge of the Sierra Maestra mountains in the centre of Granma, provincial capital **BAYAMO** is one of the most peaceful towns in Cuba. Its spotless centre is based around a pleasant park; there are near-zero levels of hassle on the streets; and, with the streets pedestrianized, even the cars are silenced.

Although a fire destroyed most of Bayamo's colonial buildings in 1869, it left the heart of town untouched, and the splendid **Iglesia de Santísimo Salvador** still presides over the cobbled **Plaza del Himno**. Elsewhere, neat rows of modern houses, dotted with pretty tree-lined parks, stand testament to a well-maintained town. Bayamo is smaller than you'd expect a provincial capital to be, and you could cram its few sights into one day, but if you've no agenda, it's better to do some gentle sightseeing, eat well and match the town's unhurried pace.

Brief history

The second of the original seven Cuban towns or *villas* founded by Diego Velázquez de Cuéllar in November 1513, Bayamo flourished during the seventeenth and eighteenth centuries when, along with its neighbour Manzanillo, it was heavily involved in dealing in contraband goods. Bayamo became one of the most prosperous towns in the country and by the nineteenth century had capitalized on the fertile plains to the west of the city, becoming an important sugar-growing and cattle-rearing area.

Influential figures like wealthy landowner Francisco Vicente Aguilera and composer Pedro Figueredo established a revolutionary cell here in 1868 to promote their call for independence from the Spanish. They were joined by **Carlos Manuel de Céspedes**, another wealthy local plantation owner, who freed his slaves and set off to war. By the end of October 1868, Céspedes's modest army of 147 had swelled to 12,000 and he had captured Bayamo and Holguín. Rather than relinquish the town, after three months of fighting, the rebels set fire to it on January 12, 1869, and watched the elegant buildings burn to the ground. Bayamo's glory days were over.

Bayamo moved into the twentieth century without fanfare, continuing to support itself by producing sugar and farming cattle. The town's last memorable moment was the unsuccessful attack on the army barracks on July 26, 1953 (see box, p.400), timed to coincide with Castro's attack in Santiago – though this happened over half a century ago, it still keeps several old-timers gossiping today.

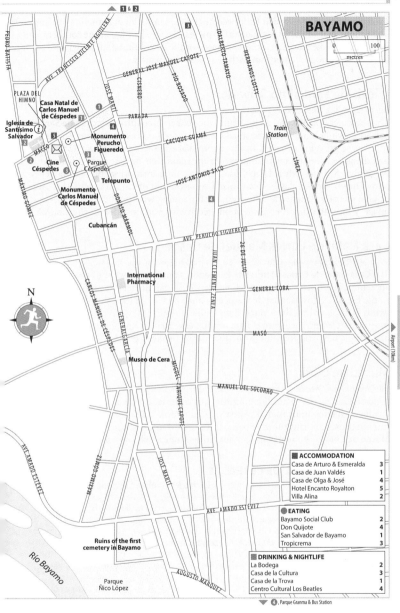

8

Airport (10km)

■ ACCOMMODATION	
Casa de Arturo & Esmeralda	3
Casa de Juan Valdés	1
Casa de Olga & José	4
Hotel Encanto Royalton	5
Villa Alina	2

● EATING	
Bayamo Social Club	2
Don Quijote	4
San Salvador de Bayamo	1
Tropicrema	3

■ DRINKING & NIGHTLIFE	
La Bodega	2
Casa de la Cultura	3
Casa de la Trova	1
Centro Cultural Los Beatles	4

▼ ④, Parque Granma & Bus Station

Parque Céspedes

Most of the sights in Bayamo are within view or easy walking distance of the central **Parque Céspedes** – also known as Plaza de la Revolución – a shiny expanse of marble ringed with palm trees, where children play and queue for rides in the goat-pulled pony cart. At the northern end is a small three-panel tribute to **Perucho Figueredo**, a local independence fighter principally remembered for writing the patriotic poem

La Bayamesa in 1868, which later became the Cuban national anthem, still sung today. The monument to **Carlos Manuel de Céspedes** (see box below), at the southern end of the plaza, is rather more grandiose: a statue of the man himself, dignified and sombre in tailcoat, on top of a podium with four bas-relief panels.

Iglesia de Santísimo Salvador

Plaza del Himno • Mon–Sat 9am–noon & 3–5pm • Free

The showpiece of Bayamo architecture, the sixteenth-century **La Iglesia de Santísimo Salvador**, which dominates the small Plaza del Himno, was one of the few buildings to survive the great fire of 1869. Inside, apple-shaped portraits of the Stations of the Cross line the walls. The impressive **mural** over the main altar depicts an incident on November 8, 1868, when Diego José Baptista, the parish priest, blessed the rebel army's newly created flag before a mixed congregation of Cuban rebels. This piece is unique in Latin America as an ecclesiastical painting with political content – the imagery indicates that the new republic received the approbation of the Church.

Casa Natal de Carlos Manuel de Céspedes

North side of Parque Céspedes • Tues–Fri 9am–5.30pm, Sat 9am–1pm & 8–10pm, Sun 10am–1pm • $1CUC

The **Casa Natal de Carlos Manuel de Céspedes** is another survivor of the fire of 1869, and contains a hotchpotch of exhibits relating to the nineteenth century in general and to the life of Carlos Manuel de Céspedes, born here in 1819. Céspedes's ceremonial sword is displayed on the ground floor, while upstairs is the *pièce de résistance*: a magnificent bronze bed with ornate oval panels, inlaid with mother-of-pearl and depicting a fantastic coastline at the foot of the bedhead panel.

Museo de Cera

Calle Calixto García no.254 e/ Masó y Manuel del Socorro • Tues–Fri 9am–5pm, Sat 10am–1pm, 7–10pm, Sun 9am–noon • $1CUC

General García, the main shopping street, is a pleasant place to stroll and catch the flavour of the town; its muted pedestrianized marble walkway makes a good foil for the fun sculptures of giant tubes of paint and the sinuous benches. Halfway down is the **Museo de Cera**, a waxworks gallery, featuring models, which include indigenous birds

---

CARLOS MANUEL DE CÉSPEDES

A key figure in the fight for independence, **Carlos Manuel de Céspedes** is much lauded in Cuba as a liberator. A wealthy plantation owner, he freed his slaves on October 10, 1868, and called for the abolition of slavery – albeit in terms least likely to alienate the wealthy landowners upon whose support he depended. Giving forth his battle cry, the *Grito de Yara*, which summoned Cubans, whether slaves or Creoles, to take arms and fight for a future free of Spain, he marched in support of the independence movement. Céspedes summed up the dissatisfaction that many Cubans felt in a long declaration which became known as the **October 10th manifesto**, nationally credited as the inception of Cuban independence because it was the first time that Cubans had been talked about in terms of a nation of people.

The newly formed army set out with the intention of capturing the nearby town of Yara, but were overtaken by a column of the Spanish army and utterly trounced, reduced to a fragment of the original 150–strong force. Undefeated, Céspedes proclaimed, "There are still twelve of us left, we are enough to achieve the independence of Cuba."

Céspedes is most remembered for the death of his son, Oscar, captured by the Spanish and subsequently shot when Céspedes refused to negotiate for peace under Spanish conditions. This act earned him the title "Padre de la Patria" (Father of the Homeland): as he famously replied to the letter requesting his surrender, "Oscar is not my only son. I am father to all the Cubans who have died to liberate their homeland."

and animals as well as personalities like Compay Segundo, Benny Moré and Ernest Hemingway, made by a local man and his sons.

Parque Ñico López

Tues–Sat 9am–noon & 1.30pm–5pm, Sun 9am–1pm • $1CUC

Bayamo's spacious walled garden, **Parque Ñico López**, landscaped with swaying palms and intersected with layers of marble steps, was arranged in the grounds of the Bayamo barracks as a tribute to Ñico López, one of the 28 men who tried to storm and capture the building on July 26, 1953.

The attack was synchronized with the assault on the Moncada barracks in Santiago (see box, p.400), partly to secure weapons for the rebel cause but primarily to prevent more of General Batista's troops being drafted in from Bayamo to Santiago. The attempt failed when the whinnying of the cavalry horses, alarmed at the sound of the rebels scrambling over the wall, aroused the sleeping soldiers, and though López escaped, later meeting up with fellow rebels in exile in Mexico, several other men died in the attack. López returned to Cuba aboard the yacht *Granma* in 1958, only to be killed a few days later in an early skirmish. The garden honours both his contribution to the cause, and, probably more crucially, his status as the man who introduced Che Guevara to Fidel Castro in 1955. López himself is commemorated by a **sculpture** in the grounds.

Inside the barracks is a rather poor **museum** giving a scant account of events accompanied by photographs of the men involved and a cutting from the following day's newspaper. You'd be better off giving it a miss and instead striking up a conversation with the old men who sometimes sit in the park, several of whom remember the attack.

ARRIVAL AND GETTING AROUND

BAYAMO

By plane Domestic flights arrive from Havana (2 weekly; 2hr) at the Aeropuerto Carlos M. de Céspedes, 10km northeast of the centre on the Holguín road, where unmetered taxis wait to bring you into town for $6–8CUC.
Airline Cubana, Martí no.52 esq. Parada (Tues & Thurs 2–4pm; ☎ 23 42 7514).
By bus and colectivo Bayamo is well served by three main roads from Las Tunas, Holguín and Santiago de Cuba; interprovincial buses pull in at the Astro terminal (☎ 23 42 7482) in the eastern outskirts of town, on the Carretera Central towards Santiago de Cuba. From here, *bicitaxis* will take you into the centre for $10–20CUP. *Colectivos* also use the Astro terminal as their unofficial base.
Destinations Camagüey (5 daily; 4hr 10min); Ciego de

Ávila (3 daily; 5hr 10min); Havana (3 daily; 14hr); Holguín (4 daily; 1hr 15min); Las Tunas (5 daily; 2hr 35min); Sancti Spíritus (5 daily; 6hr 20min); Santa Clara (3 daily; 9hr 30 min); Santiago de Cuba (5 daily; 2hr 45min).
By train The train station is about 1km east of the centre on Calle Línea esq. Calle José Antonio Saco (☎ 23 42 3056); you can catch a *bicitaxi* into the centre for around $10CUP.
Destinations Camagüey (4 weekly; 5hr 30min); Havana (4 weekly; 13hr); Manzanillo (2 daily; 3hr); Santiago de Cuba (1 daily; 4hr 15min).
By taxi Cubataxi is at Martí no.480 esq. Armando Estévez (☎ 23 42 4313).
By car Cubacar is based at *Hotel Sierra Maestra* (☎ 23 48 2990).

INFORMATION AND TOURS

Tourist information Infotur on Plaza del Himno e/ José Joaquín Palma y Padre Batista (Mon–Fri 8am–5pm; ☎ 23 42 3468) are the best bet for general information and maps.
Tours Anley Rosales Benitez at Bayamo Travel, opposite the Víazul bus station at Carretera Central 478 (☎ 05 29 2209, ⊕ bayamotravelagent.com), organizes drivers and accommodation in and around the Sierra Maestra and beyond, and offers tours, including trips to La Comandancia (from $100CUC for two people including horseriding) to La

Otilia (from $50CUC for two people). Ecotur and Flora y Fauna (see box, p.420) provide details on excursions into the Sierra Maestra.
Festivals From Jan 6, Bayamo celebrates its Semana de Cultura which culminates on Jan 12 with a commemoration and a re-enactment of the day the locals set fire to the town in 1869. The Fiesta de la Cubanía takes place between October 13–20 with fiestas, music, dancing and other cultural events.

8

ACCOMMODATION

HOTELS

Hotel Encanto Royalton Calle Maceo 53 e/ J Palma y D Mármol ☎23 42 2290, ⦿islazul.cu This lurid lemon yellow hotel has been restored and now offers 33 smart but expensive rooms, arrayed around a central courtyard and fitted out in custard cream and chocolate shades, TVs, fridges, a/c and a minibar. The choice rooms are the four at the front, with balconies overlooking Parque Céspedes. Rates include breakfast. **$70CUC**

CASA PARTICULARES

Casa de Arturo & Esmeralda Zenea no.56A e/ William Soler y Capote ☎23 42 4051, ⦿casa-bayamo.com. A top choice in Bayamo thanks to charming hosts Arturo and Esmeralda, who couldn't be more helpful in making arrangements for their guests. Great food, too, and four comfortable rooms, the best of which is at the top of the house, with its own terrace. **$25CUC**

Casa de Juan Valdés (La Casa Azul) Pio Rosado no.64 e/ Ramírez y N López ☎23 42 3324. One

well-appointed a/c room with fancy bedspread, pink marble floor and a large bathroom. There's a large living room, small kitchen area and roof terrace for guests to use, too. **$25CUC**

Casa de Olga & José Parada no.16 (altos) e/ Martí y Mármol ☎23 42 3859, ⓔyaimara.grm@infomed.sld .cu. Olga and José run a first-class B&B with two comfortable rooms off the living room of the main house. They have a great balcony from where to people-watch or drink the night away. Olga is very helpful with excursions. **$20CUC**

Villa Alina Ave. Francisco Vicente Aguilera no.240 e/ Martires y Milanés ☎23 42 4861, ⓔalvaro.grm @infomed.sld.cu. Pleasant upper-level apartment, with front-facing terrace for breakfast. The two a/c rooms have a private bathroom and television apiece, plus there's a free wake-up call from the neighbour's trio of roosters – perfect for those setting off to the mountains. A third bedroom was in the making at the time of writing. **$25CUC**

EATING

Surprisingly, for such a small town, Bayamo boasts several new **paladars**. Around the park end of General García are several stalls selling **snacks** – some of them, like the corn pretzel-style cracker, are unique to Bayamo.

Bayamo Social Club Maceo no.12, Plaza del Himno ☎23 42 2271. A new paladar run by Darien Sanchez who graduated from the local tourism school as a chef and was student of the year in 2008. The setting is basic but the Creole food is hearty. There's no fixed menu but expect tasty beef, grilled chicken and pork steaks. The menu is in *moneda nacional*, with mains at $3–6CUC. Daily 11am–midnight.

Don Quijote Ave. Antonio Maceo no.116 e/ Segunda y Mendive ☎23 48 2781. A pleasant new paladar serving up a huge spread of *comida criolla*, pastas, and seafood and shellfish. Try the house cocktail – it's a lurid blue colour but it goes down a treat. To get there, take the turning opposite the *Hotel Sierra Maestra* and then the third turning on the left; the house is immediately on the left. Daily 11am–2am.

San Salvador de Bayamo Calle Maceo no.107 e/ Martí

y Mármol ☎23 42 6942. A welcome addition to the Bayamo dining scene, this colonial-style paladar with dusty pink Moorish arches serves up a good honest spread of shellfish, kebabs, pork chops in rum, a tasty fish fillet in sweet and sour sauce, and lamb chops with raisins and ginger. Pizzas and lasagne also feature on the extensive menu, which lists prices in *moneda nacional* (mains $3–8CUC). The coconut ice cream served in a coconut is a treat. Daily 10am–11pm.

★ **Tropicrema** Figueredo e/ Libertad y Céspedes Pleasant, open-air ice-cream parlour, sometimes serving up cake as well. Tables are shared with the next person in the queue and everyone waits for everyone else to finish before leaving the table. Oddly, if they run out of ice cream they'll occasionally substitute Spam rolls. Daily 10am–10pm.

DRINKING AND NIGHTLIFE

La Bodega Plaza del Himno (no phone). An eternally popular spot behind the church, where there's beer and dancing until 2am in an intimate courtyard overlooking the Río Bayamo. Mon–Fri & Sun 9pm–1am, Sat 10pm–2am.

Casa de la Cultura General García ☎23 42 5917. Occasional evening theatre and dance performances (check the board outside for weekly listings).

Casa de la Trova Maceo no.111 (no phone). This is easily Bayamo's best live music venue. The daily programme

of traditional Cuban sounds is posted inside. Tues–Sun 10am–1am.

Centro Cultural Los Beatles Calle Zenea s/n e Figuero y Saco ☎23 42 1799. Named for the life-size statues of the fab four outside; live music is followed by disco at weekends from 8pm to midnight. Tues–Sun 7pm–midnight.

Cine Céspedes Parque Céspedes. This cinema next to the post office on shows a mix of Cuban and international films.

DIRECTORY

Banks and exchange The Banco de Crédito y Comercio at General García 101 esq. Saco (Mon–Fri 8am–3pm, Sat 8am–11am) and the CADECA at Saco no.109 e/ General García y Mármol (Mon–Sat 8.30am–4pm) change travellers' cheques and give cash advances on Visa and MasterCard.

Internet and telephones Telepunto de ETECSA, at General García no.109 (daily 8.30am–7pm), sells international and local phone cards and provides internet access for $6CUC/hr.

Medical Call ☏ 185 for a public ambulance. Bayamo's general hospital is Carlos Manuel de Céspedes, at Carretera Central (vía Santiago) y 3ra, ☏ 23 42 5012. The most central 24hr *policlínico* doctors' surgery is on Pío Rosado, and there's a 24hr pharmacy, Piloto, at General García no.53 as well as an International Pharmacy at General García s/n e/ Figueredo y Lora (Mon–Fri 8am–noon, 1–5pm, Sat 8am–noon; ☏ 23 42 9596).

Police In an emergency call ☏ 116.

Post office The post office on Parque Céspedes (Mon–Sat 8am–8pm) has a DHL service and sells phone cards.

The Sierra Maestra

Cuba's highest and most extensive mountain range, the **Sierra Maestra** stretches along the southern coast of the island, running the length of both Santiago and Granma provinces. The unruly beauty of the landscape – a vision of churning seas, undulating green-gold mountains and remote sugar fields – will take your breath away.

Access to the mountains is restricted (see box, p.420), but there are some excellent trails, most notably through the stunning cloudforest of the **Parque Nacional Turquino** to the island's highest point, Pico Turquino, at 1974m. Although a considerable part of the Sierra Maestra falls in Santiago province, Parque Nacional Turquino included, the best chance you have to do any **trekking** is to base yourself in Bayamo, where you can arrange a guide and suitable transport (see box, p.420).

The main trails begin at the lookout point of **Alto del Naranjo**, 5km southeast of *Villa Santo Domingo*, which marks the start of the mountains proper. When the mountains are off limits this is as far as many people get, but at 950m above sea level, the panoramic views are awe-inspiring. Most people, especially those planning to trek further into the mountains, make the journey up the immensely steep ascent road to Alto del Naranjo in a sturdy jeep provided by Cubataxi or Ecotur.

Pico Turquino trail

At 1974m above sea level, **Pico Turquino** stands proud as the highest point in Cuba. From Alto de Naranjo it's approximately 12km to the summit, and while it's possible to ascend and return in a day, you are better off arranging with your guide to stay overnight at the very rudimentary *Campamento de Joaquín* mountain hut and stretching the trek over a day and a half. This is not a trek for the faint-hearted: the final kilometre is a very steep slog, though not dangerous. Take something warm to wear, as temperatures plummet after nightfall and even the days are cool in the high cloudforest.

The Pico Turquino is overhung with plants and ancient tree ferns, the forest air exuding an earthy dampness and the ground oozing with thick red mud. Through the breaks in the dense foliage you can occasionally see blue-green mountain peaks and birds circling lazily above the gullies. Just before the final ascent, a short ladder to the left of the path gives a panoramic view over the surrounding landscape; it's worth grabbing the opportunity at this stage in your trek as the summit itself is often shrouded in thick clouds.

Comandancia de La Plata trail

A less taxing alternative to the Pico Turquino trail is the trek to the **Comandancia de La Plata**, 3km west of Alto de Naranjo, where Fidel Castro based his rebel

EXPLORING THE SIERRA MAESTRA

Visitors are not permitted to go trekking in the **Sierra Maestra** without a guide – if you head into the mountains on your own, you risk landing yourself in serious trouble with the authorities. Having a guide will not always guarantee entrance, however, as the routes are sometimes **closed** for various reasons – from reports of epidemics in the coffee plantations to visiting dignitaries.

INFORMATION, ACCESS AND ORGANIZED TOURS

The only places to get guaranteed **information** on access to the Sierra Maestra, including the areas in Santiago province, are the Ecotur office, in *Hotel Sierra Maestra* in Bayamo (Mon–Fri 8am–noon & 1–5pm, plus every other Sat 8am–noon; ☏ 23 48 7006, ext. 639, eagencia@ecotur.grm.tur.cu), and by calling the Centro de Visitantes (run by Flora y Fauna) in Santo Domingo, the village from where excursions begin (☏ 53 56 5349) or *Hotel Villa Santo Domingo* (see Accommodation, opposite).

Permission to access the high mountains from the Bayamo side is available from the **Parque Nacional Turquino Centro de Visitantes** (daily 7.30–8.30am; no phone), run by Flora y Fauna and located at the foothills of the mountains next door to *Villa Santo Domingo*; and through the more expensive Ecotur (see above), which also runs an office at the *Villa Santo Domingo*. **Permits** from Flora y Fauna cost $20CUC to reach Comandancia de La Plata and include guide, entrance fee and water. The jeep to Alto de Naranjo, from where the Commandancia de La Plata walk begins, is paid separately at $5CUC return if you book a Flora y Fauna tour. Flora y Fauna charges $55CUC to scale Pico Turquino in one night including transport, food, accommodation, guide and park's entrance, with the return to Santo Domingo. A two-night Turquino trek crossing the mountain finishing at Las Cuevas on the Carretera del Sur costs $70CUC including transport, food, accommodation, guide and park's entrance.

Ecotur also runs excursions into the mountains. The trip to La Plata from Santo Domingo starts at $33CUC including the jeep to Alto de Naranjo, guide, entrance fee, box lunch and water. Adding transport from Bayamo to the package costs $73CUC per person (minimum two people). One-night trips to Pico Turquino cost $68CUC including transport, guide, accommodation, park entrance and food. Ecotur also offers packages that include nights in the Villa Santo Domingo. Based in Bayamo, new private tour company Bayamo Travel (see p.417) also offer excursions in the mountains.

HIKING PRACTICALITIES

You must **arrive between 7.30 and 10.30am** on the day that you want to visit or else you may be turned back (guides arrive early to be allocated to their visitors for the day but leave swiftly if there is no one waiting). The last daily departure to the Comandancia is at 1pm (11am in the wet season). The last departure for Pico Turquino is at 9.30am year-round.

There is no public transport from Bayamo to Santo Domingo. A one-way taxi fare costs around $35CUC. Note that the obligatory jeep transport from the Centro de Visitantes to Alto de Naranjo costs $5CUC through Flora y Fauna, but $14CUC through Ecotur if you have not bought its hiking packages. Trekkers must bring their own sleeping bag for the overnight trips and sugary snacks for this trip. Everything else is provided.

---

headquarters during the Revolution. The trail is well marked and you can complete the reasonably strenuous climb in around four hours return. The headquarters are spread over two or three sites, the first of which is the very basic **hospital** (it's little more than a wooden hut) that Che Guevara founded and ran. The second site comprises the guard post, a small but worthy **museum** and the grave of a rebel who fell in battle. Most evocative are the wooden huts where the rebels lived and ate, which were covered with branches to protect them from enemy air strikes. **Castro**'s small quarters consist of a rudimentary bedroom with a simple camp bed, a kitchen, a fridge, a study and a secret trap door to escape through if he was under attack. Those wanting to take pictures of the rebel camp will need to pay an extra $5CUC at the Casa Medina rest stop, halfway along the walk.

Buey Arriba and the Comandancia de Che

Excursions to Buey Arriba and the Mando de Puesto de Che are available from Bayamo Travel (see p.417)

Fifty-four kilometres southwest of Bayamo in the Sierra Maestra is the small town of **BUEY ARRIBA**, where the **Comandancia de Che** is the starting point for a 45-minute walk uphill to the hamlet of **La Otilia**, the last rebel command post (Mando de Puesto de Che) of Che Guevara before he was dispatched to Villa Clara during Fidel Castro's 1956–59 rebel campaign. There are panoramic views of the Sierra Maestra all the way up, while the small command post is now the **Casa Museo La Otilia** (daily 7.30am–4.30; $1CUC), with displays of artefacts from Che's short stay.

In Buey Arriba itself, the **Museo Municipal** (Mon–Sat 9am–5pm, Sun 9am–noon; $1CUC; ☎23 24 3516) exhibits a white stuffed mule used by Camilo Cienfuegos.

ACCOMMODATION   SIERRA MAESTRA

Campismo La Sierrita ☎23 56 5584. Beside the Río Yara, 50km southeast of Bayamo and 14km before Santo Domingo, this rural and idyllic spot has 27 cabins with self-contained bathrooms. Call in at the Agéncia de Reservaciónes de Campismo in Bayamo (General García no.112 e/ Saco y Figueredo, Mon–Fri 8–11am & 3–7pm; ☎23 42 2425) to book with the Cubamar rep and make sure the campsite is open. If the Cubamar rep is not there you will need to book through Cubamar in Havana (☎78 33 2523), as the Campismo office does not deal with bookings by foreigners. $36CUC

Casa Sierra Maestra ☎05 26 10846. Also known as *Casa del Junco*, this is the best *casa particular* for the mountains, a welcoming house on the opposite side of the river to the Villa Santa Domingo; to get there, cross the river on the large stones downhill behind the Flora & Fauna office. The five rooms currently share bathrooms, and owner Ulises Junco and his wife Esperanza offer delicious food ($5–10CUC); just 200m upriver, there's a natural pool to soak away your cares. Horseriding excursions can be arranged ($5–10CUC), and if you're in luck you'll be there for the regular roasted pig gatherings. $20CUC

Villa Santo Domingo ☎23 56 5568. The best place to stay in the mountain area, in the foothills of the mountains (but not in a restricted area), about 68km southwest of Bayamo. Set on the banks of the Río Yara, the picturesque cabins (which now include twenty new Alpine-style villas, for which rates include breakfast) make an ideal spot to relax even if access to the mountains is denied. Cabins $45CUC, villas $70CUC

Manzanillo

Though run down and ramshackle, **MANZANILLO**, 64km west from Bayamo and 75km up the coast from Playa Las Coloradas, still possesses some charm. Now a fairly pedestrian coastal fishing village, it was established around its harbour at the end of the eighteenth century and for a time enjoyed a brisk trade in contraband goods. The sugar trade replaced smuggling as the primary business hereabouts in the nineteenth century, but the town's heyday had passed and it never grew much bigger.

Manzanillo's sole attraction these days is its fantastic **Moorish architecture**, dating from the 1910s and 1920s. The sensual buildings, all crescents, curves and brilliant tiles, are best seen in the town's central **Parque Céspedes**. Most eye-catching is the richly decorated gazebo presiding over the park, giving an air of bohemian elegance well suited to the sphinx statues in each corner and the melee of benches, palm trees and faux-nineteenth-century streetlamps. Opposite the park, the pink **Edificio Quirch** is no less splendid, although its crescent arches and tight lattice design are rather wasted on the couple of convertible-peso shops it houses.

ARRIVAL AND DEPARTURE   MANZANILLO

By plane The Aeropuerto Internacional Sierra Maestra (☎23 57 7401) is 7km from Manzanillo on Carretera a Cayo Espino, and has flights to Havana (3 weekly; 2hr 10min). Unmetered taxis charge $4–5CUC to get into town.

By train The station is 1km east of the centre.

Destinations Bayamo (2 daily; 3hr); Havana (4 weekly; 15hr); Santiago de Cuba (1 daily; 6hr).

By colectivo There are no tourist buses from Bayamo and Pilón; if you're coming from Bayamo you'll have to catch one of the *colectivo* taxis ($15–30CUC).

By taxi A one-way taxi ride from Bayamo will cost $35CUC.

INFORMATION

Information Infotur is at the *Hotel Guacanyabo*, Ave. Camilo Cienfuegos s/n (Mon–Fri 8.15am–noon & 1–4.45pm, plus alternate Saturdays; ☎ 23 57 4412). There's also an office in the Aeropuerto Internacional Sierra Maestra (☎ 23 57 4434). Both branches offer basic information.

Currency exchange Should you need to change money, head to the CADECA at Martí no.184 (Mon–Sat 8.30am–6pm, Sun 8am–1pm).

ACCOMMODATION

Casa Adrián and Tonia Mártires de Viet Nam no.49 esq. Caridad ☎ 23 57 3028. A good *casa particular* offering an independent apartment with a kitchen; tasty meals are available too. $25CUC

Parque Nacional de Demajagua

Mon–Sat 8am–5pm, Sun 8am–noon • $1CUC, photos $5CUC, videos $5CUC • There is no public transport; a taxi from Manzanillo will cost $20CUC return

Twenty kilometres south of Manzanillo, the **Parque Nacional de Demajagua** is a pleasant place to while away an hour or two. It was from here that **Carlos Manuel de Céspedes** set out to win Cuban independence from Spain (see box, p.416), and with splendid views over the bay and the cane fields, the one-time sugar plantation is a picture of serenity.

The small building housing the **museum** was built in 1968 (the centenary of the uprising), the original plantation having been completely destroyed by shells from a Spanish gunboat on October 17, 1868. The museum itself is depressingly sparse, with a brief history of the plantation forming the main part. The highlight is the first Cuban flag ever made, hand-sewn by Céspedes' mistress. The **grounds**, while not extensive, are a nice spot to relax – look out for the Demajagua bell, built into a dry-stone wall on the far side of the lawn, with which Céspedes summoned his slaves to freedom.

Parque Nacional Desembarco del Granma

South of Niquero on the coastal road, the province's southwestern tip is commandeered by the **Parque Nacional Desembarco del Granma**, which starts at **Campismo Las Coloradas** (open to Cubans only), and stretches some 20km south to the tiny fishing village of **Cabo Cruz**. The forested interior of the park is littered with trails, but its main claim to fame is that it was here, on the park's western coastline just south of Playa Las Coloradas, that the *Granma* yacht deposited Fidel Castro on December 2, 1956 (see box opposite).

Monumento Portada de la Libertad

Daily 7am–6pm • $2CUC including guide

South of Playa Las Coloradas, which is named after the murky red colour that the mangrove jungle gives to the water here, is the exact spot of the landing where Fidel Castro's rebels waded ashore marked by the **Monumento Portada de la Libertad**. Flanked on either side by mangrove forest hedged with jagged saw grass, the kilometre-long path to the monument (which starts a short way from the museum) makes a pleasant walk even for those indifferent to the Revolution, although even the most jaded cynics will find it hard to resist the guides' enthusiasm for the subject, their compelling narrative (in Spanish) bringing to life the rebels' journey through murky undergrowth and razor-sharp thicket.

The tour also takes in a life-size replica of the **yacht**, which guides can sometimes be persuaded to let you clamber aboard; and a rather spartan **museum** with photographs, maps and an emotive quotation from Castro on the eve of the crossing that neatly sums up his determination to succeed: "*Si salimos, llegamos. Si llegamos, entramos, y si entramos, triumfamos*" (If we leave, we'll get there. If we get there we'll get in, and if we get in we will win).

El Guafe

Mon–Fri 8.30am–5pm, Sat & Sun 8am–2pm • $5CUC including a guide

The interior of the Parque Nacional Desembarcoa is made up of idyllic woodland that skirts the western verge of the Sierra Maestra. From Las Coloradas you can walk to the start of **El Guafe**, one of the four trails in the park, celebrated for the intriguing stone petroglyphs found in the vicinity, the remnants of Indian culture. It's an easy and reasonably well-signposted walk – roughly a 3km circuit – which you can do on your own, although the guides have extensive knowledge of both the history of the area and the cornucopia of birds and butterflies, trees and plants you'll see along the way. Look out for the ancient cactus nicknamed "Viejo Testigo" (the Old Witness), thought to be five hundred years old and now so thick and twisted it has formed a robust, tree-like trunk.

The small, human-form **petroglyphs**, sculpted with haunting, hollowed-out eyes, are in a low-roofed cave musty with the smell of bats, probably used as a crypt by the aboriginal Indians, who carved the idols as guardians. Fragments of ceramics and a

---

THE GRANMA

8

Under constant surveillance and threat from the Batista regime following his release from prison, Fidel Castro left Havana for exile in Mexico in the summer of 1955. Along with other exiled Cubans sympathetic to his ideas, he formed the **26 July Movement** in exile – the Cuban counterpart was run by Frank País – and began to gather weapons and funds to facilitate the return to Cuba.

Castro was anxious to return as soon as possible. Leaks within the organization had already resulted in the confiscation of arms by the Mexican government and there was an ever-present threat of assassination by Batista's contacts in Mexico. By October the following year Castro had gathered enough support and money and declared himself ready to return. He bought a 58ft yacht called **Granma** from a North American couple for $15,000, and hatched a plan to sail it from Tuxpan, on the east coast of Veracruz in Mexico, to Oriente, following the tracks of José Martí – who had made a similar journey sixty years before.

At around 1.30am on November 25, 1956, with 82 men crammed into the eight-berth yacht, the *Granma* set off for Cuba. Because of the stormy weather all shipping was kept in port and the yacht had to slip past the Mexican coastguard to escape. Foul weather, cramped conditions and a malfunctioning engine meant that the journey that was supposed to take five days took eight. The plan had been to come ashore at Niquero, where Celia Sánchez, a key revolutionary, was waiting to ferry them to safety, but on December 2 they ran out of petrol just 35m from the coast, and at 6am the *Granma* capsized just south of Playa Las Coloradas. As Che later commented: "It wasn't a landing, it was a shipwreck."

Exhausted, sick and hungry, the 82 young men waded ashore only to find themselves faced with a kilometre of virtually impenetrable mangroves and sharp saw grass. They eventually made camp at Alegría de Pío, a sugar-cane zone near the coast, with the intention of resting for a few hours. It was to be a baptism of fire as Batista's troops, who had been tipped off about their arrival and had been strafing the area for several hours, came across the men and attacked. Completely unprepared, the rebels ran for their lives, scattering in all directions. Thanks to the efforts of Celia Sánchez, who had left messages at the houses of peasants sympathetic to the rebels' cause, the rebels were able to regroup two weeks later. It was hardly a glorious beginning, but the opening shots of the Revolution had been fired.

large clay jar decorated with allegorical characters were also found, supporting the theory. A second cave close to the exit of the trail houses another petroglyph known as the **Idolo del Agua** (the water idol), thought to have been carved into the rock to bless and protect the sweet water of the cave – a rarity in the area. Along the walk, look out for the tiny, iridescent green, red and blue Cartacuba bird, which has a call a bit like a grunting pig.

Parque Nacional Desembarco del Granma trails

Cubamar in Havana (☎ 78 31 2891) can arrange group excursions (minimum ten people)

Parque Nacional Desembarco del Granma's **other trails** run along the southern coastline 20–30km east of El Guafe. Highlights include the **Agua Fina cave**, roughly 20km from El Guafe, and, some 7km further east, the **Morlotte** and **El Furstete** caves as well as **Las Terrazas**, a natural coastline shelf sculpted by geographic formations to look like man-made terraces.

ACCOMMODATION   PARQUE DESEMBARCO DEL GRANMA

Campismo Las Coloradas ☎ 23 90 1126. Just outside the park, this *campismo* has simple and clean chalets with a/c and hot water, along with a restaurant and bar. Bookings are essential at weekends, when this is a favourite target for Cubans. Bookings can only be made through Cubamar in Havana or Bayamo (see p.421). At the time of writing, the campsite was only open to Cubans, though this

may well change.

Hotel Niquero Calle Martí no.100 esq. Céspedes, Niquero ☎ 23 59 2367. A basic, quiet and serviceable hotel 13km north of the park and the closest accommodation for visitors to the park. Rates include breakfast. **$28CUC**

8

Pilón

Tiny sugar town **PILÓN**, 37 kilometres southeast of Niquero and 8km west of Marea del Portillo, is like a remnant of past times, with open-backed carts laden with sugar cane zigzagging across the roads and the smell of boiling molasses enveloping the town in its thick scent. The most useful establishment in town is the local service station on the Marea del Portillo road, which sells sweets, snacks and cold drinks. It's also a good place to ask whether the Carretera del Sur to Santiago is passable.

Casa Museo Celia Sánchez Manduley

Tues–Sat 9am–5pm, Sun 9am–1pm • $1CUC

The small but engaging **Casa Museo Celia Sánchez Manduley**, erstwhile home of revolutionary Celia Sánchez, offers a ragbag of exhibits, including Taíno ceramics, shrapnel from the Wars of Independence and a photographic history of Pilón.

DRIVING THE SOUTHERN COAST ROAD

Though it suffered damage from Hurricane Sandy in late 2012, which compounded the havoc wreaked by previous hurricanes, the lonely **southern coast road** between Pilón and Santiago de Cuba offers one of the most exhilarating drives in Cuba, with the Sierra Maestra rearing up directly from the roadside, and the ocean swirling from a Caribbean postcard-blue to an indigo black. The road undulates up and down the mountainside and, at one point, due to persistent damage, has fallen into the sea; it is sometimes passable by negotiating the track and the sea. Sometimes passing inches from the ocean, skirting rockfalls and crossing or diverting via broken bridges, this is a hair-raising route, and you should always seek out local advice before setting out to drive it, either in Niquero or Pilón in the west, or in Santiago. The journey from Pilón to Santiago (where the last petrol station is) takes 6–7 hours because of the state of the road.

Pilón's beaches

There's little else to see in Pilón and even less to do, but the two beaches, **Playa Media Luna**, with beautiful views over the Sierra Maestra and a rocky coastline good for snorkelling, and the narrow white-sand **Playa Punta**, have an unruliness that's refreshingly different from the smarter resort beaches.

Marea del Portillo

Smack in the middle of Granma's southern coast, backed by a sweeping wave of mountains, is the resort of **Marea del Portillo**. Accessible from Granma's west coast and 150km southwest from Bayamo, the resort is set on a black-sand beach which looks impressive from a distance, but like a muddy field close up. It won't be most people's first choice for a beach holiday, although the white sands of tiny **Cayo Blanco** just offshore go some way to making up for this.

Appealing largely to older Canadians and Germans, as well as a few families, Marea del Portillo doesn't have the universal appeal of some resorts, especially as there is little infrastructure – just two hotels on the beach and another nearby, plus a dive shop. The surrounding countryside is beautiful, however, including the picturesque **El Salto waterfall**, and there are eighteen **dive sites**, including the *El Real* Spanish galleon.

ARRIVAL AND ACTIVITIES

MAREA DEL PORTILLO

By car Transport links to and from Marea del Portillo are diabolical – if you can rent a car before you arrive, do so, and make sure you have sufficient cash before you arrive, as the only banks in the province are in Bayamo.

Activities *Club Amigo's* Albacora dive centre (☎ 23 59 7134) rents out equipment and offers dives from $30CUC, as well as deep-sea fishing and trips to Cayo Blanco. Land-based excursions from the resort, organized by the Cubatur outlet at the hotel, include a trip to the Desembarco del Granma national park ($45CUC per person; see p.422).

ACCOMMODATION

Club Amigo Marea del Portillo Carretera Granma Km 12.5 ☎ 23 59 7121. Marea del Portillo's all-inclusive beach hotel has two restaurants, nine bars and a handsome pool area. There are double rooms and larger cabins, most of which have views over the beach. Rooms $60, cabins $92CUC

Villa Turística Punta Piedra Carretera de Pilón ☎ 23 59 7035. A further 2km along the same road from *Club Amigo Marea del Portillo*, this hotel has 13 basic rooms, including triples, and a restaurant, bar and pool, although it's not right next to the beach. Rates include breakfast. $$40CUC

Isla de la Juventud and Cayo Largo

PUNTA FRANCÉS

9

Isla de la Juventud and Cayo Largo

About 100km south of the mainland, the little-visited Isla de la Juventud (Island of Youth) is the largest of over three hundred scattered emerald islets that make up the Archipiélago de los Canarreos. Extending from the island capital of Nueva Gerona in the north to the superb diving region of Punta Francés, 70km to the southwest, the comma-shaped Juventud is bisected by a military checkpoint designed to control access to ecologically vulnerable areas. The northern region is mostly farmland, characterized by citrus orchards and mango groves, while the restricted southern swampland is rich in wildlife. Although it has an air of timeless somnolence, Isla de la Juventud was actually once a pirate haunt, ruled over for three centuries by French and English buccaneers and adventurers. Development here has been unhurried, and even today there are as many horse-drawn coaches on the roads as there are cars or trucks.

It probably won't be your first choice for a beach holiday, although it's a good place to unwind once you've visited the more flamboyant – and hectic – sights elsewhere in Cuba. With little tourist trade, Juventud's charm is anchored to its unaffected pace of life and pleasant beaches, and the lack of traffic and predominantly flat terrain make **cycling** an excellent way to explore. The single real town, **Nueva Gerona**, founded in 1830, has few of the architectural crowd-pullers that exist in other colonial towns, and so is a refreshingly low-key place to visit, easily explored over a weekend. For those keen to explore further, there are some intriguing pre-Columbian **cave paintings** in the south and, close to the capital, the museum at the abandoned **Presidio Modelo**, a prison whose most famous inmate was Fidel Castro. With a couple more small but worthy museums, some of the country's best offshore **dive sites** and one beautiful white-sand beach, Isla de la Juventud is one of Cuba's best-kept secrets.

A necklace of islets streaming 150km east, the **Archipiélago de los Canarreos** is a fantasy paradise of pearl-white sand and translucent, coral-lined shallows. While most are still desert cays too small to sustain a complex tourist structure, **Cayo Largo**, the archipelago's second-largest landmass after La Isla, is the destination of choice for most visitors to the area. Arguably Cuba's most exclusive holiday resort – if only in terms of accessibility – this comparatively tiny islet is beaten only by Varadero for package-tourist pulling power. Unlike its mainland counterpart, however, this resort is completely devoid of a genuine local population. Created in 1977 and now serving flocks of sun-worshipping Canadians and Europeans, the resort capitalizes on its flawless, 22km-long ribbon of white sand and features a marina, dive shop and a growing clique of all-inclusive hotels.

Both islands, but particularly Isla de la Juventud, have endured horrific **storm damage** over the last decade following a succession of devastating hurricanes, and though it's business as usual at the resort on Cayo Largo, some of the infrastructure on La Isla is still in a state of disrepair.

Isla de la Juventud bus routes p.432	**Latrobe's treasure** p.444
Diving off the west coast p.441	**Cayo Largo diving, fishing and boat**
Crossing the military border p.442	**excursions** p.447

MUSEO PRESIDIO MODELO

Highlights

❶ **Sierra de las Casas** The short, easy and
enjoyable trek up these low hills rewards with
some of the best views of the Isla de la
Juventud. **See p.438**

❷ **Museo Presidio Modelo** A walk around the
huge ruined cell blocks of this "Model Prison",
with its forbidding atmosphere and grim history,
is unforgettable. **See p.439**

❸ **Diving at Punta Francés** One of the premier
diving areas in Cuba, with over fifty dive sites –
from shipwrecks and caves to coral walls and
tunnels – and some stunning marine life.
See p.441

❹ **Cuevas de Punta del Este** These
atmospheric caves, once home to the Siboney
people, hold significant examples of early
pre-Columbian art, while the nearby beach
completes a day-trip. **See p.443**

❺ **Playa Francés** On a remote, upturned hook
of land, the silver sands and limpid waters here
make this the best beach on Isla de la Juventud.
See p.444

❻ **Boat trips from Cayo Largo** Hop on a
catamaran or a yacht to the outlying cays around
Cayo Largo to see the iguana colonies and snorkel
at coral reefs and deserted beaches. **See p.447**

HIGHLIGHTS ARE MARKED ON THE MAP ON P.430

9

Isla de la Juventud

A vision of fruit fields and soft beaches, it is little wonder that **Isla de la Juventud**, or "La Isla" as it's known in Cuba, allegedly captured Robert Louis Stevenson's imagination as the original desert island of *Treasure Island*. Although Christopher Columbus chanced upon the island in 1494, the Spanish had scant use for it until the nineteenth century and development unfolded at an unhurried pace. Even today the quiet, underpopulated countryside and placid towns have the air of a land waiting to awaken.

The main focus for the island's population is in the **north**, where you'll find many of the sights and the island capital of **Nueva Gerona**. Nestling up against the Sierra de las

HIGHLIGHTS

1 Sierra de las Casas
2 Museo Presidio Modelo
3 Diving at Punta Francés
4 Cuevas de Punta del Este
5 Playa Francés
6 Boat trips from Cayo Largo

ISLA DE LA JUVENTUD & CAYO LARGO

Casas, this town is satisfyingly self-contained, ambling along a couple of decades behind developments on the mainland. Spread around it is a wide skirt of low-lying fields, lined with orderly citrus orchards, fruit farms and two of the island's modest tourist attractions. Both are former prison buildings, a testament to the island's long-standing isolation. **El Abra** is a delightfully located hacienda that once held captive the nineteenth-century independence suffragist José Martí, while the **Presidio Modelo**, set up in 1926 to contain more than six thousand criminals, most famously Fidel Castro, is a contrastingly ominous-looking place. Deserted, but still a dominating presence on the island's landscape, the prison and its museum make for a fascinating excursion. There are also a couple of brown-sand beaches, **Playa Bibijagua** and **Playa Paraíso**, within easy reach of Nueva Gerona.

South from the capital are several sights that can be explored in easy day-trips. To the west of the island's second-biggest town, the rather mundane **La Fe**, are verdant botanical gardens **La Jungla de Jones**, on a long-term recovery from hurricane damage but still worth a visit. South of La Fe is a **crocodile farm** offering an excellent opportunity to study the creatures at close range. Further south still is the **military checkpoint** at Cayo Piedra, in place to conserve the marshy southern region that forms the **Siguanea Nature Reserve**, access to which is strictly controlled. South of the checkpoint on the southeast coast is one of the island's most intriguing attractions, the **pre-Columbian paintings** in the Punta del Este caves. On the west side of the south coast is the tiny hamlet of **Cocodrilo**, set on a picturesque curve of coastline and an ideal spot for swimming, while close to hand is the picture-perfect white-sand beach of **Playa El Francés**. Just offshore here you can enjoy the island's celebrated dive sites, including underwater caves and a wall of black coral, but to do so you'll need to set off from the **Marina Siguanea**, north of the protected area near the island's best hotel, the **Hotel Colony**.

Brief history

The island's earliest known inhabitants were the **Siboney** people, who are thought to have settled here around a thousand years ago. They lived close to the island's shores where they could fish and hunt, eschewing its pine-forested interior. Tools and utensils made from conch shell and bone have been found at Punta del Este, suggesting that the Siboney based themselves around the eastern caves.

By the time **Christopher Columbus** landed here in June 1494, on his second trip to the Americas, the Siboney had disappeared. Though Columbus claimed it for Spain, the Spanish Crown had little interest in the island over the next four centuries. Neither the mangrove-webbed northern coastline nor the excessively shallow southern bays afforded a natural harbour to match the likes of Havana, and the Golfo de Batabanó, separating the island from mainland Cuba, was too shallow for the overblown Spanish galleons to navigate.

Pirates and prisons

Left outside the bounds of Spanish law enforcement, the island attracted scores of pirates between the sixteenth and eighteenth centuries. It came to be known as the **Isla de Pinos** – after its plentiful pine trees, ideal for making masts and repairing ships – and, informally, as the Isla de las Cotorras, for its endemic green parrot population. Lurid stories of wine, women and warmongering were enough to keep all but the most determined settlers away, and so the pirates ruled the roost right up until the early nineteenth century, when Spanish interest was renewed in the island. However, despite a massive push by Spanish royal decree for whites to populate the island, there was comparatively little response. The Spanish authorities decided to capitalize on the island's isolation, using it as a convenient **offshore prison** during the nineteenth-century Wars of Independence, but still failed to exploit its full potential.

9

US interests

By the early twentieth century, the Spanish were ruing their indifference, as much of the property had fallen into the hands of shrewd **North American** businessmen and farmers who had waited in the wings during the troubled years. When Cuba won its independence from Spain in 1898, the island's small population allowed the North Americans to muscle in and start development unimpeded. By the 1920s a US-funded infrastructure of banks, hotels and even a prison – namely the vast Model Prison – was already in place. By the time of the Revolution the island had become a popular North American **holiday resort**.

A fruitful future

The North Americans departed following the Revolution, and the history of the island took another turn when the state's drive to create arable land established it as one of the country's major producers of fruit for export. In 1966 it became a centre for experimental **agriculture**, to which a flood of students came to work the fields and study. In 1976 the government extended this free education to **foreign students** from countries with a socialist overview, and, until the Special Period curtailed the flow, thousands of students arrived from countries like Angola, Nicaragua and South Yemen. When Cuba hosted the eleventh World Youth and Student Festival in 1978, the government changed the island's name from Isle of Pines to **Isle of Youth**, shedding the final trace of the island's rebellious past, although islanders still refer to themselves – and their national-league baseball team – as Pineros.

GETTING AROUND ISLA DE LA JUVENTUD

By car or jeep Compact Nueva Gerona is easily seen on foot but the best way to explore the rest of the island is by renting a car or jeep, since the bus network is skeletal. Cubacar is the only rental outfit in town, at José Martí esq. 32 (☎ 46 32 4432).

By bus There are bus services connecting Nueva Gerona with the rest of the island and a number of bus stops on Calle 41, the main thoroughfare through town, as well as a bus terminal of sorts on Calle 39A near the cemetery.

By taxi State taxi company Cubataxi (☎ 46 32 3121) charges $0.56CUC/km; for private taxis, look for the latter

at the Parque Guerrillero Heroico in Nueva Gerona or ask in a *casa particular*. Return taxi fares to any of the destinations around Nueva Gerona are $6–8CUC.

By bicycle The best way to see the north end of the island is by bike; there are no rental outlets, but *casas particulares* owners are often willing to loan you the family bicycle for a few convertible pesos a day.

By bicitaxi By far the most convenient way to get around the outlying areas of Nueva Gerona, *bicitaxis* can be flagged down throughout the centre. No journey should cost more than $3–4CUC.

Nueva Gerona

Isla de la Juventud's only sizeable town, **NUEVA GERONA** lies in the lee of the Sierra de las Casas, on the bank of the Río Las Casas. Whether you travel by plane or boat, this is where you'll arrive and where you're likely to be based. According to an 1819 census, the population stood at just under two hundred and it boasted just "four guano huts and a church of the same". While the town has certainly moved on

---

ISLA DE LA JUVENTUD BUS ROUTES

Buses are a reasonably reliable way of getting around the northern end of the island; the routes below cover the places you're most likely to visit. You can board them along Calle 41 or Calle 47, near Nueva Gerona's bus station.

Nueva Gerona to Playa Bibijagua Bus no.204 (4 daily each way; 30min), via Chacón (for Museo Presidio Modelo (4 daily each way; 20min).

Nueva Gerona to La Fe Bus no.431 (12 daily each way; 45min).

Nueva Gerona to Hotel Colony Bus no.40 and no.440 (4 daily each way; 2hr).

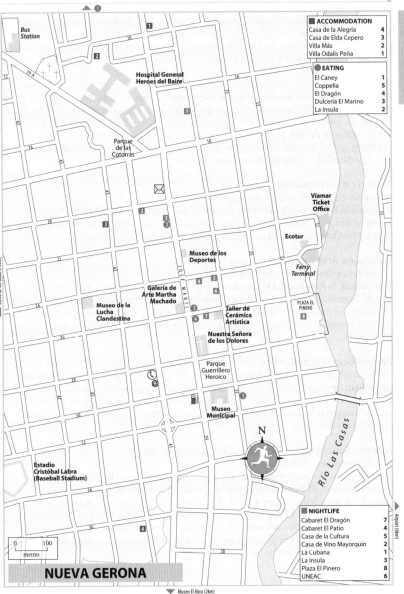

Bus Station

Hospital General Heroes del Baire

Parque de las Cotorras

Víamar Ticket Office

Ecotur

Museo de los Deportes

Ferry Terminal

Galería de Arte Martha Machado

PLAZA EL PINERO

Museo de la Lucha Clandestina

Taller de Cerámica Artística

Nuestra Señora de los Dolores

Parque Guerrillero Heroico

Museo Municipal

Estadio Cristóbal Labra (Baseball Stadium)

N

Río Las Casas

Airport (6km)

0   100
metres

NUEVA GERONA

Museo El Abra (2km)

since then, it's still a small and quirky place, with a cosiness more suited to a village than an island capital, and a sleepy peacefulness offset by the hub of action around the central streets. Even half a day here breeds a sense of familiarity, and much of the town's attraction lies in wandering its relaxed streets, where the local appetite for pestering tourists has not developed to the same levels as in other towns in Cuba. Basing yourself here and exploring the hillsides, beaches and museums around Nueva Gerona can easily keep you occupied for a couple of days.

9

Architecturally, Nueva Gerona floats in a no-man's-land between old-style colonial buildings and modern urbanity. Many of its concrete one- and two-storey buildings are painted in pastel colours, and its few older buildings, complete with stately colonnades and red-tiled roofs, add a colonial touch.

Calle José Martí

Nueva Gerona's heart lies on **Calle José Martí** (also known as Calle 39 and often referred to simply as Martí), the amiable central street that gives the town its defining character and which holds the majority of shops and restaurants. It's a good-looking strip, with the verandas of the low buildings offering welcome respite from the sun. At the northern end of the pedestrianized section, sometimes referred to as Boulevard, is a small park called the **Parque de las Cotorras**.

Museo de los Deportes

Calle José Martí e/ 22 y 24 • Tues–Sat 8am–noon & 1–5pm • Free

A couple of blocks south of Parque de las Cotorras, the tiny **Museo de los Deportes** serves as a modest tribute to local sports heroes, with sweatshirts and trophies worn and won by baseball players and other successful athletes from the island.

Galería de Arte Martha Machado

Calle José Martí esq. Calle 26 • Daily 8am–10pm • Free

The **Galería de Arte Martha Machado** has a small space for exhibitions of local art, mostly from the Naïve school, some of which is for sale. The gallery is associated with the internationally renowned artist, **Kcho** (aka Alexis Leyva Machado) who was born in Nueva Gerona. If you're in luck, your visit may coincide with a temporary exhibition of his work.

Parque Guerrillero Heroico

At the southern end of Calle José Martí, past the pedestrianized centre, is the **Parque Guerrillero Heroico**. Although unspectacular in itself – it's basically a wide slab of plaza – it's bordered by some picturesque buildings such as the handsome, pastel-yellow villa on the western side, now converted into a school, with elegant arches and wonderful stained-glass windows.

Nuestra Señora de los Dolores y San Nicolás de Barí

Parque Guerrillero Heroico • Mon–Fri 8.30am–noon • Free

Presiding over the northwestern corner of Parque Guerrillero Heroico is the ochre-coloured church of **Nuestra Señora de los Dolores y San Nicolás de Barí**, boasting a curvaceous red-tiled roof and a sturdy bell tower. The present building was completed in 1929 and is a copy of the San Lorenzo de Lucina church in Rome. The interior is disappointing: a sparsely decorated sky-blue shell houses a huddle of pews – it's only worth entering for a swift glance at the **altar** to the Virgen de la Caridad, the patron saint of Cuba, backed by the national flag.

Museo Municipal

Calle: 30 e/ 37 y 39 • Tues–Fri 9am–5pm, Sat 9am–4pm, Sun 9am–noon • $1CUC • ☎ 46 32 4582

Across Parque Guerrillero Heroico from the church is the **Museo Municipal**, housed in the old town hall, a stately colonial building with a small clocktower. Dating to 1830, this is the oldest building in Nueva Gerona. On display are portraits, weapons and naval relics illustrating the lives of the **pirates** whose activities dominated the region for over two centuries. There are also some compelling **photographs** from the early years of the twentieth century and a wonderfully retro collection of pamphlets and advertisements dating from the island's heyday as a tourist destination in the 1940s and 1950s. Also be

9

sure to look for the intricate model of **El Pinero**, the boat that ferried passengers and supplies to and from the mainland throughout the first half of the twentieth century, and which carried Fidel Castro following his release from the Presidio Modelo in 1955. The real thing can be seen sitting alongside the river at the end of Calle 26.

Museo de la Lucha Clandestina

Calle 24 e/ 43 y 45 • Tues–Fri 9am–5pm, Sat 9am–4pm, Sun 8am–noon • $1CUC

A few blocks west from Martí, the **Museo de la Lucha Clandestina** packs into a modest wooden house a surprising number of items relating to the islanders' part in the revolutionary struggle. While Cuba is stuffed with such museums, there are a couple of exhibits that actually make this one special. Look for the commemorative **photo album** compiled after the Revolution to celebrate the original band that arrived on the yacht *Granma*. Each page features photographs of two revolutionaries framed by a dramatic line drawing depicting their struggles, making them look like comic-book heroes. Also noteworthy are the 1960s **photos** of excited crowds celebrating nationalization outside banks and factories and, best of all, an ingenious fake cigar used by the rebels to smuggle messages.

ARRIVAL AND DEPARTURE

NUEVA GERONA

BY PLANE

Essentials Two daily flights (40min; $130CUC return) from Havana arrive at Rafael Cabrera Mustelier airport (☎ 46 32 2300), 10km south of the town centre. Have some small change in national pesos ready for the buses that meet the planes and run to the town centre, or take a taxi for about $7CUC.

BY FERRY

Arriving by ferry The daily catamaran ferry (2hr 45min; $50CUC each way) to Isla de la Juventud leaves from the ferry terminal at Batabanó, on the southern coast of Mayabeque province. It docks at the terminal on the Río Las Casas in Nueva Gerona (Mon–Fri 8am–noon & 2–5pm; ☎ 46 32 4415), a 5min walk from the centre. From here it's a 5min walk to the centre, or you can jump on one of the army of *bicitaxis* or horse-drawn carriages that wait to pick up passengers.

Tickets Most visitors set off for the journey to Batabanó (daily; 1hr 30min) from Havana, and as all the convertible-peso seats on the ferry may have already been sold by the

time you reach Batabanó, it's best to buy in advance in Havana. To do so, you should make an early visit (ideally before 9am) to the Oficina de la Naviera booth at Havana's Astro bus terminal (daily 7.30am–12.30pm; ☎ 7 878 1841; see p.115), where staff will sell you a bus ticket ($5CUC) and reserve your boat ticket – payment for the latter is taken at Batabanó. You'll need your passport to be allowed to travel. Return journeys are hideously oversubscribed, so buying a return tickt is highly recommended.

Leaving by ferry Leaving the island by ferry can be problematic. If you don't already already have a ferry ticket, you must go to the ticket office (☎ 46 32 4406) near the ferry terminal two hours before the scheduled departure time (daily 8am, plus 1pm Fri & Sun) on the day you plan to travel. You'll need to put yourself on the waiting list (*lista de espera*), for which you have to show your passport and pay a $2CUP charge, and then wait, sometimes several hours, until the number of no-shows (*fallos*) has been established. If there are no *fallos* then you won't be able to travel, but there are usually at least a few, and as a convertible peso-paying passenger you'll be at the top of the waiting list.

INFORMATION AND TOURS

Tourist information The only place for visitor information in town is the Ecotur office next to the ferry terminal (Mon–Fri 8am–4.30pm, Sat 8am–noon; ☎ 46 32 7101).

Travel permits and tours Ecotur's principle *raison d'être* is to administer and supervise visits to the protected

southern part of the island (see p.442), and the Nueva Gerona office sells the required permit for such trips. It also organizes excursions to La Fe, La Jungla de Jones and the Criadero de Cocodrilos, and can help with arrangements for diving trips. For information on diving you could also ring the *Hotel Colony*, on the island's southwest coast (see p.441).

ACCOMMODATION

Unless you've come for the diving, in which case you'll be based at *Hotel Colony* on the western coast of the island (see p.441), Nueva Gerona is the only base for a stay on Isla de la Juventud. The small clutch of tatty **state hotels** in and around the town has little going for them, and you're better off in one of the excellent **casas particulares** in the town itself, which are often somewhat cheaper than on the mainland.

Casa de la Alegría Calle 43 no.3602 e/ 36 y 38 ☎46 32 3664. Two pleasantly furnished double rooms close to the centre, each with a/c and private bathroom, and sharing a living room exclusively for guests. Meals are served on a large, semi-covered patio, and the hosts provide a laundry service as well. **$20CUC**

Casa de Elda Cepero Calle 43 no.2004 e/ 20 y 22 ☎46 32 2774, ✉eldacepero65@yahoo.es. Guests are given a mini apartment at the back of this house facing a lawn-covered garden. The bedroom opens onto a narrow but congenial lounge-diner which itself gives onto a covered garden patio. With an independent entrance at the side of the house, this works well as a relaxing and very private retreat. **$20CUC**

★ **Villa Más** Calle 41 no.4108 e/ 8 y 10, apto. 7

☎46 32 3544, ✉rgarcia@ijv.sld.cu. Situated behind the hospital on a dusty track where the block layout gets a bit jumbled, this hard-to-find first-floor apartment offers spotlessly clean, stylishly decorated rooms with TV and fridge. There are also two fabulous levels of roof terrace, one with a matted roof and barbecue grill, the other with views over the city and out to sea. The owner is a qualified chef and will provide meals. **$20CUC**

Villa Odalis Peña Calle 10 no.3710 esq. 39 ☎46 32 2345. Big, friendly household surrounded by pretty gardens and offering two a/c rooms, each of which has its own minibar and bathroom with an electric shower. Food is available and, unusually, vegetarian meals are a speciality. Around 300m out of town but a good choice nonetheless. **$15CUC**

EATING

As the food in the state restaurants is reliably poor, the *casas particulares* are generally the best places for a meal in town. A small concentration of uninspiring **café/restaurants** lies on José Martí, many of them closed by 8pm despite advertising longer opening hours. They are at least very cheap, between them offering burgers, pizzas and pork dishes for a national peso or two. For **snacks**, there are several options on the pedestrianized section of José Martí, including a convertible-peso supermarket between Calle 22 and Calle 24.

★ **El Caney** Calle 3ra. no.401 e/ 4 y 6 ☎46 32 5547. Open sides and a thatched roof give this lively paladar an airy feel, while the typical Cuban cuisine includes fish, pork and chicken cooked to a turn on an open grill within view. Portions are generous and well priced (around $6CUC for a main) and complimented by a very friendly owner. Daily noon–9pm.

Coppelia Calle no.37 e/ 30 y 32 (no phone). For decent ice cream head for this attractive whitewashed building a street away from Parque Guerrillermo Heroico. Flavours include the standard strawberry and chocolate with the occasional guest flavour available. Tues–Sun noon–10pm.

El Dragón José Martí esq. 26 ☎46 32 4479. Mid-range

Cuban–Chinese food in one of the only foreign-cuisine restaurants in Nueva Gerona. The house speciality is fried rice with chicken, pork and vegetables. Daily noon–8pm.

Dulcería El Marino José Martí e/ Calle 22 y Calle 24 (no phone). Particularly useful if you're heading off on a day-trip, this little bakery is a good place to stock up on sweets and pastries. Daily 10am–5.30pm.

La Insula José Martí esq. 22. A more salubrious eating environment than elsewhere in town, this is Nueva Gerona's only convertible-peso restaurant, and keeps it simple with around half a dozen classic Cuban meat dishes, such as stewed beef steak ($4.65CUC) and pork in breadcrumbs ($3.55CUC). Daily noon–9pm.

DRINKING AND ENTERTAINMENT

Not a lot happens at night in Nueva Gerona between Monday and Wednesday, but weekends can be surprisingly lively, with most of the action taking place around the half dozen blocks north of Parque Guerrillero Heroico between José Martí and the river.

Cabaret El Dragón Calle 26 e/ 37 y 39 (no phone). A large and attractive garden patio with a shiny bar, to the rear of the eponymous Chinese restaurant, where cheesy but popular live music and dance shows interchange with nights of recorded soft rock, Latin pop and salsa. Entrance $5CUP. Thurs–Sun 8pm–late.

Cabaret El Patio Calle 24 e/ José Martí y 37 (no phone). Hosts live singers and a fabulously camp small-scale cabaret in a dark and moody hall for an enthusiastic crowd. Entrance $5–10CUP, but non-Cubans are likely to be charged in CUC. Thurs–Sun 10pm–2am.

★ **Casa de la Cultura** Calle 24 esq. 37 ☎48 32 3591. Entertainment most nights, with two floors of performance

spaces, ranging from singing troupes and Afro-Cuban dancing to burlesque pantomimes and daytime children's shows. This is also the spot for catching live traditional Cuban music such as trova, son and bolero, and is most reliably lively during the week. Free. Daily, no fixed opening hours.

Casa de Vino Mayorquin Calle 41 esq. 20 (no phone). If you're feeling experimental, head for this unusual bar specializing in wines made from tropical fruits like grapefruit, orange and banana. Light meals are also served. Daily noon–8pm.

La Cubana Calle 37 e/ 16 y 18 (no phone). An outdoor bar at the end of a long, narrow patio where locals sit, chat

9

and sip cocktails, beer and soda. Daily noon–midnight.

La Insula José Martí esq. 22 ☎ 46 32 1825. The straightforward bar at this restaurant is open some evenings, and is liveliest on Sundays when it hosts a karaoke night. Entrance $2CUC, includes a one-drink *consumo*. Bar daily noon–9pm; karaoke Sun 10pm–1am.

Plaza El Pinero Calle 33 e/ 26 y 28 (no phone). Crowds gather at this open space next to the river where bands perform at weekends on a large concrete stage. Popular with the young crowd and one of the main venues for visiting bands from Havana. No fixed schedule; free.

UNEAC Calle 37 e/ 24 y 26 (no phone). The local branch of this national cultural institution has a small patio for all kinds of live music performances by aspiring and seasoned musical talent, from reggaeton and rock to guitar-strumming troubadours. No fixed schedule; free.

DIRECTORY

Banks and exchange Banco de Crédito y Comercio, José Martí no.39 esq. 18 (Mon–Fri 8am–3pm, Sat 8–11am; ☎ 46 32 2902), gives cash advances on MasterCard and Visa and changes travellers' cheques, as does the CADECA *casa de cambio* at José Martí esq. 20 (Mon–Sat 8am–6pm, Sun 8am–1pm). There are two ATMs, one at the Banco de Crédito y Comercio and one at the Banco Popular de Ahorro at José Martí esq. 26. Both only accept Visa cards and dispense $CUC.

Bookshop The nameless bookshop at José Martí esq. 22 has a range of books in Spanish and the occasional English title (Mon–Sat 8am–7pm).

Internet and telephone Public phones and internet

access are available at the Telepunto office at Calle 41 esq. 28, near Parque Guerrillero Heroico (daily 8.30am–7.30pm; $6CUC/hr).

Medical The only hospital on the island is the Héroes del Baire, on Calle 41 e/ 16 y 18. For an ambulance call ☎ 46 32 4170. The state hotels have medical posts, while the most accessible pharmacy is in the hospital grounds, facing the entrance.

Police Call ☎ 116.

Post office The main post office is on José Martí e/ 18 y 20 (Mon–Sat 8am–6pm). There's a DHL desk in the stationery shop at José Martí s/n e/ 22 y 24 (Mon–Fri 8am–noon & 1–5pm, Sat 8am–noon).

Sierra de las Casas

The best way to appreciate Nueva Gerona's diminutive scale is to take the short but exhilarating climb up the hills of the gently undulating **Sierra de las Casas** range, just to the west, for a bird's-eye view over the town and the surrounding countryside. It's under an hour's easy climb up to the highest summit, beneath which are spread the town's orderly rows of streets, curtailed by the stretch of blue beyond. To the east, below the cliff-edge, the island's flat landscape is occasionally relieved by a sparse sweep of hills; to the south, you can see the gleaming quarry which yields the stone for so many of Cuba's marble artefacts.

To get to the hills, head 500m west from Neuva Gerona's centre down Calle 24; take the first left turn and carry on another few hundred metres along a well-trodden path until you reach the foot of the first hill, marked by two lone concrete poles poking out of the ground

Cueva del Agua

24hr • Free

Before heading back to town from the Sierra de las Casas, make time to explore the underground **Cueva del Agua**, whose entrance is at the foot of the hill. The steep, narrow staircase cut from the rockbed can be slippery, so take care descending and bring a torch. There's a natural lagoon and captivating rock formations but the real treat here lies along a narrow tunnel on the right-hand side just before the mouth of the pool, where intricate, glittery stalactites and stalagmites are slowly growing into elaborate natural sculptures.

Museo El Abra

Tues–Sat 9am–4.30pm, Sun 9am–1pm • $1CUC • ☎ 46 39 6206

Around 2km southwest of Nueva Gerona, on the Carretera Siguanea – the continuation of Calle 41, which heads towards *Hotel Colony* (see p.441) – a signposted turning leads to the **Museo El Abra**, the Spanish-style hacienda where José Martí spent three months in 1870. Nestling at the foot of the Sierra de las Casas, the whitewashed farmhouse – with Caribbean-blue balustrade windows and a charming stone sundial from Barcelona – has rather more style than substance. Inside is a strained collection of inconsequential artefacts from Martí's life. Letters and documents vie for attention with his bed and a replica of the manacles from which Martí was freed on his arrival.

Although just 16 at the time of his arrest, Martí had already founded the magazine *La Patria Libre*, and his editorials contesting Spanish rule had him swiftly pegged as a dissident. On October 21, 1869, he was arrested for treason. His original sentence of six years' hard labour was mitigated and he was exiled to El Abra. Here he was permitted to serve out his sentence under the custody of family friend and farm owner José María Sardá, but within three months the Spanish governor expelled him from Cuba altogether. During his time on the island he wrote the essay *El Presidio Político en Cuba* ("The Political Prison in Cuba"), which became the seminal text of the independence struggle.

EATING

MUSEO EL ABRA

El Abra ✆ 46 32 4927. If you've got time to spare, consider heading a further 3km south along the Carretera Siguanea to the lakeside *El Abra* restaurant, whose no-frills though inexpensive *comida criolla* is redeemed somewhat by the panoramic views and the mountain backdrop. Tues–Sun 9am–6pm.

Museo Presidio Modelo

Mon–Sat 8am–4pm, Sun 8am–noon • $2CUC, photos $3CUC • To get here, turn off the road to Playa Bibijagua at the small housing scheme of Chacón

The looming bulk of the **Museo Presidio Modelo** lies 2km east of Nueva Gerona. Although this massive former prison has housed a fascinating museum for over thirty years and is now one of the most-visited sights on the island, its forbidding atmosphere has been preserved. Surrounded by guard towers, the classically proportioned governor's mansion and phalanx of wardens' villas mask the four circular cell buildings that rise like witches' cauldrons from the centre of the complex.

Commissioned by the dictator Gerardo Machado, the "Model Prison" was built in 1926 by its future inmates as an exact copy of the equally notorious Joliet Prison in the US. At one time it was considered the definitive example of efficient design, as up to six thousand prisoners could be controlled with a minimum of staff, but it soon became infamous for unprecedented levels of corruption and cruelty. The last prisoner was released in 1967 and the cell blocks have long since slid into decay, serving to increase the sense of foreboding inside.

The cell blocks

Unmanned by museum staff and falling into disrepair, the four huge cylindrical **cell blocks** still feel as oppressive as they must have been when crammed with inmates. The prisoners, housed two or more to a cell, were afforded no privacy, constantly on view through the iron bars. Note the gun slits cut into the grim tower in the dead centre of each block, allowing one guard and his rifle to control nearly a thousand inmates from a position of total safety. To really appreciate the creepy magnitude of the cell blocks, you can take the precarious narrow marble staircase to the fifth-level floor.

The prison museum

Less disturbing than the cell blocks, the **prison museum** is located in the hospital block at the back of the grounds. Knowledgeable Spanish-speaking guides take you around and will expect a small tip. The most memorable part of the museum is the dormitory where **Fidel Castro** and the rebels of the Moncada attack were sequestered on the orders of Batista, for fear of them inflaming the other prisoners with their firebrand ideas. Above each of the 26 beds is the erstwhile occupant's mug shot and a brief biography, while a piece of black cloth on each sheet symbolizes the rags the men tore from their trouser legs to cover their eyes at night, when lights were shone on them constantly as torture.

On February 13, 1954, **Batista** made a state visit to the Presidio Modelo. As he and his entourage passed their window, the rebels broke into a revolutionary anthem. As a result, Castro was confined alone in the room that now opens off the main entrance but was at the time next to the morgue, within full view of the corpses. For the early part of his forty-week sentence he was forbidden any light. Despite the prohibition, a crafty home-made lamp enabled Castro to read from his small library and to perfect the speech he had made at his defence, which was later published by the underground press as *La Historia me Absolverá* and became the manifesto of the cause.

Playa Paraíso

Not far from the Museo Presidio Modelo, a couple of beaches lie an easy bike ride away from town. Around 400m back along the main road towards Nueva Gerona from the signposted turning for the prison is the side road to **Playa Paraíso**. Just over 2km to the north, the beach is popular with locals, who call it "El Mini". The small hoop of rather grubby, seaweed-strewn sand is somewhat redeemed by its friendly atmosphere and a striking hill behind, whose shadow lengthens over the beach in the afternoon.

Playa Bibijagua

Some 4km east along the main road from Museo Presidio Modelo, **Playa Bibijagua** has an attractive grassy approach through the remains of an old hotel that's used exclusively by Cubans. Billed as a black-sand beach, it's actually a mottled brownish colour, the result of marble deposits in the sand. Although not the prettiest beach on the island, the view over a curve of coastline enveloped with pine trees is picturesque, and it has a lively atmosphere. Make sure you bring plenty of insect repellent with you to ward off the vicious sandflies.

La Fe

The island's second-largest town, **La Fe**, also known as **Santa Fe**, is 27km south of Nueva Gerona. Not much more than a handful of streets lined with housing blocks built after the Revolution, it is also the site of some mineral springs, the **Manantial de Santa Rita** (daily 24hr). A natural underground spring surfaces at the northeastern end of town, and you can join the queue of locals filling up their water bottles here from three free-flowing taps, each producing a different mineral water.

La Jungla de Jones

Daily 24hr • $6CUC

Around 3km west from La Fe, along the road that bisects the island, **La Jungla de Jones** botanical garden was home to an impressive collection of trees from all over the world until hurricanes in 2008 almost flattened it completely. A sensitive programme of replanting means that garden looks considerably less raw than at the time of the devastation, but it may take decades before its former beauty is completely restored. Nevertheless, you can still have lunch here and pick your way through the relatively wild and unkempt gardens, crisscrossed by a web of leaf-littered trails.

DIVING OFF THE WEST COAST

All the **diving** on the island is from the Marina Siguanea, but should be booked through the *buro de turismo* (daily 8am–5pm; ☏ 46 39 8181) at the *Hotel Colony*. A five-day SNSI course costs $365CUC and gives you a training day in the swimming pool, plus three dives. If you already have a diving certificate, a single dive costs $36CUC and a night dive $40CUC. There are discounted packages of six and twelve dives also available.

There are over fifty **dive sites** along a 6km strip of coast between Punta Francés and Punta Pedernales, at the western tip off the island's southern coastline, and close to Cayos Los Indios, about 30km out from the hotel, where there are two shipwrecks. The following sites are among the highlights.

El Cabezo de las Isabelitas 5km west of Playa El Francés. This shallow site has plenty of natural light and a cornucopia of fishes, including goatfish, trumpetfish and parrotfish. An uncomplicated dive, ideal for beginners.

Cueva Azul 2km west of Playa El Francés. Reaching depths of 42m, this site takes its name ("the blue cave") from the intensely coloured water. Although there are several notable types of fish to be seen, the principal thrill of this dive is ducking and twisting through the cave's crevices.

Cueva Misteriosa 4km west of Playa El Francés. You'll be provided with a lamp to explore this dark, atmospheric cave where Christmas tree worms, tarpon and a wealth of other fish species take refuge.

Los Indios Wall 5km from Cayos Los Indios. A host of stunning corals, including brain, star, fire and black coral, cling to a sheer wall that drops to the sea bed, while you can see stingrays on the bottom, some as long as 2m. There's a $10CUC supplement for this dive and you need a minimum of five people.

Pared de Coral Negro 4km northwest of Punta Francés. The black coral that gives this dive its name is found at depths of 35m, while the rest of the wall is alive with colourful sponges and brain corals, as well as several species of fish and green moray eels.

Playa Roja

Hotel Colony day-pass $5CUC, includes $3CUC *consumo*, valid from arrival until 5pm

Almost exactly 40km along the road south from Nueva Gerona is **Playa Roja**. Often referred to as Playa El Colony, it's the only decent beach on the west coast, and lies within the grounds of the only hotel in the whole southern half of the island. Built in the 1950s by the Batista regime as a casino hangout for American sophisticates, **Hotel Colony** was abandoned just weeks after its opening when Batista fled the Revolution. You can spend the day here by paying for a **day pass**, but however long you spend at the resort, make sure you come with insect repellent as mosquitoes and sandflies are ever present.

A high proportion of guests here come for the daily diving trips to Punta Francés, which are organized by the **Marina Siguanea** (see box above), 1.5km south of the hotel. Small and strictly functional, the marina is not somewhere to pass the time: there are no services other than the dive facilities and a medical post.

ARRIVAL AND DEPARTURE

PLAYA ROJA

By bus There are currently four public buses from Nueva Gerona to *Hotel Colony* (see box, p.432), at 5.30am, 11am, 2.30pm and 7pm. There is also a workers' bus ferrying hotel staff back and forth, which you can flag down on Calle 41 in Nueva Gerona; the unofficial fare is $3CUC. The best place to wait for any of these buses is opposite the ETECSA Telepunto, on the corner of Calle 41 and Calle 28.

By taxi A taxi from Nueva Gerona to the hotel should cost about $25CUC one-way.

ACCOMMODATION

Hotel Colony ☏ 46 39 8181. The only place to stay with access to Punta Francés (see p.444), this blocky hotel, with its old-fashioned decor, feels a bit dated and has suffered considerable storm damage in the last few years, but there is a reasonable swimming pool and a pleasant strip of palm-studded beach, and the sunset view from here is spectacular. Rooms are split between the main block and separate chalets (not all have sea views), and are generally clean and spacious, though with only basic facilities. **$59CUC**

9

Criadero Cocodrilo

Daily 7am–5pm • $3CUC; bring small bills as keepers rarely have change

South from La Fe, a subtle change begins to come over the terrain as the road opens up, the potholes increase and the prolific fruit groves gradually become marshy thicket. Just past the settlement of Julio Antonio Mella, 12km on, you'll come to a left turn heading to the **Criadero Cocodrilo**. Looking more like a swampy wilderness than a conventional farm, this crocodile nursery is actually, on closer inspection, teeming with reptiles. The large white basins near the entrance form the nursery for a seething mass of 4-month-old, 25cm-long snappers, surprisingly warm and soft to the touch. Nearby, what at first looks like a seed bed reveals itself to be planted with a crop of crocodile eggs that are removed from the female adults once laid, and incubated for around eighty days before hatching. Larger specimens cruise down enclosed waterways choked with lily pads and teeming with birds and butterflies.

The crocodiles are endemic to the area, but were in danger of extinction until the farm's creation. It keeps five hundred crocodiles at any one time, and periodically releases herds of them into the southern wilds when they reach seven years of age, at which point they measure about 1m in length.

The southern protected zone

Although rumours abound concerning the purpose of the military presence in the southern third of the island, its primary function is simply to conserve and restrict access to the **Siguanea nature reserve**. Parts of the reserve are completely closed to the public – you need a pass and a guide to go south of the military checkpoint at **Cayo Piedra** (see box below) – as the luxuriant vegetation of the area shelters such **wildlife** as wild deer, green parrots and the *tocororo*, Cuba's national bird.

The flat land south of the checkpoint conforms to the storybook ideal of a desert island, with caves and sinuous beaches fringing a swampy interior of mangroves and thick shrubs. It's also home to one of the most impressive sights on the island: the **pre-Columbian cave paintings** in Punta del Este, believed to date back some 1100 years, making them among the oldest in the Caribbean. Along with the caves, the most popular reasons for a visit here are the fine sand **beaches** at Punta del Este and **Punta Francés**, on opposite sides of the southern coastline.

Near Punta Francés on the island's western hook is **Cocodrilo**, a tiny hamlet whose pleasant charms are increased by a rugged granite-rock coastline that forms natural pools ideal for snorkelling. Most visitors to the beach at Punta Francés do not approach it by land along the southern coast but by boat from the *Hotel Colony* (see p.441), situated just north of the military border on the west coast. Whichever part of this area you visit, be sure to bring insect repellent with you.

CROSSING THE MILITARY BORDER

To pass the military checkpoint at Cayo Piedra you will need to buy a one-day **pass** and hire the services of a **registered guide** before you set off. The only place to organize this is the Ecotur office in Nueva Gerona (see p.436 for details). A permit and Spanish-, French-, German- or English-speaking guide costs $12CUC per person. As you'll have to make the trip from Nueva Gerona in a rental jeep (the cavernous potholes and long stretches of unpaved road necessitate a 4WD), it's a good idea to find some other people with whom to split the cost. You shouldn't encounter any difficulties at the checkpoint as long as you avail yourself of the necessary documentation – there are usually only one or two guards there to wave you past the checkpoint hut; however, should you arrive at the checkpoint without a guide and pass you will be unceremoniously turned back.

Cuevas de Punta del Este

Within walking distance of the southeast coast, 25km down a dirt track leading east from the checkpoint at Cayo Piedra, the **Cuevas de Punta del Este**, half-buried amid overgrown herbs and greenery, contain significant examples of early pre-Columbian art, pointing to an established culture on the island as early as 900 AD. These paintings are among the few remaining traces of the **Siboney** – among the first inhabitants of Cuba – who arrived from South America via other Caribbean islands between three and four millennia ago; they are thought to have died out shortly after the paintings were made.

The six caves, only two of them accessible, were discovered by accident at the turn of the twentieth century by a north American named Freeman P. Lane, who disembarked on the beach and sought shelter in one of them. The discovery made archeologists reconsider their assumption that Siboney culture was primitive, as the paintings are thought to represent a solar calendar, which would indicate a sophisticated cosmology.

Caves One and Two

On March 22 each year, the sun streams through a natural hole in the roof of **Cave One**, the largest of the group, illuminating the pictographs in a beam of sunlight. Being linked to the vernal equinox, the effect is thought to celebrate fertility and the cycle of life and death. When bones were excavated here in 1939, it became apparent that the caves' function was not only ceremonial – they had also been used for habitation and burial.

Of the 230 pictographs, the most prominent are the tight rows of concentric red-and-black circles overlapping one another on the low ceiling of Cave One. Despite creeping erosion by algae, the fading images are still very visible. Major excavation work got under way in the 1940s, when five more caves were discovered, though the paintings within are in a far worse state of repair and you'll need a keen eye to spot them. Even so, you should take a look at **Cave Two**, 500m away, where more fragments of circles are outshone by the fragile remains of a painted fish.

Playa Punta del Este

Further along the path to the Cuevas de Punta del Este, tufts of undergrowth give way to beach after a surprisingly short distance. The small white-sand strand of **Playa Punta del Este**, sown with sea grass and rimmed by mangroves, is a good spot for a refreshing dip, though it can't compare to the beauty of the other southern beaches to the west.

Playa Larga

Following the road 20km south from the Cayo Piedra checkpoint all the way to the coast, you come to the narrow wedge of sand that comprises **Playa Larga**. Though not really the best spot for a swim, it's a popular place with local fishermen from Cocodrilo, to the west, and the pretty pine-backed stretch of sand is littered with golden-pink conch shells. The beach was the landing site for several Camagüean *balseros* (rafters) intent on emigrating to the US, who arrived here in 1994 after a turbulent journey from the mainland, jubilantly believing themselves to be on North American soil, only to discover that they had not left Cuban territory.

The Carapachibey lighthouse

About 5km west of Playa Larga you can take a quick detour down a pine-lined drive to the **Carapachibey lighthouse**. Although Art Deco-like in its straight-lined simplicity, it wasn't built until 1983. At 63m in height it is supposedly the tallest lighthouse in Latin America and it's worth asking the keeper if you can make the steep climb up 280 steps to enjoy the views over the rocky coastline and turquoise sea; after dark, you can see the lights of Grand Cayman.

9

Cocodrilo

From the lighthouse, a further 20km west on the dusty road takes you to a tiny village called **COCODRILO**. This peaceful haven boasts just a few palm-wood houses and a school in front of a village green that backs onto the sea. Isolated from the north of the island by poor transport and the military checkpoint, it's a fairly rustic community seemingly unaffected by the developments of the twentieth century, albeit healthy and well educated thanks to the Revolution. Originally named Jacksonville, after one of its first families, the hamlet was founded at the beginning of the twentieth century by Cayman Islanders who came here to hunt the large numbers of turtles – now depleted – that once populated the waters and nested along the southern beaches. Some of the village's older residents still speak the English of their forefathers.

At the north end of the hamlet, cupped by a semicircle of rocky cliff, the electric-blue water of a natural **rock pool** is an excellent place to spend a few hours. It's about a 2m drop to the water below, but take care if jumping, as the pool is shallow. If you've brought equipment, it's also worth heading offshore to snorkel among the tiny, darting fish.

Punta Francés

From Cocodrilo a 10km track heads northwest to the island's most remote upturned hook of land, **Punta Francés**, where you'll find the island's top beach, **Playa Francés**. There is over 3km of beach in all, split by a sandy headland into two broad curves of silver, powdery shore ringed on one side by the lush green of a woody, palm-specked thicket and on the other by the glassy, brilliant turquoise of the Caribbean Sea. The deserted tranquillity of this private world is all part of what makes it exceptional, though this is sometimes destroyed by hordes of cruise-ship visitors. Equally attractive is the excellent **diving** offshore (see box, p.441). There is no food and drink available at the beach, as the ranch-house restaurant that once stood here was destroyed by hurricanes, though a couple of small jetties remain. A slightly easier way to get to the beach is to catch a boat from *Hotel Colony* (see p.441). Although you will be in the protected part of the island, you don't need a permit to visit Punta Francés by boat – though you are strictly prohibited from going any further than the beach.

ARRIVAL AND DEPARTURE   PUNTA FRANCÉS

By boat The boat used for diving excursions from the marina at the *Hotel Colony* also acts as a ferry between the hotel and the beach. It leaves from the hotel most days at 9am, returning at around 5pm, and you must book your journey in advance through the hotel itself ($8CUC return for non-diving hotel guests, and $15CUC for non-guests).

LATROBE'S TREASURE

The beach at Punta Francés is named after the French pirate **Latrobe**, who frequented the Ensenada de la Siguanea, on the north side of the land spit. In 1809 he captured two Spanish ships laden with gold and jewels, and made swiftly for the southern coast to hide, rightly deducing that the theft was unlikely to pass unavenged. With just enough time to bury his **treasure**, Latrobe was captured by North Americans and sent to Kingston, Jamaica, where he was promptly executed for piracy.

The whereabouts of the treasure has haunted bounty hunters ever since. The night before his execution Latrobe is supposed to have written a note to his fellow pirate Jean Lafitte, cryptically hinting that the hoard was buried ninety paces "from the mouth of the boiling spring", but Lafitte never received the note and the treasure is still hidden. Though unlikely to be anything more than romantic fancy, legend has it that the booty is buried somewhere on the coast of the Ensenada de la Siguanea.

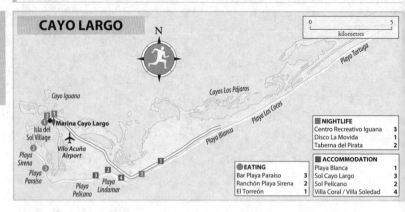

Cayo Largo

Separated from the Isla de la Juventud by 100km of sea, **Cayo Largo**, a narrow, low-lying spit of land fringed with powdery beaches and no permanent local population, is geared entirely to package-holidaymakers. The tiny islet, measuring just 25km from tip to beachy tip, caters to a steady flow of international tourists who flock here to enjoy its excellent watersports, diving and all-inclusive hotels. For a holiday cut adrift from responsibilities and the outside world, this is as good a choice as any. But while Cayo Largo is undoubtedly the stuff of exotic holiday fantasy, it's not a place to meet Cubans. There are no born-and-bred locals and the hotel staff only live on the island in shifts, so though people are as friendly as elsewhere in Cuba, the atmosphere is more than a little contrived.

Development of the cay began in 1977 when the state, capitalizing on its extensive white sands and offshore coral reefs, built the first of the small set of hotels that currently line the western and southern shores. Construction has suffered several setbacks over the last decade as the cay has been ravaged by a series of **hurricanes**, forcing a couple of the smaller hotels to close altogether. Although the cay is being steadily developed, it has a long way to go before being spoilt; indeed, the infrastructure away from the hotels is so sparse that for some the cay won't actually be developed enough, relying too heavily on the hotels themselves for entertainment and eating options. There is a small artificial "**village**" on the west of the island, which has a distinctly spurious air, consisting of just a shop, restaurants, a museum, a bank and, behind the tourist facade, blocks of workers' accommodation. The **interior** is a mixture of grassland, rocky scrub and crops of pine trees, but there is not much to see.

Isla del Sol village

Built on the southwestern coast – to optimize the pleasant view over cay-speckled waters – the artificial **Isla del Sol village** doesn't offer much of a reason to leave the resorts. Among the red-roofed ochre buildings ranged around the small but attractive **Plaza del Pirata** you'll find the obligatory tourist trappings: a shop selling cigars, postcards and sunscreen, plus a bank, museum, restaurant and bar. The main focal point is the **Marina Cayo Largo**, west of the plaza, an area that bustles with activity when motorboats dock to collect or release the sunbathers, snorkellers and divers en route to and from dive sites and beaches. For the rest of the day the village sinks into a somnolence, from which the attractions of the **Casa Museo** and **Turtle Farm** can offer a brief diversion. The museum (daily 9am–6pm; $1CUC) aims to portray Cayo Largo in its historical and biogeographical context, but though some

9

CAYO LARGO DIVING, FISHING AND BOAT EXCURSIONS

With over thirty **dive sites** in the clear and shallow waters around the cay, Cayo Largo is deservedly well known as one of Cuba's best diving areas. Particularly outstanding are the coral gardens to be found in the shallow waters around the islet, while other highlights include underwater encounters with hawksbill and sea-green turtles. The cay's **dive centre** (❶45 24 8214) at the Marina Cayo Largo offers dives for $50CUC, including all equipment and transfer to the site; prices per dive decrease with subsequent dives. Open-water SSI courses take five days and cost $395CUC.

The waters around the cays also make for excellent **fishing**, and the marina offers high-sea expeditions for $325CUC for four hours inclusive of equipment, or $485CUC for eight hours (minimum 2 people). Fly-fishing is also possible and costs $120–160CUC per person for four hours or $240–320CUC for eight hours.

The marina also runs a variety of day-long **excursions** (usually 9am–4pm) to the surrounding cays, including tiny Cayo Iguana, the nearest cay to Cayo Largo (where the eponymous reptiles can be fed by hand), Cayo Rico and the Cayos Pedrazas, 12km from the western tip of Cayo Largo. Most excursions include snorkelling at one of the surrounding coral gardens, a visit to a "natural swimming pool" where the water is only 1m deep, along with a lobster lunch and an open bar. Prices are $69–73CUC.

of the photos of hurricane damage are quite interesting, there is very little here to go on. The farm (daily 7am–noon & 1–6pm; $1CUC), just off the plaza, houses a restless collection of the wild turtles that populate the waters around the archipelago. Although they look healthy enough, their small pens seem a poor exchange for the open sea.

The beaches

There's rather more activity around the beaches to the west of Isla del Sol and along the hotel strip, where warm shallow waters lap the narrow ribbon of pale downy sand. Protected from harsh winds and rough waves by the offshore coral reef, and with over 2km of white sands, **Playa Sirena**, at the western tip of the cay, enjoys a deserved reputation as the most beautiful of all the beaches on Cayo Largo, and is consequently the busiest. This is now where all the beach watersports facilities are based. Further south along the same strand, **Playa Paraíso** is almost as attractive and popular as Sirena, with the added advantage that its shallow waters are ideal for children. Heading east, **Playa Lindamar** is a serviceable 5km curve of sand in front of the *Lindamar, Pelícano, Soledad* and *Coral* hotels and is the place to come if you're looking for some surf and wind.

For real solitude, though, you need to head off up to the eastern beaches. **Playa Blanca**, occupied at its western extremity by the *Hotel Playa Blanca*, boasts over 6km of deserted, soft beach, backed by sand dunes, and staking out your own patch shouldn't be a problem (though you'll need to bring your own refreshments as there's not an ice-cream stand in sight). Further east still, the lovely **Playa los Cocos** is seemingly endless, while far-flung **Playa Tortuga** is similarly deserted.

There are a number of **nudist beaches** on Cayo Largo, though none is officially designated as such. The nudist sections have evolved thanks to a policy of tolerance rather than outright endorsement from the Cuban authorities. Generally they are found at one end or another of each beach, as opposed to right in the middle.

ARRIVAL AND DEPARTURE
CAYO LARGO

By plane All national and international flights to Cayo Largo arrive at the tiny Vilo Acuña airport, 1km from the main belt of hotels; courtesy buses meet every flight and whisk passengers off to their hotels. Direct scheduled international flights to and from Cayo Largo have fluctuated somewhat in recent years. Air Canada and Cubana have operated weekly flights between the island and Montreal, though charter airlines are the more regular link between

9

the Vilo Acuña airport and other international airports, mostly in Canada. All domestic flights are from Havana (2 daily; 40min); note that if you come independently, you will need to book accommodation when you arrange your flight. A quicker option is to take a day-trip from Havana, which you can arrange through a number of the national travel agents (see p.142).

By boat As there is no boat service between the islands, only yacht owners – for whom the clear shallow seas, excellent fishing and serviceable marinas make it a favourite destination – can breeze in by water to the main Marina Cayo Largo on the village coastline. Although only 140km apart, there is no way to get here from Isla de la Juventud.

GETTING AROUND

The island is small enough to negotiate easily, with a single asphalt road linking the airport and the village, just 1km apart, with the hotels. The beaches to the east and west of the hotel strip are accessible via dust tracks running within a few hundred metres of the shore.

By shuttle bus Shuttle buses (free to guests) connect all the hotels with the western beaches, including Playa Sirena, and run three times daily in both directions, with the last departure from the beaches at 5pm.

By ferry A ferry ($5CUC per person) leaves from the marina in the village to Playa Sirena and Playa Paraíso twice daily at 9.30am and 11am, returning at 3pm and 5pm.

By jeep or scooter Jeep and scooter rental ($33CUC/3hr or $52CUC/24hr for jeep; $8CUC/hr or $22CUC/24hr for scooter) is available at the hotels, the latter only available for cash.

By taxi Ok Taxi (☎45 24 8245) charges around $2CUC to go the western beaches from the hotel strip.

INFORMATION

Tourist information Though there is no main tourist office on the cay, you should be able to get all the information you need from the travel agents based at the larger hotels and the hotel staff. The *Sol Pelícano* hotel (see below) has representatives from all three major Cuban travel agents: Cubatur (☎45 24 8258), Havanatur (☎45 24 8215) and Cubanacán (☎45 24 8391).

Websites There are also two informative websites, ⓦ cayolargo.net and ⓦ cayolargodelsur.cu.

Services There's a bank (Mon–Fri 8.30am–noon & 2–3.30pm, Sat & Sun 9am–noon) and a pharmacy (daily except Wed 8am–noon & 1–8pm, Wed 8am–noon & 4–10pm) at the Isla del Sol village.

ACCOMMODATION

Cayo Largo's **hotels** tend to be block-booked by overseas tour operators at a specially discounted rate, but are not cheap if you make your booking in Cuba. If you're not on a package booked from abroad then you'll have to choose your accommodation when you buy your flight in Havana, as flights and pre-booked accommodation in Cayo Largo are sold as a deal by tour operators.

Playa Blanca ☎45 24 8080, ⓦplayablanca.cu. Situated 1km east from the main cluster of hotels, the *Playa Blanca* will suit those seeking a quieter, more private hotel and beach. Rooms are of a high standard and are split between accommodation blocks and prettier two-storey villas dotted around the attractive grounds. There are two restaurants, a very simple pool, and the wooden-floor beach terrace on a rocky ledge is a nice touch. **$170CUC**

Sol Cayo Largo ☎45 24 8260, ⓦmeliacuba.com. An appealing, buzzy, Caribbean-themed hotel with airy rooms painted in tropical colours set around palm trees and rather parched lawns. With an all-inclusive buffet, beach grill and à la carte restaurants, two swimming pools, free non-motorized watersports, a health centre, tennis courts and a football field, this is the biggest and plushest place on the cay, with a clientele of twenty-something couples, families and retirees all mingling happily. **$330CUC**

Sol Pelícano ☎45 24 8333, ⓦmeliacuba.com A family-friendly luxury hotel characterized by mock-colonial architecture and a fetching five-floor lookout tower. There's a dedicated play area and children's entertainment, four all-inclusive restaurants, two swimming pools and bold two- and three-storey villas. **$300CUC**

Villa Coral/Villa Soledad ☎45 24 8111. Two hotels operating as one, with guests able to eat and use the facilities at both properties. The family-oriented *Coral* has pink-and-green accommodation blocks, divided by neat beds of sea shrubs and palms to ensure a sense of privacy. Rooms have spacious balconies and smart sun terraces with shaded seating surrounding a sparkling circular pool. The tiny, accommodation-only *Soledad* has well-kept rooms (some with a sea view) in semi-detached bungalow and eight-room blocks, and a very peaceful ambience. **$120CUC**

EATING, DRINKING AND ENTERTAINMENT

As all-inclusive accommodation packages include meals, few guests eat outside their own hotel. There are some independent **restaurants**, however, and though none are outstanding, all offer tasty fish and seafood dishes in idyllic surrounds. Similarly, the area's **bars** and **clubs** are somewhat generic and lacking in authentic Cuban flavour, but do offer the chance to venture out of the hotel grounds. A good option for a complete change of pace is the Fiesta Marán boat party ($15CUC) which takes place according to demand. Booked through any travel agent, a yacht or catamaran takes you to Playa Sirena, where you remain on board for the open bar and entertainment.

RESTAURANTS AND BEACH BARS

Bar Playa Paraíso Playa Paraíso (no phone). Snacks, cocktails, beers and soft drinks at this simple beach bar on Playa Paraíso. Daily 9am–4pm.

Ranchón Playa Sirena Playa Sirena (no phone). This decent open-air restaurant offers lobster in hot sauce ($20CUC), a lobster and shrimp mixed grill ($20CUC), and several much cheaper meat dishes such as pork loin steak ($8.50CUC). Daily 9am–4pm.

El Torreón Isla del Sol village (no phone). Choose from the tapas selection ($1.50–3.50CUC), which includes tuna bruschetta, tortilla and rolls of Serrano ham and chorizo; or the grilled meat and seafood, like skewered shrimps ($9.50CUC) and filet mignon ($10.90CUC). The grey-stone fortress-like building is rather plain inside. Daily 10am–3pm & 6pm–midnight.

BARS AND CLUBS

Centro Recreativo Iguana (no phone). Next to the *Isla del Sur* hotel, this low-key recreation centre is open until late and provides a snack bar, bowling alley, pool table and karaoke as entertainment. Daily 9am–11pm.

Disco La Movida (no phone). An open-air disco on the edge of the village and the best night spot for mixing it up with Cubans, as this is where the off-duty island staff go to party. Daily 9pm–3am.

Taberna del Pirata Isla del Sol village (no phone). Thatched-roof bar overlooking the picturesque harbour and a good spot to enjoy the cooling sea breezes while the sun sets. Daily 24hrs.

RUMBA AT CALLEJÓN DE HAMEL, CENTRO HABANA

Contexts

History

The strategic and geographical importance of Cuba to the shifting global powers of the last five centuries has dictated much of the Caribbean island's history. Formerly a stepping stone between Spain and its vast American empire, Cuba has struggled to achieve a real and lasting independence ever since, passing from Spanish colony to US satellite and, despite the nationalist Revolution of 1959, relying on economic support from the Soviet Union until the 1990s. At the start of the twenty-first century Cuba is at a crossroads, with its revolutionary, socialist ideals and achievements set firmly against survival in a capitalist global economy.

Pre-Columbian Cuba

Unlike Central America with its great Maya and Aztec civilizations, no advanced societies had emerged in Cuba by the time Columbus arrived in 1492. Although people from ancient cultures – Amerindians who had worked their way up through the Antilles from the South American mainland – had inhabited the island for thousands of years, they lived in simple dwellings and produced comparatively few artefacts and tools. It's estimated that at least one hundred thousend Amerindians were living in Cuba on the eve of the European discovery of the Americas.

The **Guanahatabey** were the first to arrive and were almost certainly living in Cuba by 3000 BC. These primitive hunter-gatherers were based in what is now Pinar del Río, often living in cave systems such as the one in Viñales. The **Siboney** arrived later and lived as fishermen and farmers, but it wasn't until the arrival of the **Taíno**, around 1100 AD, the last of the Amerindian groups to settle in Cuba, that the cultural make-up of the islanders reached a level of significant sophistication. Settling predominantly in the eastern and central regions, they lived in small villages of circular thatched-roof huts known as *bohíos*; grew tobacco, cassava, yucca and cotton; produced pottery; and practised religion. Though there is some evidence to suggest that the Taíno enslaved some of the Siboney or drove them from their home territory, they were a mostly peaceful people, largely unprepared for the conflict they were to face once the Spanish arrived.

The conquest

On October 27, 1492, **Christopher Columbus** landed on the northeastern coast of Cuba, probably in the natural harbour around which the town of Baracoa was later to emerge, though the exact spot where he first dropped anchor is hotly disputed. This first short expedition lasted only seven days, during which time Columbus marvelled at the Cuban landscape, briefly encountered the locals (who fled on seeing the new

3000 BC	2500 BC	1100 AD	1492
Guanahatabey hunter-gatherers settle in Cuba	The Siboney arrive from either modern-day Venezuela or Florida	The Taíno become last Amerindian culture to settle in Cuba	Christopher Columbus disembarks on the northern coast of modern-day Holguín province

HATUEY: THE FIRST CUBAN REBEL

The most legendary Taíno in Cuba was **Hatuey**, a bold chief who, like many others, had been forced to flee from Hispaniola after the Spanish took over the island. He led the most concerted resistance effort against the advancing colonists. The Indians fought fiercely but their initial success was cut short by the Spanish capture of Hatuey. Before burning him at the stake the Spaniards offered him salvation if he would convert to Christianity, an offer met with a flat refusal as Hatuey declared that heaven would be the last place he'd want to spend eternity if it was full of Christians.

arrivals) and left a wooden cross now preserved in the Catedral Nuestra Señora de la Asunción in Baracoa.

Columbus made a second voyage of discovery in 1494 but the first colonial expedition did not begin until late 1509, when **Diego Velázquez** – a rich settler from neighbouring Hispaniola, and the man charged with the mission by the Spanish Crown – landed near Guantánamo Bay with three hundred men. By this time the Amerindians were wary of the possibility of an invasion, word having spread via refugees from already occupied Caribbean islands.

The indigenous population did not last long once the Spanish arrived, and were either slaughtered or enslaved as the conquistadors worked their way west across Cuba. By the end of the sixteenth century, there was almost no trace of the original Cuban population left. Meanwhile, the colonizers had exhausted the small reserves of gold on the island, and interest in Cuba quickly died out as Spain expanded its territories in Central and South America, where there was far greater mineral wealth. However, as Spain consolidated its American empire, Cuba gained importance thanks to its location on the main route to and from Europe, with ports like **Havana** becoming the principal stopping-off points for ships carrying vast quantities of gold, silver and other riches across the Atlantic.

Colonization

By 1515 Velázquez had founded the first towns in Cuba, known as the **seven villas**: Baracoa, Santiago de Cuba, Bayamo, Puerto Príncipe (now Camagüey), Sancti Spíritus, Trinidad and San Cristóbal de la Habana. The population grew slowly, consisting mostly of Spanish immigrants, many from the Canary Islands, but also Italians and Portuguese. Numbers were also increased as early as the 1520s by the importation of African **slaves**, brought in to replace the dwindling indigenous population. Still, by the seventeenth century, Havana, the largest city, had only a few hundred inhabitants.

Agriculture takes hold

Many of the early settlers created huge cattle ranches, but the economy came to be based heavily on more profitable **agricultural farming**. Cassava, tropical fruits, coffee and increasingly tobacco and sugar were among the chief export products on which the colony's trade with Spain depended. As Europe developed its sweet tooth, the Spanish Crown saw its potential selling power: by the early seventeenth century the **sugar** industry had been afforded preferential treatment, subsidized and exempted from duties, and an estimated fifty sugar mills constructed.

1509	1512	1514	1519
Diego Velázquez leads the first Spanish colonization and conquest expedition to Cuba	The Spanish kill Taíno chief Hatuey and establish Cuba's first village, Baracoa	The Spanish complete their conquest of Cuba	Havana is founded at its current location, having been moved from further south

The commercial value of **tobacco**, on the other hand, was more immediate and needed no artificial stimulus. As tobacco farming expanded across the island it served to disperse the population further inland, in part because farmers sought to escape the fiscal grip of the colonial government, whose relatively scarce resources to regulate and tax the crop were concentrated in the towns and whose jurisdiction did not, effectively, apply to the Cuban interior.

Despite these developments the economic and political structure of Cuba remained relatively unchanged throughout the late sixteenth and seventeenth centuries. The island continued to be peripheral to the Spanish Empire and life evolved somewhat haphazardly, with contraband an integral part of the economy, removed from the attentions and concerns of the monarchy in Spain.

The impact of the Bourbons

When, at the beginning of the eighteenth century, the **Bourbon Dynasty** took over the throne in Spain, it sought to regain control of Spanish assets overseas, particularly in the Caribbean. The Bourbons stepped up their monopoly on trade, and in 1717 ordered that all tobacco be sold to commercial agents of the Crown sent from Spain, who added insult to injury by paying artificially low prices. Resentment from the Cuban-born tobacco farmers soon bubbled over into revolt among the growers. The subsequent **uprisings** were easily repressed by the colonial authorities, and even more restrictive measures were introduced in 1740. Discontent increased as profits for Cuban producers dropped, and the lines drawn between the *criollos* (those of Spanish descent but born in Cuba, who tended to be small-scale farmers or members of the emerging educated urban class), and the *peninsulares* (those born in Spain, who made up the ruling elite) became more pronounced.

The first half of the eighteenth century saw Cuban society become more sophisticated, as wealth on the island slowly increased. Advancements in the **cultural character** of Cuba were particularly notable during this era, partly as a result of encouragement from the Bourbons but also as a consequence of an emerging Cuban identity, unique from that of Spain. By the end of the century the colony had established its first printing press, newspaper, theatre and university.

The British occupation of Havana

Economic progress had been severely held back by the restrictive way in which Cuba, and indeed the whole Spanish Empire, was run by the Crown, forcing the colony to trade exclusively with Spain and draining the best part of the wealth away from the island into the hands of the colonial masters. This was to change in 1762 with the **British seizure of Havana**. Engaged in the Seven Years' War against Spain and France, the British sought to weaken the Spanish position by attacking Spain's possessions overseas. With Spanish attention focused in Europe, the British navy prepared a strike on the Cuban capital, control of which would strengthen their own position in the Caribbean and disrupt trade between Spain and its empire. After a six-week siege, Havana fell to the British, who immediately lifted the disabling trade restrictions and opened up new markets in North America and Europe.

Within eleven months Cuba was back in Spanish hands, exchanged with the British for Florida, but the impact of their short stay was enormous. A number of hitherto

1526	1555	1607
African slaves are brought to the island to work on sugar plantations	French corsair Jacques de Sores ransacks Havana in an era of frequent pirate attacks on Cuba's Spanish settlements	Havana is formally established as the capital of Cuba

unobtainable and rarely seen products, including new sugar machinery and consumer goods, flowed into Cuba, brought by traders and merchants who were able to do business on the island for the first time. Cubans were able to sell their own produce to a wider market and at a greater profit and, even in such a short space of time, standards of living rose, particularly in the west where much of the increased commercial activity was focused. So much had changed by the time the Spanish regained control that to revert back to the previous system of tight controls would, the Bourbons realized, provoke fierce discontent among large and powerful sections of the population. Moreover, the new Spanish king, Charles III, was more disposed to progressive reforms than was his predecessor, and the increased output and efficiency of the colony did not pass him by. **Free trade** was therefore allowed to continue, albeit not completely unchecked, transforming the Cuban economy beyond recognition.

The sugar boom

After 1762, sugar's profitability increased with the expansion of trade, causing the industry to begin operating on a much larger scale and marking a significant development in Cuban society. In 1776 the newly independent US was able to start trading directly with Cuban merchants, at the same time that the demand for sugar in Europe and the US increased.

In 1791 **revolution in Haiti** destroyed the sugar industry there and ended French control of one of its most valuable Caribbean possessions. Cuba soon took advantage of this and became the largest producer of sugar in the region. Thousands of French sugar plantation owners and coffee growers fled and settled in Cuba, bringing with them their superior knowledge of sugar production. These developments – combined with scientific advances in the sugar industry and improved transportation routes on the island – transformed the face of Cuban society. With ever-increasing portions of the land taken over for the planting of sugar cane, labour, still the most important component in the production of sugar, was needed on a vast scale. In the 1820s some sixty thousand **slaves** were brought to the island and total numbers during the first half of the nineteenth century reached over 350,000.

Reform versus independence

In the final decade of the eighteenth century and the first few decades of the nineteenth, a number of new cultural and political institutions emerged, alongside new scientific developments, all aimed specifically at improving the lives of Cubans. Though most of these changes affected only a small number of citizens, they formed the roots of a **national identity**, a conception of Cuba as a country with its own culture, its own people and its own needs, separate from those of the Spanish minority ruling class.

Slave rebellions became more common as each decade of the nineteenth century passed, symptomatic of an increasingly divided society, one which pitted *criollos* against *peninsulares*, black against white, and the less developed eastern half of the country against the more economically and politically powerful west. The sugar boom had caused Cuban society to become more stratified, creating sharper lines between the landed elite, who had benefited most from the sugar revolution, and the smaller

1713	1762	1763
The Bourbons assume power in Spain and introduce strict reforms in their colonies, centralizing power in Madrid	The English capture Havana, and occupy the city for eleven months	The English trade Havana for Florida; Spanish control of Cuba resumes

SLAVERY IN CUBA

Early Spanish colonial society was based on the **encomienda** system, whereby land and slaves were distributed to settlers by the authorities. The proportion of slaves in Cuba up until the British occupation of 1762, however, was lower than almost anywhere else in the Caribbean. Most of them worked as servants in the cities and the smaller plantations, resulting in a less impersonal relationship between slave and master. Unlike the English, who allowed their colonies to develop their own independent codes of practice, the Spanish applied the same laws governing slavery in Spain to their territories overseas. Though this did not necessarily mean that the Spanish master fed his slaves any better or punished them less brutally, it did grant slaves a degree of legal status unheard of in other European colonies. Slaves in the Spanish Empire could marry, own property and even buy their freedom, this last right known as *coartación*. By the eighteenth century there was a higher proportion of **free blacks** in Cuba than in any other Caribbean island of comparable size . Nevertheless, the life of a slave, particularly in the countryside, was a miserable existence, and for the Spanish Crown the rights of slaves were incidental at best. Spanish ordinances did as much to perpetuate slavery as they did to allow individual slaves their freedom. Laws were passed banning slaves from riding horses or from travelling long distances without their masters' permission, and preventing women slaves from keeping their children.

As the size of the **slave population** swelled in the late eighteenth and early nineteenth centuries so the conditions of slavery, particularly in the sugar industry, worsened, fuelled by the plantation owners' insatiable appetites for profit. Some slaves in the countryside continued to work on coffee and tobacco farms, but most were involved in sugar production, where **conditions** were harshest. Where before slaves had lived in collections of small huts and even been allowed to work their own small plots of land, now they were crowded into barrack buildings and all available land was turned over to sugar cane. Floggings, beatings and the use of stocks were common forms of **punishment** for even minor insubordinations, and were often used as an incentive to work harder. The whip was in constant use, employed to keep the slaves on the job and to prevent them from falling asleep, most likely during the harvest season, when they could be made to work for eighteen hours of every day for months at a time.

A large proportion of the slaves in Cuba during this period were West African Yoruba, a people with a strong military tradition, who launched frequent and fierce revolts against their oppressors. Uprisings were usually spontaneous, and frequently very violent, often involving the burning and breaking of machinery and the killing of whites. A minority of slave rebellions were highly organized and even involved whites and free blacks.

landowners, petit bourgeoisie and free blacks who had become increasingly marginalized by the dominance of large-scale sugar production.

The American Revolution of 1776 proved to be a precursor to the Wars of Independence that swept across mainland Spanish America during the initial decades of the nineteenth century. However, Cuba's own bid for self-rule was held up, partly by a period of economic prosperity, but also because most *criollos* identified more closely with the Spanish than with the black slave population who, by the start of the nineteenth century, formed a larger part of the total population than in any other colony. *Criollo* calls for reform were tempered by a fear of the slaves gaining any influence or power. The economy in Cuba relied more heavily on slavery than any of the South American states, with the livelihood of *criollos* and *peninsulares* alike dependent on its continued existence.

1790	1796	1812	1837
The first Cuban newspaper, the *Papel Periódico de La Habana*, is established	The steam engine is introduced to Cuba and employed in sugar production	The anti-slavery movement emerges in Cuba	Cuba's first railway begins operating

Nevertheless, a **reformist movement** – albeit fragmented – did emerge. There were calls, predominantly from big businessmen and well-to-do trade merchants, for fiscal reform within Spanish rule; separatists who wanted total independence; and another group still that formed an **annexationist movement** whose goal was to become part of the US, the biggest single market for Cuban sugar. There was growing support for this within the US, too, where it was felt that Cuba held tremendous strategic importance.

With the wealthier *criollos* and the *penínsulares* unwilling to push for all-out independence, the separatist cause was taken up most fervently by *criollos* of modest social origins and by free blacks. Their agenda became not just independence but social justice and, most importantly, the abolition of slavery. As the reformist movement became more radical, Spanish fear of revolution intensified; following slave rebellions in Matanzas and elsewhere in the country in the early 1840s, the colonial government reacted with a brutal campaign of repression known as **La Escalera** (the ladder), which involved tying those accused of conspiracy to a ladder and whipping him. In an atmosphere of hysteria fuelled by the fear that a nationwide slave uprising was imminent, the Spanish authorities killed hundreds of enslaved and free black suspects and arrested thousands more. At the same time, the military presence on the island grew as soldiers were sent over from Spain, and the governor's power was increased to allow repression of even the slightest sign of rebellion. The reform movement and the abolition of slavery became inextricably linked, and this fusion of ideas was embraced by reformers themselves. In 1865 the **Partido Reformista** (Reformist Party) was founded by a group of *criollo* planters, providing the most coherent expression yet of the desire for change. Among their demands were a call for Cuban representation in the Spanish parliament and equal legal status for *criollos* and *penínsulares*.

The Ten Years' War

The life of the Reformist Party proved to be a short one. Having failed to obtain a single concession from the Spanish government, it dissolved in 1867, while the reform movement as a whole suffered further blows as a new reactionary Spanish government issued a wave of repressive measures, including banning political meetings and censoring the press. Meanwhile, pro-independence groups were gaining momentum in the east, where the proportion of *criollos* to *penínsulares* was twice that in the west.

From 1866 onwards, a group of landowners, headed by **Carlos Manuel de Céspedes**, began to plot a revolution; but it had got no further than the planning stage when the colonial authorities learned of it and sent troops to arrest the conspirators. Pre-empting his own arrest on October 10, 1868, Céspedes freed the slaves working at his sugar mill, La Demajagua, near Manzanillo, effectively instigating the **Ten Years' War**, the first Cuban War of Independence. The size of the revolutionary force grew quickly as other landowners freed their slaves, and soon numbered around 1500 men. Bayamo was the first city to fall to the rebels and briefly became the headquarters of a revolutionary government. Their manifesto included promises of free trade, universal male suffrage (though this meant whites only) and the "gradual" abolition of slavery.

Support for the cause spread quickly across eastern and central parts of the country, as two of the great heroes of the Wars of Independence, the mulatto **Antonio Maceo** and

1868	1878	1886	1895
The First War of Independence begins	The Pact of Zanjón ends the First War of Independence	Slavery is abolished	The Second War of Independence commences; José Martí is killed in combat

the Dominican **Máximo Gómez**, emerged as military leaders. A much smaller insurgency movement emerged in the west, where, on the whole, the landowners remained on the side of the colonial authorities. In Havana, a teenaged **José Martí** (see p.109) was arrested and exiled after challenging Spanish rule in the newspaper Patria Libre. Then, in 1874, Céspedes was killed in battle and the revolutionary movement began to flounder, becoming increasingly fragmented as divisions between *criollos* and the peasants and ex-slaves who fought on the same side fermented distrust.

Seizing on this instability, the Spanish offered what appeared to be a compromise. The **Pact of Zanjón** was signed on February 10, 1878, and included a number of concessions on the part of the Spanish, such as increased political representation for the *criollos*. However, sections of the rebel army, led by Maceo, refused to accept the pact, asserting that none of the original demands of the rebels had been met. In 1879 this small group of rebels reignited the conflict in what became known as the **Guerra Chiquita**, the Small War. It petered out by 1880, and Maceo (along with José Martí and others) was forced into exile.

The Second War of Independence

Over the course of the next fifteen years, the reformists – among them ex-rebels – became increasingly dismayed by the Spanish government's failure to fulfil the promises made at Zanjón. Though the first phase of the **abolition of slavery** in 1880 seemed to suggest that genuine changes had been achieved, this development proved to be something of a false dawn. Slavery was replaced with the apprentice system, whereby ex-slaves were forced to work for their former owners, albeit for a small wage. It was not until 1886 that slavery was entirely abolished, while in 1890, when universal suffrage was declared in Spain, Cuba was excluded.

These years saw the independence movement build strength from outside Cuba, particularly in the US. From his base in New York, Martí worked tirelessly, visiting various Latin American countries trying to gain momentum for the idea of an independent Cuba, appealing to notions of Latin American solidarity. In 1892 he founded the **Partido Revolucionario Cubano**, or Cuban Revolutionary Party (PRC), aiming to unite the disjointed exile community and the divided independence movement on the island.

On February 24, 1895, small groups in contact with the PRC mounted armed insurrections across Cuba, beginning the **Second War of Independence**. Then, on April 1, Maceo landed in Oriente, followed a fortnight later by Martí and Gómez, who mobilized a liberation force of around six thousand Cubans. In May of the same year at Dos Ríos, Martí was killed in his first battle. Undeterred, the revolutionaries fought their way across the country; by 1897, almost the entire country save for a few heavily garrisoned towns and cities was under rebel control.

Riots in Havana gave the US the excuse they had been waiting for to send in the warship **Maine**, ostensibly to protect US citizens in the Cuban capital. On February 15, 1898, the *Maine* blew up in Havana harbour, killing 258 people; the US accused the Spanish of sabotage and so began the **Spanish–American War**. Whether the US blew up its own ship in order to justify its intervention in the War of Independence has been disputed ever since, but whatever the true cause of the explosion, it was the pretext the

1898	1899	1901
The scuppering of the US battleship *Maine* in Havana harbour triggers the start of the Spanish–American War	Spain signs the Treaty of Paris and officially relinquishes control of Cuba; the US begins its military occupation	The Cuban Constitution is ratified, but includes the Platt Amendment

US needed to enter the war. Many Cuban nationalists, believing that victory was already in their grasp, were hostile to US involvement and suspicious of its intentions, fearing an imperial-style takeover. Attempting to allay these fears, the US prepared the **Teller Amendment**, declaring that they did not intend to exercise any political power in Cuba once the war was over, their sole aim being to free the country from the colonial grip of Spain. Despite these promises, when the **Spanish surrendered** on July 17, 1898, Cuban troops were prevented by US forces from entering Santiago, where the victory ceremony took place.

The pseudo-republic

On December 10, 1898, the Spanish signed the **Treaty of Paris**, thereby handing control of Cuba, as well as Puerto Rico and the Philippines, to the US. Political power on the island lay in the hands of **General John Brooke**, who maintained a strong military force in Cuba while the US government decided what to do with the island they had coveted for so long. The voices of protest in Cuba were loud and numerous enough to convince them that annexation would be a mistake, so they opted for the next best alternative. In 1901 Cuba adopted a new constitution, devised in Washington without any Cuban consultation, which included the **Platt Amendment**, declaring that the US had the right to intervene in Cuban affairs should the independence of the country come under threat – an eventuality open to endless interpretation. The intention to keep Cuba on a short leash was made even clearer when, at the same time, a **US naval base** was established at Guantánamo Bay. On May 20, 1902, under these terms, Cuba was declared a **republic** and Tomás Estrada Palma became the first elected Cuban president.

With the economy in ruins following the war, **US investors** were able to buy up large stakes of land and business relatively cheaply. Soon three-quarters of the sugar industry was controlled by US interests, and few branches of the economy lay exclusively in Cuban hands as the North Americans invested in cigar factories, railroads, the telephone system, electricity, tourism and other industries.

The Machado era and the Depression

The first two decades of the pseudo-republic saw four corrupt Cuban presidents come and go and the US intervene on a number of occasions, either installing a governor or sending in troops. In 1925 **Gerardo Machado** was elected on the back of a series of promises he had made to clean up government. Though initially successful – he was particularly popular for his defiance of US involvement in Cuban politics – his refusal to tolerate any opposition wrecked any legitimate effort he may have made to improve the running of the country. In 1925, strikes by sugar mill and railroad workers led by **Julio Antonio Mella**, founder of the **Partido Comunista Cubano** (Cuban Communist Party), led to the assassinations of a host of political leaders. In 1928 Machado changed the constitution, extending his term in office and effectively establishing a dictatorship.

The **global economic crisis** that followed the Wall Street Crash in 1929 caused more widespread discontent, and opposition became increasingly radical. Machado ruthlessly set about trying to wipe out all opposition in a bloody and repressive

1902	1903	1906
Tomás Estrada Palma becomes the first President of the new Republic of Cuba	The lease giving the US control over Guantánamo Bay naval base is signed	US military intervention in Cuba reinstated in line with the Platt Amendment, and lasts three years

campaign. Fearing a loss of influence, the US sent in an ambassador, **Sumner Welles**, with instructions to get rid of Machado and prevent a popular uprising. As Welles set about negotiating a withdrawal of the Machado administration, a general strike across the country in late 1933, together with the loss of the army's support, which had long played an active role in informal Cuban politics, convinced the dictator that remaining in power was futile and he fled the country. Amid the chaos that followed emerged a man who was to profoundly shape the destiny of Cuba over the following decades.

The rise of Fulgencio Batista

A provisional government led by Carlos Manuel de Céspedes y Quesada filled the political vacuum left by Machado, but lasted only a few weeks. Meanwhile, a young sergeant, **Fulgencio Batista**, staged a coup within the army and replaced most of the officers with men loyal to him. Using his powerful military position he installed **Ramón Grau San Martín** as president, who went on to attempt to nationalize electricity, which was owned by a US company, and introduce progressive reforms for workers. This was too much for US President Franklin Roosevelt, who accused Grau of being a communist and refused to recognize his regime. Not wanting to antagonize the US, Batista deposed Grau and replaced him in January 1934 with **Carlos Mendieta**. Batista then continued to prop up a series of Cuban presidents until in 1940 he was himself elected.

Some of Batista's policies during his earlier years of power were met with widespread support and, despite the backing he received from the US, he was no puppet. In 1934 he presided over the dissolution of the Platt Amendment, which was replaced with a new agreement endowing Cuba with an unprecedented degree of real independence. In a move designed to harmonize some of the political groupings in Cuba and appease past opponents, in 1937 Batista released all political prisoners, while using the army to institute **health and education programmes** in the countryside and among the urban poor. By the time he lost power in 1944, ironically to Ramón Grau, Cuba was a more independent and socially just country than it had been at any other time during the pseudo-republic.

Grau showed none of the reformist tendencies that he had demonstrated during his previous short term in office and was replaced in 1948, after proving himself no less corrupt than any of his predecessors. **Carlos Prío Socarrás**, under whom very little changed, led the country until 1952 when Batista, who had left the country after his defeat in 1944, returned to fight another election. Two days before the election was to take place, Batista, fearing failure, staged a **military coup** on March 10 and seized control of the country. He subsequently abolished the constitution and went on to establish a dictatorship bearing little – if any – resemblance to his previous term as Cuban leader. Fronting a regime characterized principally by violent **repression**, **corruption** and self-indulgent **decadence**, Batista seemed to have lost any zeal he once had for social change and improvement. Organized crime became ingrained in Cuban life, particularly in Havana, where notorious American gangster Meyer Lansky controlled much of the gambling industry. During these years living conditions for the average Cuban worsened as investment in social welfare decreased.

1924	1929	1933
Gerardo Machado begins his first presidential term	Having altered the constitution, Machado begins a second term, his presidency effectively becoming a dictatorship	Machado's dictatorship is overthrown, Fulgencio Batista leads a military revolt and Ramón Grau takes up the presidency

Fidel Castro and the revolutionary movement

Among the candidates for congress in the 1952 election was **Fidel Castro**, a young lawyer who had seen his political ambitions dashed when Batista seized power for himself. Effectively frozen out of constitutional politics by Batista's intolerance of organized opposition, Castro and around 125 others, a year after the military coup, on July 26, 1953, attacked an army barracks at **Moncada** in Santiago de Cuba in a bid to topple the regime. Castro regarded the attack "as a gesture which will set an example for the people of Cuba". The attack failed miserably and those who weren't shot fled into the mountains, where they were soon caught. Castro would certainly have been shot had his captors taken him back to the barracks, but a sympathetic police sergeant kept him in the relative safety of the police jail. A trial followed in which Castro defended himself and, in his summing-up, uttered the now immortal words, "Condemn me if you will. History will absolve me." He was sentenced to fifteen years' imprisonment but had served fewer than three when Batista, feeling confident and complacent, released him, along with the other rebels, and he went into **exile**.

Now based in Mexico, Castro set about organizing a revolutionary force to take back to Cuba; among his recruits was an Argentinean doctor named **Ernesto "Che" Guevara**. They called themselves the **Movimiento 26 de Julio**, the 26th of July Movement (often shortened to **M-26-7**), after the date of the attack at Moncada. In late November 1956 Castro, Guevara and around eighty other revolutionaries set sail for Cuba in a large yacht called the *Granma*. Landing in the east at Playa Coloradas, in what is today Granma province, they were immediately attacked and suffered heavy casualties, but the dozen or so who survived headed directly for the Sierra Maestra, where they wasted no time in building up support for the cause among the local peasantry and enlisting new recruits into their army. Waging a war based on **guerrilla tactics**, the rebels were able to gain the upper hand against Batista's larger and better-equipped forces.

As the war was being fought out in the countryside, the base of support for the Revolution grew wider and wider, and an insurrectionary movement already established in the cities began a campaign of sabotage aimed at disabling the state apparatus. By the end of 1958, the majority of Cubans had sided with the rebels and the ranks of the revolutionary army had swelled. The US, sensing they were backing a lost cause, had withdrawn military support for Batista, and there were **revolts**

CUBA BEFORE CASTRO

On the eve of the Revolution, Cuba was among the most **prosperous** Latin American countries. Culturally and economically it had become intricately tied to the US, importing most of its manufactured goods from across the Florida Straits, including cars, clothes and electrical equipment – even the telephone system was North American – while the US benefited from cheap sugar, the reward for massive investment in the agricultural industry. The American **Mafia** had also gained a strong foothold in the country, predominantly in Havana, where it controlled much of the tourist industry, including the cabarets, casinos and many of the hotels. The capital was also home to a significant sized middle class. Outside the cities, however, the rural population lived in abject **poverty**, with no running water, electricity, health care or education, and hunger was not uncommon. Peasant wages were desperately low and those working on sugar farms would only draw a wage for a few months of seasonal work a year.

1934	**1940**	**1944**
Batista deposes Grau and appoints Carlos Mendieta as president	A new constitution is drafted and Batista becomes president	Ramón Grau is elected president

within the army. Realizing that he no longer exercised any authority, on January 1, 1959, Batista escaped on a plane bound for the Dominican Republic. The army almost immediately surrendered to the rebels, and Fidel Castro, who had been fighting in the east, began a **victory march** across the country, arriving in Havana seven days later on January 8, 1959.

The Cuban Revolution: the first decade

Though the Revolutionary War ended in 1959, this date marks only the beginning of what in Cuba is referred to as the Revolution. The new government appointed as its president Manuel Urrutia, but the real power lay in the hands of Fidel Castro, who, within a few months of the revolutionary triumph, took over as prime minister.

Early reforms

Fidel Castro's new government began to implement a vast programme of social and political transformation, passing more than 1500 laws in its first year. This tidal wave of change was felt most keenly in the countryside, with the intellectual and economic empowerment of rural peasants at the heart of the Revolution's objectives. The first **Agrarian Reform Law** of May 1959 established the **Agrarian Reform Institute** (INRA), which soon became a kind of government for the countryside, administering most of the rural reform programmes, including new health and educational facilities, housing developments and road construction, as well as redistribution of much of the land into the hands of the rural population and the state. By 1961 over forty percent of Cuba's farmland had been expropriated and reorganized along these lines. In 1962, in a push to eradicate **illiteracy**, the government sent more than 250,000 teachers, volunteers and schoolchildren into the countryside to teach reading and writing to the peasants. By the end of 1962 illiteracy had been slashed from 23.6 percent to 3.9 percent.

Free education for all was another key revolutionary objective, as private schools were nationalized and education until the sixth grade made compulsory, with a new programme of learning based on anti-imperialist Marxist ideology implemented. Universities proliferated, as numbers of teachers and schools multiplied. **Health**, too, saw great gains in the early years of the Revolution. A free national health service was created, and new hospitals and health centres were built, most notably in rural areas where institutional healthcare had been all but nonexistent. A new emphasis was put on preventive medicine and care in the community, while there was also investment in medical research.

Opposition and emigration

While these very real gains for large sections of the Cuban population ensured continued popular support for the new regime, not everyone was happy, and the Revolution was not without its victims in these early years. Many of those who had served under Batista, from government officials to army officers, were tried, and – with little regard for their legal rights – executed, sometimes for ideological crimes. Many moderates and liberals became increasingly **disillusioned** and isolated from the political process. Under Castro, the government had little sympathy for the constitutional framework in which the liberals felt it must operate and, appealing to what it regarded

1952	**1953**	**1956**
Batista seizes the presidency by means of a military coup	Fidel Castro and a band of rebels attack the Moncada military barracks in a failed attempt to start a revolution	Castro and 82 others disembark from the yacht *Granma* in eastern Cuba to begin a guerrilla war against Batista's regime

as the higher ideals of social justice and the interests of the collective over the individual, swept much of the legal machinery aside in its drive to eliminate opponents of the Revolution and carry out reforms. As the decade wore on, the regime became increasingly intolerant of dissenting voices, which were characterized as counter-revolutionary. By the end of the 1960s there are estimated to have been over twenty thousand **political prisoners** in Cuban jails. Gays, whose sexuality was deemed to be a product of capitalist society, were also persecuted throughout the 1960s and 1970s, with many homosexuals imprisoned and placed on "reform" programmes.

For the first few years after the rebel triumph, as Cuban-US relations soured and the Revolution radicalized, swathes of the upper and middle classes – among them landowners, doctors, lawyers and other professionals – sought refuge overseas, predominantly in the US. Between 1960 and 1962 around 200,000 **emigrants**, most of them white, left Cuba, forming large exile communities, especially in **Miami**, and setting up powerful anti-Castro organizations, intent on overthrowing Castro and returning to Cuba.

Cuba enters the Cold War

As huge sectors of Cuban industry, much of it US-owned, were **nationalized**, Washington retaliated by freezing all purchases of Cuban sugar, restricting exports to the island and then, in 1961, breaking off diplomatic relations. Counter-revolutionary forces within Cuba, some mounting terrorist campaigns in the cities, received US backing. Then, with the blessing and backing of President John F. Kennedy, an invasion was prepared. On April 17, 1961, a military force of Cuban exiles, trained and equipped in the US, landed at the **Bay of Pigs** in southern Matanzas. The revolutionaries were ready for them and the whole operation ended in failure within 72 hours (see box, p.231).

It was not until December 1961 that Fidel Castro declared himself a **Marxist–Leninist**. Whether opportunistic or, as Castro himself declared, a statement of beliefs he had always held, there was no doubt whose support he coveted at the time of his declaration, and the **Soviet Union** was only too happy to enter a pact with a close neighbour of its bitter Cold War adversary. The Soviets agreed to buy Cuban sugar at artificially high prices while selling them petroleum at well below its market value. Then, in 1962, on Castro's request, the Soviets installed over forty **missiles** on the island. Angered by this belligerent move, Kennedy declared an embargo on any military weapons entering Cuba. Soviet Premier **Nikita Khrushchev** ignored it, and Soviet ships loaded with more weapons made their way across the Atlantic. Neither side appeared to be backing down and nuclear weapons were prepared for launch in the US. A six-day stalemate followed, after which a deal was finally struck and the world breathed a collective sigh of relief – the **Cuban Missile Crisis** had passed. Khrushchev agreed to withdraw Soviet weapons from Cuba on the condition that the US would not invade the island. This triggered the tightening of the trade embargo by the US.

Economic policy in the 1960s

Reducing Cuba's dependence on sugar production was one of the central **economic policies** of the new Cuban government, and efforts were made to expand and diversify industry. However, at times revolutionary ideals outweighed realistic policy and

1959	1961
The revolutionary war is won on January 1, Batista having fled the country on New Year's Eve	A counter-revolutionary contingent attack Castro's forces at the Bay of Pigs and are defeated in 72 hours; the US declare a trade embargo on Cuba

THE POLITICS OF A ONE-PARTY STATE

Though it had several predecessors, the **Partido Comunista Cubano** or Cuban Communist Party (PCC) – the only political party in post-Revolution Cuba – was not founded until 1965, six years after Fidel Castro's victory, and did not hold its first Congress until 1975. The following year a new constitution was drawn up and approved. Castro's position as head of state became constitutionalized, thus doing away with the last vestiges of democracy. Attempts were made, on the other hand, to decentralize power by introducing an extensive system of **local government**. However, as agents of central government these local assemblies had little or no real independence.

Countless **mass organizations** provide, in theory, further avenues for grievances and the raising of issues. Widespread membership of the Committees for the Defence of the Revolution (CDR), the Union of Young Communists (UJC) and the Federation of Cuban Women (FMC), amongst other bodies, is portrayed by the government as an expression of popular support for the Revolution and its ideals. Local branches of these organizations hear local grievances and representatives pass them up to elected members at the legislative assembly. They also spearhead local campaigns, like organizing blood donation, arranging street parties and rounding up local truants. For detractors of the government, however, these organizations are the watchdogs of the regime, ensuring that at every level people are behaving as good citizens.

planning. The **mass exodus of professionals** during the early years of the decade made the transition from an essentially monocultural capitalist economy to a more diverse, industrialized yet highly centralized one extremely problematic. Until more were trained, there were simply not enough workers with the skills and experience necessary to realize such ambitious plans. Furthermore, the impact of the US embargo had been severely underestimated: the Americans had supplied machinery, raw materials and manufactured goods easily, quickly and inexpensively and, despite subsidies from the Soviet Union, the greater distances involved and less sophisticated economy of Cuba's new suppliers could not fill the hole. Following a significant drop in agricultural output, **rationing** was introduced in 1962. Attempts to produce the type of industrial goods and machinery that had previously been imported had largely failed and, following Castro's visit to the Soviet Union in 1964, during which the Russians promised to purchase 24 million tons of sugar over the next five years, the focus for the economy shifted back to **sugar**. Ambitious targets were set for each harvest, none more so than in 1970, when Castro declared that Cuba would produce ten million tons of sugar. This blind optimism was to prove disastrous, as the impossible production targets were not met, while other areas of the economy suffered from neglect and under-investment, leaving Cuba even more dependent on sugar than it had been prior to the Revolution.

Shifting sands: the 1970s and 1980s

The 1970s saw a complete reappraisal of **economic policy** and planning. A more realistic programme replaced the heady idealism of the 1960s, striking a more even balance between the role of the state, which still controlled heavy industry and the

1962	1965	1967	1976
The US and Soviet Union are brought to the brink of nuclear conflict in the Cuban Missile Crisis	The Cuban Communist Party (PCC) is created	Che Guevara is killed in Bolivia	The socialist Cuban Constitution is promulgated

THE MARIEL BOATLIFT

In March 1980, several Cubans rammed the gates of the Peruvian embassy in Havana seeking asylum. With the Peruvian authorities reluctant to hand over the perpetrators, Castro promptly removed police protection from the grounds and within 48 hours over 10,000 **asylum seekers** had crammed themselves inside the gates. Responding to this obvious build-up of tension, and seeking to rid the island of potential agitators, Castro announced that the port at Mariel bay, 25km west of Havana, would be open to anyone who wished to leave for the US. In what became known as the **Mariel Boatlift**, hundreds of small vessels crossed the straits from Miami to fetch waiting Cubans. Ever the opportunist, Castro seized on the exodus to rid Cuba of large numbers of its criminals and mental patients, releasing them from prisons and institutions to swell the ranks of exiles. Some 125,000 Cubans fled the island between April and October of 1980; the Carter administration and Castro finally agreed to end the exodus on October 31, 1980.

major pillars of the economy, and the private sector, which was expanded. With rises in the price of sugar on the world market in the first half of the decade and increased Soviet assistance, there were tangible advances in the country's economic performance. The policy changes were carried on into the next decade as the economy continued to make modest improvements.

As more private enterprise was permitted, Castro became alarmed at the number of people giving up their state jobs, and concluded that he had made a mistake. In 1986 he issued his **Rectification of Errors and Negative Tendencies** and the economy returned to centralization. With increasing sums being ploughed into defence, the economy survived only through heavy Soviet support.

The Special Period: the 1990s

The **collapse of the Soviet bloc** and subsequently the Soviet Union itself between 1989 and 1991 led to a loss of over eighty percent of Cuba's trade. In 1990, as the country stumbled into an era of extreme shortages, Fidel Castro declared, euphemistically, the beginning of the **Special Period in Times of Peace**, usually referred to simply as the Special Period (*Periodo Especial*). Food rationing became stricter, timed power cuts frequent and public transport deteriorated dramatically as the country lost almost all of its fuel imports. At the risk of undermining the Revolution's ideological basis, in August 1993, the **US dollar** was declared legal tender and the floodgates to investment from international companies were opened, most notably in the tourist and mining industries. All but the most basic products and services were sold in dollars, as the state to acquired hard currency through restaurants, hotels, supermarkets and other dollar stores. Small-scale **private enterprise** was also legalized as the face of modern-day Cuba began to take shape. Private farmers' markets became the norm, small home-based restaurants known as paladars emerged, and house owners began renting out their bedrooms to tourists.

Seizing on this moment of weakness, the US government tightened up the trade embargo even further in 1992. Thousands of Cubans risked their lives trying to escape the country across the Florida Straits in makeshift craft, and the Cuban exile

1980	1989	1990
Castro opens the port at Mariel to anyone wanting to leave the country; an exodus of 125,000 Cubans follows	The Soviet Union scales back its trade with Cuba and reduces its subsidies to the country	Castro announces a series of austerity measures as part of the Special Period

community in Miami, by now consisting of a number of well-organized and powerful political groups, rubbed its hands with glee, anticipating the imminent collapse of the Revolution and the fall of Fidel Castro.

Tales of survival from the era are by turns grotesque, comic and heroic. While stories of vendors replacing pizza cheese with melted condoms and CDR meetings called with the express purpose of ordering people to stop dining on the neighbourhood cats and dogs may be urban myths, they nonetheless represent the very desperate living conditions during the Special Period.

Emerging from crisis

As Cuba entered the new millennium it appeared to have weathered the worst of the economic storm that threatened to destroy the regime in the 1990s. However, chronic **shortages** of basic foodstuffs, household goods and medicines remained, while the advent of private enterprise allowed more distinct class-based divisions to creep back into society, still apparent today. But new **international allies** emerged, most notably Venezuela and, as left-wing governments came into power all over South and Central America, other Latin American states including Bolivia, Ecuador and Nicaragua, all now diplomatically and politically closer to Cuba than they are to the US. The special relationship with Venezuela has brought increased investment and aid, crucially in the supply of oil to the island, and the last decade has seen a significant increase in investment from Canada, Brazil, India and especially China. The latter is now Cuba's second-largest trading partner after Venezuela and has invested over US$1 billion in Cuba's nickel industry, as well as substantial amounts in tourism and public transport.

RACE RELATIONS IN CUBA

At the onset of the Revolution in 1959, Fidel Castro declared that he would eradicate racial discrimination, establishing the unacceptability of **racism** as one of the core tenets of the Revolution. He carried through his promise with legislation that threw open doors to previously white-only country clubs, beaches, hotels and universities and, more importantly, established equality in the workplace.

However, the question of race in Cuba is still a problematic issue. Official statistics put the **racial mix** at 66 percent white (of Hispanic descent), 12 percent black, 21.9 percent mulatto (mixed-race between Hispanic and black) and 0.1 percent Asian. There is, however, an obvious disparity between figures and facts, and the claims by some that as much as 70 percent of the population have some trace of black heritage seem to be closer to the truth. Some critics of the official figures claim they are a way of downplaying the importance of the black heritage.

Although institutional racism has been somewhat lessened, its existence is still apparent in the lack of black people holding the highest positions across the professional spectrum. A more recent dimension in the race question has arisen from the tourist trade. *Jineteros* and *jineteras* (hustlers, escort girls and prostitutes) are nationally perceived as exclusively Afro-Cuban, and this in turn has led to the stereotype of wealthy Afro-Cubans as prostitutes, pimps and touts, while white Cubans with money are generally assumed to be supported by relatives in Miami.

1996	1998	2006
The US trade embargo on Cuba is tightened under the terms of the Helms-Burton Law	Pope John Paul II visits Cuba	Fidel Castro is taken seriously ill and his brother Raúl assumes temporary presidential responsibilities

Raúl Castro and the new Cuba

In July 2006, with Fidel Castro convalescing after intestinal surgery, his younger brother **Raúl Castro** took over his responsibilities; in February 2008, having acted as president for eighteen months, he formally took over the presidency. In charge of the military since 1959, Raúl had a reputation as a ruthless military mastermind, a dour man compared with his charismatic older brother, portrayed as a contradictory mixture of hardliner and pragmatist. However, Raúl's presidency has been characterized as much as anything by limited but significant **reforms** that have reduced centralization and bureaucracy and increased the roles and freedoms of the private sector. Very early on in his presidency, restrictions were lifted on the private purchase of electrical consumer goods, including computers, DVD players and mobile phones. Farmers have been allowed to cultivate unused state-owned land for personal profit, but more importantly to increase productivity. Cubans can now buy and sell houses, and no longer need state permission to leave the country, just a passport.

In September 2010 Raúl Castro and his government announced the biggest **reduction to the size of the state** since the Revolution, determining that one million state-sector jobs would be cut. The process is proving to be a slow one and is still in progress, but the effects remain tangible all over Cuba. Many industries, particularly small-scale businesses, have been turned over to the private sector, turning bosses and managers into owners overnight. Hairdressers, driving instructors, art restorers and other small workplaces are now legitimate private businesses. Workers have been encouraged to set up their own businesses in one of the many professions now given legal status in the private sector, from travel agents and roofers to manicurists and carpenters, and Cubans can now employ other Cubans who are not their relatives for the first time since the Revolution.

Fundamental questions remain, not least over the **lack of social and political freedom**. With little opportunity to demonstrate or organize political opposition, widespread feelings of powerlessness and disenfranchisement remain ever-present. Cuban jails still hold **political prisoners** captive, use of the internet remains constrained and the country's small but vociferous community of bloggers, who have criticised the government in their posts, have encountered intimidation and harassment from the police and security forces. Nevertheless, the internal collapse gleefully predicted by right-wing pundits since the fall of the Soviet bloc is looking less likely than at any time in the last twenty years. There is a tangible sense of positive change in the country, as the government continues its balancing act, "updating socialism", as Raúl Castro puts it, and leading Cuba into the next phase of its incredible story.

2008	**2012**	**2013**
Raúl Castro officially becomes Cuban president and embarks on a series of liberalizing economic reforms	In October, Hurricane Sandy hits eastern Cuba; eleven people lose their lives, and 200,000 buildings are damaged	Raúl Castro declares he will stand down at the end of his second term in 2018

Cuban music and musicians

Cuba is the musical powerhouse of Latin America, the birthplace of a multitude of influential musical styles – from rumba and son to mambo and chachachá. The staggering success of the Buena Vista Social Club reminded the world of this rich musical heritage, but Cuban musical influence stretches beyond these traditional homegrown styles, with claims to roles in the history of American jazz, African rumba, Spanish and Latin American folk music and most recently Caribbean reggaeton.

The origins of most traditional Cuban musical styles are found in the east of the country, particularly in and around Santiago de Cuba, though Havana can also claim to have given birth to a number of influential music genres, and Matanzas has its own significant musical claims to fame too.

Rumba

Not to be confused with the rumba of ballroom dancing, the frenetic rhythms and dances of Cuban **rumba** are the closest contemporary Cuban music has to a direct link with the music brought to the island by African slaves. A raw music driven by drums and vocals, it emerged from the docks and sugar mills in Havana and Matanzas in the late nineteenth century. Black workers developed songs and dances by playing rhythms on cargo boxes and packing cases. Once the music became more popular, these rudimentary instruments were subsequently replaced with conga drums of several different sizes and tones along with two different kinds of wooden sticks (*claves* and *palitos*), a metal shaker (*maruga*) and specially manufactured boxes (*cajones*).

Rumba is very distinct and can sound like a cacophony of rhythm to the uninitiated, making it perhaps one of the less accessible musical styles to the foreign ear, with so many percussive elements and an absence of brass, string or wind instruments. On the other hand, rumba performances are engaging and energetic and the vocal sections, involving a leader and a responder, can be quite hypnotic. Improvisation is an integral part of the art of rumba, as is call-and-response, while the dance calls on its performers to display explosive levels of energy.

Modern rumba divides into three main dances. The **guaguancó** is a dance for a couple in a game of seduction and sexual flirtation; the **yambú** is slower and less overtly sexual, while the **columbia** is a furiously energetic solo male dance.

Rumba at its most authentic is informal and spontaneous, but the music has been extensively recorded and is widely performed. Many of the biggest names in contemporary rumba, such as **Los Muñequitos de Matanzas**, **Claves y Guaguanco** and **Los Papines**, are legendary groups formed decades ago but still going strong.

Danzón

In contrast to rumba, **danzón** is a more formal strain of Cuban music, less spontaneous and with none of the improvisations of rumba; it best represents the musical traditions brought to Cuba by the Europeans, a kind of cross between classical music and African rhythms. Danzón was born out of the instrumental music known in Cuba as **contradanza**, a style performed in ballrooms and at formal events during the nineteenth century by recreational versions of military bands.

CHARANGAS, CONJUNTOS AND ORQUESTAS TÍPICAS

The evolution from contradanza to danzón was by equal measure the transformation of **orquestas típicas** to charangas. *Orquestas típicas* were brass bands dating back to the eighteenth century and most popular in Cuba in the nineteenth century, before the success of danzón. They comprised a cornet, trombone, clarinets, a kind of elaborate bugle known as an ophicleide, violins, kettledrums, double bass and a *güiro* (a kind of scraper). These bands tended to play at formal occasions, for lines of dancers facing one another, but fell out of favour once the danzón turned the line-dance into a couple-dance, a development considered by some contemporaries as obscene and scandalous.

Though sometimes mistakenly used to denote a genre of music, a type of rhythm or a kind of dance, the term **charanga** actually describes a particular kind of band line-up. In Spanish a *charanga* is a brass band but the Cuban spin on the word has a much more specific meaning, referring to a particular set of instruments. Charanga orchestras emerged with the development of danzón in the early twentieth century and were originally known as *charangas francesas*. These bands traditionally consisted of flute, violin, piano, double bass, *güiro* and *timbal* (a type of drum). Charanga line-ups developed over the course of the twentieth century and the term is still in popular use today, though the modern-day interpretation has changed quite radically – the look and sound of La Charanga Habanera, one of the most successful salsa and timba acts of recent years, is a long way from the danzón charangas of the 1930s and 1940s. Cuban bands since the 1940s have also been referred to as **conjuntos**, though these have usually been son and subsequently salsa bands. A conjunto implies a larger, expanded version of traditional son sextets and septets and the line-up can include congas, bongos, *claves*, piano, double bass and guitars as well as trumpets.

The contradanza was adapted and reinterpreted during the course of the nineteenth century until, in 1879, a Cuban band leader in Matanzas, Miguel Failde, composed what is generally considered to be the very first danzón, though there is some dispute over this. More upbeat and tuneful than contradanza, danzón orchestras nevertheless maintained the same basis of brass and string instruments, though the flute was given greater prominence. Various other innovations were made as the style developed during the early decades of the twentieth century, evolving alongside and influencing the sound of jazz in New Orleans and elsewhere in the US. The piano later became an essential ingredient, while congas have also been incorporated, taking the style closer to what is now known as son. Notably, traditional danzón has no singing parts and is, strictly speaking, a purely **instrumental** music. It has long since fallen out of fashion, and though it is still popular with elderly Cubans who meet up at weekends in dancehalls for collective dances organized in couples, it was son that really took off and came to define the Cuban sound.

One of the all-time great Cuban bands, **Orquesta Aragón**, started out playing danzón in the 1940s before moving on to other styles in subsequent years, including chachachá and son. They still perform today both in Cuba and abroad, having toured the UK and Canada among other countries in recent years. Similar to Orquesta Aragón but formed just over sixty years later, **Charanga de Oro** set out to re-establish some of the neglected traditional styles of Cuban music and, along with other revival groups including Buena Vista Social Club and **Orquesta Barbarito Diez**, have been mainstay performers at the International Danzón Festival, which takes place in Havana around April every year.

Son

Son is the blood running through the veins of Cuban popular music. More than any other music style it represents an intrinsically Cuban blend of African and European musical elements, though it has undergone so many innovations and spawned so many sub-genres that it's difficult to talk of it as an individual musical style at all.

Though a large proportion of bands making music in Cuba today could legitimately be described as son groups, references nowadays tend to be to traditional son, with its signature sound provided by the Cuban guitar, known as the **tres**. The upright double bass and vocals, *claves*, maracas, a scraper and bongos also feature in this traditional sound.

The origins of son are in eastern Cuba and the late nineteenth century. The earliest groups to popularize the sound were sextets and subsequently, with the addition of a trumpet in the 1920s, septets. The sound was transformed in the 1940s and 1950s by **Arsenio Rodríguez**, considered by many to be the father of the modern Afro-Cuban sound. He added extra trumpets to his son band, brought in the piano and added a conga drummer, moving son closer to the sound produced by modern salsa bands, a transformation which was cemented in the 1970s by pioneering groups such as Los Van Van. Bands consisting of this larger, expanded line-up became known as conjuntos (see box opposite). This same period marked the rise of **Beny Moré**, cited by many as Cuba's greatest ever *sonero*, who was known as the "Barbarian of Rhythm". Traditional son is now in vogue again, thanks to the Buena Vista Social Club.

SON VETERANS: BUENA VISTA SOCIAL CLUB

"This is the best thing I was ever involved in," said **Ry Cooder** on the release of *Buena Vista Social Club*, the album of acoustic Cuban rhythms he recorded in Havana. Since then, *Buena Vista* has sold more than two million copies, won a Grammy award and become a live show capable of selling out New York's Carnegie Hall. Yet Cooder is the first to admit that *Buena Vista* is not really his album at all. He rightly wanted all the glory to go to the legendary Cuban veterans who were rescued from obscurity and retirement, and assembled in Havana's Egrem studio to record the album over seven days in March 1996. "These are the greatest musicians alive on the planet today, hot-shot players and classic people," Cooder said. "In my experience Cuban musicians are unique. The organization of the musical group is perfectly understood, there is no ego, no jockeying for position, so they have evolved the perfect ensemble concept."

The role of composer and guitarist **Compay Segundo** (1907–2003) was central to the project. "As soon as he walked into the studio it all kicked in. He was the leader, the fulcrum, the pivot. He knew the best songs and how to do them because he's been doing them since World War One."

Initially a clarinetist, Segundo invented his own seven-stringed guitar, known as the *armonico*, which gives his music its unique resonance. In the late 1920s he played with **Nico Saquito** before moving to Havana where he formed a duo with Lorenzo Hierrezuelo. In 1950 he formed **Compay Segundo y su Grupo**, yet by the following decade he had virtually retired from music, working as a tobacconist for seventeen years.

Rúben González (1919–2003) is described by Cooder as "the greatest piano soloist I have ever heard in my life, a cross between Thelonius Monk and Felix the Cat". Together with Líli Martínez and Peruchín, González forged the style of modern Cuban piano playing in the 1940s. He played with Enrique Jorrín's orchestra for 25 years, travelling widely through Latin America. When invited to play on *Buena Vista*, González did not even own a piano. However, since the release of his first solo album, González has toured Europe and recorded his second solo album in London. "Chanchullo" was released in 2000 to wide acclaim as critics across the board favoured the lusher, more elaborate and rhythmic material.

Other key members of the Buena Vista Club included **Omara Portuondo** (born 1930), the bolero singer known as "the Cuban Edith Piaf"; **Eliades Ochoa** (born 1946), the singer and guitarist from Santiago who leads Cuarteto Patria; and the *sonero* **Ibrahim Ferrer** (1927–2005), whose solo album Cooder produced on a return visit to Havana.

Archive footage of Segundo and González can be seen in Wim Wenders' full-length documentary feature **film**, *Buena Vista Social Club*, filmed in Cuba and at the Buena Vista concerts in Amsterdam and New York in 1998.

Nigel Williamson

Mambo

One of the most popular danzón orchestras in Cuba in the 1930s and 1940s was Arcaño y sus Maravillas, led by Antonio Arcaño. Among the orchestra's musicians was Orestes López who, in 1938, composed a tune for the band called *Mambo*. A variation on the standard danzón formula, the tune had a more African-sounding rhythm, incorporating elements of son, and was at first met by a lukewarm reaction from the Havana crowd. Within a few years, however, the sound had taken off, so much so that the Cuban pianist and bandleader **Pérez Prado** was successfully promoting his music as **mambo**, the first musician to do so.

Mambo fever hit much greater heights abroad than it ever did in the motherland, and is a rarely performed style in contemporary Cuba. Its current obscurity on the island means there are no high-profile mambo bands today, though one of the most universally loved and successful Cuban singers of all time, Beny Moré, was a prolific mambo singer. He joined Prado's band in Mexico City but returned to Cuba where he continued performing until his death in 1963. Unlike many musicians, he chose to stay in Cuba following the Revolution.

Mambo became synonymous with big bands and is a racier, louder, less elegant sound than danzón. Congas and *timbales* drums were added to danzón line-ups to create mambo orchestras. One of the biggest mambo orchestras was Beny Moré's Banda Gigante, consisting of over forty members, though performances would often involve no more than sixteen musicians. The band was hugely popular in Cuba, toured Latin America and the US and even played at the Oscars Ceremony.

Chachachá

In the late 1940s and early 1950s several members of Arcaño y Sus Maravillas defected to the more recently established **Orquesta América**, including the violinist Enrique Jorrín. Orquesta América, like most popular Cuban bands of the day, wrote mambo and danzón songs. It was while composing a danzón that Jorrín, having made several key adjustments to the structure of the song, came up with *La Engañadora*, the first ever **chachachá**. Orquesta América subsequently became known as the creators of the chachachá and were the ambassadors for the sound throughout the 1950s and beyond, as more and more bands, including Orquesta Aragón, adopted the sound. It was as the world's top chachachá band that Orquesta Aragón hit the heights of their international fame in the 1950s.

Like mambo, chachachá was tremendously popular beyond Cuban shores, particularly in the US. Jorrín himself said he composed *La Engañadora* with US audiences in mind and wanted to provide Americans with something they would find more manageable on the dancefloor, having seen them struggle with other more complex and faster Cuban dance rhythms like mambo. The name is said to have been born out of the sound made by the dancers' feet at the now defunct Silver Star club in Centro Habana when they danced to this new rhythm, their feet grazing the floor on three successive beats.

Trova

Another Cuban musical tradition to have emerged from the east of the island, **trova** grew out of the troubadour tradition of travelling musicians who would disperse news or tell stories through song. The early Cuban troubadours relied on nothing more than their voice, guitar and imagination, composing lyrics based on both romantic and patriotic themes. Nowadays, trova is typically sung with two voices in harmony and one or two guitars, and although no longer at the forefront of Cuban music, it can still be heard throughout the island in Casas de la Trova. This simple guitar-based musical tradition gave birth to the song **Guantanamera**, perhaps the best-known Cuban song, and certainly the most familiar to visitors who have spent any time in tourist bars and restaurants.

Its creator was a man named **José Pepe Sánchez**, born in Santiago de Cuba and known as the father of trova. One of his protégés, **Sindo Garay**, became a leading trova singer during the General Machado dictatorship in the 1930s and 1940s. Garay was a fixture at the *Bodeguita del Medio* bar and restaurant in Habana Vieja (see p.124), historically a meeting place for trova singers. Other greats of Cuban trova like Carlos Puebla played there, and in the run-up to the Revolution it was a popular meeting place for intellectuals and critics of Batista. There is no better place to hear the sound nowadays, however, than Santiago's Casa de la Trova (see p.408), where groups like Septeto Santiaguero, Hermanas Ferrín and Septeto de la Trova are among the regular modern performers of traditional trova.

Bolero

An offshoot of trova, Cuban **bolero** (unrelated to the Spanish musical style of the same name) is another guitar-based style but has a more lyrical, poetic and romantic slant. Like trova it is typically performed by guitar duos and two voices in harmony. It originated in Santiago de Cuba in the latter part of the nineteenth century and is said to have been the first kind of Cuban music to gain international renown. A song composed by José Pepe Sánchez, the father of trova, called *Tristeza* is credited as the first ever bolero.

In the 1920s bolero had become popular in Havana cafés and dancehalls, and performers began to include a piano in their compositions. By the 1950s, during one of its most successful decades, bolero had become more popular in Mexico than in Cuba – indeed, the centre of the bolero industry remains in Mexico to this day. Still popular in Cuba, Ibrahim Ferrer, one of the original Buena Vista Social Club singers, was an expert exponent of the bolero, as is Omara Portuondo, whose renditions of one of the classic bolero songs, *Dos Gardenias*, have a resurgence in popularity following the Buena Vista explosion.

Feelin'

The curiously named musical style known as **feelin'**, also referred to as filin, emerged in Cuba – and most particularly in Havana – during the 1940s, as a response to trends in the US jazz scene. Taking elements of American jazz and inspired by the likes of Nat King Cole and Ella Fitzgerald, Cuban musicians combined that imported sound with some of the instrumentation and structure of bolero. Where the backing track for the bolero singer is supplied by a guitarist, the archetypal feelin' soundtrack is provided by a pianist and would be categorized today as easy-listening jazz, featuring crooning singers delivering slow-paced, romantic and bluesy ballads. The English name is said to have been taken from a song sung by the American jazz vocalist Maxine Sullivan, called *I Gotta Feeling*, whose music, along with countless numbers of her contemporaries like Sarah Vaughan and Cab Calloway, reached Cuban shores via shows on the Mil Diez radio station and with black American sailors who would sell jazz records to an eager local following. Feelin' initially developed in private homes, particularly in the Cayo Hueso neighbourhood in Centro Habana, among enthusiasts who would gather together for domestic jam sessions before the style became widely popular.

Compared with trova and bolero, the two styles with which it shares the closest heritage, feelin' is underexposed in Cuba nowadays. You are most likely to hear it in those same venues where it was originally performed and which are still operating today, most usually at *El Gato Tuerto*, in the capital's Vedado district, where feelin' had its heyday during the 1950s and 1960s.

Salsa and timba

Arguably **salsa** is not a musical style at all but a catch-all term for music born and bred in the Spanish-speaking Caribbean and the Latin communities of the eastern US. Though there are countless definitions of what salsa actually is, the term was popularized as a description of a specific kind of music in the 1960s and 1970s in New York, Puerto Rico and Cuba and is undeniably a product of son. Modern salsa was created in the 1970s following innovations to son bands made by **Adalberto Alvarez**, and his band **Son 14**, and by **Juan Formell** and his legendary group **Los Van Van**, introducing changes by adding a trombone, synthesizer and drum. Cuban salsa has been tweaked in recent years to create **timba**, a version of salsa strongly associated with Havana.

Salsa and timba bands dominate Cuban popular music. Los Van Van remains at the forefront of the scene and still draws huge crowds, while fellow all-time greats La Charanga Habanera and Adalberto Alvarez are still relevant. Pioneers of a new wave of louder, more aggressive salsa bands, with grittier lyrics and a more streetwise vernacular, include **NG La Banda**, founded in 1988 but still going strong. In common with many modern-day salsa bands, they have combined salsa with elements of hip-hop, reggaeton and jazz. The group **Bamboleo** and the charismatic female vocalist **Haila** are also great performers and have been headline timba acts for a few years now, while **Maikel Blanco** and **Habana D'Primera** are two of the more recently established salsa acts to cause a real buzz.

Cuban jazz

There have been **jazz bands** in Cuba, and particularly in Havana, almost as long as they have existed in New Orleans – but quintessentially Cuban jazz, as opposed to jazz made by Cubans, emerged in the 1940s, marked by the success of the band Afro-Cubans and their lead singer Frank "Machito" Grillo. The Afro-Cubans, however, moved to New York to establish themselves in the wider consciousness of American jazz, leaving Cuban jazz as performed and developed on the island to really find its feet in the 1970s with the formation, in 1973, of the great Cuban jazz pioneers **Irakere**. Without doubt the godfather of Cuban jazz is composer and pianist **Jesús "Chucho" Valdés** who, along with Paquito D'Rivera and Arturo Sandoval, formed the backbone of Irakere. Cuban jazz tends to incorporate elements of son and other Afro-Cuban music styles. Percussion is an integral part of the sound, with the conga and bongo drums lending it its unmistakeable trademark rhythm.

Though D'Rivera and Sandoval both defected from the island in the 1980s, Havana-based Irakere is still going strong and regularly performs live. Among the leading lights of the newer generation of Cuban jazz artists is Roberto Fonseca, a virtuoso composer and master of several instruments.

Nueva trova

Nueva trova refers to the post-Revolution generation of folksy singer-songwriters who first came to prominence in the late 1960s and 1970s on a basic template of vocals and solo acoustic guitar. Nueva trova artists nowadays are a mix of solo acoustic guitar players in the traditional trova and folk moulds, as well as bands producing a slightly harder-edged sound, crossing over into rock. The style is sometimes referred to as **nueva canción** ("new song").

Nueva trova songs encompass protest and politics as well as romance and relationships, in keeping with the trova tradition. Artists have tended to be patriotic but reflective and sometimes critical of the regime. The two giants of nueva trova, considered among the founders of the movement, are **Pablo Milanés** and **Silvio Rodríguez**, both hugely popular throughout the Spanish-speaking world and still active today. Though at times critical of the regime, Milanés and Rodríguez have in fact been staunch supporters of the Revolution.

Other big names on the current nueva trova circuit are **Carlos Varela**, whose songs express some of the frustrations of the younger generation in Cuba, and **Sara González**.

Cuban rock

Rock music was actively discouraged and heavily frowned upon by the Cuban authorities in the early years of the Revolution, perceived as Yankee music and anti-revolutionary. This attitude mellowed very slowly and had softened sufficiently by 2001 for Welsh rockers the Manic Street Preachers to be able to perform at the Teatro Karl Marx in Havana, a significant breakthrough at the time. Cuba today has its share of rock musicians, and though one or two Cuban rock bands have been given record deals, on the whole they are underexposed and perform at low-key venues. As elsewhere they can be split into numerous sub-genres from soft rock to heavy metal, though the most characteristically Cuban take on rock takes its influence from the nueva trova movement. Many nueva trova artists, including Silvio Rodríguez, have written what could be described as crossover rock songs.

Santa Clara has emerged as the unofficial capital of Cuban rock, with an annual rock festival and a significant share of the country's heavy metal groups. Havana natives Santiago Feliú and Carlos Varela are among the rockier of the nueva trova artists still performing today, while Gerardo Alfonso and David Blanco are worth a listen for the latest Cuban twists on the rock formula. For something a little closer to classic rock check for Los Kent, long-time performers on the Havana rock scene.

Cuban hip-hop

Cuban hip-hop represents a refreshing alternative to the violence, misogyny and bling that have come to dominate modern hip-hop in the US and elsewhere. The music and particularly the lyrics are generally closer to the political and socially conscious rap of late 1980s and early 1990s New York hip-hop, and nothing like the formulaic gangster lyrics and ultra-polished sound of the current hip-hop celebrity. A lack of resources has, to some extent, dictated the Cuban sound, with bedroom producers drawing on whatever samples they can get their hands on, from traditional Cuban music to existing hip-hop tracks – turntables and scratch DJs are pretty much nonexistent.

Havana is the undisputed home of Cuban hip-hop. The annual Festival de Rap has been, since its inception in 1995, the biggest event in the Cuban hip-hop calendar. Its main venue, a concrete amphitheatre, is in Alamar on the eastern outskirts of Havana. Among the groups that performed at the inaugural festival were Amenaza, members of which went on to form **Orishas**, the only Cuban hip-hop group to date to have an international following and, significantly, based abroad. Most of the more innovative Cuban hip-hop artists remain outside of the mainstream. Among the privileged few groups to have recorded with Cuban-based record labels are Obsesión, Ogguere, Telmary Díaz, Fres K and Papo Record. The vast majority of groups still rely on home-made recordings and live performance to get their music heard, and some of the most respected names within the Cuban hip-hop community, such as **Los Paisanos** and the controversial **Los Aldeanos**, perform regularly around Havana.

Reggaeton and cubaton

For a while it looked as though the explosion of Cuban hip-hop groups over the last decade was going to put hip-hop firmly on the Cuban musical map. However, the momentum built up by the initial surge of rappers in Havana and elsewhere on the island was seized upon by **reggaeton** artists and it is they who have gained the

MUSICIANS TO WATCH

Gente de Zona This hugely popular trio is one of Cuba's most successful reggaeton groups and frequently plays live in Havana and around the island.

Havana D'Primera One of the most successful timba bands of recent years, touring internationally with their exciting blend of timba and jazz.

Maikel Blanco y Su Salsa Mayor One of the headline salsa bands in Havana, their billing usually attracts a large and animated crowd.

Roberto Carcassés This prodigious pianist and composer is at the forefront of Cuban jazz.

Son del Nene This exciting septet is one of the freshest exponents of the traditional Cuban sound.

Los Aldeanos This controversial hip-hop duo play live regularly in Havana and usually cause a stir with their regime-challenging lyrics.

recognition and radio airplay the hip-hop artists so craved. The sound is a combination of modern R&B, watered-down commercial reggae and dancehall with rapped lyrics. A home-grown, salsafied version of reggaeton, known as **cubaton**, is equally popular, and this kind of music is now a staple on the Havana club scene. Lyrics frequently revolve around sexual themes and have attracted controversy for their perceived vulgarity.

The first wave of Cuban reggaeton artists was led by **Eddy K**, who is still a superstar in Havana, while more recently established top performers of both reggaeton and cubaton are **Clan 537** and **Gente de Zona**.

Cuban sport

Since the 1959 Revolution Cuba has eight times finished among the top twenty in the Olympic Games' medals tables, and competes at the highest international level in an impressive number of sports. Yet uniquely, this nation of just eleven million people has achieved these levels of global success on an amateur ethos, without the kind of sponsorship, commercialization and funding common to the other world powers in sport.

Cuban sport before the Revolution

Cuba was among the first nations to take part in the **Modern Olympic Games**, competing as one of the twenty countries present in Paris in 1900. It was at these games, the second of the modern era, and four years later in St Louis, that twelve of just fourteen Olympic medals collected by Cuban competitors before the Revolution were won. All twelve medals were in **fencing**, a sport at which Cubans continue to excel, and the hero was Ramón Fonst, the first man in Olympic history to win three individual gold medals.

Most of the Cuban population, however, was alienated not only from these successes but from organized sport in general, as only the privileged classes had access to athletic facilities. The sporting infrastructure was based predominantly on private clubs, from which black Cubans were almost always banned. Class and race determined participation in sports like fencing, tennis, golf and sailing, all the exclusive domain of aristocratic organizations such as the Havana Yacht Club or the Vedado Tennis Club. Many of the most popular spectator sports, though accessible to a broader cross-section of the population, were inextricably tied up with tourism and corruption. The appeal of horse racing, dog racing, cock fighting, billiards and boxing derived mainly from **gambling**, particularly during the 1940s and 1950s when the Mafia controlled much of the infrastructure. Furthermore, on the eve of the Revolution there were only eight hundred PE teachers in a population of ten million, while just two percent of schoolchildren received any kind of formal physical education at all.

It was in **boxing** and **baseball** that popular sporting culture was most avidly expressed. These were genuinely sports for the masses, but though Cuba had one of the world's first national baseball leagues and hosted its own boxing bouts, the really big names and reputations were made in the US. Indeed, both baseball and boxing were brought to Cuba by Americans and owe much of their popularity to American commerce and organization. With such close links between the two countries during the years of the "pseudo-republic", very few talented sportsmen went unnoticed by the fight organizers and league bosses on the opposite side of the Florida Straits. Almost all the biggest names in these two sports during this period – baseball players like **Tony Pérez**, **José Cardenal** and **Tito Fuentes** and boxers such as **Benny Paret** and **Kid Chocolate** – gained their fame and fortune in the US.

Sport and the Revolution

With sport prior to 1959 characterized by corruption, social discrimination and a generally poor standing in international competitions, the revolutionary government had more than enough to get its teeth into. Led by Fidel Castro himself, who has always been a keen sportsman (see box p.476), the new regime restructured the entire system of participation.

THE FIDEL CASTRO FACTOR

According to **Fidel Castro** himself, had he not been a sportsman he would never have been a revolutionary, asserting that it was his physical training as an athlete that had allowed him to fight as a guerrilla in the revolutionary war. As early as January 1959, within a month of the rebel victory, Castro made a lengthy speech in Havana's Ciudad Deportiva and declared: "I am convinced that sporting activity is necessary for this country. It's embarrassing that there is so little sport…The Cuban results in international competitions up until now have been shameful."

Castro's own sporting prowess, attested to in widely published photographs, many of them displayed in museums and restaurants around the country, can be traced back to his high-school days at the Belen school in Havana. Castro played in Belen's basketball and baseball teams, and in 1944 was voted the top high-school athlete in the country. In his early university years the future leader continued to play basketball and baseball as well as training as a 400-metre runner, and was a proficient boxer too.

It would be naive to suppose that there has been no political motivation behind Castro's commitment to sport, but his involvement goes well beyond political gimmickry. As well as making countless speeches down the years promoting the values of sport, Castro considers the achievements in sport since the Revolution a matter of intense pride, and until ill health restricted his movements he rarely missed a chance to greet a winning team's homecoming from an overseas tournament. He has, on more than one occasion, involved himself in disputes over scandals implicating Cuban sports stars. Following the confiscation of medals from four Cuban athletes at the 1999 Pan American Games he personally appeared in a two-day televised hearing, demanding that the medals be returned.

The new ideology of sport

Like the Russians before them, the Cubans developed a new ideology around sport and its role in society. Though borrowing heavily from the Soviet model, this ideology was very much a Cuban creation. Rather than looking to Marx as a guide, the revolutionaries chose the ideas of **Baron Pierre de Coubertin**, the Frenchman responsible for the revival of the Olympic Games in 1896. Coubertin believed that one of the reasons the Ancient Greeks had reached such high levels of social and cultural achievement was the emphasis they placed on physical activity. Rejecting the neo-Marxist argument that the competitive element of sport promotes social division and elitism, the Cubans adopted Coubertin's basic premise that participation in sport was capable of bridging differences in politics, race and religion, thus encouraging feelings of brotherhood and social equality. Believing that it is not the nature of sport but the way in which it is approached and practised that would determine its effect, the Cuban state made sport one of the priorities in the transformation of society.

Sport and physical education were considered inseparable from the process of development towards Che Guevara's concept of *El Hombre Nuevo* – the New Man – one of the cornerstones of Cuban communist theory. The Cubans claim that as well as promoting better health and fitness, organized physical activities and games encourage discipline, responsibility, willpower, improved social communication skills, a cooperative spirit and internationalism, and generally contribute to a person's ethical and moral character.

Sport for all

The transformation of post-revolutionary Cuban sport began in earnest on February 23, 1961, with the creation of **INDER** (National Institute of Sport, Physical Education and Recreation), the government body responsible for carrying out programmes of sport for the masses. The first campaign was aimed at diversifying the number of sporting activities available to the public, eliminating exclusivity and involving every citizen in some kind of regular physical activity.

Sport is an integral part of the "cradle-to-grave" social welfare system born of the Revolution, and no time is wasted in introducing **children** to the benefits of physical exercise. Under the banner of slogans like "the home is the gymnasium", INDER encourages parents to actively pursue the physical health of their children, with classes in massage and physical manipulation offered for babies as young as 45 days old. Early in the morning during term time, it is common to see groups of schoolchildren doing exercises in the local parks and city squares with their teachers. These places are also where the so-called **circulos de abuelos** meet – groups of elderly people, usually past retirement age, performing basic stretches together.

In 1966 legislation was passed guaranteeing workers paid leisure time for recreational activities, and in 1967 entrance charges to sport stadiums and arenas were abolished, and remain at around one or two national pesos, well within reach of the entire population. By 1971 the number of students actively involved in one sport or another had risen from under forty thousand to just over a million, while it was estimated in a UNESCO-backed report that a further 1.2 million people were participating in some kind of regular physical exercise. The right of all Cubans to participate in physical education and organized sports was even included in several clauses of the 1976 Cuban Constitution.

Making champions

Mass participation in sport was to form the base of the Coubertin-inspired **pyramid** that underpins Cuban sport and accounts, to a large extent, for the tremendous success of Cuban sportsmen and women over the last thirty years. From primary schools to universities, physical education is a compulsory part of the curriculum and the progress of all pupils is monitored through regular **testing**. Thus, at as early as 7 or 8 years of age, the most promising young athletes can be selected for the **EIDE** (Escuelas de Iniciación Deportiva Escolar) sports schools, of which there is one in every province. Here, physiological tests, trainers' reports and interprovincial competitions all form a regular part of school life; pupils remain until they are 15 or 16. The best EIDE pupils are then selected for the **ESPA** (Escuelas Superiores de Perfeccionamiento Atlético), the elite sports schools, one stage below the National Team, which sits at the top of the pyramid. Using this structure, the Cubans have demonstrated the reciprocal relationship between the top and the bottom of the pyramid: mass participation produces world champions and, in turn, success in international competitions encourages greater numbers to practise sport.

The nurturing of potentially world-class athletes is taken so seriously in Cuba that each individual sport has to be officially sanctioned before it is recognized as suitable for competition standard. The basic principle behind this is specialization, and since the Revolution the Cubans have made sure each of their major sports is developed to a high international standard before another is introduced.

Many of the **coaches** in Cuba during the first two decades of the Revolution were supplied by other Communist bloc countries, but INDER now has its own home-grown experts. Cuban coaches have had almost as much success as the athletes they have trained, working in over forty countries, particularly Spain and throughout Latin America.

World beaters

Between the Montreal Olympics in 1976, when Cuba finished eighth, and the Atlanta Games in 1996, Cuba never fell out of the top ten in the **Olympic Games** medals tables, placing as high as fourth and fifth Moscow 1980 and Barcelona 1992 respectively. Perhaps equally impressive is Cuba's habitual second place, beaten only by the US, in the **Pan American Games**, a championship contested by all the countries of the American continent.

BASEBALL

Ironically, the most American of sports is also the most Cuban, and **baseball** stands out as one of the few aspects of US culture which the revolutionaries continued to embrace after 1959. It was introduced to the island in the late 1800s by American students studying in Cuba and by visiting sailors who would take on the local workers in Cuban dockyards. The first officially organized game took place between the Matanzas Béisbol Club and the Havana Béisbol Club on December 27, 1874; four years later, the first elite baseball league to be founded outside the US and Canada was established on the island. Frowned upon by the Spanish colonial rulers, who even banned the game for a period, baseball really took off following the end of the Spanish–American War in 1898.

US DOMINANCE

Though a national league had been established, the **Major League** in the US dominated the fortunes of the best players. Cuban and American baseball developed in tandem during the pre-revolutionary era, as the Island became a supply line to the US teams with players like Adolfo Luque, who played twelve seasons with the Cincinnati Reds from 1918, and Conrado Marrero, a pitcher with the Washington Senators in the 1950s, among the numerous Cubans to be won over by the US Major League. These were almost exclusively white players, as black Cubans suffered discrimination in both countries and were mostly restricted either to the black leagues or the Cuban league, in which Habana, Almendares, Marianao and Santa Clara were the only teams competing.

REVOLUTIONARY BASEBALL

Since 1959, Cuban baseball has transformed itself from the stepchild of the US Major League to one of the most potent, independent forces in the game. The **national league** now consists of sixteen teams instead of four and has gone from professional to amateur without losing any of the excitement that characterizes its hottest confrontations. The **national team** dominates international baseball and has done so since the early 1980s, taking three of the five **Olympic titles**, becoming ten-time victors of the **Intercontinental Cup** and winning twelve of the last fifteen biennial **World Cups**. However, the question remains as to whether Cuba's amateurs (who have rarely played in international competitions) can hold their own against the professional players of the US. The first test came in 1999 when the Baltimore Orioles made an unprecedented visit to Cuba to take on the national team. In a good-spirited game the visitors stole a 3-2 victory, but perhaps more significant than the result was the visit itself, characterized by a friendly rivalry and a mutual respect in defiance of the two nations' political antagonism. In 2006 the inaugural **World Baseball Classic** allowed both amateur and professional players from around the world to compete for their national teams, including, for the first time, Major League representatives. Cuba was knocked out in the second round in the 2009 and 2013 tournaments, and in the final in 2006.

DEFECTIONS

That Cuban players are among the best in the world is in little doubt given the success enjoyed by a number of high-profile defections to the US Major League over the years. Among the best known are **Liván Hernández**, who defected in 1995 to sign a six-million-dollar contract with the Florida Marlins, subsequently taking the team to World Series victory in 1997 and named the World Series MVP (Most Valuable Player). His brother Orlando, who was punished for his sibling's defection by being denied a place on the Olympic team that went to Atlanta in 1996, followed him by defecting in 1997, signing with the New York Yankees and pitching for the team in their three World Series victories between 1998 and 2000. Though there have been other defections since the Hernández brothers, significant talents have chosen to stay in Cuba, most famously **Omar Linares**, one of the greatest Cuban players of all time, who rejected offers of millions of dollars from Major League clubs in favour of staying with his beloved Pinar del Río in the 1990s.

Cuban boxers are among the most respected in the world, absent from the professional game on principle but kings of **amateur boxing**, reigning supreme at the AIBA World Boxing Championships since they began in 1974 and the dominant force at the Olympics for decades, although their results were disappointing in Beijing and London. Among the greats are heavyweight **Félix Savón**, six-time world champion and gold medallist at three consecutive Olympics, from 1992 to 2000; **Mario Kindelán**, a lightweight who collected two Olympic and three World Championship golds between 1999 and 2004; and the formidable heavyweight **Teófilo Stevenson**, three-time Olympic Champion and one-time potential opponent of Muhammad Ali. Stevenson was prevented from fighting the self-proclaimed "greatest of all time" by the governing body of the sport during the 1970s, which ruled it illegal for an amateur to fight a professional. Even Ali himself, in a visit to Havana in 1996, admitted that had the two ever met it would have been a close-run contest.

Cuba also has an impressive record in **track and field athletics** over the last thirty years. This small island nation has long made the result of the **Central American and Caribbean Athletics Championships** – in which Mexico, Colombia, Venezuela and Puerto Rico, among others, compete – almost a foregone conclusion, having failed to finish first only three times since 1967. One of the first Olympic track champions was **Alberto Juantorena**, who remains the only man in history to win both 400-metre and 800-metre events at the Olympic Games, achieved in Montreal in 1976. The 1990s were a successful time for Cuban athletes in the jumping events, with long jumper **Ivan Pedroso** winning his event at four consecutive World Championships and taking Olympic gold in Sydney 2000, while **Javier Sotomayor** – The Prince of Heights – has been the high jump world record holder since 1988 and took the Olympic gold medal in 1992. More recently, Cuban hurdlers have been taking the world by storm, first with **Anier García** in Sydney 2000 and then the bespectacled **Dayron Robles** in Beijing 2008, both victorious in the 110-metre hurdles.

Countless other sporting disciplines have given Cuba world and Olympic champions, including the **women's volleyball team**, Olympic gold medallists at three consecutive Games (1992, 1996 and 2000), numerous **martial arts** disciplines and **weightlifting**. Though the overall results in the 2008 and 2012 Olympic Games (28th and 16th respectively) didn't equal the heights of the 1980s and 1990s, these medal tallies nonetheless represent a country punching way above its weight in world sport.

Books and film

There are more books on almost any Cuban subject outside of Cuba than there are on the island itself. Bookstores in Cuba are half-empty and are, of course, all run by the state, so between them offer very little variety. What's more, the state-run publishing industry, brought to its knees during the economic crisis of the 1990s and still suffering from shortages, is very selective about the books that make it to print, for both practical and political reasons. Outside Cuba, Castro and Guevara have been the subjects of countless biographies by foreign authors, while you could fill a whole library with accounts and assessments of the Revolution. There's also a rich line in expat writing, from fiction to political commentary.

Cuban **films**, on the other hand, can be hard to track down outside Cuba, and on a visit to the island it's well worth delving into the Cuban cinematic works available on DVD and video, the latter format still found for sale in many music shops and bookshops. Since the Revolution, the Cuban film industry has become one of the most sophisticated and highly regarded in Latin America.

The ★ symbol indicates titles that are especially recommended.

HISTORY AND POLITICS

★ **Harlan Abrahams and Arturo Lopez-Levy** *Raúl Castro and the New Cuba*. One of the most engaging and intelligent assessments of Cuba since Raúl took over, offering a contemporary take on Cuban politics, economics and society untainted by dogma but written with a lively sense of opinion. Very readable and made more so by a broad and engaging set of interviewees that includes an artist, academic and a gay Cuban emigrant.

Soraya M. Castro Mariño and Ronald W. Pruessen *Fifty Years of Revolution*. A collection of contemporary essays on Cuban foreign relations, particularly with the US, written mostly by academics from Cuba and North America. There are some interesting opinions on and insights into future prospects for the country, some sounding a distinct note of optimism.

★ **Alfredo José Estrada** *Havana (Autobiography of a City)*. Although at times the writer lets his anti-Castro bias flavour his outlook, that doesn't detract from this meticulously researched social and architectural history, rich in fascinating vignettes in which the author traces the lineage of the city from its earliest incarnation to modern times.

★ **Richard Gott** *Cuba: A New History*. Few histories of Cuba flow off the page as fluently as this. The author has a great instinct for interesting anecdotes and information but ties his facts together so seamlessly that you never lose track of the wider narrative. Having visited Cuba regularly

for five decades, Gott also writes with considerable authority.

★ **Guillermo Cabrera Infante** *Mea Cuba*. A collection of writings on Cuba from 1968 to 1993 by a Cuban exile and opponent of the current regime. His vehement criticisms of Fidel Castro are uncompromising and can make for rather heavy reading, but there are plenty of thoughtful and eyebrow-raising commentaries from a man who is clearly passionate about his subject matter.

Louis A. Pérez, Jr. *Cuba: Between Reform and Revolution*. Superbly researched and very readable, this complete history covers pre-Columbian Cuba up to the present. It tends towards economic issues, though it's far from one-dimensional.

Julio Le Riverend *Breve Historia de Cuba*. Published in Cuba and written by one of the country's leading historians, at times this history lapses into political rhetoric and revolutionary propaganda, but it does provide some useful insights as well as information often missed by non-Cuban authors of the country's history. Also available in English.

Rosalie Schwartz *Pleasure Island – Tourism and Temptation in Cuba*. This readable and lively book charts the history of tourism and its relationship to political change in Cuba during its pre-Revolution days, drawing comparisons with its modern-day incarnation. Prostitution is examined and there is a fascinating account of the role played by the Mafia.

Julia Sweig *Cuba: What Everyone Needs To Know*. An

excellent, accessible introduction to Cuban politics, history and culture, covering a wide range of topics and themes but concentrating particularly on Cuba since 1959 and relations with the US. Balanced and thoughtful.

★ **Hugh Thomas** *Cuba: A History*. Now in its fourth decade of publication, this weighty tome remains one of the definitive histories of Cuba. Begins with the English occupation of 1762, but despite this late start this is an authoritative and exhaustive text, meticulously researched and full of fascinating facts.

Helen Yaffe *Che Guevara: The Economics of Revolution*. While much of what is written about Che Guevara focuses on his military campaigns, Yaffe's erudite account looks at the massive impact Guevara had on Cuba's economic management as a member of the Cuban government between 1959 and 1965.

BIOGRAPHY AND AUTOBIOGRAPHY

Carlos Acosta *No Way Home*. Acosta excels as a writer almost as much as he does as a ballet dancer. His detailed autobiography covers his early life in Cuba, including his childhood in the suburbs of Havana, and subsequent successes in dance companies throughout the world. The chapters that capture the feel of life in Cuba for a child in the 1980s are particularly enjoyable.

Jon Lee Anderson *Che Guevara: A Revolutionary Life*. Guevara's amazing life certainly makes a great story and, in this case, a very long one – there can be few biographies of the man as extensively researched as this. Happily this book is not ideologically driven and subsequently Guevara is portrayed in all its complexity.

Reinaldo Arenas *Before Night Falls*. Arenas's daring autobiography, smuggled out of Cuba and published abroad, is a fascinating portrayal of gay life played out under the sexually repressive mantle of 1960 and 1970s Cuba. By turns poetic, bitter and funny, the visceral and powerful prose blazes from every page.

Daisy Rubiera Castillo *Reyita: The Life of a Black Cuban Woman in the Twentieth Century*. Told in the first person to the subject's granddaughter, this simple biography creates a full picture of a life typical of many others. She relates growing up in poverty in eastern Cuba, the aftermath of slavery and racial prejudice of the 1920s and 1930s, as well as life after the Revolution.

Fidel Castro with Ignacio Ramonet *My Life*. The result of over a hundred hours of interviews with the Cuban leader between 2003 and 2005 in which Castro discusses subjects as diverse as his childhood, his revolutionary influences, his memories of Che Guevara, globalization, the environment, terrorism and the future of the Revolution. An unprecedented insight.

★ **Leycester Coltman** *The Real Fidel Castro*. Succeeds where so many biographies of the man fail in being both a balanced and a highly readable account of Castro's extraordinary life. Refreshing in its political neutrality and its animated, non-academic style, this is also a highly accessible insight into the Cuban Revolution itself.

Clive Foss *Fidel Castro*. Very readable in terms of both length and style, this is a well-balanced mini-biography of the Cuban leader, untainted by political leanings. Steers clear of the endless academic debate over Castro's political character and philosophies, focusing instead on engaging anecdotal information as well as the basic facts.

CULTURE AND SOCIETY

★ **Peter C. Bjarkman** *A History of Cuban Baseball 1864–2006*. The best of the available books on Cuban baseball, in part because it is so comprehensive and thoroughly researched, but also because it avoids the pre-Revolution bias which has sullied other accounts. Elegantly written, with infectious enthusiasm, and well illustrated too.

Stephen Foehr *Waking Up In Cuba*. An entertaining portrait of contemporary Cuba as reflected in its music and musicians. This lively account is based on the author's own encounters with a wide and intriguing range of music makers, from rappers and reggae artists to pioneers of the nueva trova movement and the Buena Vista Social Club.

★ **Rosa Lowinger and Ofelia Fox** *Tropicana Nights: The Life and Times of the Legendary Cuban Nightclub*. A thoroughly researched and expertly told story of the fabled Havana cabaret nightclub, woven into a grander narrative of the first years of the Revolution and the decade or so leading up to it. Based on testimony from an impressive list of interviewees, this is a brilliant account of how people on the ground experienced these years, and offers a compelling insight into the world of 1950s Cuban showbusiness.

Ian Lumsden *Machos, Maricones and Gays*. One of the few available books that discusses homosexuality in Cuba. A thorough and sensitive treatment, covering the history of homophobia in Cuba and such complex issues as the Cuban approach to AIDS.

Robin D. Moore *Nationalizing Blackness: Afrocubanismo and Artistic Revolution in Havana, 1920–1940*. A clear and compelling analysis of the cultural and artistic role of black Cubans during an era of prejudice, this is a good introduction to black culture in Cuba.

★ **Pepe Navarro** *La Voz del Caimán*. This engaging collection of short encounters with Cubans from all walks of life aims to portray the lives, opinions and aspirations of a society in all its complexity. Encompassing a strikingly diverse set of occupations and lifestyles, with all kinds of fascinating anecdotes and insights into modern Cuba.

Yoani Sanchez *Havana Real: One Woman Fights to Tell the Truth about Cuba Today*. Yoani Sanchez is arguably the most high-profile critic of the Cuban government still resident in Cuba. Her views, expressed via her Generation Y blog, are well written and passionate and more that a little vituperative. In this book she uses her diarist style of portraits of daily encounters with friends, foes and family to give her account of life on the underside of modern revolution.

★ **Pedro Peréz Sarduy and Jean Stubbs** (eds) *AfroCuba: An Anthology of Cuban Writing on Race, Politics and Culture*. Essays and extracts written by black Cuban writers covering religion, race relations, slavery, plantation culture and an absorbing variety of other topics. There are excerpts from plays, novels, poems and factual pieces, but some of the quality of the texts is lost in the occasionally stilted translations.

TRAVEL WRITING

Louis A. Pérez, Jr. (ed.) *Slaves, Sugar and Colonial Society: Travel Accounts of Cuba 1801–1899*. Covering a range of topics, including religion, crime, sugar and slavery, these accounts, written predominantly by US and British visitors to Cuba, provide a broad overview of Cuban society during the nineteenth century.

★ **Alan Ryan** (ed.) *The Reader's Companion to Cuba*. Twenty-three accounts by foreign visitors to Cuba between 1859 and the 1990s. A broad range of writers, including Graham Greene and Langston Hughes, covers an equally broad range of subject matter, from places and people to slavery and tourism.

Stephen Smith *The Land of Miracles: A Journey Through Modern Cuba*. Entertaining accounts of all the attention-grabbing aspects of Cuban culture – from classic cars and Santería to love hotels and Guantánamo – are surpassed by Smith's ability to pinpoint the foreigner's experience in Cuba.

Wallace and Barbara Smith *Bicycling Cuba*. Detailed specialist travel guide for cyclists by a couple who have spent over six months pedalling around Cuba. Includes some interesting and sensitively written essays as well as detailed route descriptions, airline policies on bikes and a glossary of cycling terms in Spanish.

ART, PHOTOGRAPHY AND ARCHITECTURE

Gianni Basso and Julio César Pérez Hernández *Inside Cuba*. Four hundred pages of exquisite photographs of Cuban architecture and interiors, providing not just eye-catching images but a memorable illustration of all sorts of facets of Cuban life. Dilapidated peasant housing, cigar factories, stylish civic buildings and urban residential apartments all feature.

Nathalie Bondil (ed) *Cuba: Art and History From 1868 to Today*. Produced to accompany an exhibition at the Montreal Museum of Fine Arts, this overview of modern Cuban art history is an excellent reference book, beautifully illustrated and broken down into an accessible selection of essays about key art movements and seminal artists such as Wifredo Lam.

John Comino-James *A Few Streets, A Few People*. Depicting everyday street scenes and people in the run-down Cayo Hueso district of Havana, this photo collection captures the essence of Centro Habana life, so much of it lived outdoors and on view.

Timothy Hyde *Constitutional Modernism: Architecture and Civil Society in Cuba, 1933–1959*. This academic text is stuffed with insights into the Cuban society in the period directly before the Revolution. Looking at global ideas about architecture and implantation in Cuba and subsequent public works, such as what would eventually be named the Plaza de la Revolucíon, this brings a refreshing context to this period.

Kevin Kwan *I Was Cuba*. A showcase of the fantastic photographic archive of collector Ramiro Fernández, a Havana native who left Cuba in 1960 and settled in the US. A treasure-trove of images portraying pre-Revolution Cuba, wonderfully evocative of a bygone era reaching back to the nineteenth century. Unparalleled in its content.

Christophe Loviny *Cuba by Korda*. This collection of photographs taken by Alberto Korda, the man behind the iconic portrait of Che Guevara, features numerous other classic shots, like those of Castro and his rebels in the Sierra Maestra during the Revolutionary War as well as lesser-known photos, including dramatic scenes during the Bay of Pigs invasion.

Hermes Mallea *Great Houses of Havana*. Shot by a descendant of Cuban immigrants, this beautiful coffee-table book focuses on the exquisite buildings maintained by the state as museums and "protocol houses" for foreign diplomats. As well as highlighting some design detail and architectural prowess, the photographs blow away the dusty opinion that all Cuba's colonial buildings are crumbling away.

Andreas Winkler and Sebastiaan Berger (eds) *What's New in Cuba: Images from 'Cuba: Contemporary Art'*. Many of the artists who appear in this lavishly illustrated book have shown their work at Cuba's biennial and internationally, and are considered seminal in the contemporary Cuban art movement. While there is little context on art movements within Cuba the works featured– including paintings, installations, sculpture and multimedia – give a valuable insight into which names to watch, from Tania Brugera to Felipe Dulzaides.

CUBAN FICTION

Alejo Carpentier *The Lost Steps*. One of the best-known novels by the most revered Cuban author of the twentieth century, this is a captivating story of a musician living in New York, who travels to the South American jungle and becomes enveloped in a world lost in time and cut off from civilization. Broad in scope, it's a poignant examination of the nature of happiness and the trappings of society.

⭐ **Edmundo Desnoes** *Memories of Underdevelopment*. In this novel set in 1961, the jaded narrator takes the reader through early revolutionary Cuba after his family has fled for Miami. Its bleak tone and unrelenting existentialism are in stark contrast to the euphoric portrayal of the era generally offered by the state.

Cristina García *Dreaming in Cuban*. Shot through with wit, García's moving novel about a Cuban family divided by the Revolution captures the state of mind of the exile in the US, and beautifully describes a magical and idiosyncratic Cuba.

Pedro Juan Gutiérrez *Dirty Havana Trilogy*. Disturbingly sexy and compelling, this is the story of life under Castro through the eyes of poverty-stricken Gutiérrez. Unlikely ever to be acclaimed by the Cuban Tourist Board, the narrative is as candid as it gets, airing untold stories of vice and poverty in the heart of Cuba. Very, very dirty.

⭐ **Ana Menéndez** *In Cuba I Was a German Shepherd*. Set in the netherland between Miami and Havana inhabited by displaced Cubans, these short stories comprise sensitive and achingly melancholic accounts of jealous husbands, old dreamers and fading wives, and the collection evokes both the nostalgia felt by old Cubans pining for a lost homeland and the feelings of a generation of young US Cubans living in the shadow of a never-seen Shangri-la.

Leonardo Padura *The Mario Conde Mysteries*. These award-winning detective novels broke new ground in Cuba with their gritty, truthful depictions of Havana life and of their flawed protagonist, Lieutenant Mario Conde, revitalizing a genre characterized previously by party-line-towing detectives. The plots serve as a vehicle for exploring the human condition as much as for creating suspense.

Juana Ponce de León and Esteban Ríos Rivera (eds) *Dream With No Name*. A poignant and revealing collection of contemporary short stories by writers living in Cuba and in exile. Mixing the established talent of Alejo Carpentier and Reinaldo Arenas with the younger generation of writers, this anthology covers a diversity of subjects from rural life in the 1930s to lesbian love in modern Cuba.

FILM

El Cuerno de la Abundancia (2008; dir. Juan Carlos Tabío). *The Horn of Abundance* is an insightful depiction of modern Cuban society and the pernicious effects of money on it. The story follows the inhabitants of a fictitious town who believe themselves to be poised to inherit a fortune from Spanish ancestors abroad.

Fresa y Chocolate (1994; dir. Tomás Gutiérrez Alea and Juan Carlos Tabío). The tale of an unlikely friendship between a gay artist and a pro-government student was one of the most successful Cuban films of the 1990s. Groundbreaking and controversial in Cuba – not just because one of the protagonists is gay, but because he is disillusioned with elements of life in Cuba and critical of zealous party officials. Set in Havana, this personal and political story is told with subtlety and sensitivity.

Lucia (1968; dir. Humberto Solas). Divided into three parts set respectively in 1895, 1932 and in an unspecified year in the 1960s, '196...', this seminal Cuban film traces the country's political emancipation from colonialism through the ages as seen through the eyes of three women called Lucia. Though not a polished piece of cinematography, the film is an important contribution to the Third Cinema movement of 1960s and 1970s Latin America.

La Muerte de un Burócrata (1966; dir. Tomás Gutiérrez Alea). A classic of early post-Revolution Cuban cinema from one of its most lauded directors, making it past the censors despite its critical take on the madness of Cuban bureaucracy. In this high farce the wife of a dead man buried with his work card discovers she needs the card to claim benefits she is entitled to. The plot unfolds as she seeks to exhume the body.

⭐ **Sons of Cuba** (2009; dir. Andrew Lang). Following the ups and downs of a group of young boxers at the renowned Havana Boxing Academy, this unforgettable documentary reaches way beyond its immediate subject matter – though that in itself is highly engaging – and offers a touching and sensitive portrayal of growing up in Cuba, family relationships, friendships and personal sacrifice.

Suite Habana (2003; dir. Fernando Pérez). An artful yet truthful depiction of a day in the life of thirteen Havana residents, cinematically shot but technically a documentary and, most notably, completely without dialogue. Following the routines and struggles of a broad cross-section of society, including a ballet dancer, a hospital worker and a peanut seller, this apolitical film is a touching portrait of humanity.

¡Vampiros en La Habana! (1985; dir. Juan Padrón). An entertaining and bawdy animated film set in the 1930s, which has the unlikely premise of warring European and American vampires fighting to get their fangs on a Cuban-produced formula that stops sunlight harming vampires.

Spanish

Though you are very unlikely to encounter any hostility for speaking English to Cubans, and you will usually find plenty of locals willing to attempt a conversation in English, it makes sense to learn a few basic phrases in Spanish as proficient English is not widely spoken. This is especially true if you are using local buses, as the complete lack of information means you will almost certainly have to ask for help.

Cuban Spanish bears a noticeable resemblance to the pronunciation and vernacular of the Canary Islands, one of the principal sources of Cuban immigration during the colonial era. Students of Castilian Spanish may find themselves a little thrown by all the variations in basic vocabulary in Cuba. However, though the language is full of Anglicisms and Americanisms, like *carro* instead of *coche* for car, or *queic* instead of *tarta* for cake, the Castilian equivalents are generally recognized. Be prepared also for the common Cuban habit of dropping the final letters of words and changing the frequently used -ado ending on words to -ao.

Despite these areas of confusion, the rules of **pronunciation** for all forms of Spanish are straightforward and the basic Latin American model applies in Cuba. Unless there's an accent, all words ending in d, l, r and z are stressed on the last syllable, all others on the second last. All vowels are pure and short.

a somewhere between the A sound in "back" and that in "father".

e as in "get".

i as in "police".

o as in "hot".

u as in "rule".

c is soft before E and I, hard otherwise: **cerca** is pronounced "serka".

g works the same way: a guttural H sound (like the ch in "loch") before E or I, a hard G elsewhere: **gigante** becomes "higante".

h is always silent.

j is the same sound as a guttural G: **jamón** is pronounced "hamon".

ll is pronounced as a Y: **lleno** is therefore pronounced "yeno".

n is as in English, unless it has a tilde (accent) over it, when it becomes NY: **mañana** sounds like "manyana".

qu is pronounced like the English K.

r is, technically speaking, not rolled but you will frequently hear this rule contradicted.

rr is rolled.

v sounds more like B: **vino** becomes "beano".

z is the same as a soft C: **cerveza** is thus "servesa".

SPANISH LANGUAGE BASICS

ESSENTIALS

yes	sí	open	abierto/a
no	no	closed	cerrado/a
please	por favor	with	con
thank you	gracias	without	sin
sorry	disculpe	good	buen(o)/a
excuse me	permiso, perdón	bad	mal(o)/a
Mr	señor	big	grande
Mrs	señora	small	pequeño/a, chico/a
Miss	señorita	more	más
here	aquí/acá	less	menos
there	allí	the toilets	los servicios, los baños
this	esto	ladies	señoras/damas
that	eso	gentlemen	caballeros
		I don't understand	No entiendo

I don't speak Spanish	No hablo español
I don't know	No sé

NUMBERS AND DAYS

0	cero
1	uno/una
2	dos
3	tres
4	cuatro
5	cinco
6	seis
7	siete
8	ocho
9	nueve
10	diez
11	once
12	doce
13	trece
14	catorce
15	quince
16	dieciséis
20	veinte
21	veitiuno
30	treinta
40	cuarenta
50	cincuenta
60	sesenta
70	setenta
80	ochenta
90	noventa
100	cien(to)
101	ciento uno
200	doscientos
201	doscientos uno
500	quinientos
1000	mil
2000	dos mil
first	primero/a
second	segundo/a
third	tercero/a
fourth	quarto/a
fifth	quinto/a
Monday	lunes
Tuesday	martes
Wednesday	miércoles
Thursday	jueves
Friday	viernes
Saturday	sábado
Sunday	domingo

GREETINGS AND RESPONSES

goodbye	adios/chao
hello	hola
Good morning	Buenos dias
Good afternoon/night	Buenas tardes/noches
See you later	Hasta luego
Pleased to meet you	Mucho gusto
How are you?	¿Cómo está (usted)? or ¿Cómo andas? (informal)
Not at all/You're welcome	De nada/por nada
My name is…	Me llamo…
What's your name?	¿Cómo se llama usted? or ¿Cómo te llamas? (informal)
I am English	Soy inglés(a)
…American	…americano(a)
…Australian	…australiano(a)
…Canadian	…canadiense(a)
…Irish	…irlandés(a)
…Scottish	…escosés(a)
…South African	…surafricano(a)
…Welsh	…galés(a)
…a New Zealander	…neozelandés(a)

PUBLIC TRANSPORT AND TAXIS

airport	aeropuerto
bicycle taxi	bicitaxi/ciclotaxi
bus (usually a local city bus)	guagua
bus (used more to refer to long-distance bus)	ómnibus
bus station	terminal de ómnibus
bus stop	parada
communal taxi (operates more like a bus service)	taxi colectivo; almendrón
every other day (seen on bus and train timetables)	días alternos
to hitchhike	coger botella
juggernaut-style bus	camello
non-state taxi	taxi particular; máquina
state-run taxi charging in convertible pesos	turistaxi
train station	estación de ferrocarriles
truck (a commonly used alternative to long-distance buses)	camión
I'd like a (return) ticket to…	Quisiera boleto/ pasaje (de ida y vuelta) para…
Is this the stop for…?	¿Es está la parada para…?
Is this the train for Havana?	¿Es éste el tren para La Habana?
Take us to this address	Llévenos a esta dirección

What time does it leave (arrive in…)?	¿A qué hora sale (llega a…)?
When is the next bus to…?	¿Cuándo es la próxima guagua para…?
Where can I get a taxi?	¿Dónde puedo coger un taxi?
Where does the bus to… leave from?	¿De dónde sale la guagua para…?
Where is a good place to hitchhike?	¿Dónde hay buen lugar para coger botella?

CAR RENTAL, DRIVING AND ROADS

car	carro
Could you check…?	¿Puede usted comprobar…?
…the oil	…el aceite
…the water	…el agua
…the tyres	…los neumáticos
crossroads	cruce
driver's licence	carné de conducir
Fill it up please	Llénelo por favor
Give way	Ceda el paso
I'd like to rent a car	Quisiera alquilar un carro
Is the petrol/ gasoline included?	¿Está incluida la gasolina?
main road	carretera principal
map	mapa
motorway	autopista
petrol station	gasolinera
pothole	bache
railway crossing	crucero
road	carretera
roundabout	rotonda
traffic light	semáforo

ASKING DIRECTIONS

Carry straight on	Siga todo derecho/ recto
How do I get to…?	¿Por dónde se va para llegar a…?
How far is it from here to…?	¿Qué distancia hay desde aquí hasta…?
Is it near/far?	¿Está cerca/lejos?
Is there a hotel nearby?	¿Hay un hotel aquí cerca?
Is this the right road to…?	¿Es esta la carretera para…?
Next to	Al lado de
Opposite	Frente/enfrente
Turn left/right	Doble a la izquierda/ derecha
Where does this road take us?	¿A dónde nos lleva esta carretera?
Where is…?	¿Dónde está…?

NEEDS AND ASKING QUESTIONS

Can you help me please?	Por favor, ¿me puede ayudar?
Could you speak slower please?	Por favor, ¿puede usted hablar más despacio?
Do you accept credit cards/travellers' cheques here?	¿Aceptan aquí tarjetas de crédito/ cheques de viajero?
Do you have…?	¿Tiene…?
Do you know…?	¿Sabe…?
Do you speak English?	¿Habla usted inglés?
Give me…	Deme…
How much is it?	¿Cuánto cuesta?
I'd like	Quisiera
I want	Quiero
(one like that)	(uno así)
There is (is there)?	(¿)Hay(?)
What…?	¿Qué…?
What does this mean?	¿Qué quiere deciresto?
What is there to eat?	¿Qué hay para comer?
When…?	¿Cuándo…?
What's that?	¿Qué es eso?
What's this called in Spanish?	¿Cómo se llama esto en español?
Where…?	¿Dónde…?

TIME

a day	un día
a month	un mes
a week	una semana
afternoon	tarde
half past two	dos y media
It's one o'clock	Es la una
It's two o'clock	Son las dos
later	más tarde or después
morning	mañana
night	noche
now	ahora
quarter past two	dos y cuarto
quarter to three	tres menos cuarto
today	hoy
tomorrow	mañana
tonight	esta noche
What time is it?	¿Qué hora es?
yesterday	ayer

ACCOMMODATION

air conditioning	aire acondicionado
balcony	balcón
boutique hotel	hostal
cabin complex	campismo

cabin or chalet	cabaña; bungaló, bungalow (not necessarily single storey)
Can one…?	¿Se puede…?
… camp (near) here?	¿…acampar aqui (cerca)?
Do you have a room?	¿Tiene una habitación?
…with two beds/ double bed	…con dos camas/ cama matrimonial
…facing the sea	…con vista al mar
…facing the street	…con vista a la calle
…on the ground floor	…en la planta baja
…on the first floor	…en el primer piso
Do you have anything cheaper?	¿No tiene algo más barato?
fan	el ventilador
hot/cold water	agua caliente/fria
house with rooms to rent	casa particular
It's fine, how much is it?	Está bien, ¿cuánto es?
It's for one person/ two people	Es para una persona/ dos personas
…for one night	…para una noche
It's too…	Es demasiada/o…
…expensive	…cara/o
…dark	…oscura/o
…noisy	…ruidosa/o
key	llave
laundry service	servicio de lavandería
reception	carpeta
room service	servicio de habitación
safety deposit box	caja de seguridad
swimming pool	piscina
switchboard	pizarra
The TV/radio doesn't work	No funciona el televisor/el radio
toilet/bathroom	baño
village complex	villa
We have booked a double room	Hemos reservado una habitación doble

SHOPPING, BANKS AND EXCHANGE

agromercado/ agropecuario	market selling fresh produce for national pesos
artesanía	arts and crafts
bodega	a grocery store only open to those with a corresponding state-issue ration book
bolsa negra	black market
cambio	bureau de change
casa de cambio	a bureau de change for changing convertible pesos into Cuban pesos
casa comisionista	Cuban equivalent to a pawnbroker
en efectivo	in cash
guardabolso	cloakroom for bags (usually outside shops)
habanos	Cuban cigars
humidor	box for storing and preserving cigars

SCUBA DIVING

coral reef	barrera coralina/ arrecife de coral
coral wall	pared coralina
depth	profundidad
depth gauge	profundimetro
dive sites	sitios de buceo
diver	buceador
diving gear	equipo de buceo
fins	aletas
mask	máscara
open water	mar abierto
regulator	regulador
scuba diving	buceo
shipwreck	barco hundido
snorkel	snorkel
tank	tanque
tunnel	túnel

ARCHITECTURAL AND GEOGRAPHICAL TERMS

balneario	health spa; seaside resort
cordillera	mountain range
embalse	reservoir
ingenio	sugar refinery
finca	ranch; country estate
malecón	seaside promenade
mirador	place, usually at the top of a hill or mountain, from where there are good views
mogote	boulder-like hills found only in Pinar del Río, particularly in Viñales
municipio	division of a city equivalent to a borough or electoral district
reparto	city district/ neighbourhood
taller	workshop
vega	tobacco farm
vitrales	arched stained-glass windows, unique to Cuba

CUBAN MENU READER

FOOD AND RESTAURANT BASICS

aceite	oil
ají	chilli
ajo	garlic
almuerzo	lunch
arroz	rice
azúcar	sugar
bocadillo/bocadito	sandwich
cena	dinner
cereal	cereal
combinaciones	set meals
comida criolla	Cuban/Creole food
comidas ligeras	light foods
cuenta	bill
desayuno	breakfast
ensalada	salad
entrantes	starters
entremeses	starters
guarnición	side dishes
huevos	eggs
huevos fritos	fried eggs
huevos hervidos	boiled eggs
huevos revoltillos	scrambled eggs
mantequilla	butter or margarine
mermelada	jam (UK); jelly (US)
miel	honey
mostaza	mustard
pan	bread
perro caliente	hot dog
pimienta	pepper
platos combinados	set meals
platos fuertes	mains
potaje	soup, stew
queso	cheese
sal	salt
sopa	soup
tortilla	omelette
tostada	toast
vinagre	vinegar

TABLE ITEMS

botella	bottle
carta	menu
cuchara	spoon
cucharita	teaspoon
cuchillo	knife
cuenco	bowl
mesa	table
plato	plate
servieta	napkin
tenedor	fork
vaso	glass

COOKING STYLES

al ajillo	fried with lots of garlic
a la brasa	braised
a la jardinera	with tomato sauce
a la parrilla	grilled
a la plancha	grilled
agridulce	sweet and sour
ahumado/a	smoked
al horno	baked
asado/a	roast
bien cocido/a	well done (meat)
caldoso/a	cooked with lots of stock
cazuela	stew, casserole
churrasco	grilled meat
crudo/a	raw
empanadilla	puff pastry/pie
enchilado/a	cooked in tomato sauce
estofado/a	stewed/braised
frito/a	fried
grillé	grilled
guisado/a	stewed
hervido/a	boiled
lonjas	slices/strips
poco cocinado/a	rare (meat)
regular	medium (meat)
revoltillo	scrambled
tostado/a	toasted

CUBAN DISHES

ajiaco	rich stew featuring corn and varied meats and vegetables
aporreado	beef stew with tomato and garlic
bistec uruguayo	steak covered in cheese and breadcrumbs
chicharrones	fried pork skin/ pork scratchings
congrí	rice and red beans (mixed)
empanada	pastry stuffed with meat or sometimes cheese or guava
langosta enchilada	lobster in a tomato sauce
lechón	roast pork suckling
moros y cristianos	rice and black beans
palomilla	steak fried or grilled with lime and garlic
ropa vieja	shredded stewed beef
tamale	Mexican-influenced local dish made with steamed cornflour

tasajo	shredded and jerked stewed beef
tostones	fried plantains

STREET VENDOR SNACKS

churros	long curls of fried batter covered in sugar, similar to doughnuts
coquitos	sweets made from shredded coconut and sugar
empanada de guayaba	guava jam in pastry
fritura de maíz	corn fritter
maní molido	ground-peanut bar
pan con lechón	roast chicken sandwich
papa rellena	balls of deep-fried mashed potato stuffed with mincemeat
rositas de maíz	popcorn
torreja	eggy sweet bread in syrup
tortica	shortbread biscuit
turrón de maní	peanut and syrup bar

FISH (PESCADOS) AND SEAFOOD (MARISCOS)

aguja	swordfish
anchoas	anchovies
arenque	herring
atún	tuna
bacalao	cod
calamares	squid
camarones	prawns, shrimp
cangrejo	crab
espada	swordfish
langosta	lobster
merluza	hake
pargo	red snapper (tilapia)
pulpo	octopus
salmón	salmon
tetí	small fish, local to Baracoa
trucha	trout

MEAT (CARNE) AND POULTRY (AVES)

albóndigas	meatballs
bistec	steak
brocheta	kebab
buey	beef
cabra/chivo	goat
carnero	mutton
cerdo	pork
chorizo	spicy sausage
chuleta	chop
conejo	rabbit
cordero	lamb
costillas	ribs
escalope	escalope
hamburguesa	hamburger
hígado	liver
jamón	ham
lacón	smoked pork
lomo	loin (of pork)
masas de	cubed (pork)
oveja	mutton
pato	duck
pavo	turkey
pechuga	breast
picadillo	mince
pierna	leg
pollo	chicken
rana	frog's meat
res	beef
ropa vieja	shredded beef
salchichas	sausages
sesos	brains
solomillo	sirloin
ternera	veal
tocino	bacon
venado	venison

FRUITS (FRUTAS) AND NUTS (FRUTOS SECOS)

aguacate	avocado
albaricoque	apricot
almendra	almond
avellana	hazelnut
cereza	cherry
ciruelas	prunes
coco	coconut
fresa	strawberry
fruta bomba	papaya
guayaba	guava
lima	lime
limón	lime/lemon
mamey	mamey (thick, sweet red fruit with a stone)
maní	peanut
manzana	apple
melocotón	peach
melón	melon (usually watermelon)
naranja	orange
papaya	papaya (or pawpaw)
pera	pear
piña	pineapple
plátano	banana
toronja	grapefruit
uvas	grapes

VEGETABLES (VERDURAS/VEGETALES)

aceituna	olive
berenjenas	aubergine/eggplant
boniato	sweet potato
calabaza	pumpkin
cebolla	onion
champiñón	mushroom
chícaro(nes)	pea (pulse)
col	cabbage
esparragos	asparagus
frijoles	black beans
garbanzos	chickpeas
habichuela	string beans/green beans
hongos	mushrooms
lechuga	lettuce
malanga	starchy tubular vegetable
papa	potato
papas fritas	french fries
pepino	cucumber
pimiento	capsicum pepper
quimbombo	okra
rábano	radish
remolacha	beetroot
tomate	tomato
yuca	cassava
zanahoria	carrot

SWEETS (DULCES) AND DESSERTS (POSTRES)

arroz con leche	rice pudding
…en almíbar	…in syrup
galleta	biscuit/cookie
flan	crème caramel
helado	ice cream
jimaguas	two ice-cream scoops
queik	cake
queso	cheese
merengue	meringue
natilla	custard/milk pudding/mousse
pasta de guayaba	guava jam
pay	pie (fruit)
pudín	crème caramel or hard-set flan
torta de queso	cheesecake
torta Santiago	almond tart
tortica	shortbread-type biscuit
tres gracias	three ice-cream scoops

RUMS (RONES) AND COCKTAILS (COCTELES)

Cuba Libre	rum and Coke
Cubanito	white rum, lemon juice, salt, Worcester sauce, hot sauce and crushed ice
Daiquirí	white rum, white sugar, lemon juice and crushed ice
Daiquirí Frappé	white rum, maraschino (cherry liqueur), white sugar, lemon juice and crushed ice
Habana Especial	white rum, maraschino, pineapple juice and ice
Mulata	dark rum, white sugar, lemon juice and cacao liqueur
Presidente	white rum, curaçao, grenadine and sweet white vermouth
ron…	
…añejo	dark rum, aged 7 years
…carta blanca (ron blanco)	white rum, aged 3 years
…carta oro	dark rum, aged 5 years
…gran reserva	dark rum, aged 15 years
Ron Collins	white rum, lemon juice, white sugar and soda

OTHER DRINKS (BEBIDAS)

agua	water
agua mineral	mineral water
…(con gas)	…(sparkling)
…(natural/sin gas)	…(still)
batido	milkshake
café	coffee
café con leche	coffee made with hot milk
cerveza	beer
chocolate caliente	drinking chocolate
ginebra	gin
guarapo	sugar cane pressé
jerez	sherry
jugo	juice
leche	milk
limonada natural	lemonade (fresh)
prú	fermented drink flavoured with spices
refresco	pop/fizzy drink
refresco de lata	canned pop
té	tea
té manzanillo	camomile tea
vino blanco	white wine
vino rosado	rosé wine
vino tinto	red wine
vodka	vodka
whisky	whisky

IDIOM AND SLANG

Cuban Spanish is rich in idiosyncratic words and phrases, many borrowed from English. Some of the slang is common to other Latin American countries, particularly Puerto Rico, while there are all sorts of **cubanismos** unique to the island. A number of everyday Cuban words, particularly for items of clothing, differ completely from their Castilian equivalent. These are not slang words, but equate to the same kind of differences that exist between North American and British English.

CLOTHING

blúmer knickers
camiseta vest
chor shorts
chubasquero cagoule
guayabera a traditional lightweight shirt, often with four pockets
overol dungarees
pitusa jeans
pulover T-shirt
saco a suit
tenis trainers, sneakers
yin jeans

MONEY

baro dollar/s, convertible peso/s
divisa hard currency (used in an official capacity, eg in a bank or shop)/dollars/convertible pesos
fula dollar/s, convertible peso/s
kilo/s cent/s or centavo/s
un medio five cents or centavos
moneda efectivo cash, convertible pesos
moneda nacional national currency, Cuban pesos
una peseta twenty cents or centavos

HISTORICAL TERMS

bohío thatched-roof hut as made and lived in by pre-Columbian peoples on the island
cabildo town council during the colonial era
casino Spanish social centre in the nineteenth century
cimarón escaped slave
criollo/a a pre-independence term to describe a Cuban-born Spanish person; also used to describe something as specifically or traditionally Cuban
mambí member of the nineteenth-century rebel army fighting for independence from Spain
palenque a hideout or settlement occupied by runaway slaves during the colonial period
peninsular/es Spanish-born person/s living in Cuba prior to independence
trapiche machine used in colonial era to press sugar cane

MISCELLANEOUS

asere similar to "mate" or "buddy" (usually used as an exclamation)
barbacoa two rooms created from one by building in a floor halfway up the wall to create an upper level (a popular Cuban practice)
bárbaro/a excellent, great
bolsa negra black market
CDR (Committee for the Defence of the Revolution) neighbourhood-watch groups devised to root out counter-revolutionaries
chao goodbye (never hello)
chopin convertible-peso shop, often a supermarket (an appropriation of the English "shopping")
¿Cómo andas? How's it going?
compañero/a comrade (formal); friend, mate, pal (informal)
consumo consumption; used with entrance costs to denote an entitlement of food or drink included in cost
guajiro/a person who lives in a rural area/peasant
guapo criminal or street hustler
gusano/a Cuban refugee or counter-revolutionary (pejorative)
jinetera female hustler who specifically targets tourists; prostitute ·
jinetero male hustler who specifically targets tourists
orisha A deity in Afro–Cuban religions like Santería
pa' for (shortened version of para)
paladar privately run restaurant located in the owner's home
peña musical group, jam or small concert
pepe/a tourist
pila a lot; Hay una pila de gente aqui – "There are a lot of people here"
prieto/a dark-skinned
ponchera puncture repair and bicycle maintenance workshop
posada short-term hotel renting rooms for sex
¿Qué bolá? What's up?, How's it going?
reparto neighbourhood or area of a city
sala de video venue where films are shown to the public on a television screen
socio/a mate, buddy
tonga a lot
trigueño/a light-brown-skinned
veguero tobacco farmer
yuma foreigner
zafra sugar-cane harvest

Small print and index

A ROUGH GUIDE TO ROUGH GUIDES

Published in 1982, the first Rough Guide – to Greece – was a student scheme that became a publishing phenomenon. Mark Ellingham, a recent graduate in English from Bristol University, had been travelling in Greece the previous summer and couldn't find the right guidebook. With a small group of friends he wrote his own guide, combining a highly contemporary, journalistic style with a thoroughly practical approach to travellers' needs.

The immediate success of the book spawned a series that rapidly covered dozens of destinations. And, in addition to impecunious backpackers, Rough Guides soon acquired a much broader readership that relished the guides' wit and inquisitiveness as much as their enthusiastic, critical approach and value-for-money ethos.

These days, Rough Guides include recommendations from budget to luxury and cover more than 200 destinations around the globe, as well as producing an ever-growing range of eBooks and apps.

Visit **roughguides.com** to see our latest publications.

Rough Guide credits

Editor: Polly Thomas
Layout: Anita Singh
Cartography: Rajesh Chhibber
Picture editor: Lisa Jacobs
Proofreader: Susannah Wight
Managing editor: Mani Ramaswamy
Senior editor: Alice Park
Assistant editor: Prema Dutta
Photographers: Lydia Evans, Greg Roden
Production: Charlotte Cade

Cover design: Nicole Newman, Anita Singh
Editorial assistant: Olivia Rawes
Senior pre-press designer: Dan May
Creative operations manager: Jason Mitchell
Publisher: Joanna Kirby
Operations coordinator: Helen Blount
Publishing director (Travel): Clare Currie
Commercial manager: Gino Magnotta
Managing director: John Duhigg

Publishing information

This sixth edition published November 2013 by
Rough Guides Ltd,
80 Strand, London WC2R 0RL
11, Community Centre, Panchsheel Park,
New Delhi 110017, India
Distributed by the Penguin Group
Penguin Books Ltd,
80 Strand, London WC2R 0RL
Penguin Group (USA)
345 Hudson Street, NY 10014, USA
Penguin Group (Australia)
250 Camberwell Road, Camberwell,
Victoria 3124, Australia
Penguin Group (NZ)
67 Apollo Drive, Mairangi Bay, Auckland 1310,
New Zealand
Penguin Group (South Africa)
Block D, Rosebank Office Park, 181 Jan Smuts Avenue,
Parktown North, Gauteng, South Africa 2193
Rough Guides is represented in Canada by Tourmaline
Editions Inc. 662 King Street West, Suite 304, Toronto,
Ontario M5V 1M7
Printed in Singapore by Toppan Security Printing Pte. Ltd.

512pp includes index
A catalogue record for this book is available from the
British Library
ISBN: 978-1-40936-279-1
The publishers and authors have done their best to
ensure the accuracy and currency of all the information
in **The Rough Guide to Cuba**, however, they can accept
no responsibility for any loss, injury, or inconvenience
sustained by any traveller as a result of information or
advice contained in the guide.
5 7 9 8 6 4

Help us update

We've gone to a lot of effort to ensure that the sixth
edition of **The Rough Guide to Cuba** is accurate and up-
to-date. However, things change – places get "discovered",
opening hours are notoriously fickle, restaurants and
rooms raise prices or lower standards. If you feel we've got
it wrong or left something out, we'd like to know, and if
you can remember the address, the price, the hours, the
phone number, so much the better.

Please send your comments with the subject line
"**Rough Guide Cuba Update**" to ✉ mail@uk.roughguides
.com. We'll credit all contributions and send a copy of the
next edition (or any other Rough Guide if you prefer) for
the very best emails.
Find more travel information, connect with fellow
travellers and plan your trip on ⓦ roughguides.com

ABOUT THE AUTHORS

Fiona McAuslan first visited Cuba in 1995, when she spent a year studying Spanish and Cuban history at Havana University, travelling round the island and attempting to dance salsa. Between regular visits to the country she is now a London-based journalist who writes on travel, design and lifestyle but still has two left feet.

Matt Norman lived in Havana for a year between 1995 and 1996 and has been returning regularly ever since. He will be forever indebted to the Cuban health service, and lives in South London.

Acknowledgements

Fiona McAuslan In Havana, thanks to Aurora Ampudia, Luis and Nelson for their ongoing love, support and friendship. Also in Havana, to Toby Brocklehurst for making sure that no element of the changing city escaped my notice. In Morón, to Maite Valor Morales for extensive help both in Cuba and at home. At Rough Guides thanks to Mani Ramaswamy and Alice Park for getting the project rolling and many thanks to editor Polly Thomas for approaching the edit with such care, consideration and enthusiasm – and for being a pleasure to work with. In England a special thank you to Marcus Ludewig and Marlowe McAuslan-Ludewig for ever-present laughter, love and support.

Matt Norman Biggest thanks and much love to Hildegard Milian in Havana for her hard work and dedication; and to Nimueh Rodríguez for her invaluable help. Love also to the rest of the Havana family: Miriam Rodríguez, Sinai Solé and little Ricky, Hector and Etienn. As ever I am indebted to Omelio Moreno and Mercy in Santa Clara for their generosity, kindness and fantastic cooking; to Armando

and Leonor in Cienfuegos; to Raisa Rodríguez and her sons Jorge and Javier in Matanzas for their warmth and help; and to Julio Nelson Bastida in Trinidad – thanks for the cigars and photos. Thanks also to Omar and Diana at Hostal Bahía, Maylin at Villa Lagarto and Osniel the driver in Cienfuegos; to José Fernández González for driving us around and Angel Q. Rodríguez Martínez in Santa Clara; to Reinier Toscano Orbea for all the info, Julio Muñoz, Julio Nelson Jr, David Aloma Aguila and Zobeida Rodríguez in Trinidad; to Gabriel the driver in Matanzas; to Marisol at the Barracuda Scuba Diving Centre in Varadero; and to Mandy, Miri, Luis Miguel and Gilberto Morales Pardo in Havana. Back in England, thanks to Roger Kershaw for being such a supportive and flexible manager and giving me time to get the job done; to Mani Ramaswamy, Alice Park and Lisa Jacobs at Rough Guides and especially to Polly Thomas for being such a sharp-eyed editor and a pleasure to work with. Finally, thanks and lots and lots of love to Sophie Madden for all her support, sacrifice and all those great meals.

Readers' updates

Thanks to all those readers who took the trouble to write in with their amendments and suggestions. Apologies for any misspellings or omissions.

Benet Allen; Laura Arango Roca; Jerome BellionJourdan; Carolin Berger; Yngve Borgan & Kaja Kierulf; Cathy Blake; Andy Bray; Enda Byrt; Barbara Cámbara; François Crozade; Susan Daly; David Diringer; Sr. Carlos Domínguez; Kate Feeney; Sabine Gebele; Jane Goodwin; Mike Goodwin; Oliver Goodwin; Bernard te Gussinklo; Sara Hamood; Howard Hopkins; Remco Kerssens; Peter Knight; Laura Koppenhoefer; Tobias Liechti; Younger Lewis; Suzanne M; Sherian Morgan; Julia Mörtl; Dr Heather Murray; Lynne Nettle; Michael O'Keeffe; A.W.A. Oosterbaan; Gilles Paquin; Peter Pedersen; John Radanovich; Alfred Reynolds; Hilary Roberts; Kay Rogers; Chris Sansom; Eva Sattelmayer; Sebastian Schult; Chris Turner ; Karen Urbons; Jeroen van Marle; Tom W; Rianne de Wit; Ken Woods; Werner Wynants; Xiang Yi Zhang

Photo credits

All photos © Rough Guides except the following:
(Key: t-top; c-centre; b-bottom; l-left; r-right)

p.1 Getty Images: Karsten Bidstrup (c)
p.2 4Corners: Matteo Carassale (c)
p.4 Robert Harding Picture Library: Lee Frost (t)
p.7 Getty Images: Dario Mitidieri (tl); Jeremy Woodhouse; SuperStock: Melvyn Longhurst (tr)
p.9 Alamy: MARKA (tr); Getty Images: Walter Bibikow (br)
p.11 Alamy: Jorge Royan (b); Tips Images (t)
p.12 Robert Harding Picture Library: Alvaro Leiva (t)
p.14 SuperStock: imagebroker.net (b)
p.15 Alamy: Barry Lewis (b); Getty Images: Walter Bibikow (tl)
p.16 Dorling Kindersley: Lydia Evans (tr); Fotolia: Emmanuelle Combaud (b)
p.17 Alamy: Peter Stroh (br); Fotolia: cstyle (bl); Getty Images: Alan McCord (cr); Ingolf Pompe (t)
p.18 Alamy: Chris Lewington (c); Getty Images: Ben Pipe (b); Jeremy Woodhouse (t)
p.19 Fotolia: kmiragaya (tl); SuperStock: Tips Images (b)
p.20 Alamy: EPA (br); Fotolia: kmiragaya (t)
p.21 Dorling Kindersley: Lydia Evans (tl); Getty Images: Michael Thornton (tr); Sven Creutzmann (b)
p.22 Alamy: Bert de Ruiter (cr); Fotolia: Rostislav Ageev (b); SuperStock: Fabian von Poser (cl); Toño Labra (t)
p.23 4Corners: Tim White (t); Getty Images: Walter Bibikow (bl)
p.24 4Corners: Massimo Ripani (t)
p.26 SuperStock: Marka (t)
p.64–65 4Corners: Reinhard Schmid (c)
p.67 Dorling Kindersley: Lydia Evans (t)
p.85 Getty Images: Merten Snijders (c)
p.111 Dorling Kindersley: Greg Roden (t); Lydia Evans (b)
p.141 Dorling Kindersley: Greg Roden (b); Lydia Evans (t)
p.150–151 Robert Harding Picture Library: LOOK (c)
p.153 SuperStock: Alvaro Leiva (t)
p.171 Getty Images: Tim White (b); SuperStock: Peter Schickert (t)
p.179 Getty Images: Merten Snijders (c)
p.186–187 4Corners: Reinhard Schmid (c)

p.189 Fotolia: DJ (t)
p.221 Getty Images: Grant Faint (b); SuperStock: Juan Muñoz (t)
p.225 Getty Images: Nancy Rose (c)
p.236–237 Alamy: Hermes Images (c)
p.239 Getty Images: Michael DeFreitas (t)
p.247 AWL Images: Walter Bibikow (c)
p.255 Alamy: EPH (c)
p.276–277 Fotolia: terex (c)
p.279 Getty Images: Walter Bibikow (t)
p.285 Dorling Kindersley: Lydia Evans (b); Getty Images: Ben Pipe (tr); Brent Winebrenne (tl)
p.295 Getty Images: Walter Bibikow (c)
p.306–307 Fotolia: Mariia Pazhyna (c)
p.309 Robert Harding Picture Library: LOOK (t)
p.329 Getty Images: WaterFrame (c)
p.344–345 Getty Images: Andrew Pistolesi (c)
p.347 Fotolia: Brigida Soriano (t)
p.375 SuperStock: Marka (c)
p.384–385 4Corners: Reinhard Schmid (c)
p.387 SuperStock: Fabian von Poser (t)
p.395 Getty Images: Sven Creutzmann (b); SuperStock: Photononstop (t)
p.426–427 Robert Harding Picture Library: LOOK (c)
p.429 Dorling Kindersley: Lydia Evans (t)
p.435 4Corners: Angelo Giampiccolo (t); SuperStock: Norbert Probst (b)
p.445 SuperStock: Photononstop (c)
p.450 Dorling Kindersley: Greg Roden (t)

Front cover Stained-glass window, Trinidad, SuperStock: Melvyn Longhurst
Back cover View of Havana, Fotolia: Andrey Armyagov (rb); Varadero Beach at the *Hotel Melia Las Americas*, 4Corners: Reinhard Schmid (lb); Musicians and classic car, SuperStock: Alvaro Leiva (t)

Index

Maps are marked in grey

V

W

Y

Z

Map symbols

The symbols below are used on maps throughout the book

) (	Bridge	⊥	Gardens		Waterfall
—	Wall	⚑	Military checkpoint	⚱	Museum
⋀⋀	Springs	⛺	Campsite/campismo	⊙	Statue/memorial
▲	Peak		Snorkelling		Stadium
⌃⌃	Mountain range		Fuel station		Building
◔	Cave	P	Parking		Church
⋇	Viewpoint	ⓘ	Tourist information office		Park
	Turtle nesting site	ⓒ	Telephone office		Mudflats
⌖	Lighthouse	@	Internet		Mangrove swamp/marsh
✈	Airport	✉	Post office		Beach
◆	Point of interest	⊞	Hospital		Cemetery
	Golf course				

Listings key

- ■ Accommodation
- ● Eating
- ■ Drinking / nightlife
- ● Shops / markets

ROUGH
GUIDES

SO NOW WE'VE TOLD YOU
HOW TO MAKE THE MOST
OF YOUR TIME, WE WANT
YOU TO STAY SAFE AND
COVERED WITH OUR
FAVOURITE TRAVEL INSURER

 WorldNomads.com
keep travelling safely

GET AN ONLINE QUOTE
roughguides.com/travel-insurance

RECOMMENDED BY

ROUGH
GUIDES

MAKE THE MOST OF YOUR TIME ON EARTH™